Advances in Minimum Description Length

Advances in Minimum Description Length Theory and Applications

edited by
Peter D. Grünwald
In Jae Myung
Mark A. Pitt

A Bradford Book
The MIT Press
Cambridge, Massachusetts
London, England

MIT Press books may be purchased at special quantity discounts for business or sales promotional use. For information, please email special_sales@mitpress.mit.edu or write to Special Sales Department, The MIT Press, 5 Cambridge Center, Cambridge, MA 02142.

Typeset by the authors using LATEX 2ε
Printed and bound in the United States of America

Library of Congress Cataloging-in-Publication Data

Advances in minimum description length: theory and applications / edited by Peter D. Grünwald, In Jae Myung, Mark A. Pitt.
      p. cm.   (Neural information processing series)
   Includes bibliographical references and index.
   ISBN 0-262-07262-9 (alk. paper)
   1. Minimum description length. 2. Statistics. 3. Machine learning. 4. Information theory
I. Grünwald, Peter D. II. Myung, In Jae III. Pitt, Mark A. IV. Series.

QA276.A26 2005
519.5–dc22

                                                                            2004055932

10 9 8 7 6 5 4 3 2 1

Contents

Series Foreword

The yearly Neural Information Processing Systems (NIPS) workshops bring together scientists with broadly varying backgrounds in statistics, mathematics, computer science, physics, electrical engineering, neuroscience, and cognitive science, unified by a common desire to develop novel computational and statistical strategies for information processing, and to understand the mechanisms for information processing in the brain. As opposed to conferences, these workshops maintain a flexible format that both allows and encourages the presentation and discussion of work in progress, and thus serve as an incubator for the development of important new ideas in this rapidly evolving field.

The series editors, in consultation with workshop organizers and members of the NIPS Foundation board, select specific workshop topics on the basis of scientific excelllence, intellectual breadth, and technical impact. Collections of papers chosen and edited by the organizers of specific workshops are built around pedagogical introductory chapters, while research monographs provide comprehensive descriptions of workshop-related topics to create a series of books that provides a timely, authoritative account of the latest developments in the exciting field of neural computation.

Michael I. Jordan, Sara Al. Solla, and Terrence J. Sejnowski

Preface

To be able to forecast future events, science wants to infer general laws and principles from particular instances. This process of inductive inference is the central theme in statistical modeling, pattern recognition, and the branch of computer science called "machine learning." The minimum description length (MDL) principle is a powerful method of inductive inference. It states that the best explanation (i.e., model) given a limited set of observed data is the one that permits the greatest compression of the data. Put simply, the more we are able to compress the data, the more we learn about the regularities underlying the data.

The roots of MDL can be traced back to the notion of *Kolmogorov complexity*, introduced independently by R.J. Solomonoff, A.N. Kolmogorov, and G.J. Chaitin in the 1960s. These and other early developments are summarized at the end of Chapter 1 of this book, where a brief history of MDL is presented. The development of MDL proper started in 1978 with the publication of *Modeling by the Shortest Data Description* by J. Rissanen. Since then, significant strides have been made in both the mathematics and applications of MDL. The purpose of this book is to bring these advances in MDL together under one cover and in a form that could be easily digested by students in many sciences. Our intent was to make this edited volume a source book that would inform readers about state-of-the-art MDL and provide examples of how to apply MDL in a range of research settings.

The book is based on a workshop we organized at the annual Neural Information Processing Systems (NIPS) conference held in Whistler, Canada in December 2001. It consists of sixteen chapters organized into three parts. Part I includes six introductory chapters that present the theoretical foundations of the MDL principle, its various interpretations, and computational techniques. In particular, chapters 1 and 2 offer a self-contained tutorial on MDL in a technically rigorous yet readable manner. In Part II, recent theoretical advances in modern MDL are presented. Part III begins with a chapter by J. Comley and D. Dowe that describes minimum message length (MML), a "twin sister" of MDL, and highlights the similarities and differences between these two principles. This is followed by five chapters that showcase the application of MDL in diverse fields, from bioinformatics to machine learning and psychology.

We would like to thank our editor, Bob Prior, for the support and encouragement we received during the preparation of the book. We also thank Peter Bartlett, Alex Smola, Bernhard Schölkopf, and Dale Schuurmans for providing LaTeX-macros to facilitate formatting and creation of the book. We also thank the authors for contributing papers and the referees for reviewing the manuscripts. Finally, we thank our families for putting up with our foolishness.

Peter Grünwald, In Jae Myung, Mark A. Pitt
Amsterdam and Columbus, Ohio, February 2004

I Introductory Chapters

1 Introducing the Minimum Description Length Principle

Peter Grünwald
Centrum voor Wiskunde en Informatica
Kruislaan 413
1098 SJ Amsterdam
The Netherlands
pdg@cwi.nl
www.grunwald.nl

This chapter provides a conceptual, entirely nontechnical introduction and overview of Rissanen's minimum description length (MDL) principle. It serves as a basis for the technical introduction given in Chapter 2, in which all the ideas discussed here are made mathematically precise.

1.1 Introduction and Overview

How does one decide among competing explanations of data given limited observations? This is the problem of *model selection*. It stands out as one of the most important problems of inductive and statistical inference. The minimum description length (MDL) principle is a relatively recent method for inductive inference that provides a generic solution to the model selection problem. MDL is based on the following insight: any regularity in the data can be used to *compress* the data, that is, to describe it using fewer symbols than the number of symbols needed to describe the data literally. The more regularities there are, the more the data can be compressed. Equating "learning" with "finding regularity," we can therefore say that the more we are able to compress the data, the more we have *learned* about the data. Formalizing this idea leads to a general theory of inductive inference with several attractive properties:

1. Occam's razor. MDL chooses a model that trades off goodness-of-fit on the observed data with 'complexity' or 'richness' of the model. As such, MDL embodies a form of Occam's razor, a principle that is both intuitively appealing and informally applied throughout all the sciences.

2. No overfitting, *automatically*. MDL procedures *automatically* and *inherently* protect against overfitting and can be used to estimate both the parameters and the structure (e.g., number of parameters) of a model. In contrast, to avoid overfitting when estimating the structure of a model, traditional methods such as maximum likelihood must be *modified* and extended with additional, typically ad hoc principles.

3. Bayesian interpretation. MDL is closely related to Bayesian inference, but avoids some of the interpretation difficulties of the Bayesian approach,[1] especially in the realistic case when it is known a priori to the modeler that none of the models under consideration is true. In fact:

4. No need for "underlying truth." In contrast to other statistical methods, MDL procedures have a clear interpretation independent of whether or not there exists some underlying "true" model.

5. Predictive interpretation. Because data compression is formally equivalent to a form of probabilistic prediction, MDL methods can be interpreted as searching for a model with good predictive performance on *unseen* data.

In this chapter, we introduce the MDL principle in an entirely nontechnical way, concentrating on its most important applications: model selection and avoiding overfitting. In Section 1.2 we discuss the relation between learning and data compression. Section 1.3 introduces model selection and outlines a first, 'crude' version of MDL that can be applied to model selection. Section 1.4 indicates how these crude ideas need to be refined to tackle small sample sizes and differences in model complexity between models with the same number of parameters. Section 1.5 discusses the philosophy underlying MDL, and considers its relation to Occam's razor. Section 1.7 briefly discusses the history of MDL. All this is summarized in Section 1.8.

1.2   The Fundamental Idea: Learning as Data Compression

We are interested in developing a method for *learning* the laws and regularities in data. The following example will illustrate what we mean by this and give a first idea of how it can be related to descriptions of data.

Regularity ...   Consider the following three sequences. We assume that each sequence is 10000 bits long, and we just list the beginning and the end of each sequence.

$$00010001000100010001 \quad \ldots \quad 00010001000100010001000100010001 \tag{1.1}$$

$$01110100110100100110 \quad \ldots \quad 1010111010111011000101100010 \tag{1.2}$$

$$00011000001010100000 \quad \ldots \quad 00100010000100000010000110000 \tag{1.3}$$

The first of these three sequences is a 2500-fold repetition of 0001. Intuitively, the sequence looks regular; there seems to be a simple 'law' underlying it; it might make sense to conjecture that future data will also be subject to this law, and to predict that future data will behave according to this law. The second sequence has been generated by tosses of a fair coin. It is, intuitively speaking, as "random as possible," and in this sense there is no regularity underlying it. Indeed, we cannot seem to find such a regularity either when we look at the data. The third sequence contains approximately four times as many 0s as 1s. It looks less regular, more random than the first, but it looks less random than the second. There is still some discernible regularity in these data, but of a statistical rather than of a deterministic kind. Again, noticing that such a regularity is there and predicting that future data will behave according to the same regularity seems sensible.

... and Compression We claimed that any regularity detected in the data can be used to *compress* the data, that is, to describe it in a short manner. Descriptions are always relative to some *description method* which maps descriptions D' in a unique manner to data sets D. A particularly versatile description method is a general-purpose computer language like C or PASCAL. A description of D is then any computer program that prints D and then halts. Let us see whether our claim works for the three sequences above. Using a language similar to PASCAL, we can write a program

```
for i = 1 to 2500; print "0001"; next; halt
```

which prints sequence (1.1) but is clearly a lot shorter. Thus, sequence (1.1) is indeed highly compressible. On the other hand, we show in Chapter 2, Section 2.1, that if one generates a sequence like (1.2) by tosses of a fair coin, then with extremely high probability, the shortest program that prints (1.2) and then halts will look something like this:

```
print "0111010011010000101010...1010111010111011000101100010"; halt
```

This program's size is about equal to the length of the sequence. Clearly, it does nothing more than repeat the sequence.

The third sequence lies in between the first two: generalizing $n = 10000$ to arbitrary length n, we show in Chapter 2, Section 2.1 that the first sequence can be compressed to $O(\log n)$ bits; with overwhelming probability, the second sequence cannot be compressed at all; and the third sequence can be compressed to some length αn, with $0 < \alpha < 1$.

Example 1.1 (compressing various regular sequences) The regularities underlying sequences (1.1) and (1.3) were of a very particular kind. To illustrate that *any* type of regularity in a sequence may be exploited to compress that sequence, we give a few more examples:

The Number π Evidently, there exists a computer program for generating the first n digits of π — such a program could be based, for example, on an infinite series expansion of π. This computer program has constant size, except for the specification of n which takes no more than $O(\log n)$ bits. Thus, when n is very large, the size of the program generating the first n digits of π will be very small compared to n: the π-digit sequence is deterministic, and therefore extremely regular.

Physics Data Consider a two-column table where the first column contains numbers representing various heights from which an object was dropped. The second column contains the corresponding times it took for the object to reach the ground. Assume both heights and times are recorded to some finite precision. In Section 1.3 we illustrate that such a table can be substantially compressed by first describing the coefficients of the second-degree polynomial H that expresses Newton's law, then describing the heights, and then describing the deviation of the time points from the numbers predicted by H.

Natural Language Most sequences of words are not valid sentences according to the English language. This fact can be exploited to substantially compress English text, as long as it is syntactically mostly correct: by first describing a grammar for English, and then describing an English text D with the help of that grammar [Grünwald 1996], D can be described using many fewer bits than are needed without the assumption that word order is constrained.

1.2.1   Kolmogorov Complexity and Ideal MDL

To formalize our ideas, we need to decide on a description method, that is, a formal language in which to express properties of the data. The most general choice is a general-purpose[2] computer language such as C or PASCAL. This choice leads to the definition of the *Kolmogorov complexity* [Li and Vitányi 1997] of a sequence as the length of the shortest program that prints the sequence and then halts. The lower the Kolmogorov complexity of a sequence, the *more regular* it is. This notion seems to be highly dependent on the particular computer language used. However, it turns out that for every two general-purpose programming languages A and B and every data sequence D, the length of the shortest program for D written in language A and the length of the shortest program for D written in language B differ by no more than a constant c, which does not depend on the length of D. This so-called *invariance theorem* says that, *as long as the sequence D is long enough*, it is not essential which computer language one chooses, as long as it is general-purpose. Kolmogorov complexity was introduced, and the invariance theorem was proved, independently by Kolmogorov [1965], Chaitin [1969] and Solomonoff [1964]. Solomonoff's paper, called "A Formal Theory of Inductive Inference," contained the idea that the ultimate model for a sequence of data may be identified with the shortest program that prints the data. Solomonoff's ideas were later extended by several authors, leading to an 'idealized' version of MDL [Solomonoff 1978; Li and Vitányi 1997; Gács, Tromp, and Vitányi 2001]. This idealized MDL is very general in scope, but not practically applicable, for the following two reasons:

1. *Uncomputability.* It can be shown that there exists no computer program that, for every set of data D, when given D as input, returns the shortest program that prints D [Li and Vitányi 1997].

2. *Arbitrariness/dependence on syntax.* In practice we are confronted with small data samples for which the invariance theorem does not say much. Then the hypothesis chosen by idealized MDL may depend on arbitrary details of the syntax of the programming language under consideration.

1.2.2   Practical MDL

Like most authors in the field, we concentrate here on nonidealized, practical versions of MDL that deal explicitly with the two problems mentioned above. The basic idea is to scale down Solomonoff's approach so that it does become applicable. This is achieved by using description methods that are less expressive than general-purpose computer languages. Such description methods C should be restrictive enough so that for any data sequence D, we can always compute the length of the shortest description of D that is attainable using method C; but they should be general enough to allow us to compress many of the intuitively "regular" sequences. The price we pay is that, using the "practical" MDL principle, there will always be some regular sequences which we will not be able to compress. But we already know that there can be *no* method for inductive inference at all which will always give us all the regularity there is — simply because there can be no automated method which for any sequence D finds the shortest computer program that prints D and then halts. Moreover, it will often be possible to guide a suitable choice of C by a priori knowledge we have about our problem domain. For example, below we consider a description method C that is based on the class of all polynomials, such that with the help of C we can compress all data sets which can meaningfully be seen as points on some polynomial.

1.3   MDL and Model Selection

Let us recapitulate our main insights so far:

MDL: The Basic Idea

The goal of statistical inference may be cast as trying to find regularity in the data. "Regularity" may be identified with "ability to compress." MDL combines these two insights by *viewing learning as data compression*: it tells us that, for a given set of hypotheses $\mathcal{H}$ and data set D, we should try to find the hypothesis or combination of hypotheses in $\mathcal{H}$ that compresses D most.

This idea can be applied to all sorts of inductive inference problems, but it turns out to be most fruitful in (and its development has mostly concentrated on) problems of *model selection* and, more generally, those dealing with *overfitting*. Here is a standard example (we explain the difference between "model" and "hypothesis" after the example).

Example 1.2 (Model Selection and Overfitting) Consider the points in Figure 1.1. We would like to learn how the y-values depend on the x-values. To this end, we may want to fit a polynomial to the points. Straightforward linear regression will give us the leftmost polynomial — a straight line that seems overly simple: it does not capture the regularities in the data well. Since for any set of n points there exists a polynomial of the $(n-1)$st degree that goes exactly through all these points, simply looking for the polynomial with the least error will give us a polynomial like the one in the second picture. This polynomial seems overly complex: it reflects the random fluctuations in the data rather than the general pattern underlying it. Instead of picking the overly simple or the overly complex polynomial, it seems more reasonable to prefer a relatively simple polynomial with a small but nonzero error, as in the rightmost picture. This intuition is confirmed by numerous experiments on real-world data from a broad variety of sources [Rissanen 1989; Vapnik 1998; Ripley 1996]: if one naively fits a high-degree polynomial to a small sample (set of data points), then one obtains a very good fit to the data. Yet if one *tests* the inferred polynomial on a second set of data coming from the same source, it typically fits these test data very badly in the sense that there is a large distance between the polynomial and the new data points. We say that the polynomial *overfits* the data. Indeed, all model selection methods that are used in practice either implicitly or explicitly choose a tradeoff between goodness-of-fit and

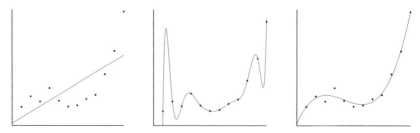

Figure 1.1 A simple, complex and tradeoff (third-degree) polynomial.

complexity of the models involved. In practice, such tradeoffs lead to much better predictions of test data than one would get by adopting the 'simplest' (one degree) or most "complex"[3] ($n-1$-degree) polynomial. MDL provides one particular means of achieving such a tradeoff.

It will be useful to make a precise distinction between "model" and "hypothesis":

Model vs. Hypothesis

We use the phrase *point hypothesis* to refer to a *single* probability distribution or function. An example is the polynomial $5x^2 + 4x + 3$. A point hypothesis is also known as a "simple hypothesis" in the statistical literature.

We use the word *model* to refer to a family (set) of probability distributions or functions with the same functional form. An example is the set of all second-degree polynomials. A model is also known as a "composite hypothesis" in the statistical literature.

We use *hypothesis* as a generic term, referring to both point hypotheses and models.

In our terminology, the problem described in Example 1.2 is a "hypothesis selection problem" if we are interested in selecting both the degree of a polynomial and the corresponding parameters; it is a "model selection problem" if we are mainly interested in selecting the degree.

To apply MDL to polynomial or other types of hypothesis and model selection, we have to make precise the somewhat vague insight "learning may be viewed as data compression." This can be done in various ways. In this section, we concentrate on the earliest and simplest implementation of the idea. This is the so-called *two-part code* version of MDL, see Figure 1.2.

Crude[4], Two-Part Version of MDL principle (Informally Stated)

Let $\mathcal{H}^{(1)}, \mathcal{H}^{(2)}, \ldots$ be a list of candidate models (e.g., $\mathcal{H}^{(k)}$ is the set of kth-degree polynomials), each containing a set of point hypotheses (e.g., individual polynomials). The best point hypothesis $H \in \mathcal{H}^{(1)} \cup \mathcal{H}^{(2)} \cup \ldots$ to explain the data D is the one which minimizes the sum $L(H) + L(D|H)$, where

- $L(H)$ is the length, in bits, of the description of the hypothesis; and

- $L(D|H)$ is the length, in bits, of the description of the data when encoded with the help of the hypothesis.

The best *model* to explain D is the smallest model containing the selected H.

Figure 1.2 The two-part MDL principle: first, crude implementation of the MDL ideas.

Example 1.3 (Polynomials, cont.) In our previous example, the candidate hypotheses were polynomials. We can describe a polynomial by describing its coefficients in a certain precision (number of bits per parameter). Thus, the higher the degree of a polynomial or the precision, the more[5] bits we need to describe it and the more 'complex' it becomes. A description of the data 'with the help of' a hypothesis means that the better the hypothesis fits the data, the shorter the description will be. A hypothesis that fits the data well gives us a lot of *information* about the data. Such information can always be used to compress the data (Chapter 2, Section 2.1). Intuitively, this is because we only have to code the *errors* the hypothesis makes on the data rather than the full data. In our polynomial example, the better a polynomial H fits D, the fewer bits we need to encode the discrepancies between the actual y-values y_i and the predicted y-values $H(x_i)$. We can typically find a very complex point hypothesis (large $L(H)$) with a very good fit (small $L(D|H)$). We can also typically find a very simple point hypothesis (small $L(H)$) with a rather bad fit (large $L(D|H)$). The sum of the two description lengths will be minimized at a hypothesis that is quite (but not too) "simple," with a good (but not perfect) fit.

1.4   Crude and Refined MDL

Crude MDL picks the H minimizing the sum $L(H) + L(D|H)$. To make this procedure well-defined, we need to agree on precise definitions for the codes (description methods) giving rise to lengths $L(D|H)$ and $L(H)$. We now discuss these codes in more detail. We will see that the definition of $L(H)$ is problematic, indicating that we somehow need to "refine" our crude MDL principle.

Definition of $L(D|H)$ Consider a two-part code as described above, and assume for the time being that all H under consideration define probability distributions. If H is a polynomial, we can turn it into a distribution by making the additional assumption that the Y-values are given by $Y = H(X) + Z$, where Z is a normally distributed noise term.

   For each H we need to define a code with length $L(\cdot \mid H)$ such that $L(D|H)$ can be interpreted as "the code length of D when encoded with the help of H." It turns out that for probabilistic hypotheses, there is only one reasonable choice for this code. It is the so-called *Shannon-Fano code*, satisfying, for all data sequences D, $L(D|H) = -\log P(D|H)$, where $P(D|H)$ is the probability mass or density of D according to H – such a code always exists; see Chapter 2, Section 2.1.

Definition of $L(H)$: A Problem for Crude MDL   It is more problematic to find a good code for hypotheses H. Some authors have simply used 'intuitively reasonable' codes in the past, but this is not satisfactory: since the description length $L(H)$ of any fixed point hypothesis H can be very large under one code, but quite short under another, our procedure is in danger of becoming arbitrary.

Instead, we need some additional principle for designing a code for $\mathcal{H}$. In the first publications on MDL [Rissanen 1978, 1983], it was advocated to choose some sort of *minimax code* for $\mathcal{H}$, minimizing, in some precisely defined sense, the shortest worst-case total description length $L(H) + L(D|H)$, where the worst case is over all possible data sequences. Thus, the MDL principle is employed at a "metalevel" to choose a code for H. However, this code requires a cumbersome discretization of the model space $\mathcal{H}$, which is not always feasible in practice. Alternatively, Barron [1985] encoded H by the shortest computer program that, when input D, computes $P(D|H)$. While it can be shown that this leads to similar code lengths, it is computationally problematic. Later, Rissanen [1984] realized that these problems could be sidestepped by using a *one-part* rather than a *two-part* *code*. This development culminated in 1996 in a completely precise prescription of MDL for many, but certainly not all, practical situations [Rissanen 1996]. We call this modern version of MDL *refined MDL*:

Refined MDL   In refined MDL, we associate a code for encoding D *not with a single $H \in \mathcal{H}$*, but with the full model $\mathcal{H}$. Thus, given model $\mathcal{H}$, we encode data not in two parts but we design a single *one-part code* with lengths $\bar{L}(D|\mathcal{H})$. This code is designed such that *whenever there is a member of (parameter in) $\mathcal{H}$ that fits the data well, in the sense that $L(D \mid H)$ is small, then the code length $\bar{L}(D|\mathcal{H})$ will also be small.* Codes with this property are called *universal codes* in the information-theoretic literature [Barron, Rissanen, and Yu 1998]. Among all such universal codes, we pick the one that is *minimax optimal* in a sense made precise in Chapter 2, Section 2.4. For example, the set $\mathcal{H}^{(3)}$ of third-degree polynomials is associated with a code with lengths $\bar{L}(\cdot \mid \mathcal{H}^{(3)})$ such that, the better the data D are fit by the best-fitting third-degree polynomial, the shorter the code length $\bar{L}(D \mid \mathcal{H})$. $\bar{L}(D \mid \mathcal{H})$ is called the *stochastic complexity* of the data given the model.

Parametric Complexity   The second fundamental concept of refined MDL is the *parametric complexity* of a parametric model $\mathcal{H}$ which we denote by $\mathbf{COMP}(\mathcal{H})$. This is a measure of the 'richness' of model $\mathcal{H}$, indicating its ability to fit random data. This complexity is related to the degrees of freedom in $\mathcal{H}$, but also to the geometric structure of $\mathcal{H}$; see Example 1.4. To see how it relates to stochastic complexity, let, for given data D, $\hat{H}$ denote the distribution in $\mathcal{H}$ which maximizes the probability, and hence minimizes the code length $L(D \mid \hat{H})$ of D. It turns out that

$$\text{Stochastic complexity of } D \text{ given } \mathcal{H} = L(D \mid \hat{H}) + \mathbf{COMP}(\mathcal{H}).$$

Refined MDL model selection between two parametric models (such as the models of first- and second-degree polynomials) now proceeds by selecting the model such that the stochastic complexity of the given data D is smallest. Although we used a one-part code to encode data, refined MDL model selection still involves a tradeoff between two terms: a goodness-of-fit term $L(D \mid \hat{H})$ and a complexity term **COMP**($\mathcal{H}$). However, because we do not explicitly encode hypotheses H anymore, there is no arbitrariness anymore. The resulting procedure can be interpreted in several different ways, some of which provide us with rationales for MDL beyond the pure coding interpretation (see Chapter 2, Sections 2.5.1–2.5.4):

1. **Counting/differential geometric interpretation.** The parametric complexity of a model is the logarithm of the number of *essentially different*, *distinguishable* point hypotheses within the model.

2. **Two-part code interpretation.** For large samples, the stochastic complexity can be interpreted as a two-part code length of the data after all, where hypotheses H are encoded with a special code that works by first discretizing the model space $\mathcal{H}$ into a set of "maximally distinguishable hypotheses," and then assigning equal code length to each of these.

3. **Bayesian interpretation.** In many cases, refined MDL model selection coincides with Bayes factor model selection based on a *noninformative prior* such as *Jeffreys' prior* [Bernardo and Smith 1994].

4. **Prequential interpretation.** Refined MDL model selection can be interpreted as selecting the model with the best predictive performance when sequentially predicting *unseen* test data, in the sense described in Chapter 2, Section 2.5.4. This makes it an instance of Dawid's [1984] *prequential* model validation and also relates it to *cross-validation* methods.

Refined MDL allows us to compare models of different functional form. It even accounts for the phenomenon that different models with the same number of parameters may not be equally "complex":

Example 1.4 Consider two models from psychophysics describing the relationship between physical dimensions (e.g., light intensity) and their psychological counterparts (e.g., brightness) [Myung, Balasubramanian, and Pitt 2000]: $y = ax^b + Z$ (Stevens's model) and $y = a \ln(x + b) + Z$ (Fechner's model) where Z is a normally distributed noise term. Both models have two free parameters; nevertheless, it turns out that in a sense, Stevens's model is more *flexible* or *complex* than Fechner's. Roughly speaking, this means there are a lot more data patterns that can be *explained* by Stevens's model than can be explained by Fechner's model. Myung and co-workers [2000] generated many samples of size 4 from Fechner's model, using some fixed parameter values. They then fitted both models to each sample. In 67% of the trials, Stevens's model fitted the data better than Fechner's, even though the latter generated the data. Indeed, in refined MDL, the 'complexity' associated with Stevens's model is much larger than the complexity associated with Fechner's, and if both models fit the data equally well, MDL will prefer Fechner's model.

Summarizing, refined MDL removes the arbitrary aspect of crude, two-part code MDL and associates parametric models with an inherent 'complexity' that does not depend on any particular description method for hypotheses. We should, however, warn the reader that we only discussed a special, simple situation in which we compared a finite number of parametric models that satisfy certain regularity conditions. Whenever the models do not satisfy these conditions, or if we compare an infinite number of models, then the refined ideas have to be extended. We then obtain a "general" refined MDL principle, which employs a combination of one-part and two-part codes.

1.5 The MDL Philosophy

The first central MDL idea is that every regularity in data may be used to compress those data; the second central idea is that learning can be equated with finding regularities in data. Whereas the first part is relatively straightforward, the second part of the idea implies that *methods for learning from data must have a clear interpretation independent of whether any of the models under consideration is "true" or not.* Quoting Rissanen [1989], the main originator of MDL:

'We never want to make the false assumption that the observed data actually were generated by a distribution of some kind, say Gaussian, and then go on to analyze the consequences and make further deductions. Our deductions may be entertaining but quite irrelevant to the task at hand, namely, to learn useful properties from the data.'
- *Jorma Rissanen, 1989*

Based on such ideas, Rissanen has developed a radical philosophy of learning and statistical inference that is considerably different from the ideas underlying mainstream statistics, both frequentist and Bayesian. We now describe this philosophy in more detail:

1. Regularity as Compression. According to Rissanen, the goal of inductive inference should be to 'squeeze out as much regularity as possible' from the given data. The main task for statistical inference is to distill the meaningful information present in the data, that is, to separate structure (interpreted as the regularity, the 'meaningful information') from noise (interpreted as the 'accidental information'). For the three sequences of Example 1.2, this would amount to the following: the first sequence would be considered as entirely regular and "noiseless." The second sequence would be considered as entirely random — all information in the sequence is accidental, there is no structure present. In the third sequence, the structural part would (roughly) be the pattern that 4 times as many 0s than 1s occur; given this regularity, the description of exactly which of all sequences with four times as many 0s than 1s occurs is the accidental information.

2. Models as Languages. Rissanen interprets models (sets of hypotheses) as nothing more than languages for describing useful properties of the data — a model $\mathcal{H}$ is *identified* with its corresponding universal code $\bar{L}(\cdot \mid \mathcal{H})$. Different individual hypotheses within the models express different regularities in the data, and may simply be regarded as *statistics*, that is, summaries of certain regularities in the data. *These regularities are present and meaningful independently of whether some $H^* \in \mathcal{H}$ is the "true state of nature" or not.* Suppose that the model $\mathcal{H}$ under consideration is probabilistic. In traditional theories, one typically assumes that some $P^* \in \mathcal{H}$ generates the data, and then 'noise' is defined as a random quantity relative to this P^*. In the MDL view 'noise' is defined relative to the model $\mathcal{H}$ as the residual number of bits needed to encode the data once the model $\mathcal{H}$ is given. Thus, noise is *not* a random variable: it is a function only of the chosen model and the *actually observed data.* Indeed, there is no place for a "true distribution" or a "true state of nature" in this view — there are only models and data. To bring out the difference to the ordinary statistical viewpoint, consider the phrase 'these experimental data are quite noisy.' According to a traditional interpretation, such a statement means that the data were generated by a distribution with high variance. According to the MDL philosophy, such a phrase means only that the data are not compressible with the currently hypothesized model — as a matter of principle, it can *never* be ruled out that there exists a different model under which the data are very compressible (not noisy) after all!

3. We Have Only the Data. Many (but not all[6]) other methods of inductive inference are based on the idea that there exists some "true state of nature," typically a distribution assumed to lie in some model $\mathcal{H}$. The methods are then designed as a means to identify or approximate this state of nature based on as little data as possible. According to Rissanen,[7] such methods are fundamentally flawed. The main reason is that the methods are designed under the assumption that the true state of nature is in the assumed model $\mathcal{H}$, which is often not the case. Therefore, *such methods only admit a clear interpretation under assumptions that are typically violated in practice.* Many cherished statistical methods are designed in this way — we mention hypothesis testing, minimum-variance unbiased estimation, several non-parametric methods, and even some forms of Bayesian inference — see Example 2.22. In contrast, MDL has a clear interpretation which *depends only on the data,* and not on the assumption of any underlying "state of nature."

Example 1.5 (Models That Are Wrong, Yet Useful) Even though the models under consideration are often wrong, they can nevertheless be very *useful.* Examples are the successful 'naive Bayes' model for spam filtering, hidden Markov models for speech recognition (is speech a stationary ergodic process? probably not), and the use of linear models in econometrics and psychology. Since these models are evidently wrong, it seems strange to base inferences on them using methods that are designed under the assumption that they contain the true distribution. To be fair, we should add that domains such as spam filtering and speech recognition are not what the fathers of modern statistics had in mind when they designed their procedures – they were usually thinking about much simpler domains, where the assumption that some distribution $P^* \in \mathcal{H}$ is "true" may not be so unreasonable.

4. MDL and Consistency. Let $\mathcal{H}$ be a probabilistic model, such that each $P \in \mathcal{H}$ is a probability distribution. Roughly, a statistical procedure is called *consistent* relative to $\mathcal{H}$ if, for all $P^* \in \mathcal{H}$, the following holds: suppose data are distributed according to P^*. Then given enough data, the learning method will learn a good approximation of P^* with high probability. Many traditional statistical methods have been designed with consistency in mind (Chapter 2, Section 2.2).

The fact that in MDL, we do not assume a true distribution may suggest that we do not care about statistical consistency. But this is not the case: we would still like our statistical method to be such that in the *idealized* case, where one of the distributions in one of the models under consideration actually generates the data, our method is able to identify this distribution, given enough data. If even in the idealized special case where a 'truth' exists within our models, the method fails to learn it, then we certainly cannot trust it to do something reasonable in the more general case, where there may not be a "true distribution" underlying the data at all. So: consistency *is* important in the MDL philosophy, but it is used *as a sanity check (for a method that has been developed without making distributional assumptions) rather than as a design principle.*

In fact, mere consistency is not sufficient. We would like our method to converge to the imagined true P^* *fast*, based on as small a sample as possible. Two-part code MDL with 'clever' codes achieves good rates of convergence in this sense (Barron and Cover [1991], complemented by Zhang [2004], show that in many situations, the rates are *minimax optimal*). The same seems to be true for refined one-part code MDL [Barron et al. 1998], although there is at least one surprising exception where inference based on the normalized maximum likelihood (NML) and Bayesian universal model behaves abnormally — see Csiszár and Shields [2000] for the details.

Summarizing this section, the MDL philosophy is quite agnostic about whether any of the models under consideration is "true", or whether something like a "true distribution" even exists. Nevertheless, it has been suggested [Webb 1996; Domingos 1999] that MDL embodies a naive belief that "simple models are a priori more likely to be true than complex models." Below we explain why such claims are mistaken.

1.6 MDL and Occam's Razor

When two models fit the data equally well, MDL will choose the one that is the "simplest" in the sense that it allows for a shorter description of the data. As such, it implements a precise form of Occam's razor – *even though as more and more data become available, the model selected by MDL may become more and more 'complex'!* Occam's razor is sometimes criticized for being either (1) arbitrary or (2) false [Webb 1996; Domingos 1999]. Do these criticisms apply to MDL as well?

"1. Occam's Razor (and MDL) Is Arbitrary" Because "description length" is a syntactic notion it may seem that MDL selects an arbitrary model: different codes would have led to different description lengths, and therefore, to different models. By changing the encoding method, we can make 'complex' things 'simple' and vice versa. This overlooks the fact we are not allowed to use just any code we like! 'Refined' MDL tells us to use a specific code, independent of any specific parameterization of the model, leading to a notion of complexity that can also be interpreted without any reference to 'description lengths' (see also Chapter 2, Section 2.9.1).

"2. Occam's Razor Is False"   It is often claimed that Occam's razor is false — we often try to model real-world situations that are arbitrarily complex, so why should we favor simple models? In the words of Webb [1996], "What good are simple models of a complex world?" [8]

The short answer is: even if the true data-generating machinery is very complex, it may be a good strategy to prefer simple models for small sample sizes. Thus, MDL (and the corresponding form of Occam's razor) is a *strategy* for inferring models from data ("choose simple models at small sample sizes"), not a statement about how the world works ("simple models are more likely to be true") — indeed, a strategy cannot be true or false; it is "clever" or "stupid." And the strategy of preferring simpler models is clever even if the data-generating process is highly complex, as illustrated by the following example:

Example 1.6 ("Infinitely" Complex Sources) Suppose that data are subject to the law $Y = g(X) + Z$ where g is some continuous function and Z is some noise term with mean 0. If g is not a polynomial, but X only takes values in a finite interval, say $[-1, 1]$, we may still approximate g arbitrarily well by taking polynomials of higher and higher degree. For example, let $g(x) = \exp(x)$. Then, if we use MDL to learn a polynomial for data $D = ((x_1, y_1), \ldots, (x_n, y_n))$, the degree of the polynomial $\ddot{f}^{(n)}$ selected by MDL at sample size n will increase with n, and with high probability $\ddot{f}^{(n)}$ converges to $g(x) = \exp(x)$ in the sense that $\max_{x \in [-1,1]} |\ddot{f}^{(n)}(x) - g(x)| \to 0$. Of course, if we had better prior knowledge about the problem we could have tried to learn g using a model class $\mathcal{M}$ containing the function $y = \exp(x)$. But in general, both our imagination and our computational resources are limited, and we may be forced to use imperfect models.

If, based on a small sample, we choose the best-fitting polynomial $\hat{f}$ within the set of *all* polynomials, then, even though $\hat{f}$ will fit the data very well, it is likely to be quite unrelated to the "true" g, and $\hat{f}$ may lead to disastrous predictions of future data. The reason is that, for small samples, the set of all polynomials is very large compared to the set of possible data patterns that we might have observed. Therefore, any particular data pattern can only give us very limited information about which high-degree polynomial best approximates g. On the other hand, if we choose the best-fitting $\hat{f}^{\circ}$ in some much smaller set such as the set of second-degree polynomials, then it is highly probable that the prediction quality (mean squared error) of $\hat{f}^{\circ}$ on future data is about the same as its mean squared error on the data we observed: the size (complexity) of the contemplated model is relatively small compared to the set of possible data patterns that we might have observed.

Therefore, the particular pattern that we do observe gives us a lot of information on what second-degree polynomial best approximates g.

Thus, (a) $\hat{f}°$ typically leads to better predictions of future data than $\hat{f}$; and (b) unlike $\hat{f}$, $\hat{f}°$ is *reliable* in that it gives a correct impression of how good it will predict future data *even if the "true" g is 'infinitely' complex*. This idea does not just appear in MDL, but is also the basis of Vapnik's [1998] structural risk minimization approach and many standard statistical methods for nonparametric inference. In such approaches one acknowledges that the data-generating machinery can be infinitely complex (e.g., not describable by a finite-degree polynomial). Nevertheless, it is still a good strategy to approximate it by simple hypotheses (low-degree polynomials) as long as the sample size is small. Summarizing:

The Inherent Difference between Under- and Overfitting

If we choose an overly simple model for our data, then the best-fitting point hypothesis within the model is likely to be almost the best predictor, within the simple model, of future data coming from the same source. If we overfit (choose a very complex model) and there is noise in our data, then, *even if the complex model contains the "true" point hypothesis*, the best-fitting point hypothesis within the model is likely to lead to very bad predictions of future data coming from the same source.

This statement is very imprecise and is meant more to convey the general idea than to be completely true. As will become clear in Chapter 2, Section 2.9.1, it becomes provably true if we use MDL's measure of model complexity; we measure prediction quality by logarithmic loss; and we assume that one of the distributions in $\mathcal{H}$ actually generates the data.

1.7   History

The MDL principle has mainly been developed by Jorma Rissanen in a series of papers starting with [Rissanen 1978]. It has its roots in the theory of *Kolmogorov* or *algorithmic* complexity [Li and Vitányi 1997], developed in the 1960s by Solomonoff [1964], Kolmogorov [1965], and Chaitin [1966, 1969]. Among these authors, Solomonoff (a former student of the famous philosopher of science, Rudolf Carnap) was explicitly interested in inductive inference. The 1964 paper contains explicit suggestions on how the underlying ideas could be made practical, thereby foreshadowing some of the later work on two-part MDL. Although Rissanen was not aware of Solomonoff's work at the time, Kolmogorov's [1965] paper did serve as an inspiration for Rissanen's [1978] development of MDL.

Another important inspiration for Rissanen was Akaike's [1973] information criterion (AIC) method for model selection, essentially the first model selection method based on information-theoretic ideas. Even though Rissanen was inspired by AIC, both the actual method and the underlying philosophy are substantially different from MDL.

MDL is much more closely related to the *minimum message length (MML) principle*, developed by Wallace and his co-workers in a series of papers starting with the groundbreaking [Wallace and Boulton 1968]; other milestones were [Wallace and Boulton 1975] and [Wallace and Freeman 1987]. Remarkably, Wallace developed his ideas without being aware of the notion of Kolmogorov complexity. Although Rissanen became aware of Wallace's work before the publication of [Rissanen 1978], he developed his ideas mostly independently, being influenced rather by Akaike and Kolmogorov. Indeed, despite the close resemblance of both methods in practice, the underlying philosophy is quite different (Chapter 2, Section 2.8).

The first publications on MDL only mention two-part codes. Important progress was made by Rissanen [1984], in which prequential codes are employed for the first time and [Rissanen 1987], introducing the Bayesian mixture codes into MDL. This led to the development of the notion of stochastic complexity as the shortest code length of the data given a model [Rissanen 1986, 1987]. However, the connection to Shtarkov's *normalized maximum likelihood code* was not made until 1996, and this prevented the full development of the notion of "parametric complexity." In the meantime, in his impressive Ph.D. thesis, Barron [1985] showed how a specific version of the two-part code criterion has excellent frequentist statistical consistency properties. This was extended by Barron and Cover [1991] who achieved a breakthrough for two-part codes: they gave clear prescriptions on how to design codes for hypotheses, relating codes with good minimax code length properties to rates of convergence in statistical consistency theorems. Some of the ideas of Rissanen [1987] and Barron and Cover [1991] were, as it were, unified when Rissanen [1996] introduced a new definition of stochastic complexity based on the *normalized maximum likelihood (NML) code* (Chapter 2, Section 2.4). The resulting theory was summarized for the first time by Barron and co-workers [1998], and is called 'refined MDL' in the present overview.

1.8   Summary and Outlook

We have discussed how regularity is related to data compression, and how MDL employs this connection by viewing learning in terms of data compression. One can make this precise in several ways; in *idealized* MDL one looks for the shortest program that generates the given data. This approach is not feasible in practice, and here we concern ourselves with *practical* MDL. Practical MDL comes in a crude version based on two-part codes and in a modern, more refined version based on the concept of *universal coding*. The basic ideas underlying all these approaches can be found in the boxes spread throughout the text.

These methods are mostly applied to model selection but can also be used for other problems of inductive inference. In contrast to most existing statistical methodology, they can be given a clear interpretation irrespective of whether or not there exists some "true" distribution generating data — inductive inference is seen as a search for regular properties in (interesting statistics of) the data, and there is no need to assume anything outside the model and the data. In contrast to what is sometimes thought, there is *no* implicit belief that 'simpler models are more likely to be true' — MDL does embody a preference for 'simple' models, but this is best seen as a strategy for inference that can be useful even if the environment is not simple at all.

In the next chapter, we make precise both the crude and the refined versions of practical MDL. For this, it is absolutely essential that the reader familiarizes him- or herself with two basic notions of coding and information theory: the relation between code length functions and probability distributions, and (for refined MDL), the idea of universal coding — a large part of Chapter 2 is devoted to these.

Notes

1. See Section 2.8.2, Example 2.22.
2. By this we mean that a universal Turing machine can be implemented in it [Li and Vitányi 1997].
3. Strictly speaking, in our context it is not very accurate to speak of "simple" or "complex" polynomials; instead we should call the *set* of first-degree polynomials "simple,' and the *set* of 100th-degree polynomials "complex."
4. The terminology 'crude MDL' is not standard. It is introduced here for pedagogical reasons, to make clear the importance of having a single, unified principle for designing codes. It should be noted that Rissanen's and Barron's early theoretical papers on MDL already contain such principles, albeit in a slightly different form than in their recent papers. Early practical applications [Quinlan and Rivest 1989; Grünwald 1996] often do use *ad hoc* two-part codes which really are 'crude' in the sense defined here.
5. See the previous endnote.
6. For example, cross-validation cannot easily be interpreted in such terms of 'a method hunting for the true distribution.'
7. My own views are somewhat milder in this respect, but this is not the place to discuss them.
8. Quoted with permission from *KDD Nuggets 96,28*, 1996.

References

Akaike, H. (1973). Information theory as an extension of the maximum likelihood principle. In B. N. Petrov and F. Csaki (Eds.), *Second International Symposium on Information Theory*, pp. 267–281. Budapest: Akademiai Kiado.

Barron, A.R. and T. Cover (1991). Minimum complexity density estimation. *IEEE Transactions on Information Theory, 37*(4), 1034–1054.

Barron, A.R. (1985). *Logically Smooth Density Estimation*. Ph. D. thesis, Department of Electrical Engineering, Stanford University, Stanford, CA.

Barron, A.R., J. Rissanen, and B. Yu (1998). The Minimum Description Length Principle in coding and modeling. Special Commemorative Issue: Information Theory: 1948-1998. *IEEE Transactions on Information Theory, 44*(6), 2743–2760.

Bernardo, J., and A. Smith (1994). *Bayesian theory.* New York: Wiley.

Chaitin, G. (1966). On the length of programs for computing finite binary sequences. *Journal of the ACM, 13,* 547–569.

Chaitin, G. (1969). On the length of programs for computing finite binary sequences: Statistical considerations. *Journal of the ACM, 16,* 145–159.

Csiszár, I., and P. Shields (2000). The consistency of the BIC Markov order estimator. *Annals of Statistics, 28,* 1601–1619.

Dawid, A. (1984). Present position and potential developments: Some personal views, statistical theory, the prequential approach. *Journal of the Royal Statistical Society, Series A, 147*(2), 278–292.

Domingos, P. (1999). The role of Occam's razor in knowledge discovery. *Data Mining and Knowledge Discovery, 3*(4), 409–425.

Gács, P., J. Tromp, and P. Vitányi (2001). Algorithmic statistics. *IEEE Transactions on Information Theory, 47*(6), 2464–2479.

Grünwald, P.D. (1996). A minimum description length approach to grammar inference. In G.Scheler, S. Wermter, and E. Riloff (Eds.), *Connectionist, Statistical and Symbolic Approaches to Learning for Natural Language Processing,* Volume 1040 in Springer Lecture Notes in Artificial Intelligence, pp. 203–216. Berlin: Springer-Verlag

Kolmogorov, A. (1965). Three approaches to the quantitative definition of information. *Problems of Information Transmission, 1*(1), 1–7.

Li, M., and P. Vitányi (1997). *An Introduction to Kolmogorov Complexity and Its Applications,* 2nd edition. New York: Springer-Verlag.

Myung, I.J., V. Balasubramanian, and M.A. Pitt (2000). Counting probability distributions: Differential geometry and model selection. *Proceedings of the National Academy of Sciences USA, 97,* 11170–11175.

Quinlan, J., and R. Rivest (1989). Inferring decision trees using the minimum description length principle. *Information and Computation, 80,* 227–248.

Ripley, B. (1996). *Pattern Recognition and Neural Networks.* Cambridge, UK: Cambridge University Press.

Rissanen, J. (1978). Modeling by the shortest data description. *Automatica, 14,* 465–471.

Rissanen, J. (1983). A universal prior for integers and estimation by minimum description length. *Annals of Statistics, 11,* 416–431.

Rissanen, J. (1984). Universal coding, information, prediction and estimation. *IEEE Transactions on Information Theory, 30,* 629–636.

Rissanen, J. (1986). Stochastic complexity and modeling. *Annals of Statistics, 14,* 1080–1100.

Rissanen, J. (1987). Stochastic complexity. *Journal of the Royal Statistical Society, Series B, 49,* 223–239. Discussion: pp. 252–265.

Rissanen, J. (1989). *Stochastic Complexity in Statistical Inquiry.* Singapore: World Scientific.

Rissanen, J. (1996). Fisher information and stochastic complexity. *IEEE Transactions on Information Theory, 42*(1), 40–47.

Solomonoff, R. (1964). A formal theory of inductive inference, part 1 and part 2. *Information and Control, 7*, 1–22, 224–254.

Solomonoff, R. (1978). Complexity-based induction systems: Comparisons and convergence theorems. *IEEE Transactions on Information Theory, 24*, 422–432.

Vapnik, V. (1998). *Statistical Learning Theory.* New York: John Wiley.

Wallace, C., and D. Boulton (1968). An information measure for classification. *Computer Journal, 11*, 185–195.

Wallace, C., and D. Boulton (1975). An invariant Bayes method for point estimation. *Classification Society Bulletin, 3*(3), 11–34.

Wallace, C., and P. Freeman (1987). Estimation and inference by compact coding. *Journal of the Royal Statistical Society, Series B, 49*, 240–251. Discussion: pp. 252–265.

Webb, G. (1996). Further experimental evidence against the utility of Occam's razor. *Journal of Artificial Intelligence Research, 4*, 397–417.

Zhang, T. (2004). On the convergence of MDL density estimation. In *Proceedings of the Seventeenth Annual Conference on Computational Learning Theory (COLT' 04).* Berlin: Springer-Verlag.

Minimum Description Length Tutorial

Peter Grünwald
Centrum voor Wiskunde en Informatica
Kruislaan 413
1098 SJ Amsterdam
The Netherlands
pdg@cwi.nl
www.grunwald.nl

This chapter provides a tutorial-style introduction to and overview of Rissanen's minimum description length (MDL) Principle. The main ideas are discussed in great conceptual and technical detail.

Plan of the Tutorial

In Chapter 1 we introduced the minimum description length (MDL) Principle in an informal way. In this chapter we give an introduction to MDL that is mathematically precise. Throughout the text, we assume some basic familiarity with probability theory. While some prior exposure to basic statistics is highly useful, it is not required. The chapter can be read without any prior knowledge of information theory. The tutorial is organized according to the following plan:

- The first two sections are of a preliminary nature:

  □ Any understanding of MDL requires some minimal knowledge of information theory — in particular the relationship between probability distributions and codes. This relationship is explained in Section 2.1.

  □ Relevant statistical notions such as 'maximum likelihood estimation' are reviewed in Section 2.2. There we also introduce the Markov chain model which will serve as an example model throughout the text.

- Based on this preliminary material, in Section 2.3 we formalize a simple version of the MDL principle, called the *crude two-part MDL principle* in this text. We explain why, for successful practical applications, crude MDL needs to be refined.

- Section 2.4 is once again preliminary: it discusses *universal coding*, the information-theoretic concept underlying refined versions of MDL.

- Sections 2.5, 2.6, and 2.7 define and discuss refined MDL. They are the key sections of the tutorial:

  □ Section 2.5 discusses basic refined MDL for comparing a finite number of simple statistical models and introduces the central concepts of *parametric* and *stochastic complexity*. It gives an *asymptotic expansion* of these quantities and interprets them from a compression, a geometric, a Bayesian, and a predictive point of view.

  □ Section 2.6 extends refined MDL to harder model selection problems, and in doing so reveals the general, unifying idea, which is summarized in Figure 2.4.

  □ Section 2.7 briefly discusses how to extend MDL to applications beyond model section.

- Having defined 'refined MDL' in Sections 2.5, 2.6, and 2.7, the next two sections place it in context:

  □ Section 2.8 compares MDL with other approaches to inductive inference, most notably the related but different *Bayesian* approach.

  □ Section 2.9 discusses perceived as well as real problems with MDL. The perceived problems relate to MDL's relation to Occam's razor; the real problems relate to the fact that applications of MDL sometimes perform suboptimally in practice.

- Finally, Section 2.10 provides a conclusion.

Reader's Guide

Throughout the text, paragraph headings reflect the most important concepts. Boxes summarize the most important findings. Together, paragraph headings and boxes provide an overview of MDL theory.

It is possible to read this chapter without having read the nontechnical overview of Chapter 1. However, we strongly recommend reading at least Sections 1.3 and 1.4 before embarking on the this chapter.

2.1   Information Theory I: Probabilities and Code Lengths

This section is a miniprimer on information theory, focusing on the relationship between probability distributions and codes. A good understanding of this relationship is essential for a good understanding of MDL. After some preliminaries, Section 2.1.1 introduces prefix codes, the type of codes we work with in MDL. These are related to probability distributions in two ways. In Section 2.1.2 we discuss the first relationship, which is related to the *Kraft inequality*: for every probability mass function P, there exists a code with lengths $-\log P$, and vice versa. Section 2.1.3 discusses the second relationship, related to the *information inequality*, which says that if the data are distributed according to P, then the code with lengths $-\log P$ achieves the minimum expected code length. Throughout the section we give examples relating our findings to our discussion of regularity and compression in Section 1.2 of Chapter 1.

Preliminaries and Notational Conventions — Codes   We use log to denote logarithm to base 2. For real-valued x we use $\lceil x \rceil$ to denote the *ceiling* of x, that is, x rounded up to the nearest integer. We often abbreviate $x_1, \ldots, x_n$ to x^n. Let $\mathcal{X}$ be a finite or countable set. A *code* for $\mathcal{X}$ is defined as a one-to-one mapping from $\mathcal{X}$ to $\cup_{n \geq 1}\{0,1\}^n$. $\cup_{n \geq 1}\{0,1\}^n$ is the set of binary strings (sequences of 0s and 1s) of length 1 or larger. For a given code C, we use $C(x)$ to denote the encoding of x. Every code C induces a function $L_C : \mathcal{X} \to \mathbb{N}$ called the *code length function*. $L_C(x)$ is the number of bits (symbols) needed to encode x using code C.

Our definition of code implies that we only consider *lossless* encoding in MDL[1]: for any description z it is always possible to retrieve the unique x that gave rise to it. More precisely, because the code C must be one-to-one, there is at most one x with $C(x) = z$. Then $x = C^{-1}(z)$, where the inverse C^{-1} of C is sometimes called a 'decoding function' or 'description method'.

Preliminaries and Notational Conventions — Probability   Let P be a probability distribution defined on a finite or countable set $\mathcal{X}$. We use $P(x)$ to denote the probability of x, and we denote the corresponding random variable by X. If P is a function on finite or countable $\mathcal{X}$ such that $\sum_x P(x) < 1$, we call P a *defective* distribution. A defective distribution may be thought of as a probability distribution that puts some of its mass on an imagined outcome that in reality will never appear.

A *probabilistic source* P is a sequence of probability distributions $P^{(1)}, P^{(2)}, \ldots$ on $\mathcal{X}^1, \mathcal{X}^2, \ldots$ such that for all n, $P^{(n)}$ and $P^{(n+1)}$ are *compatible*: $P^{(n)}$ is equal to the 'marginal' distribution of $P^{(n+1)}$ restricted to n outcomes. That is, for all $x^n \in \mathcal{X}^n$, $P^{(n)}(x^n) = \sum_{y \in \mathcal{X}} P^{(n+1)}(x^n, y)$. Whenever this cannot cause any confusion, we write $P(x^n)$ rather than $P^{(n)}(x^n)$. A probabilistic source may be thought of as a probability distribution on infinite sequences.[2] We say that the data are independently and identically distributed *(i.i.d.)* under source P if for each n, $x^n \in \mathcal{X}^n$, $P(x^n) = \prod_{i=1}^n P(x_i)$.

2.1.1   Prefix Codes

In MDL we only work with a subset of all possible codes, the so-called *prefix codes*. A prefix code[3] is a code such that no code word is a prefix of any other code word. For example, let $\mathcal{X} = \{a, b, c\}$. Then the code C_1 defined by $C_1(a) = 0$, $C_1(b) = 10$,

$C_1(c) = 11$ is prefix. The code C_2 with $C_2(a) = 0, C_2(b) = 10$ and $C_2(c) = 01$, while allowing for lossless decoding, is *not* a prefix code since 0 is a prefix of 01. The prefix requirement is natural, and nearly ubiquitous in the data compression literature. We now explain why.

Example 2.1 Suppose we plan to encode a sequence of symbols $(x_1, \ldots, x_n) \in \mathcal{X}^n$. We already designed a code C for the elements in $\mathcal{X}$. The natural thing to do is to encode $(x_1, \ldots, x_n)$ by the concatenated string $C(x_1)C(x_2) \ldots C(x_n)$. In order for this method to succeed for all n, all $(x_1, \ldots, x_n) \in \mathcal{X}^n$, the resulting procedure must define a code, that is, the function $C^{(n)}$ mapping $(x_1, \ldots, x_n)$ to $C(x_1)C(x_2) \ldots C(x_n)$ must be invertible. If it were not, we would have to use some marker such as a comma to separate the code words. We would then really be using a ternary rather than a binary alphabet.

Since we always want to construct codes for sequences rather than single symbols, we only allow codes C such that the extension $C^{(n)}$ defines a code for all n. We say that such codes have 'uniquely decodable extensions'. It is easy to see that (a) every prefix code has uniquely decodable extensions. Conversely, although this is not at all easy to see, it turns out that (b), for every code C with uniquely decodable extensions, there exists a prefix code C_0 such that for all $n, x^n \subset \mathcal{X}^n$, $L_{C^{(n)}}(x^n) = L_{C_0^{(n)}}(x^n)$ [Cover and Thomas 1991]. Since in MDL we are only interested in code *lengths*, and never in actual codes, we can restrict ourselves to prefix codes without loss of generality.

Thus, the restriction to prefix code may also be understood as a means to send concatenated messages while avoiding the need to introduce extra symbols into the alphabet.

Whenever in the sequel we speak of 'code', we really mean 'prefix code'. We call a prefix code C for a set $\mathcal{X}$ *complete* if there exists no other prefix code that compresses at least one x more and no x less then C, that is, if there exists no code C' such that for all x, $L_{C'}(x) \leq L_C(x)$ with strict inequality for at least one x.

2.1.2   The Kraft Inequality — Code Lengths and Probabilities, Part I

In this subsection we relate prefix codes to probability distributions. Essential for understanding the relation is the fact that no matter what code we use, *most sequences cannot be compressed*, as demonstrated by the following example:

Example 2.2 (Compression and Small Subsets: Example 1.2, cont.) In Example 1.2 we featured the following three sequences:

$$00010001000100010001 \ \ldots \ 00010001000100010001000100010001 \tag{2.1}$$
$$01110100110100100110 \ \ldots \ 10101110101110110000101100010 \tag{2.2}$$
$$00011000001010100000 \ \ldots \ 00100010000100000010000110000 \tag{2.3}$$

We showed that (a) the first sequence — an n-fold repetition of 0001 — could be substantially compressed if we use as our code a general-purpose programming language (assuming that valid programs must end with a `halt`-statement or a closing bracket, such codes satisfy the prefix property). We also claimed that (b) the second sequence, n independent outcomes of fair coin tosses, cannot be compressed, and that (c) the third sequence could be compressed to αn bits, with $0 < \alpha < 1$. We are now in a position to prove statement (b): strings which are 'intuitively' random cannot be substantially compressed. Let us take some arbitrary but fixed description method over the data alphabet consisting of the set of all binary sequences of length n. Such a code maps binary strings to binary strings. There are 2^n possible data sequences of length n. Only two of these can be mapped to a description of length 1 (since there are only two binary strings of length 1: '0' and '1'). Similarly, only a subset of at most 2^m sequences can have a description of length m. This means that at most $\sum_{i=1}^{m} 2^m < 2^{m+1}$ data sequences can have a description length $\leq m$. The fraction of data sequences of length n that can be compressed by more than k bits is therefore at most 2^{-k} and as such decreases exponentially in k. If data are generated by n tosses of a fair coin, then all 2^n possibilities for the data are equally probable, so the probability that we can compress the data by more than k bits is smaller than 2^{-k}. For example, the probability that we can compress the data by more than 20 bits is smaller than one in a million.

We note that *after* the data (2.2) have been observed, it is always possible to design a code which uses arbitrarily few bits to encode these data - – the actually observed sequence may be encoded as '1' for example, and no other sequence is assigned a code word. The point is that with a code that has been designed *before* seeing any data, it is virtually impossible to substantially compress randomly generated data.

The example demonstrates that achieving a short description length for the data is equivalent to identifying the data as belonging to a tiny, very *special* subset out of all a priori possible data sequences.

A Most Important Observation   Let $\mathcal{Z}$ be finite or countable. For concreteness, we may take $\mathcal{Z} = \{0, 1\}^n$ for some large n, say $n = 10000$. From Example 2.2 we know that, no matter what code we use to encode values in $\mathcal{Z}$, 'most' outcomes in $\mathcal{Z}$ will not be substantially compressible: at most two outcomes can have description length $1 = -\log 1/2$; at most four outcomes can have length $2 = -\log 1/4$, and so on. Now consider any probability distribution on $\mathcal{Z}$. Since the probabilities $P(z)$ must sum up to 1 ($\sum_z P(z) = 1$), 'most' outcomes in $\mathcal{Z}$ must have small probability in the following sense: at most 2 outcomes can have probability $\geq 1/2$; at most 4 outcomes can have probability $\geq 1/4$; at most 8 can have $\geq 1/8$-th and so on. This suggests an analogy between codes and probability distributions: each code induces a code length function that assigns a number to each z, where most z's are assigned large numbers. Similarly, each distribution assigns a number to each z, where most z's are assigned small numbers.

Probability Mass Functions correspond to Code Length Functions

Let $\mathcal{Z}$ be a finite or countable set and let P be a probability distribution on $\mathcal{Z}$. Then there exists a prefix code C for $\mathcal{Z}$ such that for all $z \in \mathcal{Z}$, $L_C(z) = \lceil -\log P(z) \rceil$. C is called the *code corresponding to P*.

Similarly, let C' be a prefix code for $\mathcal{Z}$. Then there exists a (possibly defective) probability distribution P' such that for all $z \in \mathcal{Z}$, $-\log P'(z) = L_{C'}(z)$. P' is called the *probability distribution corresponding to C'*.

Moreover C' is a *complete prefix code* iff P is proper ($\sum_z P(z) = 1$).

Thus, large probability according to P means small code length according to the code corresponding to P and vice versa.

We are typically concerned with cases where $\mathcal{Z}$ represents sequences of n outcomes; *that is, $\mathcal{Z} = \mathcal{X}^n$ ($n \geq 1$) where $\mathcal{X}$ is the sample space for one observation.*

Figure 2.1   The most important observation of this tutorial.

It turns out that this correspondence can be made mathematically precise by means of the *Kraft inequality* [Cover and Thomas 1991]. We neither precisely state nor prove this inequality; rather, in Figure 2.1 we state an immediate and fundamental consequence: *probability mass functions correspond to code length functions.* The following example illustrates this and at the same time introduces a type of code that will be frequently employed in the sequel:

Example 2.3 (Uniform Distribution Corresponds to Fixed-Length Code)
Suppose $\mathcal{Z}$ has M elements. The uniform distribution P_U assigns probabilities $1/M$ to each element. We can arrive at a code corresponding to P_U as follows. First, order and number the elements in $\mathcal{Z}$ as $0, 1, \ldots, M-1$. Then, for each z with number j, set $C(z)$ to be equal to j represented as a binary number with $\lceil \log M \rceil$ bits. The resulting code has, for all $z \in \mathcal{Z}$, $L_C(z) = \lceil \log M \rceil = \lceil -\log P_U(z) \rceil$. This is a code corresponding to P_U (Figure 2.1). In general, there exist several codes corresponding to P_U, one for each ordering of $\mathcal{Z}$. But all these codes share the same length function $L_U(z) := \lceil -\log P_U(z) \rceil$.; therefore, $L_U(z)$ is the unique code length function corresponding to P_U.

For example, if $M = 4$, $\mathcal{Z} = \{a, b, c, d\}$, we can take $C(a) = 00, C(b) = 01, C(c) = 10, C(d) = 11$ and then $L_U(z) = 2$ for all $z \in \mathcal{Z}$. In general, codes corresponding to uniform distributions assign fixed lengths to each z and are called *fixed-length* codes. To map a nonuniform distribution to a corresponding code, we have to use a more intricate construction [Cover and Thomas 1991].

In practical applications, we almost always deal with probability distributions P and strings x^n such that $P(x^n)$ decreases exponentially in n; for example, this will typically be the case if data are i.i.d., such that $P(x^n) = \prod P(x_i)$. Then $-\log P(x^n)$

New Definition of Code Length Function

In MDL we are **NEVER** concerned with actual encodings; we are only concerned with code *length* functions. The set of all code length functions for finite or countable sample space $\mathcal{Z}$ is defined as:

$$\mathcal{L}_{\mathcal{Z}} = \big\{ L : \mathcal{Z} \rightarrow [0, \infty] \mid \sum_{z \in \mathcal{X}} 2^{-L(z)} \leq 1 \big\}, \qquad (2.4)$$

or equivalently, $\mathcal{L}_{\mathcal{Z}}$ is the set of those functions L on $\mathcal{Z}$ such that there exists a function Q with $\sum_z Q(z) \leq 1$ and for all z, $L(z) = -\log Q(z)$. ($Q(z) = 0$ corresponds to $L(z) = \infty$).

Again, $\mathcal{Z}$ usually represents a sample of n outcomes: $\mathcal{Z} = \mathcal{X}^n$ ($n \geq 1$) where $\mathcal{X}$ is the sample space for one observation.

Figure 2.2   Code lengths are probabilities.

increases linearly in n and the effect of rounding off $-\log P(x^n)$ becomes negligible. Note that the code corresponding to the product distribution of P on $\mathcal{X}^n$ does not have to be the n-fold extension of the code for the original distribution P on $\mathcal{X}$ — if we were to require that, the effect of rounding off would be on the order of n. Instead, we *directly* design a code for the distribution on the larger space $\mathcal{Z} = \mathcal{X}^n$. In this way, the effect of rounding changes the code length by at most 1 bit, which is truly negligible. For this and other[4] reasons, we henceforth simply neglect the integer requirement for code lengths. This simplification allows us to *identify* code length functions and (defective) probability mass functions, such that a short code length corresponds to a high probability and vice versa. Furthermore, as we will see, in MDL we are not interested in the details of actual encodings $C(z)$; we only care about the code lengths $L_C(z)$. It is so useful to think about these as log-probabilities, and so convenient to allow for noninteger values, that we will simply *redefine* prefix code length functions as (defective) probability mass functions that can have noninteger code lengths — see Figure 2.2. The following example illustrates idealized code length functions and at the same time introduces a type of code that will be frequently used in the sequel:

Example 2.4 ('Almost' Uniform Code for the Positive Integers) Suppose we want to encode a number $k \in \{1, 2, \ldots\}$. In Example 2.3, we saw that in order to encode a number between 1 and M, we need $\log M$ bits. What if we cannot determine the maximum M in advance? We cannot just encode k using the uniform code for $\{1, \ldots, k\}$, since the resulting code would not be prefix. So in general, we will need more than $\log k$ bits. Yet there exists a prefix-free code which performs 'almost' as well as $\log k$. The simplest of such codes works as follows. k is described by a code word starting with $\lceil \log k \rceil$ 0s. This is followed by a 1, and then k is encoded using the uniform code for $\{1, \ldots, 2^{\lceil \log k \rceil}\}$. With this protocol, a decoder can first reconstruct $\lceil \log k \rceil$ by counting all 0s before the leftmost 1 in the encoding. He or she then has an upper bound on k and can use this knowledge to decode k itself. This protocol uses less than $2\lceil \log k \rceil + 1$ bits. Working with idealized, noninteger code lengths we can simplify this to $2 \log k + 1$ bits. To see this, consider the function $P(x) = 2^{-2 \log x - 1}$. An easy calculation gives

$$\sum_{x \in 1,2,\ldots} P(x) = \sum_{x \in 1,2,\ldots} 2^{-2\log x - 1} = \frac{1}{2} \sum_{x \in 1,2,\ldots} x^{-2} < \frac{1}{2} + \frac{1}{2} \sum_{x=2,3,\ldots} \frac{1}{x(x-1)} = 1,$$

so that P is a (defective) probability distribution. Thus, by our new definition (Figure 2.2), there exists a prefix code with, for all k, $L(k) = -\log P(k) = 2 \log k + 1$. We call the resulting code the 'simple standard code for the integers'. In Section 2.4 we will see that it is an instance of a so-called *universal* code.

The idea can be refined to lead to codes with lengths $\log k + O(\log \log k)$; the 'best' possible refinement, with code lengths $L(k)$ increasing monotonically but as slowly as possible in k, is known as 'the universal code for the integers' [Rissanen 1983]. However, for our purposes in this tutorial, it is good enough to encode integers k with $2 \log k + 1$ bits.

Example 2.5 (Examples 1.2 and 2.2, cont.) We are now also in a position to prove the third and final claim of Examples 1.2 and 2.2. Consider the three sequences (2.1), (2.2), and (2.3) on page 26 again. It remains to investigate how much the third sequence can be compressed. Assume for concreteness that, before seeing the sequence, we are told that the sequence contains a fraction of 1s equal to $1/5 + \epsilon$ for some small unknown ϵ. By the Kraft inequality, Figure 2.1, for all distributions P there exists some code on sequences of length n such that for all $x^n \in \mathcal{X}^n$, $L(x^n) = \lceil -\log P(x^n) \rceil$. The fact that the fraction of 1s is approximately equal to $1/5$ suggests modeling x^n as independent outcomes of a coin with bias $1/5$th. The corresponding distribution P_0 satisfies

$$-\log P_0(x^n) = \log \left(\frac{1}{5}\right)^{n_{[1]}} \left(\frac{4}{5}\right)^{n_{[0]}} = n\left[-\left(\frac{1}{5} + \epsilon\right) \log \frac{1}{5} - \left(\frac{4}{5} - \epsilon\right) \log \frac{4}{5}\right] =$$

$$n\left[\log 5 - \frac{8}{5} + 2\epsilon\right],$$

where $n_{[j]}$ denotes the number of occurrences of symbol j in x^n. For small enough ϵ, the part between parentheses is smaller than 1, so that, using the code L_0 with lengths $-\log P_0$, the sequence can be encoded using αn bits where α satisfies $0 < \alpha < 1$. Thus, using the code L_0, the sequence can be compressed by a linear amount if we use a specially designed code that assigns short code lengths to sequences with about four times as many 0s than 1s.

We note that *after* the data (2.3) have been observed, it is always possible to design a code which uses arbitrarily few bits to encode x^n — the actually observed sequence may be encoded as '1' for example, and no other sequence is assigned a code word. The point is that with a code that has been designed *before* seeing the actual sequence, given *only* the knowledge that the sequence will contain approximately four times as many 0s as 1s, the sequence is guaranteed to be compressed by an amount linear in n.

Continuous Sample Spaces   How does the correspondence work for continuous-valued $\mathcal{X}$? In this tutorial we only consider P on $\mathcal{X}$ such that P admits a density.[5] Whenever in the following we make a general statement about sample spaces $\mathcal{X}$ and

---

The P that corresponds to L minimizes expected code length

Let P be a distribution on (finite, countable or continuous-valued) $\mathcal{Z}$ and let L be defined by

$$L := \arg\min_{L \in \mathcal{L}_{\mathcal{Z}}} E_P[L(Z)]. \qquad (2.5)$$

Then L exists, is unique, and is identical to the code length function corresponding to P, with lengths $L(z) = -\log P(z)$.

Figure 2.3   The second most important observation of this tutorial.

distributions P, $\mathcal{X}$ may be finite, countable, or any subset of $\mathbb{R}^l$, for any integer $l \geq 1$, and $P(x)$ represents the probability mass function or density of P, as the case may be. In the continuous case, all sums should be read as integrals. The correspondence between probability distributions and codes may be extended to distributions on continuous-valued $\mathcal{X}$: we may think of $L(x^n) := -\log P(x^n)$ as a code length function corresponding to $\mathcal{Z} = \mathcal{X}^n$ encoding the values in $\mathcal{X}^n$ at unit precision; here $P(x^n)$ is the density of x^n according to P. See [Cover and Thomas 1991] for further details.

2.1.3   The Information Inequality — Code Lengths and Probabilities, Part II

In the previous subsection, we established the first fundamental relation between probability distributions and code length functions. We now discuss the second relation, which is nearly as important.

In the correspondence to code length functions, probability distributions were treated as mathematical objects and *nothing else*. That is, if we decide to use a code C to encode our data, this definitely does *not* necessarily mean that we assume our data to be drawn according to the probability distribution corresponding to L: we may have no idea what distribution generates our data, or conceivably, such a distribution may not even exist.[6] Nevertheless, *if* the data are distributed according to some distribution P, *then* the code corresponding to P turns out to be the optimal code to use, in an expected sense – see Figure 2.3. This result may be recast as follows: for all distributions P and Q with $Q \neq P$,

$$E_P[-\log Q(X)] > E_P[-\log P(X)].$$

In this form, the result is known as the *information inequality*. It is easily proved using concavity of the logarithm [Cover and Thomas 1991].

The information inequality says the following: suppose Z is distributed according to P ('generated by P'). Then, among all possible codes for $\mathcal{Z}$, the code with lengths $-\log P(Z)$ 'on average' gives the shortest encodings of outcomes of P. Why should we be interested in the average? The *law of large numbers* [Feller 1968] implies that, for large samples of data distributed according to P, with high P-probability, the code that gives the shortest expected lengths will also give the shortest *actual* code lengths, which is what we are really interested in. This will hold if data are i.i.d., but also more generally if P defines a 'stationary and ergodic' process.

Example 2.6 Let us briefly illustrate this. Let P^*, Q_A, and Q_B be three probability distributions on $\mathcal{X}$, extended to $\mathcal{Z} = \mathcal{X}^n$ by independence. Hence $P^*(x^n) = \prod P^*(x_i)$ and similarly for Q_A and Q_B. Suppose we obtain a sample generated by P^*. Mr. A and Mrs. B both want to encode the sample using as few bits as possible, but neither knows that P^* has actually been used to generate the sample. Mr. A decides to use the code corresponding to distribution Q_A and Mrs. B decides to use the code corresponding to Q_B. Suppose that $E_{P^*}[-\log Q_A(X)] < E_{P^*}[-\log Q_B(X)]$. Then, by the law of large numbers , with P^*-probability 1, $n^{-1}[-\log Q_j(X_1, \ldots, X_n)] \to E_{P^*}[-\log Q_j(X)]$, for both $j \in \{A, B\}$ (note $-\log Q_j(X^n) = -\sum_{i=1}^n \log Q_j(X_i)$). It follows that, with probability 1, Mr. A will need less (linearly in n) bits to encode $X_1, \ldots, X_n$ than Mrs. B.

The qualitative content of this result is not so surprising: in a large sample generated by P, the frequency of each $x \in \mathcal{X}$ will be approximately equal to the probability $P(x)$. In order to obtain a short code length for x^n, we should use a code that assigns a small code length to those symbols in $\mathcal{X}$ with high frequency (probability), and a large code length to those symbols in $\mathcal{X}$ with low frequency (probability).

Summary and Outlook   In this section we introduced (prefix) codes and thoroughly discussed the relation between probabilities and code lengths. We are now almost ready to formalize a simple version of MDL — but first we need to review some concepts of statistics.

2.2   Statistical Preliminaries and Example Models

In the next section we make precise the crude form of MDL informally presented in Section 1.3. We will freely use some convenient statistical concepts which we review in this section; for details see, for example, [Casella and Berger 1990]. We also describe the model class of *Markov chains* of arbitrary order, which we use as our running example. These admit a simpler treatment than the polynomials, to which we return in Section 2.7.

Statistical Preliminaries   A *probabilistic model*[7] $\mathcal{M}$ is a set of probabilistic sources. Typically one uses the word 'model' to denote sources of the same functional form. We often index the elements P of a model $\mathcal{M}$ using some parameter θ. In that case we write P as $P(\cdot \mid \theta)$, and $\mathcal{M}$ as $\mathcal{M} = \{P(\cdot \mid \theta) \mid \theta \in \Theta\}$, for some *parameter space* Θ. If $\mathcal{M}$ can be parameterized by some connected $\Theta \subseteq \mathbb{R}^k$ for some $k \geq 1$ and the mapping $\theta \to P(\cdot \mid \theta)$ is smooth (appropriately defined), we call $\mathcal{M}$ a *parametric model* or *family*. For example, the model $\mathcal{M}$ of all normal distributions on $\mathcal{X} = \mathbb{R}$ is a parametric model that can be parameterized by $\theta = (\mu, \sigma^2)$ where

μ is the mean and σ^2 is the variance of the distribution indexed by θ. The family of all Markov chains of all orders is a model, but not a parametric model. We call a model $\mathcal{M}$ an *i.i.d. model* if, according to all $P \in \mathcal{M}$, $X_1, X_2, \ldots$ are i.i.d. We call $\mathcal{M}$ *k-dimensional* if k is the smallest integer k so that $\mathcal{M}$ can be smoothly parameterized by some $\Theta \subseteq \mathbb{R}^k$.

For a given model $\mathcal{M}$ and sample $D = x^n$, the *maximum likelihood* (ML) P is the $P \in \mathcal{M}$ maximizing $P(x^n)$. For a parametric model with parameter space Θ, the maximum likelihood *estimator* $\hat{\theta}$ is the function that, for each n, maps x^n to the $\theta \in \Theta$ that maximizes the likelihood $P(x^n \mid \theta)$. The ML estimator may be viewed as a 'learning algorithm.' This is a procedure that, when input a sample x^n of arbitrary length, outputs a parameter or hypothesis $P_n \in \mathcal{M}$. We say a learning algorithm is *consistent* relative to distance measure d if for all $P^* \in \mathcal{M}$, if data are distributed according to P^*, then the output P_n converges to P^* in the sense that $d(P^*, P_n) \to 0$ with P^*-probability 1. Thus, if P^* is the 'true' state of nature, then given enough data, the learning algorithm will learn a good approximation of P^* with very high probability.

Example 2.7 (Markov and Bernoulli Models)   Recall that a kth-order Markov chain on $\mathcal{X} = \{0, 1\}$ is a probabilistic source such that for every $n > k$,

$$P(X_n = 1 \mid X_{n-1} = x_{n-1}, \ldots, X_{n-k} = x_{n-k}) = $$
$$P(X_n = 1 \mid X_{n-1} = x_{n-1}, \ldots, X_{n-k} = x_{n-k}, \ldots, X_1 = x_1). \quad (2.6)$$

That is, the probability distribution on X_n depends only on the k symbols preceding n. Thus, there are 2^k possible distributions of X_n, and each such distribution is identified with a *state* of the Markov chain. To fully identify the chain, we also need to specify the *starting state*, defining the first k outcomes $X_1, \ldots, X_k$. The kth-order *Markov model* is the set of all kth-order Markov chains, that is, all sources satisfying (2.6) equipped with a starting state.

The special case of the 0th-order Markov model is the *Bernoulli* or *biased coin* model, which we denote by $\mathcal{B}^{(0)}$. We can parameterize the Bernoulli model by a parameter $\theta \in [0, 1]$ representing the probability of observing a 1. Thus, $\mathcal{B}^{(0)} = \{P(\cdot \mid \theta) \mid \theta \in [0, 1]\}$, with $P(x^n \mid \theta)$ by definition equal to

$$P(x^n \mid \theta) = \prod_{i=1}^{n} P(x_i \mid \theta) = \theta^{n_{[1]}} (1 - \theta)^{n_{[0]}},$$

where $n_{[1]}$ stands for the number of 1s, and $n_{[0]}$ for the number of 0s in the sample. Note that the Bernoulli model is i.i.d. The log-likelihood is given by

$$\log P(x^n \mid \theta) = n_{[1]} \log \theta + n_{[0]} \log(1 - \theta). \quad (2.7)$$

Taking the derivative of (2.7) with respect to θ, we see that for fixed x^n, the log-likelihood is maximized by setting the probability of 1 equal to the observed frequency. Since the logarithm is a monotonically increasing function, the likelihood is maximized at the same value: the ML estimator is given by $\hat{\theta}(x^n) = n_{[1]}/n$.

Similarly, the first-order Markov model $\mathcal{B}^{(1)}$ can be parameterized by a vector $\theta = (\theta_{[1|0]}, \theta_{[1|1]}) \in [0,1]^2$ together with a starting state in $\{0,1\}$. Here $\theta_{[1|j]}$ represents the probability of observing a 1 following the symbol j. The log-likelihood is given by

$$\log P(x^n \mid \theta) = n_{[1|1]} \log \theta_{[1|1]} + n_{[0|1]} \log(1-\theta_{[1|1]}) + n_{[1|0]} \log \theta_{[1|0]} + n_{[0|0]} \log(1-\theta_{[1|0]}),$$

$n_{[i|j]}$ denoting the number of times outcome i is observed in state (previous outcome) j. This is maximized by setting $\hat{\theta} = (\hat{\theta}_{[1|0]}, \hat{\theta}_{[1|1]})$, with $\hat{\theta}_{[i|j]} = n_{[i|j]} = n_{[ji]}/n_{[j]}$ set to the conditional frequency of i preceded by j. In general, a kth-order Markov chain has 2^k parameters and the corresponding likelihood is maximized by setting the parameter $\theta_{[i|j]}$ equal to the number of times i was observed in state j divided by the number of times the chain was in state j.

Suppose now we are given data $D = x^n$ and we want to find the Markov chain that best explains D. Since we do not want to restrict ourselves to chains of fixed order, we run a large risk of overfitting: simply picking, among all Markov chains of each order, the ML Markov chain that maximizes the probability of the data, we typically end up with a chain of order $n-1$ with starting state given by the sequence $x_1, \ldots, x_{n-1}$, and $P(X_n = x_n \mid X^{n-1} = x^{n-1}) = 1$. Such a chain will assign probability 1 to x^n. Below we show that MDL makes a more reasonable choice.

2.3   Crude MDL

Based on the information-theoretic (Section 2.1) and statistical (Section 2.2) preliminaries discussed before, we now formalize a first, crude version of MDL.

Let $\mathcal{M}$ be a class of probabilistic sources (not necessarily Markov chains). Suppose we observe a sample $D = (x_1, \ldots, x_n) \in \mathcal{X}^n$. Recall 'the crude[8] two-part code MDL principle' from Chapter 1, Section 1.3, page 9:

Crude,[9] Two-Part Version of MDL principle
Let $\mathcal{H}^{(1)}, \mathcal{H}^{(2)}, \ldots$ be a set of candidate models. The best point hypothesis $H \in \mathcal{H}^{(1)} \cup \mathcal{H}^{(2)} \cup \ldots$ to explain data D is the one which minimizes the sum $L(H) + L(D|H)$, where

- $L(H)$ is the length, in bits, of the description of the hypothesis; and

- $L(D|H)$ is the length, in bits, of the description of the data when encoded with the help of the hypothesis.

The best *model* to explain D is the smallest model containing the selected H.

In this section, we implement this crude MDL principle by giving a precise definition of the terms $L(H)$ and $L(D|H)$. To make the first term precise, we must design a code C_1 for encoding hypotheses H such that $L(H) = L_{C_1}(H)$. For the second term, we must design a set of codes $C_{2,H}$ (one for each $H \in \mathcal{M}$) such that for all $D \in \mathcal{X}^n$, $L(D|H) = L_{C_{2,H}}(D)$. We start by describing the codes $C_{2,H}$.

2.3.1 Description Length of Data Given Hypothesis

Given a sample of size n, each hypothesis H may be viewed as a probability distribution on $\mathcal{X}^n$. We denote the corresponding probability mass function by $P(\cdot \mid H)$. We need to associate with $P(\cdot \mid H)$ a code, or really, just a code length function for $\mathcal{X}^n$. We already know that there exists a code with length function L such that for all $x^n \in \mathcal{X}^n$, $L(x^n) = -\log P(x^n \mid H)$. This is the code that we will pick. It is a natural choice for two reasons:

1. With this choice, the code length $L(x^n \mid H)$ is equal to minus the log-likelihood of x^n according to H, which is a standard statistical notion of 'goodness-of-fit'.

2. *If the data turn out to be distributed according to P, then* the code $L(\cdot \mid H)$ will uniquely minimize the expected code length (Section 2.1).

The second item implies that our choice is, in a sense, the only reasonable choice.[10] To see this, suppose $\mathcal{M}$ is a finite i.i.d. model containing, say, M distributions. Suppose we assign an arbitrary but finite code length $L(H)$ to each $H \in \mathcal{M}$. Suppose $X_1, X_2, \ldots$ are actually i.i.d. according to some 'true' $H^* \in \mathcal{M}$. By the reasoning of Example 2.6, we see that MDL will select the true distribution $P(\cdot \mid H^*)$ for all large n, with probability 1. This means that MDL is *consistent* for finite $\mathcal{M}$. If we were to assign codes to distributions in some other manner not satisfying $L(D \mid H) = -\log P(D \mid H)$, then there would exist distributions $P(\cdot \mid H)$ such that $L(D|H) \neq -\log P(D|H)$. But by Figure 2.1, there *must* be some distribution $P(\cdot \mid H')$ with $L(\cdot|H) = -\log P(\cdot \mid H')$. Now let $\mathcal{M} = \{H, H'\}$ and suppose data are distributed according to $P(\cdot \mid H')$. Then, by the reasoning of Example 2.6, MDL would select H rather than H' for all large n! Thus, MDL would be inconsistent even in this simplest of all imaginable cases — there would then be no hope for good performance in the considerably more complex situations we intend to use it for.[11]

2.3.2 Description Length of Hypothesis

In its weakest and crudest form, the two-part code MDL principle does not give any guidelines as to how to encode hypotheses (probability distributions). Every code for encoding hypotheses is allowed, *as long as such a code does not change with the sample size n*.

To see the danger in allowing codes to depend on n, consider the Markov chain example: if we were allowed to use different codes for different n, we could use, for each n, a code assigning a uniform distribution to all Markov chains of order $n - 1$ with all parameters equal to 0 or 1. Since there are only a finite number (2^{n-1}) of these, this is possible. But then, for each n, $x^n \in \mathcal{X}^n$, MDL would select the ML Markov chain of order $n - 1$. Thus, MDL would coincide with ML and, no matter how large n, we would overfit.

Consistency of Two-Part MDL   Remarkably, if we fix an arbitrary code for all hypotheses, identical for all sample sizes n, this is sufficient to make MDL consistent[12] for a wide variety of models, including the Markov chains. For example, let L be the length function corresponding to some code for the Markov chains. Suppose some Markov chain P^* generates the data such that $L(P^*) < \infty$ under our coding scheme. Then, broadly speaking, for every P^* of every order, with probability 1 there exists some n_0 such that for all samples larger than n_0, two-part MDL will select P^* — here n_0 may depend on P^* and L.

While this result indicates that MDL may be doing something sensible, it certainly does not justify the use of arbitrary codes - different codes will lead to preferences of different hypotheses, and it is not at all clear how a code should be designed that leads to good inferences with small, practically relevant sample sizes.

Barron and Cover [1991] have developed a precise theory of how to design codes C_1 in a 'clever' way, anticipating the developments of 'refined MDL'. Practitioners have often simply used 'reasonable' coding schemes, based on the following idea. Usually there exists some 'natural' decomposition of the models under consideration, $\mathcal{M} = \bigcup_{k>0} \mathcal{M}^{(k)}$ where the dimension of $\mathcal{M}^{(k)}$ grows with k but is not necessarily equal to k. In the Markov chain example, we have $\mathcal{B} = \bigcup \mathcal{B}^{(k)}$ where $\mathcal{B}^{(k)}$ is the kth-order, 2^k-parameter Markov model. Then *within* each submodel $\mathcal{M}^{(k)}$, we may use a fixed-length code for $\theta \in \Theta^{(k)}$. Since the set $\Theta^{(k)}$ is typically a continuum, we somehow need to discretize it to achieve this.

Example 2.8 (a Very Crude Code for the Markov Chains) We can describe a Markov chain of order k by first describing k, and then describing a parameter vector $\theta \in [0,1]^{k'}$ with $k' = 2^k$. We describe k using our simple code for the integers (Example 2.4). This takes $2 \log k + 1$ bits. We now have to describe the k'-component parameter vector. We saw in Example 2.7 that for any x^n, the best-fitting (ML) kth-order Markov chain can be identified with k' frequencies. It is not hard to see that these frequencies are uniquely determined by the counts $n_{[1|0\ldots00]}, n_{[1|0\ldots01]}, \ldots, n_{[1|1\ldots11]}$. Each individual count must be in the $(n+1)$-element set $\{0, 1, \ldots, n\}$. Since we assume n is given in advance,[13] we may use a simple fixed-length code to encode this count, taking $\log(n+1)$ bits (Example 2.3). Thus, once k is fixed, we can describe such a Markov chain by a uniform code using $k' \log(n+1)$ bits. With the code just defined we get for any $P \in \mathcal{B}$, indexed by parameter $\Theta^{(k)}$,

$$L(P) = L(k, \Theta^{(k)}) = 2 \log k + 1 + k \log(n+1),$$

so that with these codes, MDL tells us to pick the $k, \theta^{(k)}$ minimizing

$$L(k, \theta^{(k)}) + L(D \mid k, \theta^{(k)}) = 2 \log k + 1 + k \log(n+1) - \log P(D \mid k, \theta^{(k)}), \quad (2.8)$$

where the $\theta^{(k)}$ that is chosen will be equal to the ML estimator for $\mathcal{M}^{(k)}$.

Why (Not) This Code? We may ask two questions about this code. First, why did we only reserve code words for θ that are potentially ML estimators for the given data? The reason is that, given $k' = 2^k$, the code length $L(D \mid k, \theta^{(k)})$ is minimized by $\hat{\theta}^{(k)}(D)$, the ML estimator within $\theta^{(k)}$. Reserving code words for $\theta \in [0,1]^{k'}$ that cannot be ML estimates would only serve to lengthen $L(D \mid k, \theta^{(k)})$ and can never shorten $L(k, \theta^{(k)})$. Thus, the total description length needed to encode D will increase. Since our stated goal is to minimize description lengths, this is undesirable.

However, by the same logic we may also ask whether we have not reserved *too many* code words for $\theta \in [0,1]^{k'}$. And in fact, it turns out that we have: the distance between two adjacent ML estimators is $O(1/n)$. Indeed, if we had used a coarser precision, only reserving code words for parameters with distances $O(1/\sqrt{n})$, we would obtain smaller code lengths — (2.8) would become

$$L(k, \theta^{(k)}) + L(D \mid k, \theta^{(k)}) = -\log P(D \mid k, \hat{\theta}^{(k)}) + \frac{k}{2}\log n + c_k, \qquad (2.9)$$

where c_k is a small constant depending on k, but not n [Barron and Cover 1991]. In Section 2.5 we show that (2.9) is in some sense 'optimal'.

The Good News and the Bad News   The good news is (1) we have found a principled, nonarbitrary manner to encode data D given a probability distribution H, namely, to use the code with lengths $-\log P(D \mid H)$; and (2), asymptotically, *any* code for hypotheses will lead to a consistent criterion. The bad news is that we have not found clear guidelines to design codes for hypotheses $H \in \mathcal{M}$. We found some intuitively reasonable codes for Markov chains, and we then reasoned that these could be somewhat 'improved', but what is conspicuously lacking is a sound theoretical *principle* for designing and improving codes.

We take the good news to mean that our idea may be worth pursuing further. We take the bad news to mean that we do have to modify or extend the idea to get a meaningful, nonarbitrary and practically relevant model selection method. Such an extension was already suggested in Rissanen's early works [Rissanen 1978, 1983] and refined by Barron and Cover [1991]. However, in these works, the principle was still restricted to two-part codes. To get a fully satisfactory solution, we need to move to 'universal codes', of which the two-part codes are merely a special case.

2.4   Information Theory II: Universal Codes and Models

We have just indicated why the two-part code formulation of MDL needs to be refined. It turns out that the key concept we need is that of *universal coding*. Broadly speaking, a code $\bar{L}$ that is universal relative to a set of candidate codes $\mathcal{L}$ allows us to compress every sequence x^n almost as well as the code in $\mathcal{L}$ that compresses that particular sequence most. Two-part codes are universal (Section 2.4.1), but there exist other universal codes such as the Bayesian mixture code (Section 2.4.2) and the normalized maximum likelihood (NML) code (Section 2.4.3). We also discuss *universal models*, which are just the probability distributions corresponding to universal codes. In this section, we are not concerned with learning from data; we only care about compressing data as much as possible. We reconnect our findings with learning in Section 2.5.

Coding as Communication Like many other topics in coding, 'universal coding' can best be explained if we think of descriptions as *messages*: we can always view a description as a message that some sender or *encoder*, say Mr. A, sends to some receiver or *decoder*, say Mrs. B. Before sending any messages, Mr. A and Mrs. B meet in person. They agree on the set of messages that A may send to B. Typically, this will be the set $\mathcal{X}^n$ of sequences $x_1, \ldots, x_n$, where each x_i is an outcome in the space $\mathcal{X}$. They also agree upon a (prefix) code that will be used by A to send his messages to B. Once this has been done, A and B go back to their respective homes and A sends his messages to B in the form of binary strings. The unique decodability property of prefix codes implies that, when B receives a message, she should always be able to decode it in a unique manner.

Universal Coding Suppose our encoder/sender is about to observe a sequence $x^n \in \mathcal{X}^n$ which he plans to compress as much as possible. Equivalently, he wants to send an encoded version of x^n to the receiver using as few bits as possible. Sender and receiver have a set of *candidate codes* $\mathcal{L}$ for $\mathcal{X}^n$ available.[14] They believe or hope that one of these codes will allow for substantial compression of x^n. However, they must decide on a code for $\mathcal{X}^n$ before sender observes the actual x^n, and they do not know *which* code in $\mathcal{L}$ will lead to good compression of the actual x^n. What is the best thing they can do? They may be tempted to try the following: upon seeing x^n, sender simply encodes/sends x^n using the $L \in \mathcal{L}$ that minimizes $L(x^n)$ among all $L \in \mathcal{L}$. But this naive scheme will not work: since decoder/receiver does not know what x^n has been sent before decoding the message, she does not know which of the codes in $\mathcal{L}$ has been used by sender/encoder. Therefore, decoder cannot decode the message: the resulting protocol does not constitute a uniquely decodable, let alone a prefix code. Indeed, as we show below, in general *no* code $\bar{L}$ exists such that for all $x^n \in \mathcal{X}^n$, $\bar{L}(x^n) \le \min_{L \in \mathcal{L}} L(x^n)$: in words, there exists no code which, no matter what x^n is, always mimics the best code for x^n.

Example 2.9 Suppose we think that our sequence can be reasonably well compressed by a code corresponding to some biased coin model. For simplicity, we restrict ourselves to a finite number of such models. Thus, let $\mathcal{L} = \{L_1, \ldots, L_9\}$ where L_1 is the code length function corresponding to the Bernoulli model $P(\cdot \mid \theta)$ with parameter $\theta = 0.1$, L_2 corresponds to $\theta = 0.2$ and so on. From (2.7) we see that, for example,

$$L_8(x^n) = -\log P(x^n|0.8) = -n_{[0]} \log 0.2 - n_{[1]} \log 0.8$$
$$L_9(x^n) = -\log P(x^n|0.9) = -n_{[0]} \log 0.1 - n_{[1]} \log 0.9.$$

Both $L_8(x^n)$ and $L_9(x^n)$ are linearly increasing in the number of 1s in x^n. However, if the frequency n_1/n is approximately 0.8, then $\min_{L \in \mathcal{L}} L(x^n)$ will be achieved for L_8. If $n_1/n \approx 0.9$ then $\min_{L \in \mathcal{L}} L(x^n)$ is achieved for L_9. More generally, if $n_1/n \approx j/10$, then L_j achieves the minimum.[15] We would like to send x^n using a code $\bar{L}$ such that for all x^n, we need at most $\hat{L}(x^n)$ bits, where $\hat{L}(x^n)$ is defined as $\hat{L}(x^n) := \min_{L \in \mathcal{L}} L(x^n)$. Since $-\log$ is monotonically decreasing, $\hat{L}(x^n) = -\log P(x^n \mid \hat{\theta}(x^n))$. We already gave an informal explanation as to why a code with lengths $\hat{L}$ does not exist. We can now explain this more formally as follows: if such a code were to exist, it would correspond to some distribution $\bar{P}$. Then we would have for all x^n, $\bar{L}(x^n) = -\log \bar{P}(x^n)$. But, by definition, for all $x^n \in \mathcal{X}^n$, $\bar{L}(x^n) \leq \hat{L}(x^n) = -\log P(x^n|\hat{\theta}(x^n))$ where $\hat{\theta}(x^n) \in \{0.1, \ldots, 0.9\}$. Thus we get for all x^n, $-\log \bar{P}(x^n) \leq -\log P(x^n \mid \hat{\theta}(x^n))$ or $\bar{P}(x^n) \geq P(x^n \mid \hat{\theta}(x^n))$, so that, since $|\mathcal{L}| > 1$,

$$\sum_{x^n} \bar{P}(x^n) \geq \sum_{x^n} P(x^n \mid \hat{\theta}(x^n)) = \sum_{x^n} \max_{\theta} P(x^n \mid \theta) > 1, \qquad (2.10)$$

where the last inequality follows because for any two θ_1, θ_2 with $\theta_1 \neq \theta_2$, there is at least one x^n with $P(x^n \mid \theta_1) > P(x^n \mid \theta_2)$. Equation (2.10) says that $\bar{P}$ is not a probability distribution. It follows that $\bar{L}$ cannot be a code length function. The argument can be extended beyond the Bernoulli model of the example above: as long as $|\mathcal{L}| > 1$, and all codes in $\mathcal{L}$ correspond to a nondefective distribution, (2.10) must still hold, so that there exists no code $\bar{L}$ with $\bar{L}(x^n) = \hat{L}(x^n)$ for all x^n. The underlying reason that no such code exists is the fact that probabilities must sum up to something ≤ 1; or equivalently, that there exists no coding scheme assigning short code words to many different messages (see Example 2.2).

Since there exists no code which, no matter what x^n is, always mimics the best code for x^n, it may make sense to look for the next best thing: does there exist a code which, for all $x^n \in \mathcal{X}^n$, is 'nearly' (in some sense) as good as $\hat{L}(x^n)$? It turns out that in many cases, the answer is *yes*: there typically exist codes $\bar{L}$ such that no matter what x^n arrives, $\bar{L}(x^n)$ is not much larger than $\hat{L}(x^n)$, which may be viewed as the code that is best 'with hindsight' (i.e., after seeing x^n). Intuitively, codes which satisfy this property are called universal codes — a more precise definition follows below. The first (but perhaps not foremost) example of a universal code is the *two-part code* that we have encountered in Section 2.3.

2.4.1   Two-Part Codes as Simple Universal Codes

Example 2.10 (Finite $\mathcal{L}$) Let $\mathcal{L}$ be as in Example 2.9. We can devise a code $\bar{L}_{2\text{-p}}$ for all $x^n \in \mathcal{X}^n$ as follows: to encode x^n, we first encode the $j \in \{1, \ldots, 9\}$ such that $L_j(x^n) = \min_{L \in \mathcal{L}} L(x^n)$, using a uniform code. This takes $\log 9$ bits. We then encode x^n itself using the code indexed by j. This takes L_j bits. Note that in contrast to the naive scheme discussed in Example 2.9, the resulting scheme properly defines a prefix code: a decoder can decode x^n by first decoding j, and then decoding x^n using L_j. Thus, for *every possible* $x^n \in \mathcal{X}^n$, we obtain

$$\bar{L}_{2\text{-p}}(x^n) = \min_{L \in \mathcal{L}} L(x^n) + \log 9.$$

For all $L \in \mathcal{L}$, $\min_{x^n} L(x^n)$ grows linearly in n: $\min_{\theta, x^n} -\log P(x^n \mid \theta) = -n \log 0.9 \approx 0.15n$. Unless n is *very* small, no matter what x^n arises, the extra number of bits we need using $\bar{L}_{\text{2-p}}$ compared to $\hat{L}(x^n)$ is negligible.

More generally, let $\mathcal{L} = \{L_1, \ldots, L_M\}$ where M can be arbitrarily large, and the L_j can be any code length functions we like; they do not necessarily represent Bernoulli distributions anymore. By the reasoning of Example 2.10, there exists a (two-part) code such that for *all* $x^n \in \mathcal{X}^n$,

$$\bar{L}_{\text{2-p}}(x^n) = \min_{L \in \mathcal{L}} L(x^n) + \log M. \qquad (2.11)$$

In most applications $\min L(x^n)$ grows linearly in n, and we see from (2.11) that, as soon as n becomes substantially larger than $\log M$, the relative difference in performance between our universal code and $\hat{L}(x^n)$ becomes negligible. In general, we do not always want to use a uniform code for the elements in $\mathcal{L}$; note that any arbitrary code on $\mathcal{L}$ will give us an analogue of (2.11), but with a worst-case overhead larger than $\log M$ — corresponding to the largest code length of any of the elements in $\mathcal{L}$.

Example 2.11 (Countably Infinite $\mathcal{L}$) We can also construct a two-part code for arbitrary countably infinite sets of codes $\mathcal{L} = \{L_1, L_2, \ldots\}$: we first encode some k using our simple code for the integers (Example 2.4). With this code we need $2 \log k + 1$ bits to encode integer k. We then encode x^n using the code L_k. $\bar{L}_{\text{2-p}}$ is now defined as the code we get if, for any x^n, we encode x^n using the L_k minimizing the total two-part description length $2 \log k + 1 + L_k(x^n)$.

In contrast to the case of finite $\mathcal{L}$, there does *not* exist a constant c anymore such that for all $n, x^n \in \mathcal{X}^n$, $\bar{L}_{\text{2-p}}(x^n) \leq \inf_{L \in \mathcal{L}} L(x^n) + c$. Instead we have the following weaker, but still remarkable property: for all k, all n, all x^n, $\bar{L}_{\text{2-p}}(x^n) \leq L_k(x^n) + 2 \log k + 1$, so that also,

$$\bar{L}_{\text{2-p}}(x^n) \leq \inf_{L \in \{L_1, \ldots, L_k\}} L(x^n) + 2 \log k + 1.$$

For any k, as n grows larger, the code $\bar{L}_{\text{2-p}}$ starts to mimic whatever $L \in \{L_1, \ldots, L_k\}$ compresses the data most. However, the larger k, the larger n has to be before this happens.

2.4.2   From Universal Codes to Universal Models

Instead of postulating a set of candidate codes $\mathcal{L}$, we may equivalently postulate a set $\mathcal{M}$ of candidate probabilistic sources, such that $\mathcal{L}$ is the set of codes corresponding to $\mathcal{M}$. We already implicitly did this in Example 2.9.

The reasoning is now as follows: we think that one of the $P \in \mathcal{M}$ will assign a high likelihood to the data to be observed. Therefore we would like to design a code that, for all x^n we might observe, performs essentially as well as the code corresponding to the best-fitting, maximum likelihood (minimum code length) $P \in \mathcal{M}$ for x^n.

Similarly, we can think of universal codes such as the two-part code in terms of the (possibly defective; see Section 2.1 and Figure 2.1)) *distributions* corresponding to it. Such distributions corresponding to universal codes are called *universal models*. The use of mapping universal codes back to distributions is illustrated by the *Bayesian universal model* which we now introduce.

Universal Model: Twice Misleading Terminology The words 'universal' and 'model' are somewhat of a misnomer: first, these codes/models are only 'universal' relative to a restricted 'universe' $\mathcal{M}$. Second, the use of the word 'model' will be very confusing to statisticians, who (as we also do in this chapter) call a family of distributions such as $\mathcal{M}$ a 'model'. But the phrase originates from information theory, where a 'model' often refers to a single distribution rather than a family. Thus, a 'universal model' is a single distribution, representing a statistical 'model' $\mathcal{M}$.

Example 2.12 (Bayesian Universal Model) Let $\mathcal{M}$ be a finite or countable set of probabilistic sources, parameterized by some parameter set Θ. Let W be a distribution on Θ. Adopting terminology from Bayesian statistics, W is usually called a *prior distribution*. We can construct a new probabilistic source $\bar{P}_{\text{Bayes}}$ by taking a weighted (according to W) average or mixture over the distributions in $\mathcal{M}$. That is, we define for all n, $x^n \in \mathcal{X}$,

$$\bar{P}_{\text{Bayes}}(x^n) := \sum_{\theta \in \Theta} P(x^n \mid \theta)W(\theta). \tag{2.12}$$

It is easy to check that $\bar{P}_{\text{Bayes}}$ is a probabilistic source according to our definition. In case Θ is continuous, the sum gets replaced by an integral, but otherwise nothing changes in the definition. In Bayesian statistics, $\bar{P}_{\text{Bayes}}$ is called the *Bayesian marginal likelihood* or *Bayesian mixture* [Bernardo and Smith 1994]. To see that $\bar{P}_{\text{Bayes}}$ is a universal model, note that for all $\theta_0 \in \Theta$,

$$-\log \bar{P}_{\text{Bayes}}(x^n) := -\log \sum_{\theta \in \Theta} P(x^n \mid \theta)W(\theta) \leq -\log P(x^n \mid \theta_0) + c_{\theta_0}, \tag{2.13}$$

where the inequality follows because a sum is at least as large as each of its terms, and $c_\theta = -\log W(\theta)$ depends on θ but not on n. Thus, $\bar{P}_{\text{Bayes}}$ is a universal model or equivalently, the code with lengths $-\log \bar{P}_{\text{Bayes}}$ is a universal code. Note that the derivation in (2.13) only works if Θ is finite or countable; the case of continuous Θ is treated in Section 2.5.

Bayes is Better than Two-Part The Bayesian model is in a sense superior to the two-part code. Namely, in the two-part code we first encode an element of $\mathcal{M}$ or its parameter set Θ using some code L_0. Such a code must correspond to some 'prior' distribution W on $\mathcal{M}$ so that the two-part code gives code lengths

$$\bar{L}_{\text{2-p}}(x^n) = \min_{\theta \in \Theta} -\log P(x^n|\theta) - \log W(\theta), \tag{2.14}$$

where W depends on the specific code L_0 that was used. Using the Bayes code with prior W, we get, as in (2.13),

$$-\log \bar{P}_{\text{Bayes}}(x^n) = -\log \sum_{\theta \in \Theta} P(x^n \mid \theta) W(\theta) \leq \min_{\theta \in \Theta} -\log P(x^n | \theta) - \log W(\theta).$$

The inequality becomes strict whenever $P(x^n|\theta) > 0$ for more than one value of θ. Comparing to (2.14), we see that in general the Bayesian code is preferable over the two-part code: for all x^n it never assigns code lengths larger than $\bar{L}_{\text{2-p}}(x^n)$, and in many cases it assigns strictly shorter code lengths for some x^n. But this raises two important issues: (1) What exactly do we mean by 'better' anyway? (2) Can we say that 'some prior distributions are better than others'? These questions are answered below.

2.4.3   NML as an *Optimal Universal Model*

We can measure the performance of universal models relative to a set of candidate sources $\mathcal{M}$ using the *regret*:

Definition 2.13 (Regret) *Let $\mathcal{M}$ be a class of probabilistic sources. Let $\bar{P}$ be a probability distribution on $\mathcal{X}^n$ ($\bar{P}$ is not necessarily in $\mathcal{M}$). For given x^n, the* regret *of $\bar{P}$ relative to $\mathcal{M}$ is defined as*

$$-\log \bar{P}(x^n) - \min_{P \in \mathcal{M}} \{-\log P(x^n)\}. \tag{2.15}$$

The regret of $\bar{P}$ relative to $\mathcal{M}$ for x^n is the additional number of bits needed to encode x^n using the code/distribution $\bar{P}$, as compared to the number of bits that had been needed if we had used code/distribution in $\mathcal{M}$ that was *optimal ('best-fitting') with hindsight*. For simplicity, from now on we tacitly assume that for all the models $\mathcal{M}$ we work with, there is a single $\hat{\theta}(x^n)$ maximizing the likelihood for every $x^n \in \mathcal{X}^n$. In that case (2.15) simplifies to

$$-\log \bar{P}(x^n) - \{-\log P(x^n \mid \hat{\theta}(x^n))\}.$$

We would like to measure the quality of a universal model $\bar{P}$ in terms of its regret. However, $\bar{P}$ may have small (even < 0) regret for some x^n, and very large regret for other x^n. We must somehow find a measure of quality that takes into account *all* $x^n \in \mathcal{X}^n$. We take a worst-case approach, and look for universal models $\bar{P}$ with small *worst-case* regret, where the worst case is over all sequences. Formally, the *maximum* or *worst-case regret* of $\bar{P}$ relative to $\mathcal{M}$ is defined as

$$\mathcal{R}_{\max}(\bar{P}) := \max_{x^n \in \mathcal{X}^n} \left\{-\log \bar{P}(x^n) - \{-\log P(x^n \mid \hat{\theta}(x^n))\}\right\}.$$

If we use $\mathcal{R}_{\max}$ as our quality measure, then the 'optimal' universal model relative to $\mathcal{M}$, for given sample size n, is the distribution minimizing

$$\min_{\bar{P}} \mathcal{R}_{\max}(\bar{P}) = \min_{\bar{P}} \max_{x^n \in \mathcal{X}^n} \left\{-\log \bar{P}(x^n) - \{-\log P(x^n \mid \hat{\theta}(x^n))\}\right\}, \tag{2.16}$$

where the minimum is over *all* defective distributions on $\mathcal{X}^n$. The $\bar{P}$ minimizing (2.16) corresponds to the code minimizing the additional number of bits compared to code in $\mathcal{M}$ that is best in hindsight in the worst case over all possible x^n. It turns out that we can solve for $\bar{P}$ in (2.16). To this end, we first define the *complexity* of a given model $\mathcal{M}$ as

$$\mathbf{COMP}_n(\mathcal{M}) := \log \sum_{x^n \in \mathcal{X}^n} P(x^n \mid \hat{\theta}(x^n)). \qquad (2.17)$$

This quantity plays a fundamental role in refined MDL, Section 2.5. To get a first idea of why $\mathbf{COMP}_n$ is called model complexity, note that the more sequences x^n with large $P(x^n \mid \hat{\theta}(x^n))$, the larger $\mathbf{COMP}_n(\mathcal{M})$. In other words, the more sequences that can be fit well by an element of $\mathcal{M}$, the larger $\mathcal{M}$'s complexity.

Proposition 2.14 (Shtarkov 1987) *Suppose that* $\mathbf{COMP}_n(\mathcal{M})$ *is finite. Then the minimax regret (2.16) is uniquely achieved for the distribution* $\bar{P}_{\mathrm{nml}}$ *given by*

$$\bar{P}_{\mathrm{nml}}(x^n) := \frac{P(x^n \mid \hat{\theta}(x^n))}{\sum_{y^n \in \mathcal{X}^n} P(y^n \mid \hat{\theta}(y^n))}. \qquad (2.18)$$

The distribution $\bar{P}_{\mathrm{nml}}$ is known as the *Shtarkov distribution* or the *normalized maximum likelihood* (NML) distribution.

Proof   Plug in $\bar{P}_{\mathrm{nml}}$ in (2.16) and notice that for all $x^n \in \mathcal{X}^n$,

$$-\log \bar{P}(x^n) - \{-\log P(x^n \mid \hat{\theta}(x^n))\} = \mathcal{R}_{\max}(\bar{P}) = \mathbf{COMP}_n(\mathcal{M}), \qquad (2.19)$$

so that $\bar{P}_{\mathrm{nml}}$ achieves the *same* regret, equal to $\mathbf{COMP}_n(\mathcal{M})$, *no matter what* x^n *actually obtains*. Since every distribution P on $\mathcal{X}^n$ with $P \neq \bar{P}_{\mathrm{nml}}$ must satisfy $P(z^n) < \bar{P}_{\mathrm{nml}}(z^n)$ for at least one $z^n \in \mathcal{X}^n$, it follows that

$$\mathcal{R}_{\max}(P) \geq -\log P(z^n) + \log P(z^n \mid \hat{\theta}(z^n)) > \\ -\log \bar{P}_{\mathrm{nml}}(z^n) + \log P(z^n \mid \hat{\theta}(z^n)) = \mathcal{R}_{\max}(\bar{P}_{\mathrm{nml}}).$$

∎

$\bar{P}_{\mathrm{nml}}$ is quite literally a 'normalized maximum likelihood' distribution: it tries to assign to each x^n the probability of x^n according to the ML distribution for x^n. By (2.10), this is not possible: the resulting 'probabilities' add to something larger than 1. But we can normalize these 'probabilities' by dividing by their sum $\sum_{y^n \in \mathcal{X}^n} P(y^n \mid \hat{\theta}(y^n))$, and then we obtain a probability distribution on $\mathcal{X}^n$ after all.

Whenever $\mathcal{X}$ is finite, the sum $\mathbf{COMP}_n(\mathcal{M})$ is finite so that the NML distribution is well defined. If $\mathcal{X}$ is countably infinite or continuous-valued, the sum $\mathbf{COMP}_n(\mathcal{M})$ may be infinite and then the NML distribution may be undefined. In that case, there exists *no* universal model achieving constant regret as in (2.19). If $\mathcal{M}$ is parametric, then $\bar{P}_{\mathrm{nml}}$ is typically well defined as long as we suitably restrict the parameter space. The parametric case forms the basis of 'refined MDL' and is discussed at length in the next section.

Summary: Universal Codes and Models

Let $\mathcal{M}$ be a family of probabilistic sources. A *universal model in an individual sequence sense*[16] *relative to* $\mathcal{M}$, in this text simply called a 'universal model for $\mathcal{M}$', is a sequence of distributions $\bar{P}^{(1)}, \bar{P}^{(2)}, \dots$ on $\mathcal{X}^1, \mathcal{X}^2, \dots$ respectively, such that for all $P \in \mathcal{M}$, for all $\epsilon > 0$,

$$\max_{x^n \in \mathcal{X}^n} \frac{1}{n} \left\{ -\log \bar{P}^{(n)}(x^n) - [-\log P(x^n)] \right\} \leq \epsilon \text{ as } n \to \infty.$$

Multiplying both sides with n we see that $\bar{P}$ is universal if for every $P \in \mathcal{M}$, the code length difference $-\log \bar{P}(x^n) + \log P(x^n)$ increases sublinearly in n. If $\mathcal{M}$ is finite, then the two-part, Bayes and NML distributions are universal in a very strong sense: rather than just increasing sublinearly, the code length difference is bounded by a constant.

We already discussed two-part, Bayesian and minimax optimal (NML) universal models, but there several other types. We mention prequential universal models (Section 2.5.4), the *Kolmogorov* universal model, *conditionalized* two-part codes [Rissanen 2001] and Cesaro-average codes [Barron, Rissanen, and Yu 1998].

2.5   Simple Refined MDL and Its Four Interpretations

In Section 2.3, we indicated that 'crude' MDL needs to be refined. In Section 2.4 we introduced universal models. We now show how universal models, in particular the minimax optimal universal model $\bar{P}_{\text{nml}}$, can be used to define a refined version of MDL model selection. Here we only discuss the simplest case: suppose we are given data $D = (x_1, \dots, x_n)$ and two models $\mathcal{M}^{(1)}$ and $\mathcal{M}^{(2)}$ such that $\mathbf{COMP}_n(\mathcal{M}^{(1)})$ and $\mathbf{COMP}_n(\mathcal{M}^{(2)})$ (2.17) are both finite. For example, we could have some binary data and $\mathcal{M}^{(1)}$ and $\mathcal{M}^{(2)}$ are the first- and second-order Markov models (Example 2.7), both considered possible explanations for the data. We show how to deal with an infinite number of models and models with infinite $\mathbf{COMP}_n$ in Section 2.6.

Denote by $\bar{P}_{\text{nml}}(\cdot \mid \mathcal{M}^{(j)})$ the NML distribution on $\mathcal{X}^n$ corresponding to model $\mathcal{M}^{(j)}$. Refined MDL tells us to pick the model $\mathcal{M}^{(j)}$ maximizing the *normalized maximum likelihood* $\bar{P}_{\text{nml}}(D \mid \mathcal{M}^{(j)})$, or, by (2.18), equivalently, minimizing

$$-\log \bar{P}_{\text{nml}}(D \mid \mathcal{M}^{(j)}) = -\log P(D \mid \hat{\theta}^{(j)}(D)) + \mathbf{COMP}_n(\mathcal{M}^{(j)}). \tag{2.20}$$

From a coding-theoretic point of view, we associate with each $\mathcal{M}^{(j)}$ a code with lengths $\bar{P}_{\mathrm{nml}}(\cdot \mid \mathcal{M}^{(j)})$, and we pick the model minimizing the code length of the data. The code length $-\log \bar{P}_{\mathrm{nml}}(D \mid \mathcal{M}^{(j)})$ has been called the *stochastic complexity of the data D relative to model $\mathcal{M}^{(j)}$* [Rissanen 1987], whereas $\mathbf{COMP}_n(\mathcal{M}^{(j)})$ is called the *parametric complexity* or *model cost* of $\mathcal{M}^{(j)}$ (in this survey we simply call it 'complexity'). We have already indicated in the previous section that $\mathbf{COMP}_n(\mathcal{M}^{(j)})$ measures something like the 'complexity' of model $\mathcal{M}^{(j)}$. On the other hand, $-\log P(D \mid \hat{\theta}^{(j)}(D))$ is minus the maximized log-likelihood of the data, so it measures something like (minus) fit or *error* — in the linear regression case, it can be directly related to the mean squared error, Section 2.7. Thus, (2.20) embodies a tradeoff between lack of fit (measured by minus log-likelihood) and complexity (measured by $\mathbf{COMP}_n(\mathcal{M}^{(j)})$). The *confidence* in the decision is given by the code length difference

$$\left| -\log \bar{P}_{\mathrm{nml}}(D \mid \mathcal{M}^{(1)}) - [-\log \bar{P}_{\mathrm{nml}}(D \mid \mathcal{M}^{(2)})] \right|.$$

In general, $-\log \bar{P}_{\mathrm{nml}}(D \mid \mathcal{M})$ can only be evaluated numerically – the only exception I am aware of is when $\mathcal{M}$ is the Gaussian family, Example 2.20. In many cases even numerical evaluation is computationally problematic. But the reinterpretations of $\bar{P}_{\mathrm{nml}}$ we provide below also indicate that in many cases, $-\log \bar{P}(D \mid \mathcal{M})$ is relatively easy to approximate.

Example 2.15 (Refined MDL and GLRT)   Generalized likelihood ratio testing (GLRT) [Casella and Berger 1990]   tells us to pick the $\mathcal{M}^{(j)}$ maximizing $\log P(D \mid \hat{\theta}^{(j)}(D)) + c$ where c is determined by the desired Type I and Type II errors. In practice one often applies a naive variation,[17] simply picking the model $\mathcal{M}^{(j)}$ maximizing $\log P(D \mid \hat{\theta}^{(j)}(D))$. This amounts to ignoring the complexity terms $\mathbf{COMP}_n(\mathcal{M}^{(j)})$ in (2.20): MDL tries to avoid overfitting by picking the model maximizing the *normalized* rather than the ordinary likelihood. The more distributions in $\mathcal{M}$ that fit the data well, the larger the normalization term.

The hope is that the normalization term $\mathbf{COMP}_n(\mathcal{M}^{(j)})$ strikes the right balance between complexity and fit. Whether it really does depends on whether $\mathbf{COMP}_n$ is a 'good' measure of complexity. In the remainder of this section we shall argue that it is, by giving four different interpretations of $\mathbf{COMP}_n$ and of the resulting tradeoff (2.20):

1. Compression interpretation

2. Counting interpretation

3. Bayesian interpretation

4. Prequential (predictive) interpretation

2.5.1   Compression Interpretation

Rissanen's original goal was to select the model that detects the most regularity in the data; he identified this with the 'model that allows for the most compression of data x^n'. To make this precise, a code is associated with each model. The NML code with lengths $-\log \bar{P}_{\mathrm{nml}}(\cdot \mid \mathcal{M}^{(j)})$ seems to be a very reasonable choice for such a code because of the following two properties:

1. The better the best-fitting distribution in $\mathcal{M}^{(j)}$ fits the data, the shorter the code length $-\log \bar{P}_{\mathrm{nml}}(D \mid \mathcal{M}^{(j)})$.

2. No distribution in $\mathcal{M}^{(j)}$ is given a prior preference over any other distribution, since the regret of $\bar{P}_{\mathrm{nml}}(\cdot \mid \mathcal{M}^{(j)})$ is the same for all $D \in \mathcal{X}^n$ (Equation (2.19)). $\bar{P}_{\mathrm{nml}}$ is the *only* complete prefix code with this property, which may be restated as: $\bar{P}_{\mathrm{nml}}$ treats *all distributions within each $\mathcal{M}^{(j)}$ on the same footing!*

Therefore, if one is willing to accept the basic ideas underlying MDL as *first principles*, then the use of NML in model selection is now justified to some extent. Below we give additional justifications that are not directly based on data compression; but we first provide some further interpretation of $-\log \bar{P}_{\mathrm{nml}}$.

Compression and Separating Structure from Noise   We present the following ideas in an imprecise fashion — Rissanen and Tabus [2005] recently showed how to make them precise. The stochastic complexity of data D relative to $\mathcal{M}$, given by (2.20) can be interpreted as the amount of information in the data relative to $\mathcal{M}$, measured in bits. Although a one-part code length, it still consists of two terms: a term $\mathbf{COMP}_n(\mathcal{M})$ measuring the amount of *structure* or *meaningful information* in the data (as 'seen through $\mathcal{M}$'), and a term $-\log P(D \mid \hat{\theta}(D))$ measuring the amount of *noise* or *accidental information* in the data. To see that this second term measures noise, consider the regression example, Example 1.2, again. As will be seen in Section 2.7, Equation (2.40), in that case $-\log P(D \mid \hat{\theta}(D))$ becomes equal to a linear function of the mean squared error of the best-fitting polynomial in the set of kth-degree polynomials. To see that the first term measures structure, we reinterpret it below as the number of bits needed to specify a 'distinguishable' distribution in $\mathcal{M}$, using a uniform code on all 'distinguishable' distributions.

2.5.2   Counting Interpretation

The parametric complexity can be interpreted as measuring (the log of) the *number of distinguishable distributions in the model*. Intuitively, the more distributions a model contains, the more patterns it can fit well so the larger the risk of overfitting. However, if two distributions are very 'close' in the sense that they assign high likelihood to the same patterns, they do not contribute so much to the complexity of the overall model. It seems that we should measure complexity of a model in terms of the number of distributions it contains that are 'essentially different' (distinguishable), and we now show that $\mathbf{COMP}_n$ measures something like this. Consider a finite model $\mathcal{M}$ with parameter set $\Theta = \{\theta_1, \ldots, \theta_M\}$. Note that

$$\sum_{x^n \in \mathcal{X}^n} P(x^n | \hat{\theta}(x^n)) = \sum_{j=1..M} \sum_{x^n : \hat{\theta}(x^n) = \theta_j} P(x^n | \theta_j) =$$

$$\sum_{j=1..M} \left(1 - \sum_{x^n : \hat{\theta}(x^n) \neq \theta_j} P(x^n | \theta_j)\right) = M - \sum_j P(\hat{\theta}(x^n) \neq \theta_j | \theta_j).$$

We may think of $P(\hat{\theta}(x^n) \neq \theta_j | \theta_j)$ as the probability, according to θ_j, that the data look as if they come from some $\theta \neq \theta_j$. Thus, it is the probability that θ_j is *mistaken* for another distribution in Θ. Therefore, for finite $\mathcal{M}$, Rissanen's model complexity is the logarithm of the *number of distributions minus the summed probability that some θ_j is 'mistaken' for some $\theta \neq \theta_j$*. Now suppose $\mathcal{M}$ is i.i.d. By the law of large numbers [Feller 1968], we immediately see that the 'sum of mistake probabilities' $\sum_j P(\hat{\theta}(x^n) \neq \theta_j | \theta_j)$ tends to 0 as n grows. It follows that for large n, the model complexity converges to $\log M$. For large n, the distributions in $\mathcal{M}$ are 'perfectly distinguishable' (the probability that a sample coming from one is more representative of another is negligible), and then the parametric complexity $\mathbf{COMP}_n(\mathcal{M})$ of $\mathcal{M}$ is simply the log of the number of distributions in $\mathcal{M}$.

Example 2.16 (NML vs. Two-Part Codes) Incidentally, this shows that for finite i.i.d. $\mathcal{M}$, the two-part code with uniform prior W on $\mathcal{M}$, is asymptotically minimax optimal: for all n, the regret of the two-part code is $\log M$ (Equation 2.11), whereas we just showed that for $n \to \infty$, $\mathcal{R}(\bar{P}_{\text{nml}}) = \mathbf{COMP}_n(\mathcal{M}) \to \log M$. However, for small n, some distributions in $\mathcal{M}$ may be mistaken for one another; the number of *distinguishable* distributions in $\mathcal{M}$ is then smaller than the actual number of distributions, and this is reflected in $\mathbf{COMP}_n(\mathcal{M})$ being (sometimes much) smaller than $\log M$.

For the more interesting case of parametric models, containing infinitely many distributions, Balasubramanian [1997, 2005] has a somewhat different counting interpretation of $\mathbf{COMP}_n(\mathcal{M})$ as a ratio between two volumes. Rissanen and Tabus [2005] give a more direct counting interpretation of $\mathbf{COMP}_n(\mathcal{M})$. These extensions are both based on the asymptotic expansion of $\bar{P}_{\text{nml}}$, which we now discuss.

Asymptotic Expansion of $\bar{P}_{\text{nml}}$ and $\mathbf{COMP}_n$ Let $\mathcal{M}$ be a k-dimensional parametric model. Under regularity conditions on $\mathcal{M}$ and the parameterization $\Theta \to \mathcal{M}$, to be detailed below, we obtain the following asymptotic expansion of $\mathbf{COMP}_n$ [Rissanen 1996; Takeuchi and Barron 1997, 1998; Takeuchi 2000]:

$$\mathbf{COMP}_n(\mathcal{M}) = \frac{k}{2} \log \frac{n}{2\pi} + \log \int_{\theta \in \Theta} \sqrt{|I(\theta)|} d\theta + o(1) \qquad (2.21)$$

Here k is the number of parameters (degrees of freedom) in model $\mathcal{M}$, n is the sample size, and $o(1) \to 0$ as $n \to \infty$. $|I(\theta)|$ is the determinant of the $k \times k$ *Fisher information matrix*[18] I evaluated at θ. In case $\mathcal{M}$ is an i.i.d. model, I is given by

$$I_{ij}(\theta^*) := \mathrm{E}_{\theta^*}\left\{-\frac{\partial^2}{\partial\theta_i\partial\theta_j}\ln P(X|\theta)\right\}_{\theta=\theta^*}.$$

This is generalized to non-i.i.d. models as follows:

$$I_{ij}(\theta^*) := \lim_{n\to\infty}\frac{1}{n}\mathrm{E}_{\theta^*}\left\{-\frac{\partial^2}{\partial\theta_i\partial\theta_j}\ln P(X^n|\theta)\right\}_{\theta=\theta^*}.$$

Equation (2.21) only holds if the model $\mathcal{M}$, its parameterization Θ, and the sequence $x_1, x_2, \ldots$ all satisfy certain conditions. Specifically, we require:

1. $\mathbf{COMP}_n(\mathcal{M}) < \infty$ and $\int \sqrt{|I(\theta)|}d\theta < \infty$;

2. $\hat{\theta}(x^n)$ does not come arbitrarily close to the boundary of Θ: for some $\epsilon > 0$, for all large n, $\hat{\theta}(x^n)$ remains farther than ϵ from the boundary of Θ.

3. $\mathcal{M}$ and Θ satisfy certain further conditions. A simple sufficient condition is that $\mathcal{M}$ be an exponential family [Casella and Berger 1990]. Roughly, this is a family that can be parameterized so that for all x, $P(x \mid \beta) = \exp(\beta t(x))f(x)g(\beta)$, where $t : \mathcal{X} \to \mathbb{R}$ is a function of X. The Bernoulli model is an exponential family, as can be seen by setting $\beta := \ln(1-\theta) - \ln\theta$ and $t(x) = x$. Also the multinomial, Gaussian, Poisson, gamma, exponential, Zipf, and many other models are exponential families; but, for example, mixture models are not.

More general conditions are given by Takeuchi and Barron [1997, 1998] and Takeuchi [2000]. Essentially, if $\mathcal{M}$ behaves 'asymptotically' like an exponential family, then (2.21) still holds. For example, (2.21) holds for the Markov models and for AR and ARMA processes.

Example 2.17 (Complexity of the Bernoulli Model) The Bernoulli model $\mathcal{B}^{(0)}$ can be parameterized in a one-one way by the unit interval (Example 2.7). Thus, $k = 1$. An easy calculation shows that the Fisher information is given by $1/(\theta(1-\theta))$, giving $\int \sqrt{|1/\theta(1-\theta)|}d\theta = 2$. Plugging this into (2.21) gives

$$\mathbf{COMP}_n(\mathcal{B}^{(0)}) = \frac{1}{2}\log\frac{n}{2\pi} + \log 2 + o(1) = \frac{1}{2}\log n + \frac{1}{2} - \frac{1}{2}\log\pi + o(1).$$

Computing the integral of the Fisher determinant is not easy in general. Hanson and Fu [2005] compute it for several practically relevant models.

Whereas for finite $\mathcal{M}$, $\mathbf{COMP}_n(\mathcal{M})$ remains finite, for parametric models it generally grows logarithmically in n. Since typically $-\log P(x^n \mid \hat{\theta}(x^n))$ grows linearly in n, it is still the case that for *fixed* dimensionality k (i.e. for a fixed $\mathcal{M}$ that is k-dimensional) and large n, the part of the code length $-\log \bar{P}_{\mathrm{nml}}(x^n \mid \mathcal{M})$ due to the complexity of $\mathcal{M}$ is very small compared to the part needed to encode data x^n with $\hat{\theta}(x^n)$. The term $\int_\Theta \sqrt{|I(\theta)|}d\theta$ may be interpreted as the contribution of the *functional form* of $\mathcal{M}$ to the model complexity [Balasubramanian 2005]. It does not grow with n so that, when selecting between two models, it becomes irrelevant and can be ignored for *very* large n. But for small n, it can be important, as can be seen from Example 1.4, Fechner's and Stevens's model. Both models have two parameters, yet the $\int_{\Theta} \sqrt{|I(\theta)|}d\theta$-term is much larger for Fechner's than for Stevens's model. In the experiments of Myung, Balasubramanian, and Pitt [2000], the parameter set was restricted to $0 < a < \infty, 0 < b < 3$ for Stevens's model and $0 < a < \infty, 0 < b < \infty$ for Fechner's model. The variance of the error Z was set to 1 in both models. With these values, the difference in $\int_{\Theta} \sqrt{|I(\theta)|}d\theta$ is 3.804, which is non-negligible for small samples. Thus, Stevens's model contains more distinguishable distributions than Fechner's, and is better able to capture random noise in the data — as Townsend [1975] already speculated 30 years ago. Experiments suggest that for regression models such as Stevens's and Fechner's', as well as for Markov models and general exponential families, the approximation (2.21) is reasonably accurate already for small samples. But this is certainly not true for general models:

> **The Asymptotic Expansion of COMP$_n$ Should Be Used with Care!**
> Equation (2.21) does *not* hold for all parametric models; and for some models for which it does hold, the $o(1)$ term may only converge to 0 only for quite large sample sizes. Foster and Stine [1999, 2005] show that the approximation (2.21) is, in general, only valid if k is much smaller than n.

Two-Part Codes and COMP$_n(\mathcal{M})$ We now have a clear guiding principle (minimax regret) which we can use to construct 'optimal' two-part codes that achieve the minimax regret among all *two-part codes*. How do such optimal two-part codes compare to the NML code length? Let $\mathcal{M}$ be a k-dimensional model. By slightly adjusting the arguments of Barron and Cover [1991, Appendix], one can show that, under regularity conditions, the minimax optimal two-part code $\bar{P}_{2\text{-p}}$ achieves regret

$$-\log \bar{P}_{2\text{-p}}(x^n \mid \mathcal{M}) + \log P(x^n \mid \hat{\theta}(x^n)) = \frac{k}{2}\log \frac{n}{2\pi} + \log \int_{\theta \in \Theta} \sqrt{|I(\theta)|}d\theta + f(k) + o(1),$$

where $f : \mathbb{N} \to \mathbb{R}$ is a bounded positive function satisfying $\lim_{k\to\infty} f(k) = 0$. Thus, for large k, *optimally designed* two-part codes are about as good as NML. The problem with the two-part code MDL is that *in practice*, people often use much cruder codes with much larger minimax regret.

2.5.3 Bayesian Interpretation

The Bayesian method of statistical inference provides several alternative approaches to model selection. The most popular of these is based on *Bayes factors* [Kass and Raftery 1995]. The Bayes factor method is very closely related to the refined MDL approach. Assuming uniform priors on models $\mathcal{M}^{(1)}$ and $\mathcal{M}^{(2)}$, it tells us to select the model with largest marginal likelihood $\bar{P}_{\text{Bayes}}(x^n \mid \mathcal{M}^{(j)})$, where $\bar{P}_{\text{Bayes}}$ is as in (2.12), with the sum replaced by an integral, and $w^{(j)}$ is the density of the prior distribution on $\mathcal{M}^{(j)}$:

$$\bar{P}_{\text{Bayes}}(x^n \mid \mathcal{M}^{(j)}) = \int P(x^n \mid \theta) w^{(j)}(\theta) d\theta \tag{2.22}$$

$\mathcal{M}$ Is Exponential Family   Let now $\bar{P}_{\text{Bayes}} = \bar{P}_{\text{Bayes}}(\cdot \mid \mathcal{M})$ for some fixed model $\mathcal{M}$. Under regularity conditions on $\mathcal{M}$, we can perform a *Laplace approximation* of the integral in (2.12). For the special case that $\mathcal{M}$ is an exponential family, we obtain the following expression for the regret [Jeffreys 1961; Schwarz 1978; Kass and Raftery 1995; Balasubramanian 1997]:

$$-\log \bar{P}_{\text{Bayes}}(x^n) - [-\log P(x^n \mid \hat{\theta}(x^n))] = \frac{k}{2} \log \frac{n}{2\pi} - \log w(\hat{\theta}) + \log \sqrt{|I(\hat{\theta})|} + o(1) \tag{2.23}$$

Let us compare this with (2.21). Under the regularity conditions needed for (2.21), the quantity on the right of (2.23) is within $O(1)$ of $\mathbf{COMP}_n(\mathcal{M})$. Thus, the code length achieved with $\bar{P}_{\text{Bayes}}$ is within a constant of the minimax optimal $-\log \bar{P}_{\text{nml}}(x^n)$. Since $-\log P(x^n \mid \hat{\theta}(x^n))$ increases linearly in n, this means that if we compare two models $\mathcal{M}^{(1)}$ and $\mathcal{M}^{(2)}$, then for large enough n, Bayes and refined MDL select the same model. If we equip the Bayesian universal model with a special prior known as the *Jeffreys-Bernardo* prior [Jeffreys 1946; Bernardo and Smith 1994],

$$w_{\text{Jeffreys}}(\theta) = \frac{\sqrt{|I(\theta)|}}{\int_{\theta \in \Theta} \sqrt{|I(\theta)|} d\theta}, \tag{2.24}$$

then Bayes and refined NML become even more closely related: plugging (2.24) into (2.23), we find that the right-hand side of (2.23) now simply *coincides* with (2.21). A concrete example of Jeffreys' prior is given in Example 2.19. Jeffreys introduced his prior as a 'least informative prior', to be used when no useful prior knowledge about the parameters is available [Jeffreys 1946]. As one may expect from such a prior, it is invariant under continuous one-to-one reparameterizations of the parameter space. The present analysis shows that, when $\mathcal{M}$ is an exponential family, then it also leads to asymptotically minimax code length regret: for large n, *refined NML model selection becomes indistinguishable from Bayes factor model selection with Jeffreys' prior.*

$\mathcal{M}$ Is Not an Exponential Family   Under weak conditions on $\mathcal{M}$, Θ and the sequence x^n, we get the following generalization of (2.23):

$$-\log \bar{P}_{\text{Bayes}}(x^n \mid \mathcal{M}) =$$

$$-\log P(x^n \mid \hat{\theta}(x^n)) + \frac{k}{2} \log \frac{n}{2\pi} - \log w(\hat{\theta}) + \log \sqrt{|\hat{I}(x^n)|} + o(1) \tag{2.25}$$

Here $\hat{I}(x^n)$ is the so-called *observed information*, sometimes also called *observed Fisher information*; see [Kass and Voss 1997] for a definition. If $\mathcal{M}$ is an exponential family, then the observed Fisher information at x^n coincides with the Fisher information at $\hat{\theta}(x^n)$, leading to (2.23). If $\mathcal{M}$ is not exponential, then if data are distributed according to one of the distributions in $\mathcal{M}$, the observed Fisher information still converges with probability 1 to the expected Fisher information. If $\mathcal{M}$ is neither exponential nor are the data actually generated by a distribution in $\mathcal{M}$, then there may be $O(1)$-discrepancies between $-\log \bar{P}_{\mathrm{nml}}$ and $-\log \bar{P}_{\mathrm{Bayes}}$ even for large n.

2.5.4 Prequential Interpretation

Distributions as Prediction Strategies Let P be a distribution on $\mathcal{X}^n$. Applying the definition of conditional probability, we can write for every x^n:

$$P(x^n) = \prod_{i=1}^{n} \frac{P(x^i)}{P(x^{i-1})} = \prod_{i=1}^{n} P(x_i \mid x^{i-1}), \qquad (2.26)$$

so that also

$$-\log P(x^n) = \sum_{i=1}^{n} -\log P(x_i \mid x^{i-1}). \qquad (2.27)$$

Let us abbreviate $P(X_i = \cdot \mid X^{i-1} = x^{i-1})$ to $P(X_i \mid x^{i-1})$. $P(X_i \mid x^{i-1})$ (capital X_i) is the *distribution* (not a single number) of X_i given x^{i-1}; $P(x_i \mid x^{i-1})$ (lowercase x_i) is the *probability* (a single number) of actual outcome x_i given x^{i-1}. We can think of $-\log P(x_i \mid x^{i-1})$ as the *loss* incurred when predicting X_i based on the conditional distribution $P(X_i \mid x^{i-1})$, and the actual outcome turned out to be x_i. Here 'loss' is measured using the so-called *logarithmic score*, also known simply as 'log loss'. Note that the more likely x is judged to be, the smaller the loss incurred when x actually obtains. The log loss has a natural interpretation in terms of sequential *gambling* [Cover and Thomas 1991], but its main interpretation is still in terms of coding: by (2.27), the code length needed to encode x^n based on distribution P is just the *accumulated log loss incurred when P is used to sequentially predict the ith outcome based on the past $(i-1)$st outcomes*.

Equation (2.26) gives a fundamental reinterpretation of probability distributions as prediction strategies, mapping each individual sequence of *past observations* $x_1, \ldots, x_{i-1}$ to a *probabilistic prediction of the next outcome* $P(X_i \mid x^{i-1})$. Conversely, (2.26) also shows that every probabilistic prediction strategy for sequential prediction of n outcomes may be thought of as a probability distribution on $\mathcal{X}^n$: a strategy is identified with a function mapping all potential initial segments x^{i-1} to the prediction that is made for the next outcome X_i, after having seen x^{i-1}. Thus, it is a function $S : \cup_{0 \leq i < n} \mathcal{X}^i \to \mathcal{P}_{\mathcal{X}}$, where $\mathcal{P}_{\mathcal{X}}$ is the set of distributions on $\mathcal{X}$. We can now define, for each $i < n$, all $x^i \in \mathcal{X}^i$, $P(X_i \mid x^{i-1}) := S(x^{i-1})$. We can turn these partial distributions into a full distribution on $\mathcal{X}^n$ by sequentially plugging them into (2.26). The resulting distribution on $\mathcal{X}^n$ will then, of course, automatically satisfy (2.26).

Log Loss for Universal Models   Let $\mathcal{M}$ be some parametric model and let $\bar{P}$ be some universal model/code relative to $\mathcal{M}$. What do the individual predictions $\bar{P}(X_i \mid x^{i-1})$ look like? Readers familiar with Bayesian statistics will realize that for i.i.d. models, the Bayesian predictive distribution $\bar{P}_{\text{Bayes}}(X_i \mid x^{i-1})$ converges to the ML distribution $P(\cdot \mid \hat{\theta}(x^{i-1}))$; Example 2.19 provides a concrete case. It seems reasonable to assume that something similar holds not just for $\bar{P}_{\text{Bayes}}$ but for universal models in general. This in turn suggests that we may approximate the conditional distributions $\bar{P}(X_i \mid x^{i-1})$ of any 'good' universal model by the ML predictions $P(\cdot \mid \hat{\theta}(x^{i-1}))$. Indeed, we can recursively define the *maximum likelihood plug-in* distribution $\bar{P}_{\text{plug-in}}$ by setting, for $i = 1$ to n,

$$\bar{P}_{\text{plug-in}}(X_i = \cdot \mid x^{i-1}) := P(X = \cdot \mid \hat{\theta}(x^{i-1})). \tag{2.28}$$

Then

$$-\log \bar{P}_{\text{plug-in}}(x^n) := \sum_{i=1}^{n} -\log P(x_i \mid \hat{\theta}(x^{i-1})). \tag{2.29}$$

Indeed, it turns out that under regularity conditions on $\mathcal{M}$ and x^n,

$$-\log \bar{P}_{\text{plug-in}}(x^n) = -\log P(x^n \mid \hat{\theta}(x^n)) + \frac{k}{2}\log n + O(1), \tag{2.30}$$

showing that $\bar{P}_{\text{plug-in}}$ acts as a universal model relative to $\mathcal{M}$, its performance being within a constant of the minimax optimal $\bar{P}_{\text{nml}}$. The construction of $\bar{P}_{\text{plug-in}}$ can be easily extended to non-i.i.d. models, and then, under regularity conditions, (2.30) still holds; we omit the details.

We note that all general proofs of (2.30) that we are aware of show that (2.30) holds with probability 1 or in expectation for sequences generated by some distribution in $\mathcal{M}$ [Rissanen 1984, 1986, 1989]. Note that the expressions (2.21) and (2.25) for the regret of $\bar{P}_{\text{nml}}$ and $\bar{P}_{\text{Bayes}}$ hold for a much wider class of sequences; they also hold with probability 1 for i.i.d. sequences generated by sufficiently regular distributions *outside* $\mathcal{M}$. Not much is known about the regret obtained by $\bar{P}_{\text{plug-in}}$ for such sequences, except for some special cases such as if $\mathcal{M}$ is the Gaussian model.

In general, there is no need to use the ML estimator $\hat{\theta}(x^{i-1})$ in the definition (2.28). Instead, we may try some other estimator which asymptotically converges to the ML estimator — it turns out that some estimators considerably outperform the ML estimator in the sense that (2.29) becomes a much better approximation of $-\log \bar{P}_{\text{nml}}$, see Example 2.19. Irrespective of whether we use the ML estimator or something else, we call model selection based on (2.29) the *prequential* form of MDL in honor of A.P. Dawid's 'prequential analysis', Section 2.8. It is also known as 'predictive MDL'. The validity of (2.30) was discovered independently by Rissanen [1984] and Dawid [1984].

The prequential view gives us a fourth interpretation of refined MDL model selection: given models $\mathcal{M}^{(1)}$ and $\mathcal{M}^{(2)}$, MDL tells us to pick the model that minimizes the accumulated prediction error resulting from sequentially predicting future outcomes given all the past outcomes.

Example 2.18 (GLRT and Prequential Model Selection) How does this differ from the naive version of the generalized likelihood ratio test (GLRT) that we introduced in Example 2.15? In GLRT, we associate with each model the log-likelihood (minus log loss) that can be obtained by the ML estimator. This is the predictor within the model that minimizes log loss *with hindsight*, *after* having seen the data. In contrast, prequential model selection associates with each model the log-likelihood (minus log loss) that can be obtained by using a sequence of ML estimators $\hat{\theta}(x^{i-1})$ to predict data x_i. Crucially, the data on which ML estimators are evaluated has not been used in constructing the ML estimators themselves. This makes the prediction scheme 'honest' (different data are used for training and testing) and explains why it automatically protects us against overfitting.

Example 2.19 (Laplace and Jeffreys) Consider the prequential distribution for the Bernoulli model, Example 2.7, defined as in (2.28). We show that if we take $\hat{\theta}$ in (2.28) equal to the ML estimator $n_{[1]}/n$, then the resulting $\bar{P}_{\text{plug-in}}$ is not a universal model; but a slight modification of the ML estimator makes $\bar{P}_{\text{plug-in}}$ a very good universal model. Suppose that $n \geq 3$ and $(x_1, x_2, x_3) = (0, 0, 1)$ — a not so unlikely initial segment according to most θ. Then $\bar{P}_{\text{plug-in}}(X_3 = 1 \mid x_1, x_2) = P(X = 1 \mid \hat{\theta}(x_1, x_2)) = 0$, so that by (2.29),

$$- \log \bar{P}_{\text{plug-in}}(x^n) \geq - \log \bar{P}_{\text{plug-in}}(x_3 \mid x_1, x_2) = \infty,$$

whence $\bar{P}_{\text{plug-in}}$ is not universal. Now let us consider the modified ML estimator

$$\hat{\theta}_\lambda(x^n) := \frac{n_{[1]} + \lambda}{n + 2\lambda}. \tag{2.31}$$

If we take $\lambda = 0$, we get the ordinary ML estimator. If we take $\lambda = 1$, then an exercise involving beta-integrals shows that, for all i, x^i, $P(X_i \mid \hat{\theta}_1(x^{i-1})) = \bar{P}_{\text{Bayes}}(X_i \mid x^{i-1})$, where $\bar{P}_{\text{Bayes}}$ is defined relative to the uniform prior $w(\theta) \equiv 1$. Thus $\hat{\theta}_1(x^{i-1})$ corresponds to the Bayesian predictive distribution for the uniform prior. This prediction rule was advocated by the great probabilist Pierre Simon de Laplace, co-originator of Bayesian statistics. It may be interpreted as ML estimation based on an *extended* sample, containing some 'virtual' data: an extra 0 and an extra 1.

Even better, a similar calculation shows that if we take $\lambda = 1/2$, the resulting estimator is equal to $\bar{P}_{\text{Bayes}}(X_i \mid x^{i-1})$ defined relative to *Jeffreys' prior*. Asymptotically, $\bar{P}_{\text{Bayes}}$ with Jeffreys' prior achieves the same code lengths as $\bar{P}_{\text{nml}}$ (Section 2.5.3). It follows that $\bar{P}_{\text{plug-in}}$ with the slightly modified ML estimator is asymptotically indistinguishable from the optimal universal model $\bar{P}_{\text{nml}}$!

For more general models $\mathcal{M}$, such simple modifications of the ML estimator usually do not correspond to a Bayesian predictive distribution; for example, if $\mathcal{M}$ is not convex (closed under taking mixtures) then a point estimator (an element of $\mathcal{M}$) typically does not correspond to the Bayesian predictive distribution (a mixture of elements of $\mathcal{M}$). Nevertheless, modifying the ML estimator by adding some virtual data $y_1, \ldots, y_m$ and replacing $P(X_i \mid \hat{\theta}(x^{i-1}))$ by $P(X_i \mid \hat{\theta}(x^{i-1}, y^m))$ in the definition (2.28) may still lead to good universal models. This is of great practical importance, since, using (2.29), $-\log \bar{P}_{\text{plug-in}}(x^n)$ is often much easier to compute than $-\log \bar{P}_{\text{Bayes}}(x^n)$.

Summary   We introduced the refined MDL principle for model selection in a restricted setting. Refined MDL amounts to selecting the model under which the data achieve the smallest *stochastic complexity*, which is the code length according to the minimax optimal universal model. We gave an asymptotic expansion of stochastic and parametric complexity, and interpreted these concepts in four different ways.

2.6   General Refined MDL: Gluing It All Together

In the previous section we introduced a 'refined' MDL principle based on minimax regret. Unfortunately, this principle can be applied only in very restricted settings. We now show how to extend refined MDL, leading to a general MDL principle, applicable to a wide variety of model selection problems. In doing so we glue all our previous insights (including 'crude MDL') together, thereby uncovering a single general, underlying principle, formulated in Figure 2.4. Therefore, *if one understands the material in this section, then one understands the Minimum Description Length principle.*

First, Section 2.6.1, we show how to compare infinitely many models. Then, Section 2.6.2, we show how to proceed for models $\mathcal{M}$ for which the parametric complexity is undefined. Remarkably, a single, general idea resides behind our solution of both problems, and this leads us to formulate, in Section 2.6.3, a single, general refined MDL principle.

2.6.1   Model Selection with Infinitely Many Models

Suppose we want to compare more than two models for the same data. If the number to be compared is finite, we can proceed as before and pick the model $\mathcal{M}^{(k)}$ with smallest $-\log \bar{P}_{\text{nml}}(x^n \mid \mathcal{M}^{(k)})$. If the number of models is infinite, we have to be more careful. Say we compare models $\mathcal{M}^{(1)}, \mathcal{M}^{(2)}, \ldots$ for data x^n. We may be tempted to pick the model minimizing $-\log \bar{P}_{\text{nml}}(x^n \mid \mathcal{M}^{(k)})$ over all $k \in \{1, 2, \ldots\}$, but in some cases this gives unintended results. To illustrate, consider the extreme case that every $\mathcal{M}^{(k)}$ contains just one distribution. For example, let $\mathcal{M}^{(1)} = \{P_1\}, \mathcal{M}^{(2)} = \{P_2\}, \ldots$ where $\{P_1, P_2, \ldots\}$ is the set of *all* Markov chains with rational-valued parameters. In that case, $\mathbf{COMP}_n(\mathcal{M}^{(k)}) = 0$ for all k, and we would always select the ML Markov chain that assigns probability 1 to data x^n.

Typically this will be a chain of very high order, severely overfitting the data. This cannot be right! A better idea is to pick the model minimizing

$$-\log \bar{P}_{\mathrm{nml}}(x^n \mid \mathcal{M}^{(k)}) + L(k), \tag{2.32}$$

where L is the code length function of some code for encoding model indices k. We would typically choose the standard prior for the integers, $L(k) = 2 \log k + 1$ (Example 2.4). By using (2.32) we avoid the overfitting problem mentioned above: if $\mathcal{M}^{(1)} = \{P_1\}, \mathcal{M}^{(2)} = \{P_2\}, \dots$ where $P_1, P_2, \dots$ is a list of all the rational-parameter Markov chains, (2.32) would reduce to two-part code MDL (Section 2.3) which is asymptotically consistent. On the other hand, if $\mathcal{M}^{(k)}$ represents the set of kth-order Markov chains, the term $L(k)$ is typically negligible compared to $\mathbf{COMP}_n(\mathcal{M}^{(k)})$, the complexity term associated with $\mathcal{M}^{(k)}$ that is hidden in $-\log \bar{P}_{\mathrm{nml}}(\mathcal{M}^{(k)})$: thus, the complexity of $\mathcal{M}^{(k)}$ comes from the fact that for large k, $\mathcal{M}^{(k)}$ contains many distinguishable distributions, not from the much smaller term $L(k) \approx 2 \log k$.

To make our previous approach for a finite set of models compatible with (2.32), we can reinterpret it as follows: we assign uniform code lengths (a uniform prior) to the $\mathcal{M}^{(1)}, \dots, \mathcal{M}^{(M)}$ under consideration, so that for $k = 1, \dots, M$, $L(k) = \log M$. We then pick the model minimizing (2.32). Since $L(k)$ is constant over k, it plays no role in the minimization and can be dropped from the equation, so that our procedure reduces to our original refined MDL model selection method. We shall henceforth assume that we *always* encode the model index, either implicitly (if the number of models is finite) or explicitly. The general principle behind this is explained in Section 2.6.3.

2.6.2   The Infinity Problem

For some of the most common models, the parametric complexity $\mathbf{COMP}(\mathcal{M})$ is undefined. A prime example is the Gaussian location model, which we discuss below. As we will see, we can 'repair' the situation using the same general idea as in the previous subsection.

Example 2.20   (Parametric Complexity of the Normal Distributions)
Let $\mathcal{M}$ be the family of normal distributions with fixed variance σ^2 and varying mean μ, identified by their densities,

$$P(x|\mu) = \frac{1}{\sqrt{2\pi}\sigma} e^{-\frac{(x-\mu)^2}{2\sigma^2}},$$

extended to sequences $x_1, \dots, x_n$ by taking product densities. As is well-known [Casella and Berger 1990], the ML estimator $\hat{\mu}(x^n)$ is equal to the sample mean: $\hat{\mu}(x^n) = n^{-1} \sum_{i=1}^{n} x_i$. An easy calculation shows that

$$\mathbf{COMP}_n(\mathcal{M}) = \int_{x^n} P(x^n \mid \hat{\mu}(x^n)) dx^n = \infty,$$

where we abbreviated $dx_1 \ldots dx_n$ to dx^n. Therefore, we cannot use basic MDL model selection. It also turns out that $I(\mu) = \sigma^{-2}$ so that $\int_{\Theta} \sqrt{|I(\theta)|}d\theta = \int_{\mu \in \mathbb{R}} \sqrt{|I(\mu)|}d\mu = \infty$. Thus, the Bayesian universal model approach with Jeffreys' prior cannot be applied either. Does this mean that our MDL model selection and complexity definitions break down even in such a simple case? Luckily, it turns out that they can be repaired, as we now show. Barron and co-workers [1998] and Foster and Stine [2001] show that, for all intervals $[a, b]$,

$$\int_{x^n : \hat{\mu}(x^n) \in [a,b]} P(x^n \mid \hat{\mu}(x^n))dx^n = \frac{b - a}{\sqrt{2\pi}\sigma} \cdot \sqrt{n}. \qquad (2.33)$$

Suppose for the moment that it is known that $\hat{\mu}$ lies in some set $[\ K, K]$ for some fixed K. Let $\mathcal{M}_K$ be the set of conditional distributions thus obtained: $\mathcal{M}_K = \{P'(\cdot \mid \mu) \mid \mu \in \mathbb{R}\}$, where $P'(x^n \mid \mu)$ is the density of x^n according to the normal distribution with mean μ, conditioned on $|n^{-1}\sum x_i| \leq K$. By (2.33), the 'conditional' minimax regret distribution $\bar{P}_{\mathrm{nml}}(\cdot \mid \mathcal{M}_K)$ is well-defined for all $K > 0$. That is, for all x^n with $|\hat{\mu}(x^n)| \leq K$,

$$\bar{P}_{\mathrm{nml}}(x^n \mid \mathcal{M}_K) = \frac{P'(x^n \mid \hat{\mu}(x^n))}{\int_{x^n \,:\, |\hat{\mu}(x^n)| < K} P'(x^n \mid \hat{\mu}(x^n))dx^n},$$

with regret (or 'conditional' complexity),

$$\mathbf{COMP}_n(\mathcal{M}_K) = \log \int_{|\hat{\mu}(x^n)| < K} P'(x^n \mid \hat{\mu}(x^n))dx^n = \log K + \frac{1}{2}\log\frac{n}{2\pi} - \log\sigma + 1.$$

This suggests redefining the complexity of the full model $\mathcal{M}$ so that its regret depends on the area in which $\hat{\mu}$ falls. The most straightforward way of achieving this is to define a *meta-universal model* for $\mathcal{M}$, combining the NML with a two-part code: we encode data by first encoding some value for K. We then encode the actual data x^n using the code $\bar{P}_{\mathrm{nml}}(\cdot|\mathcal{M}_K)$. The resulting code $\bar{P}_{\mathrm{meta}}$ is a universal code for $\mathcal{M}$ with lengths

$$-\log \bar{P}_{\mathrm{meta}}(x^n|\mathcal{M}) := \min_K \left\{-\log \bar{P}_{\mathrm{nml}}(x^n \mid \mathcal{M}_K) + L(K)\right\}. \qquad (2.34)$$

The idea is now to base MDL model selection on $\bar{P}_{\mathrm{meta}}(\cdot|\mathcal{M})$ as in (2.34) rather than on the (undefined) $\bar{P}_{\mathrm{nml}}(\cdot|\mathcal{M})$. To make this work, we need to choose L in a clever manner. A good choice is to encode $K' = \log K$ as an integer, using the standard code for the integers. To see why, note that the regret of $\bar{P}_{\mathrm{meta}}$ now becomes

$$-\log \bar{P}_{\mathrm{meta}}(x^n \mid \mathcal{M}) - [-\log P(x^n \mid \hat{\mu}(x^n))] =$$

$$\min_{K : \log K \in \{1,2,\ldots\}} \left\{\log K + \frac{1}{2}\log\frac{n}{2\pi} - \log\sigma + 1 + 2\log\lceil\log K\rceil\right\} + 1 \leq$$

$$\log|\hat{\mu}(x^n)| + 2\log\log|\hat{\mu}(x^n)| + \frac{1}{2}\log\frac{n}{2\pi} - \log\sigma + 4 \leq$$

$$\mathbf{COMP}_n(\mathcal{M}_{|\hat{\mu}|}) + 2\log\mathbf{COMP}_n(\mathcal{M}_{|\hat{\mu}|}) + 3. \qquad (2.35)$$

If we had known a good bound K on $|\hat{\mu}|$ a priori, we could have used the NML model $\bar{P}_{\text{nml}}(\cdot \mid \mathcal{M}_K)$. With 'maximal' a priori knowledge, we would have used the model $\bar{P}_{\text{nml}}(\cdot \mid \mathcal{M}_{|\hat{\mu}|})$, leading to regret $\textbf{COMP}_n(\mathcal{M}_{|\hat{\mu}|})$. The regret achieved by $\bar{P}_{\text{meta}}$ is *almost* as good as this 'smallest possible regret-with-hindsight' $\textbf{COMP}_n(\mathcal{M}_{|\hat{\mu}|})$: the difference is much smaller than, in fact logarithmic in, $\textbf{COMP}_n(\mathcal{M}_{|\hat{\mu}|})$ itself, *no matter what x^n we observe*. This is the underlying reason why we choose to encode K with log-precision: the basic idea in refined MDL was to minimize worst-case regret, or *additional code length* compared to the code that achieves the minimal code length with hindsight. Here, we use this basic idea on a metalevel: we design a code such that the *additional regret* is minimized, compared to the code that achieves the minimal regret with hindsight.

This meta–two-part coding idea was introduced by Rissanen [1996]. It can be extended to a wide range of models with $\textbf{COMP}_n(\mathcal{M}) = \infty$; for example, if the X_i represent outcomes of a Poisson or geometric distribution, one can encode a bound on μ just as in Example 2.20. If $\mathcal{M}$ is the full Gaussian model with both μ and σ^2 allowed to vary, one has to encode a bound on $\hat{\mu}$ and a bound on $\hat{\sigma}^2$. Essentially the same holds for linear regression problems, Section 2.7.

Renormalized Maximum Likelihood   Meta–two-part coding is just one possible solution to the problem of undefined $\textbf{COMP}_n(\mathcal{M})$. It is suboptimal, the main reason being the use of two-part codes. Indeed, these two-part codes are not complete (Section 2.1): they reserve several code words for the same data $D = (x_1, \ldots, x_n)$ (one for each integer value of $\log K$); therefore, there must exist more efficient (one-part) codes $\bar{P}'_{\text{meta}}$ such that for all $x^n \in \mathcal{X}^n$, $\bar{P}'_{\text{meta}}(x^n) > \bar{P}_{\text{meta}}(x^n)$; in keeping with the idea that we should minimize description length, such alternative codes are preferable. This realization has led to a search for more efficient and intrinsic solutions to the problem. Foster and Stine [2001] consider the possibility of restricting the *parameter values* rather than the data, and develop a general framework for comparing universal codes for models with undefined $\textbf{COMP}(\mathcal{M})$. Rissanen [2001] suggests the following elegant solution. He defines the *renormalized maximum likelihood (RNML) distribution* $\bar{P}_{\text{rnml}}$. In our Gaussian example, this universal model would be defined as follows. Let $\hat{K}(x^n)$ be the bound on $\hat{\mu}(x^n)$ that maximizes $\bar{P}_{\text{nml}}(x^n \mid \mathcal{M}_K)$ for the actually given K. That is, $\hat{K}(x^n) = |\hat{\mu}(x^n)|$. Then $\bar{P}_{\text{rnml}}$ is defined as, for all $x^n \in \mathcal{X}^n$,

$$\bar{P}_{\text{rnml}}(x^n|\mathcal{M}) = \frac{\bar{P}_{\text{nml}}(x^n|\mathcal{M}_{\hat{K}(x^n)})}{\int_{x^n \in \mathbb{R}^n} \bar{P}_{\text{nml}}(x^n \mid \mathcal{M}_{\hat{K}(x^n)})dx^n}. \tag{2.36}$$

Model selection between a finite set of models now proceeds by selecting the model maximizing the *renormalized* likelihood (2.36).

Region Indifference   All the approaches considered thus far slightly prefer some regions of the parameter space over others. In spite of its elegance, even the Rissanen renormalization is slightly 'arbitrary' in this way: had we chosen the origin of the real line differently, the same sequence x^n would have achieved a different code length $-\log \bar{P}_{\mathrm{rnml}}(x^n \mid \mathcal{M})$. In recent work, Liang and Barron [2004,2005] consider a novel and quite different approach for dealing with infinite $\mathbf{COMP}_n(\mathcal{M})$ that partially addresses this problem. They make use of the fact that, while Jeffreys' *prior* is improper ($\int \sqrt{|I(\theta)|} d\theta$ is infinite), using Bayes' rule we can still compute Jeffreys' *posterior* based on the first few observations, and this posterior turns out to be a proper probability measure after all. Liang and Barron use universal models of a somewhat different type than $\bar{P}_{\mathrm{nml}}$, so it remains to be investigated whether their approach can be adapted to the form of MDL discussed here.

2.6.3 The General Picture

Section 2.6.1 illustrates that, in *all* applications of MDL, we first define a *single* universal model that allows us to code all sequences with length equal to the given sample size. If the set of models is finite, we use the uniform prior. We do this in order to be as 'honest' as possible, treating all models under consideration on the same footing. But if the set of models becomes infinite, there exists no uniform prior anymore. Therefore, we must choose a nonuniform prior/non–fixed-length code to encode the model index. In order to treat all models still 'as equally as possible', we should use some code which is 'close' to uniform, in the sense that the code length increases only very slowly with k. We choose the standard prior for the integers (Example 2.4), but we could also have chosen different priors, for example, a prior $P(k)$ which is uniform on $k = 1..M$ for some large M, and $P(k) \propto k^{-2}$ for $k > M$. Whatever prior we choose, we are forced to encode a slight preference of some models over others; see Section 2.9.1.

Section 2.6.2 applies the same idea, but implemented at a metalevel: we try to associate with $\mathcal{M}^{(k)}$ a code for encoding outcomes in $\mathcal{X}^n$ that achieves uniform (= minimax) regret for every sequence x^n. If this is not possible, we still try to assign regret as 'uniformly' as we can, by carving up the parameter space in regions with larger and larger minimax regret, and devising a universal code that achieves regret not much larger than the minimax regret achievable within the smallest region containing the ML estimator. Again, the codes we used encoded a slight preference of some regions of the parameter space over others, but our aim was to keep this preference as small as possible. The general idea is summarized in Figure 2.4, which provides an (informal) definition of MDL, but only in a restricted context. If we go beyond that context, these prescriptions cannot be used literally — but extensions in the same spirit suggest themselves. Here is a first example of such an extension:

Example 2.21 (MDL and Local Maxima in the Likelihood) In practice we often work with models for which the ML estimator cannot be calculated efficiently; or at least no algorithm for efficient calculation of the ML estimator is known. Examples are finite and Gaussian mixtures and hidden Markov models. In such cases one typically resorts to methods such as expectation-maximization (EM) or

---

GENERAL 'REFINED' MDL PRINCIPLE for Model Selection

Suppose we plan to select between models $\mathcal{M}^{(1)}, \mathcal{M}^{(2)}, \ldots$ for data $D = (x_1, \ldots, x_n)$. MDL tells us to design a universal code $\bar{P}$ for $\mathcal{X}^n$, in which the index k of $\mathcal{M}^{(k)}$ is encoded explicitly. The resulting code has two parts, the two sub-codes being defined such that

1. All models $\mathcal{M}^{(k)}$ are treated on the same footing, as far as possible: we assign a uniform prior to these models, or, if that is not a possible, a prior 'close to' uniform.

2. All distributions within each $\mathcal{M}^{(k)}$ are treated on the same footing, as far as possible: we use the minimax regret universal model $\bar{P}_{\mathrm{nml}}(x^n \mid \mathcal{M}^{(k)})$. If this model is undefined or too hard to compute, we instead use a different universal model that achieves regret 'close to' the minimax regret for each submodel of $\mathcal{M}^{(k)}$ in the sense of (2.35).

In the end, we encode data D using a hybrid two-part/one-part universal model, explicitly encoding the models we want to select between and implicitly encoding any distributions contained in those models.

Figure 2.4   The Refined MDL Principle.

gradient descent, which find a *local* maximum of the likelihood surface (function) $P(x^n \mid \theta)$, leading to a *local* maximum likelihood (LML) estimator $\dot{\theta}(x^n)$. Suppose we need to select between a finite number of such models. We may be tempted to pick the model $\mathcal{M}$ maximizing the normalized likelihood $\bar{P}_{\mathrm{nml}}(x^n \mid \mathcal{M})$. However, if we then plan to use the local estimator $\dot{\theta}(x^n)$ for predicting future data, this is *not* the right thing to do. To see this, note that, if suboptimal estimators $\dot{\theta}$ are to be used, the ability of model $\mathcal{M}$ to fit arbitrary data patterns may be severely diminished! Rather than using $\bar{P}_{\mathrm{nml}}$, we should redefine it to take into account the fact that $\dot{\theta}$ is not the global ML estimator:

$$\bar{P}'_{\mathrm{nml}}(x^n) := \frac{P(x^n \mid \dot{\theta}(x^n))}{\sum_{x^n \in \mathcal{X}^n} P(x^n \mid \dot{\theta}(x^n))},$$

leading to an adjusted parametric complexity,

$$\mathbf{COMP}'_n(\mathcal{M}) := \log \sum_{x^n \in \mathcal{X}^n} P(x^n \mid \dot{\theta}(x^n)), \qquad (2.37)$$

which, for every estimator $\dot{\theta}$ different from $\hat{\theta}$, *must* be strictly smaller than $\mathbf{COMP}_n(\mathcal{M})$.

Summary   We have shown how to extend refined MDL beyond the restricted settings of Section 2.5. This uncovered the general principle behind refined MDL for model selection, given in Figure 2.4. General as it may be, it only applies to model selection. In the next section we briefly discuss extensions to other applications.

2.7 Beyond Parametric Model Selection

The general principle as given in Figure 2.4 only applies to model selection. It can be extended in several directions. These range over many different tasks of inductive inference — we mention *prediction, transduction* (as defined in [Vapnik 1998]), *clustering* [Kontkanen, Myllymäki, Buntine, Rissanen, and Tirri 2005], and *similarity detection* [Li, Chen, Li, Ma, and Vitányi 2003]. In these areas there has been less research and a 'definite' MDL approach has not yet been formulated.

MDL *has* been developed in some detail for some other inductive tasks: *nonparametric* inference, *parameter estimation*, and *regression* and *classification* problems. We give a very brief overview of these; see [Barron, Rissanen, and Yu 1998; Hansen and Yu 2001] and, for the classification case, [Grünwald and Langford 2004].

Nonparametric Inference Sometimes the model class $\mathcal{M}$ is so large that it cannot be finitely parameterized. For example, let $\mathcal{X} = [0, 1]$ be the unit interval and let $\mathcal{M}$ be the i.i.d. model consisting of *all* distributions on $\mathcal{X}$ with densities f such that $-\log f(x)$ is a continuous function on $\mathcal{X}$. $\mathcal{M}$ is clearly 'nonparametric': it cannot be meaningfully parameterized by a connected finite-dimensional parameter set $\Theta^{(k)} \subseteq \mathbb{R}^k$. We may still try to learn a distribution from $\mathcal{M}$ in various ways, for example by *histogram density estimation* [Rissanen, Speed, and Yu 1992] or *kernel density estimation* [Rissanen 1989]. MDL is quite suitable for such applications, in which we typically select a density f from a class $\mathcal{M}^{(n)} \subset \mathcal{M}$, where $\mathcal{M}^{(n)}$ grows with n, and every $P^* \in \mathcal{M}$ can be arbitrarily well approximated by members of $\mathcal{M}^{(n)}, \mathcal{M}^{(n+1)}, \ldots$ in the sense that $\lim_{n \to \infty} \inf_{P \in \mathcal{M}^{(n)}} D(P^* \| P) = 0$ [Barron et al. 1998]. Here D is the *Kullback-Leibler* divergence [Cover and Thomas 1991] between P^* and P.

MDL Parameter Estimation: Three Approaches The 'crude' MDL method (Section 2.3) was a means of doing model selection and parameter estimation at the same time. 'Refined' MDL only dealt with selection of *models*. If instead, or at the same time, parameter estimates are needed, they may be obtained in three different ways. Historically the first suggestion [Rissanen 1989; Hansen and Yu 2001] was to simply use the refined MDL principle to pick a parametric model $\mathcal{M}^{(k)}$, and then, within $\mathcal{M}^{(k)}$, pick the ML estimator $\hat{\theta}^{(k)}$. After all, we associate with $\mathcal{M}^{(k)}$ the distribution $\bar{P}_{\text{nml}}$ with code lengths 'as close as possible' to those achieved by the ML estimator. This suggests that within $\mathcal{M}^{(k)}$, we should prefer the ML estimator. But upon closer inspection, this is not really the right thing to do: Figure 2.4 suggests using a two-part code also to select θ within $\mathcal{M}^{(k)}$; namely, we should discretize the parameter space in such a way that the resulting two-part code achieves the minimax regret among all two-part codes; we then pick the (quantized) θ minimizing the two-part code length. Essentially this approach has been worked out in detail by Barron and Cover [1991]. The resulting estimators may be called *two-part code MDL estimators*. A third possibility is to define *predictive MDL estimators* such as the Laplace and Jeffreys estimators of Example 2.19; once again, these can be understood as an extension of Figure 2.4 [Barron et al. 1998]. These second and third possibilities are more sophisticated than the first: in contrast to the ML estimates, the parameter estimates resulting from the second and third approach can be directly justfied in terms of code length minimization; although the ML estimator has been suggested in the early MDL literature, it cannot be interpreted in terms of minimizing code length and therefore, in my opinion, should not be called an MDL estimator. Not surprisingly, whereas the ML estimate is prone to overfitting as soon as the complexity of the model is not much smaller than the sample sizes, the two-part code and predictive MDL estimators give reasonable results even for very small samples [Grünwald 1998, Chapter 6].

Finally, note that if *the model $\mathcal{M}$ is finite-dimensional parametric and n is large compared to the parametric complexity of $\mathcal{M}$*, then both the two-part and the predictive MDL estimators will become indistinguishable from the ML estimators. For this reason, it has sometimes been claimed that MDL parameter estimation is just ML parameter estimation. Since for small samples, the estimates can be quite different, this statement is misleading.

Regression In regression problems we are interested in learning how the values $y_1, \ldots, y_n$ of a *regression* variable Y depend on the values $x_1, \ldots, x_n$ of the *regressor* variable X. We assume or hope that there exists some function $h : \mathcal{X} \to \mathcal{Y}$ so that $h(X)$ predicts the value Y reasonably well, and we want to learn such an h from data. To this end, we assume a set of *candidate predictors* (functions) $\mathcal{H}$. In Example 1.2, we took $\mathcal{H}$ to be the set of all polynomials. In the standard formulation of this problem, we take h to express that

$$Y_i = h(X_i) + Z_i, \tag{2.38}$$

where the Z_i are i.i.d. Gaussian random variables with mean 0 and some variance σ^2, independent of X_i. That is, we assume Gaussian noise: (2.38) implies that the conditional density of $y_1, \ldots, y_n$, given $x_1, \ldots, x_n$, is equal to the product of n Gaussian densities:

$$P(y^n \mid x^n, \sigma, h) = \left(\frac{1}{\sqrt{2\pi}\sigma} \right)^n \exp\left(-\frac{\sum_{i=1}^n (y_i - h(x_i))^2}{2\sigma^2} \right) \tag{2.39}$$

With this choice, the log-likelihood becomes a linear function of the squared error:

$$-\log P(y^n \mid x^n, \sigma, h) = \frac{1}{2\sigma^2} \sum_{i=1}^n (y_i - h(x_i))^2 + \frac{n}{2} \log 2\pi\sigma^2 \tag{2.40}$$

Let us now assume that $\mathcal{H} = \cup_{k \geq 1} \mathcal{H}^{(k)}$ where for each k, $\mathcal{H}^{(k)}$ is a set of functions $h : \mathcal{X} \to \mathcal{Y}$. For example, $\mathcal{H}^{(k)}$ may be the set of kth-degree polynomials.

When the Code length for x^n Can Be Ignored

If all models under consideration represent *conditional* densities or probability mass functions $P(Y \mid X)$, then the code length for $X_1, \ldots, X_n$ can be ignored in model and parameter selection. Examples are applications of MDL in *classification* and *regression*.

Figure 2.5 Ignoring code lengths.

With each model $\mathcal{H}^{(k)}$ we can associate a set of densities (2.39), one for each (h, σ^2) with $h \in \mathcal{H}^{(k)}$ and $\sigma^2 \in \mathbb{R}^+$. Let $\mathcal{M}^{(k)}$ be the resulting set of conditional distributions. Each $P(\cdot \mid h, \sigma^2) \in \mathcal{M}^{(k)}$ is identified by the parameter vector $(\alpha_0, \ldots, \alpha_k, \sigma^2)$ so that $h(x) := \sum_{j=0}^{k} \alpha_j x^j$. By Section 2.6.1, (2.8) MDL tells us to select the model minimizing

$$- \log \bar{P}(y^n \mid \mathcal{M}^{(k)}, x^n) + L(k), \qquad (2.41)$$

where we may take $L(k) = 2 \log k + 1$, and $\bar{P}(\cdot \mid \mathcal{M}^{(k)}, \cdot)$ is now a *conditional* universal model with small minimax regret. Equation (2.41) ignores the code length of $x_1, \ldots, x_n$. Intuitively, this is because we are only interested in learning how y *depends* on x; therefore, we do not care how many bits are needed to encode x. Formally, this may be understood as follows: we really *are* encoding the x-values as well, but we do so using a fixed code that does not depend on the hypothesis h under consideration. Thus, we are really trying to find the model $\mathcal{M}^{(k)}$ minimizing

$$- \log \bar{P}(y^n \mid \mathcal{M}^{(k)}, x^n) + L(k) + L'(x^n),$$

where L' represents some code for $\mathcal{X}^n$. Since this code length does not involve k, it can be dropped from the minimization; see Figure 2.5. We will not go into the precise definition of $\bar{P}(y^n \mid \mathcal{M}^{(k)}, x^n)$. Ideally, it should be an NML distribution, but just as in Example 2.20, this NML distribution is not well-defined. We can get reasonable alternative universal models after all using any of the methods described in Section 2.6.2; see [Barron et al. 1998] and [Rissanen 2000] for details.

'Nonprobabilistic' Regression and Classification In the approach we just described, we modeled the noise as being normally distributed. Alternatively, it has been tried to *directly* try to learn functions $h \in \mathcal{H}$ from the data, without making any probabilistic assumptions about the noise [Rissanen 1989; Barron 1990; Yamanishi 1998; Grünwald 1998; Grünwald 1999]. The idea is to learn a function h that leads to good predictions of future data from the same source in the spirit of Vapnik's [1998] *statistical learning theory*. Here prediction quality is measured by some fixed loss function; different loss functions lead to different instantiations of the procedure. Such a version of MDL is meant to be more robust, leading to inference of a 'good' $h \in \mathcal{H}$ irrespective of the details of the noise distribution.

This loss-based approach has also been the method of choice in applying MDL to *classification* problems. Here $\mathcal{Y}$ takes on values in a finite set, and the goal is to match each *feature* X (e.g., a bit map of a handwritten digit) with its corresponding *label* or *class* (e.g., a digit). While several versions of MDL for classification have been proposed [Quinlan and Rivest 1989; Rissanen 1989; Kearns, Mansour, Ng, and Ron 1997], most of these can be reduced to the same approach based on a 0/1-valued loss function [Grünwald 1998]. In recent work [Grünwald and Langford 2004] we show that this MDL approach to classification without making assumptions about the noise may behave suboptimally: we exhibit situations where no matter how large n, MDL keeps overfitting, selecting an overly complex model with suboptimal predictive behavior. Modifications of MDL suggested by Barron [1990] and Yamanishi [1998] do not suffer from this defect, but they do not admit a natural coding interpretation any longer. All in all, current versions of MDL that avoid probabilistic assumptions are still in their infancy, and more research is needed to find out whether they can be modified to perform well in more general and realistic settings.

Summary In previous sections, we have covered basic refined MDL (Section 2.5), general refined MDL (Section 2.6), and several extensions of refined MDL (this section). This concludes our technical description of refined MDL. It only remains to place MDL in its proper context: What does it *do* compared with other methods of inductive inference? And how *well* does it *perform*, compared with other methods? The next two sections are devoted to these questions.

2.8 Relations to Other Approaches to Inductive Inference

How does MDL compare with other model selection and statistical inference methods? In order to answer this question, we first have to be precise about what we mean by 'MDL'; this is done in Section 2.8.1. We then continue in Section 2.8.2 by summarizing MDL's relation to *Bayesian inference*, Wallace's *minimum message length (MML) principle*, Dawid's *prequential model validation*, *cross-validation*, and an 'idealized' version of MDL based on Kolmogorov complexity. The literature has also established connections between MDL and Jaynes's [2003] *maximum entropy principle* [Feder 1986; Li and Vitányi 1997; Grünwald 1998; Grünwald 2000; Grünwald and Dawid 2004] and Vapnik's [1998] *structural risk minimization principle* [Grünwald 1998], but there is no space here to discuss these. Relations between MDL and Akaike's *AIC* [Burnham and Anderson 2002] are subtle. They are discussed by, for example, Speed and Yu [1993].

2.8.1 What is MDL?

'MDL' is used by different authors to mean somewhat different things. Some authors use MDL as a broad umbrella term for all types of inductive inference based on data compression. This would, for example, include the 'idealized' versions of MDL based on Kolmogorov complexity and Wallaces's MML principle, to be discussed below. At the other extreme, for historical reasons, some authors use the *MDL criterion* to describe a very specific (and often not very successful) model selection criterion equivalent to the 'Bayesian information criterion' (BIC), discussed further below.

Here we adopt the meaning of the term that is embraced in the survey [Barron et al. 1998], written by arguably the three most important contributors to the field: we use MDL for general *inference based on universal models*. These include, but are not limited to approaches in the spirit of Figure 2.4. For example, some authors have based their inferences on 'expected' rather than 'individual sequence' universal models [Barron et al. 1998; Liang and Barron 2005]. Moreover, if we go beyond model selection (Section 2.7), then the ideas of Figure 2.4 have to be modified to some extent. In fact, one of the main strengths of 'MDL' in this broad sense is that it can be applied to ever more exotic modeling situations, in which the models do not resemble anything that is usually encountered in statistical practice. An example is the model of context-free grammars, already suggested by Solomonoff [1964]. In this tutorial, we call applications of MDL that strictly fit into the scheme of Figure 2.4 *refined MDL for model/hypothesis selection*; when we simply say "MDL," we mean 'inductive inference based on universal models'. This form of inductive inference goes hand in hand with Rissanen's radical MDL *philosophy*, which views learning as finding useful properties of the data, not necessarily related to the existence of a 'truth' underlying the data. This view was outlined in Chapter 1, Section 1.5. Although MDL practitioners and theorists are usually sympathetic to it, the different interpretations of MDL listed in Section 2.5 make clear that MDL applications can also be justified without adopting such a radical philosophy.

2.8.2   MDL and Bayesian Inference

Bayesian statistics [Lee 1997; Bernardo and Smith 1994] is one of the most well-known, frequently and successfully applied paradigms of statistical inference. It is often claimed that 'MDL is really just a special case of Bayes.[19'] Although there are close similarities, this is simply not true. To see this quickly, consider the basic quantity in refined MDL: the NML distribution $\bar{P}_{\text{nml}}$, Equation (2.18). While $\bar{P}_{\text{nml}}$ — although defined in a completely different manner — turns out to be closely related to the Bayesian marginal likelihood, this is no longer the case for its 'localized' version (2.37). There is no mention of anything like this code/distribution in any Bayesian textbook! Thus, it must be the case that Bayes and MDL are somehow different.

MDL as a Maximum Probability Principle   For a more detailed analysis, we need to distinguish between the two central tenets of modern Bayesian statistics: (1) Probability distributions are used to represent uncertainty and to serve as a basis for making predictions, rather than standing for some imagined 'true state of nature'. (2) All inference and decision making is done in terms of prior and posterior distributions. MDL sticks with (1) (although here the 'distributions' are primarily interpreted as 'code length functions'), but not (2): MDL allows the use of arbitrary universal models such as NML and prequential universal models; the Bayesian universal model does not have a special status among these. In this sense, Bayes offers the statistician *less* freedom in choice of implementation than MDL. In fact, MDL may be reinterpreted as a *maximum probability principle*, where the maximum is relative to some given model, in the worst case over all sequences (Rissanen [1987, 1989] uses the phrase '*global* maximum likelihood principle'). Thus, whenever the Bayesian universal model is used in an MDL application, a prior should be used that minimizes worst-case code length regret, or equivalently, maximizes worst-case relative probability. There is no comparable principle for choosing priors in Bayesian statistics, and in this respect, Bayes offers a lot *more* freedom than MDL.

Example 2.22 There is a conceptual problem with Bayes' use of prior distributions: in practice, we very often want to use models which we a priori know to be wrong; see Example 1.5. If we use Bayes for such models, then we are forced to put a prior distribution on a set of distributions which we know to be wrong — that is, we have degree-of-belief 1 in something we know not to be the case. From an MDL viewpoint, these priors are interpreted as tools to achieve short code lengths rather than degrees-of-belief and there is nothing strange about the situation, but from a Bayesian viewpoint, it seems awkward. To be sure, Bayesian inference often gives good results even if the model $\mathcal{M}$ is known to be wrong; the point is that (a) if one is a strict Bayesian, one would never apply Bayesian inference to such misspecified $\mathcal{M}$, and (b), the Bayesian theory offers no clear explanation of why Bayesian inference might still give good results for such $\mathcal{M}$. MDL provides both code length and predictive-sequential interpretations of Bayesian inference, which help explain why Bayesian inference may do something reasonable even if $\mathcal{M}$ is misspecified. To be fair, we should add that there exist variations of the Bayesian philosophy (e.g., De Finetti [1974]'s) which avoid the conceptual problem we just described.

MDL and BIC   In the first paper on MDL, Rissanen [1978] used a two-part code and showed that, asymptotically, and under regularity conditions, the two-part code length of x^n based on a k-parameter model $\mathcal{M}$ with an optimally discretized parameter space is given by

$$- \log P(x^n \mid \hat{\theta}(x^n)) + \frac{k}{2} \log n, \qquad (2.42)$$

thus ignoring $O(1)$-terms, which, as we have already seen, can be quite important. In the same year Schwarz [1978] showed that, for large enough n, Bayesian model selection between two exponential families amounts to selecting the model minimizing (2.42), ignoring $O(1)$-terms as well. As a result of Schwarz's paper, model selection based on (2.42) became known as the *BIC (Bayesian information criterion)*. Not taking into account the functional form of the model $\mathcal{M}$, it often does not work very well in practice.

It has sometimes been claimed that MDL = BIC; for example, [Burnham and Anderson 2002, p. 286] write, "Rissanen's result is equivalent to BIC". This is wrong, even for the 1989 version of MDL that Burnham and Anderson refer to —

as pointed out by Foster and Stine [2005], the BIC approximation only holds if the number of parameters k is kept fixed and n goes to infinity. If we select between nested families of models where the maximum number of parameters k considered is either infinite or grows with n, then model selection based on both $\bar{P}_{\mathrm{nml}}$ and on $\bar{P}_{\mathrm{Bayes}}$ tends to select quite different models than BIC — if k gets closer to n, the contribution to $\mathbf{COMP}_n(\mathcal{M})$ of each additional parameter becomes much smaller than $0.5 \log n$ [Foster and Stine 2005]. However, researchers who claim MDL = BIC have a good excuse: in early work, Rissanen himself used the phrase 'MDL criterion' to refer to (2.42), and unfortunately, the phrase has stuck.

MDL and MML MDL shares some ideas with the *minimum message length (MML) principle* which predates MDL by ten years. Key references are [Wallace and Boulton 1968, 1975] and [Wallace and Freeman 1987]; a long list is in [Comley and Dowe 2005]. Just as in MDL, MML chooses the hypothesis minimizing the code length of the data. But the *codes* that are used are quite different from those in MDL. First of all, in MML one *always* uses two-part codes, so that MML automatically selects both a model family and parameter values. Second, while the MDL codes such as $\bar{P}_{\mathrm{nml}}$ minimize *worst-case relative code length* (regret), the two-part codes used by MML are designed to minimize *expected absolute code length*. Here the expectation is taken over a subjective prior distribution defined on the collection of models and parameters under consideration. While this approach contradicts Rissanen's philosophy, in practice it often leads to similar results.

Indeed, Wallace and his co-workers stress that their approach is fully (subjective) *Bayesian*. Strictly speaking, a Bayesian should report his findings by citing the full posterior distribution. But sometimes one is interested in a single model or hypothesis for the data. A good example is the inference of phylogenetic trees in biological applications: the full posterior would consist of a mixture of several of such trees, which might all be quite different from each other. Such a mixture is almost impossible to interpret — to get insight into the data we need a single tree. In that case, Bayesians often use the MAP (Maximum A Posteriori) hypothesis which maximizes the posterior, or the posterior mean parameter value. Both approaches have some unpleasant properties. For example, the MAP approach is not invariant under reparameterization. The posterior mean approach cannot be used if different model families are to be compared with each other. The MML method provides a theoretically sound way of proceeding in such cases.

2.8.3 MDL, Prequential Analysis, and Cross-Validation

In a series of papers, A.P. Dawid [1984, 1992, 1997] put forward a methodology for probability and statistics based on sequential prediction which he called the *prequential approach*. When applied to model selection problems, it is closely related to MDL. Dawid proposes to construct, for each model $\mathcal{M}^{(j)}$ under consideration, a 'probability forecasting system' (a sequential prediction strategy) where the $i+1$st outcome is predicted based on either the Bayesian posterior $\bar{P}_{\mathrm{Bayes}}(\theta|x^i)$ or on some

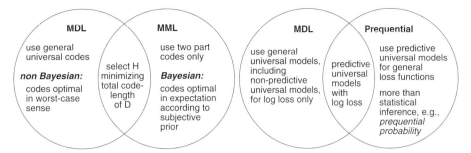

Figure 2.6   Rissanen's MDL, Wallace's MML and Dawid's Prequential Approach.

estimator $\hat{\theta}(x^i)$. Then the model is selected for which the associated sequential prediction strategy minimizes the accumulated prediction error. Related ideas were put forward by Hjorth [1982] under the name *forward validation* and Rissanen [1984]. From Section 2.5.4 we see that this is just a form of MDL — strictly speaking, *every* universal code can be thought of as a prediction strategy, but for the Bayesian and the plug-in universal models (Sections 2.5.3, 2.5.4) the interpretation is much more natural than for others.[20] Dawid mostly talks about such 'predictive' universal models. On the other hand, Dawid's framework allows adjusting the prediction loss to be measured in terms of arbitrary loss functions, not just the log loss. In this sense, it is more general than MDL. Finally, the prequential idea goes beyond statistics: there is also a 'prequential approach' to probability theory developed by Dawid [Dawid and Vovk 1999] and Shafer and Vovk [2001].

Note that the prequential approach is similar in spirit to cross-validation. In this sense MDL is related to cross-validation as well. The main differences are that in MDL and the prequential approach, (1) all predictions are done *sequentially* (the future is never used to predict the past), and (2) each outcome is predicted *exactly once*.

2.8.4   Kolmogorov Complexity and Structure Function; Ideal MDL

Kolmogorov complexity [Li and Vitányi 1997] has played a large but mostly inspirational role in Rissanen's development of MDL. Over the last fifteen years, several 'idealized' versions of MDL have been proposed, which are more directly based on Kolmogorov complexity theory [Barron 1985; Barron and Cover 1991; Li and Vitányi 1997; Vereshchagin and Vitányi 2002]. These are all based on two-part codes, where hypotheses are described using a universal programming language such as C or PASCAL. For example, in one proposal [Barron and Cover 1991], given data D one picks the distribution minimizing

$$K(P) + \big[-\log P(D)\big], \tag{2.43}$$

where the minimum is taken over *all* computable probability distributions, and $K(P)$ is the length of the shortest computer program that, when input (x, d), outputs $P(x)$ to d bits precision. While such a procedure is mathematically well-defined, it cannot be used in practice. The reason is that, in general, the P minimizing (2.43) cannot be effectively computed. Kolmogorov himself used a variation of (2.43) in which one adopts, among all P with $K(P) - \log P(D) \approx K(D)$, the P with smallest $K(P)$. Here $K(D)$ is the Kolmogorov complexity of D, that is, the length of the shortest computer program that prints D and then halts. This approach is known as the Kolmogorov *structure function* or *minimum sufficient statistic* approach [Vitányi 2005]. In this approach, the idea of separating data and noise (Section 2.5.1) is taken as basic, and the hypothesis selection procedure is defined in terms of it. The selected hypothesis may now be viewed as capturing all structure inherent in the data — given the hypothesis, the data cannot be distinguished from random noise. Therefore, it may be taken as a basis for *lossy* data compression — rather than sending the whole sequence, one only sends the hypothesis representing the 'structure' in the data. The receiver can then use this hypothesis to generate 'typical' data for it — these data should then 'look just the same' as the original data D. Rissanen views this separation idea as perhaps the most fundamental aspect of 'learning by compression'. Therefore, in recent work he has tried to relate MDL (as defined here, based on lossless compression) to the Kolmogorov structure function, thereby connecting it to lossy compression, and, as he puts it, 'opening up a new chapter in the MDL theory' [Vereshchagin and Vitányi 2002; Vitányi 2005; Rissanen and Tabus 2005].

Summary and Outlook We have shown that MDL is closely related to, yet distinct from, several other methods for inductive inference. In the next section we discuss how well it *performs* compared to such other methods.

2.9   Problems for MDL?

Some authors have criticized MDL either on conceptual grounds (the idea makes no sense) [Webb 1996; Domingos 1999] or on practical grounds (sometimes it does not work very well in practice) [Kearns et al., 1997; E. Pednault, personal communication, June 2003]. Are these criticisms justified? Let us consider them in turn.

2.9.1   Conceptual Problems: Occam's Razor

The most often heard conceptual criticisms are invariably related to Occam's razor. We have already discussed in Chapter 1, Section 1.5 why we regard these criticisms as being entirely mistaken. Based on our newly acquired technical knowledge of MDL, let us discuss these criticisms a little bit further:

1. "Occam's Razor (and MDL) Is Arbitrary" If we restrict ourselves to refined MDL for comparing a finite number of models for which the NML distribution is well-defined, then there is *nothing* arbitrary about MDL — it is exactly clear what codes we should use for our inferences. The NML distribution and its close cousins, the Jeffreys' prior marginal likelihood $\bar{P}_{\text{Bayes}}$, and the asymptotic expansion (2.21), are all invariant to continuous one-to-one reparameterizations of the model: parameterizing our model in a different way (choosing a different 'description language') does not change the inferred description lengths.

If we go beyond models for which the NML distribution is defined, or if we compare an infinite set of models at the same time, then some 'subjectivity' *is* introduced — while there are still tough restrictions on the codes that we are allowed to use, all such codes prefer some hypotheses in the model to others. If one does not have an a priori preference for any of the hypotheses, one may interpret this as some arbitrariness being added to the procedure. But this 'arbitrariness' is of an infinitely milder sort than the arbitrariness that can be introduced if we allow completely arbitrary codes for the encoding of hypotheses as in crude two-part code MDL, Section 2.3.

Things get more subtle if we are interested not in model selection (find the best order Markov chain for the data) but in infinite-dimensional estimation (find the best Markov chain parameters for the data, among the set $\mathcal{B}$ of all Markov chains of each order). In the latter case, if we are to apply MDL, we somehow have to carve up $\mathcal{B}$ into subsets $\mathcal{M}^{(0)} \subseteq \mathcal{M}^{(1)} \subseteq \ldots \subseteq \mathcal{B}$. Suppose that we have already chosen $\mathcal{M}^{(1)} = \mathcal{B}^{(1)}$ as the set of 1st-order Markov chains. We normally take $\mathcal{M}^{(0)} = \mathcal{B}^{(0)}$, the set of 0th-order Markov chains (Bernoulli distributions). But we could also have defined $\mathcal{M}^{(0)}$ as the set of all 1st-order Markov chains with $P(X_{i+1} = 1 \mid X_i = 1) = P(X_{i+1} = 0 \mid X_i = 0)$. This defines a one-dimensional subset of $\mathcal{B}^{(1)}$ that is *not* equal to $\mathcal{B}^{(0)}$. While there are several good reasons[21] for choosing $\mathcal{B}^{(0)}$ rather than $\mathcal{M}^{(0)}$, there may be no indication that $\mathcal{B}^{(0)}$ is somehow a priori more likely than $\mathcal{M}^{(0)}$. While MDL tells us that we somehow have to carve up the full set $\mathcal{B}$, it does not give us precise guidelines on how to do this – different carvings may be equally justified and lead to different inferences for small samples. In this sense, there is indeed some form of arbitrariness in this type of MDL application. But this is unavoidable: we stress that this type of arbitrariness is enforced by *all* combined model/parameter selection methods - whether they be of the structural risk minimization (SRM) type [Vapnik 1998], AIC type [Burnham and Anderson 2002], cross-validation, or any other type. The only alternative is treating all hypotheses in the huge class $\mathcal{B}$ on the same footing, which amounts to ML estimation and extreme overfitting.

2. "Occam's Razor Is False"   We often try to model real-world situations that can be arbitrarily complex, so why should we favor simple models? We gave an informal answer in Chapter 1, Section 1.6, where we claimed that *even if the true data-generating machinery is very complex, it may be a good strategy to prefer simple models for small sample sizes.*

We are now in a position to give one formalization of this informal claim: it is simply the fact that MDL procedures, with their built-in preference for 'simple' models with small parametric complexity, are typically *statistically consistent*, achieving *good rates of convergence* (page 14), whereas methods such as ML which do not take model complexity into account are typically *inconsistent* whenever they are applied to complex enough models such as the set of polynomials of each degree or the set of Markov chains of all orders. This has implications for the quality of predictions: with complex enough models, no matter how many training data we observe, if we use the ML distribution to predict future data from the same source, the prediction error we make will not converge to the prediction error that could be obtained if the true distribution were known; if we use an MDL submodel/parameter estimate (Section 2.7), the prediction error *will* converge to this optimal achievable error.

Of course, consistency is not the only desirable property of a learning method, and it may be that in some particular settings, and under some particular performance measures, some alternatives to MDL outperform MDL. Indeed this can happen – see below. Yet it remains the case that all methods I know of that deal successfully with models of arbitrary complexity have a built-in preference for selecting simpler models at small sample sizes — methods such as Vapnik's [1998] structural risk minimization, penalized minimum error estimators [Barron 1990], and the Akaike's AIC [Burnham and Anderson 2002] all trade off complexity with error on the data, the result invariably being that in this way, good convergence properties can be obtained. While these approaches measure 'complexity' in a manner different from MDL, and attach different relative weights to error on the data and complexity, the fundamental idea of finding a *tradeoff* between 'error' and 'complexity' remains.

2.9.2   Practical Problems with MDL

We just described some perceived problems about MDL. Unfortunately, there are also some real ones: MDL is not a perfect method. While in many cases the methods described here perform very well,[22] there are also cases where they perform suboptimally compared with other state-of-the-art methods. Often this is due to one of two reasons:

1. An asymptotic formula like (2.21) was used and the sample size was not large enough to justify this [Navarro 2004].

2. $\bar{P}_{\text{nml}}$ was undefined for the models under consideration, and this was solved by cutting off the parameter ranges at *ad hoc* values [Lanterman 2005].

In these cases the problem probably lies with the use of invalid approximations rather than with the MDL idea itself. More research is needed to find out when the asymptotics and other approximations can be trusted, and what is the 'best' way to deal with undefined $\bar{P}_{\text{nml}}$. For the time being, we suggest that the use of (2.21) be avoided whenever possible, and that the parameter ranges never be cut off at arbitrary values — instead, if $\textbf{COMP}_n(\mathcal{M})$ becomes infinite, then some of the methods described in Section 2.6.2 should be used. Among these, there is some – disputed – evidence that Rissanen's renormalization scheme (RNML, Section 2.6.2) does not work very well, at least in the context of wavelet denoising [Rissanen 2000].[23] Note that, whenever they are well-defined, $\bar{P}_{\text{nml}}$ and Bayesian inference with Jeffreys' prior are the preferred methods, since they both achieve the minimax regret. If they are either ill-defined or computationally prohibitive for the models under consideration, one can use a prequential method or a sophisticated two-part code such as that described by Barron and Cover [1991].

MDL and Misspecification   However, there is a class of problems where MDL is problematic in a more fundamental sense. Namely, if none of the distributions under consideration represents the data-generating machinery very well, then both MDL and Bayesian inference may sometimes do a bad job in finding the 'best' approximation within this class of not-so-good hypotheses. This has been observed in practice[24] [Kearns et al. 1997; Clarke 2002; E. Pednault, personal communication, June 2003]. Grünwald and Langford [2004] show that MDL can behave quite unreasonably for some classification problems in which the true distribution is not in $\mathcal{M}$. This is closely related to the problematic behavior of MDL for classification tasks as mentioned in Section 2.7. All this is a bit ironic, since MDL was explicitly designed *not* to depend on the untenable assumption that some $P^* \in \mathcal{M}$ generates the data. But empirically we find that while it generally works quite well if some $P^* \in \mathcal{M}$ generates the data, it may sometimes fail if this is not the case.

2.10   Conclusion

MDL is a versatile method for inductive inference: it can be interpreted in at least four different ways, all of which indicate that it does something reasonable. It is typically asymptotically consistent, achieving good rates of convergence. It achieves all this *without* having been designed for consistency, being based on a philosophy which makes no metaphysical assumptions about the existence of 'true' distributions. All this strongly suggests that it is a good method to use in practice. Practical evidence shows that in many contexts it is, in other contexts its behavior can be problematic. In my view, the main challenge for the future is to improve MDL for such cases, by somehow extending and further refining MDL procedures in a non–ad-hoc manner. I am confident that this can be done, and that MDL will continue to play an important role in the development of statistical and, more generally, inductive inference.

Further Reading   MDL can be found on the web at `www.mdl-research.org`. Good places to start further exploration of MDL are [Barron et al. 1998] and [Hansen and Yu 2001]. Both papers provide excellent introductions, but they are geared toward a more specialized audience of information theorists and statisticians, respectively. Also worth reading is Rissanen's [1989] monograph. While outdated as an introduction to MDL *methods*, this famous 'little green book' still serves as a great introduction to Rissanen's radical but appealing *philosophy*, which is described very eloquently.

Acknowledgments   I thank Jay Myung, Mark Pitt, Steven de Rooij, and Teemu Roos, who read a preliminary version of this chapter and suggested several improvements.

Notes

1. But see Section 2.8.4.

2. Working directly with distributions on infinite sequences is more elegant, but it requires measure theory, which we want to avoid here.

3. Also known as *instantaneous codes* and called, perhaps more justifiably, 'prefix-free' codes in [Li and Vitányi 1997].

4. For example, with noninteger code lengths the notion of 'code' becomes invariant to the size of the alphabet in which we describe data.

5. As understood in elementary probability, that is, with respect to Lebesgue measure.

6. Even if one adopts a Bayesian stance and postulates that an agent can come up with a (subjective) distribution for *every* conceivable domain, this problem remains: in practice, the adopted distribution may be so complicated that we cannot design the optimal code corresponding to it, and have to use some ad hoc-code instead.

7. Henceforth, we simply use 'model' to denote probabilistic models; we typically use $\mathcal{H}$ to denote sets of hypotheses such as polynomials, and reserve $\mathcal{M}$ for probabilistic models.

8. The term 'crude MDL' is not standard. It is introduced here for pedagogical reasons, to make clear the importance of having a single, unified principle for designing codes. It should be noted that Rissanen's and Barron's early theoretical papers on MDL already contain such principles, albeit in a slightly different form than in their recent papers. Early practical applications [Quinlan and Rivest 1989; Grünwald 1996] often do use ad hoc two-part codes which really are 'crude' in the sense defined here.

9. See the previous endnote.

10. But see [Grünwald 1998, Chapter 5] for more discussion.

11. See Section 1.5 of Chapter 1 for a discussion on the role of consistency in MDL.

12. See, for example [Barron and Cover 1991; Barron 1985]

13. Strictly speaking, the assumption that n is given in advance (i.e., both encoder and decoder know n) contradicts the earlier requirement that the code to be used for encoding hypotheses is not allowed to depend on n. Thus, strictly speaking, we should first encode some n explicitly, using $2\log n + 1$ bits (Example 2.4) and then pick the n (typically, but not necessarily equal to the actual sample size) that allows for the shortest three-part code length of the data (first encode n, then (k, θ), then the data). In practice this will not significantly alter the chosen hypothesis, unless for some quite special data sequences.

14. As explained in Figure 2.2, we identify these codes with their length functions, which is the only aspect we are interested in.

15. The reason is that, in the full Bernoulli model with parameter $\theta \in [0, 1]$, the maximum likelihood estimator is given by n_1/n, see Example 2.7. Since the likelihood $\log P(x^n \mid \theta)$ is a continuous function of θ, this implies that if the frequency n_1/n in x^n is approximately (but not precisely) $j/10$, then the ML estimator in the restricted model $\{0.1, \ldots, 0.9\}$ is still given by $\hat{\theta} = j/10$. Then $\log P(x^n|\theta)$ is maximized by $\hat{\theta} = j/10$, so that the $L \in \mathcal{L}$ that minimizes code length corresponds to $\theta = j/10$.

16. What we call 'universal model' in this text is known in the literature as a 'universal model in the individual sequence sense' – there also exist universal models in an 'expected sense', see Section 2.8.1. These lead to slightly different versions of MDL.

17. To be fair, we should add that this naive version of GLRT is introduced here for educational purposes only. It is not recommended by any serious statistician!

18. The standard definition of Fisher information [Kass and Voss 1997] is in terms of first derivatives of the log-likelihood; for most parametric models of interest, the present definition coincides with the standard one.

19. I have heard many people say this at many conferences. The reasons are probably historical: while the underlying philosophy has always been different, until Rissanen introduced the use of $\bar{P}_{\mathrm{nml}}$, most actual implementations of MDL 'looked' quite Bayesian.

20. The reason is that the Bayesian and plug-in models can be interpreted as probabilistic sources. The NML and the two-part code models are not probabilistic sources, since $\bar{P}^{(n)}$ and $\bar{P}^{(n+1)}$ are not compatible in the sense of Section 2.1.

21. For example, $\mathcal{B}^{(0)}$ is better interpretable.

22. We mention Hansen and Yu [2000,2001] reporting excellent behavior of MDL in regression

contexts; and Allen, Madani, and Greiner [2003], Kontkanen, Myllymäki, Silander, and Tirri [1999] and Modha and Masry [1998] reporting excellent behavior of predictive (prequential) coding in Bayesian network model selection and regression. Also, 'objective Bayesian' model selection methods are frequently and successfully used in practice [Kass and Wasserman 1996]. Since these are based on noninformative priors such as Jeffreys', they often coincide with a version of refined MDL and thus indicate successful performance of MDL.

23. To be specific, this was communicated to the author by T. Roos, U. Gather and L. Davies, and L. Russo, who all independently discovered this phenomenon. But later, T. Roos discovered that the equations given in [Rissanen 2000] ignored a substantial part of the codelength for the data, According to Roos, if the codelength is computed correctly, then the scheme works very well. At the time of writing this tutorial, Roos and co-workers and Gather and co-workers were preparing publications about the phenomenon.

24. But see Viswanathan., Wallace, Dowe, and Korb [1999] who point out that the problem of [Kearns et al. 1997] disappears if a more reasonable coding scheme is used.

References

Akaike, H. (1973). Information theory as an extension of the maximum likelihood principle. In B. N. Petrov and F. Csaki (Eds.), *Second International Symposium on Information Theory*, pp. 267–281. Budapest: Akademiai Kiado.

Allen, T.V., O. Madani, and R. Greiner (2003). Comparing model selection criteria for belief networks. Submitted for publication.

Balasubramanian, V. (1997). Statistical inference, Occam's razor, and statistical mechanics on the space of probability distributions. *Neural Computation, 9*, 349–368.

Balasubramanian, V. (2005). MDL, Bayesian inference and the geometry of the space of probability distributions. In P.D. Grünwald, I.J. Myung, and M.A. Pitt (Eds.), *Advances in Minimum Description Length: Theory and Applications.* Cambridge, MA: MIT Press.

Barron, A. (1990). Complexity regularization with application to artificial neural networks. In G. Roussas (Ed.), *Nonparametric Functional Estimation and Related Topics*, pp. 561–576. Dordrecht, the Netherlands: Kluwer.

Barron, A.R. and T. Cover (1991). Minimum complexity density estimation. *IEEE Transactions on Information Theory, 37*(4), 1034–1054.

Barron, A.R. (1985). *Logically Smooth Density Estimation.* Ph. D. thesis, Department of Electrical Engineering, Stanford University, Stanford, CA.

Barron, A.R., J. Rissanen, and B. Yu (1998). The Minimum Description Length Principle in coding and modeling. Special Commemorative Issue: Information Theory: 1948-1998. *IEEE Transactions on Information Theory, 44*(6), 2743–2760.

Bernardo, J., and A. Smith (1994). *Bayesian theory.* New York: Wiley.

Burnham, K.P., and D.R. Anderson (2002). *Model Selection and Multimodel Inference.* New York: Springer-Verlag.

Casella, G., and R. Berger (1990). *Statistical Inference.* Belmont, CA: Wadsworth.

Chaitin, G. (1966). On the length of programs for computing finite binary sequences. *Journal of the ACM, 13*, 547–569.

Chaitin, G. (1969). On the length of programs for computing finite binary sequences: Statistical considerations. *Journal of the ACM, 16*, 145–159.

Clarke, B. (2002). Comparing Bayes and non-Bayes model averaging when model approximation error cannot be ignored. Submitted for publication.

Comley, J.W., and D.L. Dowe (2005). Minimum Message Length and generalised Bayesian nets with asymmetric languages. In P.D. Grünwald, I.J. Myung, and M.A. Pitt (Eds.), *Advances in Minimum Description Length: Theory and Applications.* Cambridge, MA: MIT Press.

Cover, T., and J. Thomas (1991). *Elements of Information Theory.* New York: Wiley Interscience.

Csiszár, I., and P. Shields (2000). The consistency of the BIC Markov order estimator. *Annals of Statistics, 28*, 1601–1619.

Dawid, A. (1984). Present position and potential developments: Some personal views, statistical theory, the prequential approach. *Journal of the Royal Statistical Society, Series A, 147*(2), 278–292.

Dawid, A. (1992). Prequential analysis, stochastic complexity and Bayesian inference. In J. Bernardo, J. Berger, A. Dawid, and A. Smith (Eds.), *Bayesian Statistics*, Volume 4, pp. 109–125. Proceedings of the Fourth Valencia Meeting. Oxford, UK: Oxford University Press.

Dawid, A. (1997). Prequential analysis. In S. Kotz, C. Read, and D. Banks (Eds.), *Encyclopedia of Statistical Sciences*, Volume 1 (Update), pp. 464–470. New York: Wiley Interscience.

Dawid, A.P. and V.G. Vovk (1999). Prequential probability: Principles and properties. *Bernoulli 5*, 125–162.

De Finetti, B. (1974). *Theory of Probability. A Critical Introductory Treatment.* London: Wiley.

Domingos, P. (1999). The role of Occam's razor in knowledge discovery. *Data Mining and Knowledge Discovery, 3*(4), 409–425.

Feder, M. (1986). Maximum entropy as a special case of the minimum description length criterion. *IEEE Transactions on Information Theory, 32*(6), 847–849.

Feller, W. (1968). *An Introduction to Probability Theory and Its Applications*, 3rd edition, Volume 1. New York: Wiley.

Foster, D., and R. Stine (1999). Local asymptotic coding and the minimum description length. *IEEE Transactions on Information Theory, 45*, 1289–1293.

Foster, D., and R. Stine (2001). The competitive complexity ratio. In *Proceedings of the 2001 Conference on Information Sciences and Systems*, WP8 1-6.

Foster, D., and R. Stine (2005). The contribution of parameters to stochastic complexity. In P.D. Grünwald, I.J. Myung, and M.A. Pitt (Eds.), *Advances in Minimum Description Length: Theory and Applications*. Cambridge, MA: MIT Press.

Gács, P., J. Tromp, and P. Vitányi (2001). Algorithmic statistics. *IEEE Transactions on Information Theory, 47*(6), 2464–2479.

Grünwald, P.D. (1996). A minimum description length approach to grammar inference. In G.Scheler, S. Wermter, and E. Riloff (Eds.), *Connectionist, Statistical and Symbolic Approaches to Learning for Natural Language Processing*, Volume 1040 in Springer Lecture Notes in Artificial Intelligence, pp. 203–216. Berlin: Springer-Verlag

Grünwald, P.D. (1998). *The Minimum Description Length Principle and Reasoning under Uncertainty*. Ph. D. thesis, University of Amsterdam. Available as ILLC dissertation series 1998-03.

Grünwald, P.D. (1999). Viewing all models as 'probabilistic'. In *Proceedings of the Twelfth Annual Workshop on Computational Learning Theory (COLT' 99)*, pp. 171–182.

Grünwald, P.D. (2000). Maximum entropy and the glasses you are looking through. In *Proceedings of the Sixteenth Conference on Uncertainty in Artificial Intelligence (UAI 2000)*, pp. 238–246. San Francisco: Morgan Kaufmann.

Grünwald, P.D., and A.P. Dawid (2004). Game theory, maximum entropy, minimum discrepancy, and robust Bayesian decision theory. *Annals of Statistics, 32*(4).

Grünwald, P.D., and J. Langford (2004). Suboptimal behaviour of Bayes and MDL in classification under misspecification. In *Proceedings of the Seventeenth Annual Conference on Computational Learning Theory (COLT' 04)*.

Grünwald, P.D., I.J. Myung, and M.A. Pitt (Eds.) (2005). *Advances in Minimum Description Length: Theory and Applications*. Cambridge, MA: MIT Press.

Hansen, M., and B. Yu (2000). Wavelet thresholding via MDL for natural images. *IEEE Transactions on Information Theory, 46*, 1778–1788.

Hansen, M., and B. Yu (2001). Model selection and the principle of minimum description length. *Journal of the American Statistical Association, 96*(454), 746–774.

Hanson, A.J., and P.C.-W. Fu (2005). Applications of MDL to selected families of models. In P.D. Grünwald, I.J. Myung, and M.A. Pitt (Eds.), *Advances in Minimum Description Length: Theory and Applications*. Cambridge, MA: MIT Press.

Hjorth, U. (1982). Model selection and forward validation. *Scandinavian Journal of Statistics, 9*, 95–105.

Jaynes, E. (2003). *Probability Theory: the logic of science*. Cambridge, UK: Cambridge University Press. Edited by G. Larry Bretthorst.

Jeffreys, H. (1946). An invariant form for the prior probability in estimation problems. *Proceedings of the Royal Statistical Society (London), Series A,*

186, 453–461.

Jeffreys, H. (1961). *Theory of Probability*, 3rd edition. London: Oxford University Press.

Kass, R., and A.E. Raftery (1995). Bayes factors. *Journal of the American Statistical Association, 90*(430), 773–795.

Kass, R., and P. Voss (1997). *Geometrical Foundations of Asymptotic Inference.* New York: Wiley Interscience.

Kass, R., and L. Wasserman (1996). The selection of prior distributions by formal rules. *Journal of the American Statistical Association, 91*, 1343–1370.

Kearns, M., Y. Mansour, A. Ng, and D. Ron (1997). An experimental and theoretical comparison of model selection methods. *Machine Learning, 27*, 7–50.

Kolmogorov, A. (1965). Three approaches to the quantitative definition of information. *Problems of Information Transmission, 1*(1), 1–7.

Kontkanen, P., P. Myllymäki, W. Buntine, J. Rissanen, and H. Tirri (2005). An MDL framework for data clustering. In P.D. Grünwald, I.J. Myung, and M.A. Pitt (Eds.), *Advances in Minimum Description Length: Theory and Applications.* Cambridge, MA: MIT Press.

Kontkanen, P., P. Myllymäki, T. Silander, and H. Tirri (1999). On supervised selection of Bayesian networks. In K. Laskey and H. Prade (Eds.), *Proceedings of the Fifteenth International Conference on Uncertainty in Artificial Intelligence (UAI'99).* San Fransisco: Morgan Kaufmann.

Lanterman, A.D. (2005). Hypothesis testing for Poisson versus geometric distributions using stochastic complexity. In P.D. Grünwald, I.J. Myung, and M.A. Pitt (Eds.), *Advances in Minimum Description Length: Theory and Applications.* Cambridge, MA: MIT Press.

Lee, P. (1997). *Bayesian Statistics — an introduction.* London: Arnold & Oxford University Press.

Li, M., X. Chen, X. Li, B. Ma, and P. Vitányi (2003). The similarity metric. In *Proceedings of the fourteenth ACM-SIAM Symposium on Discrete Algorithms (SODA).*

Li, M., and P. Vitányi (1997). *An Introduction to Kolmogorov Complexity and Its Applications*, 2nd edition. New York: Springer-Verlag.

Liang, F., and A. Barron (2004). Exact minimax strategies for predictive density estimation. To appear in *IEEE Transactions on Information Theory.*

Liang, F., and A. Barron (2005). Exact minimax predictive density estimation and MDL. In P.D. Grünwald, I.J. Myung, and M.A. Pitt (Eds.), *Advances in Minimum Description Length: Theory and Applications.* MIT Press.

Modha, D.S. and E. Masry (1998). Prequential and cross-validated regression estimation. *Machine Learning, 33*(1), 5–39.

Myung, I.J., V. Balasubramanian, and M.A. Pitt (2000). Counting probability distributions: Differential geometry and model selection. *Proceedings of the National Academy of Sciences USA, 97*, 11170–11175.

Navarro, D. (2004). A Note on the Applied Use of MDL Approximations. *Neural Computation 16*, 1763–1768.

Quinlan, J., and R. Rivest (1989). Inferring decision trees using the minimum description length principle. *Information and Computation, 80*, 227–248.

Ripley, B. (1996). *Pattern Recognition and Neural Networks.* Cambridge, UK: Cambridge University Press.

Rissanen, J. (1978). Modeling by the shortest data description. *Automatica, 14*, 465–471.

Rissanen, J. (1983). A universal prior for integers and estimation by minimum description length. *Annals of Statistics, 11*, 416–431.

Rissanen, J. (1984). Universal coding, information, prediction and estimation. *IEEE Transactions on Information Theory, 30*, 629–636.

Rissanen, J. (1986). Stochastic complexity and modeling. *Annals of Statistics, 14*, 1080–1100.

Rissanen, J. (1987). Stochastic complexity. *Journal of the Royal Statistical Society, Series B, 49*, 223–239. Discussion: pp. 252–265.

Rissanen, J. (1989). *Stochastic Complexity in Statistical Inquiry.* Singapore: World Scientific.

Rissanen, J. (1996). Fisher information and stochastic complexity. *IEEE Transactions on Information Theory, 42*(1), 40–47.

Rissanen, J. (2000). MDL denoising. *IEEE Transactions on Information Theory, 46*(7), 2537–2543.

Rissanen, J. (2001). Strong optimality of the normalized ML models as universal codes and information in data. *IEEE Transactions on Information Theory, 47*(5), 1712–1717.

Rissanen, J., T. Speed, and B. Yu (1992). Density estimation by stochastic complexity. *IEEE Transactions on Information Theory, 38*(2), 315–323.

Rissanen, J., and I. Tabus (2005). Kolmogorov's structure function in MDL theory and lossy data compression. In P.D. Grünwald, I.J. Myung, and M.A. Pitt (Eds.), *Advances in Minimum Description Length: Theory and Applications.* Cambridge, MA: MIT Press.

Schwarz, G. (1978). Estimating the dimension of a model. *Annals of Statistics, 6*(2), 461–464.

Shafer, G., and V. Vovk (2001). *Probability and Finance — It's only a game!* New York: Wiley.

Shtarkov, Y.M. (1987). Universal sequential coding of single messages. *Problems of Information Transmission, 23*(3), 3–17.

Solomonoff, R. (1964). A formal theory of inductive inference, part 1 and part 2. *Information and Control, 7,* 1–22, 224–254.

Solomonoff, R. (1978). Complexity-based induction systems: Comparisons and convergence theorems. *IEEE Transactions on Information Theory, 24,* 422–432.

Speed, T. and B. Yu (1993). Model selection and prediction: Normal regression. *Annals of the Institute of Statistical Mathematics, 45*(1), 35–54.

Takeuchi, J. (2000). On minimax regret with respect to families of stationary stochastic processes (in Japanese). In *Proceedings IBIS 2000,* pp. 63–68.

Takeuchi, J., and A. Barron (1997). Asymptotically minimax regret for exponential families. In *Proceedings SITA '97,* pp. 665–668.

Takeuchi, J., and A. Barron (1998). Asymptotically minimax regret by Bayes mixtures. In *Proceedings of the 1998 International Symposium on Information Theory (ISIT 98).*

Townsend, P. (1975). The mind-body equation revisited. In C.-Y. Cheng (Ed.), *Psychological Problems in Philosophy,* pp. 200–218. Honolulu: University of Hawaii Press.

Vapnik, V. (1998). *Statistical Learning Theory.* New York: John Wiley.

Vereshchagin, N., and P.M.B. Vitányi (2002). Kolmogorov's structure functions with an application to the foundations of model selection. In *Proceedings of the 47th IEEE Symposium on the Foundations of Computer Science (FOCS'02).*

Viswanathan., M., C. Wallace, D. Dowe, and K. Korb (1999). Finding cutpoints in noisy binary sequences — a revised empirical evaluation. In *Proceedings of the Twelfth Australian Joint Conference on Artificial Intelligence,* Volume 1747 of *Lecture Notes in Artificial Intelligence (LNAI),* Sydney, Australia, pp. 405–416. New York: Springer-Verlag.

Vitányi, P.M.B. (2005). Algorithmic statistics and Kolmogorov's structure function. In P.D. Grünwald, I.J. Myung, and M.A. Pitt (Eds.), *Advances in Minimum Description Length: Theory and Applications.* Cambridge, MA: MIT Press.

Wallace, C., and D. Boulton (1968). An information measure for classification. *Computer Journal, 11,* 185–195.

Wallace, C., and D. Boulton (1975). An invariant Bayes method for point estimation. *Classification Society Bulletin, 3*(3), 11–34.

Wallace, C., and P. Freeman (1987). Estimation and inference by compact coding. *Journal of the Royal Statistical Society, Series B, 49,* 240–251. Discussion: pp. 252–265.

Webb, G. (1996). Further experimental evidence against the utility of Occam's razor. *Journal of Artificial Intelligence Research, 4,* 397–417.

Yamanishi, K. (1998). A decision-theoretic extension of stochastic complexity and its applications to learning. *IEEE Transactions on Information Theory,* *44*(4), 1424–1439.

Zhang, T. (2004). On the convergence of MDL density estimation. In *Proceedings of the Seventeenth Annual Conference on Computational Learning Theory (COLT' 04)*. Berlin: Springer-Verlag.

3 MDL, Bayesian Inference, and the Geometry of the Space of Probability Distributions

Vijay Balasubramanian
David Rittenhouse Laboratory
University of Pennsylvania
Philadelphia
PA 19104, USA
vijay@physics.upenn.edu
http://dept.physics.upenn.edu/~vbalasub

The minimum description length (MDL) approach to parametric model selection chooses a model that provides the shortest code length for data, while the Bayesian approach selects the model that yields the highest likelihood for the data. In this chapter I describe how the Bayesian approach yields essentially the same model selection criterion as MDL provided one chooses a Jeffreys prior for the parameters. Both MDL and Bayesian methods penalize complex models until a sufficient amount of data has justified their selection. I show how these complexity penalties can be understood in terms of the geometry of parametric model families seen as surfaces embedded in the space of distributions. I arrive at this understanding by asking how many different, or distinguishable, distributions are contained in a parametric model family. By answering this question, I find that the Jeffreys prior of Bayesian methods measures the density of distinguishable distributions contained in a parametric model family in a reparametrization-independent way. This leads to a picture where the complexity of a model family is related to the fraction of its volume in the space of distributions that lies close to the truth.

3.1 Introduction

Occam's razor, the principle of economy of thought invented by the scholastic philosopher William of Ockham (see, e.g., [Maurer 1982]), remains a fundamental heuristic guiding the thought of modern scientists. As a rule of thumb it states that simple explanations of a given phenomenon are to be preferred over complex ones. But why are simple explanations better? Simple explanations are certainly easier for us to understand, but is there any fundamental sense in which simple explanations are actually better at describing phenomena? Clearly, the answer to this question hinges on what the meaning of simplicity is in this context. It also has a bearing on what the physicist and mathematician Eugene Wigner called the "inexplicable effectiveness of mathematics in the natural sciences" [Wigner 1960]. Namely, mathematical models derived to fit a small amount of restricted data often correctly describe surprisingly general classes of phenomena.

In the modern context, Occam's razor has found a technical statement in the minimum description length (MDL) principle, which states that the best model of a collection of data is the one that permits the shortest description of it. In the context of statistical inference of parameteric families of models, one collects N data points and uses a statistical model to encode them as compactly as possible. Theorems from information theory then bound the length of the encoding in bits to be at least

$$SC = -\ln(X|\hat{\Theta}) + \frac{d}{2}\ln N + O(1), \qquad (3.1)$$

where X are the data, N is the number of data points, $\hat{\Theta}$ are the maximum likelihood parameters, and d is the number of parameters of the model. Rissanen has called this quantity the *stochastic complexity* of a parametric family of models [Rissanen 1984, 1986]. The first term turns out to be $O(N)$ as we discuss later, and penalizes models which assign the data low likelihood; the $O(\ln N)$ term penalizes models with many parameters. A model with lower stochastic complexity must therefore be both accurate and parsimonious. The MDL principle asserts that the best guide to the "truth" from which the data are drawn is given by the model which minimizes the stochastic complexity for describing the N available data points. This principle is *consistent* — if the truth lies in one of the model families under consideration, the $O(N)$ term in the stochastic complexity guarantees that it will eventually be selected as giving the best description of the data (see, e.g., the classic papers [Rissanen 1984, 1986; Clarke and Barron 1990; Barron and Cover 1991]).

However, at least intuitively, complexity of a parametric statistical model should involve more than just the number of parameters. For example, a good model should be robust in that it should not depend too sensitively on the choice of parameters. The purpose of this chapter is to approach model selection through a more intuitive route than coding theory. Given a collection of data drawn from some unknown distribution we can compare the quality of two parametric models by simply asking which one is more likely to have produced the data. While carrying out this procedure in Sec. 3.2, the essential step is the use of Bayes' formula to find the likelihood of a model family given the data from the likelihood of the data given the model. We then need to know the a priori likelihood that the truth is given by a model with a particular set of parameters. One might think that an unbiased choice of prior likelihood is to declare all parameter choices to be equally likely. However, we will see that this choice depends on the choice of paramterization and is therefore not suitable [Jeffreys 1961; Lee 1989].

Sec. 3.3 will argue that we can arrive at an unbiased (or reparametrization-invariant) choice of prior likelihood by demanding that all *distributions*, rather than parameters, are equally likely a priori. We will find such a prior distribution by devising a method to essentially count the different distributions that are indexed by the parameters of a model family and by weighting all of these equally. The resulting prior distribution on parameters will be the famous Jeffreys prior of Bayesian inference [Jeffreys 1961]. We will see how this prior is the reparametrization-invariant measure associated with a natural metric (the Fisher information matrix) on the space of probability distributions.

Sec. 3.4 will employ the Jeffreys' prior in a Bayesian formulation of parametric model selection. When the number of data points is large we will be able to use the techniques of "low temperature expansions" in statistical physics (see, e.g., [Ma 1985]) to evaluate the likelihood of a model given the data. Indeed, there will be several attractive analogies between quantities appearing in the inference problem and quantities like energy and temperature in physical systems, leading to useful intuition. We will see that probability theory advises us to select models that minimize the quantity

$$\chi = -\ln \mathrm{P}(X|\hat{\Theta}) + \frac{d}{2}\ln\frac{N}{2\pi} + \ln\int d\theta \sqrt{\det J(\Theta)} + \frac{1}{2}\ln\left(\frac{\det I(\hat{\Theta})}{\det J(\hat{\Theta})}\right) + O(1/N), \quad (3.2)$$

where X are the data, N is the number of data points, d is number of parameters, $\hat{\theta}$ are the maximum likelihood parameters, and J and I are analogues of the Fisher information matrix that will be explained further in the text. Notice that the $O(N)$ and $O(\ln N)$ terms coincide with stochastic complexity (3.1). The second and third terms are completely independent of the data and have been called the "geometric complexity" of the model in [Myung et al. 2000]. We will see that the third and fourth terms, both of $O(1)$, together essentially measure the fraction of the volume of a model family, as measured in the Fisher information metric, that lies close to the truth. Thus models that are "unnatural" or lack "robustness" in the sense of mostly describing hypotheses far from the truth are penalized. In this way, the Bayesian approach provides an intuitive understanding of the origin of complexity of a model in terms of the geometry of the space of distributions.

The first of the $O(1)$ terms in (3.2) appeared in Rissanen's refinement of the MDL principle [Rissanen 1996] based on a more accurate form of stochastic complexity. As we will see, the second term is relevant when the true model does not lie within the model family under consideration. An important purpose of this chapter is to provide some intuition for the origin of the MDL principle in the geometry of the space of distributions. As such, I will not strive for mathematical rigor, instead taking the approach of a physicist that the various approximations that are used will be valid under suitably general (but often unspecified!) circumstances. I will be extensively using material that appears in [Balasubramanian 1997].

3.2   The Bayesian Approach to Parametric Inference

Suppose we are given a collection of outcomes $X = \{x_1 \ldots x_N\}$, $x_i \in \mathcal{X}$ drawn independently from a density t. Suppose also that we are given two parametric families of distributions A and B and we wish to pick one of them as the model family that we will use. The Bayesian approach to this problem consists of computing the posterior conditional probabilities $P(A|X)$ and $P(B|X)$ and picking the family with the higher probability. Let A be parametrized by a set of real parameters $\Theta = \{\theta_1, \ldots \theta_d\}$. Then Bayes Rule tells us that

$$P(A|X) = \frac{P(A)}{P(X)} \int d^d\Theta \; w(\Theta) P(X|\Theta). \tag{3.3}$$

In this expression $P(A)$ is the prior probability of the model family, $w(\Theta)$ is a prior density on the parameter space, and $P(X)$ is the probability of the collection of outcomes X. I denote the measure induced by the parametrization of the d-dimensional parameter manifold as $d^d\Theta$ in a notation familiar to physicists. (For example, if x and y are real parameters, this integration measure is just $dx\,dy$.) Since we are interested in comparing $P(A|X)$ with $P(B|X)$, the probability $P(X)$ is a common factor that we may omit, and for lack of any better choice we take the prior probabilities of A and B to be equal and omit them. For the present we will assume that the model families of interest to us have compact parameter spaces so that integral over Θ occurs over a bounded domain. In applications the parameter space is often unbounded, and understanding how to deal with this situation is a vital practical issue. We return to this in Sec. 3.5. As the parameters range over their different values, a given model family sweeps out a surface, or manifold, in the space of probability distributions. This is illustrated in Fig. 3.1, which shows the space of distributions, with two model families embedded in it, one with one parameter, and the other with two. We will refer to the *parameter manifold* for, say, model family A, by the notation $\mathcal{M}_A$.

3.2.1   The Importance of Reparametrization Invariance

For the present, after dropping $P(A)$ and $P(X)$, our goal is to evaluate the posterior likelihood of a model:

$$P_{A|X} = \int_{\mathcal{M}_A} d^d\Theta \; w(\Theta) P(X|\Theta) \tag{3.4}$$

To evaluate this we must determine the prior probability of the parameters Θ of the model family, or, equivalently, determine an appropriate measure $d\mu(\Theta) = d^d\Theta \, w(\Theta)$ for integration over the parameter space. What is the correct choice of $w(\Theta)$ in the absence of adidtional prior information? Since $d\mu$ must be a probability

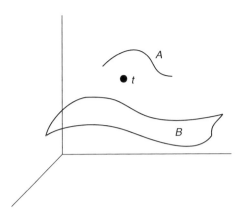

Figure 3.1 The space of probability distributions with the true data-generating distribution labeled as t. A and B label two parametric model families seen as surfaces embedded
in the space of distributions. A is a one-parameter (one-dimensional) family, while B has
two parameters.

measure, it must be that the integral over the parameter space is equal to 1:
$\int_{\mathcal{M}_A} d\mu(\Theta) = \int_{\mathcal{M}_A} d^d\Theta\, w(\Theta) = 1$. If we wish to be unbiased in our inference we
should now pick a $w(\Theta)$ that does not favor any part of the model space over
another. Frequently, it is supposed that the correct way to do this is to pick a
constant $w(\Theta)$ so that all the parameters are given equal weight a priori. The
requirement that the integral over the parameter space is 1 then gives

$$w(\Theta)\, d^d\Theta = \frac{d^d\Theta}{\int_{\mathcal{M}_A} d^d\Theta}. \tag{3.5}$$

The denominator is the volume of the parameter space as measured by the Lebesgue
measure on the parameter manifold $\mathcal{M}_A$.

Although this choice of a uniform prior seems natural, it is in fact a biased choice
in the sense that uniform priors relative to different arbitrary parametrizations can
assign different probability masses to the same subset of parameters. To illustrate
this, suppose that a model has two parameters x and y. Then (3.5) becomes

$$d^d\Theta\, w(\Theta) = \frac{dx\, dy}{\int_{\mathcal{M}_A} dx\, dy}. \tag{3.6}$$

We could have chosen to parametrize the same model in terms of $r = \sqrt{x^2 + y^2}$
and $\phi = \arctan(y/x)$. In that case, given the pair (r, ϕ) the measure (3.5) which
weights all parameter choices equally gives

$$d^d\Theta\, w(\Theta) = \frac{dr\, d\phi}{\int_{\mathcal{M}_A} dr\, d\phi}. \tag{3.7}$$

By contrast, if we change coordinates in the measure (3.6) from (x, y) to (r, ϕ), and include the Jacobian of the transformation, the measure becomes

$$d^d\Theta \, w(\Theta) = \frac{r \, dr \, d\phi}{\int_{\mathcal{M}_A} dr \, d\phi} \, . \tag{3.8}$$

Notice that (3.8) and (3.7) are not the same thing. In other words, the prescription (3.5) for giving equal weights to all parameters is itself parameter dependent and thus an undesirable method of selecting a prior distribution.

Of course, once we have picked a particular prior distribution $w(\Theta)$, Bayesian inference is reparameterization invariant, provided we remember to include the Jacobian of coordinate transformations in the integration measure as we are instructed in elementary calculus classes. The point here is that the apparently unbiased measure (3.5) that gives equal weight to all parameters is not *reparametrization-invariant* and is therefore unacceptable; if $w(\Theta)$ was uniform in the parameters, the probability of a model family given the observed data would depend on the arbitrary parametrization. We need some other way of determining an unbiased distribution of the parameter space of a model. The next section proposes that a good method is to give equal prior weight to all the *distributions* contained in a model family as opposed to all the parameters, which are only an arbitrary scheme for indexing these distributions.

3.3 Counting Probability Distributions

We would like to determine a prior probability density of the parameters of a model that implement the reasonable requirement that all *distributions*, rather than all *parameters*, are equally likely. The basic obstacle to doing this is that the parameters of a model can cover the space of distributions unevenly; some regions of parameter space might index probability distributions more "densely" than others. If this happens, the "denser" regions should be given more weight since they contain more distinguishable probability distributions. So let us ask the question, 'How do we count the number of distinct distributions in the neighborhood of a point on a parameter manifold?' Essentially, this is a question about the embedding of the parameter manifold within the space of distributions. Distinguishable choices of parameters might be indexing indistinguishable distributions (in some suitable sense) and we need to account for this to give equal weight to different distributions rather than different parameters.

To answer the question, let Θ_p and Θ_q index two distributions in a parametric family and let $X = \{x_1 \cdots x_N\}$ be drawn independently from one of Θ_p or Θ_q. In the context of model estimation, a suitable measure of distinguishability can be derived by asking how well we can guess which of Θ_p or Θ_q produced X (Fig. 3.2). Let α_N be the probability that Θ_q is mistaken for Θ_p and let β_N be the probability that Θ_p is mistaken for Θ_q. Let β_N^ϵ be the smallest possible β_N given that $\alpha_N < \epsilon$.

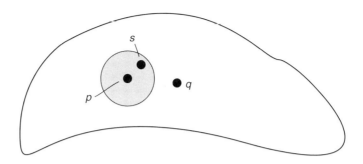

Figure 3.2 Three distributions, p, q and s are labeled in this picture of a parametric model family. The gray region indicates the neighborhood of p which contains distributions that are sufficiently similar that it will be difficult to guess which one of them produced a given sample of N data points. Thus, p and s will be *indistinguishable*, and given only N data points they should not be counted as different distributions for the purposes of statistical inference. By contrast, p and q should be treated as *distinguishable* distributions.

Then Stein's Lemma tells us that $\lim_{N\to\infty}(-1/N)\ln\beta_N^\epsilon = D(\Theta_p\|\Theta_q)$ where

$$D(p\|q) = \int dx\, p(x)\ln(p(x)/q(x)) \tag{3.9}$$

is the relative entropy between the densities p and q [Cover and Thomas 1991]. As shown in [Balasubramanian 1997, Appendix], the proof of Stein's Lemma shows that the minimum error β_N^ϵ exceeds a fixed β^* in the region where

$$\kappa/N \geq D(\Theta_p\|\Theta_q) \quad ; \quad \kappa \equiv -\ln\beta^* + \ln(1-\epsilon). \tag{3.10}$$

(This assertion is not strictly true, but will do for our purposes. See [Balasubramanian 1997, Appendix] for more details.) By taking β^* close to 1 we can identify the region around Θ_p where the distributions are not very distinguishable from the one indexed by Θ_p. As N grows large for fixed κ, any Θ_q in this region is necessarily close to Θ_p since $D(\Theta_p\|\Theta_q)$ attains a minimum of zero when $\Theta_p = \Theta_q$. Therefore, setting $\Delta\Theta = \Theta_q - \Theta_p$, Taylor expansion gives

$$D(\Theta_p\|\Theta_q) \approx \frac{1}{2}\sum_{ij} J_{ij}(\Theta_p)\Delta\Theta^i\Delta\Theta^j + O(\Delta\Theta^3) = \mathbf{\Delta\Theta}\cdot\mathbf{J}(\Theta_p)\cdot\mathbf{\Delta\Theta} + O(\Delta\Theta^3),$$
$$\tag{3.11}$$

where

$$J_{ij} = \nabla_{\phi_i}\nabla_{\phi_j}D(\Theta_p\|\Theta_p + \Phi)|_{\Phi=0} \tag{3.12}$$

is the Fisher information.[1] The second equality in (3.11) expresses the expansion

---

1. We have assumed that the derivatives with respect to Θ commute with expectations taken in the distribution Θ_p to identify the Fisher information with the matrix of second derivatives of the relative entropy.

in terms of a Fisher information matrix $\mathbf{J}$ and the vector of parameter deviations $\boldsymbol{\Delta\Theta}$.

Summary   The upshot of all of this is simple. For any given number of data points N, there is a region around Θ_p in which the distributions are not very distinguishable from the one indexed by Θ_p itself, in the sense that we would not be able to reliably guess which of these distributions the N data points really came from. As the number of data points grows, this region of indistinguishability is described by the following ellipsoid in the parameter space:

$$\frac{\kappa}{N} \geq D(\Theta_p \| \Theta_q) \approx \frac{1}{2} \sum_{ij} J_{ij}(\Theta_p) \Delta\Theta^i \Delta\Theta^j + O(\Delta\Theta^3) \qquad (3.13)$$

Here κ is given in terms of the probability of error in guessing the data-generating distribution as in (3.10) (See Fig. 3.2).

3.3.1   A Uniform Prior on Distributions

We will now devise a measure that gives equal weight to the distributions indexed by a model family as opposed to the parameters. The basic strategy is to begin by giving equal weight to every ellipsoid of the form (3.13) containing essentially indistinguishable distributions given N data points. By taking the limit $N \to \infty$ we will arrive at a measure on the parameter manifold that effectively gives equal weight to all those distributions that can be told apart or distinguished in a statistical experiment (See Fig. 3.3).

To this end, define the *volume of indistinguishability* at levels ϵ, β^*, and N to be the volume of the region around Θ_p where $\kappa/N \geq D(\Theta_p \| \Theta_q)$ so that the probability of error in distinguishing Θ_q from Θ_p is high. We find to leading order:

$$V_{\epsilon, \beta^*, N} = \left(\frac{2\pi\kappa}{N} \right)^{d/2} \frac{1}{\Gamma(d/2 + 1)} \frac{1}{\sqrt{\det J_{ij}(\Theta_p)}} \qquad (3.14)$$

If β^* is very close to 1, the distributions inside $V_{\epsilon, \beta^*, N}$ are not very distinguishable and the Bayesian prior should not treat them as separate distributions. We wish to construct a measure on the parameter manifold that reflects this indistinguishability. We also assume a principle of "translation invariance" by supposing that volumes of indistinguishability at given values of N, β^*, and ϵ should have the same measure regardless of where in the space of distributions they are centered. This amounts to an assumption that all distinguishable probability distributions are a priori on an equal footing.

An integration measure reflecting these principles of indistinguishability and translation invariance can be defined at each level β^*, ϵ, and N by covering the parameter manifold economically with volumes of indistinguishability and placing a delta function in the center of each element of the cover. This definition reflects indistinguishability by ignoring variations on a scale smaller than the covering

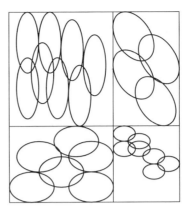

Figure 3.3 The figure shows a parameter manifold divided into four regions. In each region, the Fisher information matrix is constant, leading to a fixed shape volume of indistinguishability at any given value of N. To derive a measure on the parameter space, we partition the parameter manifold into volumes of indistinguishability as shown. (These will necessarily overlap a little.) Given only N data points we might as well consider each of these volumes as containing only a single distribution since the distributions within them cannot be told apart reliably. In effect, this converts the continuous parameter manifold into a lattice. We can then derive a prior probability density on the parameters by considering each of the discrete number of distributions representing the volumes of indistinguishability as being equally likely. As $N \to \infty$ the volumes of indistinguishability shrink, and in the continuum limit we recover the Jeffreys prior as the measure on the parameter manifold that gives equal weight all equally distinguishable distributions.

volumes and reflects translation invariance by giving each covering volume equal weight in integrals over the parameter manifold. The measure can be normalized by an integral over the entire parameter manifold to give a prior distribution. The continuum limit of this discretized measure is obtained by taking the limits $\beta^* \to 1$, $\epsilon \to 0$ and $N \to \infty$. In this limit, the measure counts distributions that are completely indistinguishable ($\beta^* = 1$) even in the presence of an infinite amount of data ($N = \infty$) [2] (see Fig. 3.3.).

To see the effect of the above procedure, imagine a parameter manifold which can be partitioned into k regions in each of which the Fisher information is constant. Let J_i, U_i, and V_i be the Fisher information, parametric volume and volume of indistinguishability in the ith region. Then the prior assigned to the ith volume by the above procedure will be

$$P_i = \frac{(U_i/V_i)}{\sum_{j=1}^k (U_j/V_j)} = \frac{U_i\sqrt{\det J_i}}{\sum_{j=1}^k U_j\sqrt{\det J_j}}. \tag{3.15}$$

Since all the β^*, ϵ, and N dependences cancel we are now free to take the continuum

2. The α and β errors can be treated more symmetrically using the Chernoff bound instead of Stein's lemma, but we will not do that here.

limit of P_i. This suggests that the prior density induced by the prescription described in the previous paragraph is

$$w(\Theta) = \frac{\sqrt{\det J(\Theta)}}{\int d^d\Theta \sqrt{\det J(\Theta)}}. \qquad (3.16)$$

By paying careful attention to technical difficulties involving sets of measure zero and certain sphere packing problems, it can be rigorously shown that the normalized continuum measure on a parameter manifold that reflects indistinguishability and translation invariance is $w(\Theta)$ or Jeffreys' prior [Balasubramanian 1996]. In essence, the heuristic argument above and the derivation in [Balasubramanian 1996] show how to "divide out" the volume of indistinguishable distributions on a parameter manifold and hence give equal weight to equally distinguishable volumes of distributions. In this sense, Jeffreys' prior is seen to be a uniform prior on the *distributions* indexed by a parametric family. The density $w(\Theta)$ is the answer to the following question: *What is the fraction of the total number of distributions indexed by a model family that is contained within an infinitesimal neighborhood of a parameter value* Θ?

Summary   We sought a measure on the parameter space, or a prior probability density, which gives equal weight to equally distinguishable probability distributions. We did this by determining a statistical notion of distinguishability that told us that it was difficult, given only N data points, to tell apart the distributions indexed by the parameters lying within the ellipsoids (3.13). Our strategy was therefore to discretize the parameter manifold into a grid of such (minimally overlapping) ellipsoids, and then to give equal prior probability to each of the distinguishable distributions located at the grid points. As the number of data points N grow large the grid points approach each other since it becomes easier to tell distributions apart when more data is available. In the limit we recover the continuum measure (3.16) on the parameter space that has effectively "divided out" redundant descriptions of the same distributions by parameters infinitesimally close to a given one (see Fig. 3.3.). Once we have committed to this prior distribution, we can work with any choice of parameters. Although (3.16) might look different given different choices, we can be sure that (3.16) always gives a fixed region of parameter space the same probability.

The Geometry of the Space of Probability Distributions   In the discussion above we derived the well-known Jeffreys prior (3.16) as a probablity density giving equal weight to all distinguishable distributions indexed by a parameter manifold. However, the form of the measure $w(\Theta) \propto \sqrt{\det J(\Theta)}$ suggests another useful interpretation. In Riemannian geometry, the infinitesimal distance Δs between two points separated by a small coordinate difference Δx^i is given by an equation:

$$\Delta s^2 = \sum_{ij} g_{ij}(x)\, \Delta x^i \, \Delta x^j \; = \boldsymbol{\Delta} x \cdot \mathbf{g} \cdot \boldsymbol{\Delta} x. \qquad (3.17)$$

This is the generalization to curved manifolds of the Pythagorean theorem and g_{ij} is called the *metric* and is for our purposes simply a matrix that varies over the surface. The second equality expresses Δs^2 in terms of a metric matrix $\mathbf{g}$ and a vector of coordinate differences $\mathbf{\Delta} x$. The corresponding measure for integrating over the curved surface is $d^d x \sqrt{\det g}$. Comparing this with (3.16) suggests strongly that in the context of statistical inference, a parameter manifold is a curved surface endowed naturally with a metric given by the Fisher information, that is, $g_{ij} = J_{ij}$ on parameter surface. From this perspective the Jeffreys prior in (3.16) has the following simple interpretation. First,

$$V(A) = \int d^d \Theta \sqrt{\det J(\Theta)} \tag{3.18}$$

measures the volume of the parameter manifold in the distinguished Fisher information metric J_{ij}. We then get a uniform prior distribution on the parameters by measuring the volume of a small region of parameters as $d^d \Theta \sqrt{\det J}$ and dividing by the total volume of the parameters so that the distribution integrates to 1.

We will not have occasion to exploit this tempting additional structure since all our results will depend on the measure $\sqrt{\det J}$. However, it is a very interesting question to consider whether the apparatus of classic differential geometry such as measures of curvature, geodesics, and other quantities play a role in statistical inference. The reader may wish to consult the works of Amari and others on information geometry (see, e.g., [Amari 1985; Amari et al. 1987]) in which Fisher information is taken seriously as a metric describing the curved geometry of parameter spaces seen as surfaces embedded in the space of all probability distributions.

3.4 Occam's Razor, MDL, and Bayesian Methods

Putting everything together we get the following expression for the Bayesian posterior probability of a parametric family in the absence of any prior knowledge about the relative likelihood of the distributions indexed by the family.

$$P_{A|X} = \frac{\int d^d \Theta \sqrt{\det J} \, \mathrm{P}(X|\Theta)}{\int d^d \Theta \sqrt{\det J}} \tag{3.19}$$

$$= \frac{\int d^d \Theta \sqrt{\det J} \exp\left[-N\left(\frac{-\ln \mathrm{P}(X|\Theta)}{N}\right)\right]}{\int d^d \Theta \sqrt{\det J}} \tag{3.20}$$

The second form of the expression is useful since the strong law of large numbers says that $(-1/N) \ln \mathrm{P}(X|\Theta) = (-1/N) \sum_{i=1}^{N} \ln \mathrm{P}(x_i|\Theta)$ converges in the almost sure sense to a finite quantity:

$$E_t\left[\frac{-\ln \mathrm{P}(x_i|\Theta)}{N}\right] = \int dx \, t(x) \ln\left(\frac{t(x)}{\mathrm{P}(x|\Theta)}\right) - \int dx \, t(x) \ln(t(x)) = D(t\|\Theta) + h(t),$$
$$\tag{3.21}$$

where $h(t)$ is the entropy of the true distribution which generates the data and $D(t|\Theta)$ is the relative entropy (3.9) between the true distribution and the one indexed by Θ. This means that as N grows large the integrand in (3.20) will be dominated by the parameter value that comes closest to the truth. Readers familiar with statistical physics will recognize the structure of these equations. The basic quantity of interest in statistical physics is the partition function

$$Z = \frac{\int d^d x \, \mu(x) e^{-\beta \, E(x)}}{\int d^d x \, \mu(x)}, \qquad (3.22)$$

where x labels the space of configurations of a physical system, $\mu(x)$ is a measure on the configuration space, $\beta \equiv 1/T$ is the inverse temperature of the system, and $E(x)$ is the energy of the configuration x [Ma 1985]. The analogy with the Bayesian posterior probability (3.20) is now clear — for example, inference with a large number N of data points is in analogy to statistical physics at a low temperature T. There are classic techniques in statistical physics to compute Z in various limits that might be useful in Bayesian statistical inference. In this chapter we are interested in studying inference where N is large. We can then borrow the well-known method of low-temperature expansions in statistical physics [Ma 1985] and apply it to the problem of evaluating (3.20).

3.4.1   Asymptotic Expansion and MDL

We will now approximately evaluate (3.20) when the number of data points is large. The method we use applies when (a) the maximum likelihood parameter $\hat{\Theta}$ which globally maximizes $P(X|\Theta)$ lies in the interior of the parameter space, (b) local maxima of $P(X|\Theta)$ are bounded away from the global maximum, and (c) both the Fisher information $J_{ij}(\Theta)$ and $P(X|\Theta)$ are sufficiently smooth functions of Θ in a neighborhood of $\hat{\Theta}$. In this case, for sufficiently large N, the integral in (3.20) is dominated by a neighborhood of the maximum-likelihood parameter $\hat{\Theta}$. We can then approximate the integrand in the neighborhood of $\hat{\Theta}$ as follows:

First, collect the measure $\sqrt{\det J}$ into the exponent as

$$P_{A|X} = \frac{\int d^d \Theta \, \exp\left[-N\left(\frac{-\ln P(X|\Theta)}{N}\right) + (1/2)\,\mathrm{Tr}\ln J(\Theta)\right]}{\int d^d \Theta \, \sqrt{\det J}}. \qquad (3.23)$$

Next, we Taylor-expand the exponent around the maximum likelihood parameter which satisfies $\nabla_{\theta_\mu} \ln P(X|\Theta) = 0$. So the Taylor expansion of the first term in the exponent begins with ∇_{θ_μ}. It is convenient to define a kind of empirical Fisher information as $I_{\mu\nu} = (-1/N)\nabla_{\theta_\mu}\nabla_{\theta_\nu} \ln P(X|\Theta)|_{\hat{\Theta}}$ so that $I_{\mu\nu}$ approaches a finite limit as $N \to \infty$.

We can then evaluate (3.23) as follows. First define a shifted integration variable

$\Phi = (\Theta - \hat{\Theta})$. Then, we can write

$$P_{A|X} = \frac{e^{-\left[\ln \mathrm{P}(X|\hat{\Theta}) - \frac{1}{2}\operatorname{Tr}\ln J(\hat{\Theta})\right]} \int d^d\Phi\, e^{-((N/2)\sum_{\mu\nu} I_{\mu\nu}\phi^\mu\phi^\nu + G(\Phi))}}{\int d^d\Theta \sqrt{\det J_{ij}}} \tag{3.24}$$

$$= \frac{e^{-\left[\ln \mathrm{P}(X|\hat{\Theta})\right]} \sqrt{\det J(\hat{\Theta})} \int d^d\Phi\, e^{-((N/2)\sum_{\mu\nu} I_{\mu\nu}\phi^\mu\phi^\nu + G(\Phi))}}{\int d^d\Theta \sqrt{\det J_{ij}}}, \tag{3.25}$$

where $G(\Phi)$ collects the cubic and higher order terms in the Taylor expansion of $\ln \mathrm{P}(X|\Theta)$ and all terms in the Taylor expansion of $\operatorname{Tr}\ln J$ around $\hat{\Theta}$. As the number of data points N gets large the integrand is very sharply peaked around $\hat{\Theta}$ and the terms collected in $G(\Phi)$ will only make subleading contributions to the integral. Indeed, we can approxime the integral as a multivariate Gaussian with a covariance matrix $N I_{\mu\nu}(\hat{\theta})$. (Some technical conditions are required as discussed in, for example, [Clarke and Barron 1990].)

When N is large, the Gaussian is very narrow and therefore the integral can be performed [Clarke and Barron 1990; Balasubramanian 1997] to give

$$-\ln P_{A|X} \equiv \chi_X(A) = -\ln \mathrm{P}(X|\hat{\theta}) + \ln\left(\frac{V(A)}{V_c(A)}\right) + O(1/N). \tag{3.26}$$

We define [Myung et al. 2000]

$$V_c(A) = \left(\frac{2\pi}{N}\right)^{d/2} \sqrt{\frac{\det J(\hat{\theta})}{\det I(\hat{\theta})}}. \tag{3.27}$$

$V_c(A)$ is essentially the volume of a small ellipsoid around $\hat{\theta}$ within which the probability of the data $\mathrm{P}(X|\Theta)$ is appreciable. Specifically, $V_c(A)$ only differs by a numerical factor from the volume of a region where $\mathrm{P}(X|\Theta) \geq \lambda \mathrm{P}(X|\hat{\Theta})$ for any λ close to 1. As such, it measures the volume of distinguishable distributions in A that come close to the truth, as measured by predicting the data X with good probability.

The ratio $V_c(A)/V(A)$ penalizes models which occupy a small volume close to the truth *relative to* the total volume of the model. The second term expands to

$$C = \ln\left(\frac{V(A)}{V_c(A)}\right) = \frac{d}{2}\ln\left(\frac{N}{2\pi}\right) + \ln\int d\theta \sqrt{\det J(\theta)} + \frac{1}{2}\ln\left(\frac{\det I(\hat{\theta})}{\det J(\hat{\theta})}\right). \tag{3.28}$$

In Bayesian model selection, C functions as a penalty for complexity.

Assembling everything, when selecting between two model families, A and B, probability theory instructs to compute

$$\chi_X = -\ln \mathrm{P}(X|\hat{\theta}) + \frac{d}{2}\ln\frac{N}{2\pi} + \ln\int d\theta \sqrt{\det J(\theta)} + \frac{1}{2}\ln\left(\frac{\det I(\hat{\theta})}{\det J(\hat{\theta})}\right) + O(1/N) \tag{3.29}$$

for each family given the data X. The observed data are more likely to have come from the model family with a smaller χ. We will interpret this as a manifestation of Occam's razor and the MDL principle and will explain how the various terms in (3.29) arise from the geometry of the parameter space of the model family.

Interpretation: Occam's Razor   The first term in (3.29) is the maximum log-likelihood of the data given a model and therefore measures how accurately the model is able to describe the data. This term is $O(N)$ since, as we discussed, $(1/N)\ln(\mathrm{P}(X|\hat{\Theta})$ approaches a finite limit. This happens because probabilities multiply and this causes the probability of any given sample to decrease exponentially with the sample size. In any case, for sufficiently large N this $O(N)$ term always dominates and therefore with enough data the most accurate model family is chosen by Bayesian methods.

As we described, the remaining three terms arise in our analysis essentially as a measurement of the fraction of the volume of a model's parameter space that lies close to truth. The first and second terms in C are independent of the true distribution as well as the data, and therefore represent an intrinsic property of the model family. The term proportional to $d/2$ arises because as the number of data points increases the radius of the region near the maximum likelihood parameter that gives a good description of the data shrinks in proportion to $1/N$ so that the volume of this region shrinks as $(1/N)^{d/2}$, as in (3.27). As discussed earlier, the integral $\int d^d\Theta \sqrt{\det J(\Theta)}$ measures, in a sense, the volume of distinguishable distributions that the model can describe. Thus the third term in (3.29) penalizes models that are less constrained, in the sense of describing a greater variety of distributions. Finally, the fourth term in (3.29) penalizes models that are not robust in the sense that they depend very sensitively of the choice of parameters. The covariance matrix I determines how rapidly the integrand of $P_{A|X}$ falls off around the maximum likelihood parameter. So, if I is large, we have a situation as in Fig. 3.4a where the model gives a good description of the data only for very restricted parameters. Conversely if I is small, there is large basin of parameters that describes the data well. The ratio $\det I/\det J$ appears because how narrow or wide the the "good" region of a model family is should really be determined with respect to the natural measure on the parameter manifold, which we have argued to be the Fisher information matrix.

Note that if the truth actually lies within the model family, $I \to J$ as the amount of data N increases, essentially because of the law of large numbers. Thus, up to corrections that decrease with N, the $\ln(\det I/\det J)$ term vanishes in this case. Interestingly, it is easy to show by explicit computation that the same thing happens for exponential families $(\mathrm{P}(x|\vec{\theta}) = q(x)e^{-\vec{\theta}\cdot\vec{f}(x)}/Z$, where q and $\vec{f}$ are any suitable functions and Z normalizes the distribution) since I is independent of the data in this case [Grünwald 2005]. So up to terms suppressed by powers of N, the "robustness term" in (3.29) does not affect comparisons of exponential families between each other or with a model containing the truth. We interpret this by saying that all exponential families, as well as all families that contain the truth are equally robust, or insensitive to the choice of parameters. Nevertheless, the robustness term can either be positive or negative for other parametric families relative to a given true distribution, and so it does play an important role in comparisons with and between other kinds of model families.

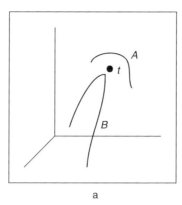 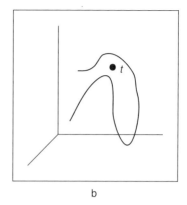

a   b

Figure 3.4 In box a, model B comes very close to the true distribution at one point, but is mostly far away. Model A is close to truth for many choices of its parameters. When the amount of data is small, MDL will tend to prefer A because this model is more robust and not enough data have accumulated to identify a specific distribution in B as coming close to the truth. As the number of data points increases, however, B will eventually be preferred. Box b illustrates a situation where a single model family will have two local maxima in the log-likelihood it assigns the data – it comes close to the truth in two regions of the parameter space. When the number of data points is small, one region (the more robust one) will dominate the Bayesian posterior, and as the number of data points increases, the other region (the more accurate one) will dominate.

The MDL model selection criterion [Rissanen 1996] chooses the statistical model that minimizes the sum of the first three terms in (3.29). Note that if the true distribution lies within the considered model family, $J(\hat{\theta})$ approaches $I(\hat{\theta})$ as N grows large, and consequently $\ln(V(f)/V_c(f))$ becomes equal to the complexity penalty in the MDL selection criterion. This shows that as the sample size grows, the log of the Bayesian posterior probability of a model family $(-\ln \mathrm{P}(f|y))$ coincides with MDL when the truth lies in the model family. Therefore, selecting the most probable model is essentially equivalent to choosing the model that gives the MDL of the data, and the Bayesian complexity C coincides with Rissanen's modified stochastic complexity [Rissanen 1996]. It would be very nice to give an adequate interpretation of the final term in (3.29) in the context of the coding theory that gives rise directly to the MDL criterion.

To summarize, we have arrived at an intuitive geometric interpretation of the meaning of complexity in the MDL and Bayesian approaches to model selection: *"complexity" measures the ratio of the volume occupied by distinguishable distributions in a model that come close to the truth relative to the volume of the model as a whole.* The apparent complexity of a model's functional form in a particular parametrization and even the number of parameters in a model are simply components of this general understanding of how probability theory incorporates complexity in statistical inference.

3.5   Some Challenges

This chapter is appearing in the proceedings of a workshop which described both theoretical developments and practical applications of the MDL techniques (see, e.g., [Myung et al. 2001]). The principal obstacle to the general application of the results presented here is that we were obliged to assume a bounded parameter space in order to make sense of the Jeffreys prior and consequently of the second term in the complexity penalty (3.28) which involved an integral over the parameter space. Actually the problem is not really that the parameter space can be unbounded, but that the integral

$$\int d^d\Theta\sqrt{\det J} \tag{3.30}$$

can diverge. This can even happen with a bounded parameter space if the Fisher information J_{ij} becomes infinite sufficiently quickly in some region. In either case, the situation is that there are "too many" candidate hypotheses included in the model family. One simple way to deal with this situation is to bound the domain of parameters in such a way that (3.30) is finite. In this case, we should consider the added variables describing how the parameter space is bounded as parameters of the model themselves and one might imagine doing a "meta-Bayesian analysis" to determine them. Another promising approach is to declare that we are only practically interested in those distributions which assign a probability greater than some small ϵ to the observed data. This will naturally give a bounded domain of parameters describing the data with a reasonable probability. Then we can repeat the entire analysis of this paper for such bounded domains. I hope to report on this approach in a future publication.

Another interesting issue that has been avoided both here and elsewhere in the literature is what happens when there are multiple local likelihood maxima for a given model family. This would arise in a situation such as the one depicted in Fig. 3.4b where the model family approaches the two distributions in two locations. In such a circumstance $-\ln P_{A|X}$ will be a sum of multiple contributions like the one in (3.26) each arising from a saddlepoint of the exponent in (3.23). This sort of situation occurs often in statistical physics and will lead here to an analogue the fascinating phenomenon of *phase transitions* — as the number of data points increases, one saddlepoint or another will suddenly come to dominate the log-likelihood of the model family, leading to potentially very different descriptions of the data.

3.6 Acknowledgment

This work was prepared with the support of NSF grant PHY-0331728.

References

Amari, S.I. (1985). *Differential Geometrical Methods in Statistics*. Berlin: Springer-Verlag.

Amari, S.I., O.E. Barndorff-Nielsen, R.E. Kass, S.L. Lauritzen, and C.R. Rao (1987). *Differential Geometry in Statistical Inference*, Volume 10. Institute of Mathematical Statistics Lecture Note-Monograph Series, Hayward, CA.

Balasubramanian, V. (1996). A geometric formulation of Occam's razor for inference of parametric distributions. Princeton University Physics Preprint PUPT-1588, January 1996 and preprint No. adap-org/9601001 from http://arXiv.org/

Balasubramanian, V. (1997). Statistical inference, Occam's razor and statistical mechanics on the space of probability distributions. *Neural Computation*, *9*(2).

Barron, A.R., and T.M. Cover (1991). Minimum complexity density estimation. *IEEE Transactions on Information Theory*, *37*(4):1034–1054.

Clarke, B.S., and A.R. Barron (1990). Information-theoretic asymptotics of Bayes methods. *IEEE Transactions on Information Theory*, *36*(3):453–471.

Cover, T.M., and J.A. Thomas (1991). *Elements of Information Theory*. New York: Wiley

Grünwald, P.D. (2005). Minimum description length tutorial. Chapter 2 of this book.

Jeffreys, H. (1961). *Theory of Probability*, 3rd edition. Oxford, UK: Oxford University Press.

Lee, P.M. (1989). *Bayesian Statistics: An Introduction*. Oxford, UK: Oxford University Press.

Ma, S.K. (1985). *Statistical Mechanics*. Teanick, NJ: World Scientific.

Maurer, A.A. (1982). *Medieval Philosophy*. Toronto: Pontifical Institute of Medieval Studies.

Myung, I.J., V. Balasubramanian, and M.A. Pitt (2000). Counting probability distributions: Differential geometry and model selection. *Proceedings of the National Academy of Sciences USA*, *97*(21), 11170–11175.

Myung, I.J., M.A. Pitt, S. Zhang, and V. Balasubramanian (2001). The use of MDL to select among computational models of cognition. In T.K. Leen, T.G, Dietterich and V. Tresp (eds.), *Advances in Neural Information Processing*

Systems 13, pp. 38–44. Cambridge, MA: MIT Press

Rissanen, J. (1984) Universal coding, information, prediction and estimation. *IEEE Transactions on Information Theory 30*(4), 629–636.

Rissanen, J. (1986). Stochastic complexity and modelling. *Annals of Statistics 14*(3):1080–1100.

Rissanen, J. (1996). Fisher information and stochastic complexity. *IEEE Transactions on Information Theory, 42*(1), 40–47.

Wigner, E. (1960). The unreasonable effectiveness of mathematics in the natural sciences. *Communications in Pure and Applied Mathematics, 13*(1).

4   Hypothesis Testing for Poisson vs. Geometric Distributions Using Stochastic Complexity

Aaron D. Lanterman
School of Electrical and Computer Engineering
Georgia Institute of Technology
Mail Code 0250
Atlanta, GA 30332
lanterma@ece.gatech.edu
http://users.ece.gatech.edu/˜lanterma

We illustrate the concept of hypothesis testing using stochastic complexity, in the modern sense of normalized maximum likelihood codes, via the simple example of deciding whether a Poisson or a geometric model better matches the collected data. The Poisson model is generally found to have more power in describing data than the geometric model. Hence, the Poisson model is more harshly penalized by the stochastic complexity criterion.

The integral of the square root of the Fisher information of both the Poisson and geometric models is found to be infinite. Hence, the allowed parameter range must be restricted somehow to make this integral finite. Some of the consequences of this are explored.

4.1   Introduction

Since the seminal work of Wallace and Boulton [1968] and Rissanen [1978], many researchers have developed increasingly sophisticated approaches to model selection under the general terms *minimum description length* (MDL) and *minimum message length* (MML). The differences between various approaches that have been proposed over the years are at times subtle, at other times profound, and quite often simultaneously subtle and profound [Lanterman 2001]. The most recent version of MDL uses a concept of *stochastic complexity* based on *normalized maximum likelihood (NML)* codes [Barron, Rissanen, and Yu 1998].

The purpose of this chapter is twofold:

1. Newcomers who simply wish to apply these ideas to their own work often find the writings by the founding fathers of MDL and MML dense and impenetrable. We feel that the literature needs more concrete examples, explained on a nonintimidating level. Also, much of the MDL-MML literature revolves around the omnipresent Gaussian distribution; we would like to encourage more research on non-Gaussian examples.

With these goals in mind, this entire chapter revolves around the simple hypothesis test of deciding whether a set of N data points $\mathbf{x}^N = (x_1, x_2, \ldots x_N) \in \mathbb{N}^n$ was drawn from a Poisson or geometric distribution. The choice of the Poisson distribution was motivated by the author's long-term curiosity about applying ideas from MDL to regularizing Poisson intensity estimates in emission tomography [Snyder and Miller 1985; Politte and Snyder 1988; Snyder, Miller, Thomas, and Politte 1987]. The geometric distribution was chosen simply because it is another familiar discrete distribution. The MDL viewpoint does not require us to assume that the data were actually drawn from one of the proposed models; it just tries to find the model that best fits the data. Nevertheless, we will explore the resulting procedures via Monte Carlo simulations where the data really are generated by one of the two models.

2. In the 1996 paper that outlines the refined notion of stochastic complexity [Rissanen 1996], Rissanen writes that it concludes "a decade long search." However, as we shall see in Section 4.4.2, the stochastic complexity, which is essentially a code length, is actually infinite for many useful models! Some solutions to this quandary have been proposed, which we will review in Section 4.4.2. However, none of these solutions have the same elegance or sense of "conclusion" as the original notion of the NML code and its related theorems. Hence, in our opinion, the search is not quite over.

Both the Poisson and geometric distributions investigated here yield infinite stochastic complexity in their raw form, and the choices we make in dealing with this problem have a substantive impact on the results. We hope this chapter prompts further research into developing new versions of the stochastic complexity criterion that will handle these difficulties in a conceptually pleasing fashion.

4.1.1   The Poisson and Geometric Distributions

Poisson and geometric random variables are nonnegative and discrete-valued; hence, our summaries of results in the literature will generally be written in terms of probability mass functions (indicated with capital letters such as P) and summations. These results will generally hold for continuous-valued data as well by simply replacing probability mass functions with densities and sums with integrals.

The Poisson probability mass function, parameterized by an intensity θ, is given by

$$P_P(x:\theta) = \frac{e^{-\theta}\theta^x}{x!} \tag{4.1}$$

for $x \in \mathbb{N}$, the set of natural numbers $0, 1, 2, \cdots$. The Poisson distribution has mean θ. A particular realization x might represent the number of caffeine-craving customers arriving at a coffee shop between 8:30 and 9:30 AM.

The geometric probability mass function can be parameterized in a couple of equivalent ways. We parameterize it by a "probability of tails" parameter θ, and define the density as

$$P_G(x:\theta) = \theta^x(1-\theta) \tag{4.2}$$

for $x \in \mathbb{N}$. Here, a particular realization x represents the number of tails that appear in a series of coin flips before the first 'heads' appears.[1] Our geometric distribution has mean $\theta/(1-\theta)$.

In later sections, we will be using different kinds of asymptotic expansions. Some technical conditions need to hold for these expansions to be valid. Fortunately, the Poisson and geometric distributions are both exponential families [Poor 1994], which implies that the maximum likelihood (ML) estimators, log-likelihood ratios, and Fisher information that we discuss later will be easy to compute. In addition, provided that the range of the parameter space is restricted to a compact (i.e. closed and bounded) subset of $\Re$, the asymptotic expansions we need are valid.

4.2 Review of Hypothesis Testing

4.2.1 Simple Hypothesis Testing

Suppose for a moment that the parameters describing the hypothesized Poisson and geometric distributions, θ_P and θ_G respectively, are known exactly. Standard statistical detection theory [Van Trees 1968; Poor 1994] would proceed by computing the ratio of the probability mass functions of the data (called the likelihood ratio) and comparing it to a threshold τ:

$$\frac{\prod_{i=1}^{N} P_P(x_i:\theta_P)}{\prod_{i=1}^{N} P_G(x_i:\theta_G)} \underset{<}{\overset{>}{\gtrless}} \tau \tag{4.3}$$

We choose the Poisson model if the likelihood ratio is greater than τ, and declare the geometric model if the likelihood ratio is less than τ.

---

1. Some other versions make θ a probability of heads, and/or make x the total number of flips *including* the first heads, in which case $x \in \{1, 2, \cdots\}$. Our parameterization in terms of a "failure" probability is a bit unusual, but it will make some of our later equations less cumbersome.

We can equivalently use a log-likelihood ratio test:

$$\sum_{i=1}^{N} L_P(x_i : \theta_P) - \sum_{i=1}^{N} L_G(x_i : \theta_G) \underset{<}{\overset{>}{\gtrless}} \ln \tau \overset{\text{df}}{=} \eta, \qquad (4.4)$$

where the log-likelihoods are $L_P = \ln P_P$ and $L_G = \ln P_G$. The log-likelihood ratio sometimes has a more aesthetically pleasing form, and is often more stable to compute numerically. Conveniently, LRT may refer to either a "likelihood ratio test" or a "log-likelihood ratio test."

There are several schools of thought in choosing η. One is the Neyman-Pearson criterion, which chooses η to achieve a desired "probablity of false alarm" P_{FA}; one simply lives with the resulting "probablity of detection" P_D (or vice versa).[2] Radar systems are often designed with such criteria. Another approach takes a Bayesian viewpoint, and assigns prior probabilities to the two hypotheses, as well as subjective costs associated with wrong decisions.

Deciding upon the costs and prior probabilities in the Bayesian setting, or the desired P_{FA} (sometimes called the "significance level," which often seems to be pulled out of a magic hat) in the Neyman-Pearson setting, can often feel rather arbitrary. If we start with the Bayesian viewpoint and consider equal prior probabilities and equal costs, then $\tau = 1$, or equivalently $\eta = 0$, and we choose the hypothesis with higher probability. This intuitive approach is often called "maximum likelihood detection."

The log-likelihood for a set of N independent outcomes for the Poisson and geometric distributions is given by

$$L_P(\theta) = -N\theta + \ln(\theta) \sum_{i=1}^{N} x_i - \sum_{i=1}^{N} \ln x_i!$$

$$= -N\theta + N \ln(\theta) \bar{x} - \sum_{i=1}^{N} \ln x_i!, \qquad (4.5)$$

$$L_G(\theta) = \ln(\theta) \sum_{i=1}^{N} x_i + N \ln(1 - \theta)$$

$$= N[\bar{x} \ln(\theta) + \ln(1 - \theta)], \qquad (4.6)$$

where $\bar{x} = \sum_{i=1}^{N} x_i / N$ is the sample average.

---

2. The "probability of miss" is $1 - P_D$. The terms "detection," "false alarm," and "miss" are the legacy from detection theory's military roots, although the terms are often used more broadly. In the example in (4.3), a "false alarm" occurs when the LRT declares the sample to be Poisson-distributed when it is really geometric-distibuted; a "miss" occurs when the LRT declares the distribution of the sample to geometric when it is really Poisson. Statisticians often prefer a more neutral nomenclature; what we call "false alarms" and "misses" they call Type I and Type II errors, respectively. I can never seem to remember which is Type I and which is Type II, and my own roots lie in military applications, which explains my preference for "false alarms" and "misses."

4.2.2 Hypothesis Testing with Unknown Parameters

It is often unrealistic to assume that parameters such as θ_P and θ_G would be known in advance. Such cases are often referred to as *composite* hypothesis testing problems. If the parameters can be treated as realizations of a random variable, a prior density on the parameters may be proposed, and the parameters integrated out, yielding a simple hypothesis test. However, it may be unrealistic to assume such a prior, and statisticians from the frequentist school often object to the prior on philosophical grounds, whatever the prior might be.

If the parameter must be treated as nonrandom, in practice it is common to estimate the parameters based on the data, and plug those estimates $\hat{\theta}(\mathbf{x}^N)$ into (4.4) and use them as if they were the true parameter values, yielding a *generalized likelihood (or log-likelihood) ratio test*:

$$\frac{\prod_{i=1}^{N} P_P(x_i : \hat{\theta}_P(\mathbf{x}^N))}{\prod_{i=1}^{N} P_G(x_i : \hat{\theta}_G(\mathbf{x}^N))} \underset{<}{\overset{>}{\sim}} \tau, \quad \sum_{i=1}^{N} L_P(x_i : \hat{\theta}_P(\mathbf{x}^N)) - \sum_{i=1}^{N} L_G(x_i : \hat{\theta}_G(\mathbf{x}^N)) \underset{<}{\overset{>}{\sim}} \ln \tau \overset{\text{df}}{=} \eta \tag{4.7}$$

Maximum likelihood estimators are most often used. If these are difficult to compute, other estimators, such as method-of-moments estimators, might be explored. Luckily, the ML estimators of the Poisson and the geometric distributions are easily computed. The first derivatives of the log-likelihoods for the two models are

$$\frac{\partial}{\partial \theta} L_P(\theta) = N \left(-1 + \frac{\bar{x}}{\theta_P} \right), \tag{4.8}$$

$$\frac{\partial}{\partial \theta_G} L_G(\theta_G) = N \left[\frac{\bar{x}}{\theta_G} - \frac{1}{1 - \theta_G} \right]. \tag{4.9}$$

Equating (4.9) and (4.8) with zero yields the ML estimates:

$$\hat{\theta}_P(\mathbf{x}^N) = \bar{x}, \; \hat{\theta}_G(\mathbf{x}^N) = \frac{\bar{x}}{\bar{x} + 1}. \tag{4.10}$$

4.3 Some Models Have an Unfair Advantage

Figure 4.1 shows the result of Monte Carlo experiments designed to compute probabilities of correct decision. For each point on the graphs, 40,000 runs were conducted to estimate the probability. The solid lines show results from the log-likelihood ratio test (4.4) when the parameters are known exactly. The dashed lines show results from the generalized log-likelihood ratio test (GLRT) (4.7), where the parameters are unknown. Both the LRT and GLRT are compared to a threshold of $\eta = 0$. Hence, in each case, we pick the model with the largest likelihood, which seems reasonable.

To make the hypothesis testing problem difficult, we pick θ_G and θ_P so that the mean of the data under each model is the same. Recall the mean of the Poisson distribution is just θ_P. If we are given a particular θ_P, we can make the mean of the geometric distribution match by setting $\theta_G = \theta_P/(\theta_P + 1)$. For convenience, we will often use θ_P to indicate the desired mean of the data in our simulations, and will assume that θ_G has been adjusted to match. We employ conventions like this throughout the chapter.

In the graphs on the top row of Figure 4.1, the shapes on the lines indicate what "true" model the data were generated from, either Poisson ("stars") or geometric ("squares"). The left graph shows the case where we fix the data mean at 5, and change the number of outcomes N. The right graph shows the case where we fix the number of outcomes at 6, and change the data mean.

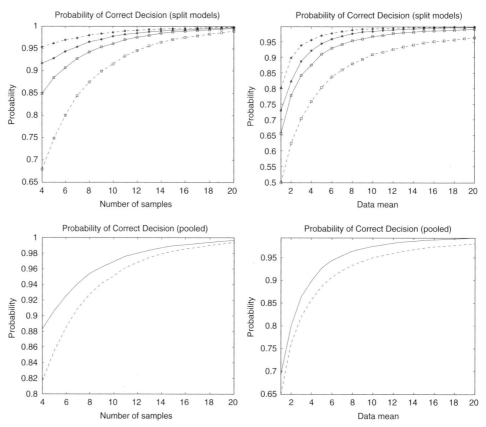

Figure 4.1 Probability of correct decision of the LRT, in which the parameters are known *(solid line)*, and the GLRT in which they are estimated. In the top row, the symbols indicate whether the data are generated by the Poisson ("star") or geometric model ("square") model. The lower row gives the average over the Poisson and geometric cases. In the left column, the number of outcomes is varied along the horizontal axis, and the data mean is fixed at 5. In the right column, the number of outcomes is fixed at 6, and the data mean is varied instead.

Notice something odd happens when we go from the LRT to the GLRT. The probability of correctly identifying a geometric model went down. In the GLRT, we do not know the exact parameters, and must estimate them, so we might expect some loss of performance. However, the probability of correctly identifying a Poisson model *went up*. This does not really compensate for the loss of performance when the geometric model is true, though. As shown in the bottom row of Figure 4.1, if we pool both the Poisson-true and geometric-true cases together and average the "star" and "square" lines in the graphs on the top row, the total probability of correct identification in the GLRT case is less than in the LRT case.

Recall that while the log-likelihood ratio test can be derived from many different optimality criteria (such as the Neyman-Pearson criteria), the GLRT does not enjoy as firm a theoretical footing. The GLRT is an intuitive and reasonable test, and there are many asymptotic results concerning its behavior [Bahadur 1967; Groeneboom and Oosterhoff 1977], but its behavior for small samples is difficult to predict. In some cases, we have only an unknown parameter under one of the hypotheses, and under the other hypothesis (usually the null hypothesis), all the parameters are known. In these cases, we can modify the threshold η to achieve a particular desired P_{FA}, and make a plot of the resulting P_D as a function of the unknown parameters under the other hypothesis to get a feel for how the detector operates. This approach may not always be satisfactory, as picking a particular P_{FA} may feel arbitrary. Also, in some cases (as in the Poisson vs. geometric problem discussed in this chapter), we have unknown parameters under both hypotheses, and there is no obvious procedure for picking the threshold. Hence, we are inclined to seek a more theoretically grounded approach.

In searching for a new tactic, one might first wonder why a procedure that picks the model with the greatest log-likelihood after plugging in parameter estimates seems to favor the Poisson model over the geometric model. Our intuition tells us the Poisson model is somehow more powerful than the geometric model, and that it deserves to be penalized in some way to compensate for its extra power. In a sense, the Poisson model can more readily describe a wider variety of distributions than the geometric model. This notion is made precise in [Myung, Balasubramanian, and Pitt 2000]. This extra power means that the Poisson model can sometimes fit data from the geometric model better than the geometric model itself. (The opposite can also happen, but is much less likely.) Characterizing the descriptive power of models, and crafting new kinds of hypothesis tests based on these characterizations, are among the goals of stochastic complexity described in the next section.

4.4   Stochastic Complexity

Let our sample be represented by the vector $\mathbf{x}$, which contains a fixed number of outcomes. A "good" model allows us to encode the data $\mathbf{x}$ efficiently. If we have several different statistical models $P_1(\mathbf{x})$, $P_2(\mathbf{x})$, $P_3(\mathbf{x})$, and so on to choose from, Shannon's information theory [Cover and Thomas 1991; Hansen and Yu 2001] tells us we should choose the model k for which the code length[3] $-\ln P_k(\mathbf{x})$ is the smallest, or equivalently, for which $P_k(\mathbf{x})$ is the largest[4]. Shannon's theorems make sense when $\mathbf{x}$ takes values in a discrete set. Continuous data can be handled via discretization. Choosing a small code length is entirely consistent with the "maximum likelihood" hypothesis test described in Section 4.2.1.

At first glance, the presence of unknown parameters (possibly vectors, with dimension varying from model to model) does not appear to be a problem. It seems deceptively reasonable to just replace the unknown parameters with their ML estimates, and simply choose from among the $P_1(\mathbf{x} : \hat{\theta}_1(\mathbf{x}))$, $P_2(\mathbf{x} : \hat{\theta}_2(\mathbf{x}))$, $P_3(\mathbf{x} : \hat{\theta}_3(\mathbf{x}))$, and so on, but caution is required, as making the plugged-in parameter a function of $\mathbf{x}$ means that $P_k(\mathbf{x} : \hat{\theta}_k(\mathbf{x}))$ are not probability mass functions (or densities, in the case of continuous data) anymore! Shannon's theorems want probability distributions. Hence, we normalize the $P_k(\mathbf{x} : \hat{\theta}_k(\mathbf{x}))$ to get something that sums up to 1, called the *normalized maximum likelihood* (NML) density:

$$P_{NML}(\mathbf{x}) = \frac{P(\mathbf{x} : \hat{\theta}(\mathbf{x}))}{\sum_{\tilde{\mathbf{x}} \in \mathcal{X}} P(\tilde{\mathbf{x}} : \hat{\theta}(\tilde{\mathbf{x}}))}, \qquad (4.11)$$

where we have suppressed explicit notation of the model k. We can then apply Shannon's theory and choose that model based on what gives us the shortest NML code. This notion actually dates back to Shtarkov's 1987 work on coding individual sequences [Shtarkov 1987]. Its link to the minimum description length principle was later recognized by Rissanen [1996]. Procedures based on this code boast a dizzying arsenal of universal optimality properties [Rissanen 2001].

The negative logarithm of (4.11) is called the *stochastic complexity*:

$$SC = -\ln P(\mathbf{x} : \theta) + PC, \qquad (4.12)$$

where the second term is called the *parametric complexity*:

$$PC = \ln \sum_{\tilde{\mathbf{x}} \in \mathcal{X}} P(\tilde{\mathbf{x}} : \hat{\theta}(\tilde{\mathbf{x}})) \qquad (4.13)$$

---

3. To stay consistent with the typical practice in statistics, we generally use natural logarithms, and hence usually measure information and code lengths in terms of "nats." One can convert from nats to the more traditional base-2 logarithm "bits" of information theory by dividing by $\ln 2$.

4. In such a procedure, one should also technically encode which model k is chosen. One can think of this as an initial sequence of bits telling a decoder which model to use; these bits arrive before the information for $\mathbf{x}$, encoded with that model, is sent. If the number of possible models is finite, one can encode k using the same number of bits for each k, in which case the addition of this prefix does not change the choice of model at all. If the number of possible models is infinite, the situation is slightly trickier, but the number of bits in the prefix code is typically negligible anyway. Hence, this chapter does not consider this issue any further.

The MDL principle says we should choose the model with the smallest stochastic complexity. From a maximum likelihood viewpoint, we can think of the parametric complexity as a penalty we must pay for not knowing the parameter exactly. In older "two-part" versions of MDL [Rissanen 1978, 1983, 1986, 1987a], the ML estimate is explicitly coded with a certain degree of precision that is optimal in some predetermined sense, and the number of bits used to encode the ML estimate to a certain precision can be thought of as a rough estimate of the parametric complexity. The newer NML code abandons the notion of a separate stage of encoding the parameter and the associated artificial notion of truncating it to some precision. As shown in [Rissanen 1996, p. 42], NML substantially refines the estimate of the stochastic complexity by removing a redundancy in the two-part code.

In all but a few special cases, computing parametric complexity according to (4.13) is difficult. Under certain technical conditions, in the case of independent, identically distributed data, Theorem 1 of [Rissanen 1996] shows that it can be asymptotically approximated by

$$PC \approx APC = \frac{k}{2} \ln \frac{N}{2\pi} + \ln \int_{\Theta} \sqrt{\det I(\theta)} d\theta, \qquad (4.14)$$

where k is the number of free parameters, N is the number of outcomes, and $I(\theta)$ is the Fisher information matrix *for one outcome*. The element of the Fisher information matrix at row r and column c *for N outcomes* is given by

$$I_{rc}(\theta) = -E_\theta \left[\frac{\partial^2}{\partial \theta_r \partial \theta_c} \ln P(\mathbf{x} : \theta) \right]. \qquad (4.15)$$

If the data are independently and identically distributed (i.i.d.) according to θ, then the Fisher information matrix for N outcomes is simply N times the Fisher information matrix for one outcome. The subscript on the E indicates that the expectation over $\mathbf{x}$ is being taken assuming a particular value of θ. [We have made a slight abuse of notation; previously, subscripts on θ were used to index different models k, but in (4.15) subscripts are used to index particular elements in a parameter vector θ.] Although similar approximations are available in many non-i.i.d. cases, we will stick with the i.i.d. case for simplicity [Takeuchi 2000]). In Section 4.4.2, we will see that the denominator of (4.11) and the integral in (4.14) are infinite for many useful models, and hence require special care.

If N is large, then the *APC* asymptotically approaches the simple formula most often associated with MDL: $(k/2) \ln N$. The process of choosing a model by minimizing

$$- \ln P(\mathbf{x} : \hat{\theta}) + (k/2) \ln N \qquad (4.16)$$

goes by several names, such as the Bayesian information criterion (BIC) and the Schwarz [1978] information criterion (SIC). Notice that naively pulling out the simple $(k/2) \ln N$ formula would not help us in our example, as both the Poisson and geometric models have the same number of parameters. Thinking a bit further outside the box, one could imagine a small sample-size case where a model with, say, two parameters may actually have less parametric complexity, and hence less descriptive power, than a model with one parameter. In such cases blindly invoking the $(k/2) \ln N$ term would be quite misleading [Grünwald 2005].

4.4.1   Fisher Information Computations

The second derivatives of the Poisson and geometric log-likelihoods are

$$\frac{\partial^2}{\partial \theta_P^2} L_P(\theta_P) = -N \frac{\bar{x}}{\theta_P^2}, \tag{4.17}$$

$$\frac{\partial^2}{\partial \theta_G^2} L_G(\theta_G) = -N \left[\frac{\bar{x}}{\theta_G^2} + \frac{1}{(1 - \theta_G)^2} \right]. \tag{4.18}$$

The Fisher information associated with estimating θ_P and θ_G is given by

$$I_P(\theta_P) = -E_{\theta_P} \left[\frac{\partial^2}{\partial \theta_P^2} L(\theta_P) \right] = N \frac{E[\bar{x}]}{\theta_P^2} = \frac{N}{\theta_P}, \tag{4.19}$$

$$I_G(\theta_G) = -E_{\theta_G} \left[\frac{\partial^2}{\partial \theta_G^2} L(\theta_G) \right] = N \frac{\theta_G}{\theta_G^2(1 - \theta_G)} + \frac{N}{(1 - \theta_G)^2} = \frac{N}{(1 - \theta_G)^2 \theta_G}. \tag{4.20}$$

The indefinite integrals of the square roots of the Fisher information for the Poisson and geometric models needed for computing the approximate parametric complexity (4.14) are

$$\int \sqrt{I_P(\theta_P)} d\theta_P = \int \sqrt{\frac{1}{\theta_P}} d\theta_P = 2\sqrt{\theta_P}, \tag{4.21}$$

$$\int \sqrt{I_G(\theta_G)} d\theta_G = \int \sqrt{\frac{1}{(1 - \theta_G)^2 \theta_G}} d\theta_G = \int \frac{1}{(1 - \theta_G)\sqrt{\theta_G}} d\theta_G$$

$$= \ln \left(\frac{1 + \sqrt{\theta_G}}{1 - \sqrt{\theta_G}} \right). \tag{4.22}$$

Note that (4.21) and (4.22) refer once again to the Fisher information for *one* outcome.

4.4.2   Misbehaving Integrals

When computing stochastic complexity, we would like to integrate over the full possible range of the parameters, here $\theta_P \in [0, \infty)$ and $\theta_G \in [0, 1]$. In some cases, such as the independent finite-alphabet process of Example 1 of [Rissanen 1996], we can do so without any trouble. However, in many other cases, the integral in (4.14), when taken over the full parameter range, is not finite! This conundrum is encountered in the exponential and Gaussian cases in Examples 2 and 3 of [Rissanen 1996], as well as the Poisson and geometric models considered here.

Finding a satisfying way of taming models with "infinite" stochastic complexity is an active research topic. At least five approaches have appeared in the literature:

1. As suggested by Rissanen [1996, p. 328], we could simply restrict the parameter

range to lie over a particular region where we suspect that the "true" value lives that also allows the integral to be finite. Myung et al. [2000] take this tactic, writing: "We will always cut off the ranges of parameters to ensure that $V(f)$ [the authors' term for the integral of the square root of the Fisher information] is finite. These ranges should be considered as part of the functional form of the model." Upon contemplation, this approach does not seem at all satisfactory, since choosing the parameter range a priori smacks of the sort of arbitrary choice that the MDL philosophy seeks to avoid. To illustrate the conceptual difficulties with arbitrary parameter space restriction, we consider this approach in Section 4.5.

2. Rissanen [1996, Section 5] suggests a more sophisticated approach, where we consider an increasing sequence of subsets $\Theta(1) \subset \Theta(2) \subset \ldots \subset \Theta$. In computing stochastic complexity using this scheme, for a given $\mathbf{x}$, we pick the smallest k such that $\hat{\theta}(\mathbf{x}) \in \Theta(k)$. The integral in (4.14) is computed over $\Theta(k)$ instead of the full Θ, and an additional $l^\star(k)$ bits are added to "encode" the particular k.[5] The resulting complexity measure is dependent on the particular $\Theta(1), \Theta(2), \ldots$ sequence we choose. The set sequence choice is somewhat arbitrary, so this approach feels only slightly more pleasing than Approach 1.

3. In some cases, it may be possible to let the limits of the parameter range be "hyperparameters," and one can form another level of NML code by normalizing over the hyperparameters. If this new normalization is not finite, the process can be repeated. This rather elegant technique was proposed by Rissanen. In the case of the additive Gaussian models, three iterations of this procedure are sufficient [Rissanen 2000]. This is far more satisfactory than the application of Approach 2 to the Gaussian problem (using an increasing set sequence and $l^\star$) seen in Example 3 of [Rissanen 1996]. Such a tactic can be tried in other situations, but it is not clear at present that it will always be successful. There may be cases where each iteration yields a need for another set of hyperparameters and the procedure does not terminate. This issue needs much further exploration.

4. Liang and Barron [2004,2005] consider location and scale parameters in Gaussian regression problems. They show that if one conditions on a fixed initial observation, say x_1, many of the normalization difficulties illustrated in this chapter can be avoided. Although Barron and Liang come at the problem from a Bayesian viewpoint with uniform improper priors, their results can be closely related to the NML approaches discussed in this chapter, making them ripe avenues for future research.

5. Finally, we mention the intriguing *competitive complexity ratio* approach devised by Stine and Foster [2000]. Although their work was motivated by the trouble of infinite parametric complexity that is the focus of this chapter, it may be misleading to think of the competitive complexity ratio approach as a "patch" of NML like Approaches 2 and 3 above. Instead, Stine and Foster pose a different problem.

---

5. We are using $l^\star(k)$ to denote the "log-star" described by Rissanen [1983], which is approximately $\log k + 2 \log \log k$.

They consider parametric complexity under the constraint of side information restricting the range, as in Approach 1, which they call *conditional parametric complexity*. However, they go a step further by considering a family of restricted ranges, which allows them to formulate an *unconditional parametric complexity*. Stine and Foster write, "One means to bound the parametric complexity in this model is to incorporate bounds as part of the code itself [as in Approach 3]... Rather than consider various means of incorporating information about the parameter space $\Theta_{[a,b]}$ directly into the code, we instead consider a competitive analysis of how well a realizable code fares when compared to a code that *knows* features of the true parameter space." This approach is still not entirely free of some arbitrary choices, as the competitive complexity ratio depends on the family of potential side information chosen. As an example, in investigating the Gaussian location problem, Stine and Foster compute different competitive complexity ratios depending on whether the restricting sets (which contain the origin) are allowed to be nonsymmetric or forced to be symmetric. These comments should not be construed as criticisms; we feel Stine and Foster's work is definitely a step in the right direction.

We spent some time attempting to apply Approaches 3, 4, and 5 to the Poisson and geometric distributions discussed here, but did not make much progress, and hence leave such explorations as a direction for future work.

The integrals for our models have no problem at the lower limits of $\theta_G = 0$ and $\theta_P = 0$. However, the indefinite integrals evaluate to infinity at the upper limit of $\theta_G = 1$ and $\theta_P = \infty$. Hence, we will restrict θ_G and θ_P to the ranges $0 \le \theta_G \le \theta_G^{(top)} < 1$ and $0 \le \theta_P \le \theta_P^{(top)} < \infty$. Of course, much may depend on our choice of $\theta_G^{(top)}$ and $\theta_P^{(top)}$. The approximate parametric complexities (4.14) for both models are

$$APC_P = \frac{1}{2} \ln \frac{N}{2\pi} + \ln 2\sqrt{\theta_P^{(top)}} = \frac{1}{2} \ln \frac{N}{2\pi} + \ln 2 + \frac{1}{2} \ln \theta_P^{(top)}, \tag{4.23}$$

$$APC_G = \frac{1}{2} \ln \frac{N}{2\pi} + \ln \left[\ln \left(\frac{1 + \sqrt{\theta_G^{(top)}}}{1 - \sqrt{\theta_G^{(top)}}} \right) \right]. \tag{4.24}$$

4.4.3   Comparing Approximate and Exact Formulas

One may wonder how accurate an approximation (4.14) is of the true parametric complexity (4.13). For $N > 1$, computing (4.13) for our Poisson and geometric models is rather messy, so let us first consider the simple extreme case of $N = 1$.

In the single-outcome case, we can write

$$P_P(x : \hat{\theta}_P(x)) = \frac{e^{-\hat{\theta}_P(x)}\hat{\theta}_P(x)^x}{x!} = \frac{e^{-x}x^x}{x!}, \tag{4.25}$$

$$P_G(x : \hat{\theta}_G(x)) = [\hat{\theta}_G(x)]^x[1 - \hat{\theta}_G(x)]$$

$$= \left(\frac{x}{x+1}\right)^x \left(1 - \frac{x}{x+1}\right) = \frac{x^x}{(x+1)^{x+1}}. \tag{4.26}$$

Recall that the integrals of the square roots of the Fisher information given in the left hand sides of (4.21) and (4.22) are infinite when evaluated over the full parameter ranges. As we might expect, when (4.25) and (4.26) are plugged into the exact parametric complexity formula (4.13), the sums over $x \in \mathbb{N}$ are infinite too.

We sum over restricted sets

$$\mathcal{X}_P(\theta_P^{(top)}) = \{x \in \mathbb{N} : \hat{\theta}_P(x) \le \theta_P^{(top)}\} = \{x \in \mathbb{N} : x \le \theta_P^{(top)}\}, \tag{4.27}$$

$$\mathcal{X}_G(\theta_G^{(top)}) = \{x \in \mathbb{N} : \hat{\theta}_G(x) \le \theta_G^{(top)}\} = \left\{x \in \mathbb{N} : \frac{x}{x+1} \le \theta_G^{(top)}\right\}$$

$$= \left\{x \in \mathbb{N} : x \le \frac{\theta_G^{(top)}}{1 - \theta_G^{(top)}}\right\}. \tag{4.28}$$

To avoid numerical difficulties,[6] we rearrange the sums of (4.25) over (4.27) and (4.26) over (4.28) as

$$NML_P = \sum_{x=0}^{\lfloor \theta_P^{(top)} \rfloor} \frac{e^{-x}x^x}{x!} = \sum_{x=0}^{\lfloor \theta_P^{(top)} \rfloor} \exp[-x + x\ln(x) - \ln\gamma(x+1)], \tag{4.29}$$

$$NML_G = \sum_{x=0}^{\left\lfloor \frac{\theta_G^{(top)}}{1-\theta_G^{(top)}} \right\rfloor} \frac{x^x}{(x+1)^{x+1}}$$

$$= \sum_{x=0}^{\left\lfloor \frac{\theta_G^{(top)}}{1-\theta_G^{(top)}} \right\rfloor} \exp[x\ln(x) - (x+1)\ln(x+1)]. \tag{4.30}$$

The left panel of Figure 4.2 plots the exact parametric complexity (ln of (4.29)) against the approximate parametric complexity (4.23) for the Poisson model for $0 < \theta_P^{(top)} \le 1000$ with $N = 1$. The two lines follow one another rather closely. In spite of the fact that the approximate stochastic complexity is based on asymptotic arguments, it seems to do quite well even for $N = 1$. The right panel zooms in on a portion of the plot for $0 < \theta_P^{(top)} \le 30$.

To see how the approximation improves as N increases for the Poisson model, Figure 4.3 compares exact parametric complexity computed via a brute-force summation for $N = 2$ (left panel) and $N = 3$ (right panel) against the approximate

---

6. We compute $\ln\gamma(x+1)$ using MATLAB's built-in `gammaln` function.

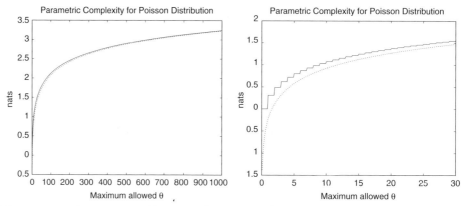

Figure 4.2   Approximate *(dotted line)* and exact *(solid line)* single-outcome parametric complexity of the Poisson model for $0 < \theta_P^{(top)} \le 1000$ *(left panel)* and $0 < \theta_P^{(top)} \le 30$ *(right panel)*.

parametric complexity for $0 < \theta_P^{(top)} \le 30$. Notice that the approximation improves with increasing N.

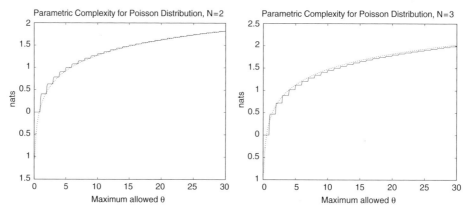

Figure 4.3   Approximate *(dotted line)* and exact *(solid line)* single-outcome parametric complexity of the geometric model for $0 < \theta_P^{(top)} \le 30$ for $N = 2$ *(left panel)* and $N = 3$ *(right panel)*.

For $N = 1$, the exact and approximate parametric complexity formulas only seem to match for the geometric model for $\theta_G^{(top)}$ close to 1, as shown in Figure 4.4. Also notice that for $\theta_G^{(top)}$ lower than around 0.7, the approximate formula gives a negative answer, which is not sensible. However, as N increases, the approximation rapidly becomes more reasonable. This can be seen in Figure 4.5, which shows comparisons for the geometric model computed for $N = 2$ and $N = 3$ via a brute-force summation.

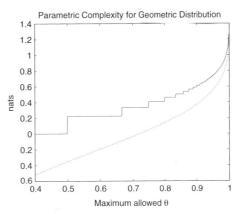

Figure 4.4 Approximate *(dotted line)* and exact *(solid line)* single-outcome parametric complexity of the geometric model for $0.4 \le \theta_G^{(top)} \le 0.999$.

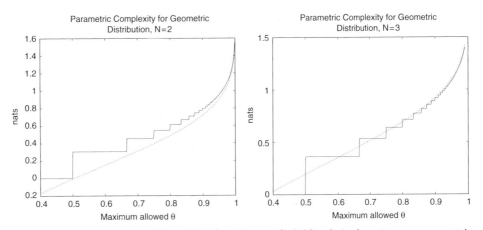

Figure 4.5 Approximate *(dotted line)* and exact *(solid line)* single-outcome parametric complexity of the geometric model for $0.4 \le \theta_G^{(top)} \le 0.999$ for N=2 *(left panel)* and $0.4 \le \theta_G^{(top)} \le 0.99$ for $N = 3$ *(right panel)*. The range for the $N = 3$ case was shrunk a bit on the right, from 0.999 to 0.99, so the computations would not take too long.

Notice the stairstep nature of the exact formula (solid line) in Figure 4.4 and the right panel of Figure 4.2, which results from the "floor" operation in (4.29) and (4.30).

Clearly, the choice of $\theta_P^{(top)}$ makes a big difference in the complexity of the Poisson model, and may be a source of concern. Choosing $\theta_G^{(top)}$ seems less problematic, as one can pick a $\theta_G^{(top)}$ very close to 1 and cover most interesting possible values of θ_G without the parametric complexity going through the roof. For instance, for $N = 1$, if we take $\theta_G^{(top)} = 1 - 10^{-6}$, we get $SC_G \approx 1.8043$ and $ASC_G \approx 1.8025$. Taking $\theta_G^{(top)} = 1 - 10^{-7}$ instead gives $SC_G \approx 1.9348$ and $ASC_G \approx 1.9435$.

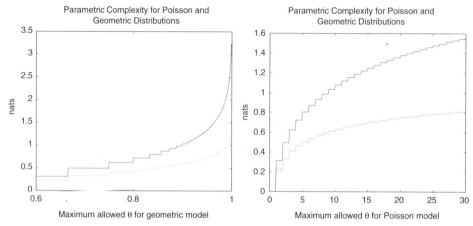

Figure 4.6   The left panel shows exact parametric complexity for the geometric (dotted line) and Poisson (solid line) models for $N = 1$. The geometric model complexity is computed with $\theta_G^{(top)}$, as shown on the horizontal axis. The equivalent Poisson model complexity is computed with $\theta_P^{(top)} = \theta_G^{(top)}/(1 - \theta_G^{(top)})$ to match the means of the Poisson and geometric distributions at the top of their parameter ranges. The right panel is similar; the only difference is that the $\theta_P^{(top)}$ is plotted on the horizontal axis, and the equivalent geometric model complexity is computed with $\theta_G^{(top)} = \theta_P^{(top)}/(1 + \theta_P^{(top)})$.

By way of comparison, consider that $\theta_G = 1 - 10^{-7}$ corresponds to a geometric distribution with a mean of 10^7. Remember θ_P is the mean of the Poisson distribution. If we compute the approximate parametric complexity for the Poisson model with $\theta_P^{(top)} = 10^7$ and $N = 1$, we get $ASC_P = 7.8333$. The Poisson model has $7.8333 - 1.9435 = 5.8898$ more nats of "descriptive power." Venturing down this path a little further, Figure 4.6 plots the exact parametric complexity for the geometric model [ln of (4.29)] for a range of $\theta_G^{(top)}$ (dotted line) for $N = 1$. In the left panel, for each $\theta_G^{(top)}$ along the horizontal axis, the exact parametric complexity for the Poisson model [ln of (4.30)] is also shown (solid line), using $\theta_P^{(top)} = \theta_G^{(top)}/(1 - \theta_G^{(top)})$, chosen so that the maximum allowed values of θ_G and θ_P give matching means, which we will call the "top" mean.[7] Notice that the amount by which the Poisson parametric complexity exceeds the geometric stochastic complexity increases with θ_G (or equivalently, increases with the "top" mean.) We continue this convention in the next section. The right panel is similar, except that $\theta_P^{(top)}$ is plotted on the horizontal axis, and a $\theta_G^{(top)}$ is chosen to match the mean.

---

7. We choose the ranges this way to try to put the models on equal footing. The choice of matching the "top" mean makes intuitive sense, but is admittedly somewhat arbitrary. We could try matching specific quantiles, such as medians.

4.5   Results of Including Stochastic Complexity

The left panels of Figure 4.7 show probabilities of correct decision as a function of the sample size N for a true data mean of 5 under each model. The solid line shows the result of the LRT assuming the correct parameters are known. The dashed line gives the results of the GLRT. The dots, pluses, and crosses, show the result for the minimum stochastic complexity criterion, using values for $\theta_P^{(top)}$ and $\theta_G^{(top)}$ shown in Table 4.1. The right panels of the table show the difference in approximate stochastic complexities, which is an estimate of how much extra descriptive power the Poisson model enjoys over the geometric model.

Table 4.1   Values of $\theta_P^{(top)}$ and $\theta_G^{(top)}$ used in Figure 4.7.

symbol	$\theta_P^{(top)}$	$\theta_G^{(top)}$	$APC_P - APC_G$
·	$10^{1.25} - 1 \approx 16.7828$	$1 - 10^{-1.25} \approx 0.9438$	0.6598 nats
+	$10^{2.25} - 1 \approx 55.2341$	$1 - 10^{-2.25} \approx 0.9944$	1.3991 nats
×	$10^3 - 1 = 999$	$1 - 10^{-3} = 0.9990$	2.0310 nats

Notice in the top left panel of Figure 4.7, corresponding to data generated under the Poisson model, that choosing $\theta_P^{(top)} = 10^{1.25} - 1$ (corresponding to 'dots') seems to pull the GLRT performance *down* to that provided by the original LRT. In exchange, we get better performance when data are generated by the geometric model, as shown in the middle left panel, where the dotted line lies above the dashed line (although it is still not as good as that given by the LRT assuming known parameters, which is shown by the solid line).

On the other hand, notice in the middle panel that if we set $\theta_P^{(top)} = 10^{2.25} - 1$ (corresponding to "pluses"), that performance of the GLRT is pulled *up* to that given by the original LRT. The compromise, as seen in the top left panel, is that the test on Poisson data now operates even worse that it did under the original LRT.

Taking $\theta_P^{(top)} = 10^3 - 1$ (corresponding to 'crosses') gives even worse performance in the Poisson case (upper left panel), in exchange for performance in the geometric case (middle left panel) that is even better than that given by the original LRT.

The lower left panel gives the average of the upper left and middle left panels. The lines with the 'dots' and the 'pluses' (corresponding to $\theta_P^{(top)} = 10^{1.25} - 1$ and $10^{1.75} - 1$, respectively) happen to lie very close to one another. They give better performance, in this average sense, than the GLRT, but as expected, they do not do quite as well as the original LRT in which the true parameter values are exactly known. Interestingly, taking $\theta_P^{(top)} = 10^3 - 1$ does not improve average performance over the raw GLRT; it appears such a choice excessively punishes the Poisson model. One must be careful, however, of interpreting this lower left panel too literally; the average is only a meaningful measure if the two models are equally

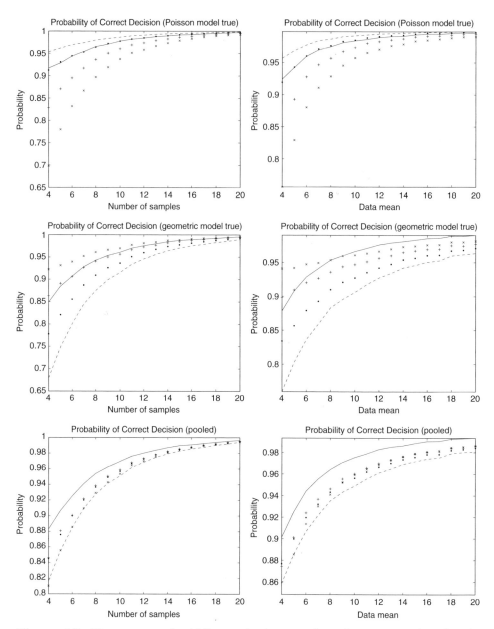

Figure 4.7 The upper and middle panels correspond to data generated under the Poisson and geometric models, respectively. The original LRT and raw GLRT results are shown by the solid and dashed lines. The dots, pluses, and crosses show results from a detector based on the approximate stochastic complexity criterion (see text for details). The lower row gives the average of the first two rows. In the left column, the mean is fixed at 5, and the number of outcomes is varied. In the right column, the sample mean is varied, and the number of outcomes is kept fixed at 6.

likely a priori, which is just the sort of Bayesian-sounding statement the stochastic complexity agenda seeks to avoid.

The panels on the right of Figure 4.7 are analogous to the panels on the left, except this time we keep the sample size fixed at $N = 5$, and change the true data mean θ_P.

Notice that the performance for data generated by the geometric and Poisson models is heavily influenced by our choice of the parameter region. To explore this further, Figures 4.8 and 4.9 show the probability of correct detection where the horizonal axis specifies the "top" mean $\theta_P^{(top)}$. The rows are analogous to those in Figure 4.7; the top two rows consider data generated by the Poisson (top row) and geometric (middle row) models, and the bottom row is the average of the top two rows. Figure 4.8 shows results for a sample size $N = 3$, and Figure 4.9 shows results for a sample size $N = 10$. The left and right panels of each figure show the cases for $E[x_i] = 5$ and $E[x_i] = 10$, respectively.

4.6   Toward a Solution to the Range Selection Problem

The previous section vividly illustrates that we cannot wish away the problem of infinite stochastic complexity by a priori restricting ranges of integration. Choosing the "top" value in the previous section wound up being equivalent to sliding the threshold of a GLRT-style test.

We made several attempts to implement Approach 2 described in Section 4.4.2, where a series of subsets of parameter ranges are considered, and the particular subset chosen is encoded. We tried numerous choices of subsets, yet none seemed satisfactory, as the resulting performance curves (analogous to Figure 4.7) exhibited disturbing discontinuities associated with the juncture points of the subsets, and generally seemed to perform worse than the original GLRT. The results along that direction were discouraging (and Rissanen himself seems to have abandoned that path in general), so we do not report them here.

Upon hearing about those results, Peter Grünwald suggested a "smoothed" variation of that approach that appears promising. Imagine that we let the top end of the parameter range under each model correspond to exactly the ML estimate of the parameter under that model. In each case, note that the emprical mean is a sufficient statistic for that ML estimate. We can now imagine encoding that empirical mean using some arbitrarily precise scheme; the key is to suppose we use the *same scheme* resulting in the *same number of bits* under each hypothesis, so the contributions need not be considered. One could rightfully argue that we could have just applied the same hand waving to the original ML parameter estimate itself, and that all we have done here is to shuttle the hand waving to a deeper stage. In spite of those objections, the pudding-manifest proof realized in the dotted lines of Figure 4.10 has an intriguing flavor. Notice that the dotted line in the middle right panel follows the solid line (corresponding to the known parameters). This behavior contrasts with the various fixed-parameter-range performance curves shown in the

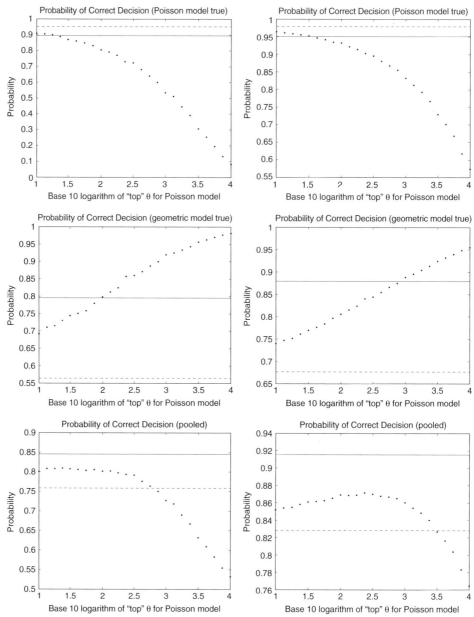

Figure 4.8 Probability of correct decision for $N = 3$, estimated using 40,000 Monte Carlo runs. The parameters θ_G and θ_P are chosen so that either $E[x_i] = 5$ *(left)* or $E[x_i] = 10$ *(right)*. The top two rows show the probability of correct decision where the data are generated according to the Poisson model *(top row)* and the geometric model *(bottom row)*. The bottom row shows the average of the probabilities given in the top two rows for a generic "probability of correct decision," supposing that the Poisson and geometric models are equally likely. The solid line shows the result of the LRT test, assuming the true parameters are known. The dashed line shows the result of the GLRT, in which ML estimates are substituted for true parameters. The dotted line shows the result of the stochastic complexity criterion as a function of the "top" of the parameter range.

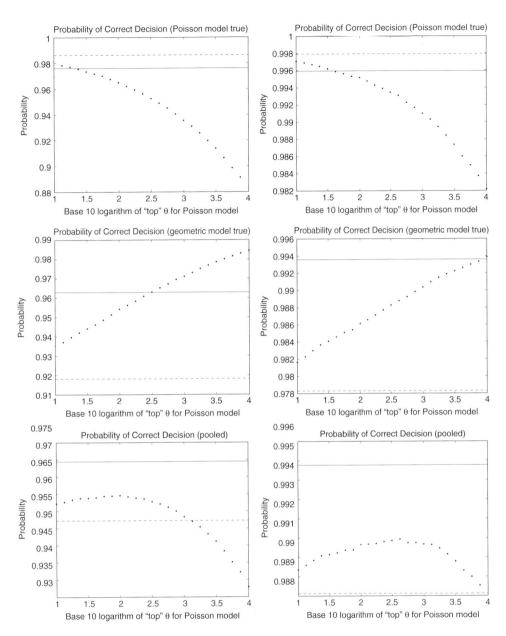

Figure 4.9   Probability of correct decision for $N = 10$, estimated using 40,000 Monte Carlo runs. The parameters θ_G and θ_P are chosen so that either $E[x_i] = 5$ *(left)* or $E[x_i] = 10$ *(right)*. The top two rows show the probability of correct decision where the data are generated according to the Poisson model *(top row)* and the geometric model *(bottom row)*. The bottom row shows the average of the probabilities given in the top two rows for a generic "probability of correct decision," supposing that the Poisson and geometric models are equally likely. The solid line shows the result of the LRT, assuming the true parameters are known. The dashed line shows the result of the GLRT, in which ML estimates are substituted for true parameters. The dotted line shows the result of the stochastic complexity criterion as a function of the "top" of the parameter range.

middle panel on the right of Figure 4.7, where the crosses, pluses, and dots lie above *or* below the curve depending on the target data mean selected for each particular experiment. In a sense, the behavior seen in the corresponding panel in Figure 4.10 is more *stable*; the dotted curve lies slightly below the LRT curve *throughout the full set of data means shown*. Similar observations could be made about the middle panels on the left of Figures 4.7 and 4.10.

Out of curiosity, for one last experiment, we tried letting the top end of the Poisson parameter range correspond to the maximum value in the data set instead of the mean (with the geometric parameter chosen appropriately to match, as we have done throughout the chapter). Using these ranges yields the lines with the crosses shown in Figure 4.10. This procedure seems to punish the Poisson model and favor the geometric model, perhaps overly so. Notice the crosses waver both above and below the solid (GLRT) line; hence this procedure does not enjoy the stability of behavior relative to the true parameter value discussed in the previous paragraph.

4.7   Concluding Contemplations

We embarked on this chapter with the intention and hope of "solving" the problem of infinite parametric complexity for at least one interesting non-Gaussian case. Alas, after twenty-some pages, a *completely satisfying* solution for this simple case of Poisson vs. geometric hypothesis testing (e.g., something as tasty as Rissanen's solution for the Gaussian regression, listed as Approach 3 in Section 4.4.2) has eluded us. That approach, along with Approaches 4 and 5 mentioned in the same section, would be good approaches to focus on in continuing this work.

Acknowledgments

I thank the editors for inviting me to be a panelist in a discussion at the workshop that led to this book and for inviting me to contribute a chapter. I would particularly like to thank Peter Grünwald for his extensive and deep comments on several successive drafts of this chapter and for not strangling me when I missed deadline after deadline.

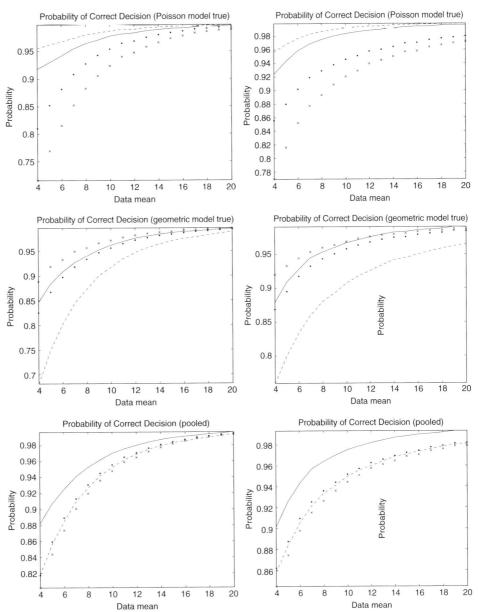

Figure 4.10 The upper and middle panels correspond to data generated under the Poisson and geometric models, respectively. The original LRT and raw GLRT results are shown by the solid and dashed lines. The dots and crosses show results obtained using the approximate stochastic complexity expression with restricted ranges. The dots correspond to taking the top value of the parameter range to be $\bar{x}$, the empirical mean of the data, under the Poisson hypothesis, and taking the top value to be the equivalent $\theta_G^{(top)} = \bar{x}/(\bar{x}+1)$ under the geometric hypothesis. The crosses correspond to taking the top value of the parameter range to be x_{MAX}, the maximum value of the data, under the Poisson hypothesis, and taking the top value to be the equivalent $\theta_G^{(top)} = x_{MAX}/(x_{MAX}+1)$ under the geometric hypothesis. The lower row gives the average of the first two rows. In the left panels, the mean is fixed at 5, and the number of outcomes is varied. In the right panels, the sample mean is varied, and the number of outcomes is kept fixed at 6. This figure is analogous to Figure 4.7.

References

Bahadur, R. (1967). An optimal property of the likelihood ratio statistic. In *Proceedings of the Fifth Berkeley Symposium on Mathematical Statistics and Probability*, Volume 1, pp. 13–16.

Barron, A.R., J. Rissanen, and B. Yu (1998). The Minimum Description Length Principle in coding and modeling. Special Commemorative Issue: Information Theory: 1948-1998. *IEEE Transactions on Information Theory, 44*(6), 2743–2760.

Cover, T., and J. Thomas (1991). *Elements of Information Theory.* New York: Wiley Interscience.

Groeneboom, P., and J. Oosterhoff (1977). Bahadur efficiency and probabilities of large deviations. *Statistica Neerlandica, 31*, 1–24.

Grünwald, P.D. (2005). Tutorial on MDL. In P.D. Grünwald, I.J. Myung, and M.A. Pitt (Eds.), *Advances in Minimum Description Length: Theory and Applications.* Cambridge, MA: MIT Press.

Hansen, M., and B. Yu (2001). Model selection and the principle of minimum description length. *Journal of the American Statistical Association, 96*, 746–774.

Lanterman, A. (2001). Schwarz, Wallace, and Rissanen: Intertwining themes in theories of model order estimation. *International Statistical Review 69*(2), 185–212.

Liang, F., and A. Barron (2004). Exact minimax strategies for predictive density estimation. To appear in *IEEE Transactions on Information Theory.*

Liang, F., and A. Barron (2005). Exact minimax predictive density estimation and MDL. In P.D. Grünwald, I.J. Myung, and M.A. Pitt (Eds.), *Advances in Minimum Description Length: Theory and Applications.* MIT Press.

Myung, I.J., V. Balasubramanian, and M.A. Pitt (2000). Counting probability distributions: Differential geometry and model selection. *Proceedings of the National Academy of Sciences USA, 97*, 11170–11175.

Politte, D., and D. Snyder (1988). The use of constraints to eliminate artifacts in maximum likelihood image estimation for emission tomography. *IEEE Transactions on Nuclear Science, 35*(1), 608–610.

Poor, V. (1994). *An Introduction to Signal Detection and Estimation*, 2nd edition. New York: Spinger-Verlag.

Rissanen, J. (1978). Modeling by shortest data description. *Automatica, 14*, 465–471.

Rissanen, J. (1983). A universal prior for integers and estimation by minimum description length. *Annals of Statistics, 11*(2), 416–431.

Rissanen, J. (1986). Stochastic complexity and modeling. *Annals of Statistics,*

$14(3)$, 1080–1100.

Rissanen, J. (1987). *Minimum Description Length Principle*, Volume 5, pp. 523–527. New York: Wiley.

Rissanen, J. (1996). Fisher information and stochastic complexity. *IEEE Transactions on Information Theory, $42(1)$*, 40–47.

Rissanen, J. (2000). MDL denoising. *IEEE Transactions on Information Theory, $46(7)$*, 2537–2543.

Rissanen, J. (2001). Strong optimality of the normalized ML models as universal codes and information in data. *IEEE Transactions on Information Theory, $47(5)$*.

Schwarz, G. (1978). Estimating the dimension of a model. *Annals of Statistics, $6(2)$*, 461–464.

Shtarkov, Y. (1987). Universal sequential coding of single messages. *Problems of Information Transmission, $23(3)$*, 3–17.

Snyder, D., and M. Miller (1985). The use of sieves to stabilize images produced with the EM algorithm for emission tomography. *IEEE Transactions on Nuclear Science, 32*, 3864–3872.

Snyder, D., M. Miller, J.L.J. Thomas, and D. Politte (1987). Noise and edge artifacts in maximum likelihood reconstruction for emission tomography. *IEEE Transactions on Medical Imaging, $6(3)$*, 228–237.

Stine, R. and D. Foster (2000). The competitive complexity ratio. In *Conference on Information Sciences and Systems*.

Takeuchi, J.(2000). On minimax regret with respect to families of stationary stochastic processes [in Japanese]. In *Proceedings of IBIS 2000*, pp. 63–68.

Van Trees, H. L. (1968). *Detection, Estimation and Modulation Theory, Part I*. New York: Wiley.

Wallace, C., and D. Boulton (1968). An information measure for classification. *Computer Journal $11(2)$*, 195–209.

5   Applications of MDL to Selected Families of Models

Andrew J. Hanson
Computer Science Department
Indiana University
Bloomington, Indiana 47405
USA
hanson@cs.indiana.edu

Philip Chi-Wing Fu
Department of Computer Science
The Hong Kong University of Science and Technology
Clear Water Bay, Hong Kong
cwfu@cs.ust.hk

Evaluating models that approximate complex data distributions is a core problem in data understanding. In this pedagogical review, we describe how the minimum description length (MDL) principle can be applied to evaluate the *relative appropriateness* of distinct models that defy conventional comparison methods, including models that are obscurely equivalent under functional transformations and inequivalent models with the same number of parameters. The MDL principle provides a concrete approach to identifying models that fit the data, avoid overfitting the noise, and embody no more functional complexity in the model itself than is necessary. New results on the geometric complexity of several families of useful models are derived, and illustrative examples are worked out in detail.

5.1   Introduction

The world of experimental science is replete with applications that require suitable approximations in order to model complex data sets that contain excessive apparent detail due to noise. Signal analysis, image analysis, shape detection, modeling data from psychological observations, modeling data from physical observations, and so

forth, are only a few of the examples that spring immediately to mind. As each
new research paper develops yet another clever technique or proposes yet another
functional class of models, one bothersome question remains: how can we distinguish
among different approaches? What criterion besides the author's word do we have
to conclude that one model is better than another? In other words, how do we
distinguish a *suitable* approach from an *optimal* approach? Our purpose in this
chapter is to present a core collection of data models analyzed so that the minimum
description length (MDL) principle can be used, *after* a parameter choice has been
selected, as a possible means of *comparing the appropriateness of distinct models*.
We outline the practices of MDL for a general scientific audience, derive new results
for the geometric complexity of common classes of functional models, and provide
a selection of illustrations suitable for a variety of modeling and data reduction
problems.

The Idea in a Nutshell   The conundrum that leads us to the ideas presented in
this chapter is simply this: suppose you do a least squares fit to a proposed model for
a data sample. You suspect that the 10th-order polynomial you used to fit the data
is in fact *nonsense*, even if it has *really* low variance, because you have good reason
to believe that a cubic polynomial process actually generated the data. You confirm
this by checking your 10th-order fit against another attempt at the measurement,
and it is ridiculously bad, even though the fit to the first sample was superb. If you
check the new data against a cubic fit to the old data, it will *still* be an appropriate
fit. *How do you figure this out* a priori *when you cannot* take *a second sample?* The
MDL method described here shows how this can be accomplished in well-behaved
situations. The essence of the entire argument is illustrated in figures 5.2, 5.3, and
5.4, which show explicitly that the "best" model using MDL, the lowest point on
the graph, is also typically the "right" model, the one used secretly to simulate the
noisy data; the lowest-variance models are *almost always* wrong.

General Background   The minimum description length principle appears first in
the work of Rissanen [1983, 1986, 1989] where it arose in the information-theoretic
analysis of stochastic processes. Over the years, a number of refinements have ap-
peared, many also due to Rissanen and his collaborators (see, e.g., [Leclerc 1989;
Fua and Hanson 1991; Mehta, Rissanen, and Agrawal 1995; Rissanen 1996; Balasubramanian 1997; Aggrawal, Gehrke, Gunopulos, and Raghavan 1998; Rissanen 1999;
Myung, Forster, and Browne 2000; Myung 2000; Myung, Balasubramanian, and
Pitt 2000; Myung, Pitt, Zhang, and Balasubramanian 2001; Hansen and Yu 2001;
Rissanen 2001a; Pitt, Myung, and Zhang 2002; Leclerc, Luong, and Fua 2003]).
The definitive formulation, answering many questions regarding comparison with
alternative approaches, is found in [Rissanen 2001b]. The underlying idea is simply to stretch information theory to its limits, and to evaluate all the parts of a
data description in the same universal language: the number of bits needed in the
description. Thus an excessively simple model would require few bits for its own
description, but many bits to describe the deviations of the data from the model,

while an excessively complex model could describe the data flawlessly, but would require a huge self-description. Less obvious is the fact that two models with the same number of parameters can differ substantially in the measure of the "descriptive power" of their functional spaces, and the appropriateness of a particular model can be distinguished on that basis as well. If this is done carefully, the theory is insensitive to reparameterizations of the models, a potential source of endless confusion and controversy. Also of interest to some classes of problems is the fact that both the model for the data sample and the model for its error process enter into the evaluation. Thus one intuitively expects the evaluation of all modeling problems to involve a compromise including the model's parameters, the form of its statistical noise, and a description of the intrinsic complexity of the modeling function itself. The best compromise is the most elegant description, the minimal overall amount of required information, the concrete mathematical formulation of Occam's razor.

At this time, there are still some open questions regarding the uniqueness of the "geometric cost" that permits the calculation of the relative complexity of two models, the handling of small, as opposed to nearly infinite, data samples, and an annoying arbitrariness in the choice of model parameter volumes. However, practical calculations using formulas valid for asymptotically large data samples and a functional metric based on the Fisher information matrix are straightforward in practice and exhibit the most essential desired properties: the results are independent of functional reparameterizations of the models, and favor models that generalize to other samples from the same distribution, as opposed to deceptively accurate models that are in fact overfitting the noise.

5.2   Computing Model Description Length

The fundamental description-length or "cost" formula that we will use, loosely following [Myung et al. 2000; Myung et al. 2001; Pitt et al. 2002], takes this form:

$$D = F + G \,, \tag{5.1}$$

which can be read as

> "**D**escription-length **equals F**it **plus G**eometry."

The first term quantifies the "goodness-of-fit" to the data and takes the general form

$$F = -\ln f(y|\hat{\theta}) \,. \tag{5.2}$$

To compute this term, we must have some means of making a specific numerical choice for the fitted values $\{\hat{\theta}\}$ of the model parameters. We will restrict our treatment here to models of the form

$$y = g(\theta, \mathbf{x}) \quad \text{with an error model} \,, \tag{5.3}$$

describing the dependent (measured) variable y in terms of a set of model parameters $\{\theta\}$ and the independent variables $\mathbf{x}$. Various error models such as additive noise models and multiplicative noise models could be specified; normal-distributed Gaussian additive noise is the most common choice.

The function $f(y|\theta)$ is a user-chosen statistical likelihood function corresponding to the model of (5.3) with its error process, and the $\{\hat{\theta}\}$ are model parameters fixed by some (typically maximum likelihood) fitting procedure. F is thus an information-theoretic measure corresponding to the number of bits of description length attributable to inaccuracy: if $f \approx 0$, the data are not well-described by $\{\hat{\theta}\}$, whereas if $f \approx 1$, the description is ideal. (Note: we will use natural logarithms denoted by "ln" throughout, although technically perhaps $\log_2$ should be used to express all description lengths directly in bits.)

If we have a *sample*, $\{y_n(\mathbf{x}), n = 1, \ldots, N\}$, then we evaluate $f(y|\hat{\theta})$ as the product of the probabilities for each individual *outcome* y_n at the fixed parameter values $\hat{\theta}$ found from the maximum likelihood fit to the hypothesized model $g(\theta, \mathbf{x})$:

$$f(y|\hat{\theta}) \rightarrow f(\{y_n\}|\hat{\theta}) \equiv \prod_{n=1}^{N} f(y_n|\hat{\theta}). \qquad (5.4)$$

This makes explicit the intuition that F quantifies the cost of describing the deviation of the set of N measured outcomes in the sample $\{y_n(\mathbf{x})\}$ from the maximum likelihood fit. A critical feature of the approach is that the error distribution *must* be specified to completely define the model; MDL can in fact theoretically distinguish between identical models with *differing* statistical error generation processes.

The second term is the "geometric term" (technically the *parametric complexity* of the model),

$$G = +\frac{K}{2} \ln \frac{N}{2\pi} + \ln \int_{\mathrm{Vol}} d^K\theta \sqrt{\det I(\theta)} \,, \qquad (5.5)$$

where K is the number of parameters and $\{\theta_k, k = 1, \ldots, K\}$ is the parameter set of the model having Vol as the domain of the entire K-dimensional parameter space integration for the model being considered. $I(\theta)$ is the $K \times K$ Fisher information matrix averaged over the data samples, but with each y replaced by its expectation; the computation of $I(\theta)$ is complex, and is discussed in detail just below. Note that we have chosen to use uppercase K to denote the number of model parameters, while many authors use lowercase k for this quantity; we reserve k for the running index over the set of model parameters.

Intuitively, $I(\theta)$ has many properties of a metric tensor, and in fact $d^K\theta \sqrt{\det I}$ has precisely the form of a reparameterization-invariant volume element $d^K\mathbf{x} \sqrt{g}$ familiar from Riemannian geometry and general relativity. This volume element effectively allows us to count the number of distinct probability distributions the model can generate (see the discussion in [Pitt et al. 2002] and related citations).

The Fisher information matrix   We now attend to the definition of the Fisher information matrix and the rest of the machinery required to carry out explicit computations of $I(\theta)$, as well as working out a standard example that will serve as our model throughout the rest of the chapter.

First, we define the general notion of an expectation of a function $h(y)$ with respect to a statistical likelihood function as follows:

$$E(h(y)) = \int dy \, h(y) \, f(y|\theta) \qquad (5.6)$$

Thus, any coefficient in a polynomial expansion of $h(y)$ will be multiplied by the expectation corresponding to the appropriate mth moment,

$$E(y^m) = \int dy \, y^m \, f(y|\theta). \qquad (5.7)$$

To compute the Fisher information matrix, one begins by considering the expectation of the second derivative of the chosen log-likelihood function for continuous variables and parameters,

$$L_{ij}(\theta, \mathbf{x}) = E\left(\frac{\partial^2}{\partial\theta_i\partial\theta_j}\left[-\ln f(y|\theta, \mathbf{x})\right]\right) , \qquad (5.8)$$

where we explicitly include the possible dependence of f on the dependent variable $\mathbf{x}$ through $g(\theta, \mathbf{x})$. When the expectation is computed, the dependent variable y is integrated out; however, the values of the dependent variables $\mathbf{x}$ remain, and, in particular, will be known for each outcome of a particular sample $\{y_n\}$. This leads to the definition of the Fisher information matrix, which is the average of L_{ij} over the actually obtained outcomes in the data sample; using (5.4) to expand $\ln f(y|\theta)$ as the sum of the logs of the individual components for the dependent variable y_n measured at the location $\mathbf{x}_n$ in the space of independent variables, we obtain the basic definition

$$
\begin{aligned}
I_{ij}(\theta) &= \frac{1}{N}\sum_{n=1}^{N} L_{ij}(\theta, \mathbf{x}_n)\\
&= \frac{1}{N}\sum_{n=1}^{N} E\left(\frac{\partial^2}{\partial\theta_i\partial\theta_j}\left[-\ln f(y|\theta, \mathbf{x}_n)\right]\right)
\end{aligned}
\qquad (5.9)
$$

for the Fisher information matrix of a measured sample.

The Normal Distribution   The easiest way to understand $I(\theta)$ is to choose a specific error model and work out an example. The Gaussian describing the usual normal distribution,

$$f(y|\theta, \mathbf{x}) = \frac{1}{\sigma\sqrt{2\pi}} \exp\left(-\frac{1}{2\sigma^2}(y - g(\theta, \mathbf{x}))^2\right) , \qquad (5.10)$$

is by far the most common error distribution, and is easy to compute with. The error is modeled by the Gaussian width σ, and the relevant expectations may be computed explicitly:

$$E(1|\mathbf{x}) = 1$$
$$E(y|\mathbf{x}) = g(\theta, \mathbf{x})$$
$$E(y^2|\mathbf{x}) = \sigma^2 + g(\theta, \mathbf{x})^2$$
$$\cdots \tag{5.11}$$

The first step toward calculating the Fisher information matrix for the normal distribution is to differentiate (5.10) and apply the expectation formulas of (5.11) to find

$$L_{ij}(\theta, \mathbf{x}) = -\frac{1}{\sigma^2} E(y - g(\theta, \mathbf{x})) \, \partial_i \, \partial_j \, g(\theta, \mathbf{x}) + \frac{1}{\sigma^2} \partial_i g(\theta, \mathbf{x}) \partial_j g(\theta, \mathbf{x})$$
$$= 0 + \frac{1}{\sigma^2} \frac{\partial g(\theta, \mathbf{x})}{\partial \theta_i} \frac{\partial g(\theta, \mathbf{x})}{\partial \theta_j} \; . \tag{5.12}$$

We obtain the corresponding Fisher information matrix by computing the average over outcomes,

$$I_{ij}(\theta) = \frac{1}{N} \sum_{n=1}^{N} L_{ij}(\theta, \mathbf{x}_n) = \frac{1}{N\sigma^2} \sum_{n=1}^{N} \partial_i g_n(\theta) \partial_j g_n(\theta) \; , \tag{5.13}$$

where we use the convenient abbreviation $g_n(\theta) = g(\theta_1, \ldots, \theta_K; \mathbf{x}_n)$. Note that the $\{\theta\}$ are free variables, not the maximum likelihood values, since we must integrate over their domains; however, the values $\{\hat{\theta}\}$ may still be of importance, since they can in principle determine the dominant contribution to the integral. In addition, it is important to realize that $\det I$ will vanish unless the number N of linearly independent measurements is at least equal to the dimension of the parameter space, $N \geq K$; the geometric term is undefined unless there are enough measurements to determine a fit to the model parameters.

When computing the determinant in the integral of the geometric term for the normal distribution, it is sometimes convenient to rearrange the terms in (5.13) using

$$\ln \int d^K \theta \, \sqrt{\det I(\theta)} = \ln \int d^K \theta \, \sqrt{\left(\frac{1}{N\sigma^2}\right)^K} \sqrt{\det | \sum_n \partial_i g_n(\theta) \partial_j g_n(\theta) |}$$
$$= -\frac{K}{2} \ln N\sigma^2 + \ln \int d^K \theta \, \sqrt{\det | \sum_n \partial_i g_n(\theta) \partial_j g_n(\theta) |} \; .$$

This permits us to cancel the factors of N and re-express the geometric term as

$$G = \frac{K}{2} \ln \frac{N}{2\pi} - \frac{K}{2} \ln N\sigma^2 + \ln \int d^K \theta \, \sqrt{\det | \sum_n \partial_i g_n(\theta) \partial_j g_n(\theta) |}$$
$$= -K \ln \sigma\sqrt{2\pi} + \ln \int d^K \theta \, \sqrt{\det | \sum_n \partial_i g_n(\theta) \partial_j g_n(\theta) |} \; . \tag{5.14}$$

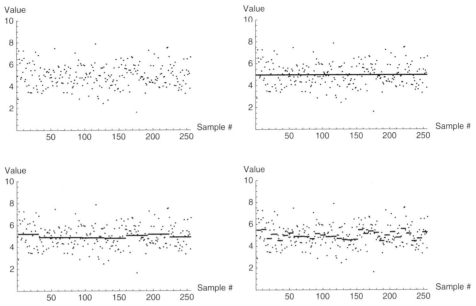

Figure 5.1   Top left: Data set generated from a constant plus noise (identical to the $N = K$-parameter "perfect" piecewise fit). Top right: Single-parameter mean value fit. Bottom left: Overfitting with an evenly spaced set of 8 piecewise constants. Bottom right: Overfitting with 32 piecewise constants.

5.3   Piecewise Constant Models

Suppose that a particular data set is sampled at intervals corresponding to power-of-two subdivisions of the domain. Then we can identify the "simplest" model – the global mean, the most complex model, where each data point is itself a model parameter, and a complete set (the binary tree) of power-of-two models between these two extremes. We now treat each in turn.

Global Mean Model   The simplest possible model is just a constant

$$y = \mu$$

(plus noise) corresponding to the simulated data shown in figure 5.1(top left). A least squares fit to the data gives the maximum likelihood solution

$$\hat{\mu} = \frac{1}{N} \sum_{n=1}^{N} y_n,$$

as shown in figure 5.1(top right). $\hat{\mu}$ is expected to be very close to the value of μ used to simulate the data, but will virtually never match it exactly. The cost of representing the deviations from this fit is given by

$$F = -\ln f(\{y_n\}|\hat{\mu})$$

$$= -\ln \prod_{n=1}^{N} \frac{1}{\sigma\sqrt{2\pi}} \exp(-(y_n - \hat{\mu})^2/2\sigma^2)$$

$$= N \ln \sigma\sqrt{2\pi} + \frac{1}{2\sigma^2} \sum_{n=1}^{N} (y_n - \hat{\mu})^2.$$

$$= N \ln \sigma\sqrt{2\pi} + \frac{N}{2\sigma^2}(\text{variance}) \ . \qquad (5.15)$$

Since $K = 1$ and the Fisher matrix is 1×1, we have simply

$$I(\mu) = \frac{1}{N} \sum_{n=1}^{N} \frac{1}{\sigma^2} = \frac{1}{\sigma^2} \ , \qquad (\text{ Note: } \left(\frac{\partial\mu}{\partial\mu}\right)^2 = 1 \ )$$

so the geometric term [from either (5.5) or (5.14)] becomes

$$G = \frac{K}{2} \ln \frac{N}{2\pi} + \ln \frac{1}{\sigma} \int_{\min}^{\max} d\mu$$

$$= \frac{1}{2} \ln \frac{N}{2\pi} + \ln \frac{\mu_{\max} - \mu_{\min}}{\sigma} \ . \qquad (5.16)$$

Data-Perfect Model   On the other hand, the most complex model is effectively no model at all, the model with one parameter for each measured value ($K = N$),

$$y = \sum_{n=1}^{N} y_n \delta(x, x_n) \ ,$$

where $\delta(x, x_n)$ is the Kronecker delta (unity for $x = x_n$, zero otherwise). There is nothing to fit: assuming the choice of $\{x_n\}$ is a regularly-spaced sequence, so $\{x_n\}$ is not a choice of parameters, then we have N parameters $\{y_n\}$; if the $\{x_n\}$ are specified independently in the measurement, then we would have $2N$ parameters, $\{(x_n, y_n)\}$. For simplicity, we treat the former case, so the model graph is the same as the data plot in figure 5.1(top left), and

$$F = -\ln f(\{y_n\}|\{y_n\})$$

$$= N \ln \sigma\sqrt{2\pi} + \frac{1}{2\sigma^2} \sum_{n=1}^{N} (y_n - y_n)^2$$

$$= N \ln \sigma\sqrt{2\pi} + 0 \ . \qquad (5.17)$$

As promised, this has no cost corresponding to deviations of the data from the model. The Fisher information matrix, however, is now $N \times N$, and [from (5.12)]

$$
\begin{aligned}
L_{ij} &= \frac{1}{\sigma^2} \left(\sum_n \frac{\partial(y_n \delta(x, x_n))}{\partial y_i} \right) \left(\sum_{n'} \frac{\partial(y_{n'} \delta(x, x_{n'}))}{\partial y_j} \right) \\
&= \frac{1}{\sigma^2} \delta(x, x_i) \delta(x, x_j)
\end{aligned}
\tag{5.18}
$$

$$
I_{ij} = \frac{1}{N\sigma^2} \sum_{n=1}^{N} \delta(x_n, x_i) \delta(x_n, x_j) = \frac{1}{N\sigma^2} \delta(i, j) \ .
\tag{5.19}
$$

This is tricky because $\sum_{n=1}^{N} \delta(x_n, x_i) \delta(x_n, x_j)$ equals 1 only if i equals j, so it equals $\delta(i, j)$. Since $K = N$ and $\delta(i, j)$ represents the $N \times N$ identity matrix, the geometric contribution (assuming identical parameter domain sizes V) is [from (5.5)]

$$
\begin{aligned}
G &= \frac{N}{2} \ln \frac{N}{2\pi} + \ln \underbrace{\int_V \cdots \int_V}_{N} d^N \mathbf{y} \sqrt{\det \frac{1}{N\sigma^2} \delta(i, j)} \\
&= \frac{N}{2} \ln \frac{N}{2\pi} - \frac{N}{2} \ln N + \ln \frac{V^N}{\sigma^N} \\
&= +\frac{N}{2} \ln \frac{1}{2\pi} + N \ln \frac{V}{\sigma} \ .
\end{aligned}
\tag{5.20}
$$

Binary-Tree Model   Data are often approximated by a binary tree generated by applying recursive two-element box filters. We can represent an entire family of models in this fashion, each with 2^M parameters, where $M = 0$ is the single parameter (global mean) model treated first, and $M = \log_2 N$ ($N = 2^M$) is the zero-error model. The models each take the form

$$
y = \sum_{n=1}^{N} g_n(M) \delta(x, x_n) \ .
$$

The power-of-two subdivision is represented by requiring the $g_n(M)$'s to be repeated $N/2^M$ times, and defining the 2^M independent parameters to be $\{z_n(M), n = 1, \ldots, 2^M\}$. The best-fit values $\hat{\mathbf{z}}$ then are computed from the means over the repeated occurrences (e.g., the box-filtered means at each level). To be explicit, if $\{y_n\}$ is a sample, the M independent parameter sets giving the best fit at each level are

$M = \log_2 N$	$\rightarrow$	$\hat{z}_n = y_n$
$M = \log_2(N/2)$	$\rightarrow$	$\hat{z}_1 = (\hat{g}_1 = \hat{g}_2) = (1/2)(y_1 + y_2),$
		$\hat{z}_2 = (\hat{g}_3 = \hat{g}_4) = (1/2)(y_3 + y_4), \ldots$
$M = \log_2(N/4)$	$\rightarrow$	$\hat{z}_1 = (\hat{g}_1 = \hat{g}_2 = \hat{g}_3 = \hat{g}_4) =$
		$(1/4)(y_1 + y_2 + y_3 + y_4), \ldots$
$\ldots$	$\ldots$	$\ldots$
$M = 0$	$\rightarrow$	$\hat{z}_1 = (\hat{g}_1 = \ldots = \hat{g}_n) = \hat{\mu}$

In figure 5.1, we show a single data set generated by a distribution with constant mean along with the fits for $M = 0$, $M = 3$, and $M = 5$, respectively, to illustrate overfitting.

The goodness-of-fit term becomes

$$F(M) = -\ln \prod_{n=1}^{N} f(y_n | \hat{\mathbf{z}}(M))$$

$$= N \ln \sigma \sqrt{2\pi} + \frac{1}{2\sigma^2} \sum_{n=1}^{N} (y_n - \hat{z}_{m(n)}(M))^2, \tag{5.21}$$

where $m(n) = \lceil n2^M / N \rceil$, so the $\hat{z}_m(M)$ are understood as the 2^M independent constants (not N independent values) giving the best-average fit to the measurements at binary-tree level M.

The geometric term, which gives the measure of the functional space spanned by the $z_m(M)$ considered as *variable* parameters, is based on the $2^M \times 2^M$ matrix

$$I_{ij}(M) = \frac{1}{N\sigma^2} \sum_{n=1}^{N} \left[\frac{\partial}{\partial z_i} \left(\sum_{l=1}^{N} z_{m(l)}(M)\delta(x_n, x_l) \right) \right.$$

$$\left. \frac{\partial}{\partial z_j} \left(\sum_{l'=1}^{N} z_{m(l')}(M)\delta(x_n, x_{l'}) \right) \right]$$

$$= \frac{1}{\sigma^2 2^M} \delta(i, j) , \tag{5.22}$$

where we have used the fact that $N/2^M$ occurrences of $z_m(M)$ are replicated at the level M. (Each of the two inner summations will produce $N/2^M$ terms that have different indices for the same z, which we might write as $[z_i \, \delta(x_n, x_{(iN)/(2^M)}) + \ldots]$ and $[z_j \, \delta(x_n, x_{(jN)/(2^M)}) + \ldots]$, respectively; when we differentiate, multiply, and sum, we obtain $N/2^M$ copies of the $\delta(i, j)$ term in (5.19).)

Thus, with $K = 2^M$ and $\delta(i, j)$ representing the $2^M \times 2^M$ identity matrix, we have (assuming identical parameter domain sizes V) [similar to (5.20)],

$$G(M) = +\frac{2^M}{2} \ln \frac{N}{2\pi} + \ln \underbrace{\int_V \cdots \int_V}_{2^M} d^{2^M} \mathbf{z} \sqrt{\det \frac{\delta(i, j)}{2^M \sigma^2}}$$

$$= +\frac{2^M}{2} \ln \frac{N}{2\pi} + \ln V^{2^M} + \frac{1}{2} \ln \left(\frac{1}{2^M \sigma^2} \right)^{2^M}$$

$$= \frac{2^M}{2} \ln \frac{N}{2\pi \, (2^M)} + 2^M \ln \frac{V}{\sigma} , \tag{5.23}$$

and, for the Mth level binary-tree model, the total description length is

$$D(M) = F(M) + G(M)$$

$$= N \ln \sigma \sqrt{2\pi} + \frac{1}{2\sigma^2} \sum_{n=1}^{N} (y_n - \hat{z}_{m(n)}(M))^2$$

$$+ \frac{2^M}{2} \ln \frac{N}{2\pi \, (2^M)} + 2^M \ln \frac{V}{\sigma} \,. \tag{5.24}$$

This form shows explicitly the transition from (5.16), with $M = 0$, to (5.20), with $2^M = N$.

Quadtrees, Octrees, etc.   The binary tree model for piecewise constant 1D data can be easily extended to higher dimensions. For D-dimensional data, the corresponding model is a piecewise constant 2^D-tree ($D = 2$ being a quadtree, $D = 3$ being an octree, etc.). For simplicity, we assume N^D data samples over all D dimensions. We define the model as

$$A(x, y, \dots) = \sum_{ij\dots}^{N^D} z_{m(ij\dots)}(M)\delta(x, x_i)\delta(y, y_j)\dots \,.$$

Then the data-fitting term becomes

$$F(M, D) = -\ln \prod_{ij\dots}^{N^D} f(A_{ij\dots}|\hat{\mathbf{z}}(M)) \tag{5.25}$$

$$= N^D \ln \sigma \sqrt{2\pi} + \frac{1}{2\sigma^2} \sum_{ij\dots}^{N^D} (A_{ij\dots} - \hat{z}_{m(ij\dots)})^2 \,.$$

The number of parameters is $K = (2^M)^D$ and the $K \times K$ Fisher matrix is

$$I_{ij\dots,i'j'\dots} = \frac{1}{\sigma^2} \left(\frac{1}{2^M} \right)^D \delta(ij\dots,i'j'\dots) \,,$$

where $i, j, \dots$ now range to 2^M instead of N. The geometry term is

$$G(M, D) = \frac{2^{MD}}{2} \ln \frac{N}{2\pi \, (2^{MD})} + 2^{MD} \ln \frac{V}{\sigma} \,, \tag{5.26}$$

which generalizes (5.24) for $D = 1$. One could even apply this approach to the *independent* modeling of *each* level of a signal's resolution hierarchy to achieve optimal compression.

Numerical Experiments   The principal motivation for the MDL approach is to distinguish between a *good fit* and *overfitting* to achieve what is referred to in the statistics and pattern recognition literature as *generalization*. If the model does not generalize, then additional data sets with the same statistics will *not* be well-described, indicating the presence of an excessively complex model that conforms to the random noise patterns of one isolated sample. We can test this by generating

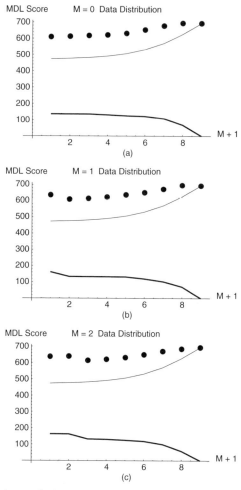

Figure 5.2 Comparison of the variance contribution $F - $ const *(heavy curve)*, the geometric contribution $G + $ const *(light curve)*, and their sums $D(M)$ *(heavy dots)* as a function of level M for three different data distributions: *(top)* Original data generated by a single mean, $M = 0$. *(middle)* Original data generated by two means, $M = 1$. *(bottom)* Original data generated by four means, $M = 2$.

a 256-element sample normally distributed about a mean of zero with $\sigma = 1$, and allowed parameter values $[-3, 3]$ so that $V = 6$ (ambiguities can arise if V/σ is too small). For $M = 0$, the fit to the single parameter is $\hat{z} = \hat{\mu} = (1/N)\sum y_n$; for $M = 1$, we can determine $\hat{z}_1$ and $\hat{z}_2$ to be the means for the left and right halves of the data, and so on.

In figure 5.2(a), we compare the variance term $(F(M) - $ const$)$ (the heavy curve) vs. $(G(M) + $ const$)$ (the light curve) as a function of M, and show the summed description length $D(M)$ as black dots. In figure 5.2(b), we repeat the process, except that the data are distributed about a "true" $M = 1$ model, with means 0

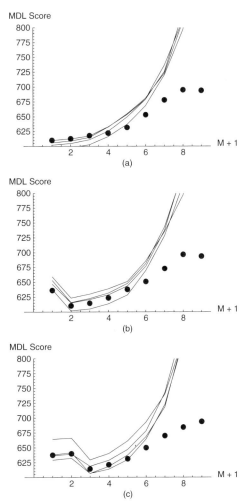

Figure 5.3   MDL cost as a function of binary-tree level M for the model for four data set samplings and three different models. The heavy dots are the same points $D(M)$ as in figure 5.2 and denote the costs of the model used to determine the maximum likelihood parameters used in evaluating curves for the remaining models. (a) Original data are distributed about a single mean ($M = 0$); (b) two means ($M = 1$); (c) four means ($M = 2$).

and 1 for the left and right halves of the data. figure 5.2(c) shows the results for an $M = 2$ model, with means $(0, 1, 0, 1)$. We can now explicitly see the tradeoff between the data fit and the model description: the minimum sum occurs as promised for the true model.

Curiously, we see that the drastic drop in the data error for the "perfect" N-parameter model gives it a slight statistical edge over its neighbors. However, this is an illusory advantage: if we generate several *additional* data sets with the same distributions and evaluate them against the set of fits $\{\hat{\mathbf{z}}(M)\}$ determined by the original data sets, we see the results in figure 5.3. The overfitted models with excess parameters are extremely poor descriptions of the abstract data distribution. The minimal models generalize perfectly, and the overfitted models are terrible generalizations.

We conclude that choosing the model with the minimum description length avoids both the traps of underfitting and overfitting, and suggests the selection of models close to those generated by the actual data rather than being confused by models with artificially low variance. In principle, models with different statistical distributions and parameter-space geometry can also be distinguished, though noncompact parameter spaces require some externally imposed assumptions [Myung et al. 2000; Pitt et al. 2002].

5.4   Continuous Linear Models

Polynomial Functions   Polynomials form the simplest class of differentiable models beyond the piecewise-constant models of the previous section, and can be extended to include piecewise continuous splines in principle. If we choose K-parameter polynomial models of the form

$$y = \sum_{k=0}^{K-1} a_k x^k \tag{5.27}$$

and then carry out a least squares fit to get the maximum likelihood parameter estimates $\hat{a}_k$, the data-fitting term for N outcomes $\{(x_n, y_n)\}$ is

$$F(K) = N \ln \sigma \sqrt{2\pi} + \frac{1}{2\sigma^2} \sum_{n=1}^{N} \left(y_n - \sum_{k=0}^{K-1} \hat{a}_k (x_n)^k \right)^2 , \tag{5.28}$$

and the $K \times K$ geometric term matrix with $i, j = 0, \dots, K-1$, is

$$
\begin{aligned}
I_{ij} &= \frac{1}{N\sigma^2} \sum_{n=1}^{N} \frac{\partial}{\partial a_i} \left(\sum_{k=0}^{K-1} a_k (x_n)^k \right) \frac{\partial}{\partial a_j} \left(\sum_{k'=0}^{K-1} a_{k'} (x_n)^{k'} \right) \\
&= \frac{1}{N\sigma^2} \sum_{n=1}^{N} (x_n)^i (x_n)^j \;\; = \;\; \frac{1}{N\sigma^2} \sum_{n=1}^{N} (x_n)^{(i+j)} .
\end{aligned} \tag{5.29}
$$

The geometric term becomes

$$
\begin{aligned}
G(K) &= +\frac{K}{2} \ln \frac{N}{2\pi} + \ln \underbrace{\int_V \cdots \int_V}_{K} d^K a \sqrt{\det \left[\frac{1}{N\sigma^2} \sum_{n=1}^{N} (x_n)^{(i+j)} \right]} \\
&= -\frac{K}{2} \ln 2\pi + K \ln \frac{V}{\sigma} + \frac{1}{2} \ln \det \left[\sum_{n} (x_n)^{(i+j)} \right] ,
\end{aligned} \tag{5.30}
$$

where we assumed the same domain size V for each parameter. The determinant vanishes even for linearly independent outcomes unless $N \geq K$, excluding under-

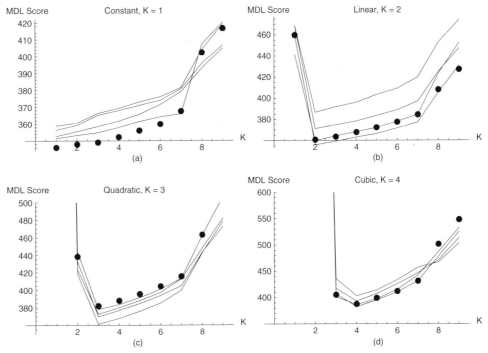

Figure 5.4 The lowest MDL cost as a function of the number of fitted polynomial parameters K for one data sample *(heavy dots)* selects the generating model, as well as generalizing to four additional data samples *(curves)*. (a) The simulated data are normally distributed about a constant function; (b) linear function; (c) quadratic function; (d) cubic function.

determined models. Note that, unlike the piecewise constant case, $G(K)$ now has an explicit data dependence.

In the specific case where there are sufficiently many outcomes so that the sum in (5.30) approximates a Monte Carlo integration over some domain, say $a \leq x \leq b$, we can explicitly compute the last term in (5.30), with $\Delta x \approx (b - a)/N$, as

$$\frac{1}{2} \ln \det \frac{N}{b - a} \left[\frac{b^{i+j+1} - a^{i+j+1}}{i + j + 1} \right] .$$

We remark on the close relationship of the resulting matrix to the notoriously ill-conditioned Hilbert matrix, which is exact if $a = 0$ and $b = 1$.

An identical exercise to that in figure 5.3 can now be carried out. In figure 5.4, we show the cost of fits up to $K = 9$ (8th power) for samples generated using constant, linear, quadratic, and cubic models with normally distributed error. We observed that the relative magnitudes of the standard deviation in the error model and the scale of x can affect whether the correct polynomial order is unambiguously selected. Here we used $\sigma = 1$, $a_k = 1$, and $0 \leq x \leq 3$ with 256 outcomes. We see that the optimal K is that used to generate the data.

Orthonormal Functions If we replace the power series by a set of normalized orthogonal polynomials, we would write

$$y = \sum_{k=0}^{K-1} a_k h_k(x) \;, \tag{5.31}$$

where the orthogonality relation between h_k and its conjugate $\overline{h}_k$, using integration domain U, is by definition

$$\int_U dx\, \overline{h}_k(x) h_{k'}(x) = \delta_{k,k'} \;, \tag{5.32}$$

so that we may *formally* determine the expansion coefficients from the integrals

$$a_k = \int_U dx\, \overline{h}_k(x) y(x) \;. \tag{5.33}$$

Here we in principle have a *choice* of methods to determine the optimal coefficients $\{\hat{a}_k\}$:

- *Maximum likelihood.* The model (5.31) can be fit using least squares methods like any other function. This method is probably preferred for sparse data distributions.
- *Projection. Provided* the samples are appropriately distributed or can be selected in such a way that the discretely sampled version of the projection (5.33) is a good approximation to the analytic integral, we can take $\Delta x \approx U/N$, and write

$$\hat{a}_k \approx \frac{U}{N} \sum_{n=1}^{N} \overline{h}_k(x_n) y_n \;. \tag{5.34}$$

The polynomials themselves form our first example of this class of functions if we normalize the Legendre polynomials appropriately, for example,

$$Q_0(x) = \sqrt{\frac{1}{2}} \cdot 1$$
$$Q_1(x) = \sqrt{\frac{3}{2}} \cdot x$$
$$Q_2(x) = \sqrt{\frac{5}{2}} \cdot \left(\frac{3}{2}x^2 - \frac{1}{2} \right)$$
$$\vdots$$

with integration range $-1 \leq x \leq 1$. Choosing the model sequence up to some maximum K as

$$y = a_0 \sqrt{\frac{1}{2}} + a_1 \sqrt{\frac{3}{2}} x + a_2 \sqrt{\frac{5}{2}} \left(\frac{3}{2}x^2 - \frac{1}{2} \right) + \cdots \;, \tag{5.35}$$

we can choose either the *least squares fit* or the *projection* to determine the model coefficients; the projection can be computed using

$$\hat{a}_0 = \frac{2}{N} \sum_{n=1}^{N} \sqrt{\frac{1}{2}} y_n$$

$$\hat{a}_1 = \frac{2}{N} \sum_{n=1}^{N} \sqrt{\frac{3}{2}} x_n y_n$$

$$\hat{a}_2 = \frac{2}{N} \sum_{n=1}^{N} \sqrt{\frac{5}{2}} \left(\frac{3}{2} x_n^2 - \frac{1}{2} \right) y_n$$

$$\vdots$$

Given the model (5.35) and the coefficients $\{\hat{\mathbf{a}}\}$, we can compute $f(y|\hat{\mathbf{a}})$ and thus F and G almost exactly as we did for the polynomial example leading to figure 5.4, and we expect similar results if the samples are sufficiently well behaved.

Other examples of this class include the discrete sine-cosine series, $(1/\sqrt{\pi}) \cos j\theta$ and $(1/\sqrt{\pi}) \sin j\theta$ for $j \neq 0$, and $(1/\sqrt{2\pi})$ for $j = 0$, where, for example,

$$\int_{U=2\pi} d\theta \left(\frac{1}{\sqrt{\pi}} \cos j\theta \right) \left(\frac{1}{\sqrt{\pi}} \cos j'\theta \right) = \delta_{j,j'} , \tag{5.36}$$

and the spherical harmonic series with basis functions $Y_{lm}(\theta, \phi)$, detailed below.

Remark The calculation of the geometric term of the description length for orthonormal functions has one notable peculiarity. If we assume a real basis, so $\overline{h} = h$ (e.g., the cosine), the Fisher matrix can be reduced to

$$I_{ij} = \frac{1}{N\sigma^2} \sum_{n=1}^{N} h_i(x_n) h_j(x_n) . \tag{5.37}$$

Remarkably, just as we saw for the projection, (5.33), this is essentially a Monte Carlo approximation to the orthogonality integral, (5.32), if the samples are appropriately distributed. Therefore, as $N \to$ (large) (which is, indeed, the condition for the validity of many of the MDL formulas we are using), with $\Delta x \approx U/N$, then

$$I_{ij} \approx \frac{1}{N\sigma^2} \frac{N}{U} \delta_{i,j} . \tag{5.38}$$

If $V_K = \prod_k \int da_k$, then the geometric term is just

$$G = \frac{K}{2} \ln \frac{N}{2\pi U} + \ln \frac{V_K}{\sigma^K}. \tag{5.39}$$

If we assume identical parameter domains, then we can also make the simplification $V_K = (V)^K$.

Similar classes of functions such as wavelets would give results exactly analogous to our findings for orthogonal expansions:

$$
\begin{aligned}
I_{ij} &= \frac{1}{N\sigma^2} \sum_{n=1}^{N} W_i(x_n) W_j(x_n) \\
&\approx \frac{1}{N\sigma^2} \frac{N}{U} \int_U dx\, W_i(x) W_j(x) \\
&\approx \frac{1}{N\sigma^2} \frac{N}{U} H_{ij} \,,
\end{aligned}
\tag{5.40}
$$

so

$$
G = \frac{K}{2} \ln \frac{N}{2\pi U} + \ln \frac{V_K}{\sigma^K} + \frac{1}{2} \ln \det H_{ij} \,,
\tag{5.41}
$$

for some appropriately defined integration domains and overlap functions H_{ij}.

Explicit Example: Real Spherical Harmonics Suppose that we have a model for a radially varying spherical data set that we wish to expand around a fixed origin using an unknown optimal number L of spherical harmonics. Then we can express this radial function for sampled values of the angular coordinates (θ, ϕ) on an ordinary sphere as

$$
y = r(\theta, \phi) = \sum_{l=0}^{L} \sum_{m=-l}^{+l} \left(c_{lm} Y_{lm}^c(\theta, \phi) + s_{lm} Y_{lm}^s(\theta, \phi) \right) \,,
\tag{5.42}
$$

where Y_{lm}^c and Y_{lm}^s are the cosine-like and sine-like real spherical harmonics (see, e.g., the web page `http://mathworld.wolfram.com/SphericalHarmonic.html`, [Arfken 1985], or [Ritchie and Kemp 1999] for full details). Note that $\{c_{lm}, s_{lm}\}$ are the model parameters that we previously denoted by $\{\theta\}$, while (θ, ϕ) now corresponds to "physics convention" polar coordinates with $(x = r\cos\phi\sin\theta,\ y = r\sin\phi\sin\theta,\ z = r\cos\theta)$ in order to have the correct correspondence to the conventions for $Y_{lm}(\theta, \phi)$: we take $0 \le \phi < 2\pi$, $0 \le \theta \le \pi$, so the integration volume element $d\Omega = d\cos\theta\, d\phi$ has total volume 4π. Our task is to determine the optimal value L of the last useful term in the harmonic series for a body of data using MDL.

For each value of L in a set of attempted data descriptions with $L = 0, 1, 2, 3, \ldots$, we determine by some suitable means (e.g., least squares fit or projection) a corresponding set of optimal model parameters $\{\hat{c}_{lm}, \hat{s}_{lm}\}$ from the data. The goodness-of-fit term in the MDL expression with normal statistics becomes

$$
\begin{aligned}
F &= -\sum_{n=1}^{N} \ln f\left(r(\theta_n, \phi_n) | \{\hat{c}_{lm}, \hat{s}_{lm}\} \right) \\
&= N \ln \sigma\sqrt{2\pi} + \\
&\quad \frac{1}{2\sigma^2} \sum_{n=1}^{N} \left(r(\theta_n, \phi_n) - \sum_{lm} \left(\hat{c}_{lm} Y_{lm}^c(\theta_n, \phi_n) + \hat{s}_{lm} Y_{lm}^s(\theta_n, \phi_n) \right) \right)^2 ,
\end{aligned}
\tag{5.43}
$$

and the geometric complexity term is

$$G = \frac{K}{2} \ln \frac{N}{2\pi} + \ln \int d\{c_{lm}\} \int d\{s_{lm}\} \sqrt{\det I(\{c_{lm}, s_{lm}\})} \ . \tag{5.44}$$

We remark that for even functions, only the c_{lm} survive, and so $K = (L+1)^2$; for odd functions, the $l = 0$ term is absent, and so technically $K = (L+1)^2 - 1$; for mixed functions, we would therefore expect $K = 2(L+1)^2 - 1$ parameters. We will leave K unspecified to allow appropriate adjustments for particular data sets.

Expanding the Fisher information matrix, we can explicitly write the terms as

$$\det I_{lm,l'm'}(\{c_{lm}, s_{lm}\}) =$$

$$\det \frac{1}{N\sigma^2} \begin{bmatrix} \sum_{n=1}^{N} Y_{lm}^c(\theta_n, \phi_n) Y_{l'm'}^c(\theta_n, \phi_n) & \sum_{n=1}^{N} Y_{lm}^c(\theta_n, \phi_n) Y_{l'm'}^s(\theta_n, \phi_n) \\ \sum_{n=1}^{N} Y_{lm}^s(\theta_n, \phi_n) Y_{l'm'}^c(\theta_n, \phi_n) & \sum_{n=1}^{N} Y_{lm}^s(\theta_n, \phi_n) Y_{l'm'}^s(\theta_n, \phi_n) \end{bmatrix}$$

$$= \left(\frac{1}{N\sigma^2}\right)^K \det \sum_{n=1}^{N} \begin{bmatrix} Y_n^c Y_n^c & Y_n^c Y_n^s \\ Y_n^s Y_n^c & Y_n^s Y_n^s \end{bmatrix} \ . \tag{5.45}$$

Thus we can write the geometric contribution as follows:

$$G = \frac{K}{2} \ln \frac{N}{2\pi} - \frac{K}{2} \ln N\sigma^2 + \ln \int d\{c_{lm}\} \int d\{s_{lm}\} + \frac{1}{2} \ln \det \sum_{n=1}^{N} \begin{bmatrix} Y_n^c Y_n^c & Y_n^c Y_n^s \\ Y_n^s Y_n^c & Y_n^s Y_n^s \end{bmatrix}$$

If we denote the parameter integrals as, for example, $\int dc_{lm} = C_{lm}$, we can finally write

$$G = -K \ln \sigma \sqrt{2\pi} + \sum_{lm} \ln C_{lm} + \sum_{lm} \ln S_{lm} + \frac{1}{2} \ln \det \sum_{n=1}^{N} \begin{bmatrix} Y_n^c Y_n^c & Y_n^c Y_n^s \\ Y_n^s Y_n^c & Y_n^s Y_n^s \end{bmatrix} . \tag{5.46}$$

If, as noted above, the sampled values should provide an approximation to the orthogonality relation integral

$$\int d\Omega \, Y_{lm}^c Y_{l'm'}^c = [\text{identity matrix}]_{lm,l'm'} \ ,$$

then with $\Delta\Omega \approx 4\pi/N$, we can obtain the approximate result

$$G = -K \ln \sigma \sqrt{2\pi} + \sum_{lm} \ln C_{lm} + \sum_{lm} \ln S_{lm} + \frac{1}{2} \ln \left(\frac{N}{4\pi}\right)^K$$

$$= -K \ln \sigma \sqrt{2\pi} + \sum_{lm} \ln C_{lm} + \sum_{lm} \ln S_{lm} + \frac{K}{2} \ln \frac{N}{4\pi} \ . \tag{5.47}$$

Observations We can see that it is almost trivial to *test* to see whether or not least squares fitting should be performed rather than numerical projection for orthogonal polynomials: for projection to be a valid approximation, the numerical sum over the independent variables must give a (user-definable) sufficient approximation to the orthogonality relation for the bare basis functions, independent of any measured data or model selection.

We note also that if *complex* functions such as the classical spherical harmonics are used instead of the real cosine-like and sine-like harmonic combinations, one finds experimentally that it is necessary to use complex conjugate pairs of Y_{lm}'s in the matrix $I_{lm,l'm'}$ to get positive definite numerical results.

If *continuous* Fourier expansions are used as models, the determination of quantities such as the functional integrals over the coefficients required in the MDL procedure appears to be an open question for future research.

5.5   Gaussian Models

Our examples so far have all been linear in the coefficients, so that the derivatives in the Fisher matrix computation eliminate the parameter dependence, and nothing particularly interesting happens in the integration. In this section, we treat a new class, the Gaussian models, which are very important data models in their own right, and exhibit new and nontrivial behavior in their parameter derivatives. Unfortunately, it is also much more difficult to determine reliable least squares fits; a single Gaussian's parameters can be determined by a polynomial least squares fit to the logarithm, but sums of Gaussians require more general methods such as Levenberg-Marquardt optimization (see, e.g., [Bates and Watts 1988]).

We choose as our general model a sum of $K/3$ Gaussians, with K parameters in total, of the following form:

$$y = g(x, \theta) = \sum_{k=1}^{K/3} a_k \exp\left(-\frac{(x - b_k)^2}{2c_k^2}\right) \tag{5.48}$$

This can easily be generalized to use a D-dimensional independent variable $\mathbf{x}$ by extending b_k to a D-dimensional vector $\mathbf{b}_k$. This increases the number of parameters per Gaussian to $2 + D$ instead of 3.

The calculation of the description length follows the usual procedure: assume that the Gaussian distribution itself has random errors described by a normal distribution with standard deviation σ and carry out a least squares fit procedure to get the maximum likelihood parameter estimates $\{\hat{a}_k, \hat{b}_k, \hat{c}_k\}$. (We assume the total error model is given by a single σ, though we could choose different ones for different values of K if we wished.) The data-fitting term for N outcomes $\{(x_n, y_n)\}$ is

$$F(K) = N \ln \sigma \sqrt{2\pi}$$

$$+ \frac{1}{2\sigma^2} \sum_{n=1}^{N} \left(y_n - \sum_{k=1}^{K/3} \hat{a}_k \exp\left(-\frac{(x_n - \hat{b}_k)^2}{2\hat{c}_k^2}\right) \right)^2 . \tag{5.49}$$

The $K \times K$ geometric term matrix is

$$
I_{ij} = \frac{1}{N\sigma^2} \sum_{n=1}^{N}
\begin{bmatrix}
A_1(x_n) \\
B_1(x_n) \\
C_1(x_n) \\
\vdots
\end{bmatrix}
\otimes
\begin{bmatrix}
A_1(x_n) & B_1(x_n) & C_1(x_n) & \cdots
\end{bmatrix} ,
\tag{5.50}
$$

where

$$
A_k(x) = \frac{\partial g}{\partial a_k} = e^{\frac{-(x-b_k)^2}{2\,c_k^2}}
$$

$$
B_k(x) = \frac{\partial g}{\partial b_k} = \frac{a_k\,(x-b_k)}{c_k^2}\,e^{\frac{-(x-b_k)^2}{2\,c_k^2}}
$$

$$
C_k(x) = \frac{\partial g}{\partial c_k} = \frac{a_k\,(x-b_k)^2}{c_k^3}\,e^{\frac{-(x-b_k)^2}{2\,c_k^2}} .
$$

We denote the allowed integration domains by $a_{\min} \le a \le a_{\max}$, $b_{\min} \le b \le b_{\max}$, $c_{\min} \le c \le c_{\max}$, and note that, for each triple of parameters, there is an overall factor of a^4/c^{10} in the determinant of I_{ij}; thus the argument of the logarithm in $G(K)$ is an integral of the form

$$
V(K) = \int d^{K/3}\mathbf{a} \int d^{K/3}\mathbf{b} \int d^{K/3}\mathbf{c} \sqrt{\prod_{k=1}^{K/3} a_k^4/c_k^{10}\, \det\left[\text{sum of exponentials}\right]}
$$

$$
= \prod_{k=1}^{K/3} \int da_k\, a_k^2 \int db_k \int dc_k\, c_k^{-5} \sqrt{\det\left[\text{sum of exponentials}\right]} .
$$

5.6   Models with the Same Number of Parameters

For completeness, we summarize here the comparison of the Fechner and Stevens models presented by Pitt et al. [2002]; these models each have only two parameters, and the problem of whether one or the other is a better description of a given body of psychophysics data had long been an unanswerable question. We shall see that, while standard analysis overwhelmingly favors one model over the other, no matter what the source of the data, MDL can clearly distinguish them.

Goodness-of-Fit for the Fechner and Stevens Models   The Fechner model,

$$
y = a \ln(x + b) ,
$$

and the Stevens model,

$$
y = ax^b ,
$$

both have two parameters and can in principle describe the same data. Assuming corresponding probability distributions

$$f^{\mathrm{F}}(y|a,b) = \frac{1}{\sigma\sqrt{2\pi}} \exp{-\frac{1}{2\sigma^2}\left(y - a\ln(x+b)\right)^2}$$

$$f^{\mathrm{S}}(y|a,b) = \frac{1}{\sigma\sqrt{2\pi}} \exp{-\frac{1}{2\sigma^2}\left(y - ax^b\right)^2} \,,$$

the goodness-of-fit term for a body of data with maximum likelihood parameters $(\hat{a}, \hat{b})$ is

$$F_{\text{Fechner GOF}} = -\ln f(\{y_n\}|\hat{a}, \hat{b})$$

$$= N\ln\sigma\sqrt{2\pi} + \frac{1}{2\sigma^2}\sum_{n=1}^{N}(y_n - \hat{a}\ln(x_n + \hat{b}))^2$$

$$= N\ln\sigma\sqrt{2\pi} + \frac{N}{2\sigma^2}(\text{variance}) \tag{5.51}$$

for the Fechner model, with an obvious analogous expression for the Stevens model.

Geometric Terms The geometric term is easily seen to take the general form

$$L_{ij}(a,b,\mathbf{x}) = \frac{1}{\sigma^2}\begin{bmatrix} (\frac{\partial}{\partial a}g(a,b,\mathbf{x}))^2 & \frac{\partial}{\partial a}g(a,b,\mathbf{x}) \cdot \frac{\partial}{\partial b}g(a,b,\mathbf{x}) \\ \frac{\partial}{\partial a}g(a,b,\mathbf{x}) \cdot \frac{\partial}{\partial b}g(a,b,\mathbf{x}) & (\frac{\partial}{\partial b}g(a,b,\mathbf{x}))^2 \end{bmatrix} \,.$$

For the Fechner model, with $E(y_n) = a\ln(b+x_n)$, the relevant matrix term becomes

$$L_{ij}^{\text{Fechner}}(a,b,x_n) = \frac{1}{\sigma^2}\begin{bmatrix} (\ln(b+x_n))^2 & a\frac{\ln(b+x_n)}{b+x_n} \\ a\frac{\ln(b+x_n)}{b+x_n} & \frac{a^2}{(b+x_n)^2} \end{bmatrix} \,, \tag{5.52}$$

while for the Stevens model, with $E(y_n) = ax_n^b$, the matrix is

$$L_{ij}^{\text{Stevens}}(a,b,x_n) = \frac{1}{\sigma^2}\begin{bmatrix} x_n^{2b} & ax_n^{2b}\ln x_n \\ ax_n^{2b}\ln x_n & a^2 x_n^{2b}(\ln x_n)^2 \end{bmatrix} \,. \tag{5.53}$$

For sample sizes two or greater, we average over the values of x_n to find the corresponding 2×2 matrix

$$I_{ij}(a,b) = \frac{1}{N}\sum_{n=1}^{N} L_{ij}(a,b,x_n) \,. \tag{5.54}$$

The geometric term for each model is determined from the integral over the $K = 2$–dimensional parameter space in the expression

$$G = \ln\frac{N}{2\pi} + \ln\int da \int db \sqrt{\det I(a,b)} \,. \tag{5.55}$$

Thus we find for the Fechner model, $y = a \ln(x + b)$,

$$G_{\text{Fechner}} = -\ln 2\pi\sigma^2 + \ln \int a \, da \int F(b) \, db$$

$$F^2(b) = \left(\sum_{n=1}^{N} (\ln(x_n + b))^2 \right) \left(\sum_{n=1}^{N} (x_n + b)^{-2} \right) - \left(\sum_{n=1}^{N} \frac{\ln(x_n + b)}{(x_n + b)} \right)^2, \quad (5.56)$$

and for the Stevens model, $y = ax^b$,

$$G_{\text{Stevens}} = -\ln 2\pi\sigma^2 + \ln \int a \, da \int S(b) \, db$$

$$S^2(b) = \left(\sum_{n=1}^{N} (x_n)^{2b} \right) \left(\sum_{n=1}^{N} (x_n)^{2b} (\ln x_n)^2 \right) - \left(\sum_{n=1}^{N} (x_n)^{2b} \ln x_n \right)^2. \quad (5.57)$$

Comparison and Analysis The comparison of these two two-parameter models can now be seen to reduce to the comparison of the two integrals over b: we may assume that, if the model choice is ambiguous, the two variance terms are comparable, and that the overall contribution of the scaling coefficient a is also the same. Hence the difference is

$$\Delta_{(\textbf{Stevens} - \textbf{Fechner})} = \ln \int S(b) \, db - \ln \int F(b) \, db . \quad (5.58)$$

Pitt et al. [2002] observe that the integral over b from $(0 \to \infty)$ diverges for $S(b)$, requiring an ad hoc choice of finite integration domain, while the integral converges for $F(b)$, so no such choice is necessary. With a reasonable choice of integration domain $(0 \le b \le 3$, to be precise), and random samples drawn from the Stevens and Fechner distributions, respectively, the full MDL cost equation clearly prefers the model that created the distribution, while the Stevens model is overwhelmingly chosen over the Fechner model in all cases if only the goodness-of-fit is taken into account.

5.7 Remarks and Future Work

The minimum description length criterion for model selection has the remarkable property that it can be formulated in a way – for example, using the Fisher information matrix as a metric – that does not depend in any essential way on reparameterizations of the models; unlike many standard methods, the MDL procedures presented here are not deceived by disguises, and so confusions that can arise from subtle transformations are avoided. Furthermore, it is often possible to distinguish a priori among competing models to select the model that was most likely to have produced the original distribution, even when a much lower maximum likelihood fitting error results from overfitting with a more complex model.

However, there are a number of overall problems to be addressed in practical applications of the method. Among these, we note particularly the following:

- *Parameter ranges.* As we have seen in many examples, such as the Stevens model, the parameter values must often be restricted to obtain finite integrals for the geometric term. This technically invalidates the reparameterization invariance. This problem is well-known and various attempts have been made to address it: Rissanen [1996], for example, discusses the issue and suggests possible correction terms; other solutions (I.J. Myung, personal communication) might be to approximate the integral over the determinant using the value of the determinant at the maximum likelihood point (though this again invalidates reparameterization invariance), or to seek alternative metrics to replace the Fisher information matrix, optimally selected according to some metacriteria that are consistent with the rest of the MDL procedure. An elegant solution for regression problems has been found by Liang and Barron (see Chapter 7 in this book); see also Lanterman (Chapter 4).

- *Sample sizes.* The MDL formalism that is the basis for the equations we have used is the result of a very sophisticated mathematical analysis, and is valid only for asymptotically large sample sizes. The accuracy of the basic formulas is therefore suspect for the frequently occurring case of small samples. Correction terms are known, but just how to handle small data samples has not been completely understood.

- *Model complexity computation.* The mathematical foundation of the geometric complexity terms we have used is deeply rooted in the mathematics of functional forms, functional integrals, and functional measures (see, e.g., [Balasubramanian 1997]); while these methods are used extensively in relativistic quantum field theory for simple subclasses of integrands, the general analysis is very poorly understood and lies at the limits of current mathematical methods. There are very likely many details, such as the treatment of unusual probability distributions and error distributions, that remain to be properly analyzed.

Acknowledgments

We are indebted to In Jae Myung, Yvan Leclerc, and Pascal Fua for helpful comments. A.J.H. is particularly grateful to Pascal Fua for his kind hospitality at the École Polytechnique Fédérale de Lausanne while this work was being completed, and C.W.F. thanks P.A. Heng and T.T. Wong for their corresponding hospitality at the Chinese University of Hong Kong. As this manuscript was being prepared, we learned with great sadness that Yvan Leclerc, an old friend and one of the pioneers of practical MDL applications, had passed away; he will be missed.

References

Aggrawal, R., J. Gehrke, D. Gunopulos, and P. Raghavan (1998). Automatic subspace clustering of high dimensional data for data mining applications. In *Proceedings of ACM SIGMOD International Conference on Managment of*

Data, pp. 94–105.

Arfken, G. (1985). Sections 12.6 and 12.9: Spherical harmonics and integrals of the products of three spherical harmonics. In *Mathematical Methods for Physicists*, 3rd edition. Orlando, FL: Academic Press.

Balasubramanian, V. (1997). Statistical inference, Occam's razor, and statistical mechanics on the space of probability distributions. *Neural Computation, 9*, 349–368.

Bates, D.M., and D.G. Watts (1988). *Nonlinear Regression and Its Applications.* New York: Wiley.

Fua, P., and A. Hanson (1991). An optimization framework for feature extraction. *Machine Vision and Applications, 4*, 59–87.

Hansen, M.H., and B. Yu (2001). Model selection and the principle of minimum description length. *Journal of the American Statistical Association, 96*(454), 746–774.

Leclerc, Y. (1989). Constructing simple stable description for image partitioning. *International Journal of Computer Vision, 3*, 73–102.

Leclerc, Y., Q. Luong, and P. Fua (2003). Self-consistency and MDL: A paradigm for evaluating point correspondences and detecting change.

Mehta, M., J. Rissanen, and R. Agrawal (1995). MDL-based decision tree pruning. In *International Conference on Knowledge Discovery in Databases and Data Mining (KDD-95)*, pp. 216–221. Cambridge, MA: AAAI Press.

Myung, I. (2000). The importance of complexity in model selection. *Journal of Mathematical Psychology, 44*(1), 190–204.

Myung, I., V. Balasubramanian, and M. Pitt (2000). Counting probability distributions: Differential geometry and model selection. *Proceedings of the National Academy of Sciences USA, 97*(21), 11170–11175.

Myung, I., M. Forster, and M. Browne (Eds.), (2000). A special issue on model selection. *Journal of Mathematical Psychology, 44*.

Myung, I.J., M.A. Pitt, S. Zhang, and V. Balasubramanian (2001). The use of MDL to select among computational models of cognition. In *Advances in Neural Information Processing Systems 13*. Cambridge, MA: MIT Press.

Pitt, M.A., I.J. Myung, and S. Zhang (2002). Toward a method of selecting among computational models of cognition. *Psychological Review, 109*(3), 472–491.

Rissanen, J. (1983). A universal prior for integers and estimation by minimal description length. *Annals of Statistics, 11*, 416–431.

Rissanen, J. (1986). Stochastic complexity and modeling. *Annals of Statistics, 14*(3), 1080–1100.

Rissanen, J. (1989). *Stochastic Complexity in Statistical Inquiry.* Teaneck, NJ: World Scientific.

Rissanen, J. (1996). Fisher information and stochastic complexity. *IEEE Trans-*

actions on Information Theory, 42, 40–47.

Rissanen, J. (1999). Hypothesis selection and testing by the MDL principle. *Computer Journal, 42,* 260–269.

Rissanen, J. (2001a). Lectures on statistical modeling theory. Available at http://www.cs.tut.fi/~rissanen/papers/lectures.ps.

Rissanen, J. (2001b). Strong optimality of the normalized ML models as universal codes and information in data. *IEEE Transactions on Information Theory, 47* (5), 1712–1717.

Ritchie, D., and G. Kemp (1999). Fast computation, rotation, and comparison of low resolution spherical harmonic molecular surfaces. *Journal of Computational Chemistry 20,* 383–395; http://www.math.chalmers.se/ kemp/publications/.

6   Algorithmic Statistics and Kolmogorov's Structure Functions

Paul Vitányi
CWI, Kruislaan 413
1098 SJ Amsterdam, The Netherlands
paulv@cwi.nl, http://www.cwi.nl/˜paulv

A nonprobabilistic foundation for model selection and prediction can be based on Kolmogorov complexity (algorithmic information theory) and Kolmogorov's structure functions (representing all stochastic properties of the data). A distinguishing feature is the analysis of goodness-of-fit of an individual model for an individual data string. Among other things it presents a new viewpoint on the foundations of maximum likelihood and minimum description length. We provide a leasure introduction to the central notions and results.

"To each constructive object corresponds a function $\Phi_x(k)$ of a natural number k —the log of minimal cardinality of x-containing sets that allow definitions of complexity at most k. If the element x itself allows a simple definition, then the function Φ drops to 1 even for small k. Lacking such definition, the element is "random" in a negative sense. But it is positively "probabilistically random" only when function Φ having taken the value Φ_0 at a relatively small $k = k_0$, then changes approximately as $\Phi(k) = \Phi_0 - (k - k_0)$." — [A.N. Kolmogorov 1974]

6.1   Introduction

Naively speaking, Statistics deals with gathering data, ordering and representing data, and using the data to determine the process that causes the data. That this viewpoint is a little too simplistic is immediately clear: suppose that the true cause of a sequence of outcomes of coin flips is a 'fair' coin, where both sides come up with equal probability. It is possible that the sequence consists of 'heads' only. Suppose that our statistical inference method succeeds in identifying the true cause (fair coin flips) from these data. Such a method is clearly at fault: from an all-heads sequence a good inference should conclude that the cause is a coin with a heavy bias toward 'heads', irrespective of what the true cause is. That is, a good inference method must assume that the data are "typical" for the cause—that is, we do not aim at finding the "true" cause, but at finding a cause for which the data are as "typical" as possible. Such a cause is called a *model* for the data. But what if the data consist of a sequence of precise alternations "head–tail"? This is as unlikely an outcome of a fair coin flip as the all-heads sequence. Yet, within the coin-type models we have no alternative to choosing a fair coin. But we know very well that the true cause must be different. For some data it may not even make sense to ask for a "true cause." This suggests that truth is not our goal; but within given constraints on the model class we try to find the model for which the data are most "typical" in an appropriate sense, the model that best "fits" the data. Considering the available model class as a magnifying glass, finding the best-fitting model for the data corresponds to finding the position of the magnifying glass that best brings the object into focus. In the coin-flipping example, it is possible that the data have no sharply focused model, but within the allowed resolution—ignoring the order of the outcomes but only counting the number of 'heads'—we find the best model.

Classically, the setting of statistical inference is as follows: We carry out a probabilistic experiment of which the outcomes are governed by an unknown probability distribution P. Suppose we obtain as outcome the data sample x. Given x, we want to recover the distribution P. For certain reasons we can choose a distribution from a set of acceptable distributions only (which may or may not contain P). Intuitively, our selection criteria are that (1) x should be a "typical" outcome of the distribution selected, and (2) the selected distribution has a "simple" description. We need to make the meaning of "typical" and "simple" rigorous and balance the requirements (1) and (2). In probabilistic statistics one analyzes the average-case performance of the selection process.For traditional problems, dealing with frequencies over small sample spaces, this approach is appropriate. But for current novel applications, average relations are often irrelevant, since the part of the support of the probability density function that will ever be observed has about zero measure. This is the case in, for example, complex video and sound analysis. There arises the problem that for individual cases the selection performance may be bad although the performance is good on average, or vice versa. There is also the problem of what probability means, whether it is subjective, objective, or exists at all. Kolmogorov's proposal outlined strives for the firmer and less contentious ground expressed in finite combinatorics and effective computation.

We embark on a systematic study of model selection where the performance is related to the individual data sample and the individual model selected. It turns out to be more straightforward to investigate models that are finite sets first, and then generalize the results to models that are probability distributions. To simplify matters, and because all discrete data can be binary-coded, we consider only data samples that are finite binary strings. Classic statistics has difficulty in expressing the notion of an individual "best" model for an individual data sample. But the lucky confluence of information theory, theory of algorithms, and probability leads to the notion of Kolmogorov complexity—the notion of information content in an individual object, and it allows us to express and analyze the novel notion of the information in one individual object (e.g., a model) about another individual object (e.g., the data). Development of this theory allows us to precisely formulate and quantify how well a particular model fits a particular piece of data, a matter which formerly was judged impossible.

6.2 Algorithmic Statistics

In 1965 A.N. Kolmogorov combined the theory of computation and a combinatorial approach to information theory into a proposal for an objective and absolute definition of the information contained by an individual finite object, commonly represented by a finite binary string. This is to be contrasted with the average notion of the entropy of a random source as proposed by C. Shannon [1948]. The theory of "Kolmogorov complexity" has turned out to be ubiquitously applicable [Li and Vitányi 1997]. Continuing this train of thought, as perhaps the last mathematical innovation of an extraordinary scientific career, Kolmogorov [1974] proposed a refinement, which, in J. Rissanen's phrasing, "permits extraction of a desired amount of properties from the data, leaving the remainder as something like noise. The properties are modeled by a finite set that includes the data string, which amounts to modeling data by uniform distribution, and the amount of properties is measured by the Kolmogorov complexity of the description of the finite set involved." This proposal can be viewed as one to found statistical theory on finite combinatorial principles independent of probabilistic assumptions, as the relation between the individual data and its explanation (model), expressed by Kolmogorov's structure function. While these notions have been studied intermittently over the years, and have been described in articles and in Cover and Thomas's influential textbook [Cover and Thomas 1991], as well as our own [Li and Vitányi 1997], they have been previously but poorly understood. Recently, however, the situation has been changed through a sequence of results concerning the "algorithmic" sufficient statistic, and its relation with the corresponding probabilistic notion in [Gács, Tromp, and Vitányi 2001], and a comprehensive body of results concerning Kolmogorov's so-called 'structure function' in [Vereshchagin and Vitányi 2002]. The purpose of this chapter is to briefly outline the basic notions involved and the significance of the main results obtained.

Basic Notions of the Theory   We want to describe every individual finite binary sequence x in two parts, one part being the model description (properties, the meaning of the data) and one part being the data-to-model code (the remaining random "noise"). It is convenient to consider models that are finite sets of finite binary strings, and a contemplated model for x contains x as one of its elements. It turns out that the results are true for more sophisticated models like computable probability density functions. An example of the data-to-model code of x with respect to the model S is the index of x in the lexicographic enumeration of the elements of S. The description of the model, typically a program that generates the model, is called a "statistic." The following properties of how a model S relates to sequence x are crucial:

- *Typicality:* Is x a typical or random element of S?
- *Optimality:* We call S optimal for x if the two-part description of x based on model S is minimal (among all potential two-part descriptions).

A shortest description (or program) for an optimal set S is called an 'algorithmic statistic' for x. The developments in the chapter are based on imposing a constraint on the number of bits allowed to describe the model (the amount of desired properties). Let α indicate the maximum number of bits allowed to describe the model. For fixed α, we consider selection of a model for x in three ways, characterized by three different functions:

1. Selection based on the minimum randomness deficiency function (what we shall argue is the *model fitness* estimator) $\beta_x(\alpha)$;

2. selection based on using Kolmogorov's structure function (what we shall argue is the *maximum likelihood* (ML) estimator) $h_x(\alpha)$; and

3. selection based on the shortest two-part code length (what we shall argue is the minimum description length MDL estimator) $\lambda_x(\alpha)$.

Method 1 is based on the notion of 'typicality' and basically selects the model S for which the data x look most typical. In a precise mathematical sense, stated below in terms of Kolmogorov complexity, this implies that S is a model of 'best fit' for x. So method 1 gives us the proper model for x. Unfortunately, it turns out that method 1 is too difficult to apply. But we can obtain our goal in a roundabout manner: Method 2 selects a model S—containing data x—that minimizes the data-to-model code length that maximally can occur for a string in S. It is useful to explain the notion of data-to-model code length by example. For data string $x = 00\ldots0$ of length n and the large-cardinality but small-complexity model $\{0,1\}^n$, the data-to-model code length is at about n bits since there are elements in S that require n bits to be singled out. Using the small-cardinality but potentially high-complexity model $\{x\}$, the data-to-model code length is $O(1)$. This data-to-model code length may be very different from the shortest way to describe x in a model like $\{0,1\}^n$, which is $O(1)$ bits, since x is the lexicographically first element in $\{0,1\}^n$. Method 3 selects the model S such that the total two-part description length, consisting of one part describing S containing x, and the second part describing the maximal data-to-model code of a string in S, is minimized. We will establish, in a mathematically rigorous manner, that the minimax procedure in methods 2 and 3 result in correct selection according to the criterion of method 1. The methods are not equivalent: selection according to method 1 does not imply a correct choice according to the criteria of either method 2 or method 3; and method 3 doesn't imply a correct choice according to the criterion of method 2.

Outline of the Results   Kolmogorov's structure function, its variations and its relation to model selection, have obtained some notoriety, but no previous comprehension. Before, it has always been questioned why Kolmogorov chose to focus on the mysterious function h_x, rather than on a more evident function denoted as β_x. The main result, in [Vereshchagin and Vitányi 2002], with the beauty of truth, justifies Kolmogorov's intuition. One way to phrase it is this: The structure function determines all stochastic properties of the data in the sense of determining the best-fitting model at every model-complexity level. One easily stated consequence is: For all data x, both method 2 (which below is interpreted as the maximum likelihood estimator) and method 3 (which can be viewed as a minimum description length estimator) select a model that satisfies the best-fit criterion of method 1 (the best-explanation estimator) *in every case* (and not only with high probability). In particular, when the "true" model that generated the data is not in the model class considered, then the ML or MDL estimator still give a model that "best fits" the data, among all the models in the contemplated class. This notion of "best explanation" and "best fit" is understood in the sense that the data are "most typical" for the selected model in a rigorous mathematical sense that is discussed below. A practical consequence is as follows: while the best fit [a model that witnesses $\beta_x(\alpha)$] cannot be computationally monotonically approximated up to any significant precision, we can monotonically minimize the two-part code [find a model witnessing $\lambda_x(\alpha)$], or the one-part code [find a model witnessing $h_x(\alpha)$] and thus monotonically approximate *implicitly* the best-fitting model, [Vereshchagin and Vitányi 2002]. But this should be sufficient: we want the best model rather than a number that measures its goodness. We show that—within the obvious constraints—every graph is realized by the structure function of some data. This means that there are data of each conceivable combination of stochastic properties. All these results are not completely precise: they hold up to a logarithmic additive error. They usher in an era of statistical inference that is *always* (almost) best rather than *expected*.

Reach of Results   In Kolmogorov's initial proposal, as in this work, models are finite sets of finite binary strings, and the data are one of the strings (all discrete data can be binary-encoded). The restriction to finite set models is just a matter of convenience: the main results generalize to the case where the models are arbitrary computable probability density functions and, in fact, other model classes. Since our results hold only within additive logarithmic precision, and the equivalences of the relevant notions and results between the model classes hold up to the same precision, the results hold equally for the more general model classes.

The generality of the results is at the same time a restriction. In classic statistics one is commonly interested in model classes that are partially poorer and partially richer than the ones we consider. For example, the class of Bernoulli processes, or k-state Markov chains, is poorer than the class of computable probability density functions of moderate maximal Kolmogorov complexity α, in that the latter may contain functions that require far more complex computations than the rigid syntax of the former classes allows. Indeed, the class of computable probability density functions of even moderate complexity allows implementation of a function mimicking a universal Turing machine computation. On the other hand, even the lowly Bernoulli process can be equipped with a noncomputable real bias in $(0, 1)$, and hence the generated probability density function over n trials is not a computable function. This incomparability between the algorithmic model classes studied here, and the statistical model classes studied traditionally, means that the current results cannot be directly transplanted to the traditional setting. Indeed, they should be regarded as pristine truths that hold in a Platonic world that can be used as a guideline to develop analogues in model classes that are of more traditional concern, as in [Rissanen 2002]. See also Remark 6.9 below.

6.3 Preliminaries

Let $x, y, z \in \mathcal{N}$, where $\mathcal{N}$ denotes the natural numbers and we identify $\mathcal{N}$ and $\{0, 1\}^*$ according to the correspondence

$$(0, \epsilon), (1, 0), (2, 1), (3, 00), (4, 01), \ldots$$

Here ϵ denotes the *empty word*. The *length* $|x|$ of x is the number of bits in the binary string x, not to be confused with the *cardinality* $|S|$ of a finite set S. For example, $|010| = 3$ and $|\epsilon| = 0$, while $|\{0, 1\}^n| = 2^n$ and $|\emptyset| = 0$. The emphasis is on binary sequences only for convenience; observations in any alphabet can be so encoded in a way that is 'theory neutral'.

A binary string y is a *proper prefix* of a binary string x if we can write $x = yz$ for $z \neq \epsilon$. A set $\{x, y, \ldots\} \subseteq \{0, 1\}^*$ is *prefix-free* if for any pair of distinct elements in the set neither is a proper prefix of the other. A prefix-free set is also called a *prefix code*. There is a special type of prefix code, the *self-delimiting code*, that has the added property of being *effective* in the sense that there is an algorithm that, starting at the beginning of the code word, scanning from left to right, can determine where the code word ends. A simple example of this is the code that encodes the source word $x = x_1 x_2 \ldots x_n$ by the code word

$$\bar{x} = 1^n 0 x.$$

Using this code we define the standard self-delimiting code for x to be $x' = \overline{|x|} x$. It is easy to check that $|\bar{x}| = 2n + 1$ and $|x'| = n + 2 \log n + 1$. We can extend this code to pairs of strings: Let $\langle \cdot \rangle$ be a standard invertible effective one-one encoding from $\mathcal{N} \times \mathcal{N}$ to a subset of $\mathcal{N}$. For example, we can set $\langle x, y \rangle = x' y$ or $\langle x, y \rangle = \bar{x} y$. We can iterate this process to define $\langle x, \langle y, z \rangle \rangle$, and so on.

Kolmogorov Complexity For precise definitions, notation, and results, see [Li and Vitányi 1997]. Informally, the Kolmogorov complexity, or algorithmic entropy, $K(x)$ of a string x is the length (number of bits) of a shortest binary program (string) to compute x on a fixed reference universal computer (such as a particular universal Turing machine). Intuitively, $K(x)$ represents the minimal amount of information required to generate x by any effective process. The conditional Kolmogorov complexity $K(x|y)$ of x relative to y is defined similarly as the length of a shortest program to compute x, if y is furnished as an auxiliary input to the computation. For technical reasons we use a variant of complexity, so-called prefix complexity, which is associated with Turing machines for which the set of programs resulting in a halting computation is prefix-free. We realize prefix complexity by considering a special type of Turing machine with a one-way input tape, a separate work tape, and a one-way output tape. Such Turing machines are called *prefix* Turing machines. If a machine T halts with output x after having scanned all of p on the input tape, but not further, then $T(p) = x$ and we call p a *program* for T. It is easy to see that $\{p : T(p) = x, x \in \{0,1\}^*\}$ is a *prefix code*. In fact, because the algorithm (in this case a Turing machine T) determines the end of the code word for the source word x (i.e., the program p such that $T(p) = x$), this code is in fact *self-delimiting*. Let $T_1, T_2, \ldots$ be a standard enumeration of all prefix Turing machines with a binary input tape, for example the lexicographic length-increasing ordered syntactic prefix Turing machine descriptions, [Li and Vitányi 1997], and let $\phi_1, \phi_2, \ldots$ be the enumeration of corresponding functions that are computed by the respective Turing machines (T_i computes ϕ_i). These functions are the *partial recursive* functions or *computable* functions (of effectively prefix-free encoded arguments). The Kolmogorov complexity of x is the length of the shortest binary program from which x is computed.

Definition 6.1 The *prefix Kolmogorov complexity* of x is

$$K(x) = \min_{p,i}\{|\bar{i}| + |p| : T_i(p) = x\}, \tag{6.1}$$

where the minimum is taken over $p \in \{0,1\}^*$ and $i \in \{1, 2, \ldots\}$. For the development of the theory we actually require the Turing machines to use *auxiliary* (also called *conditional*) information, by equipping the machine with a special read-only auxiliary tape containing this information at the outset. Then, the *conditional version* $K(x \mid y)$ of the prefix Kolmogorov complexity of x given y (as auxiliary information) is defined similarly as before, and the unconditional version is set to $K(x) = K(x \mid \epsilon)$.

One of the main achievements of the theory of computation is that the enumeration $T_1, T_2, \ldots$ contains a machine, say $U = T_u$, that is computationally universal in that it can simulate the computation of every machine in the enumeration when provided with its index. Expressing an index i by the shortest self-delimiting code i^* (if there is more then one such code, then the notation is disambiguated in a standard manner that need not concern us here) for i usable by U, we have $U(\langle y, i^* p \rangle) = T_i(\langle y, p \rangle)$ for all i, p, y. We fix one such machine and designate it as the *reference universal prefix Turing machine*. Using this universal machine it is easy to show [Vereshchagin and Vitányi 2002]

$$K(x \mid y) = \min_q \{|q| : U(\langle y, q \rangle) = x\} + O(1) \tag{6.2}$$

$$K(x) = \min_q \{|q| : U(q) = x\} + O(1).$$

Remark 6.2 A prominent property of the prefix-freeness of the set of programs for the reference prefix Turing machine U is that we can interpret $2^{-K(x)}$ as a probability distribution. By the fundamental Kraft's inequality — see, for example, [Cover and Thomas 1991; Li and Vitányi 1997], we know that if $l_1, l_2, \ldots$ are the code word lengths of a prefix code, then $\sum_x 2^{-l_x} \leq 1$. Hence,

$$\sum_x 2^{-K(x)} \leq 1. \tag{6.3}$$

This leads to the notion of universal distribution—a rigorous form of Occam's razor—which implicitly plays an important part in the present exposition. The functions $K(\cdot)$ and $K(\cdot \mid \cdot)$, though defined in terms of a particular machine model, are machine independent up to an additive constant and acquire an asymptotically universal and absolute character through Church's thesis, from the ability of universal machines to simulate one another and execute any effective process. The Kolmogorov complexity of an individual object was introduced by Kolmogorov [1965] as an absolute and objective quantification of the amount of information in it. The information theory of Shannon [1948], on the other hand, deals with *average* information *to communicate* objects produced by a *random source*. Since the former theory is much more precise, it is surprising that analogues of theorems in information theory hold for Kolmogorov complexity, be it in somewhat weaker form, see [Li and Vitányi 1997].

Precision   It is customary in this area to use "additive constant c" or equivalently "additive $O(1)$ term" to mean a constant, accounting for the length of a fixed binary program, independent of every variable or parameter in the expression in which it occurs. In this chapter we use the prefix complexity variant of Kolmogorov complexity for convenience. Actually some results are easier to prove for plain complexity. Most results presented here are precise up to an additive logarithmic term, which means that they are valid for plain complexity as well—prefix complexity exceeds plain complexity by at most a logarithmic additve term. Thus, our use of prefix complexity is important for "fine details" only.

Meaningful Information   The information contained in an individual finite object (like a finite binary string) is measured by its Kolmogorov complexity—the length of the shortest binary program that computes the object. Such a shortest program contains no redundancy: every bit is information; but is it meaningful information? If we flip a fair coin to obtain a finite binary string, then with overwhelming probability that string constitutes its own shortest program. However, also with overwhelming probability, all the bits in the string are meaningless information, random noise. On the other hand, let an object x be a sequence of observations of heavenly bodies. Then x can be described by the binary string pd, where p is the description of the laws of gravity, and d the observational parameter setting: we can divide the information in x into meaningful information p and accidental information d. The main task for statistical inference and learning theory is to distil the meaningful information present in the data. The question arises whether it is possible to separate meaningful information from accidental information, and if so, how. The essence of the solution to this problem is revealed when we rewrite (6.1) via (6.2) as follows:

$$K(x) = \min_{p,i}\{|\bar{i}| + |p| : T_i(p) = x\} \qquad (6.4)$$
$$= \min_{p,i}\{2|i| + |p| + 1 : T_i(p) = x\},$$
$$= \min_{p,i}\{K(i) + |p| : T_i(p) = x\} + O(1),$$

where the minimum is taken over $p \in \{0,1\}^*$ and $i \in \{1,2,\ldots\}$. In the last step we use first the equality according to (6.2), then that the fixed reference universal prefix Turing machine $U = T_u$ with $|u| = O(1)$, and finally that $U(i^*p) = T_i(p)$ for all i and p. Here i^* denotes the shortest self-delimiting program for i; therefore $|i^*| = K(i)$. The expression (6.4) emphasizes the two-part code nature of Kolmogorov complexity. In the example

$$x = 101010101010101010101010$$

we can encode x by a small Turing machine printing a specified number of copies of the pattern "01" which computes x from the program "13." This way, $K(x)$ is viewed as the shortest length of a two-part code for x, one part describing a Turing machine T, or *model*, for the *regular* aspects of x, and the second part describing the *irregular* aspects of x in the form of a program p to be interpreted by T. The regular, or "valuable," information in x is constituted by the bits in the "model" while the random or "useless" information of x constitutes the remainder. This leaves open the crucial question: How to choose T and p that together describe x? In general, many combinations of T and p are possible, but we want to find a T that describes the meaningful aspects of x.

Data and Model   We consider only finite binary data strings x. Our model class consists of Turing machines T that enumerate a finite set, say S, such that on input $p \leq |S|$ we have $T(p) = x$ with x the pth element of T's enumeration of S, and $T(p)$ is a special *undefined* value if $p > |S|$. The "best-fitting" model for x is a Turing machine T that reaches the minimum description length in (6.4). Such a machine T embodies the amount of useful information contained in x, and we have divided a shortest program x^* for x into parts $x^* = T^*p$ such that T^* is a shortest self-delimiting program for T. Now suppose we consider only low-complexity finite-set models, and under these constraints the shortest two-part description happens to be longer than the shortest one-part description. For example, this can happen if the data are generated by a model that is too complex to be in the contemplated model class. Does the model minimizing the two-part description still capture all (or as much as possible) meaningful information? Such considerations require study of the relation between the complexity limit on the contemplated model classes, the shortest two-part code length, and the amount of meaningful information captured.

6.4   Algorithmic Sufficient Statistic

In the following we will distinguish between "models" that are finite sets, and the "shortest programs" to compute those models that are finite strings. Such a shortest program is in the proper sense a statistic of the data sample as defined before. In a way this distinction between "model" and "statistic" is artificial, but for now we prefer clarity and unambiguousness in the discussion.

We first need a definition. Denote the *complexity of the finite set S* by $K(S)$—the length (number of bits) in the shortest binary program p from which the reference universal prefix machine U computes a listing of the elements of S and then halts. That is, if $S = \{x_1, \ldots, x_n\}$, then $U(p) = \langle x_1, \langle x_2, \ldots, \langle x_{n-1}, x_n \rangle \ldots \rangle \rangle$. Another concept we need is $K(x|S)$, the length of the shortest binary program that computes x from a listing of all the elements of S. We are now about to formulate the central notions 'x is typical for S' and 'S is optimal for x'.

6.4.1   Typical Elements

Consider a string x of length n and prefix complexity $K(x) = k$. We identify the *structure* or *regularity* in x that is to be summarized with a set S of which x is a *random* or *typical* member: given S containing x, the element x cannot be described significantly shorter than by its maximal length index in S, that is, $K(x \mid S) \geq \log |S| + O(1)$. Formally,

Definition 6.3 Let $\beta \geq 0$ be an agreed-upon, fixed, constant. A finite binary string x is a *typical* or *random* element of a set S of finite binary strings, if $x \in S$ and

$$K(x \mid S) \geq \log |S| - \beta. \tag{6.5}$$

We will not indicate the dependence on β explicitly, but the constants in all our inequalities ($O(1)$) will be allowed to be functions of this β.

This definition requires a finite S. In fact, since $K(x \mid S) \leq K(x) + O(1)$, it limits the size of S to $O(2^k)$. Note that the notion of typicality is not absolute but depends on fixing the constant implicit in the O-notation.

Example 6.4 Consider the set S of binary strings of length n whose every odd position is 0. Let x be an element of this set in which the subsequence of bits in even positions is an incompressible string. Then x is a typical element of S (or by some abuse of language we can say S is typical for x). But x is also a typical element of the set $\{x\}$.

6.4.2 Optimal Sets

Let x be a binary data string of length n. For every finite set $S \ni x$, we have $K(x) \leq K(S) + \log |S| + O(1)$, since we can describe x by giving S and the index of x in a standard enumeration of S. Clearly this can be implemented by a Turing machine computing the finite set S and a program p giving the index of x in S. The size of a set containing x measures intuitively the number of properties of x that are represented: The largest set is $\{0,1\}^n$ and represents only one property of x, namely, being of length n. It clearly "underfits" as explanation or model for x. The smallest set containing x is the singleton set $\{x\}$ and represents all conceivable properties of x. It clearly "overfits" as explanation or model for x.

There are two natural measures of suitability of such a set as a model for x. We might prefer either the simplest set, or the smallest set, as corresponding to the most likely structure 'explaining' x. Both the largest set $\{0,1\}^n$ [having low complexity of about $K(n)$] and the singleton set $\{x\}$ [having high complexity of about $K(x)$], while certainly statistics for x, would indeed be considered poor explanations. We would like to balance simplicity of model vs. size of model. Both measures relate to the optimality of a two-stage description of x using a finite set S that contains it. Elaborating on the two-part code,

$$K(x) \leq K(x, S) \leq K(S) + K(x \mid S) + O(1) \qquad (6.6)$$
$$\leq K(S) + \log |S| + O(1),$$

where only the final substitution of $K(x \mid S)$ by $\log |S| + O(1)$ uses the fact that x is an element of S. The closer the right-hand side of (6.6) gets to the left-hand side, the better the description of x is. This implies a tradeoff between meaningful model information, $K(S)$, and meaningless "noise" $\log |S|$. A set S (containing x) for which (6.6) holds with equality,

$$K(x) = K(S) + \log |S| + O(1), \qquad (6.7)$$

is called *optimal*. A data string x can be typical for a set S without that set S being optimal for x. This is the case precisely when x is typical for S (i.e., $K(x|S) = \log S + O(1)$) while $K(x, S) > K(x)$.

6.4.3 Sufficient Statistic

A *statistic* of the data $x = x_1 \ldots x_n$ is a function $f(x)$. Essentially, every function will do. For example, $f_1(x) = n$, $f_2(x) = \sum_{i=1}^{n} x_i$, $f_3(x) = n - f_2(x)$, and

$f_4(x) = f_2(x)/n$, are statistics. A "sufficient" statistic of the data contains all information in the data about the model. In introducing the notion of sufficiency in classic statistics, Fisher [1922] stated: "The statistic chosen should summarize the whole of the relevant information supplied by the sample. This may be called the Criterion of Sufficiency ... In the case of the normal curve of distribution it is evident that the second moment is a sufficient statistic for estimating the standard deviation." For example, in the Bernoulli model (repeated coin flips with outcomes 0 and 1 according to fixed bias), the statistic f_4 is sufficient. It gives the mean of the outcomes and estimates the bias of the Bernoulli process, which is the only relevant model information. For the classic (probabilistic) theory see, for example, [Cover and Thomas 1991]. In [Gács et al. 2001] an algorithmic theory of sufficient statistic (relating individual data to individual model) was developed and its relation to the probabilistic version established. The algorithmic basics are as follows: Intuitively, a model expresses the essence of the data if the two-part code describing the data consisting of the model and the data-to-model code is as concise as the best one-part description.

Mindful of our distinction between a finite set S and a program that describes S in a required representation format, we call a shortest program for an optimal set with respect to x an *algorithmic sufficient statistic* for x. Furthermore, among optimal sets, there is a direct tradeoff between complexity and log size, which together sum to $K(x) + O(1)$. Equality (6.7) is the algorithmic equivalent dealing with the relation between the individual sufficient statistic and the individual data sample, in contrast to the probabilistic notion in, for example, [Cover and Thomas 1991].

Example 6.5 It can be shown that the set S of Example 6.4 is also optimal, and so is $\{x\}$. Sets for which x is typical form a much wider class than optimal sets for x: the set $\{x, y\}$ is still typical for x but with most y it will be too complex to be optimal for x.

For a perhaps less artificial example, consider complexities conditional on the length n of strings. Let y be a random string of length n, let S_y be the set of strings of length n which have 0s exactly where y has, and let x be a random element of S_y. Then x has about 25% 1s, so its complexity is much less than n. The set S_y has x as a typical element, but is too complex to be optimal, since its complexity (even conditional on n) is still n.

An algorithmic sufficient statistic is a sharper individual notion than a probabilistic sufficient statistic. An optimal set S associated with x (the shortest program computing S is the corresponding sufficient statistic associated with x) is chosen such that x is maximally random with respect to it. That is, the information in x is divided in a relevant structure expressed by the set S, and the remaining randomness with respect to that structure, expressed by x's index in S of $\log |S|$ bits. The shortest program for S is itself alone an algorithmic definition of structure, without a probabilistic interpretation.

Optimal sets with the shortest program (or rather that shortest program) is the *algorithmic minimal sufficient statistic* of x. Formally, this is the shortest program that computes a finite set S such that (6.7) holds.

Example 6.6 (Sufficient Statistic) Let us look at a coin toss example. Let k be a number in the range $0, 1, \ldots, n$ of complexity $\log n + O(1)$ given n and let x be a string of length n having k 1s of complexity $K(x \mid n, k) \geq \log \binom{n}{k}$ given n, k. This x can be viewed as a typical result of tossing a coin with a bias about $p = k/n$. A two-part description of x is given by the number k of 1s in x first, followed by the index $j \leq \log |S|$ of x in the set S of strings of length n with k 1s. This set is optimal, since $K(x \mid n) = K(x, k \mid n) = K(k \mid n) + K(x \mid k, n) = K(S) + \log |S|$.

Example 6.7 (Hierarchy of Sufficient Statistics) In a picture such as the 'Mona Lisa', to borrow an example from [Cover and Thomas 1991], we can be interested in the image depicted, but also in the underlying color pattern or pattern of brush strokes. Each of these aspects suggest that there is a particular "model level" at which there is a sufficient statistic for that aspect. An expert trying to attribute a painting may aim at finding sufficient statistics for many such aspects. This is the intuition we try to capture. Let us now try to obtain a formal version of a situation with many sufficient statistics.

All the information in an object, like a picture, is described by a binary string x of length, say, $n = ml$. Chop x into l substrings x_i ($1 \leq i \leq l$) of equal length m each. Let k_i denote the number of 1s in x_i. Each such substring metaphorically represents a patch of, say, color. The intended color, say cobalt blue, is indicated by the number of 1s in the substring. The actual color depicted may be typical cobalt blue or less typical cobalt blue. The smaller the randomness deficiency of substring x_i in the set of all strings of length m containing precisely k_i 1s, the more typical x_i is, the better it achieves a typical cobalt blue color. The metaphorical "image" depicted by x is $\pi(x)$, defined as the string $k_1 k_2 \ldots k_l$ over the alphabet $\{0, 1, \ldots, m\}$, the set of colors available. We can now consider several statistics for x.

Let $X \subseteq \{0, 1, \ldots, m\}^l$ (the set of possible realizations of the target image), and let Y_i for $i = 0, 1, \ldots, m$ be the set of binary strings of length m with i 1s (the set of realizations of target color i). Consider the set

$$S = \{y : \pi(y) \in X, y_i \in Y_{k_i} \text{ for all } i = 1, \ldots, l\}$$

One possible application of these ideas is to gauge how good the picture is with respect to the given summarizing set S. Assume that $x \in S$. The set S is then a statistic for x that captures both the colors of the patches and the image, that is, the total picture. If the randomness deficiency $\delta(x \mid S)$ is small, then S is a sufficient statistic of x. This means that x perfectly expresses the meaning aimed for by the image and the true color aimed for in every one of the color patches.

Another possible application of the theory is to find a good summarization of the meaningful information in a given picture. Let x be a string, and let $S \ni x$ be the set above that has all the randomness deficiencies equal zero. Clearly, S summarizes the relevant information in x since it captures both image and coloring, that is, the total picture. But we can distinguish more sufficient statistics. The set

$$S_1 = \{y : \pi(y) \in X\}$$

is a statistic that captures only the image. It can be sufficient only if all colors used in the picture x are typical (have small randomness deficiency). The set

$$S_2 = \{y : y_i \in Y_{k_i} \text{ for all } i = 1, \ldots, l\}$$

is a statistic that captures the color information in the picture. It can be sufficient only if the image is typical. Finally, the set

$$A_i = \{y : y_i \in Y_{k_i}\}$$

is a statistic that captures only the color of patch y_i in the picture. It can be sufficient only if $K(i) \approx 0$ and all the other color applications and the image are typical.

6.5   Structure Functions

We will prove that there is a close relation between functions describing three, a priori seemingly unrelated, aspects of modeling individual data, depicted in Figure 6.1.

6.5.1   Model Fitness

For every finite set $S \subseteq \{0,1\}^*$ containing x we have

$$K(x|S) \leq \log |S| + O(1). \tag{6.8}$$

Indeed, consider the self-delimiting code of x consisting of its $\lceil \log |S| \rceil$ bit long index of x in the lexicographic ordering of S. This code is called *data-to-model code*. The lack of typicality of x with respect to S is the amount by which $K(x|S)$ falls short of the length of the data-to-model code. The *randomness deficiency* of x in S is defined by

$$\delta(x|S) = \log |S| - K(x|S), \tag{6.9}$$

for $x \in S$, and ∞ otherwise. The *minimal randomness deficiency* function is

$$\beta_x(\alpha) = \min_S \{\delta(x|S) : S \ni x, \ K(S) \leq \alpha\}, \tag{6.10}$$

where we set $\min \emptyset = \infty$. If $\delta(x|S)$ is small, then x may be considered as a *typical* member of S. This means that S is a "best" model for x—a most likely explanation.

There are no simple special properties that single it out from the majority of elements in S. We therefore like to call $\beta_x(\alpha)$ the *best-fit estimator*. This is not just terminology: if $\delta(x|S)$ is small, then x satisfies *all* properties of low Kolmogorov complexity that hold with high probability for the elements of S. To be precise [Vereshchagin and Vitányi 2002]: Consider strings of length n and let S be a subset of such strings. We view a *property* of elements in S as a function $f_P : S \to \{0,1\}$. If $f_P(x) = 1$, then x has the property represented by f_P and if $f_P(x) = 0$, then x does not have the property.

1. If f_P is a property satisfied by all x with $\delta(x|S) \leq \delta(n)$, then f_P holds with probability at least $1 - 1/2^{\delta(n)}$ for the elements of S.

2. Let f_P be any property that holds with probability at least $1 - 1/2^{\delta(n)}$ for the elements of S. Then, every such f_P holds simultaneously for every $x \in S$ with $\delta(x|S) \leq \delta(n) - K(f_P|S) - O(1)$.

Example 6.8 (Lossy Compression) The function $\beta_x(\alpha)$ is relevant to lossy compression (used, e.g., to compress images). Assume we need to compress x to α bits where $\alpha \ll K(x)$. Of course this implies some loss of information present in x. One way to select redundant information to discard is as follows: Find a set $S \ni x$ with $K(S) \leq \alpha$ and with small $\delta(x|S)$, and consider a compressed version S' of S. To reconstruct an x', a decompresser uncompresses S' to S and selects at random an element x' of S. Since with high probability the randomness deficiency of x' in S is small, x' serves the purpose of the message x as well as does x itself. Let us look at an example. To transmit a picture of "rain" through a channel with limited capacity α, one can transmit the indication that this is a picture of the rain and the particular drops may be chosen by the receiver at random. In this interpretation, $\beta_x(\alpha)$ indicates how "random" or "typical" x is with respect to the best model at complexity level α—and hence how "indistinguishable" from the original x the randomly reconstructed x' can be expected to be.

6.5.2   Maximum Likelihood

Kolmogorov at a conference in Tallinn, Estonia, 1974 (no written version) and in a talk at a meeting at the Moscow Mathematical Society in the same year, of which the abstract [Kolmogorov 1974] is reproduced at the beginning of this chapter (the only writing by Kolmogorov about this circle of ideas), proposed the following function: The *Kolmogorov structure* function h_x of given data x is defined by

$$h_x(\alpha) = \min_S \{\log |S| : S \ni x, \ K(S) \leq \alpha\}, \qquad (6.11)$$

where $S \ni x$ is a contemplated model for x, and α is a non-negative integer value bounding the complexity of the contemplated S's. Clearly, the Kolmogorov structure function is nonincreasing and reaches $\log |\{x\}| = 0$ for $\alpha = K(x) + c_1$ where c_1 is the number of bits required to change x into $\{x\}$. For every $S \ni x$ we have (6.6), and hence $K(x) \leq \alpha + h_x(\alpha) + O(1)$; that is, the function $h_x(\alpha)$ never decreases more than a fixed independent constant below the diagonal *sufficiency*

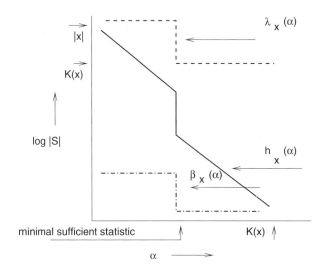

Figure 6.1   Structure functions $h_x(i), \beta_x(\alpha), \lambda_x(\alpha)$, and minimal sufficient statistic.

line L defined by $L(\alpha) + \alpha = K(x)$, which is a lower bound on $h_x(\alpha)$ and is approached to within a constant distance by the graph of h_x for certain α's (e.g., for $\alpha = K(x) + c_1$). For these α's we thus have $\alpha + h_x(\alpha) = K(x) + O(1)$; a model corresponding to such an α (witness for $h_x(\alpha)$) is a sufficient statistic, and it is *minimal* for the least such α (see above and [Cover and Thomas 1991; Gács, Tromp, and Vitányi 2001]).

Following Kolmogorov we analyzed a canonical setting where the models are finite sets. As Kolmogorov himself pointed out, this is no real restriction: the finite sets model class is equivalent, up to a logarithmic additive term, to the model class of probability density functions, as studied in [Shen 1983; Gács, Tromp, and Vitányi 2001]. The model class of *computable probability density functions* consists of the set of functions $P : \{0,1\}^* \to [0,1]$ with $\sum P(x) = 1$. "Computable" means here that there is a Turing machine T_P that, given x and a positive rational ϵ, computes $P(x)$ with precision ϵ. The (prefix) complexity $K(P)$ of a computable (possibly partial) function P is defined by $K(P) = \min_i\{K(i) : $ Turing machine T_i computes $P\}$. A string x is typical for a distribution P if the randomness deficiency $\delta(x \mid P) = -\log P(x) - K(x \mid P)$ is small. The conditional complexity $K(x \mid P)$ is defined as follows. Say that a function A approximates P if $|A(y, \epsilon) - P(y)| < \epsilon$ for every y and every positive rational ϵ. Then $K(x \mid P)$ is the minimum length of a program that given every function A approximating P as an oracle prints x. Similarly, P is c-optimal for x if $K(P) - \log P(x) \leq K(x) + c$. Thus, instead of the data-to-model code length $\log|S|$ for finite set models, we consider the data-to-model code length $-\log P(x)$ (the Shannon-Fano code). The value $-\log P(x)$ measures also how likely x is under the hypothesis P and the mapping $x \mapsto P_{\min}$ where $P_{\min}$ minimizes $-\log P(x)$ over P with $K(P) \leq \alpha$ is a *maximum likelihood estimator*, (figure 6.2). Our results thus imply that that maximum likelihood estimator always

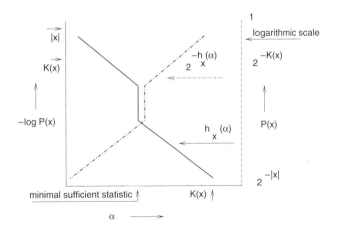

Figure 6.2 Structure function $h_x(i) = \min_P\{-\log P(x) : P(x) > 0, \; K(P) \leq i\}$ with P a computable probability density function, with values according to the left vertical coordinate, and the maximum likelihood estimator $2^{-h_x(i)} = \max\{P(x) : P(x) > 0, \; K(P) \leq i\}$, with values according to the right-hand side vertical coordinate.

returns a hypothesis with minimum randomness deficiency.

It is easy to show that for every data string x and a contemplated finite set model for it, there is an almost equivalent computable probability density function model. Conversely, for every data string x and a contemplated computable probability density function model for it, there is a finite set model for x that has no worse complexity, randomness deficiency, and worst-case data-to-model code for x, up to additive logarithmic precision (see [Vereshchagin and Vitányi 2002]).

6.5.3 Minimum Description Length

The length of the minimal two-part code for x consisting of the model cost $K(S)$ and the length of the index of x in S, the complexity of S upper bounded by α, is given by the *MDL function* or *MDL estimator*:

$$\lambda_x(\alpha) = \min_S\{\Lambda(S) : S \ni x, \; K(S) \leq \alpha\}, \tag{6.12}$$

where $\Lambda(S) = \log|S| + K(S) \geq K(x) - O(1)$ is the total length of two-part code of x with help of model S. Clearly, $\lambda_x(\alpha) \leq h_x(\alpha) + \alpha + O(1)$, but a priori it is still possible that $h_x(\alpha') + \alpha' < h_x(\alpha) + \alpha$ for $\alpha' < \alpha$. In that case $\lambda_x(\alpha) \leq h_x(\alpha') + \alpha' < h_x(\alpha) + \alpha$. However, in [Vereshchagin and Vitányi 2002] it is shown that $\lambda_x(\alpha) = h_x(\alpha) + \alpha + O(\log n)$ for all x of length n. Even so, this does not mean that a set S that witnesses $\lambda_x(\alpha)$ in the sense that $x \in S$, $K(S) \leq \alpha$, and $K(S) + \log|S| = \lambda_x(\alpha)$, also witnesses $h_x(\alpha)$. It can be the case that $K(S) \leq \alpha - r$ and $\log|S| = h_x(\alpha) + r$ for arbitrarily large $r \leq n$.

This function $\lambda_x(\alpha)$ is the celebrated two-part MDL code length with the model code length restricted to at most α.

6.6   Overview of Results

The most fundamental result in [Vereshchagin and Vitányi 2002] is the equality

$$\beta_x(\alpha) = h_x(\alpha) + \alpha - K(x) = \lambda_x(\alpha) - K(x), \qquad (6.13)$$

which holds within logarithmic additive terms in argument and value. Additionally, every set S that witnesses the value $h_x(\alpha)$ (or $\lambda_x(\alpha)$), also witnesses the value $\beta_x(\alpha)$ (but not vice versa). It is easy to see that $h_x(\alpha)$ and $\lambda_x(\alpha)$ are upper semicomputable (Definition 6.12 below); but we have shown [Vereshchagin and Vitányi 2002] that $\beta_x(\alpha)$ is neither upper nor lower semicomputable (not even within a great tolerance). A priori there is no reason to suppose that a set that witnesses $h_x(\alpha)$ (or $\lambda_x(\alpha)$) also witnesses $\beta_x(\alpha)$, for *every* α. But the fact that they do, vindicates Kolmogorov's original proposal and establishes h_x's preeminence over β_x.

Remark 6.9 What we call 'maximum likelihood' in the form of h_x is really 'maximum likelihood under a complexity constraint α on the models' as in $h_x(\alpha)$. In statistics, it is a well-known fact that maximum likelihood often fails (dramatically overfits) when the models under consideration are of unrestricted complexity (e.g., with polynomial regression with Gaussian noise, or with Markov chain model learning, maximum likelihood will always select a model with n parameters, where n is the size of the sample—and thus typically, maximum likelihood will dramatically overfit, whereas, for example, MDL typically performs well). The equivalent, in our setting, is that allowing models of unconstrained complexity for data x, say complexity $K(x)$, will result in the ML estimator $h_x(K(x) + O(1)) = 0$—the witness model being the trivial, maximally overfitting, set $\{x\}$. In the MDL case, on the other hand, there may be a long constant interval with the MDL estimator $\lambda_x(\alpha) = K(x)$ ($\alpha \in [\alpha_1, K(x)]$) where the length of the two-part code does not decrease anymore. Selecting the least complexity model witnessing this function value we obtain the, very significant, algorithmic *minimal* sufficient statistic. In this sense, MDL augmented with a bias for the least complex explanation, which we may call the 'Occam's razor MDL', is superior to maximum likelihood and resilient to overfitting. If we do not apply bias in the direction of simple explanations, then MDL may be just as prone to overfitting as is ML. For example, if x is a typical random element of $\{0,1\}^n$, then $\lambda_x(\alpha) = K(x) + O(1)$ for the entire interval $K(n) + O(1) \leq \alpha \leq K(x) + O(1) \approx n$. Choosing the model on the left side, of simplest complexity, of complexity $K(n)$ gives us the best fit with the correct model $\{0,1\}^n$. But choosing a model on the right side, of high complexity, gives us a model $\{x\}$ of complexity $K(x) + O(1)$ that completely overfits the data by modeling all random noise in x (which in fact in this example almost completely consists of random noise).

Thus, it should be emphasized that 'ML = MDL' really only holds if complexities are constrained to a value α (that remains fixed as the sample size grows—note that in the Markov chain example above, the complexity grows linearly with the sample size); it certainly does not hold in an unrestricted sense (not even in the algorithmic setting).

Remark 6.10 In a sense, h_x is more strict than λ_x: a set that witnesses $h_x(\alpha)$ also witnesses $\lambda_x(\alpha)$ but not necessarily vice versa. However, at those complexities α where $\lambda_x(\alpha)$ drops (a little bit of added complexity in the model allows a shorter description), the witness set of λ_x is also a witness set of h_x. But if λ_x stays constant in an interval $[\alpha_1, \alpha_2]$, then we can tradeoff complexity of a witness set vs. its cardinality, keeping the description length constant. This is of course not possible with h_x where the cardinality of the witness set at complexity α is fixed at $h_x(\alpha)$.

The main result can be taken as a foundation and justification of common statistical principles in model selection such as maximum likelihood or MDL. The structure functions λ_x, h_x, and β_x can assume all possible shapes over their full domain of definition (up to additive logarithmic precision in both argument and value); see [Vereshchagin and Vitányi 2002]. [This establishes the significance of (6.13), since it shows that $\lambda_x(\alpha) \gg K(x)$ is common for x, α pairs—in which case the more or less easy fact that $\beta_x(\alpha) = 0$ for $\lambda_x(\alpha) = K(x)$ is not applicable, and it is a priori unlikely that (6.13) holds: Why should minimizing a set containing x also minimize its randomness deficiency? Surprisingly, it does!] We have exhibited a—to our knowledge first—natural example, β_x, of a function that is not semicomputable but computable with an oracle for the halting problem.

Example 6.11 (**"Positive" and "Negative" Individual Randomness**) In [Gács et al. 2001] we showed the existence of strings for which essentially the singleton set consisting of the string itself is a minimal sufficient statistic. While a sufficient statistic of an object yields a two-part code that is as short as the shortest one-part code, restricting the complexity of the allowed statistic may yield two-part codes that are considerably longer than the best one-part code (so the statistic is insufficient). In fact, for every object there is a complexity bound below which this happens—but if that bound is small (logarithmic) we call the object "stochastic" since it has a simple satisfactory explanation (sufficient statistic). Thus, Kolmogorov [1974] (see abstract) makes the important distinction of an object being random in the "negative" sense by having this bound high (they have high complexity and are not typical elements of a low-complexity model), and an object being random in the "positive, probabilistic" sense by both having this bound small and itself having complexity considerably exceeding this bound [like a string x of length n with $K(x) \geq n$, being typical for the set $\{0,1\}^n$, or the uniform probability distribution over that set, while this set or probability distribution has complexity $K(n) + O(1) = O(\log n)$]. We depict the distinction in Figure 6.3. In simple terms: a data string of high Kolmogorov complexity is *positively random* if the simplest satisfactory explanation (sufficient statistic) has low complexity, and it therefore is the typical outcome of a simple random process. Another data string of the same

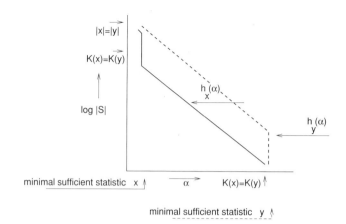

Figure 6.3 Data string x is "positive random" or "stochastic" and data string y is "negative random" or "nonstochastic".

length and the same complexity is *negatively random* if the simplest satisfactory explanation (sufficient statistic) has high complexity: it can only be the typical outcome of a complex random process.

In [Vereshchagin and Vitányi 2002] it is shown that for every length n and every complexity $k \leq n + K(n) + O(1)$ (the maximal complexity of x of length n) and every $\alpha \in [0, k]$, there are x's of length n and complexity k such that the minimal randomness deficiency $\beta_x(i) \geq n - k \pm O(\log n)$ for every $i \leq \alpha \pm O(\log n)$ and $\beta_x(i) \pm O(\log n)$ for every $i > \alpha \pm O(\log n)$. Therefore, the set of n-length strings of every complexity k can be partitioned in subsets of strings that have a Kolmogorov minimal sufficient statistic of complexity $\Theta(i \log n)$ for $i = 1, \ldots, k/\Theta(\log n)$. For instance, there are n-length nonstochastic strings of almost maximal complexity $n - \sqrt{n}$ having significant $\sqrt{n} \pm O(\log n)$ randomness deficiency with respect to $\{0,1\}^n$ or, in fact, every other finite set of complexity less than $n - O(\log n)$!

6.7   Relation to MDL

1. Consider the following algorithm based on the MDL principle. Given x, the data to explain, and α, the maximum allowed complexity of explanation, we search for programs p of length at most α that print a finite set $S \ni x$. Such pairs (p, S) are possible explanations. The *best explanation* is defined to be the (p, S) for which $\delta(x|S)$ is minimal. Since the function $\delta(x|S)$ is not computable, we cannot find the best explanation in a finite amount of time. Another reason for this is that the programs use unknown computation time and thus we can never be certain that we have found all possible explanations.

Compare this indirect method with the direct one: after step t of dovetailing select (p, S) for which $\log|S| - K^t(x|S)$ is minimum among all programs p that up to this time have printed a set S containing x, where $K^t(x|S)$ is the approximation of $K^t(x|S)$ obtained after t steps of dovetailing, that is, $K^t(x|S) = \min\{|q| : U$ on input $\langle q, S \rangle$ prints x in at most t steps$\}$. Let (q_t, B_t) stand for that model. This time the same hypothesis can be declared best twice. However, from some moment onward the explanation (q_t, B_t) which is declared best does not change anymore.

Why do we prefer the indirect method to the direct one? The explanation is that in practice we deal often with t that are much less than the time of stabilization of both L_t and B_t. For small t, the model L_t is better than B_t in the following respect: L_t has some guarantee of goodness, as we know that $\delta(x|L_t) + K(x) \leq |p_t| + \log|L_t| + O(1)$. That is, we know that the sum of deficiency of x in L_t and $K(x)$ is less than some known value. In contrast, the model B_t has no guarantee of goodness at all: we do not know any upper bound neither for $\delta(x|B_t)$, nor for $\delta(x|B_t) + K(x)$.

Our result in [Vereshchagin and Vitányi 2002] implies that the indirect method of MDL gives not only some guarantee of goodness but also that, in the limit, that guarantee approaches the value it upper-bounds, that is, approaches $\delta(x|L_t) + K(x)$, and $\delta(x|L_t)$ itself is not much greater than $\delta(x|B_t)$ (except for some values of α called "critical" in [Vereshchagin and Vitányi 2002].) That is, in the limit, the method of MDL will yield an explanation that is only a little worse than the best explanation.

2. If $S \ni x$ is a smallest set such that $K(S) \leq \alpha$, then S can be converted into a best strategy of complexity at most α, to predict the successive bits of x given the preceding 1s, see the "snooping curve" example in [Vereshchagin and Vitányi 2002]. Interpreting "to explain" as "to be able to predict well," MDL in the sense of sets witnessing $\lambda_x(\alpha)$ gives indeed a good explanation at every complexity level α.

3. In statistical applications of MDL [Rissanen 1983], minimum message length (MML) [Wallace and Freeman 1987], and related methods, one selects the model in a given model class that minimizes the sum of the model code length and the data-to-model code length; in modern versions one chooses the model that minimizes the data-to-model code length (ignoring the model code length). In [Vereshchagin and Vitányi 2002] we have shown that these methods are almost equivalent in the case when the model class consists of *all* the models with certain model-complexity constraints. In contrast, ultimate compression of the two-part code, proposed in [Vitányi and Li 2000], may be achieved by a model for which the data are not typical, even when the model class consists of *all* the models with certain model-complexity constraints. By ultimate compression of the two-part code we mean minimizing $K(A) + K(x|A)$ over all models in the model class. For instance, let x be a string of length n and complexity about $n/2$ for which $\beta_x(O(\log(n))) = n/4 + O(\log(n))$. Such a string exists by the results in [Vereshchagin and Vitányi 2002]. Moreover, let the model class consist of all finite sets containing x of complexity at most $\alpha = O(\log n)$. Then for the model $A_0 = \{0, 1\}^n$ we have $K(A_0) = O(\log n)$ and $K(x|A_0) = n/2 + O(\log n)$; thus the

sum $K(A_0) + K(x|A_0) = n/2 + O(\log n)$ is minimal up to a term $O(\log n)$. However, the randomness difficiency of x in A_0 is about $n/2$, which is much bigger than the minimum $\beta_x(O(\log(n)) \approx n/4$. For the model A_1 witnessing $\beta_x(O(\log(n)) \approx n/4$ we also have $K(A_1) = O(\log n)$ and $K(x|A_1) = n/2 + O(\log n)$. However, it has smaller cardinality, $\log|A_1| = 3n/4 + O(\log n)$, and hence smaller randomness deficiency.

The same happens also for other model classes. Consider, for instance, as the model class, the Bernoulli processes with rational bias p for outcome "1" ($0 \le p \le 1$) to generate binary strings of length n. Suppose we look for the model minimizing the code length of the model plus data given the model: $K(p|n) + K(x|p, n)$. Let the data be $x = 00\ldots 0$. Then the model corresponding to probability $p = \frac{1}{2}$ compresses the data code to $K(x \mid n, p) = O(1)$ bits and $K(p|n) = O(1)$. But we find about the same code length if we take $p' = 0$. Thus we have no basis to distinguish between the two, while obviously the second possibility is preferable. This shows that ultimate compression of the two-part code, here resulting in $K(p|n) + K(x|n, p)$, may yield a model P for which the data have large randomness deficiency ($-\log P(x) - K(x \mid n, p) = n$ for $p = \frac{1}{2}$) and hence are atypical.

However, in the structure functions $h_x(\alpha)$ and $\lambda_x(\alpha)$ the data-to-model code for the model $p = \frac{1}{2}$ is $-\log P(x) = -\log(\frac{1}{2})^n = n$ bits, while $p = 0$ results in $-\log 1^n = 0$ bits. Choosing the shortest data-to-model code results in the minimal randomness deficiency, as in (the generalization to probability distributions of) our main theorem in [Vereshchagin and Vitányi 2002].

4. Another question arising in MDL or ML estimation is its performance if the "true" model is not part of the contemplated model class. Given certain data, why would we assume they are generated by probabilistic or deterministic processes? They have arisen by natural processes most likely not conforming to mathematical idealization. Even if we can assume the data arose from a process that can be mathematically formulated, such situations arise if we restrict modeling of data arising from a "complex" source (a conventional analogue being data arising from $2k$-parameter sources) by "simple" models (a conventional analogue being k-parameter models). Again, our main result in [Vereshchagin and Vitányi 2002] shows that, within the class of models of maximal complexity α, under these constraints we still select a simple model for which the data are maximally typical. This is particularly significant for data x if the allowed complexity α is significantly below the complexity of the Kolmogorov minimal sufficient statistic, that is, if $h_x(\alpha) + \alpha \gg K(x) + c$. This situation is potentially common, for example, if we have a small data sample generated by a complex process. For a data sample that is very large relative to the complexity of the process generating it, this will typically not be the case and the structure function will drop to the sufficiency line early on.

Relation to Maximum Likelihood Estimation   The algorithm based on the ML principle is similar to the algorithm of the previous example. The only difference is that the currently best (p, S) is the one for which $\log|S|$ is minimal. In this case the limit hypothesis $\tilde{S}$ will witness $h_x(\alpha)$ and we obtain the same corollary: $\delta(x|S) \le \beta_x(\alpha - O(\log n)) + O(\log n)$.

6.8   Computability Questions

How difficult is it to compute the functions h_x, λ_x, β_x, and the minimal sufficient statistic? To express the properties appropriately we require the notion of functions that are not computable, but which can be approximated monotonically by a computable function.

Definition 6.12 A function $f : \mathcal{N} \rightarrow \mathcal{R}$ is *upper semicomputable* if there is a Turing machine T computing a total function ϕ such that $\phi(x, t+1) \leq \phi(x, t)$ and $\lim_{t \to \infty} \phi(x, t) = f(x)$. This means that f can be computably approximated from above. If $-f$ is upper semicomputable, then f is lower semicomputable. A function is called *semicomputable* if it is either upper semicomputable or lower semicomputable. If f is both upper semicomputable and lower semicomputable, then we call f *computable* (or recursive if the domain is integer or rational).

Semicomputability gives no speed-of-convergence guaranties: even though the limit value is monotonically approximated we know at no stage in the process how close we are to the limit value. The functions $h_x(\alpha), \lambda_x(\alpha), \beta_x(\alpha)$ have finite domain for given x and hence can be given as a table—so formally speaking they are computable. But this evades the issue: there is no algorithm that computes these functions for given x and α. Considering them as two-argument functions we show the following (we actually quantify these statements):

- The functions $h_x(\alpha)$ and $\lambda_x(\alpha)$ are upper semicomputable but they are not computable up to any reasonable precision.
- Moreover, there is no algorithm that given x^* and α finds $h_x(\alpha)$ or $\lambda_x(\alpha)$.
- The function $\beta_x(\alpha)$ is not upper or lower semicomputable, not even to any reasonable precision, but we can compute it given an oracle for the halting problem.
- There is no algorithm that given x and $K(x)$ finds a minimal sufficient statistic for x up to any reasonable precision.

The precise forms of these quite strong noncomputability and nonapproximability results are given in [Vereshchagin and Vitányi 2002].

Acknowledgment

I thank Peter Gács, John Tromp, and Nikolai Vereshchagin, my co-authors of [Gács, Tromp, and Vitányi 2001; Vereshchagin and Vitányi 2002].

References

Cover, T., and J. Thomas (1991). *Elements of Information Theory*. New York: Wiley Interscience.

R.A. Fisher (1922). On the mathematical foundations of theoretical statistics, *Philosophical Transactions of the Royal Society of London, Series A, 222*, 309–368.

Gács, P., J. Tromp, and P. Vitányi (2001). Algorithmic statistics. *IEEE Transactions on Information Theory, 47*(6), 2464–2479.

Kolmogorov, A. (1965). Three approaches to the quantitative definition of information. *Problems of Information Transmission, 1*(1), 1–7.

Kolmogorov, A.N. (1974). Complexity of algorithms and objective definition of randomness, *Uspekhi Matematicheskikh Nauk 294*, 155. (Russian abstract of talk at Moscow Math. Soc. meeting 4/16/1974. Translated by L.A. Levin in November 2002.)

Li, M., and P. Vitányi (1997). *An Introduction to Kolmogorov Complexity and Its Applications*, 2nd edition. New York: Springer-Verlag.

Rissanen, J. (1983). A universal prior for integers and estimation by minimum description length. *Annals of Statistics, 11*, 416–431.

Rissanen, J. (2002). Kolmogorov's Structure Function for Probability Models, Proceedings of IEEE Information Theory Workshop 2002, pp. 98–99. Piscataway, NJ: IEEE Press.

Shannon, C.E. (1948). The mathematical theory of communication. *Bell Systems Technical Journal, 27*, 379–423, 623–656.

Shen, A.Kh. (1983). The concept of (α, β)-stochasticity in the Kolmogorov sense, and its properties [in Russian]. *Soviet Mathematics Doklady, 28*(1), 295–299.

Shen, A.Kh. (1999). Discussion on Kolmogorov complexity and statistical analysis. *The Computer Journal, 42*(4), 340–342.

Vereshchagin, N., and P.M.B. Vitányi (2002). Kolmogorov's structure functions with an application to the foundations of model selection. In *Proceedings of the 47th IEEE Symposium on the Foundations of Computer Science (FOCS'02)*. Submitted to *IEEE Transactions on Information Theory.*

Vitányi, P.M.B., and M. Li (2000). Minimum description length induction, Bayesianism, and Kolmogorov complexity, *IEEE Transactions on Information Theory,462*, 446–464.

Wallace, C., and P. Freeman (1987). Estimation and inference by compact coding. *Journal of the Royal Statistical Society, Series B, 49*, 240–251. Discussion: pp. 252–265.

II Theoretical Advances

7 Exact Minimax Predictive Density Estimation and MDL

Feng Liang
Institute of Statistics and Decision Sciences
Duke University
Durham, NC 27708-0251 USA
feng@stat.duke.edu

Andrew Barron
Department of Statistics
Yale University
New Haven, CT 06520 USA
andrew.barron@yale.edu

The problems of predictive density estimation with Kullback-Leibler loss, optimal universal data compression for minimum description length (MDL) model selection, and the choice of priors for Bayes factors in model selection are interrelated. Research in recent years has identified procedures which are minimax for risk in predictive density estimation and for redundancy in universal data compression. Here, after reviewing some of the general story, we focus on the case of location families. The exact minimax procedures use an improper uniform prior on the location parameter. We illustrate use of the minimax optimal procedures with data previously used in a study of robustness of location estimates. Plus we discuss applications of minimax MDL criteria to variable selection problems in regression.

7.1 Introduction

Suppose we are about to transmit a data string $y = (y_1, \ldots, y_n)$ and we assume that the underlying data-generating process is some distribution from a parametric family with probability density function $p(y \mid \theta)$ depending on a d-dimensional parameter vector θ taking values in $\Theta \subset \mathbb{R}^d$. If the parameter θ were known to us, by Shannon coding theory, the ideal code length would be equal to $\log 1/p(y \mid \theta)$

where for now we ignore the requirement of integer code length and finite precision representation of the numbers. Such a code length is optimal in the following two senses: first, it is the shortest code on average, giving entropy as the shortest expected code length; second, it is competitively optimal [Barron, Rissanen and Yu 1998; Cover and Thomas 1991]. Without the knowledge of θ, we in fact code the data with some other distribution, say $q(y)$ with code length $\log 1/q(y)$. The corresponding excess average code length (*expected redundancy*) is given by the Kullback-Leibler divergence:

$$\mathbb{E}_{y|\theta} \log \frac{p(y \mid \theta)}{q(y)} \tag{7.1}$$

A minimax optimal coding strategy is one that achieves the minimax expected redundancy equal to

$$\min_q \max_\theta \mathbb{E}_{y|\theta} \log \frac{p(y \mid \theta)}{q(y)}. \tag{7.2}$$

By a result from decision theory [Ferguson 1967; Davisson and Leon-Garcia 1980; Gallager 1979; Haussler 1997], the minimax code length (7.2) agrees with the maximin value

$$\max_w \min_q \int w(\theta)\, \mathbb{E}_{y|\theta} \log \frac{p(y \mid \theta)}{q(y)}\, d\theta = \max_w \int w(\theta)\, \mathbb{E}_{y|\theta} \log \frac{p(y \mid \theta)}{p_w(y)}\, d\theta,$$

where w is a prior distribution on Θ and p_w is the corresponding Bayes mixture (marginal) density $p_w(y) = \int w(\theta)p(y \mid \theta)d\theta$ which minimizes the Bayes average redundancy $R_w(q) = \int w(\theta)\mathbb{E}_{y|\theta} \log p(y \mid \theta)/q(y)d\theta$. Thus the mixture density $p_w(y)$ provides the optimal code length $\log 1/p_w(y)$ for model selection by description length criteria. Likewise, the mixture density $p_w(y)$ is also the key ingredient in Bayes factors for model selection.

Previous work has shown that the mixture code p_{w_J} with Jeffreys' prior w_J (proportional to the root of the determinant of the Fisher information matrix) is asymptotically minimax when the square root of the determinant of the information matrix is integrable [Clarke and Barron 1990; Clarke and Barron 1994; Rissanen 1996]. However, for some cases, including location families, the Jeffreys' prior is improper (the root determinant of the information matrix is not integrable) and the minimax redundancy is infinite.

We may express both $q(y)$ and $p(y \mid \theta)$ in the predictive form. For example, the joint density $q(y) = q(y_1, \ldots, y_n)$ is given by

$$q(y) = \prod_{m=0}^{n-1} q(y_{m+1} \mid y^m), \quad y^m = (y_1, \ldots, y_m).$$

Then we have the following identity

$$\mathbb{E}_{y|\theta} \log \frac{p(y \mid \theta)}{q(y)} = \mathbb{E}_{y|\theta} \log \frac{\prod_m p(y_{m+1} \mid y^m, \theta)}{\prod_m q(y_{m+1} \mid y^m)}$$

$$= \sum_m \mathbb{E}_{y|\theta} \log \frac{p(y_{m+1} \mid y^m, \theta)}{q(y_{m+1} \mid y^m)}. \tag{7.3}$$

Each term on the right side of (7.3) is the Kullback-Leibler risk of the predictive density estimator for the $(m + 1)$th observation based on the previous m observations, $q(\cdot \mid y^m)$. That is, the expected redundancy (7.1) is precisely the accumulated Kullback-Leibler risk of the sequence of predictive density estimators. The connection between optimal coding and statistical estimation is not a surprise because we know that codes correspond to probability distributions by the fundamental Kraft inequality [Cover and Thomas 1991].

For each m, a minimax strategy can be constructed by specifying the predictive distribution $\{q_m^*(\cdot \mid y^m)\}$ which is the solution of

$$\min_q \max_\theta \ \mathbb{E}_{y^{m+1}|\theta} \log \frac{p(y_{m+1} \mid y^m, \theta)}{q(y_{m+1} \mid y^m)}. \tag{7.4}$$

Here we summarize some of our recent results reported in [Liang and Barron 2002] in which we studied certain transformation families, including location families, scale families and combined location and scale families. There we showed that when conditioning on sufficiently many initial observations ($m \geq d$), the minimax redundancy is finite and is achieved by a particular generalized Bayes rule. For example, for location families, the minimax procedure is generalized Bayes using the uniform (Lebesgue) prior. Though the priors are improper, the posterior based on enough initial observations are proper (i.e., $\int p(y^m \mid \theta)w(\theta)d\theta$ is finite for each y^m). The product of those sequential minimax estimators, $q_m^*(y_{m+1} \mid y^m)q_{m+1}^*(y_{m+2} \mid y^{m+1}) \cdots q_{n-1}^*(y_n \mid y^{n-1})$, specifies a valid predictive density for $(y_{m+1}, \ldots, y_n)$ conditioning on the previous m observations. In general, this product is not the minimax solution of the total expected redundancy for the future $(n - m)$ observations,

$$\min_q \max_\theta \mathbb{E}_{y^n|\theta} \log \frac{p(y_{m+1}, \ldots, y_n \mid y^m, \theta)}{q(y_{m+1}, \ldots, y_n \mid y^m)}, \tag{7.5}$$

because the values of θ which maximize the risk in (7.4) may differ at various m. Thus the sum of individual minimax risks is an upper bound on the minimax total risk in (7.5). Nevertheless, for location and scale problems, we exhibit a constant risk minimax procedure, so it simultaneously provides a minimax solution for both the individual risk and the total risk (7.5), and in such cases the sum of the individual minimax risks is equal to the minimax total.

When we report predictive density estimates, as we do in section 7.3, it is convenient to do so through the value of the log reciprocal, $\log_2 1/q^*(y_{m+1} \mid y^m)$, not only because they add up nicely to give the total code length but also because informally it will show, for unusual values of y_i, a degree to which that value is surprising and thereby forces a longer description.

The minimum description length (MDL), as a criterion in model selection, was introduced by Rissanen [1978] (see review papers by Barron, Rissanen and Yu [1998], and by Hansen and Yu [2001]). The idea of MDL is to first represent each model by a universal distribution and then choose the one with the shortest description length for the observed data. In this framework, a good model is the one that captures most features of the data and hence can describe the data in a short code. Our results on exact minimaxity of predictive density estimation provide a means to construct the underlying universal coding scheme for MDL, with the code length achieving the minimax redundancy.

As in other papers in this collection, and in the above-mentioned review papers, there has been a trend in recent years to compare universal procedures not to the code length $\log 1/p(y|\theta)$ that would have been the best for a hypothetical distribution governing the data [as in the traditional definition of redundancy as given in (7.1)], but rather to study the regret $\log 1/q(y) - \log 1/p(y|\hat{\theta}(y))$ in which the universal code length $\log 1/q(y)$ is compared to the shortest code length with hindsight $\min_\theta \log 1/p(y|\theta)$, corresponding to the maximum likelihood estimate $\hat{\theta}(y)$. For any strategy q, if one takes the expected value of this regret it differs from the expected redundancy by an amount $E_{y|\theta} \log p(y|\hat{\theta}(y))/p(y|\theta)$. Now, in general, this difference could depend on θ. However, for location and scale families we find that this difference between expected regret and expected redundancy is a constant (independent of θ, as well as independent of q), and the same conclusion of constancy of the expected difference holds in our setting in which one conditions on an initial set of observations. Thus our procedures for location and scale families, which are exactly minimax for expected redundancy (Kullback-Leibler risk) are also exactly minimax for expected regret.

The editors have asked that we also comment further about the nature of asymptotic expressions for regret and Kullback-Leibler risk, and how, if at all, our exact minimax procedures relate to those asymptotics. For independent and identically distributed (i.i.d.) sampling from smooth parametric families, as we have said, the Bayes procedures with Jeffreys' prior provide asymptotically minimax expected regret and expected redundancy, provided the square root of the determinant of the Fisher information $I(\theta)$ is integrable [Clarke and Barron 1990; Clarke and Barron 1994; Rissanen 1996; Barron, Rissanen and Yu 1998]. In that case, with no need to condition on initial data, the total code length has expected regret that is asymptotically of the form $(d/2)\log(n/2\pi) + \log\int |I(\theta)|^{1/2} + o(1)$, where d is the parameter dimension and $o(1)$ tends to zero as the sample size n tends to infinity as shown in [Clarke and Barron 1990; Clarke and Barron 1994]. The same asymptotics hold also for the minimax individual sequence regret, as reviewed in [Barron et al. 1998], though as mentioned there it requires substantial modification of Jeffreys' prior when outside exponential families.

Continuing with our focus on expected regret or expected redundancy (Kullback-Leibler risk) incorporating conditioning on a initial sample of size m, we see that if m as well as n is large, then taking the difference in the risk expressions at the final size n and the initial size m, many of the terms cancel away, leaving a conditional redundancy of $(d/2)\log n/m + o(1)$ where $o(1)$ tends to zero as m and $n > m$ tends to infinity. However, unlike the total redundancy, such asymptotic differences do not reveal much role for the choice of procedure, as the results of [Clarke and Barron 1990, 1994] show that $(d/2)\log n/m + o(1)$ is the asymptotic conditional redundancy of Bayes procedures for all choices of smooth prior. A considerably more refined asymptotic analysis is in [Hartigan 1998] where he shows that the Kullback-Leibler risk for one-step ahead predictive density estimation with a sample of size k has asymptotic expression $(d/2)(1/k) + c(\theta, w)/k^2 + o(1/k)^2$, where $c(\theta, w)$ depends in a somewhat complicated way on the parameter value and the derivative of the log of the prior density $w(\theta)$ as well as the form of the parametric family. Summing Hartigan's risk expression for k from m to n permits a refined conditional redundancy expression of the form $(d/2)\log n/m + 2c(\theta, w)/m + o(1/m)$ that is sensitive to the choice of procedure (through the choice of the prior w). Thus the asymptotics of expected conditional redundancy, as well as the Kullback-Leibler risk, motivate Hartigan's study of the minimax properties of $c(\theta, w)$ initiated in [Hartigan 1998] (one may see also [Aslan 2002; Emerson 2002]). For each family one has a differential inequality to solve to determine if a suggested level C is indeed a minimax bound (i.e., one addresses whether there is a prior w such that $c(\theta, w) \le C$ for all θ). It is reassuring that the priors shown in our work to be exact minimax for finite sample sizes in the special cases of location and scale families do fit in Hartigan's theory as asymptotically minimax.

The remainder of the chapter is arranged as follows: in section 7.2 we summarize ideas from [Liang and Barron 2002] showing the minimaxity for the case of location families. In section 7.3, we show how to use our result to calculate the MDL criterion value to do model selection on some real data sets, which were used before in a study of robustness by Stigler [1977]. The application of variable selection in a linear regression model is discussed in section 7.4 and some additional discussion is given in section 7.5.

7.2   Exact Minimax Coding Strategy

In this section, we summarize the derivation of the minimax procedure q^* for location families. It is the simplest case among the transformation families covered by us in [Liang and Barron 2002].

Suppose the observations $y^{m+1} = (y_1, \ldots, y_{m+1})$ are from a location family, that is,

$$y_i = z_i + \theta,$$

for $i = 1, \ldots, m + 1$, where $\theta \in \mathbb{R}^d$ is an unknown location parameter and $z^{m+1} = (z_1, \ldots, z_{m+1})$ has a known distribution with a joint density denoted by

p_0. Then the density for y^{m+1} is given by

$$p(y^{m+1} \mid \theta) = p_0(y^{m+1} - \theta),$$

where $y^{m+1} - \theta$ is a shorthand notation for $(y_1 - \theta, \ldots, y_{m+1} - \theta)$. From now on, we will use p_0 and p as generic expressions for their corresponding marginal and conditional densities. For example, $p_0(z_{m+1})$ denotes the marginal density for z_{m+1} and $p_0(z_{m+1} \mid z^m)$ denotes the conditional density for z_{m+1} given z_1 through z_m.

Without any knowledge of θ, the predictive distribution we use for coding y_{m+1} is denoted by $q(\cdot \mid y^m)$. The expected redundancy (or the *risk* for predictive density estimation) is equal to

$$\mathbb{E}_{y^{m+1}|\theta} \log \frac{p_0(y_{m+1} - \theta)}{q(y_{m+1} \mid y^m)}. \tag{7.6}$$

Let us first focus on the class of *location-invariant* predictive density estimators. For any number $a \in \mathbb{R}^d$, a location-invariant estimator q satisfies the following equality:

$$q(y_{m+1} \mid y^m) = q(y_{m+1} - a \mid y^m - a) \tag{7.7}$$

Supposing our estimator q is location invariant, we can apply the invariance property (7.7) with $a = y_1$ to (7.6) and obtain

$$\mathbb{E}_{y^{m+1}|\theta} \log \frac{p_0(y_{m+1} - \theta)}{q(y_{m+1} - y_1 \mid 0, y_2 - y_1, \ldots, y_m - y_1)}$$
$$= \mathbb{E} \ \log \frac{p_0(y_{m+1} - \theta)}{q(u_m \mid 0, u_1, \ldots, u_{m-1})}, \tag{7.8}$$

where $u_i = y_{i+1} - y_1$, for $i = 1, \ldots, m$. Notice that u_i is also equal to $z_{i+1} - z_1$ which has a density not depending on the unknown parameter θ. Let $p_u(u_m \mid u^{m-1})$ denote the density for u_m given u^{m-1} derived from p_0. We have the quantity (7.8) equal to

$$\mathbb{E} \ \log \frac{p_0(y_{m+1} - \theta)}{p(u_m \mid u^{m-1})} + \mathbb{E}_{u^{m-1}} \Big[\mathbb{E}_{u_m} \log \frac{p_u(u_m \mid u^{m-1})}{q(u_m \mid 0, u^{m-1})} \Big].$$

Notice that the second term in the above quantity is an expected Kullback-Leibler divergence which is always bigger than or equal to zero and is equal to zero if and only if

$$q(u_m \mid 0, u^{m-1}) = p_u(u_m \mid u^{m-1}). \tag{7.9}$$

Re-expressing in terms of the y_i's and applying the invariance property of q, we have that(7.9) is equivalent to

$$q(y_{m+1} \mid y^m) = p_u(y_{m+1} - y_1 \mid y_2 - y_1, \ldots, y_m - y_1).$$

So the best invariant estimator q^* is the one equal to the right side of the above equality. This analysis for the best invariant density estimator with Kullback-Leibler loss is analogous to that originally given by Pitman [1939] (cf. [Ferguson 1967, pp.

186–187]) for finding the best invariant estimator of θ with squared error loss.

To get a final expression for q^*, we calculate $p_u(u_m \mid u^{m-1}) = p(u^m)/p(u^{m-1})$ and replace u_i by $y_{i+1} - y_1$. Since $u_i = z_{i+1} - z_1$, the joint density for $(z_1, u_1, \ldots, u_{m-1})$ is equal to $p_0(z_1, u_1 + z_1, \ldots, u_{m-1} + z_1)$. Integrating out z_1, we obtain the joint density $p_u(u^{m-1})$ which, when re-expressed in terms of y_i's, is

$$\int p_0(y_1 - \theta, y_2 - \theta, \ldots, y_m - \theta)d\theta = \int p(y^m \mid \theta)d\theta.$$

So the best invariant estimator q^* is equal to

$$q^*(y_{m+1} \mid y^m) = \frac{\int p(y^{m+1} \mid \theta)d\theta}{\int p(y^m \mid \theta)d\theta}, \tag{7.10}$$

which can be interpreted as the generalized Bayes procedure with the uniform (improper) prior $w(\theta)$ constant on $\mathbb{R}^d$ (Lebesgue measure) for location families.

To show that the best invariant estimator q^* is minimax among all the estimators, we use a result from decision theory (see [Ferguson 1967]) that constant risk plus extended Bayes implies minimax. The constant risk is a consequence of the location invariance property of q^*.

For a procedure q to be an extended Bayes means that there exists a sequence of Bayes procedures $\{p_{w_k}\}$ with proper priors w_k such that their Bayes risk differences $R_{w_k}(q) - R_{w_k}(p_{w_k})$ go to zero, as $k \to \infty$. Recall that the Bayes procedure p_{w_k} is

$$p_{w_k}(y_{m+1} \mid y^m) = \frac{\int_\Theta p(y^{m+1} \mid \theta)w_k(\theta)d\theta}{\int_\Theta p(y^m \mid \theta)w_k(\theta)d\theta},$$

and the Bayes risk $R_{w_k}(q)$ is

$$R_{w_k}(q) = \int w_k(\theta)\mathbb{E}_{y^{m+1}\mid\theta} \log \frac{p(y_{m+1} \mid y^m, \theta)}{q(y_{m+1} \mid y^m)}d\theta.$$

The Bayes risk difference for q^* is

$$R_{w_k}(q^*) - R_{w_k}(p_{w_k}) = \mathbb{E}_{y^{m+1}}^{w_k} \log \frac{p_{w_k}(y_{m+1} \mid y^m)}{q^*(y_{m+1} \mid y^m)},$$

where $\mathbb{E}_{y^{m+1}}^{w_k}$ means the expectation is taken with respect to the Bayes mixture $p_{w_k}(y^{m+1})$.

By the chain rule of information theory, the Bayes risk difference is bounded by the total risk difference conditioning on only one observation, without loss of generality, say y_1, and this total risk difference is

$$\mathbb{E}_{y^{m+1}}^{w_k} \log \frac{p_{w_k}(y_2, \ldots, y_{m+1} \mid y_1)}{q^*(y_2, \ldots, y_{m+1} \mid y_1)}$$
$$= \mathbb{E}_{y^{m+1}}^{w_k}[-\log \frac{\int p(y^{m+1} \mid \theta)w_k(\theta)\frac{1}{w_k(\theta)}d\theta}{\int p(y^{m+1})w_k(\theta)d\theta}] + \mathbb{E}_{y_1}^{w_k}[-\log \int p(y_1 \mid \theta)w_k(\theta)d\theta], \tag{7.11}$$

where we use the fact that the density for y_1 given θ, $p(y_1 \mid \theta) = p_0(y_1 - \theta)$, is also a density for θ by the symmetry between y_1 and θ, hence $\int p(y_1 \mid \theta)d\theta = 1$.

Invoking Jensen's inequality ($g(\mathbb{E}X) \leq \mathbb{E}g(X)$ for a convex function g) for both terms in (7.11), we obtain the Bayes risk difference is less than or equal to

$$\int w_k(\theta) \log w_k(\theta) d\theta - \mathbb{E}_{y_1}^{w_k} \int p_0(y_1 - \theta) \log w_k(\theta) d\theta. \tag{7.12}$$

By choosing the prior w_k to be normal with mean zero and variance k and changing variables, we finally express the bound (7.12) as C/k where C is a constant, the second moment of the distribution of z_1. So the Bayes risk difference goes to zero when k goes to infinity, provided that the distribution p_0 has finite second moment. The paper by Liang and Barron [2002] goes further to show the extended Bayes property under a weaker logarithmic moment condition and for other transformation families.

Note that for location families, when conditioning on any one observation, say the ith, the minimax predictive density for the rest of the observations is

$$\frac{\int p(y^n \mid \theta) d\theta}{\int p(y_i \mid \theta) d\theta},$$

which reduces to $\int p(y^n \mid \theta) d\theta$ since the denominator is equal to 1 for location families. Thus we obtain the same value no matter which single observation one conditions on.

Similar analysis in [Liang and Barron 2002] shows that in combined location and scale families, a minimax predictive density estimator is the generalized Bayes estimator using a uniform prior for location and log-scale, made proper by conditioning on the first two observations. Location and scale families of random variables take the form $y_i = \sigma z_i + \theta$ with probability densities of the form $p(y_i \mid \theta, \sigma) = \frac{1}{\sigma} p_0(\frac{y_i - \theta}{\sigma})$. In an independent sampling model the likelihood takes the form $p(y^n \mid \theta, \sigma) = \prod_{i=1}^n p(y_i \mid \theta, \sigma)$. Conditioning on the first two observations the minimax density for (prediction or coding of) the rest of the observations is $\int \int p(y^n \mid \theta, \sigma) d\theta d\sigma / \sigma$ divided by the corresponding value for two observations $\int \int p(y_1, y_2 \mid \theta, \sigma) d\theta d\sigma / \sigma$. This joint predictive density for $y_3, \ldots, y_n$ factors into predictive densities for each y_{m+1} given y^m as before. Each of these predictive densities takes the form $\int \int p(y_{m+1} \mid \theta, \sigma) w(\theta, \sigma \mid y^m) d\theta d\sigma$ where $w(\theta, \sigma \mid y^m)$ is the posterior distribution corresponding to our optimal prior.

We illustrate the use of this posterior for minimax predictive density estimation, location estimation, and model selection, in the next section.

7.3   Model Selection in Robust Estimation

We often encounter the problem of estimating the location parameter for some data. The sample mean is a good estimator when the data satisfy the normality assumption, but it can be a very bad one when the data are actually from a heavy-tailed distribution like the Cauchy. The predictive densities are used in formulation of optimal criteria for selection among various shapes of the density to use in the location problem.

Various robust estimators for the location parameter, such as the sample median, have been proposed and compared [Andrews et al. 1997; Huber 1981; Stigler 1977]. The mean, as a location estimator, works well for data from normal-like distribution because the sample mean is the maximum likelihood estimator (MLE) of the location. Some other robust estimates also correspond to the MLE of certain distributions. We use the mean of the minimax predictive density estimator, $\int \tilde{y} q^*(\tilde{y} \mid y^m) d\tilde{y}$, which arose importantly in the work of Pitman [1939]. It is the mean of the posterior density of θ using the uniform prior (when z has mean 0), which Pitman showed to be the minimax estimator of location with squared error loss. It is a nice confluence of decision-theoretic properties that the minimax estimator of location is the mean of the minimax predictive density estimator.

Next we pick some data sets which have been used before in comparing performances for different robust procedures and calculate the exact minimax MDL for various models to see which one is preferred and to see whether our model selection result is consistent with the results from the robustness study. Here we focus attention on five families of densities: normal, double exponential, Huber, uniform, and Cauchy. The double exponential density is $p(y \mid \theta) = p_0(y - \theta)$ with

$$p_0(y) = \frac{1}{2} e^{-|y|}.$$

Its MLE is the sample median. The Huber's density [Huber 1981, page 71] is $p(y \mid \theta) = p_0(y - \theta)$ with

$$p_0(y) = \begin{cases} C e^{-y^2/2}, & |y| \leq k, \\ C e^{-k|y|+k^2/2}, & |y| > k, \end{cases}$$

where $k = 1.5$. Its MLE is known as the Huber P15 estimator, which is the solution of

$$\sum_{i=1}^{n} \min(k, \max(-k, y_i - \theta)) = 0.$$

For the uniform density with a parameterized center and range, the MLE estimate of location is the midrange of the sample. These maximum likelihood estimates are not the focus of our attention, but because of the tradition of their use we will compare our minimax procedures to plug-in MLE estimates.

The data sets we use in this paper are from Stigler's study for robust location estimators [Stigler 1977]. They are all taken from famous experiments such as eighteenth-century attempts to determine the distance from the earth to the sun and the density of the earth, and nineteenth-century attempts to determine the speed of light. Though the focus in Stigler is on location estimation, one still needs to decide what scale to use for the various families of densities in constructing one's estimates. A rough cut would be to plug in maximum likelihood values. Here we advocate minimax predictive densities, description lengths, and parameter estimates for the combined location and scale families. As we have said the corresponding minimax predictive density is generalized Bayes using a uniform prior on the location and log-scale parameters. A side benefit of these exact minimax rules is that the tail of the predictive distribution tends to be heavier than with plug-in rules, so that the minimax procedure is more robust. Indeed, in [Liang and Barron 2002] we showed that for the normal, the minimax predictive rule is in the heavier-tailed T family of distribution. Even for the uniform density, which has no tails (and is terrible for plug-in rules as we shall see), the minimax estimator has infinite tails of polynomial decay.

For the 20 data sets we calculated our estimates for various families: normal, Huber, double exponential, Cauchy, and uniform. We find that generally the minimax estimators for the normal, Huber, and double exponential work well. Indeed, despite the presence of a few outliers, with the minimax procedures the normal family is competitive to a greater degree than one might have thought, so there is not as much need to resort to Huber's density or the two-sided exponential to achieve some robustness. Even the uniform does better than one might have thought. As for the Cauchy, we find that it is not supported by the data. In that aspect we agree with the conclusion of Stigler who said, "... the data sets considered tend to have slightly heavier tails than the normal, but that a view of the world through Cauchy-colored glasses may be overly-pessimistic."

Table 7.1 shows more detailed results on model selection for one of Stigler's data sets (table 4, data set 5) with $n = 21$ observations, which are from Short's 1763 determinations of the parallax of the sun. We focus the reader's attention first on the columns headed "minimax". Each entry denotes the log reciprocal of the minimax predictive density, $\log_2[1/q^*(y_i \mid y^{i-1})]$, for the ith observation conditioning on the previous $(i-1)$ observations, using the indicated family of density. Since combined location and scale families are considered here, we have to condition on at least two observations, that is, $i = 3, 4, \ldots, 21$. The totals used for model selection are $\log_2[1/q^*(y_3, \ldots, y_n \mid y_1, y_2)]$, which have interpretations both for minimax code length (MDL) and for Bayes factors. Plug-in type estimators, $p(y_i \mid \hat{\theta}_{i-1}, \hat{\sigma}_{i-1})$, have also been used, where $\hat{\theta}_{i-1}$ and $\hat{\sigma}_{i-1}$ are the MLE based on the previous $i - 1$ observations. The product of the plug-in rules arose in the prequential approach to statistical inference studied by Dawid [1984, 1991] and in the MDL criteria in Rissanen [1984, 1989]. For comparison purposes, we include them in Table 7.1 too. For this data set, the description lengths based on minimax predictive densities are much shorter than those based on MLE plug-in densities. The two outliers, 10.04 and 10.48, apparently have larger contributions to the totals than the other observations. Surprisingly, the description length for the 5th observation, 9.71, is pretty long, especially for the coding strategies using plug-in densities. This is because, without knowing the true parameters, 9.71 does look like an outlier among the first 5 observations, even though it is not among all the 21 observations. We can see that all the minimax predictive densities handled this situation much better than plug-in densities, because they have already taken the unknown location and scale into consideration by averaging. The extreme case is uniform: using MLE

Table 1. PREDICTIVE DENSITY ESTIMATES

Contributions of each observation to total code lengths

y_i	Huber's Density		Normal		Double Exp		Cauchy		Uniform	
	plug-in	minimax	plug-in	minimax	plug-in	minimax	plug-in	minimax	plug-in	minimax
8.43	-	-	-	-	-	-	-	-	-	-
9.09	-	-	-	-	-	-	-	-	-	-
8.5	2.24	1.81	0.17	1.12	0.54	1.06	0.35	0.92	-0.6	0.99
8.44	2.33	1.52	0.02	0.56	-1.60	0.11	2.79	-1.02	-0.6	0.4
9.71	9.13	1.81	10.86	4.06	47.28	4.55	14.92	5.60	∞	3.96
8.07	3.49	1.65	2.00	1.89	6.03	1.73	7.45	3.78	∞	2.73
8.36	2.27	1.45	0.73	1.00	-0.46	0.51	1.90	1.00	0.71	1.2
8.6	1.99	1.41	0.38	0.64	0.24	0.25	3.38	0.79	0.71	1.13
9.11	3.39	1.47	0.93	1.06	5.64	1.94	6.27	8.79	0.71	1.08
8.66	1.99	1.40	0.26	0.47	-0.19	0.19	2.07	1.97	0.71	1.04
8.58	2.03	1.39	0.23	0.41	-1.41	-0.12	1.05	1.94	0.71	1
9.54	6.41	1.59	2.93	2.52	7.50	3.47	6.43	2.51	0.71	0.98
8.34	2.59	1.42	0.81	0.91	0.49	0.60	1.83	2.02	0.71	0.95
8.55	2.08	1.39	0.34	0.47	-0.99	-0.13	0.86	1.89	0.71	0.94
9.03	2.67	1.41	0.54	0.64	2.39	1.42	4.48	1.98	0.71	0.92
10.04	8.91	1.90	6.30	4.90	8.39	5.03	6.91	11.74	∞	4.87
9.04	2.22	1.39	0.55	0.66	1.65	1.17	3.24	2.57	0.98	1.16
8.71	2.02	1.38	0.43	0.53	-0.33	0.16	0.76	2.54	0.98	1.15
10.48	10.03	2.27	8.00	6.21	8.70	5.72	6.45	3.39	∞	6.37
8.31	2.89	1.45	1.31	1.36	0.93	1.11	1.41	2.64	1.27	1.42
8.67	2.06	1.38	0.71	0.80	-0.52	0.21	0.44	2.53	1.27	1.41
Total	70.76	29.49	37.50	30.21	84.25	28.97	72.99	57.58	∞	33.7
$\hat{\theta}$	8.80	8.94	8.87	8.87	8.66	8.66	8.59	8.80	9.28	9.28

Table 7.1: Log reciprocal of predictive densities (description lengths) for Short's 1763 determinations of the parallax of the sun (in seconds of a degree). Short's data are listed in the 1st column (from [Stigler 1977], data set 5 in Table 4). The rows show the contributions of each observation to the code length or log Bayes factor. They are included to compare how plug-in and minimax procedures respond to observations which are outliers compared to those that came before. The row labelled Total provides total code lengths or log Bayes factors for model selection. The $\hat{\theta}$ row gives location estimates based on all 21 observations. For plug-in density estimation, these are the sample mean, Huber's P15 the sample median, and the Cauchy MLE, and for minimax estimation, these are the mean of the predictive densities (Pitman estimators).

plug-in densities, we will have infinity description length once the new observation is outside the range of the previous ones. Note that, for the minimax procedure, the total description length $\log_2[1/q^*(y_3, \ldots, y_n \mid y_1, y_2)]$ does not depend on the order of which the $n - 2$ observations $y_3, \ldots, y_n$ are presented, while for plug-in procedure, it does. We randomly permuted the 21 observations 1000 times and calculated the corresponding description length based on plug-in and minimax for normal and double exponential. We found that the description lengths based on minimax procedures are much less variant than those based on plug-in procedures.

Further remarks on some practicalities of data compression and prediction may be helpful. The data were, of course, not given as infinite precisions real numbers, but rather they were given to the nearest hundredth. These correspond naturally to intervals of width $1/100$ for each observation. The probabilities of these intervals would be the integrals of the densities. Since the densities here do not change perceptibly over these small intervals, the probability is the computed density value times the interval width. Correspondingly, one can report log-reciprocal probabilities from Table 7.1 simply by adding $\log_2 100$ to the entries for each observation. These sum to give the total $\log_2[1/\text{Prob}(y_3, \ldots, y_n|y_1, y_2)]$, which, when rounded up to an integer, is the length in bits of the Shannon code for $y_3, \ldots, y_n$ given the value of y_1, y_2.

For model selection, one may inspect which of the five minimax predictive distributions provides the shortest $l(y^n) = \log_2 1/q^*(y_3, \ldots, y_n|y_1, y_2)$. Then to convert this to a code length, one adds $(n-1)\log_2 100$ to convert it to log reciprocal probabilities as required for the Shannon code, and one adds two or three extra bits to communicate which of the five models is used in the final description.

We recommend, before committing to a model selection, that one consider instead the use of model averaging for data compression and prediction. Indeed as we now briefly demonstrate, model averaging provides a shorter code length. To explain, let $\pi(\cdot)$ be a distribution on the model index M, and let $\log 1/\text{Prob}(y \mid M) + \log 1/\pi(M)$ be the total code length for the data using a selected model $M = \hat{M}$, where the term $\log 1/\pi(M)$ is to describe which model is used. On the other hand, if we encode the data with respect to the mixture distribution, it yields code length $\log 1/\sum_M \text{Prob}(y \mid M)\pi(M)$ which is always shorter, because the sum is always greater than any of its terms. The relative contribution of an individual term to the sum is given by its posterior weight $\pi(M \mid y) = \pi(M)\text{Prob}(y|M)/\sum_{M'} \pi(M')\text{Prob}(y|M')$. When this weight for a selected model $\hat{M}$ is nearly 1, the mixture code and the model selection–based code have essentially the same length. Otherwise it is advantageous to code with the mixture.

For the example problem, we have five models $M = 1, 2, \ldots, 5$, we use $\pi(M) = 1/5$, and the total code lengths are all computed conditional on two observations. For the given data, none of these five individual models stands out as giving much higher probability (shorter code length) than the others as seen in the row labeled "Totals". Therefore, coding with respect to the mixture will be better than with model selection.

The corresponding approach for prediction in statistics is called Bayesian model averaging (BMA) [Hoeting, Madigan, Raftery and Volinsky 1999]. The model averaging can be implemented in one path through the data via a Bayesian update. At observation $i + 1$, the partial product $q^*(y_3, \ldots, y_i \mid y_1, y_2, M)$ is updated for each of the models. It is used to give posterior weights $\pi(M \mid y^i)$ for each model in the predictive density:

$$q_{ave}(y_{i+1} \mid y^i) = \sum_M \pi(M \mid y^i) q^*(y_{i+1} \mid y^i, M)$$

The final predictive density estimator is $q_{ave}(y \mid y^n)$ and the corresponding final location estimator is then $\hat{\theta}_{ave} = \sum_M \hat{\theta}_M \pi(M \mid y^n)$, where $\hat{\theta}_M$ is the minimax location estimator (Pitman estimator) associated with the predictive density $q^*(y \mid y^n, M)$ for the component M. In our case, the weights $\pi(M \mid y^n)$ are proportional to $2^{-l(y^n \mid M)}$ where the values for $l(y^n \mid M)$ are given in the row of totals in table 7.1. For these data the final location estimate is $\hat{\theta}_{ave} = 8.80$.

The posterior mean parameter estimates we computed here for each model are, as we said, Pitman's estimators, which are minimax in each family for the squared error loss. One may also consider parameter estimators that are minimax for the loss function one obtains by restricting the Kullback-Leibler divergence to members of a given family. For location and scale parameters the minimax estimates in this case turn out to be, for each sample y^m, the choice of parameter value δ that provides a member of the family closest in Kullback-Leibler divergence (KL) to the minimax predictive density $q^*(\cdot | y^m)$. For example, for location estimation with the two-sided exponential the minimax estimator is the median of this predictive density (rather than the median of the sample). For the normal, of course, the restriction of KL to the location family reproduces the squared error so the minimax procedure with this loss remains the posterior mean of predictive density.

7.4 Variable Selection in Linear Regression

Consider a linear regression model where we have observations y_i and the corresponding possible explanatory variables (also called covariates, predictors, or regressors) $x_{i1}, \ldots, x_{id}$. We use γ to index the possible subsets of the d variables, and $x_{i\gamma}$ to denote the column vector of the covariates in γ. Given a subset of variables γ, the observations are modeled by

$$y_i = x_{i\gamma}^t \theta_\gamma + \epsilon_i,$$

where θ_γ is a vector of unknown parameters with dimension equal to d_γ, the size of the subset γ. We all know that the more variables one includes in the regression model, the better will be the fit to the data, at the possible expense of generalizability to new cases. Such a phenomenon is called "overfitting". To avoid it, statisticians look for a subset of variables to achieve a tradeoff between fitting errors and model complexity.

If we assume the error ϵ_i has a density function p_0, then the density for y_i is given by

$$p(y \mid \theta, \gamma) = p_0(y - x_{i\gamma}^t \theta_\gamma).$$

Such a distribution family is a generalized location family. Similar analysis to what we did for location families can be applied and it reveals, as shown in [Liang and Barron 2002], that the exact minimax predictive density estimator q^* is the Bayes estimator with uniform prior over the parameter space $\mathbb{R}^{d_\gamma}$, conditioning on $m \geq d_\gamma$ observations.

In ordinary regression models, we often assume that the random error ϵ_i's are normal$(0, \sigma^2)$. Consider first the case that σ^2 is known. The corresponding minimax MDL criterion for variable selection chooses the subset of variables, γ, such that one minimizes

$$\mathrm{MDL}_\gamma = \frac{1}{2\sigma^2}[\mathrm{RSS}_N(\gamma) - \mathrm{RSS}_m(\gamma)] + \frac{1}{2}\log\frac{|(S_N(\gamma)|}{|S_m(\gamma)|},$$

where $S_m(\gamma) = \sum_{i=1}^m x_{i\gamma}x_{i\gamma}^t$ and $\mathrm{RSS}_m(\gamma) = \|y - x_\gamma^t\hat{\theta}_{\gamma,m}\|^2$, respectively, are the information matrix and the residual sum of squares using m observations. Similarly for $S_N(\gamma)$ and $\mathrm{RSS}_N(\gamma)$. Here $|\cdot|$ denotes the determinant. For model selection, we evaluate the criterion for various choices of explanatory variables x_γ (provided $d_\gamma \leq m$), and pick the one that minimizes this optimal description length criterion.

When σ^2 is unknown, we found in [Liang and Barron 2002] that the minimax procedure q^* is a generalized Bayes procedure with a uniform prior on the location and log-scale parameters and the corresponding MDL criterion is given by

$$\frac{N - d_\gamma}{2}\log\mathrm{RSS}_N(\gamma) - \frac{m - d_\gamma}{2}\log\mathrm{RSS}_m(\gamma) + \frac{1}{2}\log\frac{|S_N(\gamma)|}{|S_m(\gamma)|} - \log\frac{\Gamma(\frac{N-d_\gamma}{2})}{\Gamma(\frac{m-d_\gamma}{2})}.$$

7.5 Some Additional Discussion

The priors we showed to provide the exact minimax MDL criterion (uniform on location and log-scale parameters) were suggested earlier by researchers from other perspectives. For example, it is related to the intrinsic Bayes factor (IBF) introduced by Berger and Pericchi [1996] for the Bayesian model selection. Again, the prior is improper. So they condition on a training sample. The minimal size of the conditioning data for our minimax MDL result agrees with the minimal size of training sample in the IBF, which is the smallest number among those which provide proper predictive densities. Our work provides decision-theoretic optimality (for Kullback risk) of the given choice of priors for IBF and MDL.

The concept of conditioning arises very naturally in time series analysis and in the framework of *prediction without refitting* (see Speed and Yu [1993]) where it is of interest to do prediction for some future data based on an initial data set. But when the data does not come with natural order, it is not clear how to implement the exact MDL because of its dependency on the initial data set. An approach considered by Rissanen [1989] is to average over all possible subsets of observations of size as the conditioning observations. However, as he points out, the exact description length interpretation is then lost. A similar problem is encountered in defining intrinsic Bayes factors by Berger and Pericchi [1996]. To remove the dependence and increase the stability for the training sample, Berger and Pericchi proposed different averages (such as arithmetic, geometric, and median) over all possible training samples. Such an approach can be carried over to the exact MDL, but the description length interpretation may be lost.

The initial observations are used to convert the improper prior to a proper posterior. Therefore one way to avoid conditioning is to find a minimax Bayes procedure which is based on a proper prior. Our recent result [Liang 2002] has shown that there exists a proper Bayes minimax predictive density estimator with smaller risk than q^* everywhere provided that the dimension is bigger than 4, for normal location families.

Under current investigation is the extent to which the proper Bayes minimax density estimation solution extends to the regression setting. One special case is when the initial design matrix S_m and the total design matrix S_N are proportional to each other. Then a proper prior can be used to assign a description length for the whole data with the property that after the description of the first m observations, the description of the rest is minimax optimal (as well as proper Bayes). Moreover, compared to the minimax code with uniform prior, it provides everywhere smaller (conditional) description length. It is under current investigation whether this result can be extended to more general design matrices.

References

Andrews, D.F., P.J. Bickel, F.R. Hampel, P.J. Huber, W.H. Rogers, and J. W. Tukey (1972). *Robust Estimates of Location: Survey and Advances*. Princeton NJ: Princeton University Press.

Aslan, M. (2002). *Asymptotically Minimax Bayes Predictive Densities*. Ph.D. dissertation, Yale University, New Haven, CT: 2002.

Barron, A.R., J. Rissanen, and B. Yu (1998). The minimum description length principle in coding and modeling. *IEEE Transactions on Information Theory 44*, 2743–2760.

Berger, J.O. (1980). *Statistical Decision Theory: Foundations, Concepts, and Methods*. New York: Springer-Verlag.

Berger, J.O., and L.R. Pericchi (1996). The intrinsic Bayes factor for model selection and prediction. *Journal of the American Statistical Association 91*, 109–122.

Clarke, B.S., and A.R. Barron (1990). Information-theoretic asymptotics of Bayes methods. *IEEE Transactions on Information Theory 36*, 453–471.

Clarke, B.S., and A.R. Barron (1994). Jeffreys' prior is asymptotically least favorable under entropy risk. *Journal of Statistical Planning and Inference 41*,37–60.

Cover, T., and J. Thomas (1991). *Elements of Information Theory.* New York: Wiley.

Davisson, L.D., and A. Leon-Garcia (1980). A source matching approach to finding minimax codes. *IEEE Transactions on Information Theory 26*, 166–174.

Dawid, A.P. (1984). Present position and potential developments: Some personal views, statistical theory, the prequential approach. *Journal of the Royal Statistical Society, Series A, 147*, 278–292.

Dawid, A.P. (1991). Prequential analysis, stochastic complexity and Bayesian inference. Bayesian statistics 4, *Proceedings of the Fourth Valencia International Meeting.* Oxford, UK: Clarendon Press.

Emerson. J. (2002). *Asymptotic Admissibility and Bayesian Estimation.* Ph.D. dissertation, Yale University, New Haven, CT: 2002.

Ferguson, T.S. (1967). *Mathematical Statistics, a Decision Theoretic Approach.* New York: Academic Press.

Gallager, R. (1979). Source coding with side information and universal coding. Technical Report LIDS-P-937, MIT Laboratory Information and Decision Systems, Cambridge, MA.

Hansen, M., and B. Yu (2001). Model selection and the minimum description length principle. *Journal of the American Statistical Association, 96*, 746–774.

Hartigan, J. (1998). The maximum likelihood prior. *The Annals of Statistics, 26*(6), 2083–2103.

Haussler, D. (1997). A general minimax result for relative entropy. *IEEE Transactions on Information Theory, 43*(4), 1276–1280.

Huber, P.J. (1981). *Robust Statistics.* New York: Wiley.

Hoeting, J.A., D. Madigan, A.E. Raftery, and C.T. Volinsky (1999). Bayesian model averaging: A tutorial. *Statistical Science, 14*(4), 382–417.

Liang, F. (2002). *Exact minimax strategies for predictive density estimation and data compression.* Ph.D. dissertation, Yale University, New Haven, CT: 2002.

Liang, F., and A.R. Barron (2002). Exact minimax strategies for predictive density estimation, data compression and model selection. Accepted by *IEEE Transactions on Information Theory.* Summary appears in *Proceedings of the 2002 IEEE International Symposium on Information Theory.*

Pitman, E.J.G. (1939). The estimation of location and scale parameters of a continuous population of any given form. *Biometrika, 30*.

Rissanen, J. (1978). Modeling by shortest data description. *Automatica 14*, 465–471.

Rissanen, J. (1984). Universal coding, information, prediction and estimation. *IEEE Transactions on Information Theory 30*, 629–636.

Rissanen, J (1989). *Stochastic Complexity in Statistical Inquiry*. Singapore: World Scientific.

Rissanen, J. (1996). Fisher information and stochastic complexity. *IEEE Transactions on Information Theory 42*, 40–47.

Speed, T. and B. Yu. (1993) Model selection and prediction: normal regression. *Journal of the Institute of Statistical Mathematics 45*, 35–54.

Stigler, S.M. (1977). Do robust estimators work with real data? *Annals of Statistics*, 5(6), 1055–1098.

8 The Contribution of Parameters to Stochastic Complexity

Dean P. Foster and Robert A. Stine
Department of Statistics
The Wharton School of the University of Pennsylvania
Philadelphia, PA 19104-6302
foster@wharton.upenn.edu and stine@wharton.upenn.edu

We consider the contribution of parameters to the stochastic complexity. The stochastic complexity of a class of models is the length of a universal, one-part code representing this class. It combines the length of the maximum likelihood code with the parametric complexity, a normalization that acts as a penalty against overfitting. For models with few parameters relative to sample size, $k \ll n$, the parametric complexity is approximately $\frac{k}{2} \log n$. The accuracy of this approximation, however, deteriorates as k grows relative to n, as occurs in denoising, data mining, and machine learning. For these tasks, the contribution of parameters depends upon the complexity of the model class. Adding a parameter to a model class that already has many produces a different effect than adding one to a model class that has few. In denoising, for example, we show that the parametric complexity leads to an adaptive model selection criterion. We also address the calculation of the parametric complexity when the underlying integration is unbounded over the natural parameter space, as in Gaussian models.

8.1   Introduction, Terminology, and Notation

Parametric probability distributions p_θ provide a rich set of models for data compression, coding, and prediction. The parameters that distinguish these models often have clear physical ties to the underlying data, and so provide a comforting sense of reality and interpretation. The parameters can be linked to arrival rates, averages of underlying stochastic processes, or effects of exogenous influences that one seeks to control. When linked to a data-generating mechanism, both the number and values of the parameters θ take on substantive meaning that guides the choice of values for these tuning constants. When stripped of this connection and expanded in number, however, the choice of the best parameterization for p_θ becomes an alluring impediment. Modern computing makes it all too easy to expand the dimension of θ by adding superfluous parameters that promise much but deliver little. Indeed, overparameterized models that have been optimized to obtain the closest fit to data not only obscure any ties to an underlying data-generating mechanism but also predict poorly. Complex models found by automatic searches through massive data warehouses – data mining – nonetheless rule the day in modeling many phenomena. To choose one of these requires an automated criterion, and stochastic complexity stands out with appeal from many perspectives.

The routine use of stochastic complexity as a criterion to choose among complex models faces serious hurdles, however. These challenges arise in determining how to penalize for overparameterized models. Stochastic complexity appeared about 20 years ago [Rissanen 1986] and was found to possess a variety of optimality properties that spurred its use in hard problems. This optimality, though, lay in identifying parameters in models whose dimension remains fixed while the number of data records, n, expands. In data mining, the complexity of a model – reflected in the number of parameters – grows with the amount of data. The larger the data warehouse, the larger and more complex the variety of models one considers. If the dimension of θ grows with n, the standard asymptotic heuristics for stochastic complexity no longer obtain. For example, the familiar assessment of $\frac{1}{2}\log n$ per parameter no longer holds. Also, to make the procedure workable (in particular, to bound a key normalization), various artificial constraints have to be placed on the underlying probability models. These constraints can be provided in various forms with subtle implications for the choice of an optimal model.

We adopt the following notation and terminology that emphasize the connection between prefix codes and stochastic complexity. The response of interest is a sequence of n values $\mathbf{y} = (y_1, \ldots, y_n)$, with each y_i a point in some data space D so that $\mathbf{y} \in D^n = D \times D \times \cdots \times D$. Our examples set D to $\{0, 1\}$ for binary data and to the real line $\mathbb{R}$ in the Gaussian case. We assume that the space of possible outcomes D is known. Rephrased as a problem in coding, the objective of model selection is to represent $\mathbf{y}$ using the shortest possible uniquely decodable prefix code. Here, "shortest possible" typically has one of two meanings. In a worst-case analysis, the chosen code for $\mathbf{y}$ is the solution of a minimax problem. Let A

denote a prefix-coding algorithm. For any $\mathbf{y} \in D^n$, the codebook associated with A represents $\mathbf{y}$ using $\ell(A(\mathbf{y}))$ bits; an inverse lookup gives the decoding. A worst-case analysis seeks a code whose length attains the minimax rate

$$\min_A \max_{\mathbf{y} \in D^n} \ell(A(\mathbf{y})) \, . \tag{8.1}$$

Alternatively, one can define the best code as that with the shortest length with respect to some expectation [Barron, Rissanen, and Yu 1998].

The "models" that we study here are parametric probability distributions for the data, and so we will identify a specific codebook by its associated distribution. Because of the Kraft inequality, we can associate any prefix code with a (sub)probability distribution over D^n. Given a choice of parameters θ in some space Θ, p_θ identifies the codebook for $\mathbf{y}$ implied by, say, arithmetic coding of $\mathbf{y}$ using the probability $p_\theta(\mathbf{y})$. Implicit in our notation is that one knows the form of the mapping that takes θ into a probability. For example, p_{μ,σ^2} could denote the normal distribution with mean μ and variance σ^2. One often collects a family of these models into classes, and here we use the term "library" for a collection of codebooks indexed by $\theta \in \Theta$,

$$\mathcal{L}(\Theta) = \{p_\theta : \theta \in \Theta\} \, . \tag{8.2}$$

Continuing with the Gaussian illustration, if $\Theta = \mathbb{R} \times \mathbb{R}^+$, then we have the independently and identically distributed (i.i.d.) Gaussian library

$$\mathcal{G}(\Theta) = \left\{ p_{\mu,\sigma^2} : p_{\mu,\sigma^2}(\mathbf{y}) = \frac{e^{-\sum(y_i - \mu)^2/2}}{(2\pi\sigma^2)^{n/2}}, \mu \in \mathbb{R}, \sigma^2 > 0 \right\} \, . \tag{8.3}$$

Calligraphic letters denote libraries; we use $\mathcal{L}$ to denote a generic library and use $\mathcal{B}$ and $\mathcal{G}$ for specific libraries. Notice that although any codebook p_θ identifies a prefix code for $\mathbf{y}$, a library $\mathcal{L}(\Theta)$ does not. We cannot encode $\mathbf{y}$ using $\mathcal{L}(\Theta)$ alone; either we must identify a specific $p_\theta \in \mathcal{L}(\Theta)$ or unify the library into a single codebook.

The following section defines stochastic complexity as the length of a prefix code for $\mathbf{y}$ obtained by an "encyclopedia," a special codebook that represents a library. We introduce a special name for this codebook to distinguish it from the codebooks implied by parametric models p_θ that make up a library. With the terminology complete, Section 8.2 concludes with a guide to the rest of this chapter.

8.2   MDL and Stochastic Complexity

The *minimum description length* (MDL) criterion seeks the best library (model class) for encoding a particular sequence $\mathbf{y}$. The task is not to find the best individual codebook per se, but rather to identify a library. Since we assume that the mapping of parameters to codebooks p_θ has known form (given θ), the problem becomes one of choosing the parameter space Θ rather than the form of

p_θ. For example, we consider the problem of picking from regression models that are distinguished by the number of predictors rather than the comparison of linear regression to, say, other classes of generalized linear models.

To implement MDL thus requires a measure of how well a library can represent $\mathbf{y}$. Intuitively, one can proceed by first finding the maximum likelihood codebook in $\mathcal{L}(\Theta)$, say $p_{\hat{\theta}(\mathbf{y})}$. Since this codebook is indexed in a manner than depends upon $\mathbf{y}$, however, we cannot simply encode the data using the codebook $p_{\hat{\theta}(\mathbf{y})}$ alone because the receiver would not know which of the codebooks in $\mathcal{L}(\Theta)$ to use for the decoding. Two-part codes provide an obvious solution: identify the codebook in $\mathcal{L}(\Theta)$ by prefixing the code obtained by $p_{\hat{\theta}(\mathbf{y})}$ with another code identifying $\hat{\theta}(\mathbf{y})$. Through some clever arguments reviewed in [Rissanen 1989], Rissanen shows that one achieves a shorter overall code by coarsely identifying $\hat{\theta}(\mathbf{y})$. The use of two-part codes, however, introduces two problems. First, it is often neither easy nor obvious to decide how to round $\hat{\theta}(\mathbf{y})$; the discrete "spiral" codes given in [Rissanen 1983] illustrate some of the difficulties. Second, two-part codes are not "Kraft-tight"; the resulting implicit probability on D^n sums to less than 1.

Stochastic complexity addresses both problems. First, it provides a direct construction that removes the subjective choice of how to encode $\hat{\theta}(\mathbf{y})$. Second, stochastic complexity encodes $\mathbf{y}$ with an efficient, one-part code. The underlying construction is rather natural: normalize the maximum likelihood code $p_{\hat{\theta}(\mathbf{y})}$ so that it becomes a probability. Since the data itself determine the maximum likelihood estimator (MLE), $p_{\hat{\theta}(\mathbf{y})}$ is not a subprobability,

$$\int_{D^n} p_{\hat{\theta}(\mathbf{y})}(\mathbf{y})d\mathbf{y} > 1 \ ,$$

(assuming a continuous model) and hence cannot define a prefix code for $\mathbf{y}$. The code length exceeds $\log 1/p_{\hat{\theta}}(\mathbf{y})$ in order to identify which codebook in $\mathcal{L}(\Theta)$ was used to represent the data. Rather than tack on a code that identifies $\hat{\theta}(\mathbf{y})$, one can instead convert the library back into a codebook. We distinguish these unified libraries from the parametric codebooks p_θ by calling them *encyclopedias*. The length of the code for $\mathbf{y}$ given by an encyclopedia is obtained by normalizing $p_{\hat{\theta}(\mathbf{y})}$ to generate a probability over D^n. This normalization requires us to divide by precisely the same integral that shows that $p_{\hat{\theta}(\mathbf{y})}$ is not a probability,

$$C\left(\mathcal{L}, \Theta, D^n\right) = \int_{D^n} p_{\hat{\theta}(\mathbf{y})}(\mathbf{y})d\mathbf{y} \ , \quad \text{where} \quad \hat{\theta}(\mathbf{y}) = \arg\max_{\theta \in \Theta} p_\theta(\mathbf{y}) \ . \tag{8.4}$$

Though this notation is cumbersome, we need these arguments to distinguish different forms of this normalization. The one-part code obtained from the resulting encyclopedia encodes $\mathbf{y}$ using the normalized maximum likelihood (NML) probability, denoted

$$g_{\mathcal{L}(\Theta)}(\mathbf{y}) = \frac{p_{\hat{\theta}(\mathbf{y})}(\mathbf{y})}{C\left(\mathcal{L}, \Theta, D^n\right)} \ . \tag{8.5}$$

The NML encyclopedia possesses many advantages. Not only can $g_{\mathcal{L}(\Theta)}$ be computed routinely without the need to round the MLE, the resulting Kraft-tight code obtains the minimax rate (8.1) [Shtarkov 1987].

The stochastic complexity of the library $\mathcal{L}(\Theta)$ for representing $\mathbf{y}$ is defined to be the length of the code provided by the resulting NML encyclopedia $g_{\mathcal{L}(\Theta)}$,

$$L(\mathbf{y}; \mathcal{L}, \Theta, D^n) = \log C(\mathcal{L}, \Theta, D^n) + \log \frac{1}{p_{\hat{\theta}(\mathbf{y})}(\mathbf{y})} \ , \quad \hat{\theta}(\mathbf{y}) \in \Theta \ . \qquad (8.6)$$

The MDL criterion then picks the library that minimizes the stochastic complexity. The log of the normalizing constant, $\log C(\mathcal{L}, \Theta, D^n)$, is known as the *parametric complexity* of the library. It compensates for overfitting an excessive number of parameters; thus it acts like a penalty term.

The use of stochastic complexity can often be simplified by using a particularly simple asymptotic approximation for the parametric complexity. The underlying asymptotic analysis fixes the dimension of the parameter space Θ and lets the length n tend to infinity. Under suitable regularity conditions, it follows that [Rissanen 1996]

$$\log C(\mathcal{L}, \Theta, D^n) = \frac{\dim(\Theta)}{2} \log \frac{n}{2\pi} + \log \int_{\Theta} |I(\theta)|^{1/2} d\theta + o(1), \qquad (8.7)$$

where $I(\theta)$ is the asymptotic Fisher information matrix with elements

$$I_{ij}(\theta) = \lim_{n \to \infty} -\frac{1}{n} \frac{\partial^2 \log p_\theta(y)}{\partial \theta_i \partial \theta_j} \ . \qquad (8.8)$$

The leading summand of (8.7) suggests that, in regular problems, the addition of each parameter increases the stochastic complexity by about $\frac{1}{2} \log n$. This interpretation motivates the common association of MDL with the Bayesian information criterion (BIC) whose penalty also grows logarithmically in n.

This approximation is both appealing and effective when used in the context of comparing a sequence of nested models of small dimension. For example, it works well in choosing among low-order polynomials or autoregressions (although comparisons tend to favor other criteria if prediction is the objective). For choosing among models of large dimension, such as those we use to predict credit risk [Foster and Stine 2002], however, the classic formulation of MDL (i.e., penalizing by the number of parameters times $\frac{1}{2} \log n$) no longer applies. For parameter-rich, data-mining models, this approximation no longer offers a useful measure of the complexity of the class.

The next three sections investigate the role of parameters in stochastic complexity, with an emphasis on models with many parameters. In Section 8.3, we consider the role of parameters in the Bernoulli library, a library that can be converted into an encyclopedia. We show that the contribution of a parameter depends on the complexity of the model itself; adding a parameter to a model with many adds less than adding one to a model with few. In Sections 8.4 and 8.5, we consider the parametric complexity of encyclopedias for Gaussian libraries. Section 8.4 considers methods for bounding the parametric complexity of a low-dimension Gaussian library, and

Section 8.5 considers high-dimensional models associated with denoising.

8.3 Parameters and the Bernoulli Library

We begin our discussion of stochastic complexity by choosing a context in which it all works. For this section, the data are binary with $D = \{0,1\}$. Codebooks for $\mathbf{y} \in \{0,1\}^n$ in the usual library $\mathcal{B}$ define probabilities of the form

$$p_\theta(\mathbf{y}) = \theta^{\sum y_i} (1-\theta)^{n-\sum y_i}, \tag{8.9}$$

with the parameter space $\Theta = [0,1]$. Given a binary sequence $\mathbf{y}$, the library $\mathcal{B}([0,1])$ of i.i.d. codebooks fixes θ for all i; larger parameter spaces allow this probability to vary over observations. In either case, we can compute the parametric complexity explicitly and see how the dimension of Θ affects the stochastic complexity.

The existence of a sufficient statistic simplifies this calculation. Under the assumed model class, the data are modeled as a realization of a sequence of independent Bernoulli random variables. Let $S_n = \sum_i Y_i$ denote the sum of these hypothetical random variables, and let $\hat{\theta} = S_n/n$ denote the MLE for θ. The sufficiency of S_n for θ allows us to factor the distribution of $\mathbf{Y} = (Y_1, \ldots, Y_n)$ into the product of the distribution of S_n and that of $\mathbf{Y}$ conditional on S_n (which is thus free of θ). Using these sufficiency arguments, the normalizing constant is

$$\begin{aligned}
C(\mathcal{B}, [0,1], \{0,1\}^n) &= \sum_{\mathbf{y}} p_{\hat{\theta}(\mathbf{y})}(\mathbf{y}) \\
&= \sum_{s=0}^{n} p_{\hat{\theta}(\mathbf{y})}(S_n = s) \sum_{\mathbf{y}:\hat{\theta}(\mathbf{y})=s/n} p(\mathbf{y} \mid S_n = s) \\
&= \sum_{s=0}^{n} p_{\hat{\theta}(\mathbf{y})}(S_n = s) \\
&= \sum_{s=0}^{n} \binom{n}{s}(s/n)^s(1-s/n)^{n-s}, \tag{8.10}
\end{aligned}$$

where p without a subscript denotes a probability distribution that is free of parameters. If we use Stirling's formula to approximate the factorials in (8.10), we obtain

$$\binom{n}{s}(s/n)^s(1-s/n)^{n-s} \approx \frac{\sqrt{n}}{\sqrt{2\pi s(n-s)}}.$$

This approximation is quite accurate except near the boundaries of the parameter space. (The approximation has singularities for $s = 0, n$, but the actual summands are 1. A Poisson approximation is more accurate at the extremes than this, essentially, normal approximation.) Integrating the approximation gives

$$C(\mathcal{B}([0,1]), [0,1], \{0,1\}^n) = \frac{\sqrt{n}}{\sqrt{2\pi}} \int_0^n \frac{1}{\sqrt{s(n-s)}} ds + O(1) = \sqrt{\frac{n\pi}{2}} + O(1). \tag{8.11}$$

The error in this approximation is about 2/3.

The stochastic complexity (8.6) of the i.i.d. library $\mathcal{B}([0,1])$ for $\mathbf{y}$ is thus the sum of the code length for $\mathbf{y}$ plus the parametric complexity,

$$L(\mathbf{y}; \mathcal{B}, [0,1], \{0,1\}^n) = \tfrac{1}{2} \log \tfrac{n\pi}{2} + \log 1/p_{\hat{\theta}(\mathbf{y})}(\mathbf{y}) + O(1/\sqrt{n}) \ .$$

The parametric complexity agrees with the asymptotic approximation (8.7). The one parameter θ contributes about $\tfrac{1}{2} \log n$ the stochastic complexity.

The stochastic complexity of $\mathcal{B}(\Theta)$ is invariant of one-to-one transformations of Θ, even if such a transformation makes Θ unbounded. For example, if we write p_θ in the canonical form of an exponential family, then

$$p_\theta(y) = e^{y \log \theta/(1-\theta) + \log 1 - \theta}, \quad y = 0, 1,$$

or

$$p_\eta(y) = e^{y \, \eta + \psi(\eta)}, \quad y = 0, 1,$$

with $\eta = \log \theta/(1 - \theta)$, the log of the odds ratio. Expressed in this form, the parameter space becomes $\mathbb{R}$. The stochastic complexity remains the same, though, since transforming the parameter space does not change the likelihood obtained by the various codebooks. The MLE for η is $\hat{\eta} = \log \hat{\theta}/(1 - \hat{\theta})$ and

$$\sum_{\mathbf{y}} p_{\hat{\eta}(\mathbf{y})}(\mathbf{y}) = \sum_{\mathbf{y}} p_{\hat{\theta}(\mathbf{y})}(\mathbf{y}) \ .$$

The contribution of a parameter does change, however, if we expand Θ to dimensions on the order of the number of observations. While artificial, perhaps, in this context, the use of stochastic complexity in data mining requires one to assess and compare models of large dimension. With a richer class of models, we no longer obtain an appealing separation of parameters from data. In such problems, the asymptotic approximation (8.7) fails because the dimension of Θ grows with n. An alternative, local asymptotic analysis leads to a rather different characterization of the amount to penalize for each parameter, one for which the penalty is proportional to the number of parameters rather than $\log n$ [Foster and Stine 1999].

Consider the "saturated" Bernoulli library $\mathcal{B}$ with the parameter space extended to $\Theta = [0,1] \times [0,1] \times \cdots \times [0,1] = [0,1]^n$, allowing one parameter for each observation. The MLE for $\theta^n = (\theta_1, \ldots, \theta_n)$ is $\hat{\theta}^n(\mathbf{y}) = \mathbf{y}$. As a result, the length of the maximum likelihood code for $\mathbf{y}$ collapses to zero,

$$\log \frac{1}{p_{\hat{\theta}^n(\mathbf{y})}(\mathbf{y})} = \log 1 = 0 \ .$$

The parametric complexity of $\mathcal{B}([0,1]^n)$ now comprises *all* of the stochastic complexity of the encyclopedia, with all of the information from the data concentrated in the parameters,

$$\log C(\mathcal{B}, [0,1]^n, \{0,1\}^n) = \log \sum_{\mathbf{y}} p_{\hat{\theta}^n(\mathbf{y})}(\mathbf{y}) = \log 2^n = n \ .$$

Each parameter contributes just 1 bit, not $\frac{1}{2}\log n$, to the complexity of $\mathcal{B}([0,1]^n)$. Parameters in libraries for which the dimension of Θ is $O(n)$ evidently add less to the complexity than those in models of small, fixed dimension.

The concentration of the stochastic complexity into the parametric complexity leads to a dilemma when one then tries to use stochastic complexity to choose among model classes. The stochastic complexity of the saturated library $\mathcal{B}([0,1]^n)$ is n, agreeing with the expected stochastic complexity of the very different, "null" library $\mathcal{B}(\{\frac{1}{2}\})$ which fixes $\theta_i = \frac{1}{2}$ for all i. On average, stochastic complexity cannot distinguish the saturated library that varies θ to match each observation from a dogmatic "null" library that treats the data as i.i.d. noise. Models that treat the data as pure signal have the same stochastic complexity (on average) as those which treat the data as pure noise. Rissanen [2000] encounters such ambiguity between "signal" and "noise" when using MDL in the denoising problem where the dimension of the class of models is on the order of n.

8.4   Complexity of the Gaussian Library

The parametric complexity of many libraries is unbounded, and as a result one must deviate from the clean definition of stochastic complexity that we have illustrated so far. Perhaps the most important cases of this phenomenon are the Gaussian libraries $\mathcal{G}(\Theta)$ introduced in (8.3). The codebooks in a Gaussian library model $\mathbf{y}$ as though it were a realization of random variables $Y_i \stackrel{\text{i.i.d.}}{\sim} N(\mu, \sigma^2)$. A Gaussian library cannot be converted into an encyclopedia like those representing a Bernoulli library $\mathcal{B}$. The asymptotic approximation to the parametric complexity (8.7) reveals the problem: the Fisher information (8.8) for μ is constant but the natural range for this parameter is $\mathbb{R}$. To see the problem more clearly, though, we will avoid this approximation and work directly from the definition.

Assume for the moment that $\sigma^2 = 1$ is known and focus on the one-parameter library with unknown mean,

$$\mathcal{G}(\mathbb{R}) = \{p_\mu : p_\mu(\mathbf{y}) = \frac{e^{-\sum(y_i - \mu)^2/2}}{(2\pi)^{n/2}}, \ \mu \in \mathbb{R}\} \ .$$

Following [Barron et al. 1998], the parametric complexity is most easily found by once again using the sufficiency of the sample average $\overline{Y} = \sum Y_i/n$ for μ. Modeled as a sample of normals, the distribution of $\mathbf{y}$ factors into

$$p_\mu(\mathbf{y}) = p_\mu(\overline{y}) \, p(\mathbf{y}|\overline{y})$$

where $p(\mathbf{y}|\overline{y})$ is the conditional distribution of $\mathbf{y}$ given $\overline{Y}$, and thus is free of μ. The distribution of the sufficient statistic is $N(\mu, \sigma^2/n)$,

$$p_\mu(\overline{y}) = \left(\frac{n}{2\pi\sigma^2}\right)^{1/2} e^{-\frac{n}{2\sigma^2}(\overline{y}-\mu)^2} \ .$$

When we set $\mu = \overline{y}$ in the NML distribution, this density reduces to a constant,

$$p_{\overline{y}}(\overline{y}) = \left(\frac{n}{2\pi\sigma^2}\right)^{1/2} \ . \tag{8.12}$$

Since the parametric complexity $\log C(\mathcal{G}, \mathbb{R}, \mathbb{R}^n)$ (with both Θ and D set to the real line) is unbounded, we cannot use stochastic complexity as defined as a criterion for model selection.

One approach to this dilemma is to bound the parametric complexity by constraining Θ. For example, the parametric complexity is finite if we constrain Θ to the ball of radius $R > 0$ around the origin, $\Theta_R = \{\mu : -R \leq \mu \leq R\}$. It is important to note that R is a constant chosen prior to looking at the data. This constraint has no effect on the range of data; it only limits the values allowed for μ and its MLE,

$$\hat{\mu}_R(\mathbf{y}) = \begin{cases} -R, & \overline{y} < -R \ , \\ \overline{y}, & -R \leq \overline{y} \leq R \ , \\ R, & R < \overline{y} \ . \end{cases}$$

The parametric complexity of $\mathcal{G}(\Theta_R)$ is then 1 plus a multiple of the radius of the parameter space,

$$\begin{aligned} C(\mathcal{G}, \Theta_R, \mathbb{R}^n) &= \int_{\mathbb{R}^n} p_{\hat{\mu}_R(\mathbf{y})}(\overline{y}) p(\mathbf{y}|\overline{y}) d\mathbf{y} \\ &= 2 \int_R^\infty \left(\frac{n}{2\pi\sigma^2}\right)^{1/2} e^{-(\overline{y}-R)^2/2} \ d\overline{y} + \int_{-R}^R \left(\frac{n}{2\pi\sigma^2}\right)^{1/2} \ d\overline{y} \\ &= 1 + \frac{2\sqrt{n}R}{\sqrt{2\pi\sigma^2}} \ . \end{aligned} \tag{8.13}$$

The addition of 1 in (8.13) arises from integrating over those $\mathbf{y}$ for which the MLE lies on the boundary of Θ_R. The associated stochastic complexity for an arbitrary $\mathbf{y} \in \mathbb{R}^n$ is then

$$\begin{aligned} L_{\mathcal{G}(\Theta_R)}(\mathbf{y}) &= \log C(\mathcal{G}, \Theta_R, \mathbb{R}^n) + \log 1/p_{\hat{\mu}_R(\mathbf{y})}(\mathbf{y}) \\ &= \log(1 + \frac{2\sqrt{n}R}{\sqrt{2\pi\sigma^2}}) + \log 1/p_{\overline{y}}(\mathbf{y}) + K(p_{\overline{y}}\|p_{\hat{\mu}_R}) \ . \end{aligned}$$

The last term $K(p_{\overline{y}}\|p_{\hat{\mu}})$ is the Kullback-Leibler divergence between the distribution $p_{\hat{\mu}}$, which uses the constrained MLE, and $p_{\overline{y}}$, which uses the unconstrained sample average,

$$K(p\|q) = \int_{D^n} p(\mathbf{y}) \ \log \frac{p(\mathbf{y})}{q(\mathbf{y})} \ d\mathbf{y} \ .$$

This approach allows us to use stochastic complexity as before, with a single encyclopedia representing a library. The sender and receiver can agree to a particular choice of R prior to encoding $\mathbf{y}$. Stine and Foster [2000] label (8.13) the *unconditional parametric complexity*.

This unconditional approach introduces a problem, however, into the use of stochastic complexity as the criterion for MDL. One must decide prior to observing $\mathbf{y}$ how to constrain Θ. Restricting μ to lie in Θ_R may seem natural, but certainly other choices are possible. [Stine and Foster 2000] propose a competitive analysis to pick optimal constraints, but here we consider an alternative method that bounds the parametric complexity in a rather different manner. This alternative *constrains the data* rather than the parameter space.

The most common method for bounding the parametric complexity constrains the data space D^n rather than Θ. Let D_R^n denote the subset of $\mathbb{R}^n$ for which the average of $\mathbf{y}$ lies inside Θ_R,

$$D_R^n = \{\mathbf{y} : \mathbf{y} \in \mathbb{R}^n, -R \leq \overline{y} \leq R\} . \tag{8.14}$$

Under this constraint, the normalizing constant becomes

$$C(\mathcal{G}, \mathbb{R}, D_R^n) = \int_{D_R^n} p_{\overline{y}}(\mathbf{y}) \, dy = \frac{2\sqrt{n}R}{\sqrt{2\pi\sigma^2}} , \tag{8.15}$$

which is one less than the constant obtained by constraining the parameter space. Notice that restricting $\mathbf{y}$ to D_R^n implies a constraint on Θ as well,

$$C(\mathcal{G}, \mathbb{R}, D_R^n) = C(\mathcal{G}, \Theta_R, D_R^n) .$$

To distinguish such implicit constraints on Θ from those set externally, our notation omits the implicit constraints on Θ when induced by those placed on $\mathbf{y}$.

When constraining $\mathbf{y}$, one must ensure that $\mathbf{y}$ lies in D_R^n or else the library lacks a codebook for the data. Thus, in applications, one replaces the a priori bound R by a data-dependent constraint, say $R(\mathbf{y})$. $R(\mathbf{y})$ is usually chosen so that the unconstrained MLE lies in the implicit parameter space, $\overline{y} \in \Theta_{R(\mathbf{y})}$. This measure of complexity, however, ignores the fact that the receiver needs to know $\overline{y}$. A feature of $\mathbf{y}$ has "leaked out" of the normalization process and must be encoded separately. Constraining Θ directly produces a "one-volume" encyclopedia that generates a prefix code for $\mathbf{y}$. Constraining the data space D^n leads to a "multi-volume" encyclopedia that cannot generate a prefix code — the receiver does not know which of the volumes to use to decode the message. Consequently, one must add to the stochastic complexity the length of a prefix that identifies $R(\mathbf{y})$,

$$L(\mathbf{y}; \mathcal{G}, \mathbb{R}, D_{R(\mathbf{y})}^n) = \ell(R(\mathbf{y})) + \log\left(\frac{2\sqrt{n}R(\mathbf{y})}{\sqrt{2\pi\sigma^2}}\right) + \log 1/p_{\overline{y}}(\mathbf{y}) .$$

The length of the code for $R(\mathbf{y})$ lies outside the framework of the underlying NML model, and thus this approach sacrifices its minimax optimality. In a one-parameter model, the addition of a code for $R(\mathbf{y})$ has little effect on the selection of a model by MDL, especially when formulated along the lines of, say, $R(\mathbf{y}) = 2^{2k(\mathbf{y})}$ for some integer $k(\mathbf{y})$ as in [Rissanen 2000]. The next section shows, however, that the impact of "leaking information" outside the NML normalization grows as one adds more parameters.

Before moving to models of large dimension, the presence of data-dependent bounds introduces other problems as well. In particular, the form of the data-driven constraints can determine whether a library has infinite or finite complexity. We illustrate this aspect of data-driven constraints by introducing an unknown variance σ^2. To avoid singularities in the likelihood, it is natural to bound σ^2 away from zero, say $0 < \sigma_0^2 \leq \sigma^2$.

With σ^2 estimated from $\mathbf{y}$, the parametric complexity depends upon how one constrains $\mathbf{y}$. If $\mathbf{y}$ is constrained so that $\overline{y} \in \Theta_R$, the parametric complexity is infinite unless we introduce an upper bound for σ^2. Barron et al. [1998] and Hansen and Yu [2001] employ this type of constraint. If instead $\mathbf{y}$ is constrained by restricting $\overline{y}$ to a region defined on a standardized scale, say $\overline{y} \in \Theta_{z\sigma/\sqrt{n}}$ as in [Rissanen 1999], then the parametric complexity is finite, *without* the need for an upper bound on σ^2. This effect of the "shape" of the constraints does not appear if we constrain the parameter space rather than the data.

We begin again with the factorization of the likelihood $p_{\mu,\sigma^2}(\mathbf{y})$ implied by sufficiency. The statistics $\overline{Y}$ and $S^2 = \sum(Y_i - \overline{Y})^2/n$ are independent and jointly sufficient for μ and σ^2. The Gaussian likelihood thus factors into a product of three terms,

$$p_{\mu,\sigma^2}(\mathbf{y}) = p(\mathbf{y}|\overline{y}, s^2)\, p_{\mu,\sigma^2}(\overline{y})\, p_{\sigma^2}(s^2)\,,$$

where $p_{\sigma^2}(s^2)$ denotes the chi-squared density of S^2,

$$
\begin{aligned}
p_{\sigma^2}(s^2) &= \frac{\left(\frac{ns^2}{\sigma^2}\right)^{\alpha-1} e^{-ns^2/2\sigma^2}}{\Gamma(\alpha)2^\alpha}\frac{n}{\sigma^2}\\
&= \frac{c_n}{\sigma^2}\left(\frac{s^2}{\sigma^2}\right)^{\alpha-1} e^{-ns^2/2\sigma^2}\,,
\end{aligned}
\tag{8.16}
$$

where the constants c_n and α are

$$c_n = \frac{n^\alpha}{\Gamma(\alpha)2^\alpha}\,,\quad \alpha = \frac{n-1}{2}\,. \tag{8.17}$$

The conditional density of the data $p(Y|\overline{Y}, S^2)$ given $\overline{Y}$ and S^2 is free of μ and σ^2.

Now let $\hat{D}^n$ denote a subset of $\mathbb{R}^n$ for which the MLE lies within $\hat{\Theta}$. Given this constraint, the parametric complexity is the log of the following integral:

$$
\begin{aligned}
C(\mathcal{G}, \Theta, \hat{D}^n) &= \int_{\hat{\Theta}}\int_{\hat{D}^n} p(\mathbf{y}|\overline{y}, s^2)p_{\overline{y},s^2}(\overline{y})\, p_{s^2}(s^2)d\mathbf{y}\, d\overline{y}\, ds^2\\
&= k_n \int_{\hat{\Theta}}\left(\frac{1}{s^2}\right)^{3/2} d\overline{y}\, ds^2\,,
\end{aligned}
\tag{8.18}
$$

where k_n collects constants from the chi-squared and normal densities,

$$k_n = c_n \frac{\sqrt{n}e^{-n/2}}{\sqrt{2\pi}} = \frac{n^{\alpha+1/2}e^{-n/2}}{\sqrt{2\pi}\,\Gamma(\alpha)\,2^\alpha} \ . \tag{8.19}$$

To see how the form of the constraints affects the parametric complexity, we just plug them into the integral (8.18) and evaluate. With $\mathbf{y}$ constrained so that $\overline{y} \in \Theta_R$ and $s^2 \geq \sigma_0^2$, the integral splits as

$$\int p_{\overline{y},s^2(\mathbf{y})}(\mathbf{y})d\mathbf{y} = k_n \int_{-R}^{R} d\overline{y} \int_{\sigma_0^2}^{\infty} \left(\frac{1}{s^2}\right)^{3/2} ds^2 = k_n \frac{2\,R}{\sigma_0^2} \ .$$

The conditional parametric complexity is finite. On the other hand, with $\mathbf{y}$ constrained so that $\overline{y}$ lies within a standardized range (e.g., we plan to encode data whose mean lies within 20 standard errors of zero), the parametric complexity is infinite,

$$\int p_{\overline{y},s^2(\mathbf{y})}(\mathbf{y})d\mathbf{y} = k_n \int_{\sigma_0^2}^{\infty} \int_{-zs/\sqrt{n}}^{zs/\sqrt{n}} \left(\frac{1}{s^2}\right)^{3/2} d\overline{y}\, ds^2 = 2k_n z \int_{\sigma_0^2}^{\infty} \frac{1}{s^2}\, ds^2 \ .$$

One can bound the complexity in this case by adding a further constraint to the data that restricts $\mathbf{y}$ to those sequences for which, say, $s^2 \leq \sigma_1^2$.

Bounding the parametric complexity by constraining $\mathbf{y}$ thus gives two rather different measures of the complexity of these Gaussian libraries. Consider the effect of restricting $\mathbf{y}$ to those sequences for which $s^2 \leq \sigma_1^2$. If $\mathbf{y}$ is also constrained so that $\overline{y}$ is bounded on the standardized scale, the parametric complexity is a multiple of $\log\left(\sigma_1^2/\sigma_0^2\right)$. If $\overline{y}$ is bounded directly, the parametric complexity is a multiple of $1/\sigma_0^2 - 1/\sigma_1^2$. One tends to infinity with σ_1^2, whereas the other remains finite.

Unconditional bounds, in contrast, give the same answer whether μ is restricted directly or on a standardized scale. In either case, the parametric complexity is unbounded. Denote the constrained parameter space by

$$\Theta_R^{\sigma_1^2} = \{(\mu, \sigma^2): \ -R \leq \mu \leq R, \sigma_0^2 \leq \sigma^2 \leq \sigma_1^2\} \ .$$

Let $\hat{\theta}$ denote the MLE for this space. These constraints are "rectangular" in the sense that

$$\hat{\theta} = (\hat{\mu}, \hat{\sigma}^2) = \left(\min(\max(-R, \overline{y}), R), \min(\max(\sigma_0^2, s^2), \sigma_1^2)\right) \ .$$

If $(\overline{y}, s^2)$ lies outside of $\Theta_R^{\sigma_1^2}$, then one obtains the MLE by projecting this point perpendicularly onto the boundary of $\Theta_R^{\sigma_1^2}$. When $(\overline{y}, s^2)$ violates both constraints, the projected point is a "corner" of $\Theta_R^{\sigma_1^2}$ [e.g., one corner is (R, σ_1^2)]. For these rectangular bounds, the normalizing constant is

$$C(\mathcal{G}, \Theta_R^{\sigma_1^2}, \mathbb{R}^n) = \int_{\mathbb{R}^n} p_{\hat{\mu},\hat{\sigma}^2}(\mathbf{y})\, d\mathbf{y}$$

$$\geq \int_{\mathbf{y}:\sigma_0^2 \leq s^2 \leq \sigma_1^2} p_{\hat{\mu},s^2}(\mathbf{y})\, d\mathbf{y}$$

$$= \int_{\sigma_0^2}^{\sigma_1^2} p_{s^2}(s^2) \left(1 + \frac{2\sqrt{n}R}{\sqrt{2\pi s^2}}\right) ds^2$$

$$= c_n e^{-n/2} \int_{\sigma_0^2}^{\sigma_1^2} \frac{1}{s^2} ds^2 + 2k_n R \left(\frac{1}{\sigma_0^2} - \frac{1}{\sigma_1^2}\right)$$

$$= c_n e^{-n/2} \left(\log \frac{\sigma_1^2}{\sigma_0^2}\right) + 2k_n R \left(\frac{1}{\sigma_0^2} - \frac{1}{\sigma_1^2}\right).$$

Notice that $C(\mathcal{G}, \Theta_R^{\sigma_1^2}, \mathbb{R}^n)$ has both the log of the ratio of the bounds for σ^2 as well as the difference of the ratios. Thus, $C(\mathcal{G}, \Theta_R^{\sigma_1^2}, \mathbb{R}^n)$ tends to infinity with σ_1^2.

A similar calculation shows that the normalizing constant also tends to infinity when the constraints for μ are specified on the standardized scale. If we restrict μ to $\Theta_{z\sigma/\sqrt{n}}$, the projections of $(\overline{y}, s^2)$ onto the parameter space are no longer rectangular. Nonetheless, we can show that the normalization again tends to infinity. Regardless of the location of $\overline{y}$, the probability at the MLE is at least as large as that at a restricted location, $p_{\hat{\mu}, \hat{\sigma}^2} \geq p_{0, \hat{\sigma}^2}$. Consequently, the normalizing constant is bounded below as follows:

$$
\begin{aligned}
C(\mathcal{G}, \Theta_{z\sigma/\sqrt{n}}^{\sigma_1^2}, \mathbb{R}^n) &= \int_{\mathbb{R}^n} p_{\hat{\mu}, \hat{\sigma}^2}(\mathbf{y})\, d\mathbf{y} \\
&\geq \int_{\mathbb{R}^n} p_{0, \hat{\sigma}^2}(\mathbf{y})\, d\mathbf{y} \\
&\geq \int_{\mathbf{y}:\sigma_0^2 \leq s^2 \leq \sigma_1^2} p_{0, s^2}(\mathbf{y})\, d\mathbf{y} \\
&= \int_{\sigma_0^2}^{\sigma_1^2} p_{s^2}(s^2) ds^2 \\
&= c_n e^{-n/2}\, \log \frac{\sigma_1^2}{\sigma_0^2}.
\end{aligned}
$$

Again, the normalizing constant tends to infinity as σ_1^2 grows.

8.5   Complexity of Libraries with High Dimension

We consider the use of MDL in the so-called denoising problem. In denoising, the response $\mathbf{y}$ is modeled as a weighted average of selected orthogonal signal vectors $\{W_j^n\}_{j=1}^n$ plus Gaussian noise,

$$\mathbf{Y} = \sum_{j \in \gamma} \beta_j W_j^n + \sigma \epsilon^n, \quad \epsilon_i \overset{\text{i.i.d.}}{\sim} N(0,1). \tag{8.20}$$

The range of the summation is a set of indices $\gamma \subset \{1, \dots, n\}$ that indicates which of the signal vectors have nonzero coefficients. If $j \in \gamma$, then W_j^n affects $\mathbf{y}$; otherwise, the inclusion of W_j^n only adds noise to a fitted reconstruction. The signal vectors might be wavelets, sines and cosines, or any other orthogonal basis for $\mathbb{R}^n$. The problem in denoising is to identify γ; ideally, the reconstruction requires only a small subset of the signal vectors when the basis is well-chosen. Thus, denoising amounts to variable selection in an orthogonal regression in which one has just as many *possible* predictors as observations.

Because the signal vectors are orthogonal, these models have a convenient canonical form. We can rotate any family of signal vectors into the standard basis for $\mathbb{R}^n$ in which $W_j^n = e_j^n = (0, \ldots, 1_j, 0, \ldots, 0)$. When (8.20) is re-expressed in this way, the underlying probability model becomes the multivariate normal location model, $\mathbf{Y} = \mu^n + \sigma\,\epsilon$ for $\mu^n \in \mathbb{R}^n$. The libraries used in denoising thus generalize the i.i.d library (8.3) by greatly expanding the parameter space

$$\mathcal{G}(\Theta) = \{p_{\mu^n} : p_{\mu^n}(\mathbf{y}) = \frac{e^{-\sum(y_i - \mu_i)^2/2}}{(2\pi)^{n/2}}, \mu^n \in \Theta\}. \qquad (8.21)$$

Each codebook in $\mathcal{G}(\Theta)$ describes $\mathbf{y}$ as a collection of independent, normal random variables, $Y_i \sim N(\mu_i, 1)$, $i = 1, \ldots, n$. The trick is to figure out which $\mu_i \neq 0$. We include the saturated library that allows one parameter per observation and duck some of the boundary problems described in the prior section by fixing $\sigma^2 = 1$. Obviously, one would need to estimate σ^2 in an application. In wavelet denoising [Donoho and Johnstone 1994], σ^2 can be estimated quite well from the coefficients of the $n/2$ most localized basis elements.

Our interest lies in using stochastic complexity as the criterion for picking the best dimension for the parameter space. As a first step, consider libraries that are identified by a given set γ of nonzero means. Let $\Theta_\gamma = \{\mu^n : \mu^n \in \mathbb{R}^n, \mu_i = 0, i \notin \gamma\}$ denote a $q = |\gamma|$ dimension subspace of $\mathbb{R}^n$. If γ^c denotes the complement of γ relative to $\{1, 2, \ldots, n\}$, then $\mathcal{G}(\Theta_\gamma)$ contains codebooks for the following models:

$$\mathcal{G}(\Theta_\gamma) = \{p_{\mu^n} : p_{\mu^n}(\mathbf{y}) = \frac{e^{-(\sum_\gamma (y_i - \mu_i)^2 + \sum_{\gamma^c} y_i^2)/2}}{(2\pi)^{n/2}}\} \qquad (8.22)$$

Given γ, we can introduce constraints like those considered in the prior section to obtain the parametric complexity. It remains to identify γ. If we think of representing γ using a vector of Boolean indicators, then the ideas of Section 8.2 become relevant. The stochastic complexity of $\mathcal{B}([0,1])$ for an observed sequence of n i.i.d. Boolean random variables is approximately $\frac{1}{2}\log n + \log\binom{n}{q}$. If we presume γ, then the resulting stochastic complexity omits the cost of identifying the coordinates of the nonzero parameters.

Rissanen [2000] handles this task by presuming all 2^n models are equally likely and adds an n-bit code for γ to the complexity of $\mathcal{G}(\Theta_\gamma)$ for all γ. Because this addition adds the same amount to the stochastic complexity for every parameter space, it has no effect on the selection of the best library. This approach does, however, imply a strong bias toward models with about $n/2$ nonzero parameters, as though $\gamma_i \overset{\text{i.i.d.}}{\sim}$ Bernoulli($\frac{1}{2}$). If instead we incorporate more of γ into the NML normalization, we discover that stochastic complexity adapts to the number of nonzero parameters.

One way to retain more of the complexity with the NML normalization is to presume one has an a priori ordering of the basis elements, for example [Barron et al. 1998]. This approach is adopted, for example, when MDL is used to pick the order of a nested sequence of polynomial regressions. Typically, one does not compare all possible polynomials, but rather only compares an increasing sequence of nested models: a linear model to a quadratic model, a quadratic to a cubic, and so forth. For the canonical denoising problem, this knowledge is equivalent to being given an ordering of the parameters, say,

$$\mu_{(1)}^2 \le \mu_{(2)}^2 \le \cdots \le \mu_{(n)}^2 .$$

While natural for polynomial regression, such knowledge seems unlikely in denoising.

To retain the coordinate identification within an encyclopedia, we aggregate indexed libraries $\mathcal{G}(\Theta_\gamma)$ into larger collections. Again, let $q = |\gamma|$ denote the number of nonzero parameters and let

$$\Theta_q = \cup_{|\gamma|=q} \Theta_\gamma$$

denote the union of q-dimensional subspaces of $\mathbb{R}^n$. Our goal is to select the best of aggregated library $\mathcal{G}(\Theta_q)$. Said differently, our representative encyclopedia has a volume for each $q = 1, \ldots, n$. The use of such an encyclopedia for coding requires only q, not γ itself, to be specified externally. Because any reasonable code for positive integers assigns roughly equal-length codes to $q = 15$ and $q = 16$, say, the leakage of q outside of the encyclopedia has minimal effect on the use of stochastic complexity in MDL. We can encode q in $O(\log n)$ bits, whereas γ requires $O(n)$ bits.

Like other Gaussian libraries, the parametric complexity of $\mathcal{G}(\Theta_q)$ is unbounded without constraints. To specify these, let

$$y_{(1)}^2 < y_{(2)}^2 < \cdots < y_{(n)}^2$$

denote the data ordered in increasing magnitude. The MLE $\hat{\mu}_q^n \in \Theta_q$ matches the largest q elements $y_{(n-q+1)}, \ldots, y_{(n)}$ and sets the others to zero, implying

$$p_{\hat{\mu}_q^n}(\mathbf{y}) = \frac{e^{-(y_{(1)}^2 + \cdots + y_{(n-q)}^2)/2}}{(2\pi)^{n/2}} .$$

In order to bound the parametric complexity, we constrain $\mathbf{y}$. For $x \in \mathbb{R}^n$, let $\|x\|^2 = \sum_i x_i^2$ denote the Euclidean norm. Following [Rissanen 2000], we constrain the data to those $\mathbf{y}$ for which the MLE lies in a ball of radius $\sqrt{q}R$ around the origin,

$$D_{q,R}^n = \{\mathbf{y} : \|\hat{\mu}_q^n(\mathbf{y})\| \le \sqrt{q}\,R\} .$$

As with one-dimensional Gaussian models, a prefix code must include a code for R as well as q to identify the appropriate encyclopedia. (For denoising, $q\,R^2$ constrains the "regression sum of squares" that appears in the numerator of the standard F-test of a least squares regression. In particular, R^2 is *not* the R-squared statistic often seen in regression output.)

The parametric complexity of the library $\mathcal{G}(\Theta_q)$ is the log of the integral of the maximum likelihood density over the restricted range $D^n_{q,R}$. We estimate this complexity by partitioning the normalizing integral into disjoint subsets for which the same coordinates form $\hat{\mu}^n_q$. The subset of nonzero parameters γ is fixed over each of these subsets, and the integrals over these subsets are identical. Since there are $\binom{n}{q}$ partitions of the indices that fix γ, the parametric complexity is $\binom{n}{q}$ times the integral for the convenient subset in which the maximum of the $n-q$ smaller elements, $m_q(\mathbf{y}) = \max(y^2_1, \ldots, y^2_{n-q})$, is smaller than the minimum of the q larger elements, $M_q(\mathbf{y}) = \min(y^2_{n-q+1}, \ldots, y^2_n)$. Note that $m_q(\mathbf{y}) < M_q(\mathbf{y})$. We then obtain

$$C\left(\mathcal{G}, \Theta_q, D^n_{q,R}\right) = \int_{D^n_{q,R}} p_{\hat{\mu}^n_q}(\mathbf{y})\, d\mathbf{y}$$

$$= \binom{n}{q} \int_{\|y_{n-q+1}, \ldots, y_n\|^2 < qR^2} \frac{F_{n-q}(M_q(\mathbf{y}))}{(2\pi)^q} dy_{n-q+1} \cdots dy_n, \quad (8.23)$$

where $F_k(x)$ is the integral

$$F_k(x) = \int_{y^2_1, \ldots, y^2_k < x} \frac{e^{-(y^2_1 + \cdots + y^2_k)/2}}{(2\pi)^{k/2}} dy_1 \cdots dy_k . \quad (8.24)$$

This integral resembles the cumulative distribution of a chi-squared random variable, but the range of integration is "rectangular" rather than spherical.

The presence of a partition between the largest q elements of $\mathbf{y}$ and the remaining $n-q$ elements in this integration makes it difficult to compute the exact stochastic complexity, but we can still get useful upper and lower bounds. The upper bound is easier to find, so we start there. If we expand the range of integration in $F_{n-q}(x)$ to all of $\mathbb{R}^{n-q}$, the integral is just that of a q-dimensional normal density and so $F_{n-q}(x) \leq 1$. Thus, for this bound the inner integral expressed as F_{n-q} in (8.23) is just 1, and the constraints together with the binomial coefficient give an upper bound for the normalizing constant,

$$C\left(\mathcal{G}, \Theta_q, D^n_{q,R}\right) \leq \binom{n}{q} \int_{\|y_{n-q+1}, \ldots, y_n\|^2 < qR^2} dy_{n-q+1} \cdots dy_n$$

$$= \binom{n}{q} V_q(\sqrt{q}R) , \quad (8.25)$$

where $V_k(r)$ denotes the volume of the ball of radius r in $\mathbb{R}^k$,

$$V_k(r) = \frac{r^k \pi^{k/2}}{(\frac{k}{2})!} .$$

The lower bound results from further constraining the range of integration in (8.23). Rather than integrate over all boundaries between the smaller $n-q$ terms and the larger q, we integrate over a single boundary at $2\log(n-q)$, $m_q(\mathbf{y}) \leq 2\log(n-q) \leq M_q(\mathbf{y})$. The choice of $2\log(n-q)$ as the point of separation follows from the observation that $2\log(n-q)$ is an almost sure bound for the largest squared normal in a sample of $n - q$. If $Z_1, \ldots, Z_n \overset{\text{i.i.d.}}{\sim} N(0, 1)$ and we set

$$P(\max(Z_1^2, \ldots, Z_n^2) < 2 \log n) = \omega_n \, ,$$

then $\lim_{n \to \infty} \omega_n = 1$ [Leadbetter, Lindgren, and Rootzen 1983]. It follows that

$$
\begin{aligned}
C\left(\mathcal{G}, \Theta_q, D_{q,R}^n\right) &\geq \binom{n}{q} \int_{2 \log(n-q) \leq \|y_{n-q+1}, \ldots, y_n\|^2 < q\, R^2} dy_{n-q+1} \cdots dy_n \\
&= \binom{n}{q} A_q(\sqrt{2 \log(n-q)}, \sqrt{q}R) \, ,
\end{aligned}
\tag{8.26}
$$

where $V_q(r_1, r_2)$ with two arguments denotes the volume of the annulus of inner radius r_1 and outer radius r_2 in $\mathbb{R}^q$,

$$V_q(r_1, r_2) = V_q(r_2) - V_q(r_1) \, .$$

Combining (8.25) with (8.26), the parametric complexity of the model class with q nonzero parameters is bounded between

$$\binom{n}{q} V_q(\sqrt{2 \log n}, \sqrt{q}R) \leq C\left(\mathcal{G}_q, \Theta_q, D_{q,R}^n\right) \leq \binom{n}{q} V_q(\sqrt{q}R) \, . \tag{8.27}$$

A further approximation to these bounds provides insight into the contribution of parameters to the stochastic complexity of high-dimensional models. In practice, a data-driven constraint, say $R(\mathbf{y})$, replaces R to ensure the encyclopedia can encode $\mathbf{y}$. For q of moderate size, the volume of the annulus in the lower bound of (8.27) is small in comparison to that of the ball itself; heuristically, most of the volume of a sphere in $\mathbb{R}^q$ lies near the surface of the sphere. Following this line of reasoning and approximating the logs of factorials as $\log k! \approx k \log k$ (omitting constants unaffected by q), we obtain an expression for the parametric complexity that is easy to interpret,

$$
\begin{aligned}
\log C\left(\mathcal{G}, \Theta_q, D_{q,R(\mathbf{y})}^n\right) &\approx \log \binom{n}{q} + q \log R(\mathbf{y}) \\
&\approx q \log \frac{n}{q} + q \log R(\mathbf{y}) \, ,
\end{aligned}
\tag{8.28}
$$

which is reasonable for $q \ll n$.

Consider two situations, one with q large, nonzero μ_i and the other with q smaller, nonzero parameters. For the "strong-signal" case, assume that the nonzero parameters in μ^n are all much larger than the almost sure bound $\sqrt{2 \log n}$. In particular, assume that these $\mu_i = O(\sqrt{n})$,

$$\text{Strong signal:} \quad \mu_i^2 \approx c\, n \, , \quad i \in \gamma, \quad \Rightarrow \quad R^2 = c\, n \, .$$

For the "weak-signal" case, we assume the effects are all near the noise threshold,

$$\text{Weak signal:} \quad \mu_i^2 \approx 2 \log n \, , \quad i \in \gamma, \quad \Rightarrow \quad R^2 = c \log n \, .$$

For coding data with strong signal, the approximation (8.28) to the parametric complexity resembles the approximation obtained by the standard asymptotic analysis of models with small, fixed dimension. In particular, $\frac{q}{2}\log n$ dominates the approximation (8.28) if $R^2 = O(n)$. This similarity is natural. Given a fixed, parametric model with finitely many parameters, the standard analysis lets $n \to \infty$ while holding the model fixed. Thus, the estimation problem becomes much like our strong-signal case: with increasing samples, the standard errors of estimates of the fixed set of parameters fall at the rate of $1/\sqrt{n}$, and the underlying "true model" becomes evident. The term $q \log R$ dominates the approximation (8.28), implying a penalty of $\frac{1}{2}\log n$ as the model grows from dimension q to $q+1$, just as in (8.7).

The penalty for adding a parameter is rather different when faced with weak signals. In such cases, the approximation (8.28) suggests a penalty that resembles those obtained from adaptive thresholding and empirical Bayes. With $R = O(\log n)$, $q \log n/q$ dominates the approximate parametric complexity (8.28). This type of penalty appears in various forms of so-called adaptive model selection. For choosing q out of p possible parameters, one can motivate an adaptive model selection criterion that contains a penalty of the form $q \log p/q$ from information theory [Foster and Stine 1996], multiple comparisons [Abramovich, Benjamini, Donoho, and Johnstone 2000], and empirical Bayes [George and Foster 2000].

8.6   Discussion

So, what is the asymptotic contribution of parameters to the stochastic complexity of a model? Unfortunately, the answer appears to be that "it depends." Ideally, the parametric complexity is a fixed measure of the "complexity" of a class of models, or library. Because the idealized parametric complexity is invariant of $\mathbf{y}$, it offers a clear assessment of how the fit (namely, the maximum of the log-likelihood) of a model can overstate the ability of such models to represent data. In models with rich parameterizations, the parametric complexity sometimes increases at the familiar rate of $\frac{1}{2}\log n$ per parameter (one-parameter Bernoulli, high-signal denoising), but at other times grows dramatically slower. The cost per parameter is only 1 in the saturated Bernoulli model and about $\log n/q$ in low-signal denoising. The latter problem, finding the subtle, yet useful parameters from a large collection of possible effects seems, to us, most interesting and worthy of further study.

Adaptive criteria that vary the penalty for adding a parameter have demonstrated success in applications. For example, we have built predictive models for credit risk that consider on the order of 100,000 features as predictors [Foster and Stine 2002]. The model was identified using a variation on the adaptive rule suggested in the weak-signal denoising problem. Such applications of adaptive rules require other important considerations that we have not addressed here. In particular, modeling with an adaptive rule requires careful estimation of the standard error of parameters. In modeling credit risk, the introduction of several spurious predictors leads to bias in the estimate of the effects of subsequent predictors and a cascade of overfitting.

References

Abramovich, F., Y. Benjamini, D. Donoho, and I. Johnstone (2000). Adapting to unknown sparsity by controlling the false discovery rate. Technical report 2000–19, Department of Statistics, Stanford University, Stanford, CA.

Barron, A.R., J. Rissanen, and B. Yu (1998). The minimum description length principle in coding and modeling. *IEEE Transactions on Information Theory*, *44*, 2743–2760.

Donoho, D.L. and I.M. Johnstone (1994). Ideal spatial adaptation by wavelet shrinkage. *Biometrika*, *81*, 425–455.

Foster, D.P. and R.A. Stine (1996). Variable selection via information theory. Technical report discussion paper 1180, Center for Mathematical Studies in Economics and Management Science, Northwestern University, Chicago.

Foster, D.P. and R.A. Stine (1999). Local asymptotic coding. *IEEE Transactions on Information Theory*, *45*, 1289–1293.

Foster, D.P. and R.A. Stine (2002). Variable selection in data mining: Building a predictive model for bankruptcy. Submitted for publication.

George, E.I. and D.P. Foster (2000). Calibration and empirical Bayes variable selection. *Biometrika*, *87*, 731–747.

Hansen, M.H. and B. Yu (2001). Model selection and the principle of minimum description length. *JASA*, *96*, 746–774.

Leadbetter, M.R., G. Lindgren, and H. Rootzen (1983). *Extremes and Related Properties of Random Sequences and Processes*. New York: Springer-Verlag.

Rissanen, J. (1983). A universal prior for integers and estimation by minimum description length. *Annals of Statistics*, *11*, 416–431.

Rissanen, J. (1986). Stochastic complexity and modeling. *Annals of Statistics*, *14*, 1080–1100.

Rissanen, J. (1989). *Stochastic Complexity in Statistical Inquiry*. Singapore: World Scientific.

Rissanen, J. (1996). Fisher information and stochastic complexity. *IEEE Transactions on Information Theory*, *42*, 40–47.

Rissanen, J. (1999). Hypothesis selection and testing by the MDL principle. *Computer Journal*, *42*, 260–269.

Rissanen, J. (2000). MDL denoising. *IEEE Transactions on Information Theory*, *46*, 2537–2543.

Shtarkov, Y.M. (1987). Universal sequential coding of single messages. *Problems of Information Transmission 23*, 3–17.

Stine, R.A. and D.P. Foster (2000). The competitive complexity ratio. In *2000 Conference on Information Sciences and Systems*, pp. WP8 1–6. Princeton University, Princeton, NJ.

9 Extended Stochastic Complexity and Its Applications to Learning

Kenji Yamanishi

NEC Corporation,
1-1, 4-chome, Miyazaki, Miyamae-ku, Kawasaki, Kanagawa 216-8555, Japan.
E-mail: k-yamanisi@cw.jp.nec.com
http://www.labs.nec.co.jp/DTmining/members/yamanishi/index_e.html

Rissanen has introduced stochastic complexity to define the amount of information in a given data sequence relative to a given hypothesis class of probability densities, where the information is measured in terms of a logarithmic loss associated with universal data compression. We introduce the notion of *extended stochastic complexity* (ESC) and demonstrate its effectiveness in design and analysis of learning algorithms in online prediction and batch-learning scenarios. ESC can be thought of as an extension of Rissanen's stochastic complexity to the decision-theoretic setting where a general real-valued function is used as a hypothesis and a general loss function is used as a distortion measure.

As an application of ESC to online prediction, we show that a sequential realization of ESC produces an online prediction algorithm called Vovk's aggregating strategy, which can be thought of as an extension of the Bayes algorithm. We introduce the notion of the minimax relative cumulative loss as the performance measure of online prediction and show that ESC can be a minimax solution to the minimax relative cumulative loss, which is attained by the aggregating strategy.

As an application of ESC to batch-learning, we show that a batch-approximation of ESC induces a batch-learning algorithm called the minimum L-complexity algorithm (MLC), which is an extension of the minimum description length (MDL) principle. We derive upper bounds on the statistical risk for MLC, which are least to date. Through ESC we give a unifying view of the most effective learning algorithms that have recently been explored in machine learning theory.

9.1   Introduction

Rissanen [1986, 1987, 1989, 1996] introduced the notion of *stochastic complexity* (SC) to define the amount of information included in a data sequence relative to a given class of probability mass functions or probability densities. Now let $\mathcal{H}_k = \{p_\theta(\cdot) : \theta \in \Theta_k \subset \mathbf{R}^k\}$ be a class of probability densities or probability mass functions, which we call a *hypothesis class*, where each p_θ, which we call a *hypothesis*, is specified by a k-dimensional real-valued parameter θ over the parameter space Θ_k. Let $\pi(\theta)$ be a prior density of θ over Θ_k. The SC of a data sequence $D^m = D_1 \cdots D_m$ relative to $\mathcal{H}_k$ is defined as

$$-\ln \int d\theta \pi(\theta) p_\theta(D^m),$$

which can be interpreted as the shortest code length of D^m with respect to the hypothesis class $\mathcal{H}_k$.[1] This quantity is a generalization of Shannon's information [Shannon 1948], which is defined as the negative logarithm of the probability value of the data sequence relative to a hypothesis, in the sense that SC is defined relative to a class of hypotheses, while Shannon's information is defined relative to a single hypothesis.

Rissanen has proved in [Rissanen 1986, 1987,1989, pp. 58–97] that SC plays an essential role in contexts of statistical inference specifically in the following two senses:

1. *A tight lower bound on the total predictive code length:* Consider the online stochastic prediction process (see e.g., [Rissanen 1983, 1984; Dawid 1991; Yamanishi 1995], defined as follows: An example is sequentially given; $D_1, D_2, \cdots, D_t, \cdots$, and at each time t a learner is to predict a probability density (or a probability mass function) $\hat{p}_t(D)$ of the occurrence of D_t before seeing it, based on the past sequence $D_1 \cdots D_{t-1}$. After prediction, the learner receives a correct value D_t, and the distortion of the prediction is measured in terms of the *logarithmic loss* defined by $-\ln \hat{p}_t(D_t)$, which is equivalent to the *predictive code length* for D_t (see [Rissanen 1983, 1984,1986]).The cumulative prediction loss over the course of predictions can be considered as the total predictive code length. It has turned out in [Rissanen 1986, 1987, 1989, pp. 67–73], that the SC of a data sequence relative to a given hypothesis class is the asymptotically greatest lower bound on the total predictive code length, for most sequences and most $\theta \in \Theta_k$. Therefore, the process of sequentially approximating SC may induce an online prediction algorithm for which the cumulative logarithmic loss is asymptotically minimal. Such algorithms that sequentially approximate SC include the Bayes algorithm (see e.g., [Clarke

---

1. In [Rissanen 1987, 1989, pp. 58-67, 1996], Rissanen defined the SC in several different manners, although all of them are unified as a concept of the shortest code length of a data sequence with the help of a given class of probability densities. Here we adopt the definition of SC in [Rissanen 1987, 1989, p. 59].

and Barron 1990]) and the online maximum likelihood prediction algorithm (see [Yamanishi 1995, 1997]).

2. *A basis for the MDL principle:* A model selection criterion to approximate SC in a nonpredictive way induces the *minimum description length (MDL) principle* (see [Rissanen 1978]), which asserts that the best hypothesis which explains the generation of the data is that which can best compress the data as well as the hypothesis itself. That is, the MDL principle can be thought of as the process of batch-approximation of SC using the two step coding (the first step is to encode the hypothesis, and the second step is to encode the data sequence relative to the hypothesis). It is known from [Barron and Cover 1991; Yamanishi 1992a] that the MDL principle produces an estimator which almost surely converges to the true density with the highest rate in some parametric settings.

In addition to the above two respects, the effectiveness of SC in the universal hypothesis testing scenario has been reported in [Rissanen 1987, 1989, pp. 107–121] and [Yamanishi 1992b].

Notice that SC is defined in the scenario in which a hypothesis takes a form of a probability density and the distortion of prediction is measured in terms of the logarithmic loss. This setting is quite natural for almost statistical and information-theoretic formulations such as Shannon's information theory because it gives a clear coding-theoretic interpretation of the logarithmic loss. However, we may often be interested in the decision-theoretic setting (see e.g., [Berger 1985]) in which a hypothesis is a general real-valued function and the distortion of prediction is measured in terms of a general loss function other than the logarithmic loss. Such a situation may occur in real problems, including pattern recognition, function estimation, curve fitting, game theory, and so on. It would be natural to expect that a notion analogous to SC may exist in a more general decision-theoretic setting and would play an essential role there.

The primary contribution of this chapter is, according to [Yamanishi 1998a], to extend SC into the general decision-theoretic scenario as above and to demonstrate the effectiveness of the extended notion in design and analysis of learning algorithms in online prediction and batch-learning scenarios. We name this extended notion the *extended stochastic complexity* [Yamanishi 1998a], which we denote as ESC. By showing that the most effective learning algorithms can be derived from the processes of approximating ESC, we give a unifying view of designing decision-theoretic learning algorithms.

Let $\mathcal{H}_k = \{f_\theta(x) : \theta \in \Theta_k \subset \mathbf{R}^k\}$ be a k-dimensional parametric class of real-valued functions and $\pi(\theta)$ be a prior density function over the parameter space Θ_k. Let L be a given loss function where $L(y, f_\theta(x))$ denotes the loss value for predicting y with $f_\theta(x)$. For a given positive number $\lambda > 0$, ESC of a data sequence $D^m = D_1 \cdots D_m$ ($D_t = (x_t, y_t)$, $t = 1, \cdots, m$) relative to $\mathcal{H}_k$ is formally defined as

$$-\frac{1}{\lambda} \ln \int d\theta \pi(\theta) \exp\left(-\lambda \sum_{t=1}^m L(y_t, f_\theta(x_t))\right).$$

For the online prediction problem, we show in Section 9.3 that the process of a sequential realization of ESC induces Vovk's *aggregating strategy* [Vovk 1990], which has been explored extensively in computational learning theory. The *Bayes algorithm* (see e.g., [Clarke and Barron 1990]) can be reduced to the special case of the aggregating strategy. Kivinen and Warmuth [1994] and Haussler, Kivinen, and Warmuth [1995] investigated the performance of the aggregating strategy only when the hypothesis class is finite. We rather investigate it in the case where the hypothesis class is continuous (see also the work by Freund [1996]). We further define the notion of relative cumulative loss (RCL) by the difference between the cumulative loss for any online prediction algorithm and that for the best assignment in a given hypothesis class. Then we show that the worst-case relative cumulative loss for the aggregating strategy is upper-bounded by $(k \ln m)/2\lambda^* + C$ where λ^* is a constant depending on the loss function, C depends on the hypothesis class, and m is the sample size. Then we show that under certain conditions ESC is a minimax solution to RCL within error $o(\ln m)$.

For the batch-learning problem, we consider a hypothesis selection criterion to approximate ESC in a nonpredictive way. The criterion chooses from a given sequence of examples a hypothesis such that the weighted sum of the empirical loss for the hypothesis and the description length for the hypothesis is minimized. We call a learning algorithm based on this hypothesis-selection criterion the *minimum L-complexity algorithm* (MLC) [Yamanishi 1998a] for the loss function L. MLC can be thought of as an extension of the *MDL learning algorithm* (see [Rissanen 1989, pp. 79–93, pp. 155–167],[Barron and Cover 1991],[Yamanishi 1992a]), and is closely related to Barron's *complexity regularization algorithm* [Barron 1991], which we denote as CR. Actually, in the case where the hypothesis is a probability density and the distortion measure is the logarithmic loss function, MLC is equivalent to the MDL learning algorithm. For the quadratic loss function, MLC is equivalent to CR, but, for general bounded loss functions, MLC is given in a more general form than CR in order to give a unifying strategy regardless of the loss functions used. We analyze how well MLC works in terms of its statistical risk. We prove that for general bounded loss functions, under certain conditions for the target distribution, MLC has the same upper bounds on the statistical risk as those obtained for CR in [Barron 1991], which are least to date.

The rest of this chapter is organized as follows: Section 9.2 gives a brief review of the notions of stochastic complexity and minimax regret. Section 9.3 gives a formal definition of ESC and shows its applications to designing an online prediction algorithm and its analysis. Section 9.4 shows an application of ESC to designing a batch-learning algorithm and its analysis. Section 9.5 makes concluding remarks.

9.2   Stochastic Complexity and Minimax Regret

We start by giving a formal setting of sequential stochastic prediction. Let $\mathcal{Y}$ be an alphabet, which can be either discrete or continuous. We first consider the simplest case where $\mathcal{Y}$ is finite. Observe a sequence $y_1, y_2, \cdots$ where each $y_t (t = 1, 2, \cdots)$ takes a value in $\mathcal{Y}$. A *stochastic prediction algorithm* $\mathcal{A}$ performs as follows: At each round $t = 1, 2, ...,$ $\mathcal{A}$ assigns a probability mass function over $\mathcal{Y}$ based on the past sequence $y^{t-1} = y_1 \cdots y_{t-1}$. The probability mass function can be written as a conditional probability $P(\cdot | y^{t-1})$. After the assignment, $\mathcal{A}$ receives an outcome y_t and suffers a *logarithmic loss* defined by $-\ln P(y_t | y^{t-1})$. This process goes on sequentially. Note that $\mathcal{A}$ is specified by a sequence of conditional probabilities: $\{P(\cdot | y^{t-1}) : t = 1, 2, ..\}$. After observing a sequence $y^m = y_1 \cdots y_m$ of length m, $\mathcal{A}$ suffers a *cumulative logarithmic loss* $\sum_{t=1}^{m} \left(-\ln P(y_t | y^{t-1}) \right)$ where $P(\cdot | y_0) = P_0(\cdot)$ is given. Note that the logarithmic loss $-\ln P(y_t | y^{t-1})$ can be interpreted as the Shannon code length for y_t given y^{t-1}, hence the cumulative logarithmic loss can be interpreted as the total code length for y^m when they are sequentially encoded.

The goal of stochastic prediction is to make the cumulative loss as small as possible. We introduce a reference set of prediction algorithms, which we call a *hypothesis class*, then evaluate the cumulative loss for any algorithm relative to it. For sample size m, we define the *worst-case regret* for $\mathcal{A}$ relative to a hypothesis class $\mathcal{H}$ by

$$R_m(\mathcal{A} : \mathcal{H}) \overset{\text{def}}{=} \sup_{y^m} \left(\sum_{t=1}^{m} \left(-\ln P(y_t | y^{t-1}) \right) - \inf_{f \in \mathcal{H}} \sum_{t=1}^{m} \left(-\ln f(y_t | y^{t-1}) \right) \right),$$

which means the worst-case difference between the cumulative logarithmic loss for $\mathcal{A}$ and the minimum cumulative logarithmic loss over $\mathcal{H}$. Further, we define the *minimax regret* for sample size m by

$$R_m(\mathcal{H}) = \inf_{\mathcal{A}} R_m(\mathcal{A} : \mathcal{H}),$$

where the infimum is taken over all stochastic prediction algorithms. In the analysis of the minimax regret we require no statistical assumption for the data-generation mechanism, but rather consider the worst case with respect to sequences.

Notice here that for any m, a stochastic prediction algorithm specifies a joint probability mass function by

$$P(y^m) = \prod_{t=1}^{m} P(y_t | y^{t-1}). \tag{9.1}$$

Thus the minimax regret is rewritten as

$$R_m(\mathcal{H}) = \inf_{P} \sup_{y^m} \ln \frac{\sup_{f \in \mathcal{H}} f(y^m)}{P(y^m)}.$$

Shtarkov [1987] showed that the minimax regret is attained by the joint probability mass function under the *normalized maximum likelihood*, defined as follows:

$$P(y^m) = \frac{\sup_{f \in \mathcal{H}} f(y^m)}{\sum_{y^m} \sup_{f \in \mathcal{H}} f(y^m)},$$

and then the minimax regret amounts to be

$$R_m(\mathcal{H}) = \ln \sum_{y^m} \sup_{f \in \mathcal{H}} f(y^m). \tag{9.2}$$

The quantity (9.2) is also called the *parametric complexity* [Rissanen 1996].

Specifically consider the case where the joint distribution is given by a product of probability mass function belonging to a parametric hypothesis class given by $\mathcal{H}_k = \{P_\theta(\cdot) : \theta \in \Theta_k\}$ where Θ_k is a k-dimensional compact set in $\mathbf{R}^k$. Let $\hat{\theta}$ be the maximum likelihood estimator (MLE) of θ from y^m (i.e., $\hat{\theta} = \arg\max_{\theta \in \Theta} P_\theta(y^m)$ where $P_\theta(y^m) = \prod_{t=1}^{m} P_\theta(y_t \mid y^{t-1})$). Rissanen [1996] proved that under the condition that the central limit theorem holds for MLE uniformly over Θ_k, $R_m(\mathcal{H}_k)$ is asymptotically expanded as follows:

$$R_m(\mathcal{H}_k) = \frac{k}{2} \ln \frac{m}{2\pi} + \ln \int \sqrt{|I(\theta)|} d\theta + o(1), \tag{9.3}$$

where $I(\theta) \overset{\text{def}}{=} (\lim_{m \to \infty}(1/m)E_\theta[-\partial^2 \ln P_\theta(y^m)/\partial\theta_i\partial\theta_j])_{i,j}$ denotes the Fisher information matrix and $o(1)$ goes to zero uniformly with respect to y^m as m goes to infinity. Note that the regularity condition required for (9.3) to be satisfied is weakened in recent work (see e.g., [Takeuchi and Barron 1998]).

For a given sequence y^m and $\mathcal{H}_k$, the negative log-likelihood for y^m under the joint probability mass function that attains the minimax regret is called the *stochastic complexity* of y^m (relative to $\mathcal{H}_k$) [Rissanen 1987, 1989,1996],which we denote as $SC(y^m)$. That is, an asymptotic expansion of SC is given by

$$SC(y^m) = -\ln P_{\hat{\theta}}(y^m) + \frac{k}{2} \ln \frac{m}{2\pi} + \ln \int \sqrt{|I(\theta)|} d\theta + o(1). \tag{9.4}$$

Choose $\mathcal{A}$ as the *Bayesian prediction strategy* such that

$$P(\cdot|y^{t-1}) = \int P(\theta|y^{t-1})P_\theta(\cdot)d\theta$$

for each t where $\pi(\theta)$ is a prior density of θ and

$$P(\theta|y^{t-1}) = \pi(\theta) \prod_{j=1}^{t-1} P_\theta(y_j \mid y^{j-1}) / \int \pi(\theta) \prod_{j=1}^{t-1} P_\theta(y_j \mid y^{j-1})d\theta$$

is a posterior density of θ.

Then it is easily checked that its cumulative logarithmic loss for y^m amounts to be

$$L(y^m) = -\ln \int \pi(\theta) \prod_{t=1}^{m} P_\theta(y_t)d\theta. \tag{9.5}$$

If we choose an appropriate prior such as Jeffreys' prior [Clarke and Barron 1994],

$$\pi(\theta) = \sqrt{|I(\theta)|} / \int \sqrt{|I(\theta)|} d\theta,$$

or its modified variants, then (9.5) asymptotically coincides with (9.4) (see [Takeuchi and Barron 1998]). We call (9.5) the *stochastic complexity of the mixture form*. In the following sections, we present an extension of the SC as a solution to the minimax regret formulation to nonlogarithmic loss cases.

9.3   ESC and Minimax RCL

9.3.1   Minimax Relative Cumulative Loss

In this subsection we extend the notion of SC to a general decision-theoretic scenario.

For a positive integer n, let $\mathcal{X}$ be a subset of $\mathbf{R}^n$, which we call the *domain*. Let $\mathcal{Y} = \{0,1\}$ or $\mathcal{Y} = [0,1]$, which we call the *range*. Let $\mathcal{Z} = [0,1]$ or $\mathcal{Z}$ be a set of probability mass functions over $\mathcal{Y}$. We call $\mathcal{Z}$ the *decision space*. We set $\mathcal{D} = \mathcal{X} \times \mathcal{Y}$. We write an element in $\mathcal{D}$ as $D = (x,y)$. Let $L : \mathcal{Y} \times \mathcal{Z} \to \mathbf{R}^+ \cup \{0\}$ be a loss function.

A *sequential prediction algorithm* $\mathcal{A}$ performs as follows: At each round $t = 1, 2, \cdots$, $\mathcal{A}$ receives $x_t \in \mathcal{X}$ then outputs a predicted result $z_t \in \mathcal{Z}$ on the basis of $D^{t-1} = D_1 \cdots D_{t-1}$ where $D_i = (x_i, y_i)$ $(i = 1, \cdots, t-1)$. Then $\mathcal{A}$ receives the correct outcome $y_t \in \mathcal{Y}$ and suffers a loss $L(y_t, z_t)$. Hence $\mathcal{A}$ defines a sequence of maps: $\{f_t : t = 1, 2, \cdots\}$ where $f_t(x_t) = z_t$. A *hypothesis class* $\mathcal{H}$ is a set of sequential prediction algorithms.

Below we define the measure of performance of sequential prediction.

Definition 9.1 *For sample size m, for a hypothesis class $\mathcal{H}$, let $\mathcal{D}^m(\mathcal{H})$ be a subset of $\mathcal{D}^m$ depending on $\mathcal{H}$. For any sequential prediction algorithm $\mathcal{A}$, we define the worst-case relative cumulative loss (RCL) for $\mathcal{A}$ by*

$$\mathcal{R}_m(\mathcal{A} : \mathcal{H}) \stackrel{\mathrm{def}}{=} \sup_{D^m \in \mathcal{D}^m(\mathcal{H})} \left(\sum_{t=1}^m L(y_t, z_t) - \min_{f \in \mathcal{H}} \sum_{t=1}^m L(y_t, f_t(x_t)) \right),$$

where z_t denotes the output of $\mathcal{A}$ at the tth round. We define the minimax RCL *by*

$$\mathcal{R}_m(\mathcal{H}) = \inf_{\mathcal{A}} \mathcal{R}_m(\mathcal{A} : \mathcal{H}), \qquad (9.6)$$

where the infimum is taken over all sequential prediction algorithms.

Consider the special case where $\mathcal{X} = \emptyset, \mathcal{Y} = \{0,1\}, \mathcal{Z} =$ the set of probability mass functions over $\mathcal{Y}$, and the loss function is the logarithmic loss: $L(y, P) = -\ln P(y)$. We can easily check that in this case the minimax RCL (9.6) is equivalent with the minimax regret (9.3).

Hereafter, we consider only the case where $\mathcal{Z} = [0,1]$, that is, the prediction is made deterministically. Below we give examples of loss functions for this case.

$$L(y, z) = (y - z)^2 \quad \text{(square loss)}, \tag{9.7}$$

$$L(y, z) = |y - z|^\alpha \quad \text{(alpha loss, } \alpha > 0), \tag{9.8}$$

$$L(y, z) = y \ln \frac{y}{z} + (1 - y) \ln \frac{1 - y}{1 - z} \quad \text{(entropic loss)}, \tag{9.9}$$

$$L(y, z) = \frac{1}{2} \left((\sqrt{y} - \sqrt{z})^2 + \left(\sqrt{1 - y} - \sqrt{1 - z} \right)^2 \right) \quad \text{(Hellinger loss)}, \tag{9.10}$$

$$L(y, z) = \frac{1}{2}(-(2y - 1)(2z - 1) + \ln(e^{2z-1} + e^{-2z+1}) + B) \quad \text{(logistic loss)}, \tag{9.11}$$

where $B = \ln(1 + e^{-2})$. The square loss is most suitable for classical regression problems and curve-fitting problems. The alpha loss with $\alpha \neq 2$, logistic loss, and entropic loss may be used for measuring distortion in the problems of pattern recognition and sequential decision making.

9.3.2   Extended Stochastic Complexity

According to [Yamanishi 1998a], we formally extend the notion of stochastic complexity of the mixture form to introduce extended stochastic complexity.

Definition 9.2 *Let μ be a probability measure on a hypothesis class $\mathcal{H}$. For a given loss function L, for $\lambda > 0$, for a sequence $D^m \in \mathcal{D}^m$, we define the* extended stochastic complexity *(ESC) of D^m relative to $\mathcal{H}$ by*

$$I(D^m : \mathcal{H}) \overset{\text{def}}{=} -\frac{1}{\lambda} \ln \int e^{-\lambda \sum_{t=1}^m L(y_y, f_t(x_t))} \mu(df). \tag{9.12}$$

We may assume that the hypothesis class can be written in a parametric form as $\mathcal{H} = \mathcal{H}_k$ or that $\mathcal{H} = \cup_k \mathcal{H}_k$ where $\mathcal{H}_k = \{f_\theta : \theta \in \Theta_k \subset \mathbf{R}^k\}$ $(k = 1, 2, \cdots)$, in which $f_\theta \in \mathcal{H}_k$ is specified by a k-dimensional parameter vector $\theta = (\theta_1, \cdots, \theta_k)$, and Θ_k is a k-dimensional compact set of real-valued parameter vectors. The range of k can be either finite or infinite. We denote a prior probability mass function on the set $\{1, 2, \cdots\}$ as $\pi(k)$ and a prior density function over Θ_k as $\pi(\theta) = \pi_k(\theta)$. Hereafter, for $D = (x, y) \in \mathcal{D}$, for $f \in \mathcal{H}$, we denote the loss $L(y, f(x))$ or $L(y, f(\cdot|x))$ as $L(D : f)$ for the sake of notational simplicity. Then (9.12) can be written as follows:

$$I(D^m : \mathcal{H}_k) \overset{\text{def}}{=} -\frac{1}{\lambda} \ln \int d\theta \pi(\theta) \exp \left(-\lambda \sum_{t=1}^m L(D_t : f_\theta) \right) \tag{9.13}$$

(Note: The integrability of $\pi(\theta) \exp(-\lambda \sum_{t=1}^m L(D_t : f_\theta))$ with respect to θ for all D^m is assumed.)

In the case where the hypothesis class is a class of conditional probability mass functions and the distortion measure is the logarithmic loss function, letting $\lambda = 1$,

ESC is written as

$$I(D^m : \mathcal{H}_k) = -\ln \int d\theta \pi(\theta) \prod_{t=1}^{m} f_\theta(y_t | x_t), \tag{9.14}$$

which coincides with Rissanen's *stochastic complexity* (SC, see [Rissanen 1986, 1987, 1989, pp. 58–67], of the mixture form for the case where each y_t ($t = 1, 2, \cdots$) is independently generated.

Let $\mathcal{H} = \cup_k \mathcal{H}_k$. Then each hypothesis is specified by k as well as θ, where θ and k make a hierarchical structure. Then ESC as in (9.13) is changed to the following form:

$$I(D^m : \mathcal{H}) \overset{\text{def}}{=} -\frac{1}{\lambda} \ln \sum_k \pi(k) \int d\theta \pi_k(\theta) \exp\left(-\lambda \sum_{t=1}^{m} L(D_t : f_\theta)\right) \tag{9.15}$$

9.3.3   The Aggregating Strategy

In this subsection we introduce an online prediction algorithm called the aggregating strategy on the basis of the sequential decomposition property of ESC.

For a loss function L, we define $L_0(z)$ and $L_1(z)$ by $L_0(z) \overset{\text{def}}{=} L(0, z)$ and $L_1(z) \overset{\text{def}}{=} L(1, z)$, respectively. We make the following assumption for L.

Assumption 9.3 *The loss function L satisfies:*
1. $L_0(z)$ and $L_1(z)$ are twice continuously differentiable with respect to z. $L_0(0) = L_1(1) = 0$. For any $0 < z < 1$, $L_0'(z) > 0$ and $L_1'(z) < 0$.
2. Define λ^* by

$$\lambda^* \overset{\text{def}}{=} \left(\sup_{0<z<1} \frac{L_0'(z)L_1'(z)^2 - L_1'(z)L_0'(z)^2}{L_0'(z)L_1''(z) - L_1'(z)L_0''(z)}\right)^{-1}. \tag{9.16}$$

Then $0 < \lambda^* < \infty$.
3. Let $G(y, z, w) = \lambda^*(L(y, z) - L(y, w))$. For any $y, z, w \in [0, 1]$, $\partial^2 G(y, z, w)/\partial y^2 + (\partial G(y, z, w)/\partial y)^2 \geq 0$.

Under Assumption 9.3, according to [Kivinen and Warmuth 1994; Haussler et al. 1995], we define the *generalized inverse function* of L_0 by $L_0^{-1}(L_0(z)) = z$ for $0 \leq z \leq 1$ and $L_0^{-1}(z) \geq 1$ for $z \geq L_0(1)$. Similarly we define the generalized inverse function of L_1 by $L_1^{-1}(L_1(z)) = z$ for $0 \leq z \leq 1$ and $L_1^{-1}(z) \leq 0$ for $z \geq L_1(0)$.

Example 9.4 For the entropic loss function as in (9.9), we see that $L_0(z) = -\ln(1 - z)$ and $L_1(z) = -\ln z$. Then we have $L_0^{-1}(z) = 1 - e^{-z}$ and $L_1^{-1}(z) = e^{-z}$. A simple calculation yields $\lambda^* = 1$. We see that Assumption 9.3 holds for L.

Example 9.5 For the quadratic loss function as in (9.7), we see that $L_0(z) = z^2$ and $L_1(z) = (1 - z)^2$. Then we have $L_0^{-1}(z) = \sqrt{z}$ and $L_1^{-1}(z) = 1 - \sqrt{z}$. A simple calculation yields $\lambda^* = 2$. We see that Assumption 9.3 holds for L.

Example 9.6 For the Hellinger loss function as in (9.10), we see that $L_0(z) = 1 - \sqrt{1-z}$ and $L_1(z) = 1 - \sqrt{z}$. Then we have $L_0^{-1}(z) = 2z - z^2$ $(0 \leq z \leq 1)$, $L_0^{-1}(z) = 1$ $(z \geq 1)$ and $L_1^{-1}(z) = (1-z)^2 (0 \leq z \leq 1)$, $L_1^{-1}(z) = 0$ $(z \leq 0)$. A simple calculation shows $\lambda^* = \sqrt{2}$. We see that the conditions 1 and 2 in Assumption 9.3 hold, but the condition 3 does not hold.

Example 9.7 For the logistic loss function as in (9.27), we see that $L_0(z) = (1/2)\ln((e^{2(2z-1)} + 1)/(1 + e^{-2}))$ and $L_1(z) = (1/2)\ln((1 + e^{-2(2z-1)})/(1 + e^{-2}))$. Then we have $L_0^{-1}(z) = 1/2 + (1/4)\ln((1 + e^{-2})e^{2z} - 1)$ and $L_1^{-1}(z) = 1/2 - (1/4)\ln((1 + e^{-2})e^{2z} - 1)$. A simple calculation yields $\lambda^* = 2$. We see that Assumption 9.3 holds for L.

We start with the following lemma on the sequential decomposition property of ESC to motivate the aggregating strategy.

Lemma 9.8 *For any D^m, the ESC of D^m relative to $\mathcal{H}_k$ can be written as follows:*

$$I(D^m : \mathcal{H}_k) = \sum_{t=1}^{m} L(y_t \mid D^{t-1}, x_t), \tag{9.17}$$

where

$$L(y_t \mid D^{t-1}, x_t) \stackrel{\text{def}}{=} -\frac{1}{\lambda} \ln \int d\theta \pi(\theta \mid D^{t-1}) \exp\left(-\lambda L(D_t : f_\theta)\right), \tag{9.18}$$

$$\pi(\theta \mid D^{t-1}) \stackrel{\text{def}}{=} \frac{\pi(\theta) \exp\left(-\lambda \sum_{j=1}^{t-1} L(D_j : f_\theta)\right)}{\int d\theta \pi(\theta) \exp\left(-\lambda \sum_{j=1}^{t-1} L(D_j : f_\theta)\right)}. \tag{9.19}$$

Here we let $\pi(\theta|D^0) = \pi(\theta)$ and $L(D_0 : f_\theta) = 0$.

Proof Observe first that plugging $\pi(\theta \mid D^{t-1})$ into $L(y_t \mid D^{t-1}, x_t)$ yields

$$L(y_t \mid D^{t-1}, x_t) = -\frac{1}{\lambda} \ln \frac{\int d\theta \pi(\theta) \exp\left(-\lambda \sum_{j=1}^{t} L(D_j : f_\theta)\right)}{\int d\theta \pi(\theta) \exp\left(-\lambda \sum_{j=1}^{t-1} L(D_j : f_\theta)\right)}$$
$$= I(D^t : \mathcal{H}_k) - I(D^{t-1} : \mathcal{H}_k).$$

Summing $L(y_t \mid D^{t-1}, x_t)$ with respect to t gives

$$\sum_{t=1}^{m} L(y_t \mid D^{t-1}, x_t) = I(D^m : \mathcal{H}_k) - I(D^0 : \mathcal{H}_k) = I(D^m : \mathcal{H}_k),$$

where we have used the fact that $I(D^0 : \mathcal{H}_k) = 0$. $\qquad\square$

A variant of Kivinen and Warmuth's version of the aggregating strategy for the case of $\mathcal{Y} = [0, 1]$, which we denote by AGG, is described as follows:

Algorithm AGG

Let $\mathcal{H}_k, L, \pi$, and $\lambda > 0$ be given.

At each time t, on receiving x_t, compute $\Delta_t(0) \stackrel{\text{def}}{=} L(0|D^{t-1}, x_t)$ and $\Delta_t(1) \stackrel{\text{def}}{=} L(1|D^{t-1}, x_t)$ where the notation of $L(y|D^{t-1}, x_t)$ $(y = 0, 1)$ follows (9.18). Then predict y_t with any value $\hat{y}_t$ satisfying

$$L_1^{-1}(\Delta_t(1)) \leq \hat{y}_t \leq L_0^{-1}(\Delta_t(0)). \tag{9.20}$$

If no such $\hat{y}_t$ exists, the algorithm fails. We write $\hat{y}_t = \text{AGG}_t(x_t)$.

After prediction, the correct outcome y_t is received.

Note that if $L_1^{-1}(\Delta_t(1)) \leq L_0^{-1}(\Delta_t(0))$ holds, then $\hat{y}_t$ satisfying (9.20) is given by, for example,

$$\hat{y}_t = \frac{1}{2} \left(L_1^{-1}(\Delta_t(1)) + L_0^{-1}(\Delta_t(0)) \right).$$

We say that L is λ-*realizable* when AGG never fails for λ. Haussler and co-workers [1995] proved that in the case of $\mathcal{Y} = \{0, 1\}$, under the conditions 1 and 2 in Assumption 9.3, L is λ-realizable if and only if $\lambda \leq \lambda^*$ for λ^* as in (9.16).

Kivinen and Warmuth [1994] proved that if L satisfies condition 3 in Assumption 9.3, then for $\hat{y}_t = \text{AGG}_t(x_t)$ satisfying (9.20), for all $y_t \in [0, 1]$, the following inequality holds:

$$L(D_t : \text{AGG}_t) \leq L(y_t|D^{t-1}, x_t). \tag{9.21}$$

Summing both sides of (9.21) with respect to t leads to an upper bound on the cumulative loss for AGG using $\mathcal{H}_k$:

$$\sum_{t=1}^{m} L(D_t : \text{AGG}_t) \leq \sum_{t=1}^{m} L(y_t|D^{t-1}, x_t) = I(D^m : \mathcal{H}_k).$$

Here we have used Lemma 9.8 to derive the last equation. This leads to the following theorem.

Theorem 9.9 *Under Assumption 9.3, for any D^m, for any $\lambda \geq \lambda^*$, the cumulative loss for AGG is upper-bounded by $I(D^m : \mathcal{H})$.*

Theorem 9.9 implies that the cumulative loss for the aggregating strategy is upper-bounded by the ESC for any sequence.

In the special case of online stochastic prediction where the logarithmic loss function is used as a distortion measure, letting $\lambda = 1$, (9.18) and (9.19) are written as follows:

$$L(y_t \mid D^{t-1}, x_t) = -\ln \int d\theta \pi(\theta \mid D^{t-1}) f_\theta(y_t|x_t), \tag{9.22}$$

$$\pi(\theta \mid D^{t-1}) = \frac{\pi(\theta) \prod_{j=1}^{t-1} f_\theta(y_j|x_j)}{\int d\theta \pi(\theta) \prod_{j=1}^{t-1} f_\theta(y_j|x_j)} \tag{9.23}$$

Equation (9.23) is the Bayes posterior density of θ, and (9.22) is the code length of the Bayes code based on the mixture density: $\bar{f}(y|x_t) \overset{\text{def}}{=} \int d\theta \pi(\theta \mid D^{t-1}) f_\theta(y|x_t)$. Hence the prediction for which the loss at time t is $L(y_t \mid D^{t-1}, x_t)$ is realized by an algorithm that outputs a density $\bar{f}(y|x_t)$ at each time t. This algorithm is called the *Bayes algorithm* (see, e.g., [Clarke and Barron 1990]).

9.3.4   Asymptotic Bounds on Minimax RLC

This subsection makes a connection between minimax RCL and ESC through the analysis of the aggregating strategy. We make the following assumption for $L, \mathcal{H}_k$, and π.

Assumption 9.10 *The following conditions hold for $L, \mathcal{H}_k$, and π:*
1. The parametrization of the class $\mathcal{H}_k = \{f_\theta : \theta \in \Theta_k\}$ is one-to-one, that is, if $\theta_1 \neq \theta_2$, then the corresponding f_{θ_1} and f_{θ_2} are distinct.
2. For any D, $L(D : f_\theta)$ is twice continuously differentiable with respect to θ.
3. For a given D^m and $\theta \in \Theta_k$, define a matrix $\hat{J}(\theta)$ for which the (i,j)th component is given by

$$\hat{J}_{i,j}(\theta) \overset{\text{def}}{=} \frac{1}{m}\left(\left.\frac{\partial^2 \sum_{t=1}^m L(D_t : f_\theta)}{\partial\theta_i \partial\theta_j}\right|_\theta\right).$$

Let $\mathcal{D}^m(\Theta_k) \subset \mathcal{D}^m$ be a set of all D^m satisfying that for D^m, there exists $\hat{\theta} \in \Theta_k$ such that the minimum of $\sum_{t=1}^m L(D_t : f_\theta)$ over Θ_k is attained by $\hat{\theta}$, and $\partial \sum_{t=1}^m L(D_t : f_\theta)/\partial\theta|_{\theta=\hat{\theta}} = 0$. Then for $d = d_m$ such that $d_m > k$, $\lim_{m\to\infty} d_m = \infty$ and $\lim_{m\to\infty}(d_m/m) = 0$, $\hat{J}(\theta)$ is continuous with respect to θ in $|\hat{\theta} - \theta| \leq \sqrt{d_m/m}$ uniformly over all data sequences $D^m \in \mathcal{D}^m(\Theta_k)$ where the norm $|\cdot|$ denotes the Euclidean norm.
4. Let $\mu(D^m : \theta)$ be the largest eigenvalue of $\hat{J}(\theta)$. For d_m as in condition 3, there exists a constant $0 < \mu < \infty$ such that for all m,

$$\sup_{D^m} \sup_{\theta:|\theta-\hat{\theta}|<(d_m/m)^{1/2}} \mu(D^m : \theta) \leq \mu.$$

5. Let $N_m \overset{\text{def}}{=} \{\theta \in \Theta_k : |\theta-\hat{\theta}| \leq \sqrt{d_m/m}\}$ and $N'_m \overset{\text{def}}{=} \{\theta \in \mathbf{R}^k : |\theta-\hat{\theta}| \leq \sqrt{d_m/m}\}$. Then for some $0 < r < 1$, for all sufficiently large m, $vol(N_m) \geq r \times vol(N'_m)$ where $vol(S)$ is Lebesgue volume of S.
6. For some $\underline{c} > 0$, for any $\theta \in \Theta$, $\pi(\theta) \geq \underline{c}$.

The following lemma gives an upper bound on ESC for the worst case. It shows that the ESC is within error $(k/2\lambda)\ln m$ of the least cumulative loss. It is proven using the technique of Laplace method.

Lemma 9.11 [Yamanishi 1998a] *Under   Assumption 9.10 for* $\mathcal{H}_k, L,$ *and* π*, for any* $\lambda > 0$*,*

$$I(D^m : \mathcal{H}_k) \leq \sum_{t=1}^{m} L(D_t : f_{\hat{\theta}}) + \frac{k}{2\lambda} \ln \frac{m\lambda\mu}{2\pi} + \frac{1}{\lambda} \ln(1/r\underline{c}) + o(1), \qquad (9.24)$$

where $o(1)$ *goes to zero uniformly in* $D^m \in \mathcal{D}^m(\Theta_k)$ *as* m *goes to infinity. The notation of* $\hat{\theta}, \mu, r,$ *and* $\underline{c}$ *follows Assumption 9.10.*

(See Appendix for the proof.)

Combining Theorem 9.9 with Lemma 9.11 leads to the following asymptotic upper bound on the minimax RCL.

Theorem 9.12 *Under Assumptions 9.3 and 9.10,*

$$\mathcal{R}_m(\mathcal{H}_k) \leq \frac{k}{2\lambda^*} \ln \frac{m\lambda^*\mu}{2\pi} + \frac{1}{\lambda^*} \ln \frac{1}{r\underline{c}} + o(1), \qquad (9.25)$$

where $\mathcal{D}^m(\mathcal{H})$ *as in (9.6) is set to* $\mathcal{D}^m(\Theta_k)$ *as in Assumption 9.10.*

Theorem 9.12 shows that the minimax RCL is within error $O(1)$ of $(k/2\lambda^*) \ln m$.

In order to investigate how tight (9.25) is, we derive an asymptotic lower bound on the minimax RCL.

Theorem 9.13 [Yamanishi 1998b; Vovk 1998]. *When* L *is the entropic loss or the square loss, for some regularity condition for* $\mathcal{H}$*,*

$$\mathcal{R}_m(\mathcal{H}_k) \geq \left(\frac{k}{2\lambda^*} - o(1) \right) \ln m. \qquad (9.26)$$

Furthermore, if a hypothesis class is restricted to be a finite subset of $\mathcal{H}_k$*, then for any loss function* L *satisfying Assumption 9.3, for some regularity condition for* $\mathcal{H}_k$ *and* L*, (9.26) holds.*

(See Appendix for the proof.)

We see from Theorems 9.12 and 9.13 that the ESC can be thought of as a minimax solution to RCL within error of $o(\ln m)$. It is formally summarized as follows:

Corollary 9.14 *Let*

$$\mathcal{I}_m(\mathcal{H}_k) \stackrel{\text{def}}{=} \sup_{D^m \in \mathcal{D}^m(\Theta)} \left(I(D^m : \mathcal{H}_k) - \min_{\theta} \sum_{t=1}^{m} L(y_t, f_\theta(x_t)) \right).$$

Then under the conditions as in Theorems 9.12 and 9.13,

$$\lim_{m \to \infty} \frac{|\mathcal{I}_m(\mathcal{H}_k) - \mathcal{R}_m(\mathcal{H}_k)|}{\ln m} = 0.$$

Corollary 9.14 implies that the relation between ESC and the minimax RCL is an analogue of that between SC and the minimax regret. This gives a rationale that ESC is a natural extension of SC.

Example 9.15 Let $\Theta_k = \{\theta = (\theta_1, \cdots, \theta_k) \in [0,1]^k : \theta_1^2 + \cdots + \theta_k^2 \leq 1\}$. Let a hypothesis class be $\mathcal{H}_k = \{f_\theta(x) = \theta^T x : X \in \mathcal{X}, \theta \in \Theta_k\}$. Let the distortion measure be the quadratic loss function as in (9.7). Then Assumption 9.10 holds, and we can set $\mu = 2k$ and $r = 1/2^k$. (Note that the estimate of r would be further improved.) If we set π to be the uniform density over Θ_k, we can set $\underline{c} = 2^k \Gamma(1 + k/2)/\pi^{k/2}$ where Γ denotes the gamma function.

For given D^m, let

$$\hat{\theta} = (\hat{J})^{-1} \frac{1}{m} \sum_{t=1}^{m} y_t x_t$$

where $\hat{J}$ is a matrix for which the (i,j)th component is given by $(1/m) \sum_{t=1}^{m} x_t^{(i)} x_t^{(j)}$. Let $\mathcal{D}^m(\Theta_k) = \{D^m \in \mathcal{D}^m : \hat{J} \text{ is regular and } \hat{\theta} \in \Theta_k\}$. Then for all $D^m \in \mathcal{D}^m(\Theta_k)$, the worst-case RCL for AGG with respect to D^m is upper-bounded by

$$\frac{k}{4} \ln \frac{2mk}{\pi} + \frac{1}{2} \ln \frac{\pi^{k/2}}{\Gamma(1 + k/2)} + o(1).$$

Example 9.16 Let $\mathcal{X} = \{1\}$ and $\mathcal{Y} = \mathcal{Z} = [0,1]$. Let a hypothesis class be $\mathcal{H} = \{f_\theta(x) = \theta x = \theta : \theta \in \Theta\}$ where $\Theta = [0,1]$. Let the distortion measure be the logistic loss function, for which the form rescaled for $\mathcal{Y} = \mathcal{Z} = [0,1]$ is given by

$$L(y,z) = \frac{1}{2} \left(-(2y-1)(2z-1) + \ln \left(e^{2z-1} + e^{-2z+1} \right) - B \right),$$

where $B = \ln(1 + e^{-2})$. Then it is easy to check that Assumption 9.10 holds, and that we can set $\mu = 2$ and $r = 1/2$. If we set π to be the uniform density over Θ, we can set $\underline{c} = 1$.

For given D^m, let

$$\hat{\theta} = 1/2 + (1/4) \ln \left(\left(1 + (1/m) \sum_{t=1}^{m} (2y_t - 1) \right) \Big/ \left(1 - (1/m) \sum_{t=1}^{m} (2y_t - 1) \right) \right).$$

Let $\mathcal{D}^m(\Theta) = \{D^m \in \mathcal{D}^m : \hat{\theta} \in \Theta\}$. Then for all $D^m \in \mathcal{D}^m(\Theta)$, the worst-case RCL for AGG with respect to D^m is upper-bounded by

$$\frac{1}{4} \ln \frac{2m}{\pi} + \frac{1}{2} \ln 2 + o(1).$$

Example 9.17 Let $\mathcal{X} = \{1\}, \mathcal{Y} = \{0,1\}$, and $\mathcal{Z} = [0,1]$. Let a hypothesis class be $\mathcal{H} = \{f_\theta(x) = \theta x = \theta : \theta \in \Theta\}$ where $\Theta = [\varepsilon, 1-\varepsilon]$ for $0 < \varepsilon < 1/2$. Let the distortion measure be the Hellinger loss function as in (9.10) for $(y,z) \in \mathcal{Y} \times \mathcal{Z}$.

Then we can confirm that Assumption 9.10 holds and we can set $\mu = (1/2)F(\varepsilon)$ and $r = 1/2$, where $F(\varepsilon) = 1/\varepsilon^{3/2} + 1/(1 - \varepsilon)^{3/2}$. If we set π to be the uniform density over Θ, then $\underline{c} = 1/(1 - 2\varepsilon)$.

For given D^m, let

$$\hat{\theta} = \left(\sum_{t=1}^{m} \sqrt{y_t} \right)^2 \Bigg/ \left(\left(\sum_{t=1}^{m} \sqrt{y_t} \right)^2 + \left(\sum_{t=1}^{m} \sqrt{1 - y_t} \right)^2 \right).$$

Let $\mathcal{D}^m(\Theta) = \{ D^m \in \mathcal{D}^m : \hat{\theta} \in \Theta \}$. Then for all $D^m \in \mathcal{D}^m(\Theta)$, the worst-case RCL for AGG with respect to D^m is upper-bounded by

$$\frac{1}{2\sqrt{2}} \ln \frac{\sqrt{2} m F(\varepsilon)}{4\pi} + \frac{1}{\sqrt{2}} \ln 2(1 - 2\varepsilon) + o(1).$$

Example 9.18 Let $\mathcal{X}$ be a bounded subset of $\mathbf{R}^n$ for a given positive integer n. Let $\mathcal{Y} = \{0, 1\}$ and let $\mathcal{Z}$ be a set of all probability mass functions over $\{0, 1\}$. Let $\mathcal{S} = \{S_i\}$ be a set of subsets of $\mathcal{X}$ such that $\cup_i S_i = \mathcal{X}$, $S_i \cap S_j = \emptyset (i \neq j)$, and $|\mathcal{S}| = k$. Let $\Theta_k = [0, 1]^k$. Let a hypothesis class $\mathcal{H}_k$ be a set of conditional probability mass functions defined by $\mathcal{H}_k = \{ f_\theta(1|x) = 1 - f_\theta(0|x) = \theta_i \text{ if } X \in S_i \ (i = 1, \cdots, k) : \theta = (\theta_1, \cdots, \theta_k) \in \Theta_k, \mathcal{S} = \{S_i\} \}$. That is, the hypothesis f_θ defines a rule that $y = 1$ occurs with probability θ_i and $y = 0$ occurs with probability $1 - \theta_i$ for x that fell into the region S_i $(i = 1, \cdots, k)$. These types of conditional probability mass functions are called *stochastic rules with finite partitioning* (see [Yamanishi 1992a]). Let the distortion measure be the quadratic loss function: $L(y, f(\cdot|x)) = (1 - f(y|x))^2$ for $y \in \mathcal{Y}$ and $f(\cdot|X) \in \mathcal{Z}$. Then by Assumption 9.10 $\mathcal{D}^m(\Theta_k) = \mathcal{D}^m$. We can set $\mu = 2$ and $r = 1/2^k$. If we set π to be the uniform density over Θ_k, we can set $\underline{c} = 1$.

Consider $\mathcal{H}$ as a class of real-valued functions through $f_\theta(x) = f_\theta(1|x)$. For all $D^m \in \mathcal{D}^m$, the worst-case RCL for AGG with respect to D^m is upper-bounded by

$$\frac{k}{4} \ln \frac{2m}{\pi} + \frac{k}{2} \ln 2 + o(1),$$

where m_i is the number of examples for which x fell into S_i $(i = 1, \cdots, k)$ and m_{1i} is the number of examples for which $y = 1$ and x fell into S_i $(i = 1, \cdots, k)$.

9.4   Applications of ESC to Batch-Learning

9.4.1   Batch-Learning Model

In this subsection we consider an application of ESC to the design and analysis of a batch-learning algorithm. In general, a *batch-learning algorithm* (see, e.g., [Haussler 1992]) is an algorithm that takes as input a sequence of examples: $D^m = D_1 \cdots D_m \in \mathcal{D}^*$ $(D_t = (x_t, y_t), \ t = 1, \cdots, m)$ and a hypothesis class $\mathcal{H}$, and then outputs a single hypothesis belonging to $\mathcal{H}$.

Let $\mathcal{F}$ be a set of all functions from $\mathcal{X}$ to $\mathcal{Z}$ in the case where $\mathcal{Z} \subset \mathbf{R}$, or let $\mathcal{F}$ be a set of all conditional probability densities (probability mass functions) over $\mathcal{Y}$ for given $x \in \mathcal{X}$ in the case where $\mathcal{Z}$ is a set of conditional probability densities (probability mass functions) over $\mathcal{Y}$ for given $x \in \mathcal{X}$. Suppose that each D is independently drawn according to the target distribution P over $\mathcal{D}$. For a hypothesis $f \in \mathcal{H}$, we define a *generalization loss* of f with respect to P by

$$\Delta_P(f) \stackrel{\text{def}}{=} E_P[L(D:f)] - \inf_{h \in \mathcal{F}} E_P[L(D:h)],$$

where E_P denotes the expectation taken for the generation of $D = (x,y)$ with respect to P. For sample size m, we also define a *statistical risk* for a batch-learning algorithm $\mathcal{A}$ as the expected value of the generalization loss:

$$E\left[\Delta_P(\hat{f})\right],$$

where $\hat{f}$ is an output of $\mathcal{A}$, which is a random variable depending on the input sequence D^m, and the expectation E is taken for the generation of D^m with respect to $P(D^m)$. Our goal is to design a batch-learning algorithm for which the statistical risk is as small as possible.

9.4.2   The Minimum L-Complexity Algorithm

Next we consider a batch-approximation of ESC by a single hypothesis to motivate a batch-learning algorithm. We now approximate the integral in (9.13) by quantizing Θ_k. For a k-dimensional parametric hypothesis class $\mathcal{H}_k = \{f_\theta : \theta \in \Theta_k \subset \mathbf{R}^k\}$, let $\Theta_k^{(m)}$ be a finite subset of Θ_k depending on sample size m. We define $\mathcal{H}_k^{(m)} (\subset \mathcal{H}_k)$ by $\mathcal{H}_k^{(m)} \stackrel{\text{def}}{=} \{f_\theta : \theta \in \Theta_k^{(m)}\}$. We refer $\Theta_k^{(m)}$ to as a *quantization* of Θ_k. Similarly, we refer $\mathcal{H}_k^{(m)}$ to as a *quantization* of $\mathcal{H}_k$. We call a map $\tau_m : \Theta_k \to \Theta_k^{(m)}$ a *truncation*. Similarly, we also call a map $\mathcal{H}_k \to \mathcal{H}_k^{(m)}$ defined by $f_\theta \in \mathcal{H}_k \to f_{\tau_m(\theta)} \in \mathcal{H}_k^{(m)}$ a *truncation*. For $\theta \in \Theta_k^{(m)}$, let $S(\theta) \stackrel{\text{def}}{=} \{\theta' \in \Theta_k : \tau_m(\theta') = \theta\}$, which is a set of real-valued points which are truncated to θ by τ_m.

Choosing τ_m so that for each $\theta \in \Theta_k^{(m)}$, the Lebesgue measure of $S(\theta)$ goes to zero as m increases to infinity, we may consider an approximation of ESC by the quantity $J(D^m : \mathcal{H}_k)$ defined as follows:

$$J(D^m : \mathcal{H}_k) \stackrel{\text{def}}{=} -\frac{1}{\lambda} \ln \sum_{\theta \in \Theta_k^{(m)}} W(\theta) \exp\left(-\lambda \sum_{t=1}^{m} L(D_t : f_\theta)\right),$$

where $W(\theta) \stackrel{\text{def}}{=} \int_{\theta' \in S(\theta)} \pi(\theta') d\theta'$ for a given prior density $\pi(\theta)$. The quantity

$J(D^m : \mathcal{H}_k)$ can be upper-bounded as follows:

$$J(D^m : \mathcal{H}_k) \leq -\frac{1}{\lambda} \ln \max_{\theta \in \Theta_k^{(m)}} W(\theta) \exp\left(-\lambda \sum_{t=1}^{m} L(D_t : f_\theta)\right)$$

$$= \min_{\theta \in \Theta_k^{(m)}} \left\{ \sum_{t=1}^{m} L(D_t : f_\theta) - \frac{1}{\lambda} \ln W(\theta) \right\}.$$

Notice here that $W(\theta)$ can be thought of as a probability mass of θ over $\Theta_k^{(m)}$ since $\sum_{\theta \in \Theta_k^{(m)}} W(\theta) = 1$. Hence $-\ln W(\theta)$ can be interpreted as the code length for θ. This implies that letting L_m be any function: $\Theta_k^{(m)} \to \mathbf{R}^+$ satisfying Kraft's inequality: $\sum_{\theta \in \Theta_k^{(m)}} e^{-L_m(\theta)} \leq 1$, we can upper-bound $J(D^m : \mathcal{H}_k)$ by

$$\min_{\theta \in \Theta_k^{(m)}} \left\{ \sum_{t=1}^{m} L(D_t : f_\theta) + \frac{1}{\lambda} L_m(\theta) \right\}. \tag{9.27}$$

This argument can be easily extended to a batch-approximation of ESC relative to a union set $\mathcal{H} = \cup_k \mathcal{H}_k$ with respect to k. That is, ESC of the form of (9.15) can be approximated by

$$\min_{k} \min_{\theta \in \Theta_k^{(m)}} \left\{ \sum_{t=1}^{m} L(D_t : f_\theta) + \frac{1}{\lambda} L_m(\theta, k) \right\}, \tag{9.28}$$

where $L_m(\cdot, \cdot)$ is a function: $\cup_k \Theta_k^{(m)} \times \{1, 2, \cdots\} \to \mathbf{R}^+$ satisfying $\sum_k \sum_{\theta \in \Theta_k^{(m)}} e^{-L_m(\theta, k)} \leq 1$.

From the above discussion we see that the best batch-approximation of ESC can be realized by a single hypothesis that minimizes the weighted sum of the empirical loss for the hypothesis with respect to D^m and the code length for the hypothesis. This fact motivates a batch-learning algorithm that produces from a data sequence D^m a hypothesis that attains the minimum of (9.28). For a loss function L, we name this algorithm the *minimum L-complexity algorithm* [Yamanishi 1998a], which we denote by MLC.

In order to define MLC, we have to fix a method of quantization for Θ_k. A question arises as to how finely we should quantize a continuous parameter space to approximate ESC best. The optimal quantization scale can be obtained similarly with the argument in [Rissanen 1989, pp. 55–56] as follows: Let $\delta = (\delta_1, \cdots, \delta_m)$ be the maximal quantization scale around the truncated value $\tau_m(\hat{\theta})$ of $\hat{\theta}$ where $\hat{\theta} = \arg\min_{\theta \in \Theta_k} \sum_{t=1}^{m} L(D_t : f_\theta)$ with $\partial \sum_{t=1}^{m} L(D_t : f_\theta)/\partial\theta|_{\theta=\hat{\theta}} = 0$. Applying Taylor's expansion of $L(D_t : f_{\hat{\theta}+\delta})$ around $\hat{\theta}$ up to the second order, we have

$$\sum_{t=1}^{m} L(D_t : f_{\hat{\theta}+\delta}) = \sum_{t=1}^{m} L(D_t : f_{\hat{\theta}}) + \frac{m}{2} \delta^T \Sigma \delta + mo(\delta^2),$$

where $\Sigma = ((1/m)(\partial^2 \sum_{t=1}^{m} L(D_t : f_\theta)/(\partial\theta_i \partial\theta_j)|_{\theta=\hat{\theta}})$. Since the code length for δ is given by $-\sum_i \ln \delta_i + O(1)$, the minimization of a type of (9.27) requires that

$$\sum_{t=1}^{m} L(D_t : f_{\hat{\theta}}) + \frac{m}{2} \delta^T \Sigma \delta - \frac{1}{\lambda} \sum_i \ln \delta_i$$

be minimized with respect to δ. Supposing that Σ is positive definite, it can be verified that the minimum is attained by δ such that $\prod_{i=1}^{k} \delta_i = \Theta \left(1/(\lambda m)^{k/2} |\Sigma|^{1/2} \right)$. This quantization scale δ also ensures that the minimum loss over $\Theta_k^{(m)}$ is within $O(k^2)$ of that over Θ_k. This nature for the fineness of quantization may be formalized as follows:

Assumption 9.19 *There exists a quantization of $\mathcal{H}_k$ such that for some $0 < B < \infty$, for all m, for all $D^m = D_1 \cdots D_m \in \mathcal{D}^*$, the following inequality holds:*

$$\min_{\theta \in \Theta_k^{(m)}} \sum_{t=1}^{m} L(D_t : f_\theta) \leq \inf_{\theta \in \Theta_k} \sum_{t=1}^{m} L(D_t : f_\theta) + Bk^2, \qquad (9.29)$$

where $\Theta_k^{(m)}$ is a quantization of Θ_k for sample size m.

We are now ready to give a formal definition of MLC.

Algorithm MLC
Let $\mathcal{H} = \cup_k \mathcal{H}_k$ and L be given. For each k, for each m, fix a quantization $\mathcal{H}_k^{(m)}$ of $\mathcal{H}_k$ and let $\mathcal{H}^{(m)} = \cup_k \mathcal{H}_k^{(m)}$. For each m, fix $L_m : \mathcal{H}^{(m)} \to \mathbf{R}^+$ satisfying

$$\sum_{f \in \mathcal{H}^{(m)}} e^{-L_m(f)} \leq 1, \qquad (9.30)$$

and λ, which may depend on m.
Input: $D^m \in \mathcal{D}^*$
Output: $\hat{f} \in \mathcal{H}^{(m)}$ such that

$$\hat{f} = \arg \min_{f \in \mathcal{H}^{(m)}} \left\{ \sum_{t=1}^{m} L(D_t : f) + \frac{1}{\lambda} L_m(f) \right\}. \qquad (9.31)$$

In the case where the hypothesis class is a class of probability densities and the distortion measure is the logarithmic loss function, MLC coincides with the statistical model selection criterion called the *minimum description length (MDL) principle* (see [Rissanen 1978, 1984, 1986, 1987, 1989, pp. 79–92]).

MLC is closely related to Barron's *complexity regularization algorithm* ([Barron 1991]), which we denote by CR. Barron showed that CR takes the same form as (9.31) with respect to the quadratic loss function and the logarithmic loss function. For other bounded loss functions, however, Barron took CR to have the following different form of

$$\hat{f} = \arg \min_{f \in \mathcal{H}^{(m)}} \left\{ \sum_{t=1}^{m} L(D_t : f) + \frac{1}{\lambda} (m L_m(f))^{1/2} \right\}, \qquad (9.32)$$

where λ is a positive constant. This form was taken to ensure bounds on the statistical risk of $\hat{f}$ by the method of analysis in [Barron 1991], and no longer has interpretation as an approximation of ESC. Unlike CR of the form of (9.32), MLC offers a unifying strategy that always takes the form of (9.31) regardless of a loss function and λ.

9.4.3   Analysis of MLC

We analyze MLC by giving upper bounds on its statistical risk.

Theorem 9.20 [Yamanishi 1998a] *Suppose that for some $0 < C < \infty$, for all D, for all $f \in \mathcal{H}$, $0 \le L(D : f) \le C$. Let $h(\lambda) \stackrel{\text{def}}{=} (e^{\lambda C} - 1)/C$. Assume that for the sequence $D^m = D_1, \cdots, D_m \in \mathcal{D}^*$, each D_t is independently drawn according to the unknown target distribution P. Let $\mathcal{H}^{(m)}$ be a quantization of $\mathcal{H}$. Then for any $\lambda > 0$, the statistical risk for MLC using $\mathcal{H} = \cup_k \mathcal{H}_k$ is upper-bounded as follows:*

$$E\left[\Delta_P(\hat{f})\right] < \inf_{f \in \mathcal{H}^{(m)}} \left\{ C^2 h(\lambda) + \Delta_P(f) + \frac{(L_m(f) + 1)}{mh(\lambda)} \right\} \qquad (9.33)$$

(See Appendix for the proof.)

Note that bound (9.33) is general in the sense that it holds for all $\lambda > 0$, while Barron's CR of the form (9.32) has an upper bound on its statistical risk:

$$\inf_{f \in \mathcal{H}^{(m)}} \left\{ \Delta_P(f) + const \left(\frac{L_m(f)}{m}\right)^{1/2} \right\}, \qquad (9.34)$$

under some constraints of λ. As will be seen in Corollary 9.21, however, MLC also leads to the square-root regularization term (with respect to m) after making necessary adjustments to λ to obtain the least upper bound on its statistical risk. In the end, MLC has the same performance as CR, while MLC has generality and allowance of the criterion to take the form of (9.31) rather than (9.32).

Let $\mathcal{F}$ be a set of all functions from $\mathcal{X}$ to $\mathcal{Z}$ or a set of conditional probability densities or conditional probability mass functions over $\mathcal{Y}$ for given $X \in \mathcal{X}$. Assume that for a given target distribution P, there exists a function f^* that attains the minimum of $E_P[L(D : f)]$ over all f in $\mathcal{F}$. Letting $\mathcal{H}_k \subset \mathcal{F}$ be a k-dimensional parametric class, the *parametric case* is the case where f^* is in $\mathcal{H}_k$ for some finite k. The *nonparametric case* is the case where f^* is not in $\mathcal{H}_k$ for any $k < \infty$. Below, as a corollary of Theorem 9.20, we give upper bounds on the statistical risk for MLC both for the parametric and nonparametric cases.

Corollary 9.21 [Yamanishi 1998a] *Suppose that for each k, $\mathcal{H}_k$ and L satisfy Assumption 9.19 and that for the quantization of $\mathcal{H}_k$ satisfying (9.29), any quantization scale $\delta = (\delta_1, \cdots, \delta_k)$ satisfies $\prod_{i=1}^{k} \delta_i = \Theta(1/(\lambda m)^{k/2})$. Suppose also that $L_m(f)$ takes a constant value over $\mathcal{H}_k^{(m)}$.*

Parametric case: *Assume that for the target distribution P, for some $k^* < \infty$, f^* is in $\mathcal{H}_{k^*}$ and is written as f_{θ^*}. Then letting $\lambda = (1/C)\ln(1 + C((\ln m)/m)^{1/2}) = O(((\ln m)/m)^{1/2})$, we have the following upper bound on the statistical risk for MLC:*

$$E[\Delta_P(\hat{f})] = O\left(\left(\frac{\ln m}{m}\right)^{1/2}\right) \tag{9.35}$$

Nonparametric case: *Assume that for the target distribution P, for some $\alpha > 0$, for each k, the optimal hypothesis f^* can be approximated by a k-dimensional subclass $\mathcal{H}_k$ of $\mathcal{H}$ with error: $\inf_{f \in \mathcal{H}_k} \Delta_P(f) = O(1/k^\alpha)$. Then letting $\lambda = (1/C)\ln(1 + C((\ln m)/m)^{1/2})$, we have the following upper bound on the statistical risk for MLC:*

$$E[\Delta_P(\hat{f})] = O\left(\left(\frac{\ln m}{m}\right)^{\alpha/(2(\alpha+1))}\right) \tag{9.36}$$

In the special case where α is known to MLC in advance, letting $\lambda = (1/C)\ln(1 + C((\ln m)/m)^{\alpha/(2\alpha+1)})$, we have the following upper bound on the statistical risk for MLC:

$$E[\Delta_P(\hat{f})] = O\left(\left(\frac{\ln m}{m}\right)^{\alpha/(2\alpha+1)}\right) \tag{9.37}$$

(See Appendix for the proof.)

For the parametric case, the convergence rate bound (9.35) coincides with that obtained for Barron's CR with respect to m (see [Barron 1991]). This bound is fastest to date. For the nonparametric case, (9.37) is slightly better than (9.36) and coincides with that obtained for CR in [Barron 1991], which is fastest to date.

9.5   Concluding Remarks

We have introduced ESC as an extension of stochastic complexity to the decision-theoretic setting where a general real-valued function is used as a hypothesis and a general loss function is used as a distortion measure. Through ESC we have given a unifying view of the design and analysis of the learning algorithms which have turned out to be most effective in batch-learning and online prediction scenarios.

For the online prediction scenario, a sequential realization of ESC induces the aggregating strategy. This corresponds to the fact that a sequential realization of SC induces the Bayes algorithm for the specific case where the hypothesis class is a class of probability densities and the distortion measure is the logarithmic loss. We have derived an upper bound on the worst-case relative cumulative loss for the aggregating strategy and showed that under certain conditions ESC is a minimax solution to the relative cumulative loss.

For the batch-learning scenario, a batch-approximation of ESC using a single hypothesis induces the learning algorithm MLC, which is a formal extension of the MDL learning algorithm.

We have derived upper bounds on the statistical risk for MLC with respect to general bounded loss functions. It has turned out that MLC has the least upper bounds (to date) on the statistical risk by tuning λ optimally. It remains for future study to derive a tight lower bound on the statistical risk for MLC to compare it with our upper bounds.

Through this chapter we have built a theory with respect to bounded loss functions. However, it is not necessarily applied to unbounded loss functions. Rissanen [2003] has recently developed a theory of stochastic complexity with respect to unbounded nonlogarithmic loss functions to derive a general form of tight lower bounds for nonlogarithmic loss functions. Combining our theory with Rissanen's would lead to a significant generalization of stochastic complexity.

9.6 Appendix: Proofs

9.6.1 Proof of Lemma 9.11

The key technique for proving Lemma 9.11 is *Laplace's method*, which is a method for approximating an integral by that over a small neighborhood of the parameter value which attains the maximum of the quantity to be integrated (see e.g., [De Bruijn 1958],[Clarke and Barron 1990]). We first prove (9.24) based on the proof of Theorem 2.3 in [Clarke and Barron 1990], which effectively makes use of the Laplace method to approximate the Bayesian marginal density.

Let $d = d_m$ satisfy that $d_m > k$, $\lim_{m \to \infty} (d_m/m) = 0$ and $\lim_{m \to \infty} d_m = \infty$ and let $\delta_m = \sqrt{d_m/m}$. For a given sequence D^m in $\mathcal{D}^m(\Theta_k)$, let $\hat{\theta} = \arg\min_{\theta \in \Theta_k} \sum_{t=1}^m L(D_t : f_\theta)$ and $N_{\delta_m} \overset{\text{def}}{=} \{\theta \in \Theta_k : |\theta - \hat{\theta}| \le \delta_m\}$ where $|\cdot|$ is the Euclidean norm. Observe first that for $\theta \in N_{\delta_m}$, a Taylor's expansion of $L(D^m : f_\theta)$ around $\hat{\theta}$ up to the second order is evaluated as follows: Let ξ be a parameter value such that $|\xi - \hat{\theta}| \le |\theta - \hat{\theta}|$. Under Assumption 9.10, by the continuity of the second derivatives and the uniform continuity of $\hat{J}(\theta)$, and the condition that the largest eigenvalue of $\hat{J}(\theta)$ is uniformly upper-bounded by μ in a neighborhood of $\hat{\theta}$, for sufficiently large m, for all $D^m \in \mathcal{D}^m(\Theta_k)$, the following inequality holds:

$$L(D^m : f_\theta) = L(D^m : f_{\hat{\theta}}) + \frac{m}{2}(\theta - \hat{\theta})^T \hat{J}(\xi)(\theta - \hat{\theta})$$

$$\le L(D^m : f_{\hat{\theta}}) + \frac{m\mu}{2} \sum_{i=1}^k (\theta_i - \hat{\theta}_i)^2. \tag{9.38}$$

We can upper-bound $I(D^m : \mathcal{H}_k)$ using (9.38) as follows:

$$
I(D^m : \mathcal{H}_k)
$$
$$
= -\frac{1}{\lambda} \ln \int \pi(\theta) \exp\left(-\lambda L(D^m : f_\theta)\right) d\theta
$$
$$
\leq -\frac{1}{\lambda} \ln \int_{N_{\delta_m}} \pi(\theta) \exp\left(-\lambda L(D^m : f_\theta)\right) d\theta
$$
$$
\leq -\frac{1}{\lambda} \ln \int_{N_{\delta_m}} \pi(\theta) \exp\left(-\lambda L(D^m : f_{\hat\theta}) - (\lambda\mu m/2)\sum_{i=1}^{k}(\theta_i - \hat\theta_i)^2\right) d\theta
$$
$$
\leq L(D^m : f_{\hat\theta}) - \frac{1}{\lambda}\ln\pi(\underline{\theta}) + \frac{1}{\lambda}\ln\int_{N_{\delta_m}}\exp\left(-(\lambda\mu m/2)\sum_{i=1}^{k}(\theta_i - \hat\theta_i)^2\right) d\theta,
$$

where $\underline{\theta}$ is the parameter value such that $\pi(\theta)$ is at minimum in N_{δ_m}. Note that $\pi(\theta)$ is uniformly lower-bounded by $\underline{c}$ over Θ_k and thus $-(1/\lambda)\ln\pi(\underline{\theta}) \leq -(1/\lambda)\ln\underline{c}$.

In order to evaluate the quantity $\int_{N_{\delta_m}}\exp\left(-(\lambda\mu m/2)\sum_{i=1}^{k}(\theta_i - \hat\theta_i)^2\right) d\theta$, define $N'_{\delta_m} \stackrel{\text{def}}{=} \{\theta \in \mathbf{R}^k : |\theta - \hat\theta| \leq \delta_m\}$. Under condition 11, we see

$$
\int_{N_{\delta_m}}\exp\left(-(\lambda\mu m/2)\sum_{i=1}^{k}(\theta_i - \hat\theta_i)^2\right) d\theta
$$
$$
\geq r\int_{N'_{\delta_m}}\exp\left(-(\lambda\mu m/2)\sum_{i=1}^{k}(\theta_i - \hat\theta_i)^2\right) d\theta
$$
$$
\geq r\left(1 - \frac{k}{d_m}\right)\left(\frac{2\pi}{m}\right)^{k/2}\left(\sqrt{(\lambda\mu)^k}\right)^{-1}.
$$

Hence we obtain

$$
I(D^m : \mathcal{H}_k) \leq L(D^m : f_{\hat\theta}) + \frac{k}{2\lambda}\ln\frac{m\lambda\mu}{2\pi} + \frac{1}{\lambda}\ln(1/\underline{c}) - \frac{1}{\lambda}\ln r\left(1 - \frac{k}{d_m}\right).
$$

Letting d_m go to infinity, we have

$$
I(D^m : \mathcal{H}_k) \leq L(D^m : f_{\hat\theta}) + \frac{k}{2\lambda}\ln\frac{m\lambda\mu}{2\pi} + \frac{1}{\lambda}\ln(1/r\underline{c}) + o(1),
$$

where the $o(1)$ term tends to zero uniformly over $\mathcal{D}^m(\Theta_k)$ as m goes to infinity, and μ does not depend on D^m. This completes the proof of (9.24). $\square$

9.6.2   Proof of Theorem 9.13

Let $\mathcal{P}^m$ be the set of all probability distributions over $\mathcal{D}^m$ such that $P(\mathcal{D}^m(\Theta_k)) = 1$. Observe that for any probability distribution $P^* \in \mathcal{P}^m$,

$$
\inf_A \sup_{D^m \in \mathcal{D}^m(\Theta)} R(A : D^m) \geq \sup_{P \in \mathcal{P}^m} \inf_A E_P[R(A : D^m)]
$$
$$
\geq \inf_A E_{P^*}\left[\sum L(y_t.\hat y_t)\right] - E_{P^*}\left[\min_{\theta\in\Theta} L(y_t, f_\theta(x_t))\right], \quad (9.39)
$$

where E_P denotes the expectation taken for the generation of D^m with respect to P. Hence the proof can be reduced to bounding the both terms of (9.39) by choosing a specific distribution for P^*. We choose the mixture density for P^* as indicated below. Similar proof techniques are partly used in [Vovk 1998]. We attempt to unify them by offering a method applied commonly to the entropic loss and the square loss.

First we prove (9.26) for the entropic loss in the case of $k = 1$. Let $x_* \in \mathcal{X}$ be such that for all $y^m = y_1 \cdots y_m \in \mathcal{Y}^m$, $\hat{\theta} = \arg\min_\theta \sum_{t=1} L(y_t, f_\theta(x_*))$ satisfies $\partial \sum_{t=1} L(y_t, f_\theta(x_*))|_{\theta=\hat{\theta}} = 0$, and $\hat{\theta}$ is uniquely determined. There exists such x_* under Assumption 9.10. Define the probability distribution P^* so that it is decomposed as $P^*(D^m) = P_{\mathcal{X}}^*(x^m) P_{\mathcal{Y}}^*(y^m)$ (i.e., x^m and y^m are independent.) Here

$$
P_{\mathcal{X}}^*(x^m) = \begin{cases} 1 & x^m = x_* \cdots x_* \\ 0 & \text{otherwise}, \end{cases}
$$

and

$$
P_{\mathcal{Y}}^*(y^m) = \int \pi(\theta) \prod_{i=1}^m P(y_i|\theta) d\theta,
$$

where

$$
P(y|\theta) = \begin{cases} f_\theta(x_*) & y = 1 \\ 1 - f_\theta(x_*) & y = 0 \end{cases}
$$

and π is a given prior density over Θ. Then the conditional probability distribution of $y_t \in \{0, 1\}$ for given $y^{t-1} = y_1 \cdots y_{t-1}$ is given by

$$
P(y|y^{t-1}) = P^*(y^{t-1} y_t) / P^*(y^{t-1})
$$
$$
= \int P(y_t|\theta) P(\theta|y^{t-1}) d\theta,
$$

where

$$
P(\theta|y^{t-1}) = \frac{\pi(\theta) \prod_{i=1}^{t-1} P(y_i|\theta)}{\int \pi(\theta) \prod_{i=1}^{t-1} P(y_i|\theta) d\theta}.
$$

Observe that for the entropic loss L, for P^* as above,

$$
\inf_A E_{P^*} \left[\sum_{t=1}^m L(y_t, \hat{y}_t) \right] = E_{P^*} \left[-\sum_{t=1}^m \ln P(y_t|y^{t-1}) \right].
$$

Notice here that by choosing Jeffreys' prior as in Section 9.2 for π,

$$
P(1|y^{t-1}) = \left(\sum_{j=1}^{t-1} y_j + 1 \right) / t. \tag{9.40}
$$

Then we see that for all y^m,

$$-\sum_{t=1}^{m} \ln P(y_t|y^{t-1}) \geq -\sum_{t=1}^{m} \ln P(y_t|\hat{\theta}) + \frac{1}{2}(1-o(1))\ln m, \qquad (9.41)$$

where $\hat{\theta} = \arg\min_{\theta\in\Theta}\left(-\sum_{t=1}^{m}\ln P^*(y_t|\theta)\right)$.

Hence we have

$$\inf_{A} E_{P^*}\left[\sum_{t=1}^{m} L(y_t,\hat{y}_t)\right] - E_{P^*}\left[\min_{\theta\in\Theta} L(y_t,f_\theta(x_t))\right] \geq \frac{1}{2}(1-o(1))\ln m.$$

Plugging this into (9.39) yields (9.26) with $k=1$ and $\lambda^*=1$. This result can be straightforwardly extended into the case where θ is multidimensional.

Next we prove (9.26) for the square loss in the case of $k=1$. We use the same notation for $P^*, P(y|\theta)$ and $P(y_t|y^{t-1})$ as the entropic loss case. The idea of the proof is basically the same as that for the entropic loss. Then we see

$$E_{P^*}\left[\min_{\theta\in\Theta} L(y_t,f_\theta(x_t))\right] = E_{P^*}\left[\sum_{t=1}^{m} y_t^2 - \frac{1}{m}\left(\sum_{t=1}^{m} y_t\right)^2\right]. \qquad (9.42)$$

Here we take an expectation of each y_t with respect to $P(y|\theta)$, then take an expectation of the sum with respect to $\pi(\theta)$ to see that (9.42) is given as follows:

$$E_{P^*}\left[\sum_{t=1}^{m} y_t^2 - \frac{1}{m}\left(\sum_{t=1}^{m} y_t\right)^2\right] = m\int \pi(\theta)P(1|\theta)P(0|\theta)d\theta + O(1) \qquad (9.43)$$

On the other hand, we have

$$\inf_{A} E_{P^*}\left[\sum_{t=1}^{m} L(y_t,\hat{y}_t)\right] = E_{P^*}\left[\sum_{t=1}^{m}(y_t - P(1|y^{t-1}))^2\right].$$

Here we can plug an approximation

$$P(1|y^{t-1}) \approx \sum_{j=1}^{t-1} y_j/(t-1)$$

into (9.44) and take an expectation of each y_t with respect to $P(y|\theta)$ and then take an expectation of the sum with respect to $\pi(\theta)$ to see that the expectation of (9.42) with respect to P^* is given as follows:

$$E_{P^*}\left[\sum_{t=1}^{m}(y_t - P(1|y^{t-1}))^2\right] = (m + \ln m)\int \pi(\theta)P(1|\theta)P(0|\theta)d\theta + O(1) \qquad (9.44)$$

Let $\pi(\theta)$ be the prior density over Θ that puts a large probability mass on the neighborhood of θ such that $P(1|\theta) = 1/2$. Then (9.44) is lower-bounded by

$$m\int \pi(\theta)P(1|\theta)P(0|\theta)d\theta + (1/4 - o(1))\ln m.$$

Plugging this bound and (9.43) into (9.39) yields (9.26) with $k = 1$ and $\lambda^* = 2$. This result can be straightforwardly extended into the case where θ is multi-dimensional. See [Yamanishi 1998b] for further generalization with respect to general loss functions $\qquad\qquad\qquad\qquad\qquad\qquad\qquad\qquad\qquad\qquad\qquad$ $\square$

9.6.3   Proof of Theorem 9.20

We abbreviate $\sum_{t=1}^{m} L(D_t : f)$ as $L(D^m : f)$. Choose $\bar{f} \in \mathcal{H}^{(m)}$ arbitrarily. Let $\hat{f}$ be an output of MLC.

First note that if $\Delta_P(\hat{f}) > \varepsilon$, then the hypothesis that attains the minimum of the quantity: $\lambda L(D^m : f) + L_m(f)$ over $\mathcal{H}^{(m)}$ lies in the range $\{f \in \mathcal{H}^{(m)} : \Delta_P(f) > \varepsilon\}$. Thus $Prob[\Delta_P(\hat{f}) > \varepsilon]$ is upper-bounded as follows:

$$Prob\left[\Delta_P(\hat{f}) > \varepsilon\right]$$

$$\leq Prob\left[\min_{f \in \mathcal{H}^{(m)}:\Delta_P(f)>\varepsilon} \{\lambda L(D^m : f) + L_m(f)\} \leq \lambda L(D^m : \bar{f}) + L_m(\bar{f})\right]$$

$$= Prob\left[\max_{f \in \mathcal{H}^{(m)}:\Delta_P(f)>\varepsilon} e^{-\lambda L(D^m:f)-L_m(f)} \geq e^{-\lambda L(D^m:\bar{f})-L_m(\bar{f})}\right]$$

$$\leq \sum_{f \in \mathcal{H}^{(m)}:\Delta_P(f)>\varepsilon} Prob\left[e^{-\lambda L(D^m:f)-L_m(f)} \geq e^{-\lambda L(D^m:\bar{f})-L_m(\bar{f})}\right] \qquad (9.45)$$

Next we evaluate the probability (9.45). Let E be the set of D^m satisfying the event that $e^{-\lambda L(D^m:f)-L_m(f)} \geq e^{-\lambda L(D^m:\bar{f})-L_m(\bar{f})}$. For all $f \in \mathcal{H}^{(m)}$, we have

$$Prob\left[e^{-\lambda L(D^m:f)-L_m(f)} \geq e^{-\lambda L(D^m:\bar{f})-L_m(\bar{f})}\right]$$

$$= \int_{D^m \in E} dP(D^m)$$

$$\leq \int_{D^m \in E} dP(D^m) \frac{e^{-\lambda L(D^m:f)-L_m(f)}}{e^{-\lambda L(D^m:\bar{f})-L_m(\bar{f})}}$$

$$\leq e^{-L_m(f)+L_m(\bar{f})} \int dP(D^m) e^{-\lambda L(D^m:f)+\lambda L(D^m:\bar{f})}$$

$$= e^{-L_m(f)+L_m(\bar{f})} \left(\int dP(D) e^{-\lambda(L(D:f)-L(D:\bar{f}))}\right)^m. \qquad (9.46)$$

Here we have used the independence assumption for D to derive the last equation.

We use the following key lemma to further evaluate (9.46).

Lemma 9.22 *For f satisfying $\Delta_P(f) > \varepsilon$,*

$$\int dP(D) e^{-\lambda(L(D:f)-L(D:\bar{f}))} < \exp\left[-h(\lambda)\left(\varepsilon - \left(C^2 h(\lambda) + \Delta_P(\bar{f})\right)\right)\right], \qquad (9.47)$$

where $h(\lambda) = (e^{\lambda C} - 1)/C$.

By plugging (9.47) into (9.46), and then the resulting inequality into (9.45), we can upper-bound $Prob[\Delta_P(\hat{f}) > \varepsilon]$ as follows:

$$Prob[\Delta_P(\hat{f}) > \varepsilon] < e^{L_m(\bar{f})}e^{-mh(\lambda)(\varepsilon - (C^2 h(\lambda) + \Delta_P(\bar{f})))} \sum_{f \in \mathcal{H}^{(m)}: \Delta_P(f) > \varepsilon} e^{-L_m(f)}$$

$$\leq \exp\left[-mh(\lambda)\left(\varepsilon - \left(C^2 h(\lambda) + \Delta_P(\bar{f}) + \frac{L_m(\bar{f})}{mh(\lambda)}\right)\right)\right], \quad (9.48)$$

where the last inequality follows from the fact: $\sum_{f \in \mathcal{H}^{(m)}: \Delta_P(f) > \varepsilon} e^{-L_m(f)} \leq \sum_{f \in \mathcal{H}^{(m)}} e^{-L_m(f)} \leq 1$ by (9.30). Letting $\varepsilon' = \varepsilon - (C^2 h(\lambda) + \Delta_P(\bar{f}) + L_m(\bar{f})/mh(\lambda))$, (9.48) is written as

$$Prob\left[\Delta_P(\hat{f}) - \left(C^2 h(\lambda) + \Delta_P(\bar{f}) + \frac{L_m(\bar{f})}{mh(\lambda)}\right) > \varepsilon'\right] < e^{-mh(\lambda)\varepsilon'}.$$

Hence the statistical risk for MLC is upper-bounded as follows:

$$E[\Delta_P(\hat{f})] < C^2 h(\lambda) + \Delta_P(\bar{f}) + \frac{L_m(\bar{f})}{mh(\lambda)} + \int_0^\infty e^{-mh(\lambda)\varepsilon'} d\varepsilon'$$

$$= C^2 h(\lambda) + \Delta_P(\bar{f}) + \frac{L_m(\bar{f}) + 1}{mh(\lambda)} \quad (9.49)$$

Since (9.49) holds for all $\bar{f} \in \mathcal{H}^{(m)}$, we obtain (9.33) by minimizing the left-hand side of (9.49) with respect to $\bar{f}$ over $\mathcal{H}^{(m)}$. This completes the proof of (9.33).   □

Proof (of Lemma 9.22): We start with the following two formulas:

Sublemma 9.23 *For $0 < C < \infty$, for $\lambda > 0$,*

$$e^{-\lambda x} \leq 1 - \frac{1 - e^{-\lambda C}}{C} x \quad (0 \leq x \leq C), \quad (9.50)$$

$$e^{-\lambda x} \leq 1 - \frac{e^{\lambda C} - 1}{C} x \quad (-C \leq x \leq 0). \quad (9.51)$$

Let $V(D : f, \bar{f}) \stackrel{\text{def}}{=} L(D : f) - L(D : \bar{f})$ and $\Delta(f \parallel \bar{f}) \stackrel{\text{def}}{=} E_P[V(D : f, \bar{f})]$. Then $-C \leq V(D : f, \bar{f}) \leq C$. Thus making use of (9.50) and (9.51), we obtain the following upper bound on $\int dP(D)e^{-\lambda(L(D:f)-L(D:\bar{f}))}$:

$$\int dP(D)e^{-\lambda(L(D:f)-L(D:\bar{f}))}$$

$$= \int_{D:V(D:f,\bar{f})\geq 0} dP(D)e^{-\lambda V(D:f,\bar{f})} + \int_{D:V(D:f,\bar{f})<0} dP(D)e^{-\lambda V(D:f,\bar{f})}$$

$$\leq \int_{D:V(D:f,\bar{f})\geq 0} dP(D)\left(1 - \frac{1 - e^{-\lambda C}}{C} V(D:f,\bar{f})\right)$$

$$+ \int_{D:V(D:f,\bar{f})<0} dP(D)\left(1 - \frac{e^{\lambda C} - 1}{C} V(D:f,\bar{f})\right)$$

$$(9.52)$$

Let $C_1 \stackrel{\text{def}}{=} (1 - e^{-\lambda C})/C$, $C_2 \stackrel{\text{def}}{=} (e^{\lambda C} - 1)/C$, and $h(f, \bar{f}) \stackrel{\text{def}}{=} \int_{D:V(D:f,\bar{f})\geq 0} dP(D)$

$V(D : f, \bar{f})(\le C)$. Then (9.52) can be further upper-bounded as follows:

$$\int_D dP(D)e^{-\lambda(L(D:f)-L(D:\bar{f}))}$$

$$\le 1 - C_1 \int_{D:V(D:f,\bar{f})\ge 0} dP(D)V(D : f, \bar{f}) - C_2 \int_{D:V(D:f,\bar{f})<0} dP(D)V(D : f, \bar{f})$$

$$= 1 - C_2\Delta(f \parallel \bar{f}) + (C_2 - C_1)h(f, \bar{f})$$

$$\le 1 - C_2\Delta(f \parallel \bar{f}) + (C_2 - C_1)C$$

$$= 1 - C_2\Delta_P(f) + C_2\Delta_P(\bar{f}) + (C_2 - C_1)C, \tag{9.53}$$

where (9.53) follows from the relation: $\Delta(f \parallel \bar{f}) = \Delta_P(f) - \Delta_P(\bar{f})$. Further note that $(C_2 - C_1)C = (e^{\lambda C} - 1)^2/e^{\lambda C} > 0$ and $(C_2 - C_1)C = C^2 C_2^2/e^{\lambda C} \le C^2 C_2^2$. Thus we have the following inequality for any f such that $\Delta_P(f) > \varepsilon$:

$$\int dP(D)e^{-\lambda(L(D:f)-L(D:\bar{f}))}$$

$$< 1 - C_2\varepsilon + C^2 C_2^2 + C_2\Delta_P(\bar{f})$$

$$\le \exp\left[-C_2\left(\varepsilon - \left(C^2 C_2 + \Delta_P(\bar{f})\right)\right)\right], \tag{9.54}$$

where (9.54) follows from the fact that for any $A > 0$, $1 - Ax \le e^{-Ax}$. Rewriting C_2 in (9.54) as $h(\lambda)$ yields (9.47). This completes the proof of Lemma 9.22. □

9.6.4 Proof of Corollary 9.21

First consider the parametric case where f^* is written as $f_{\theta^*} \in \mathcal{H}_{k^*}$ for some k^*. For each k, let $\mathcal{H}_k^{(m)}$ be a quantization of $\mathcal{H}_k$ with quantization scale δ such that $\prod_{i=1}^k \delta_i = \Theta(1/(\lambda m)^{k/2})$ for sample size m. Let $\bar{f}^*$ be the truncation of $f^* \in \mathcal{H}_{k^*}$. Then we see that $L_m(\bar{f}^*) = O(k^* \ln(m\lambda)) = O(k^* \ln m)$. If we set $\lambda = (1/C) \ln(1 + C((\ln m)/m)^{1/2})$, then we have $h(\lambda) = O(((\ln m)/m)^{1/2})$. Under Assumption 9.19 we can use the fact that $\Delta_P(f^*) = 0$ to upper-bound the statistical risk as follows:

$$E\left[\Delta_P(\hat{f})\right] < C^2 h(\lambda) + \Delta_P(f^*) + \frac{(L_m(\bar{f}^*) + \lambda B(k^*)^2 + 1)}{mh(\lambda)} = O\left(\left(\frac{\ln m}{m}\right)^{1/2}\right),$$

which yields (9.35).

Next consider the nonparametric case where $\inf_{f \in \mathcal{H}_k} \Delta_P(f) = O(1/k^\alpha)$. We obtain the following bound on the statistical risk for MLC:

$$E\left[\Delta_P(\hat{f})\right] < \min_k \inf_{f_\theta \in \mathcal{H}_k^{(m)}} \left\{C^2 h(\lambda) + \Delta_P(f_\theta) + \frac{(L_m(\bar{f}_\theta) + \lambda B k^2 + 1)}{mh(\lambda)}\right\}$$

$$= O\left(\min_k \left(\left(\frac{\ln m}{m}\right)^{1/2} + \frac{1}{k^\alpha} + k\left(\frac{\ln m}{m}\right)^{1/2}\right)\right)$$

$$= O\left(\left(\frac{\ln m}{m}\right)^{\alpha/2(\alpha+1)}\right), \tag{9.55}$$

which yields (9.36). The minimum in (9.55) is attained by $k = O((m/\ln m)^{1/2(\alpha+1)})$. Bound (9.37) can be obtained similarly with (9.36). $\qquad\square$

References

Barron, A.R. (1991). Complexity regularization with application to artificial neural networks. In G. Roussas (Ed.), *Nonparametric Functional Estimation and Related Topics,* pp. 561–576. Boston: Kluwer Academic.

Barron, A.R., and T. Cover (1991). Minimum complexity density estimation. *IEEE Transactions on Information Theory,* 37, pp.1034–1054.

Berger, J.O. (1985). *Statistical Decision Theory and Bayesian Analysis.* New York: Springer-Verlag.

Clarke, B.S., and A.R. Barron (1990). Information-theoretic asymptotics of Bayes methods. *IEEE Transactions on Information Theory,* 36, 453–471.

Clarke, B.S., and A.R. Barron (1994). Jeffreys prior is asymptotically least favorable under entropy risk. *Journal of Statistical Planning and Inference,* 41, 37–60.

Cesa-Bianchi, N., Y. Freund, D.P. Helmbold, D. Haussler, R. Schapire, and M.K. Warmuth (1993). How to use expert advice. In *Proceedings of the Twenty-fifth ACM Symposium on Theory of Computing,* New York: ACM Press, pp. 429-438.

Dawid, A. (1991). Statistical theory: The prequential approach. *Journal of the Royal Statistical Society Series A,* 147, 278–292.

De Bruijn, N.G. (1958). *Asymptotic Methods in Analysis.* New York:Dover.

Freund, Y. (1996). Predicting a binary sequence almost as well as the optimal biased coin. In *Proceedings of the Ninth ACM Conference on Computational Learning Theory,* New York: ACM Press, 89–98.

Haussler, D. (1992). Generalizing the PAC model for neural net and other learning applications. *Information and Computation,* 100, 78–150.

Haussler, D., J. Kivinen, and M.K. Warmuth (1995). Tight worst-case loss bounds for predicting with expert advice. In *Computational Learning Theory: Second European Conference, EuroCOLT'95,* New York: Springer-Verlag, pp.69–83.

Kivinen, J., and M. Warmuth (1994). Using experts for predicting continuous outcomes. In *Computational Learning Theory: EuroCOLT'93,* Oxford, UK: pp. 109–120.

Rissanen, J. (1978). Modeling by shortest data description. *Automatica,* 14, 465–471.

Rissanen, J. (1983). A universal data compression system. *IEEE Transactions on Information Theory,* 29, 656–664.

Rissanen, J. (1984). Universal coding, information, prediction, and estimation. *IEEE Transactions on Information Theory, 30,* 629–636.

Rissanen, J. (1986). Stochastic complexity and modeling. *Annals of Statistics, 14,* 1080–1100.

Rissanen, J. (1987). Stochastic complexity. *Journal of the Royal Statistical Society Series B, 49*(3), 223–239.

Rissanen, J. (1989). *Stochastic Complexity in Statistical Inquiry.* Singapore: World Scientific.

Rissanen, J. (1996). Fisher information and stochastic complexity. *IEEE Transactions on Information Theory, 42*(1), 40–47.

Rissanen, J. (2003). Complexity of simple nonlogarithmic loss functions. *IEEE Transactions on Information Theory, 49*(2), 476–484.

Shannon, C.E. (1948). A mathematical theory of communications. *Bell Systems Technical Journal, 47,* 147–157.

Shtarkov, Y.M. (1987). Universal sequential coding of single messages. *Problems of Information Transmission, 23*(3), 3–17.

Takeuchi, J. and A.R. Barron (1998). Asymptotically minimax regret by Bayes mixture. *Proceedings of 1998 IEEE International Symposium on Information Theory.*

Vovk, V.G. (1990). Aggregating strategies. In *Proceedings of the Third Annual Workshop on Computational Learning Theory,* pp.371–386. San Francisco: Morgan Kaufmann.

Vovk, V.G. (1998). Competitive online linear regression. In *Proceedings of Advances in NIPS'98,* pp. 364–370. Cambridge, MA: MIT Press.

Yamanishi, K. (1992a). A learning criterion for stochastic rules. *Machine Learning, 9,* 165–203.

Yamanishi, K. (1992b). Probably almost discriminative learning. *Machine Learning, 18,* 23–50.

Yamanishi, K. (1994a). Generalized stochastic complexity and its applications to learning. In *Proceedings of the 1994 Conference on Information Science and Systems,* Volume 2, pp.763–768.

Yamanishi, K. (1994b). The minimum L-complexity algorithm and its applications to learning non-parametric rules. In *Proceedings of the Seventh Annual ACM Conference on Computational Learning Theory,* pp.173–182. New York: ACM Press,

Yamanishi, K. (1995). A loss bound model for on-line stochastic prediction algorithms. *Information and Computation, 119*(1), 39–54.

Yamanishi, K. (1997). On-line maximum likelihood prediction with respect to general loss functions. *Journal of Computer and System Sciences, 55*(1), 105–118.

Yamanishi, K. (1998a). A decision-theoretic extension of stochastic complexity and its approximation to learning. *IEEE Transactions on Information Theory*, 44, 1424–1439.

Yamanishi, K. (1998b). Minimax relative loss analysis for sequential prediction algorithms using parametric hypotheses. In *Proceedings of 1998 ACM Annual Conference on Computational Learning Theory*, pp. 32–43. New York: ACM Press.

10   Kolmogorov's Structure Function in MDL Theory and Lossy Data Compression

Jorma Rissanen
Helsinki Institute for Information Technology,
Tampere and Helsinki Universities of Technology, Finland, and
University of London, England
Jrrissanen@aol.com

Ioan Tabus
Tampere University of Technology
Institute of Signal Processing
Tampere, Finland
tabus@cs.tut.fi

This chapter describes an extension of the minimum description length (MDL) theory inspired by Kolmogorov's structure function in the algorithmic theory of complexity. As in the MDL theory the models for the data are parametric distributions instead of programs in the algorithmic theory, and the results will be directly applicable to modeling problems. While the MDL principle gives the best code length by jointly describing the model and the remaining 'noise', we now get a similar decomposition when the code length of the model is restricted by a parameter. This gives a rate-distortion type of curve, which not only applies to modeling but also suggests a rate-distortion theory different from Shannon's, which we discuss in a preliminary manner.

10.1   Introduction

The Kolmogorov complexity of a data sequence in the algorithmic theory of information is defined to be the length of a shortest program in a universal programming language that generates the sequence. Although such a program takes advantage of all the regular features in the data that the language permits, it does not separate these features from the in general noisy data nor makes plain what they are. Clearly, what we mean by a 'model' of data is precisely the regular features. In an unpublished work (see [Vereshchagin and Vitányi 2001] and [Cover and Thomas 1991]), Kolmogorov introduced an extension of the complexity which not only isolates the regular features but also provides a yardstick for the amount of noise that a desired amount of features leaves unexplained.

The minimum description length (MDL) theory was patterned after the algorithmic theory but with a far less powerful language in which to represent the regular features in data, namely, a class of probability models. Because the models must be capable of being fitted to data they must be finitely describable and hence in the end parametric. The role of Kolmogorov complexity is played by the stochastic complexity [Rissanen 1996], which does make plain the structure of the optimal model and its number of parameters but not the necessary quantization of the real valued parameters.

In this chapter we apply Kolmogorov's ideas of the extended complexity to probability models, and we obtain a new chapter in the MDL theory. An interesting outcome of this work is a new theory of rate distortion, which we discuss in a preliminary way.

10.2   Kolmogorov Structure Function

Our work is based on Kolmogorov's unpublished ideas, which we learned from a recent paper by Vereshchagin and Vitányi [2001]. The ideas are perhaps easiest understood in the original framework of the algorithmic information theory, which we summarize.

The *Kolmogorov complexity* of a string $x = x^n = x_1, \ldots, x_n$, relative to a universal computer U, is defined as

$$K(x) = \min_{p(x)} |p(x)|,$$

where $|p(x)|$ is the length of a self-delimiting program in the language that generates the string [Solomonoff 1964; Kolmogorov 1965], see also Chapter 6 by Paul Vitányi in this book. Such a program is a code word of the string, which can be decoded by running the program. Since no program is a prefix of another, the set of them defines a prefix code.

Kolmogorov defined a *model* of the string x to be a finite set S that includes the string. This corresponds to intuition in that all strings in the set share a common model. The Kolmogorov complexity $K(x)$ is the shortest code length of the string without any separation of its properties from the 'noise', as it were, which most strings we are interested in have. It is clear that the measure of the amount of the properties of the string extracted by the set S is $K(S)$. But how to measure the remaining amount of noise? One might think that it could be done by the conditional complexity or code length $K(x|S)$, but this is not right, because $K(x|S)$ would take advantage of other possible properties in the string not captured by S. Also, one could not obtain the idea of Kolmogorov sufficient statistic; see, for instance, [Cover and Thomas 1991]. To ensure that no further properties are used, Kolmogorov took the code length $\log|S|$ to measure the amount of the remaining 'noise', and he defined the following *structure function*,

$$h_x(\alpha) = \min_{S \ni x}\{\log|S| : K(S) \le \alpha\}, \qquad (10.1)$$

of the parameter α. The minimizing set S_α extracts all properties from x on the level α; that is, with 'model cost' (= code length needed to describe S) not exceeding α. Notice, too, that $\log|S| \doteq \max_{y \in S} K(y|S)$, where by $\doteq$ ($\dot\ge$) we mean equality (inequality) up to a constant not depending on the length of y, as it's usually done in the algorithmic theory of information.

Clearly, $h_x(\alpha)$ is a decreasing function of α. The amount $K(x) - \alpha$, defining the so-called *sufficiency line*, is a lower bound for the structure function, and there is a special value $\bar\alpha$ defined as

$$\bar\alpha = \min\{\alpha : h_x(\alpha) + \alpha \doteq K(x)\}. \qquad (10.2)$$

The two-part code length

$$h_x(\bar\alpha) + \bar\alpha$$

represents the Kolmogorov *minimal sufficient statistics decomposition*, in which $S_{\bar\alpha}$ represents all learnable properties of x that can be captured by finite sets leaving $h_x(\bar\alpha)$ as the code length for noninformative 'noise'.

10.3   Probability Model Classes

Because the Kolmogorov complexity is noncomputable we want to apply the preceding notions, suitably modified, to the classes of parametric density or probability functions as models:

$$\mathcal{M}_\gamma = \{f(x^n; \theta, \gamma) : \theta \in \Omega_\gamma \subseteq R^k\}, \quad \mathcal{M} = \bigcup \mathcal{M}_\gamma,$$

where γ is a structure index such as the indices of some of the rows of a regressor matrix and $\theta = \theta_1, \ldots, \theta_k$, k depending on γ. For much of the discussion the structure index will be constant, and to simplify notations we write $f(x^n; \theta)$ for $f(x^n; \theta, \gamma)$. We mention that in the MDL theory the traditional 'nonparametric' models are not accepted. The reason is that unlike the parametric models they cannot be fitted to data, and in this theory there is no need for 'true' or imagined data generating distributions modeled by nonparametric distributions. In fact, we make no assumption about the data that they be samples from any distribution.

In order to define the structure function for the probability models we need to replace $K(x)$ by the *stochastic complexity* as the negative logarithm of the normalized maximum likelihood (NML) density function and the model cost $K(S)$ by the shortest code length $L(\theta^d, k)$ for quantized parameters θ^d and their number k. Further, we replace the set S by the set of 'typical' strings $f(\cdot; \theta^d)$.

10.3.1   Stochastic Complexity

Consider the normalized maximum likelihood (NML) density function

$$\hat{f}(x^n; \mathcal{M}_\gamma) = \frac{f(x^n; \hat{\theta}(x^n))}{C_n} \tag{10.3}$$

$$C_n = \int_{\hat{\theta}(y^n) \in \Omega^\circ} f(y^n; \hat{\theta}(y^n)) dy^n \tag{10.4}$$

$$= \int_{\hat{\theta} \in \Omega^\circ} g(\hat{\theta}; \hat{\theta}) d\hat{\theta},$$

where Ω° is the interior of $\Omega = \Omega_\gamma$, assumed to be compact, and $g(\hat{\theta}; \theta)$ is the density function on statistic $\hat{\theta}(x^n)$ induced by $f(y^n; \theta)$.

The NML density function, which clearly is universal in the model class considered, solves two minimax problems. The first, due to Shtarkov [1987], is as follows:

$$\min_q \max_{y^n} \log \frac{f(y^n; \hat{\theta}(y^n))}{q(y^n)}$$

It also solves the second minimax problem [Rissanen 2001],

$$\min_q \max_g E_g \log \frac{f(X^n; \hat{\theta}(X^n))}{q(X^n)} = \min_q \max_g E_g [\log 1/q(X^n) - \log 1/f(X^n; \hat{\theta}(X^n))],$$

where q and g range over any set of distributions that include $\hat{f}(x^n; \mathcal{M}_\gamma)$

Proof   The second minimax problem is equivalent with

$$\min_q \max_g D(g\|q) - D(\hat{f}\|g) + \log C_n \geq \max_g \min_q \ldots = \log C_n,$$

where $D(g\|q)$ denotes the Kullback-Leibler distance. The equality is reached for $\hat{q} = \hat{g} = \hat{f}$.   ∎

It is seen that the second minimax problem and its solution generalize Shannon's noiseless coding theorem in that the minimax code defined by the NML density function mimics the worst-case data-generating distribution, while in Shannon's theorem the optimal prefix code must mimic the data-generating distribution. Also, Shannon's theorem follows if we take the model class as a singleton set.

These properties of the NML density function can be strengthened such that if we restrict the data-generating density function g to the model class, then the minimax value cannot be beaten for any code except for g in a set whose volume shrinks to zero as $n \to \infty$ [Rissanen 2001].

Because of these results the definition of

$$-\log \hat{p}(x^n; \mathcal{M}_\gamma) = -\log p(x^n; \hat{\theta}(x^n), \gamma) + \log C_{n,\gamma} \qquad (10.5)$$

as the *stochastic complexity* of x^n, given $\mathcal{M}_\gamma$, is well justified [Rissanen 1996]; we also reintroduced the structure index γ.

Consider the generalization of the so-called Fisher information matrix,

$$J(\theta) = \lim_{n \to \infty} -n^{-1} \{ E_\theta \frac{\partial^2 \log f(X^n; \theta, \gamma)}{\partial \theta_i \partial \theta_j} \}, \qquad (10.6)$$

which we assume to be positive definite, bounded, and bounded away from the origin of a coordinate system in Ω in which the parameters $\theta = \theta_1, \dots, \theta_k$ are defined. We also assume its elements to be continuous. Under the main condition that the central limit theorem is satisfied by the model class in the sense that the distribution of $\hat{\theta}(x^n) - \theta$ converges to the normal distribution of mean zero and covariance $J^{-1}(\theta)$, we have the estimate [Rissanen 1996]

$$-\log \hat{f}(x^n; \mathcal{M}_\gamma) = -\log f(x^n; \hat{\theta}(x^n), \gamma) + \frac{k}{2} \log \frac{n}{2\pi} + \log \int_\Omega |J(\theta)|^{1/2} d\theta + o(1). \qquad (10.7)$$

10.3.2 A Partition of Ω

We want to have a partition of the compact parameter space into curvilinear hyperrectangles such that the Kullback-Leibler distance between the models $f_i = f(y^n; \theta^i)$ and $f_j = f(y^n; \theta^j)$, defined by the centers of two adjacent rectangles $\theta^i = \theta(i)$ and $\theta^j = \theta(j)$, is the same for any pair. We do not actually need to construct it because we only need some properties of it. In practice such a partition can be approximately obtained in various ways. To achieve this apply Taylor's expansion to the two adjacent models, which gives

$$D(f_i \| f_j) = \frac{n}{2} (\theta^j - \theta^i)' J(\tilde{\theta})(\theta^j - \theta^i),$$

where $\tilde{\theta}$ is a point between θ^i and θ^j. Next, consider the factorization of $J(\theta)$ as

$$J(\theta) = P'(\theta) \Lambda(\theta) P(\theta),$$

where $P(\theta)$ is an orthogonal matrix of rows $e_i'(\theta)$ defined by the unit length (column) eigenvectors $e_i(\theta)$ of $J(\theta)$, and Λ is a diagonal matrix defined by the eigenvalues $\lambda_i(\theta)$ of $J(\theta)$.

The eigenvectors and eigenvalues define at any point in Ω a set of curves $u_1(t), \dots, u_k(t)$, like geodesics, parameterized by a scalar t, both positive and negative, as the solution to the differential equations

$$du_i(t)/dt = \lambda_i^{-1}(u_i(t)) e_i(u_i(t)),$$

with the initial conditions $u_i(0) = \theta$. The tangents of the curves at θ are orthogonal.

We see that if $J(\theta)$ is a constant matrix the curves $u_i(t) = t\lambda_i^{-1}e_i$ are just extensions of the unit vectors e_i and hence straight lines.

The edges of a k-dimensional curvilinear rectangle are defined by 2^k corners, at each of which k geodesics intersect. We want to control the edges and hence the volume of these rectangles with a parameter d. Consider a hyperellipsoid centered at $\bar{\theta}$,

$$\delta' J(\bar{\theta})\delta = \sum_i^k \lambda_i(\bar{\theta})(\delta' e_i(\bar{\theta}))^2 = d/n, \tag{10.8}$$

where $\delta = \theta - \bar{\theta}$. It encloses a rectangle of maximum volume,

$$V = \left(\frac{4d}{nk}\right)^{k/2} |J(\bar{\theta})|^{-1/2}, \tag{10.9}$$

whose edge lengths are

$$s_i(\bar{\theta}) = \left(\frac{4d}{nk\lambda_i(\bar{\theta})}\right)^{1/2}. \tag{10.10}$$

We want the edges of the curvilinear rectangles to have lengths such that the Euclidean distance between their endpoints is s_i to the precision required for the desired maximum volume. For large n the volume of the curvilinear rectangle, centered at $\bar{\theta}$, will be V in (10.9) to within an error not exceeding $O(n^{-k})$.

Let the origin be a corner z_1, from which k geodesics emanate. Create k edges along these geodesics such that the Euclidean distance between their endpoint and the origin is $s_i(0)$, for $i = 1, \ldots, k$. Denote the endpoints by $z_2, \ldots, z_{k+1}$. There are k surfaces of dimensionality $k - 1$ defined by the geodesics of type

$$u_1(t), \ldots, u_{i-1}(t), 0, u_{i+1}(t), \ldots, u_k(t)$$

starting at every point of the ith edge. These sides of the rectangle include the origin and every $k-1$ collection of the corners $z_2, \ldots, z_{k+1}$, and they define one half of the $2k$ sides of the rectangle. We then move to the next corner, where the edge lengths not already assigned are set to their values (10.10). Complete the construction by defining the remaining k sides in terms of the geodesics starting along the edges of the previously constructed sides.

By a similar construct we create the next layers of curvilinear rectangles and we get a partition $\Pi = \{B_{i,n}(d) : i = 1, \ldots, N_d\}$ of Ω by the curvilinear rectangles with their centers θ^i, except at the boundary, which may cut a portion off the rectangles.

We need to define a center of the curvilinear rectangle so defined. We take it as the center $\bar{\theta}$ of the ellipsoid (10.8) for which the sum of the Euclidean distance from the corners to the ellipsoid is minimized. Call this center θ^1 and the curvilinear rectangle as the cell $B_{1,n}(d)$. It is clear that as $n \to \infty$ the edges of the rectangle converge to straight lines and the distances from the corners to the ellipsoid to zero.

10.3.3   Code Length for Models

If the central limit theorem (CLT) holds for $\hat{\theta}(y^n)$ we have the convergence, (10.7),

$$C_n \left(\frac{2\pi}{n} \right)^{k/2} \to \int_\Omega |J(\theta)|^{1/2} d\theta.$$

Consider the *canonical* 'prior' density function for $\hat{\theta}$,

$$w(\hat{\theta}) = \frac{g(\hat{\theta}; \hat{\theta})}{\int_\Omega g(\theta; \theta) d\theta}, \qquad (10.11)$$

which in the limit becomes Jeffreys' prior:

$$w(\hat{\theta}) = \frac{|J(\hat{\theta})|^{1/2}}{\int_\Omega |J(\theta)|^{1/2} d\theta}$$

This defines a probability distribution for the centers θ^i, which tends to a *uniform* one as n grows:

$$q_d(\theta^i) = \int_{B_{i,n}(d)(\theta^i)} w(\theta) d\theta \qquad (10.12)$$

$$\frac{q_d(\theta^i)}{w(\theta^i)|B_{i,n}(d)|} \to 1 \qquad (10.13)$$

$$\frac{q_d(\theta^i)}{\left(\frac{2d}{\pi k} \right)^{k/2} C_n^{-1}} \to 1 \qquad (10.14)$$

Here $|B_{i,n}(d)|$ denotes the volume of $B_{i,n}(d)$. With this approximation we get the code length for the model, defined by the center θ^i,

$$L_d(\theta^i) \cong \frac{k}{2} \log \frac{\pi k}{2d} + \log C_n. \qquad (10.15)$$

This also gives the number of rectangles partitioning Ω:

$$C_n \left(\frac{k\pi}{2d} \right)^{k/2}$$

10.4   Structure Function

We consider the set $X_{i,n}(d)$ of strings y^n such that $\hat{\theta}(y^n) \in B_{i,n}(d)$ as the set of typical strings of the model defined by θ^i. Just as $\log |S|$ is the code length of the worst-case sequence in S, we need the code length of the worst-case sequence y^n in $X_{i,n}(d)$, which is obtained by the Taylor series expansion as follows:

$$-\log f(y^n; \theta^i, \gamma) = -\log f(y^n; \hat{\theta}(y^n), \gamma) + \frac{1}{2} d, \qquad (10.16)$$

where y^n denotes a sequence for which

$$n(\hat{\theta}(y^n) - \theta^i)' \hat{J}(\tilde{\theta}^i)(\hat{\theta}(y^n) - \theta^i) = d.$$

Here $\hat{J}(\hat{\theta})$ is the empirical Fisher information matrix

$$\hat{J}(\hat{\theta}) = -n^{-1}\{\frac{\partial^2 \log f(y^n; \hat{\theta}, \gamma)}{\partial \hat{\theta}_j \partial \hat{\theta}_k}\}, \qquad (10.17)$$

and $\tilde{\theta}^i$ is a point between θ^i and $\hat{\theta}(y^n)$. We also assume that for all data sequences such that $\hat{\theta}(y^n)$ falls within $B_{i,n}(d)$ the empirical $\hat{J}(\hat{\theta}(y^n))$ converges to $\hat{J}(\hat{\theta})$ as $\hat{\theta}(y^n) \to \hat{\theta}$.

Suggested by this we define the structure function for the model class $\mathcal{M}_\gamma$ as follows:

$$h_{x^n}(\alpha) = \min_d\{-\log f(x^n; \hat{\theta}(x^n), \gamma) + \frac{1}{2}d : L_d(\theta^i) \leq \alpha\}, \qquad (10.18)$$

For the minimizing d the inequality will have to be satisfied with equality,

$$\alpha = \frac{k}{2}\log\frac{\pi k}{2d} + \log C_{n,\gamma},$$

and with the asymptotic approximation (10.15) we get

$$d_\alpha = \frac{\pi k}{2}C_{n,\gamma}^{2/k}e^{-2\alpha/k}, \qquad (10.19)$$

and

$$h_{x^n}(\alpha) = -\log f(x^n; \hat{\theta}(x^n), \gamma) + d_\alpha/2. \qquad (10.20)$$

We may ask for the values of α for which the structure function is closest to the sufficiency line defined by

$$-\log \hat{f}(x^n; \mathcal{M}_\gamma) - \alpha,$$

which amounts to the minimization of the two-part code length

$$\min_\alpha\{h_{x^n}(\alpha) + \alpha\}. \qquad (10.21)$$

With (10.20) and (10.19) we get the minimizing α as

$$\bar{\alpha} = \frac{k}{2}\log\frac{\pi}{2} + \log C_{n,\gamma}, \qquad (10.22)$$

and $d_{\bar{\alpha}} = k$. We then get the *universal sufficient statistics decomposition* of the model class $\mathcal{M}_\gamma$,

$$h_{x^n}(\bar{\alpha}) + \bar{\alpha} = -\log f(x^n; \hat{\theta}(x^n), \gamma) + \frac{k}{2} + \frac{k}{2}\log\frac{\pi}{2} + \log C_{n,\gamma}, \qquad (10.23)$$

in the spirit of Kolmogorov's sufficient statistics. In particular, the two last terms correspond to the code length for the model $K(S)$ in the algorithmic theory. These terms also represent the optimal amount of information one can extract from the string with the model class $\mathcal{M}_\gamma$, leaving the first two terms, $h_{x^n}(\bar{\alpha})$, as the code length of whatever remains in the data, the 'noise'. This is something of a figure of speech, because we have not split the data sequence x^n into 'noise' and the model. Such a separation turns out to be an intriguing problem, leading to a theory of lossy data compression to be discussed below. The models for which the values of α are larger than $\bar{\alpha}$ also extract all the information from the data, but in so doing they try to explain some of the noise, as it were. The interesting models correspond to the range $\alpha \leq \bar{\alpha}$, for they incorporate a portion of the learnable properties for a smaller 'model cost', the code lengh for the optimal model on that level, and they leave a greater amount as unexplained noise. We mention that in [Balasubramanian 1997], $C_{n,\gamma}$ was given the interpretation of the number of optimally *distinguishable* models from data x^n in a somewhat intricate sense. In a very real sense the number of the centers θ^i of the cells $B_{i,n}(d)$ can also be viewed as optimally distinguishable, and the two numbers are seen to differ for large n only slightly.

We next turn to the model class $\mathcal{M} = \bigcup_\gamma \mathcal{M}_\gamma$. To deal with that we need a distribution for γ. We take this as $1/|\Gamma|$, where Γ is the set of the relevant structures. For many cases it is enough to take the code length for γ simply as $\log n$, which is what we do here. In general the choice of the distribution for γ can be an intricate issue. The structure function is now

$$h_{x^n}(\alpha) = \min_{d,\gamma}\{-\log f(x^n; \hat{\theta}(x^n), \gamma) + \frac{1}{2}d : L_d(\theta_i) + \log n \leq \alpha\}. \qquad (10.24)$$

For each γ the minimizing value for d is

$$d_{\alpha,\gamma} = \frac{\pi k}{2}(nC_{n,\gamma})^{2/k}e^{-2\alpha/k},$$

and it is reached when the code length for the optimal model is α. To get an idea of the behavior of $d_{\alpha,\gamma}$ when $\gamma = k$ we use the asymptotic formula (10.7) for $C_{n,\gamma}$, which gives

$$d_{\alpha,\gamma} = \frac{k}{4}n^{1+2/k}e^{-2\alpha/k}(\int_\theta |J(\theta)|)^{2/k}.$$

For a fixed $\alpha = O(\log n)$ this is seen to be an increasing function of k, roughly as $O(k)$. The structure function then is given by

$$h_{x^n}(\alpha) = \min_{\gamma<n}\{-\log f(x^n; \hat{\theta}(x^n), \gamma) + \frac{1}{2}d_{\alpha,\gamma}\} = -\log f(x^n; \hat{\theta}(x^n), \hat{\gamma}) + \frac{1}{2}d_{\alpha,\hat{\gamma}}, \qquad (10.25)$$

where $\bar{\gamma}$ with $\bar{k}$ parameters is the minimizing value as a function of α. There is generally a well-defined minimum.

The minimum of the two-part code length $h_{x^n}(\alpha) + \alpha$ over α is

$$\min_{d,\gamma}[-\log f(x^n; \hat{\theta}(x^n), \gamma) + \frac{1}{2}d + L_d(\theta_i) + \log n]. \qquad (10.26)$$

For each γ the minimizing value for d is $\hat{d} = k$, as before, and we are left with the minimization

$$\min_{\gamma}\{-\log \hat{f}(x^n; \gamma) + \log n + \frac{k}{2} \log \frac{\pi e}{2}\}.$$

Letting $\hat{\gamma}$ denote the smallest of the minimizing structures and $\hat{k}$ the number of parameters in it, we get

$$h_{x^n}(\hat{\alpha}) = -\log f(x^n; \hat{\theta}(x^n), \hat{\gamma}) + \hat{k}/2, \qquad (10.27)$$

where

$$\hat{\alpha} = \frac{\hat{k}}{2} \log \frac{\pi}{2} + \log(nC_{n,\hat{\gamma}}). \qquad (10.28)$$

This gives the *universal sufficient statistics decomposition* of the model class $\mathcal{M}$:

$$h_{x^n}(\hat{\alpha}) + \hat{\alpha} = -\log f(x^n; \hat{\theta}(x^n), \hat{\gamma}) + \frac{\hat{k}}{2} + \log(nC_{n,\hat{\gamma}}) + \frac{\hat{k}}{2} \log \frac{\pi}{2} \qquad (10.29)$$

As above, $h_{\mathbf{x}^n}(\alpha)$ stays above the sufficiency line $L(\alpha) = -\log \hat{f}(x^n; \hat{\gamma}) + d_{\alpha,\gamma}/2$, the distance between the two minimized at the point $\hat{\alpha}$.

There remains one more case to consider, namely, the case where we are interested only in selecting the structure of the model rather than both the structure and the values of the parameters. If we use the simple distribution $1/n$ for the structure as in the previous case we get the structure function as

$$h_{x^n}(\alpha) = \min_{\gamma < n}\{-\log f(x^n; \hat{\theta}(x^n), \gamma) : \log C_{n,\gamma} + \log n \le \alpha\}. \qquad (10.30)$$

Of special interest is the value for α that minimizes $h_{x^n}(\alpha) + \alpha$, which amounts to the MDL principle in the stochastic complexity form:

$$\min_{\gamma < n}\{-\log f(x^n; \hat{\theta}(x^n), \gamma) + \log C_{n,\gamma}\} \qquad (10.31)$$

In conclusion, the theory of the structure functions defined gives strong support to the MDL principle in any of its forms, because it permits a formalization of the learnable information and its separation from uninformative noise, which is what the purpose of all modeling should be. Curiously enough, it also explains the riddle in traditional statistics of why one should accept the maximum likelihood estimates of the parameter values but not of their number. In this theory, neither of these estimates are acceptable. Rather, they are replaced by the MDL estimates.

10.5   Lossy Data Compression

The development above provides a different approach to lossy data compression from Shannon's rate-distortion theory. Let $X_{i,n}(d)$ be the inverse image of $B_{i,n}(d)$

under $\hat{\theta}(z^n)$. The idea is to construct the distorted sequences $\hat{x}^n$ as a subset of $X_{i,n}(d)$ defining the codebook.

10.5.1   Regression Models

We first consider the simple case where the model class is rich enough that we can take the codebook for each γ and d to consist of the single sequence, the mode

$$\hat{x}^n = \max_{y^n} f(y^n; \theta^i, \gamma).$$

Then, clearly, the code length of $\hat{x}^n$ equals $L_d(\theta^i) + \log n$, and the difference between the distorted sequence and x^n shrinks to zero when we let the number of parameters k grow and d shrink. This happens in regression problems, where the regressor matrix is of size $n \times n$ so that we have a transformation $x^n \leftrightarrow \theta^n$. With quadratic errors the model class consists of Gaussian density functions,

$$f(x^n | W; \theta, \gamma) = \frac{1}{(2\pi\tau)^{n/2}} e^{-(1/\tau) \sum_{t=1}^{n} (x_t - \bar{x}_t)^2}, \tag{10.32}$$

where $W = \{w_{i,t}\}$ is the regressor matrix and

$$\bar{x}_t = \sum_{i \in \gamma} \theta_i w_{i,t},$$

and γ is a set of indices of the rows of W. When the least squares coefficients $\hat{\theta}(x^n)$ are quantized to the centers of the cells $B_{i,n}(d)$, the distorted sequence $\hat{x}^n$ is indeed given by the mode

$$\hat{x}_t = \sum_{j \in \gamma} \theta_j^i w_{j,t}, \tag{10.33}$$

where $\theta^i = \theta_1^i, \ldots, \theta_k^i$ is the center of the cell that includes $\hat{\theta}(x^n)$.

When the regressor matrix is orthonormal, as is the case with certain wavelets, the optimal index set γ consists of the indices of the optimal number of the largest squared coefficients in the wavelet transform [Rissanen 2000], and the code length $L_d(\theta^i) + \log n = \alpha$ equals the code length for the distorted string. The amount of distortion is determined by the pair (d, k), which also determines $h_{x^n}(\alpha)$, and this as a function of α corresponds to the rate-distortion curve. An important difference is that this curve is defined for each sequence rather than in the mean distortion, and the whole technique gives a universal lossy compression, relative to the given Gaussian class. For another approach to universal lossy data compression, see [Zhang and Kontoyannis 2001].

10.5.2   Binary Sequences with Hamming Distance

We consider next the remaining cases where the model classes are not rich enough to permit the construction of the distorted sequence entirely in the parameter space.

To be specific we consider the case of binary strings, for which the natural distortion measure is the Hamming distance. We shall deal with it as if the model class in question were a Bernoulli class, but we may use it only to generate the distorted strings.

For the class of Bernoulli models with the parameter θ for the probability of the symbol 1 we take the parameter space as $[0, 1]$, even though the Fisher information $J(\theta) = 1/(\theta(1 - \theta))$ is infinite at 0 and 1. This is because we will consider binary strings x^t of short length $t \leq 64$, and no center of the partition $\Pi_t = \{B_{i,t}\}$ will be too close to the endpoints of the interval. We will not use the parameter d, and we take the lengths of the equivalence classes by (10.9) for the optimal value $d = 1$ as

$$|B_{i,t}| - \frac{2}{\sqrt{t}}(\theta^i(1 - \theta^i)^{1/2}.$$

We also place the center of the largest equivalence class at $\theta = 1/2$. Write the centers as $i_1/t, i_2/t, \ldots$. Instead of defining a distorted string for the center i_ν/t by the mode of $P(x^t; i_\nu/t)$ we map the center into the set of strings $S(i_\nu/t)$ of length t with i_ν 1s. We describe first a fast and simple algorithm to give the codebook $S_m(i_\nu/t)$ of size m, which may be compared with a lower bound to be defined.

In $S(i_\nu/t)$, sorted in an increasing lexical order, take the subset of m equally spaced strings as the codebook $S_m(i_\nu/t)$. In other words, the ordinals of these strings are $s, 2s, \ldots, ms$, where

$$s = \lfloor \binom{t}{i_\nu}/m \rfloor.$$

The ordinals, written in binary, serve as the code words $C(\hat{x}^t)$, from which the strings in the codebook can be decoded by the last-in first-out (LIFO) arithmetic decoding process [Rissanen 1976; Rissanen 1979]. This is done recursively. Starting with $\hat{x} = i, \hat{x}'$, where the first symbol $i = 0$ or $i = 1$, as the case may be, decode $i = 1$, if and only if

$$C(i, \hat{x}') \geq A(i, \hat{x}') = \binom{|\hat{x}'|}{n_1(\hat{x})}, \tag{10.34}$$

which leaves the string $\hat{x}'$ to be decoded ; we use the notation $n_i(\hat{x})$ for the number of 1s in $\hat{x}$ and $|\hat{x}|$ for its length. The process then continues by the recursions

$$C(\hat{x}') = C(0, \hat{x}') \tag{10.35}$$

$$C(\hat{x}') = C(1, \hat{x}') - A(1, \hat{x}') \tag{10.36}$$

$$A(\hat{x}') = \frac{n_i(\hat{x}') + 1}{|\hat{x}'| + 1} A(i, \hat{x}'). \tag{10.37}$$

For a string x^t let the maximum likelihood estimate $\hat{\theta}(x^t) = \sum_j x_j/t$ fall in the i_ν'th equivalence class. Take the distorted sequence $\hat{x}^t$ as the first sequence in the codebook $S_m(i_\nu/t)$ that is closest to x^t in the Hamming distance.

One can encode $\hat{x}^t$ with about $L(\hat{x}^t) = \log m + \log N_t$ bits, where N_t is the number of equivalence classes in Π_t. However, depending on the data sequence x^n

the distorted string $\hat{x}^n$ as a concatenation of the segments $\hat{x}^t$ may be encoded with shorter code length, for instance by the Lempel-Ziv algorithm or by Algorithm Context.

The distortion for string x^t is defined as follows [Rissanen 1989; Grünwald 1998]: Let

$$P(x|\hat{x}) = \frac{2}{3}2^{-\delta(x,\hat{x})}$$

be a probability distribution for $\hat{x} = 0$ and $\hat{x} = 1$, defined by the Hamming distance. Extend these by independence to sequences $P(x^t|\hat{x}^t)$. Then put

$$h'_{x^t}(\alpha_0) = \min_{\hat{x}^t \in S_m(i_\nu/t)} \{-\log P(x^t|\hat{x}^t) : \frac{n_1(x^t)}{t} \in B_{i_\nu,t},\, L(\hat{x}^t) \le t\alpha_0\} \tag{10.38}$$

$$= \min_{\hat{x}^t \in S_m(i_\nu/t)} \{\sum_{j=1}^{t} \delta(x_j,\hat{x}_j) + t\log\frac{3}{2} : \frac{n_1(x^t)}{t} \in B_{i_\nu,t},\, L(\hat{x}^t) \le t\alpha_0\}. \tag{10.39}$$

Since $S_m(i_\nu/t)$ is not the optimal codebook of size m we use the notation $h'_{x^t}(\alpha)$ for the resulting structure function; we also wrote $\alpha = t\alpha_0$. In particular, if we wish to model the data locally by a Bernoulli class, then $L(\hat{x}^t) = \log m + \log N_t$. The structure function for the entire sequence x^n is given by

$$h'_{x^n}(\alpha_0) = \sum_t \min_{\hat{x}^t \in S_m(i_\nu/t)} \{\sum_{j=1}^{t} \delta(x_j,\hat{x}_j) + t\log\frac{3}{2} : \frac{n_1(x^t)}{t} \in B_{i_\nu,t},\, L(\hat{x}^n) \le n\alpha_0\}. \tag{10.40}$$

Notice that this is a little different from the sum of the structure functions $h'_{x^t}(\alpha_0)$ of the segments x^t, because $L(\hat{x}^n)$ may be a bit shorter than the sum of the code lengths for the segments.

We next describe the optimal codebook and the resulting rate distortion curve. Consider the inverse image $X_{i_\nu,t} = \{z^n : n_1(z^n)/t \in B_{i_\nu,t}\}$, and its Voronoi partition defined by the Hamming distance and a codebook $X_m(i_\nu,t) \subset X_{i_\nu,t}$ of size m. Notice that the codebook now is not restricted to be a subset of $S(i_\nu/t)$. That is, the equivalence classes are defined by

$$D_{i_\nu,t}(\hat{x}^t) = \{z^t : \frac{n_1(z^t)}{t} \in B_{i_\nu,t},\, \hat{z}^t = \hat{x}^t, \hat{x}^t \in X_m(i_\nu,t)\}.$$

In words, $D_{i_\nu,t}(\hat{x}^t)$ is the set of all sequences z^t which are closest to $\hat{x}^t$ in the codebook $X_m(i_\nu,t)$. Now introduce the following quantity:

$$h_{x^t}(\alpha_0, X_m(i_\nu,t)) = \min_{\hat{x}^t \in X_m(i_\nu,t)} \{\log|D_{i_\nu,t}(\hat{x}^t)| : x^t \in D_{i_\nu,t}(\hat{x}^t), \log m + \log N_t \le t\alpha_0\}$$

Notice that with this we measure the amount of distortion with the logarithm of the size of the smallest set of the closest sequences to $\hat{x}^t$. In the extreme case where the codebook includes all the sequences in $X_{i_\nu,t}$ and $\hat{x}^t = x^t$, the size of $D_{i_\nu,t}(\hat{x}^t)$ is unity, and its logarithm is zero, as it should be. Similarly, if $m = 1$, both the distortion and the size of $D_{i_\nu,t}(\hat{x}^t)$ are maximum. Define the optimal codebook

$\hat{X}_m(i_\nu, t)$ as the solution of the minimax problem

$$\min_{X_m(i_\nu,t)} \max_{x^t \in X_{i_\nu,t}} h_{x^t}(\alpha_0, X_m(i_\nu, t)) =$$

$$\min_{X_m(i_\nu,t)} \max_{\hat{x}^t \in X_m(i_\nu,t)} \{\log|D_{i_\nu,t}(\hat{x}^t)| : \log m + \log N_t \le t\alpha_0\}.$$

The structure function $h_{x^t}(\alpha_0)$ is defined for the optimal codebook as $h_{x^t}(\alpha_0; \hat{X}_m(i_\nu, t))$, and it is seen to be the minimax value

$$h_{x^t}(\alpha_0) = \min_{X_m(i_\nu,t)} \max_{\hat{x}^t \in X_m(i_\nu,t)} \{\log|D_{i_\nu,t}(\hat{x}^t)| : \log m + \log N_t \le t\alpha_0\}$$

$$\ge \log \sum_{\frac{i}{t} \in B_{i_\nu,t}} \binom{t}{i} - t\alpha_0 + \log N_t. \tag{10.41}$$

We assumed here that $L(\hat{x}^t) = \log m + \log N_t$. The second inequality follows from the fact that for all partitions into m blocks the maximum block size cannot be smaller than the number of strings in $X_{i_\nu,t}$ divided by m.

10.6 Experiments

We take for our experiments a DNA sequence, formed of four bases, A,C,G, and T, which we represent as $A = 00$, $T = 01$, $C = 10$, G=11. For long DNA sequences, C and G bases tend to have similar occurrence frequencies, and the same applies to A and T. Hence the first bit in the basis representation discriminates between the {A,T} and the {C,G} groups. The precise location of a 0 or 1 bit along the so obtained binary string is not of interest as much as the local density of 0s and 1s as well as the relative ratio of the densities of the two groups. Hence, this information could well be obtained from a lossy compression of the sequence of 0s and 1s modeled as a locally Bernoulli source. The DNA sequence, called $HUMGHCSA$, contains 66495 bases, and we construct a binary sequence of their first symbols giving a binary sequence of the same length.

Since we do not have a priori knowledge about the precise value of the window width, t, we experiment with three cases: $t = 16, 32$, and 64. With the partition algorithm and the segment lengths given by (10.5.2) we obtain for $t = 16$ $N_t = 5$ classes, centered at $i_\nu \in \{1,4,8,12,15\}$; $N_t = 9$ classes for $t = 32$, centered at $i_\nu \in \{1,2,6,11,16,21,26,30,31\}$; and $N_t = 11$ classes for $t = 64$, centered at $i_\nu \in \{2,5,10,17,24,32,40,47,54,59,62\}$.

In order to have similar values of $\alpha = \log_2 m + \log_2 N_t$, we select different values for $m = m_t$ in the three cases of t, namely $m_{16}^4 \approx m_{32}^2 \approx m_{64}$. This way, when encoding a 64-bits-long string, we use $\log_2 m_{64}$ bits for the index in the codebook $S_{m_{64}}$, and since we address four times the codebook $S_{m_{16}}$, each index having the length $\log_2 m_{16}$ we need almost the same amount $4\log_2 m_{16} = \log_2 m_{64}$ to encode the same 64-bits-long string using windows of length 16. However, the values of α will have to be adjusted for the three values of t, due to differences in N_t.

The experiment was performed for six different values of m_t such that we cover the practical range of the α values, α/n between .13 and .31 (Figure 10.1). The smallest nontrivial codebook was taken as $m_{16} = 2$, and the largest $m_{64} = 1024$. We also consider an adaptive algorithm for choosing the best window width. The extra cost in α will be $\log_2 3$ bits needed for the specification of the window width $t \in \{16, 32, 64\}$ that performed best (in distortion sense) over each segment of 64 symbols. Due to the extra cost no significant decrease in the distortion was obtained, and the best window width was found to be $t = 64$, at all values of α.

To illustrate the visual similarity of the original and the lossy reconstructed sequences, we display in Figure 10.2 a short subsequence from both. The symbol 1 is represented by a black line and 0 by a white line. It can be seen that the local densities of the two symbol values are well preserved, which demonstrates the validity of the very fast and simple distortion algorithm resulting from this method.

We find the structure function corresponding to the minmax solution $h_{x^n}(\alpha)$ for the string x^n by splitting it into subsequences x^t, and we obtain the lower bound curves represented in Figure 10.3 for $t \in \{16, 32, 64\}$. We observe that the curves are parallel, and the higher the window width the closer the curves are to the sufficiency line $h(\alpha_{NML}) + \alpha_{NML} - \alpha$, which goes through the point $(\alpha_{NML}, h(\alpha_{NML}))$. Here $\alpha_{NML} = \sum_t \log_2 C_t$ and $h(\alpha_{NML}) = \sum_t -n_1(x^t) \log_2 n_1(x^t) - (t - n_1(x^t)) \log_2(t - n_1(x^t))$ for $t = 64$ correspond to the NML code.

For the small window width $t = 16$ it is also possible to count the cardinalities of the Voronoi cells $D_{i_\nu, t}(\hat{x}^t)$ for the suboptimal, but practically implementable, codebook $S_m(i_\nu/t)$, and we can evaluate $h_{x^t}(\alpha_0; S_m(i_\nu/t))$. We show in Figure 10.4 the three curves, $h'_{x^t}(\alpha_0)$, $h_{x^t}(\alpha_0; S_m(i_\nu/t))$, and $h_{x^t}(\alpha_0)$. The suboptimal codebooks are seen to almost achieve the lower bound.

Figure 10.1 The curve $h'_{x^n}(\alpha)$ for a sequence x^n of $n = 66495$ bits, for different values of the local window width $t \in \{16, 32, 64\}$ or variable according to the least distortion. Also shown is the line $h(\alpha)$ passing through the point $(\alpha_{NML}, h(\alpha_{NML}))$ marked by a diamond, corresponding to the NML code for $t = 64$.

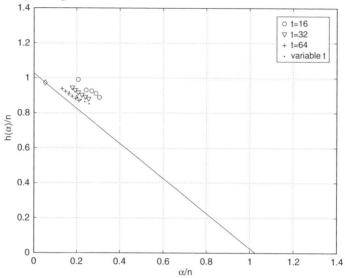

Figure 10.2 The first 1000 samples of the original binary sequence *(bottom)* and the lossy recovery of it *(top)* at a rate $\alpha/n = 0.21$ bits per symbol.

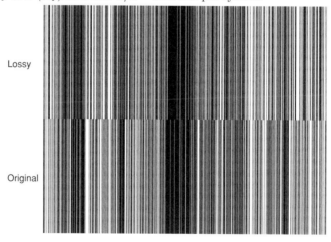

Figure 10.3 The lower bound $h_{x^n}(\alpha)$ for a sequence x^n of $n = 66495$ bits, for different values of the local window width $t \in \{16, 32, 64\}$. Also shown is the line $h(\alpha) + \alpha$ passing through the point $(\alpha_{NML}, h(\alpha_{NML}))$ corresponding to the NML code for $t = 64$.

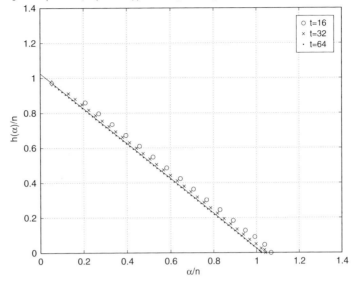

Figure 10.4 The curves $h_{x^t}(\alpha_0)$ *(Plot 1)*, $h'_{x^t}(\alpha_0)$ *(Plot 2)* and $h_{x^t}(\alpha_0; S_m(i_\nu/t))$ *(Plot 3)* for a sequence x^n of $n = 66495$ bits and $t = 16$. Also shown is the line $h(\alpha) + \alpha$ passing through the point $(\alpha_{NML}, h(\alpha_{NML}))$ marked by a diamond, corresponding to the NML code for $t = 64$.

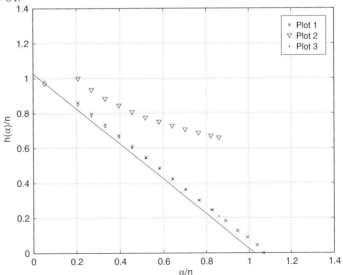

References

Balasubramanian, V. (1997). Statistical inference, Occam's razor and statistical mechanics on the space of probability distributions. *Neural Computation*, *9*(2), 349–268.

Cover, T., and J. Thomas (1991). *Elements of Information Theory*. New York: Wiley.

Grünwald, P. (1998). *The Minimum Description Length Principle and Reasoning under Uncertainty*. *ILLC Dissertation Series* 1998–03, University of Amsterdam.

Kolmogorov, A.N. (1965). Three approaches to the quantitative definition of information. *Problems of Information Transmission*, *1*(1), 1–7.

Rissanen, J. (1976). Generalized Kraft inequality and arithmetic coding. *IBM Journal of Research and Development*, *20*(3), 198–203.

Rissanen, J. (1979). Arithmetic codings as number representations. *Acta Polytechnica Scandinavica*, 31, 44–51.

Rissanen, J. (1989). *Stochastic Complexity in Statistical Inquiry*. Singapore: World Scientific.

Rissanen, J. (1996). Fisher information and stochastic complexity. *IEEE Transactions on Information Theory*, *42*(1), 40–47.

Rissanen, J. (2000). MDL denoising. *IEEE Transactions on Information Theory*, *46*(7), 2537–2543.

Rissanen, J. (2001). Strong optimality of the normalized ML models as universal codes and information in data. *IEEE Transactions on Information Theory*, *47*(5), 1712–1717.

Shtarkov, Yu. M. (1987). Universal sequential coding of single messages. *Problems of Information Transmission*, *23*(3), 3–17.

Solomonoff, R. (1964). A formal theory of inductive inference, part 1 and part 2. *Information and Control*, *7*, 1–22, 224–254.

Vereshchagin, N., and P. Vitányi (2002). Kolmogorov's structure functions with an application to the foundation of model selection. In *Proceedings of the 47th IEEE Symposium on the Foundations of Computer Science (FOCS'02)*.

Zhang, J., and I. Kontoyannis (2002). Arbitrary source models and Bayesian codebooks in rate-distortion theory. *IEEE Transactions on information theory*, *48*(8), 2226–2290.

III   Practical Applications

11   Minimum Message Length and Generalized Bayesian Nets with Asymmetric Languages

Joshua W. Comley
School of Computer Science and Software Engineering
Monash University
Clayton Campus
Victoria 3800
Australia

David L. Dowe
School of Computer Science and Software Engineering
Monash University
Clayton Campus
Victoria 3800
Australia

This chapter describes the minimum message length (MML) principle, including its relationship to the subsequent minimum description length (MDL) principle. A brief discussion of the history and development of MML is given, including 'strict MML' (SMML) and some of its approximations. After addressing some common misconceptions about MML, we present a novel application of MML to the inference of generalized Bayesian networks, using decision trees to supply conditional probability distributions. Unlike many Bayesian network applications, the new generalized Bayesian networks presented in this chapter are capable of modeling a combination of discrete and continuous attributes. This demonstrates the power of information-theoretic approaches, such as MML, which are able to function over both discrete probability distributions and continuous probability densities. Furthermore, we give examples of asymmetric languages in which the desired target attribute is best modeled implicitly rather than as an explicit output attribute. Last, we provide some preliminary results and suggest several possible directions for further research.

11.1   Introduction

Minimum message length (MML) is an information-theoretic Bayesian principle of inductive inference, machine learning, statistical inference, econometrics, and "data mining" which was developed by Chris Wallace and David Boulton in a series of six journal papers from 1968 to 1975, including several explicit articulations of the MML principle (see, e.g., [Wallace and Boulton 1968, p. 185, sec. 2]; [Boulton and Wallace 1970, p. 64, col. 1]; [Boulton and Wallace 1973, sec. 1, col. 1]; [Boulton and Wallace 1975, sec. 1, col. 1]; [Wallace and Boulton 1975, sec. 3]). (David Boulton then published his Ph.D. thesis [Boulton 1975] in this area.)

Given a data set, D, we wish to find the most probable hypothesis, H — that is, that which maximizes $P(H|D)$. By Bayes' theorem, the posterior probability of H is the product of the prior probability of H and the likelihood function of D given H divided by the marginal probability of the observed data, D — that is, $P(H|D) = (1/P(D)) \times P(H) \times P(D|H)$, where the marginal probability $P(D)$ is given by $P(D) = \sum_H P(H) \cdot P(D|H)$ or $P(D) = \int_H P(H) \cdot P(D|H) \, dH$. Recall from elementary information theory that an event of probability p_i can be optimally encoded by a code word of length $l_i = -\log p_i$. Because $P(D)$ is a function of D independent of the hypothesis, H, maximising $P(H|D)$ is equivalent to maximising the product of the two probabilities $P(H) \times P(D|H)$, which is in turn equivalent to minimising $-\log P(H) - \log P(D|H)$, the length of a two-part message transmitting, first, H and then D given H (see, e.g., [Wallace and Boulton 1968, p. 185, sec. 2]; [Boulton and Wallace 1970, p. 64, col. 1]; [Boulton and Wallace 1973, sec. 1, col. 1]; [Boulton and Wallace 1975, sec. 1, col. 1]; [Wallace and Boulton 1975, sec. 3]).

In the remainder of this chapter, we define strict MML (SMML) and then deal with several issues pertaining to MML. These include dealing with some common (unfortunate) misconceptions in the literature about MML, Kolmogorov complexity, Bayesianism, statistical invariance, and statistical consistency. We also present in Section 11.3.1 a conjecture [Dowe, Baxter, Oliver, and Wallace 1998, p. 93]; [Wallace and Dowe 1999a, p. 282]; [Wallace and Dowe 2000, p. 78] of David Dowe's relating some of these concepts. In Section 11.4, we mention the issue of inference vs. prediction and the merits of logarithmic scoring in probabilistic prediction. We tersely (due to space constraints) survey some MML literature, relate it to our understanding of current minimum description length (MDL) writings and raise the issue of MML as a universal principle of Bayesian inference. Given the many (unfortunate) misconceptions some authors seem to have about the extensive MML literature and its original concepts, and given the above-mentioned historical precedence of MML over MDL, we have cited several instances where — at least at the time of writing — MML is apparently state-of-the-art.

Subsequently and in Section 11.4.4, we then discuss comparatively new work on the second author's notion of inverse learning (or implicit learning) [Dowe and Wallace 1998; Comley and Dowe 2003] and the first author's refinements thereof [Comley and Dowe 2003], including setting the asymmetric languages in a framework of generalized Bayesian networks and investigating search algorithms. We believe that this is an advance of much substance and potential.

11.2   The Strict Minimum Message Length Principle

The strict minimum message length (strict MML, or SMML) principle was first introduced in [Wallace and Boulton 1975], from which we largely borrow in this section. The relationship of strict MML with algorithmic information theory is given in [Wallace and Dowe 1999a], and various other descriptions and applications of it are given in [Wallace and Freeman 1987; Wallace 1996; Wallace and Dowe 1999b; Farr and Wallace 2002; Fitzgibbon, Dowe, and Allison 2002a].

A point estimation problem is a quadruple $\{H, X, h, f\}$ such that H is a parameter space (assumed to be endowed with a field of subsets), X is a set of possible observations, and h is a given prior probability density function with respect to a measure, $d\theta$, on the parameter space H such that $\int_H h(\theta)\, d\theta = 1$.

f is the known conditional probability function $f : (X, H) \to [0, 1] : f(x, \theta) = f(x|\theta)$, where $\sum_i f(x_i|\theta) = 1$ for all $\theta \in H$.

A solution to a point estimation problem is a function $m : X \to H$ with $m(x) = \theta$. Recalling from Section 11.1, that $r(x) = \int_H h(\theta)f(x|\theta)\, d\theta$ is the marginal probability of a datum, x, we note that $\sum_{x \in X} r(x) = 1$ and that the posterior distribution, $g(\cdot|\cdot)$, is given by $g(\theta|x) = h(\theta) \cdot f(x|\theta)/\int_H h(\theta) \cdot f(x|\theta)d\theta = h(\theta)f(x|\theta)/r(x)$.

We assume that the set, X, of possible observations is countable. (We suspect the even stronger result(s) that it is probably even recursively enumerable and perhaps even recursive.) Given that X is countable, so, too, is $H^* = \{m(x) : x \in X\}$, that is, we can say $H^* = \{\theta_j : j \in N\}$. We can then define $c_j = \{i : m(x_i) = \theta_j\}$ for each $\theta_j \in H^*$, and $C = \{c_j : \theta_j \in H^*\}$. Given some fixed H^* as just defined, we assign finite prior probabilities $q_j = \sum_{i \in c_j} r(x_i) = \sum_{i:m(x_i)=\theta_j} r(x_i)$ to the members θ_j of H^* and then, for each $x \in X$, we choose $m(x)$ to be that $\theta \in H^*$ which maximize $p(x|h)$ and in turn minimizes the expected length of the codebook (given this H^*).

This defines $m^* : x \to H^*$, which we can then take to be our solution to $\{H, X, h, f\}$, provided that we have indeed selected the correct H^*.

For each c_j we choose the point estimate θ_j to minimize $-\sum_{x_i : i \in c_j} r(x_i) \cdot \log f(x_i|\theta_j)$. For each H^* the average two-part message length is

$$\left(-\sum_j (q_j \cdot \log q_j) \right) + \left(-\sum_j \sum_{i \in c_j} \left(q_j \cdot \frac{r(x_i)}{q_j} \cdot \log f(x_i|\theta_j) \right) \right).$$

In essence the larger the data groups the shorter the average length of the first part of the message but the longer the average length of the second part. We choose the c_j to minimize the expected two-part message length of the codebook. Having thus chosen the codebook given datum x, the SMML estimate is the θ_j representing the code block including x.

11.3   Invariance and Consistency of MML, and Some Common Misconceptions

11.3.1   Maximum a Posteriori (MAP) and MML

One common misconception among some authors is that the MML estimate is supposedly the same as the posterior mode – or maximum a posteriori (MAP) – estimate. To the contrary, when dealing with continuous distributions, MAP maximizes the posterior *density* (not a probability) [Wallace and Boulton 1975, p. 12]; [Wallace and Dowe 1999a, p. 279 sec. 6.1.1]; [Wallace and Dowe 1999c, p. 346]; [Wallace and Dowe 2000, secs. 2 and 6.1] and is typically not invariant, whereas MML maximizes the posterior *probability* and is invariant[Wallace and Boulton 1975] [Wallace and Freeman 1987, p, 243]; [Wallace 1996, sec. 3.5 and elsewhere]; [Dowe, Baxter, Oliver, and Wallace 1998, secs. 4.2 and 6]; [Wallace and Dowe 1999a, secs. 6.1 and 9]; [Wallace and Dowe 1999c, secs. 1 and 2]; [Wallace and Dowe 2000, p. 75, sec. 2 and p. 78–79]. A method of parameter estimation is said to be (statistically) invariant if for all one-to-one transformations t, $t(\hat{\theta}) = t(\hat{\theta})$, that is, the point estimate in the transformed parameter space is equal to the transformation of the original point estimate.

For further cases highlighting the difference between MML and MAP which also show MML outperforming MAP, see, for example, [Dowe, Oliver, Baxter, and Wallace 1995; Dowe, Oliver, and Wallace 1996], (for polar and cartesian coordinates on the circle and sphere respectively), and [Wallace and Dowe 1999b, secs. 1.2 and 1.3].

MAP and MML when all attributes are discrete   On some occasions, all attributes are discrete – such as if we were interested only in the topology of a decision tree and the attributes which were split on (and possibly also the most likely class in each leaf [Quinlan and Rivest 1989]) without being interested in the additional inference of the class probabilities [Wallace and Patrick 1993; Tan and Dowe 2002; Comley and Dowe 2003; Tan and Dowe 2003] in each leaf. In these cases, where all attributes are discrete, like MML, MAP will also maximize a probability rather than merely a density. For many MML approximations, in these cases, both MAP and MML will optimize the same objective function and obtain the same answer. It is a subtle point, but *even in these* cases, MAP will generally be different from the strict MML inference scheme [Wallace and Boulton 1975; Wallace and Freeman 1987; Wallace and Dowe 1999a] of Sections 11.2 and 11.3.3 (which partitions in data space) and to the 'fairly strict MML' scheme (which is similar to strict MML but instead partitions in parameter space). The subtle point centers on the fact that the construction of the strict (or fairly strict) codebook is done in such a way as to minimize the expected message length [Wallace and Dowe 1999a, sec. 6.1]. Consider two distinct hypotheses available as MAP inferences which happen to be very similar (e.g., in terms of Kullback-Leibler distance) and suppose – for the sake of argument – that they have almost identical prior probability. If these are merged into one, the prior probability of the resultant hypothesis will have about twice the prior probability – resulting in its being about 1 bit cheaper in the first part of the message – than either of the unmerged alternatives. If the expected additional cost to the second part of the message from the merging is more than compensated for by the expected saving from the first part, then such a merging would take place in the construction of the MML codebook. So, we recall from Section 11.3.1 that MAP is different from MML when continuous-valued attributes and probability densities are involved. But – as we have just explained – even in the rare case when all attributes are discrete and only probabilities (and no densities) are involved, then – although some approximations to MML would yield MAP – we *still* find that MML is generally different from MAP. Whereas the MAP, maximum likelihood (ML), and Akaike's information criterion (AIC) estimates are statistically inconsistent for a variety of parameter estimation problems (e.g., Neyman-Scott [Dowe and Wallace 1997] and linear factor analysis [Wallace 1995; Wallace and Freeman 1992]), the two-part structure of MML messages leads to MML's general statistical consistency results [Barron and Cover 1991; Wallace 1996]; [Wallace and Freeman 1987, Sec. 2, p 241]. We note in passing Dowe's related question [Dowe, Baxter, Oliver, and Wallace 1998, p. 93]; [Wallace and Dowe 1999a, p. 282]; [Wallace and Dowe 2000, p. 78] as to whether only (strict) MML and possibly also closely related Bayesian techniques (such as minimising the expected Kullback-Leibler distance [Dowe, Baxter, Oliver, and Wallace 1998]) can generally be both statistically invariant and statistically consistent.

11.3.2   "The" Universal Distribution and Terms "of Order One"

In its most general sense (of being akin to Kolmogorov complexity or algorithmic information-theoretic complexity), MML uses the priors implicit in the particular choice of universal Turing machine [Wallace and Dowe 1999a, sec. 7 and elsewhere]. We agree with other authors [Rissanen 1978, p. 465]; [Barron and Cover 1991, sec. IV, pp. 1038–1039]; [Vitanyi and Li 1996][Li and Vitanyi 1997, secs 5.5 and 5.2]; [Vitanyi and Li 2000] about the relevance of algorithmic information theory (or Kolmogorov complexity) to MDL and MML. However, a second common misconception is either an implicit assumption that there is one unique universal distribution, or at least something of a cavalier disregard for quantifying the (translation) terms "of order one" and their relevance to inference and prediction. We note that there are countably infinitely many distinct universal Turing machines and corresponding universal (prior) distributions. As such, the relevance of the Bayesian choice of prior or Turing machine or both should be properly understood [Wallace and Dowe 1999a, secs. 2.4 and 7].

11.3.3   Strict MML Codebook, Expected Length and Actual Lengths

A third, related, common misconception concerns the construction of the MML codebook in SMML. Given the likelihood function(s) and the Bayesian prior(s), without having seen any data, we construct the MML codebook as in Section 11.2 so as to minimize the expected length of the two-part message [Wallace and Boulton 1975, secs. 3.1 - 3.3]; [Wallace and Freeman 1987, sec. 3]; [Wallace 1996]; [Wallace and Dowe 1999a, secs. 5 and 6.1]; [Wallace and Dowe 1999b, secs. 1.2 and 1.3]. This typically results in coding blocks which are partitions of the *data* space. (One can only record countably different measurement values, and it is reasonable to assume that any continuous-valued measurement is made to some accuracy, ϵ. As such, its value can be encoded with a finite code length.) With the MML codebook now thus chosen, given data D, we choose hypothesis, H, so as to minimize the length of the two-part message. This should clarify that common misconception about SMML and the MML codebook. The strict MML principle has been applied to problems of binomial distributions [Wallace and Boulton 1975, sec. 5]; [Wallace and Freeman 1987, sec. 3]; [Farr and Wallace 2002] and a restricted cut-point segmentation problem [Fitzgibbon et al. 2002a] (which, like the Student T distribution, would appear to have no sufficient statistics other than the data themselves), but is generally computationally intractable. In practice, we consider approximations to a partitioning of the *parameter* space, such as the invariant point estimator of [Wallace and Freeman 1987, sec. 5, a usable estimator]; [Wallace and Dowe 1999a, sec. 6.1.2, practical MML]; [Wallace and Dowe 1999c, p. 346, col. 2] – and sometimes others, as discussed below.

Tractable Approximations to Strict MML   The invariant point estimator of [Wallace and Freeman 1987, sec. 5, a usable estimator]; [Wallace and Dowe 1999a, sec. 6.1.2, practical MML]; [Wallace and Dowe 1999c, p. 346, col. 2] is based on a quadratic approximation to the Taylor expansion of the log-likelihood function and the assumption of the prior being approximately locally uniform. Despite the many and vast successes (e.g. [Wallace and Dowe 1993; Dowe, Oliver, and Wallace 1996; Dowe and Wallace 1997; Oliver and Wallace 1991; Oliver 1993; Tan and Dowe 2002; Tan and Dowe 2003; Wallace and Dowe 2000; Edgoose and Allison 1999; Wallace and Korb 1999; Baxter and Dowe 1996; Wallace 1997; Vahid 1999; Viswanathan and Wallace 1999; Fitzgibbon, Dowe, and Allison 2002b; Comley and Dowe 2003]) of the Wallace and Freeman [1987] approximation [Wallace and Freeman 1987, sec. 5]; [Wallace and Dowe 1999a, sec. 6.1.2], it *is* an approximation, and its underlying assumptions are sometimes strained [Wallace and Dowe 1999c, p. 346, col. 2] (or at least appear to be [Grünwald, Kontkanen, Myllymaki, Silander, and Tirri 1998]) – leading us to new approximations. These include Dowe's invariant MMLD approximation and Fitzgibbon's modification(s) [Fitzgibbon et al. 2000a,b], Wallace's numerical thermodynamic entropy approximation [Wallace 1998], and others (e.g. [Wallace and Freeman 1992; Wallace 1995]).

We note that the standard deviation σ of measurements of accuracy ϵ (as in Section 11.2 and 11.3.3) is generally assumed ([Wallace and Dowe 1994, sec. 2.1]; [Comley and Dowe 2003, sec. 9]) to be bounded below by 0.3ϵ or $\epsilon/\sqrt{12}$.

11.4   MML as a Universal Principle, Prediction and MDL

11.4.1   Brief History of Early MML Papers, 1968–1975

These first six MML papers [Wallace and Boulton 1968; Boulton and Wallace 1969, 1970, 1973, 1975; Wallace and Boulton 1975] from Section 11.1 and David Boulton's 1975 Ph.D. thesis [Boulton 1975] were variously concerned with univariate or multivariate multinomial distributions [Boulton and Wallace 1969; Wallace and Boulton 1975], multivariate Gaussian distributions, mixture modeling (or clustering or cluster analysis or intrinsic classification or unsupervised learning) of such distributions [Wallace and Boulton 1968; Boulton and Wallace 1970; Boulton and Wallace 1975; Boulton 1975] and even hierarchical mixture modeling of such distributions [Boulton and Wallace 1973]. We also see the introduction [Boulton and Wallace 1970, p. 63] of the (term) *nit*, where 1 nit $= \log_2 e$ bits. The nit has also been referred to as a *nat* in subsequent MDL literature, and was known to Alan M. Turing as a *natural ban* (see, e.g., [Hodges 1983, pp. 196–197] for *ban*, *deciban*, and *natural ban*). These units can be used not only to measure message length and description length but also to score probabilistic predictions.

11.4.2   Inference, Prediction, Probabilistic Prediction and Logarithmic Scoring

Two equivalent motivations of MML are, as given in Section 11.1, (1) to maximize the posterior *probability* (*not* a density – see Section 11.3.1) and, equivalently, (2) to minimize the length of a two-part message.

The second interpretation (or motivation) of MML can also be thought of in terms of Occam's razor [Needham and Dowe 2001]. Both these interpretations can be thought of as inference to the best (single) explanation. Prediction [Solomonoff 1964, 1996, 1999] is different from inductive inference (to the best explanation) in that prediction entails a weighted Bayesian averaging of all theories, not just the best theory [Solomonoff 1996; Dowe, Baxter, Oliver, and Wallace 1998]; [Wallace and Dowe 1999a, sec. 8]; [Wallace and Dowe 1999c, sec. 4]. Thus, despite the many successes described in this chapter, MML is not directly concerned with prediction.

Probabilistic Prediction and Logarithmic Scoring   A prediction which gives only a predicted class (e.g., class 2 is more probable than class 1) or mean (e.g., $\hat{\mu} = 5.2$) conveys less information than one giving a probability distribution — such as $(\hat{p}_1 = 0.3, \hat{p}_2 = 0.7)$ or $N(\hat{\mu} = 5.2, \hat{\sigma}^2 = 2.1^2)$ — whereas a probabilistic prediction, such as $(0.3, 0.7)$, also gives us the predictively preferred class (class 2) as a byproduct. To paraphrase it more bluntly, the current literature could be said to contain all too many methods endeavoring to tune their "right"/"wrong" predictive accuracy with scant regard to any probabilistic predictions. A first obvious shortcoming of such an approach will be its willingness to "find" (or "mine") spurious patterns in data which is nothing more than 50% : 50% random noise.

One criterion of scoring functions for probabilistic predictions is that the optimal expected long-term return should be gained by using the true probabilities, if known. The logarithmic scoring function achieves this, and has been advocated and used for binomial [Good 1952; Good 1968; Dowe, Farr, Hurst, and Lentin 1996]; [Vovk and Gammerman 1999, sec. 3], multinomial [Dowe and Krusel 1993]; [Tan and Dowe 2002, sec. 4]; [Tan and Dowe 2003, sec. 5.1], and other distributions (e.g., Gaussian [Dowe et al. 1996]). Interestingly, Deakin has noted several cases of scoring functions other than logarithmic achieving this criterion for multinomial distributions [Deakin 2001]. Nonetheless, we prefer the logarithmic scoring function for the added reason of its relation to log-likelihood, the sum of the logarithms of the probabilities being the logarithm of the product of the probabilities, in turn being the logarithm of the joint probability.

The predictive estimator which minimizes the expected (negative) log-likelihood function is known as the minimum expected Kullback-Leibler distance (MEKLD) estimator [Dowe et al. 1998]. Theoretical arguments [Solomonoff 1964; Dowe et al. 1998] and intuition suggest that the SMML estimator (recall Sections 11.2 and 11.3.3) will come very close to minimising the expected Kullback-Leibler distance.

11.4.3   MML, MDL, and Algorithmic Information Theory

The relation between MML [Wallace and Boulton 1968; Wallace and Freeman 1987; Wallace and Dowe 1999a] and MDL [Rissanen 1978, 1987, 1999b] has been discussed in [Wallace and Freeman 1987; Rissanen 1987] and related articles in a 1987 special issue of the *Journal of the Royal Statistical Society*, in [Wallace and Dowe 1999a,b,c; Rissanen 1999a,b,c] and other articles [Dawid 1999; Clarke 1999; Shen 1999; Vovk and Gammerman 1999; Solomonoff 1999], in a 1999 special issue of the *Computer Journal*, and elsewhere. For a discussion of the relationship between strict MML (SMML) (see Sections 11.2 and 11.3.3) and the work of Solomonoff [1964], Kolmogorov [1965], and Chaitin [1966], see [Wallace and Dowe 1999a].

We reiterate the sentiment [Wallace and Dowe 1999c] that, in our opinion, MDL and MML agree on many, many points. We also acknowledge that from the perspective of someone who knew relatively little about MDL and MML, the disagreements between MDL and MML would appear to be both infrequent and minor [Wallace and Dowe 1999c]. Having said that, we now venture to put forward some concerns about some MDL coding schemes.

Efficiency and Reliability of Coding Schemes and of Results   Recalling Section 11.4.2, the predictive reliability of MDL and MML will depend very much upon the coding schemes used. In [Quinlan and Rivest 1989; Wallace and Patrick 1993] and [Kearns, Mansour, Ng, and Ron 1997; Viswanathan, Wallace, Dowe, and Korb 1999], we respectively see a decision tree inference problem and a problem of segmenting a binary process in which the original coding schemes [Kearns et al. 1997; Quinlan and Rivest 1989] had their results improved upon by corresponding improvements in the relevant coding schemes [Viswanathan et al. 1999; Wallace and Patrick 1993]. Reinterpreting the Occam's razor measure of decision tree simplicity from the node count in [Murphy and Pazzani 1994] to a message length measure in [Needham and Dowe 2001] likewise gives improved results.

While the principle and spirit of the 1978 MDL coding scheme [Rissanen 1978] live on, it is generally acknowledged in more recent MDL writings and elsewhere (see, e.g., [Wallace and Dowe 1999a, p. 280, col. 2]) to have been substantially improved upon.

In conclusion, we ask the reader wishing to use an MDL or MML coding scheme to note that the reliability of the results will be highly dependent upon the reliability of the coding scheme.

Further Comments on Some Other MDL Coding Schemes   While MML is openly and subjectively Bayesian and known to be so, many often either assert that MDL is Bayesian or ask whether or not it is (see, e.g., [Vitanyi and Li 1996]; [Dawid 1999, p. 323, col. 2, sec. 4, sec. 5]; [Clarke 1999, sec. 2]; [Vitanyi and Li 2000]). Some would contend that a parameter space restriction [Rissanen 1999b, p. 262, col. 2] was also invoking a prior — namely, that the values of the parameters cannot lie in the prohibited area (cf. [Dawid 1999, p. 325, col. 2]).

The Jeffreys 'prior' [Jeffreys 1946] uses the Fisher information as though it were a Bayesian prior, thus depending upon the sensitivity of the measuring instruments and observational protocol used to obtain the data [Lindley 1972; Bernardo and Smith 1994]; [Dowe, Oliver, and Wallace 1996, p. 217]. This would appear to be able to lead to situations where the prior beliefs one uses in modeling the data depend upon the strength or location of the measuring instrument [Dowe, Oliver, and Wallace 1996, p. 217]; [Wallace and Dowe 1999a, sec. 2.3.1] (see also [Wallace and Freeman 1987, Sec. 1, p241]; [Wallace and Dowe 1999a, sec. 5, p. 277, col. 2] for other concerns). The Jeffreys 'prior' has been used in comparatively recent MDL work [Rissanen 1996a,b], raising some of the above concerns. The Jeffreys 'prior' also does not always normalise (e.g., [Wallace and Dowe 1999b, secs. 2.3.2 – 2.3.4]). We understand that Liang and Barron [2005] and Lanterman [2005] partially address this problem. The notion of complete coding in MDL [Rissanen 1996a; Dom 1996]; [Grünwald, Kontkanen, Myllymaki, Silander, and Tirri 1998, sec. 4] would appear to be in danger of contravening the convergence conditions of the two-part message form from [Barron and Cover 1991].

Some other comments on some MDL coding schemes and suggested possible remedies for some of the above concerns are given in [Wallace and Dowe 1999c, sec. 2] and [Wallace and Dowe 1999b, sec. 3].

11.4.4   MML as a Universal Principle

The second author founded and (in 1996) chaired the Information, Statistics and Induction in Science (ISIS) conference (see, e.g., [Rissanen 1996b; Solomonoff 1996; Wallace 1996; Vitanyi and Li 1996; Dowe and Korb 1996]) because of a belief in the universal relevance of MML to problems in induction and the philosophy of science. Recalling Section 11.4.3, we suspect that the editors and perhaps also many of the other authors in this book might well have similar beliefs.

The relevance of MML to inductive inference is clear, but let us summarize. MML has been used for parameter estimation for a variety of distributions [Wallace and Boulton 1968; Boulton and Wallace 1969; Wallace and Dowe 1993; Dowe, Oliver, and Wallace 1996; Dowe and Wallace 1997; Wallace and Dowe 2000], and for supervised learning [Wallace and Patrick 1993; Oliver and Wallace 1991; Oliver 1993; Vahid 1999; Tan and Dowe 2002; Tan and Dowe 2003] and unsupervised learning (clustering or mixture modeling) [Wallace and Boulton 1968; Wallace 1986; Wallace and Dowe 1994; Wallace and Dowe 2000; Edgoose and Allison 1999], hierarchical clustering [Boulton and Wallace 1973], inference of probabilistic finite state automata (PFSAs) or hidden Markov models (HMMs) [Wallace and Georgeff 1983], Markov models of clustering [Edgoose and Allison 1999], linear and polynomial regression [Baxter and Dowe 1996; Wallace 1997; Viswanathan and Wallace 1999; Vahid 1999; Fitzgibbon et al. 2002b], segmentation problems [Viswanathan et al. 1999; Fitzgibbon et al. 2002a], factor analysis [Wallace and Freeman 1992; Wallace 1995], clustering with factor analysis [Edwards and Dowe 1998], and so on. It should be added that the success of MML in some of the above problems is emphatic. We also recall the statistical invariance and statistical consistency of MML from Section 11.3.

MML or closely related work has also been applied to genome analysis [Allison, Wallace, and Yee 1990; Dowe, Oliver, Dix, Allison, and Wallace 1993; Dowe, Allison, Dix, Hunter, Wallace, and Edgoose 1996; Edgoose, Allison, and Dowe 1996], psychology [Kissane, Bloch, Dowe, R.D. Snyder andP. Onghena, and Wallace 1996], causal networks [Wallace and Korb 1999], Bayesian networks (sec. 11.4.4 in this book and [Comley and Dowe 2003]), Goodman's "Grue" paradox [Solomonoff 1996], financial market (in)efficiency [Dowe and Korb 1996], and cognitive science and IQ tests [Dowe and Hajek 1998; Hernandez-Orallo and Minaya-Collado 1998; Dowe and Oppy 2001]; [Sanghi and Dowe 2003, sec. 5.2].

We now proceed throughout the remainder of this chapter to discuss comparatively new work on the second author's notion of inverse learning (or implicit learning) [Dowe and Wallace 1998; Comley and Dowe 2003] and the first author's refinements thereof [Comley and Dowe 2003], including setting the asymmetric languages in a framework of generalized Bayesian networks and investigating search algorithms. sectionMML, Generalized Joint Distributions, and Implicit Learning

11.4.5 Generalized Bayesian Networks

We now describe an application of MML to the inference of generalized Bayesian networks. This is an extension of the idea of 'inverse learning' or 'implicit learning' proposed by Dowe in [Dowe and Wallace 1998], and further developed by Comley in [Comley and Dowe 2003]. In this domain we deal with multivariate data, where each item X (also known as a thing, case, or record) has k attributes (also referred to as

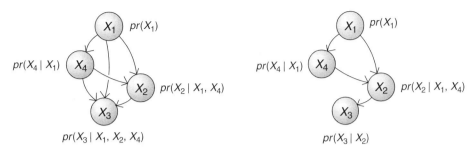

Figure 11.1 Examples of Bayesian network structures, illustrating the probability distributions supplied in each node. On the left is a fully connected network, while the network on the right is partially connected. Notice here that X_3 is conditionally independent of X_1 and X_4 given X_2.

variables or fields), denoted here as $X_1, \ldots, X_k$. We wish to model the statistical relationships between attributes when presented with a set of n such data. We may want to do this to be able to predict one of the attributes when given values for the others, or simply because we are interested in the interattribute correlations.

The graphical structure of Bayesian networks makes them an intuitive and easily interpreted representation of the relationships between attributes. A Bayesian network is a directed acyclic graph (DAG) with one node corresponding to each attribute. Each node provides a conditional probability distribution of its associated attribute given the attributes associated with its parent nodes. Figure 11.1 shows example network structures for $X = \{X_1, X_2, X_3, X_4\}$. For a general introduction to Bayesian network theory, see [Russell and Norvig 1995, chap. 15, sec. 5].

Bayesian networks model the joint distribution over all attributes, and express this as a product of the conditional distributions in each node. In the case of a fully connected Bayesian network (see Figure 11.1), the joint distribution $P(X_1 \& X_2 \& \ldots \& X_k)$ is modeled as $P(X_1) \cdot P(X_2|X_1) \ldots P(X_k|X_1, \ldots, X_{k-1})$. In practice, however, Bayesian networks are rarely fully connected, and make use of conditional independencies to simplify the representation of the joint distribution (see Figure 11.1).

Although — in the abstract sense — the conditional probability distribution of a node can take any form at all, many Bayesian network methods simply use conditional probability tables, and are limited by the restriction that all attributes must be discrete. Others [Scheines, Spirtes, Glymour, and Meek 1994; Wallace and Korb 1999] model only continuous attributes, describing an attribute as a linear combination of its parent attributes. Here we show how information-theoretic approaches like MML can be used, together with decision tree models, to build a general class of networks able to handle many kinds of attributes. We use decision trees to model the attribute in each node, as they tend to be a compact and powerful representation of conditional distributions, and are able to efficiently express context-specific independence [Boutilier, Friedman, Goldszmidt, and Koller 1996]. It should be noted that any conditional model class could be used, so long as MML message lengths can be formulated for it. An MML coding scheme for basic decision trees is given in [Wallace and Patrick 1993], which refines an earlier coding scheme suggested in [Quinlan and Rivest 1989]. A variant of this scheme is summarized in Section 11.4.7.

11.4.6 Development and Motivation of Implicit Learning

The idea of implicit learning (or inverse learning) by MML presented here builds on material originally proposed by Dowe in [Dowe and Wallace 1998]. That work involved only two attributes, or at most two groups of attributes. Comley [Comley and Dowe 2003] later refined the implicit learning MML coding scheme (given in Section 11.4.7) and generalized the idea to handle more than two attribute groups, relating it to Bayesian networks.

Although the two-attribute case is a simple one, it provides informative examples of the benefits of implicit learning. The idea is that we have a class of conditional models that we are comfortable with and know how to use. We can use this to accurately model one attribute X_1 as a probabilistic function of the other attribute, X_2. But imagine it is actually X_2 that we wish to predict, given X_1. Using Bayes' rule, and coupling our model of $P(X_1|X_2)$ with a 'prior' model of $P(X_2)$, we can form a model of the joint distribution $P(X_1 \& X_2) = P(X_2) \cdot P(X_1|X_2)$. By taking a cross-sectional 'slice' from this composite joint model, we can then extract the conditional probability $P(X_2|X_1)$.

For example, take the case where X_1 and X_2 are both continuous variables, where X_2 is generated from the Gaussian distribution $N(10, 1)$ and X_1 is in turn generated from $(X_2)^3 + N(0, 1)$. Suppose our model language is the class of univariate polynomials of the form

$$X_2 = a_0 + a_1 X_1 + a_2 (X_1)^2 + a_3 (X_1)^3 + \cdots + a_d (X_1)^d + N(0, \sigma^2) \text{ for some degree } d$$

and we wish to predict X_2 given X_1. If such a technique were to model X_2 as an *explicit* probabilistic function of X_1, it could not express — let alone discover — the true conditional relationship $X_2 = \left(X_1 + N(0, 1)\right)^{\frac{1}{3}}$, as this is outside its model language. However we can use the same model language to *implicitly* state X_2's dependence on X_1 using the joint distribution and Bayes' rule as follows:

$$P(X_2|X_1) = \frac{P(X_1 \& X_2)}{P(X_1)} \tag{11.1}$$

$$= \frac{\left(P(X_2) \cdot P(X_1|X_2)\right)}{\int_{z \in X_2^*} P(z) \cdot P(X_1|z)}, \tag{11.2}$$

where $P(X_2)$ is given by $X_2 = 10 + N(0, 1)$, and $P(X_1|X_2)$ is given by $X_1 = (X_2)^3 + N(0, 1)$. The point here is that the given model language cannot explicitly express $P(X_2|X_1)$. It can, however, express both $P(X_2)$ and $P(X_1|X_2)$, which can be used together to define $P(X_2|X_1)$ implicitly.

Many other circumstances exist where our target attribute is not necessarily best modeled as an explicit probabilistic function of the remaining attributes. Consider two continuous attributes, X_1 and X_2, which come from a two-dimensional mixture model [Wallace and Dowe 2000; McLachlan and Peel 2000]. While one could attempt to do a linear or polynomial regression of the target attribute, X_1, as a function of X_2, one would do best to acknowledge the mixture model and then model X_1 as a cross section (given X_2) of the mixture distribution. (Indeed, in this example X_1 and X_2 could equally well be groups of attributes [Dowe and Wallace 1998]). The point is that with a restricted model language one cannot always accurately estimate the desired conditional probability distribution, and it may be beneficial to implicitly model the target attribute by estimating the joint distribution. The generality of MML makes it an ideal tool for doing this. The consistency results of MML [Barron and Cover 1991; Wallace 1996; Wallace and Dowe 1999a; Wallace and Dowe 1999c], [Wallace and Freeman 1987, sec. 2, p. 241] suggest strongly that — quite crucially — it will converge to the best possible representation of the joint distribution.

The idea of implicit modeling was in fact first inspired by the problem of protein secondary structure prediction based on a known amino acid sequence. Learning a conditional model of the secondary structure sequence given the amino acid sequence is difficult, but the secondary structure sequence is far from random and can be easily modeled by itself. This model can be paired with a conditional model of the amino acids given the secondary structures, forming a joint distribution from which secondary structure can be predicted.

11.4.7 MML Coding of a General Bayesian Network

Recall from Section 11.1 the two-part format of the MML message - first stating the hypothesis H, then data D in light of this hypothesis. These two parts reflect a Bayesian approach where the cost of stating H is $-\log\left(\mathrm{P}(H)\right)$, $\mathrm{P}(H)$ being our prior belief that H is the true hypothesis, and D is transmitted using some optimal code based on the probabilities supplied by H. The H corresponding to the shortest overall message is chosen, as it maximizes the joint probability $\mathrm{P}(H\&D)$. Since D is held constant and we are only choosing from competing Hs this also corresponds to choosing the H with the highest posterior probability $\mathrm{P}(H|D)$. This subsection details how one might construct such a message for the general Bayesian networks proposed here.

The first part of the message, our hypothesis, must include the structure of the network — that is, the (partial) node ordering and connectivity — and the parameters required for the conditional probability distribution in each node. There are many possible ways in which one could do this; we describe one below.

We start by asking how many possible network structures there are. For k attributes there are $k!$ different fully connected structures (or total node orderings). But this does not take into account the number of partially connected networks. A total ordering has $\binom{k}{2} = (k^2 - k)/2$ directed arcs (each of which may or may not be present in a partially connected network). So there are $2^{(k^2-k)/2}$ possible arc configurations for each of the $k!$ total orderings, leaving us with $k!\ 2^{(k^2-k)/2}$ possible network structures. We can assign each of these an equal prior probability of $\left(k!\ 2^{(k^2-k)/2}\right)^{-1}$.

Note now, though, that many of the partially connected structures will actually correspond to the *same* network (Figure 11.2). As we wish to choose between distinct networks it is important to treat these equivalent network representations as a single hypothesis. If we were to ignore this, the hypothesis' prior probability will be split among its equivalent representations, each of which would be inappropriately expensive. So from each group G of equivalent structures we choose one representative and assign it the prior probability of $c_G\left(k!\ 2^{(k^2-k)/2}\right)^{-1}$ where c_G is the cardinality of group G. This means that network structures with many equivalent representations are assigned a higher prior probability. Note that the coding scheme was chosen primarily for its simplicity, rather than being motivated by any belief that these structures are really more likely. For some applications it may be worth using a less 'biased' scheme, even if this is computationally more difficult.

Let us now calculate $len(S)$, the number of bits required to encode a network structure S (remembering that we are yet to transmit the conditional probability distribution parameters for each node).

$$len(S) = -\log_2\left(\mathrm{P}(S)\right) \tag{11.3}$$

$$= -\log_2\left(\frac{c_G}{k!2^{\frac{k^2-k}{2}}}\right) \tag{11.4}$$

$$= \log_2(k!) + \log_2\left(2^{\frac{k^2-k}{2}}\right) - \log_2(c_G) \tag{11.5}$$

$$= \log_2(k!) + \frac{k^2-k}{2} - \log_2(c_G) \tag{11.6}$$

Now that we have stated the node ordering and connectivity, we can transmit the parameters for the conditional distribution in each node. Nodes can express their conditional probability distributions using any of a wide variety of model classes — for example, conditional probability tables, polynomial regressions, and so on; here we use a rather general class of decision tree, described below.

The leaves of the tree may model either continuous-valued attributes using Gaussian density functions, or discrete-valued attributes using multistate distributions. Branch (test) nodes are capable of performing a binary split on a continuous-valued attribute (using a cut point) or a multiway split on a discrete-valued attribute (one subtree per possible value). Once a discrete-valued attribute has been tested in a branch, no sub-tree may test this attribute again (as the outcome of such a test is already known). However, a continuous attribute may still be tested by a branch even if a parent branch has already tested it, as a different cut point can be used to further partition the data. The coding scheme used for these trees is similar to that presented in [Wallace and Patrick 1993].

We transmit the topology in a depth-first fashion as a string of code words —

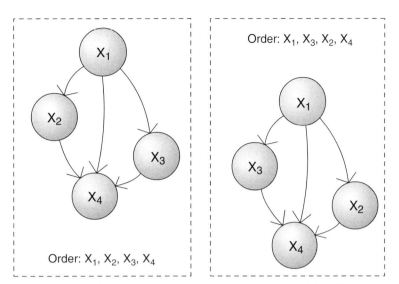

Figure 11.2   Two equivalent partially connected networks with different total node orderings.

each either 'branch' or 'leaf'. The probability of the root node being a branch is $n_A/(n_A+1)$ where n_A is the number of input attributes for the tree. The probability of any other node being a branch is taken to be $1/a$ where a is the 'arity' of the node's parent. The probability of a leaf is obviously one minus the probability of a branch. For a tree where all tests have a binary outcome, stating 'branch' or 'leaf' each cost one bit.[1] After each 'branch' code word, we state which of the input attributes is tested there. This costs $\log_2(n'_A)$ bits where n'_A is the number of input attributes that could be tested at that node. n'_A is equal to n_A at the root of the tree, but decreases by one in any path when a discrete attribute is tested (as further testing of the same discrete attribute is prohibited). If it is a continuous attribute we are testing, we also need to encode the associated cutpoint c. For this we use a scheme outlined in [Comley and Dowe 2003, sec. 3.1], and used prior to that in the software associated with [Wallace and Patrick 1993] and [Kornienko, Dowe, and Albrecht 2002, sec. 4.1].

Each 'leaf' code word is followed by the parameters for the model in that leaf — either μ and σ for a Gaussian distribution, or $\mathrm{P}(v_1),\ldots,\mathrm{P}(v_{m-1})$ for an m-state distribution (where the target attribute can take the values $v_1,\ldots,v_m$). Wallace and Boulton [1968] and Boulton and Wallace [1969] give well-behaved priors and coding schemes for both of the Gaussian and multistate models respectively.

This completes the transmission of H. We now transmit the data, D, one attribute at a time according to the node ordering of the network specified in H. For

----

1. Except at the root of the tree where $\mathrm{P}(branch) = n_A/(n_A + 1)$

each attribute X_i, we can build an optimal code book based on the conditional probability distribution in the relevant node. We use this code book in conjunction with the attributes already sent to encode X_i. We thus achieve our two-part MML message.

If our H is a complicated network with high connectivity and large decision trees it will be expensive to transmit, but can achieve high compression of the training data, allowing us to state D very efficiently. At the other extreme oversimplified networks can be encoded cheaply, but may not fully exploit the correlations that exist in the data, making the transmission of D expensive. Minimising our two-part MML message corresponds to our intuitive wish to find a tradeoff between unjustifiably complicated models that overfit the data, and overly simplistic models that fail to recognize important patterns. The level of complexity we can accept in our models increases with the size of our (training) data.

11.4.8 Symmetric (Invertible) Languages

It is interesting to note that some families of conditional distribution are symmetric with respect to node ordering — that is, any probabilistic relationship $P(X_i) = f(X_j, X_k)$ can also be expressed as $P(X_j) = g(X_i, X_k)$, or $P(X_k) = h(X_i, X_j)$, where f, g, and h are all in the family of conditional distributions. Put another way, the inverse of any model in the language is also in the language.

For Bayesian networks using such distributions, the node ordering has no effect on the family of joint distributions able to be expressed, provided that the connectivity of the network remains the same. In other words, reversing the direction of one or more arcs in a network will have no impact on the distributions it is able to represent. The choice of node ordering for such a network is somewhat arbitrary in the sense that it should not alter the joint distribution inferred.[2] This is in fact the case for the typical Bayesian network where all attributes are discrete and modeled by conditional probability tables. Another example of a model language able to be inverted without altering the joint distribution is that where all attributes are continuous and modeled as a linear combination of their parents, plus some Gaussian noise term. This is shown below:

$$X_i = a_1 P_1 + a_2 P_2 + \cdots + a_p P_p + N(\mu, \sigma^2),$$

where $P_1, \ldots P_p$ are the p parent attributes of X_i.

Although one can still do implicit learning with such languages, if the aim is simply to extract the conditional distribution, say $P(X_i | X \setminus \{X_i\})$, from the inferred network, then one will do just as well to simply learn this conditional distribution outright rather than go to the trouble of inferring an entire Bayesian network. This idea is investigated by Ng and Jordan in [Ng and Jordan 2002], which is con-

---

2. In the case of causal networks the node ordering is often dictated by the user's notion of causality, or extra temporal information.

cerned with generative-discriminative model pairs. That work concerns two equivalent representations of a conditional probability distribution: one modeled explicitly (discriminative), and the other modeled implicitly via a joint distribution (generative). Ng and Jordan compare the performance of the generative and discriminative models, focusing on the efficiency of each and the asymptotic error rates. In this chapter we are interested in *asymmetric* languages — that is, situations where we are unable to express (or work with) the discriminative equivalent of a generative model. Thus the discriminative and generative models compared here do not really qualify as 'pairs' — the generative model is a more general case that can describe distributions unavailable to the discriminative model.

11.4.9   Inferring the Node Order

As mentioned in Section 11.4.8, some networks use conditional distribution languages that are symmetric with regard to node order. Altering the node order of such a network will not change the family of joint distributions able to be expressed.

If, however, we use asymmetric conditional models — for example, the class of decision trees described in Section 11.4.7 — then the order of the nodes can have a significant impact on the nature of the joint distribution.

Consider the simple case where we have only two attributes — a binary-valued attribute X_b and a continuous-valued attribute X_c. Using the decision tree language just mentioned, there are two ways to build a joint distribution over $(X_b \& X_c)$ — one using the ordering X_b, X_c and the other using the ordering X_c, X_b. These are illustrated in Figure 11.3. When we construct our MML message (using the coding scheme in Section 11.4.7), one of these networks will be cheaper than the other. So, in the case of such an asymmetric model language, MML provides us with a natural way of inferring node ordering. The node ordering in this example is not to be interpreted causally. We are simply choosing the ordering which provides us with the best family of joint distributions. For research pertaining to MML and causal networks, see, for example, [Wallace and Korb 1999].

11.4.10   An Efficient Search for Network Structure

Section 11.4.9 explained that, when using asymmetric conditional models, node ordering and connectivity can have a significant impact on the nature of the joint distribution. We show here how we can use this to our advantage when searching for the best network structure.

We begin by searching over the space of total node orderings. As mentioned in Section 11.4.7, there are $k!$ possible total orderings, where k is the number of attributes. Clearly we would like to avoid learning all the corresponding networks. First, we use the MML decision tree scheme discussed in Section 11.4.7 to build k decision tree models, $DT_1, \ldots, DT_k$, where DT_i models X_i and treats the other attributes as input. Note that just because X_j is an input attribute to DT_i does not necessarily mean that it is tested at any branches.

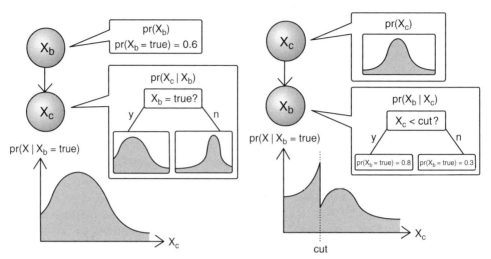

Figure 11.3 Two networks, each representing a different joint distribution over $X_b \& X_c$. This figure shows the difference that node order can make to the nature of the joint distribution when dealing with asymmetric Bayesian networks. Two networks are depicted - one on the left with the ordering (X_b, X_c), and one on the right with the ordering (X_c, X_b). To the right of each node we depict the conditional probability distributions it contains. Below each network is a (rough) graph showing how, when $X_b = true$, $P(X)$ varies with X_c. NOTE: This figure is not drawn accurately or to scale — it is intended only to give an idea of the behavior of our class of asymmetric networks.

We can now establish a list of independencies, and one- and two-way dependencies. If DT_i does not test X_j, and DT_j does not test X_i then we can conclude that X_i and X_j are independent (at least in the presence of the other attributes) and there is not likely to be much benefit in directly connecting the corresponding nodes.

If DT_i *does* test X_j, but DT_j does *not* test X_i, then we establish a one-way dependency. This is particularly useful in formulating partial ordering constraints. Here we assert that there is little use in placing a connection from X_i to X_j in the network, as we are not able to express X_j's dependency on X_i. There is, however, some benefit in a connection directed from X_j to X_i, because we can see from examining DT_i that we *can* express some dependency of X_i on X_j. Given these considerations, it makes sense to try to place X_i after X_j in the total node ordering.

If DT_i tests X_j, and DT_j also tests X_i, then we conclude that there is a two-way dependency between X_i and X_j. This tells us that a connection between the corresponding nodes will probably be useful, but does not tell us which way this link should be directed, and hence does not shed any light on sensible total node orderings.

We now build a list L of useful directed links. For each one-way dependency from X_i to X_j, we add $X_i \to X_j$ to the list. For each two-way dependency between X_g and X_h, we add both $X_g \to X_h$ and $X_h \to X_g$ to the list.

Now we give each possible fully connected network structure a score equal to the number of directed links in L that it exhibits. We keep only those structures with an equal highest score. For each of these structures, we remove any links that do not feature in L, creating a set of partially-connected structures, many of which will now be equivalent. For each group of equivalent structures we record the cardinality, and keep only one representative. We can now build a list of the conditional probability distributions required. Many of these will be used in more than one network, and there is no need to learn them more than once. For example, two networks may both model X_j as a probabilistic function of the same set of parent attributes, $P(X_j)$. The corresponding decision tree need only be learned once.

After learning all decision trees required (using the MML approach outlined in Section 11.4.7), we cost each network according to the scheme presented in Section 11.4.7. The cheapest network is chosen to represent our joint distribution.

While this method generally works well, it is not guaranteed to produce the optimal network structure. The two paragraphs below outline two potential downfalls.

Falsely Detecting Dependencies Consider an attribute X_a depending on a Boolean attribute X_b, and, *if X_b is true*, also depending on X_c. We conclude from this that X_a depends on both X_b and X_c, and that the corresponding directed links are worthwhile. Imagine now that we go with the ordering X_c, X_a, X_b. Suddenly the link $X_c \rightarrow X_a$ is useless — we cannot detect any dependency of X_a on X_c without the presence of X_b. It would be better to have removed this link, but it is too late because the structure (and connectivity) is decided before the trees are inferred, and it is only when we infer the trees that we discover $DT_{a|c}$ does not test X_c.

Failing to Detect a Dependency If some attributes are highly correlated, they may 'overshadow' each other. For example, X_a has a strong dependency on X_b, and a weaker (but still important) dependency on X_c. The decision tree DT_a tests X_b at the root node, nicely partitioning the classes. Each leaf now decides not to bother testing X_c, due to fragmentation of data, and the minimal extra purity gained. So we conclude that X_a does not depend on X_c, but in fact this independence is conditional on X_b being present. Imagine an ordering X_c, X_a, X_b where we would decide to remove the link $X_c \rightarrow X_a$. Now our encoding of X_a will not benefit from any correlations.

Another cause of this error is that in the presence of many input attributes, stating which attribute is to be tested at any branch becomes expensive. A 'borderline' branch may be rejected on this basis whereas in the actual network (where there are fewer input attributes) it will be cheaper to state that branch and it may be accepted.

11.4.11 A Coding Scheme for 'Supervised' Networks

We present in this subsection an alternative to the MML costing scheme given in Section 11.4.7. This alternative scheme can be used when we know, before inferring the network, which attribute it is that we wish to predict. This is often the case in practical classification situations, where there is usually a particular attribute of interest which is difficult to measure, that we want to predict based on the rest of the (more easily) observed attributes. In this subsection we will refer to such an attribute as the 'target' attribute, and label it as X_t.

This scheme focuses on learning an accurate *conditional* distribution of X_t given $X \setminus \{X_t\}$, as opposed to learning an accurate joint distribution over all of X. Wettig, Grünwald, Roos, Myllymäki, and Tirri [2003] refer to networks that result from such schemes as 'supervised' networks, and to networks that have attempted instead to optimize the joint distribution as 'unsupervised' networks. We adopt this terminology, as it draws attention to the role of networks and their distributions in classification tasks.

If we had a universal language for our conditional probability distributions (CPDs), able to represent any conditional distribution at all, then we could do no better than to optimize the joint distribution over X. In other words, if one is able to perfectly model the joint distribution, then this will also yield (by taking the appropriate 'cross section') the best conditional distribution for any attribute. In practical situations, however, we cannot usually find such a perfect representation of the joint distribution, and the best joint distribution able to be expressed may not in fact correspond to the best conditional distribution for X_t.

For the asymmetric networks presented here, the structure, connectivity, and parameters required to represent the best joint distribution may differ significantly from those required to represent the best conditional distribution of X_t. We expect, when the task is to predict or classify X_t that the supervised network will produce better results.

Our proposed MML scheme for supervised networks differs only slightly from that for unsupervised networks presented in Section 11.4.7. The major difference is that the supervised scheme assumes that the values for $X \setminus \{X_t\}$ are common knowledge, and need not be included in the message. We transmit the network structure and the decision tree parameters in exactly the same manner. In the supervised scheme, though, we do not transmit the data values of $X \setminus \{X_t\}$. After decoding the network the receiver may use it, together with the values for $X \setminus \{X_t\}$, to derive a CPD $pr(X_t | X \setminus \{X_t\})$. It is by using this distribution that the values of our target attribute, X_t, are transmitted.

11.4.12   An Example Network

Figure 11.4 shows a network and one of the CPDs learned from the well-known iris data set.

Figure 11.5 summarizes the performance of various classifiers on the iris data set. The classifiers are:

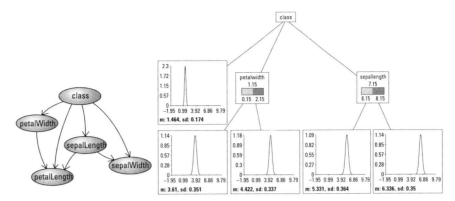

Figure 11.4   On the left is a Bayesian network learned from the iris data set using the MML approach presented in this chapter. On the right is the decision tree used to give a probability density over *petalLength*, given values of the parent attributes — *petalWidth*, *class*, and *sepalLength*.

- **MML-DT:** This is a decision tree tool that infers models from the class of decision trees described in Section 11.4.7. It uses an MML costing metric (see Section 11.4.7) similar to that in [Wallace and Patrick 1993] and a look-ahead-0 greedy search algorithm. This method is equivalent to a supervised network where all nontarget attributes are parents of the target attribute.

- **C5:** C5 [Quinlan] (and its forerunner, C4.5) are popular decision tree tools used for classification. C5 does not use the MML principle and is widely used as a performance benchmark in classification problems.

- **unsup-net:** This is the algorithm presented in this chapter for learning unsupervised asymmetric Bayesian networks.

- **sup-net:** This is the modified algorithm (see Section 11.4.11) that learns supervised asymmetric Bayesian networks.

The results in Figure 11.5 are from a series of ten-fold cross-validation experiments using the *iris* data set, available from [Blake and Merz 1998]. In all, 10 experiments were performed, for a total of 100 learning tasks for each method. In each experiment, each method's performance was averaged over the 10 test sets to yield a score, *s*. The graph shows the best, worst, and average values of *s* for each classifier. These results show the two MML asymmetric Bayesian network classifiers performing favorably, on average achieving a lower classification error than the decision trees. This is an example of a situation in which we do better by modeling the target attribute, implicitly using a joint distribution – rather than building an explicit conditional model like the two decision tree classifiers.

11.4.13   Issues for Further Research

The asymmetric Bayesian networks presented in this chapter have already produced encouraging results [Comley and Dowe 2003], and raise several interesting areas

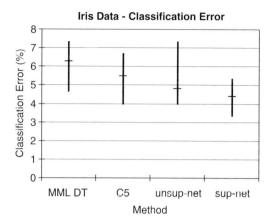

Figure 11.5 Best, average and worst performance of four classification tools on the *iris* data set.

for further research. We feel it would be beneficial to investigate other classes of asymmetric models, for example a multivariate version of the polynomial regression described in Section 11.4.6.

Another issue for future research relates to the estimation of Gaussian density functions in the leaves of decision trees modeling continuous attributes. The probability distribution for a discrete attribute tested by such a decision tree is partly determined by the ratio of these Gaussian distributions. When the estimated variance is small, this ratio can become very large and yield extreme probabilities for certain values of the discrete (target) attribute. This issue is discussed in more detail in [Comley and Dowe 2003]. In [Ng and Jordan 2002] the problem is avoided to some degree by fixing the variance at a value estimated from the entire training set, and allowing only the mean to vary as a function of the discrete target attribute. This seemingly has the effect of avoiding small variance estimates, and producing less dramatic ratios of Gaussian distributions.

Finally, we believe that the network structure coding scheme and search strategy presented in this chapter could be further refined, and have begun work on a promising variation based on incrementally adding directed links to an initially unordered, empty network.

11.5 Summary

This chapter has described minimum message length (MML) — a statistically invariant information-theoretic approach to Bayesian statistical inference dating back to Wallace and Boulton Wallace and Boulton [1968] — and highlighted some of the differences between MML and the subsequent minimum description length (MDL) principle. Furthermore, in Section 11.3, we have addressed several common misconceptions regarding MML, and (in Section 11.3.1) we mentioned Dowe's question as to whether Bayesianism is inherently necessary to guarantee statistical invariance and consistency.

This chapter has also presented an application of MML to a general class of Bayesian network that uses decision trees as conditional probability distributions. It can efficiently express context-specific independence, and is capable of modeling a combination of discrete and continuous attributes. We have suggested that when we know which attribute is to be predicted, it may be better to use a 'supervised' network rather than an 'unsupervised' one. We have proposed a modification to our algorithm to allow for this.

The main contribution here, other than extending Bayesian networks to handle continuous *and* discrete data, is the identification of 'asymmetric' networks, and the proposal of an efficient scheme to search for node order and connectivity.

11.6 Acknowledgments

We thank Peter Grünwald and the other editors both for the opportunity to write this chapter and for editorial feedback. David L. Dowe humbly thanks his dear mother, family and friends for their support for this work and his every endeavor.

References

Allison, L., C. S. Wallace, and C. Yee (1990). When is a string like a string? In *Proceedings of the International Symposium on Artificial Intelligence and Mathematics*.

Barron, A.R., and T.M. Cover (1991). Minimum complexity density estimation. *IEEE Transactions on Information Theory*, *37*, 1034–1054.

Baxter, R.A., and D.L. Dowe (1996). Model selection in linear regression using the MML criterion. Technical report 96/276, Department of Computer Science, Monash University, Clayton, Victoria, Australia.

Bernardo, J., and A. Smith (1994). *Bayesian Theory*. New York: Wiley.

Blake, C., and C. Merz (1998). UCI repository of machine learning databases. Department of Information and Computer Sciences, University of California, Irvine. See also `http://www.ics.uci.edu/~mlearn/MLRepository.html`.

Boulton, D. (1975). *The Information Criterion for Intrinsic Classification*. Ph.D. thesis, Department of Computer Science, Monash University, Clayton, Victoria, Australia.

Boulton, D.M., and C.S. Wallace (1969). The information content of a multistate distribution. *Journal of Theoretical Biology*, *23*, 269–278.

Boulton, D.M., and C.S. Wallace (1970). A program for numerical classification.

Computer Journal, 13(1), 63–69.

Boulton, D.M., and C.S. Wallace (1973). An information measure for hierarchic classification. *Computer Journal, 16*(3), 254–261.

Boulton, D.M. and C.S. Wallace (1975). An information measure for single-link classification. *Computer Journal, 18*(3), 236–238.

Boutilier, C., N. Friedman, M. Goldszmidt, and D. Koller (1996). Context-specific independence in Bayesian networks. In *Uncertainty in Artificial Intelligence: Proceedings of the Twelfth Conference (UAI-1996)*, pp. 115–123. San Francisco, CA :Morgan Kaufmann.

Chaitin, G.J. (1966). On the length of programs for computing finite sequences. *Journal of the Association for Computing Machinery, 13*, 547–569.

Clarke, B. (1999). Discussion of the papers by Rissanen, and by Wallace and Dowe. *Computer Journal, 42*(4), 338–339.

Comley, J.W. and D.L. Dowe (2003). General Bayesian networks and asymmetric languages. In *Proceedings of the Second Hawaiian International Conference on Statistics and Related Fields.*

Dawid, A.P. (1999). Discussion of the papers by Rissanen and by Wallace and Dowe. *Computer Journal, 42*(4), 323–326.

Deakin, M.A.B. (2001). The characterisation of scoring functions. *Journal of the Australian Mathematical Society, 71*, 135–147.

Dom, B. E. (1996). MDL estimation for small sample sizes and its application to linear regression. Technical report RJ 10030 (90526), IBM Almaden Research Center, San Jose, CA.

Dowe, D.L., L. Allison, T. Dix, L. Hunter, C. Wallace, and T. Edgoose (1996). Circular clustering of protein dihedral angles by minimum message length. In *Proceedings of the First Pacific Symposium on Biocomputing (PSB-1)*, Mauna Lani, HI, U.S.A., pp. 242–255. Singapore: World Scientific.

Dowe, D.L., R.A. Baxter, J.J. Oliver, and C.S. Wallace (1998). Point estimation using the Kullback-Leibler loss function and MML. In *Proceedings of the Second Pacific Asian Conference on Knowledge Discovery and Data Mining (PAKDD'98)*, Melbourne, Australia, pp. 87–95. Berlin: Springer Verlag.

Dowe, D.L., G.E. Farr, A. Hurst, and K.L. Lentin (1996). Information-theoretic football tipping. In N. de Mestre (Ed.), *Third Australian Conference on Mathematics and Computers in Sport*, Bond University, Queensland, Australia, pp. 233–241. See also http://www.csse.monash.edu.au/~footy .

Dowe, D.L., and A.R. Hajek (1998). A non-behavioural, computational extension to the Turing Test. In *Proceedings of the International Conference on Computational Intelligence and Multimedia Applications (ICCIMA'98)*, Gippsland, Australia, pp. 101–106.

Dowe, D.L., and K.B. Korb (1996). Conceptual difficulties with the efficient market hypothesis: Towards a naturalized economics. In D. Dowe, K. Korb, and

J. Oliver (Eds.), *Proceedigns of the Conference on Information, Statistics and Induction in Science (ISIS'96)*, Melbourne, Australia, pp. 212–223. Singapore: World Scientific.

Dowe, D.L. and N. Krusel (1993). A decision tree model of bushfire activity. Technical report 93/190, Department of Computer Science, Monash University, Clayton, Victoria 3800, Australia.

Dowe, D.L., J.J. Oliver, R.A. Baxter, and C.S. Wallace (1995). Bayesian Estimation of the von Mises concentration parameter. In *Proceedings of the Fifteenth International Workshop on Maximum Entropy and Bayesian Methods (MaxEnt '95)*, Santa Fe, NM. Boston: Kluwer.

Dowe, D.L., J.J. Oliver, T.I. Dix, L. Allison, and C.S. Wallace (1993). A decision graph explanation of protein secondary structure prediction. In *Proceedings of the 26th Hawaii International Conference on System Sciences (HICSS-26)*, Volume 1, Maui, HI, pp. 669–678. Los Alamitos, CA: IEEE Computer Society Press.

Dowe, D.L., J.J. Oliver, and C.S. Wallace (1996). MML estimation of the parameters of the spherical Fisher distribution. In *Proceedings of the Seventh International Workshop on Algorithmic Learning Theory (ALT'96)*, Sydney, Australia, pp. 213–227. Volume 1160 of *Lecture Notes in Artificial Intelligence (LNAI)*. Berlin: Springer Verlag.

Dowe, D.L., and G.R. Oppy (2001). Universal Bayesian inference? *Behavioral and Brain Sciences*, *24*(4), 662–663.

Dowe, D.L. and C.S. Wallace (1997). Resolving the Neyman-Scott problem by Minimum Message Length. In *Computing Science and Statistics — Proceedings of the 28th Symposium on the Interface*, Sydney, Australia, pp. 614–618.

Dowe, D.L., and C.S. Wallace (1998). Kolmogorov complexity, minimum message length and inverse learning. In *Proceedings of the Fourteenth Australian Statistical Conference (ASC-14)*, Gold Coast, Queensland, Australia, p. 144.

Edgoose, T., and L. Allison (1999). MML Markov classification of sequential data. *Statistics and Computing*, *9*(4), 269–278.

Edgoose, T., L. Allison, and D.L. Dowe (1996). An MML classification of protein structure that knows about angles and sequence. In *Proceedings of Third Pacific Symposium on Biocomputing (PSB-98)*, Mauna Lani, HI, pp. 585–596. Singapore: World Scientific.

Edwards, R., and D. Dowe (1998). Single factor analysis in MML mixture modeling. In *Proceedings of the Second Pacific Asian Conference on Knowledge Discovery and Data Mining (PAKDD'98)*, Melbourne, Australia, pp. 96–109. Berlin: Springer Verlag.

Farr, G.E., and C.S. Wallace (2002). The complexity of strict minimum message length inference. *Computer Journal*, *45*, 285–292.

Fitzgibbon, L., D. Dowe, and L. Allison (2002a). Change-point estimation using new minimum message length approximations. In *Proceedings of the Seventh Pacific Rim International Conference on Artificial Intelligence (PRICAI-2002)*, pp. 244–254. Volume 2417 of *Lecture Notes in Artificial Intelligence (LNAI)*. Berlin: Springer-Verlag.

Fitzgibbon, L., D. Dowe, and L. Allison (2002b). Univariate polynomial inference by Monte Carlo message length approximation. In *Proceedings of the 19th International Conference on Machine Learning (ICML-2002)*, pp. 147–154. San Francisco: Morgan Kaufmann.

Good, I.J. (1952). Rational decisions. *Journal of the Royal Statistical Society, Series B, 14*, 107–114.

Good, I. J. (1968). Corroboration, explanation, evolving probability, simplicity, and a sharpened razor. *British Journal of Philosophy of Science, 19*, 123–143.

Grünwald, P., P. Kontkanen, P. Myllymaki, T. Silander, and H. Tirri (1998). Minimum encoding approaches for predictive modeling. In *Proceedings of the Fourteenth International Conference on Uncertainty in Artificial Intelligence (UAI98)*, pp. 183–192.

Hernandez-Orallo, J., and N. Minaya-Collado (1998). A formal definition of intelligence based on an intensional variant of algorithmic complexity. In *Proceedings of the International Symposium on Engineering of Intelligent Systems (EIS'98)*, pp. 244–254.

Hodges, A. (1983). *Alan Turing : The Enigma*. New York: Simon & Schuster.

Jeffreys, H. (1946). An invariant form for the prior probability in estimation problems. *Proceedings of the Royal Society of London A, 186*, 453–454.

Kearns, M., Y. Mansour, A.Y. Ng, and D. Ron (1997). An experimental and theoretical comparison of model selection methods. *Machine Learning Journal, 27*, 7–50.

Kissane, D., S. Bloch, D. Dowe, D.M.R.D. Snyder, P. Onghena, and C. Wallace (1996). The Melbourne family grief study, I: Perceptions of family functioning in bereavement. *American Journal of Psychiatry, 153*, 650–658.

Kolmogorov, A.N. (1965). Three approaches to the quantitative definition of information. *Problems of Information Transmission, 1*, 4–7.

Kornienko, L., D.L. Dowe, and D.W. Albrecht (2002). Message length formulation of support vector machines for binary classification - a preliminary scheme. In *Proceedings of the 15th Australian Joint Conference on Artificial Intelligence*, Canberra, Australia, 2-6 December 2002, pp. 119–130. Volume 2557 of *Lecture Notes in Artificial Intelligence (LNAI)*. Berlin: Springer Verlag, 2002.

Lanterman, A.D. (2005). Hypothesis testing for Poisson versus geometric distributions using stochastic complexity. In P.D. Grünwald, I.J. Myung, and M.A. Pitt (Eds.), *Advances in Minimum Description Length: Theory and Applications*. Cambridge MA: MIT Press, 2005.

Li, M. and P. Vitanyi (1997). *An Introduction to Kolmogorov Complexity and its*

Applications (2nd ed.). Springer-Verlag.

Liang, F. and Barron, A. (2005). Exact minimax predictive density estimation and MDL. In P. D. Grünwald, I. J. Myung, and M. A. Pitt (Eds.), *Advances in Minimum Description Length: Theory and Applications*. MIT Press, 2004.

Lindley, D. (1972). Bayesian statistics, a review. *SIAM*, 71.

McLachlan, G., and D. Peel (2000). Finite mixture models. *Wiley Series in Probability and Statistics*. New York: Wiley.

Murphy, P., and M. Pazzani (1994). Exploring the decision forest: An empirical investigation of Occam's razor in decision tree induction. *Journal of Artificial Intelligence, 1*, 257–275.

Needham, S.L. and D.L. Dowe (2001). Message length as an effective Ockham's razor in decision tree induction. In *Proceedings of the Eighth International Workshop on Artificial Intelligence and Statistics (AISTATS 2001)*, Key West, FL, pp. 253–260.

Ng, A.Y. and M.I. Jordan (2002). On discriminative vs. generative classifiers: A comparison of logistic regression and naive Bayes. In T.G. Dietterich, S. Becker, and Z. Ghahramani (Eds.), *Advances in Neural Information Processing Systems 14*. Cambridge, MA: MIT Press.

Oliver, J.J. (1993). Decision graphs - an extension of decision trees. In *Proceedings of the Fourth International Workshop on Artificial Intelligence and Statistics*, pp. 343–350. Extended version available as technical report 173, Department of Computer Science, Monash University, Clayton, Victoria, Australia.

Oliver, J.J. and C.S. Wallace (1991). Inferring decision graphs. In *Proceedings of Workshop 8 — Evaluating and Changing Representation in Machine Learning IJCAI-91*.

Quinlan, J.R. C5.0. Available at `http://www.rulequest.com`.

Quinlan, J.R. and R.L. Rivest (1989). Inferring decision trees using the Minimum Description Length Principle. *Information and Computation, 80*(3), 227–248.

Rissanen, J.J. (1978). Modeling by shortest data description. *Automatica, 14*, 465–471.

Rissanen, J.J. (1987). Stochastic complexity. *Journal of the Royal Statistical Society (Series B), 49*, 260–269.

Rissanen, J.J. (1996a). Fisher information and stochastic complexity. *IEEE Transactions on Information Theory, 42*(1), 40–47.

Rissanen, J. J. (1996b). A universal regression model. In D. Dowe, K. Korb, and J. Oliver (Eds.), *Proceedings of the Conference on Information, Statistics and Induction in Science (ISIS'96)*, Melbourne, Australia, p. 4. Singapore: World Scientific.

Rissanen, J.J. (1999a). Discussion of paper "Minimum message length and Kolmogorov complexity" by C. S. Wallace and D. L. Dowe. *Computer Journal,*

42, 327–329.

Rissanen, J.J. (1999b). Hypothesis selection and testing by the MDL principle. *Computer Journal 42*, 223–239.

Rissanen, J.J. (1999c). Rejoinder. *Computer Journal, 42*, 343–344.

Russell, S., and P. Norvig (1995). *Artificial Intelligence: a Modern Approach.* Prentice Hall.

Sanghi, P. and D.L. Dowe (2003). A computer program capable of passing I.Q. tests. In *Proceedings of the Joint International Conference on Cognitive Science*, UNSW, Sydney, Australia.

Scheines, R., P. Spirtes, C. Glymour, and C. Meek (1994). *Tetrad II: User's Manual.* Hillsdale, NJ: Lawrence Erlbaum.

Shen, A. (1999). Discussion on Kolmogorov complexity and statistical analysis. *Computer Journal, 42*(4), 340–342.

Solomonoff, R.J. (1964). A formal theory of inductive inference. *Information and Control 7*, 1–22,224–254.

Solomonoff, R.J. (1996). Does algorithmic probability solve the problem of induction? In D. Dowe, K. Korb, and J. Oliver (Eds.), *Proceedings of the Conference on Information, Statistics and Induction in Science (ISIS'96)*, Melbourne, Australia, pp. 7–8. Singapore: World Scientific.

Solomonoff, R.J. (1999). Two kinds of probabilistic induction. *Computer Journal, 42*(4), 256–259.

Tan, P.J. and D.L. Dowe (2002). MML inference of decision graphs with multi-way joins. In *Proceedings of the Fifteenth Australian Joint Conference on Artificial Intelligence*, Canberra, Australia, pp. 131–142. Volume 2557 of *Lecture Notes in Artificial Intelligence (LNAI)*. Berlin: Springer-Verlag.

Tan, P.J., and D.L. Dowe (2003, December). MML inference of decision graphs with multi-way joins and dynamic attributes In *Proceedings of the Sixteenth Australian Joint Conference on Artificial Intelligence (AI'03)*, Perth, Australia.

Vahid, F. (1999). Partial pooling: A possible answer to "To pool or not to pool". In R. Engle and H. White (Eds.), *Festschrift in Honor of Clive Granger*, pp. 410–428. Chapter 17. Oxford, UK: Oxford University Press.

Viswanathan, M., and C.S. Wallace (1999). A note on the comparison of polynomial selection methods. In *Proceedings of Uncertainty 99: the Seventh International Workshop on Artificial Intelligence and Statistics*, Fort Lauderdale, FL, pp. 169–177. San Francisco: Morgan Kaufmann.

Viswanathan, M., C.S. Wallace, D.L. Dowe, and K.B. Korb (1999). Finding cutpoints in noisy binary sequences - a revised empirical evaluation. In *Proceedings of the Twelfth Australian Joint Conference on Artificial Intelligence.* Volume 1747 of *Lecture Notes in Artificial Intelligence (LNAI)*, Sydney, Australia, pp. 405–416.

Vitányi, P., and M. Li (1996). Ideal MDL and its relation to Bayesianism. In D. Dowe, K. Korb, and J. Oliver (Eds.), *Proceedings of the Conference on Information, Statistics and Induction in Science (ISIS'96)*, Melbourne, Australia, pp. 405–416. Singapore: World Scientific.

Vitányi, P., and M. Li (2000). Minimum description length induction, Bayesianism, and Kolmogorov complexity. *IEEE Transactions on Information Theory, 46*(2), 446–464.

Vovk, V., and A. Gammerman (1999). Complexity approximation principle. *Computer Journal, 42*(4), 318–322. [special issue on Kolmogorov complexity].

Wallace, C.S. (1986). An improved program for classification. In *Proceedings of the Ninth Australian Computer Science Conference (ACSC-9)*, Volume 8, pp. 357–366.

Wallace, C.S. (1995). Multiple factor analysis by MML estimation. Technical report 95/218, Deptartment of Computer Science, Monash University, Clayton, Victoria, Australia.

Wallace, C.S. (1996). False oracles and SMML estimators. In D. Dowe, K. Korb, and J. Oliver (Eds.), *Proceedings of the Information, Statistics and Induction in Science (ISIS '96) Conference*, Melbourne, Australia, pp. 304–316. Singapore: World Scientific. Also Technical Rept 89/128, Department of Computer Science, Monash University, Clayton, Victoria, Australia, June 1989.

Wallace, C.S. (1997). On the selection of the order of a polynomial model. Technical report, Department of Computer Science, Royal Holloway College, London, England.

Wallace, C.S. (1998). Intrinsic classification of spatially correlated data. *Computer Journal, 41*(8), 602–611.

Wallace, C.S., and D.M. Boulton (1968). An information measure for classification. *Computer Journal, 11*, 185–194.

Wallace, C.S., and D.M. Boulton (1975). An invariant Bayes method for point estimation. *Classification Society Bulletin, 3*(3), 11–34.

Wallace, C.S., and D.L. Dowe (1993). MML estimation of the von Mises concentration parameter. Technical report 93/193, Department of Computer Science, Monash University, Clayton, Victoria, Australia.

Wallace, C.S., and D.L. Dowe (1994). Intrinsic classification by MML — the Snob program. In *Proceedings of the Seventh Australian Joint Conference on Artificial Intelligence*, University of New England, Armidale, Australia, pp. 37–44.

Wallace, C.S., and D.L. Dowe (1999a). Minimum message length and Kolmogorov complexity. *Computer Journal, 42*(4), 270–283. [special issue on Kolmogorov Complexity].

Wallace, C.S., and D.L. Dowe (1999b). Refinements of MDL and MML coding. *Computer Journal, 42*(4), 330–337. [special issue on Kolmogorov complexity].

Wallace, C.S., and D.L. Dowe (1999c). Rejoinder. *Computer Journal, 42*(4), 345–347.

Wallace, C.S., and D.L. Dowe (2000). MML clustering of multi-state, Poisson, von Mises circular and Gaussian distributions. *Statistics and Computing, 10*(1), 73–83.

Wallace, C.S., and P.R. Freeman (1987). Estimation and inference by compact coding. *Journal of the Royal Statistical Society Series B, 49*, 240–252.

Wallace, C.S., and P.R. Freeman (1992). Single factor analysis by MML estimation. *Journal of the Royal Statistical Society Series B, 54*(1), 195–209.

Wallace, C.S., and M.P. Georgeff (1983). A general objective for inductive inference. Technical report 83/32, Department of Computer Science, Monash University, Clayton, Victoria, Australia.

Wallace, C.S., and K.B. Korb (1999). Learning linear causal models by MML sampling. In A. Gammerman (Ed.), *Causal Models and Intelligent Data Management*, pp. 89–111. Berlin: Springer Verlag.

Wallace, C.S., and J.D. Patrick (1993). Coding decision trees. *Machine Learning, 11*, 7–22.

Wettig, H., P. Grünwald, T. Roos, P. Myllymäki, and H. Tirri (2003). When discriminative learning of Bayesian network parameters is easy. Proceedings of the Eighteenth International Joint Conference on Artificial Intelligence (IJCAI 2003), Acapulco, Mexico, pp. 491–496.

12 Simultaneous Clustering and Subset Selection via MDL

Rebecka Jörnsten
Department of Statistics
Rutgers University
501 Hill Center
PISCATAWAY, NJ, 08854
USA
rebecka@stat.rutgers.edu
http://www.stat.rutgers.edu/~rebecka

Bin Yu
Department of Statistics
UC Berkeley
367 Evans Hall
Berkeley, CA, 94720
USA
binyu@stat.berkeley.edu
http://www.stat.berkeley.edu/~binyu

Model selection in regression is a popular subject, with applications in many different fields. Minimum description length (MDL) criteria for regression have received much attention in statistics and recently "gMDL" was shown to bridge AIC and BIC [Hansen and Yu 2001]. However, traditionally only the code length of the response variable has been considered in the MDL model selection literature.

The microarray technology allows for the simultaneous monitoring of thousands of genes for each sample. The emergence of this technology is changing the game of regression modeling because of the existence of thousands of covariates or gene expressions while the sample size is usually less than a hundred. Certain preprocessing or organization of the gene expression vector is necessary and often carried out by clustering analysis. That is, the high-dimensional gene expression data can be used to study similarities of gene expression profiles across different samples to form a gene clustering. The clusters may be indicative of genetic pathways. Parallel to gene clustering is the important application of sample classification based on all or selected gene expressions. The gene clustering and sample classification are often undertaken separately, or in a directional manner (one as an aid for the other). However, such separation of these two tasks may occlude informative structure in the data.

In this chapter, we review an algorithm developed by Jörnsten and Yu [2003] for the simultaneous clustering of genes and subset selection of gene clusters for sample classification. The clustering and selection criterion is based on the MDL principle and developed first for linear regression models, and then applied to classification problems through optimal scoring. For the first time, an MDL code length is given for both explanatory variables (genes) and response variables (sample class labels). The final output of the algorithm is a sparse and interpretable classification rule based on cluster centroids or the closest genes to the centroids. One gene expression data set and two simulation studies are used to show the effectiveness of this algorithm.

Gene expression data have recently received attention in the MDL literature. Tabus, Rissanen, and Astola [2003] focus on the classification problem, comparing different subsets of genes based on their ability to predict the class labels. Here, the full matrix of gene expression data is assumed known by both encoder and decoder, bypassing the need to model the structure of the explanatory variables. Discrete regression models are built from subsets of coarsely quantized expression values and evaluated using the normalized maximum likelihood (NML) code length. The quantization step simplifies the NML computation, a reduction that is similar in spirit to the exact (permutation) tests for logistic regression that appeared in the late 1980s [Hirji, Mehta, and Patel 1987]. Li and Zha [2002] also form predictive models of class labels, but begin by clustering the expression data. Their approach builds on the discriminant vector quantization (DVQ) encoding method and is loosely inspired by the MDL framework. Unlike Tabus et al. [2003], DVQ operates on both the space of explanatory variables and the class labels simultaneously. Coding is based on a normal mixture model, and a variant of the classical expectation-maximization (EM) algorithm is proposed for training (an algorithm that is similar to the so-called 'classification' EM). Beginning with Jornsten [2001], we have argued that simultaneous clustering and classification offers better insights into the nature of gene expression data. The DVQ method of Li and Zha [2002] is one embodiment of this idea. In this chapter, we illustrate our approach to the problem.

12.1 Introduction

Microarray technology has had a profound impact on statistical research today. Traditional methods for testing, classification, and feature selection do not always fit the bill for this application. Consequently, many new methodologies have been developed with microarray data as the motivational source. In this section we present an introduction to the technology itself. We describe how gene expression data are obtained from microarray images. We also give a brief outline of the most important tasks involved in the analysis of gene expression data.

With the conclusion of the Human Genome Project and other sequencing projects, the next step is to assign biological function to identified DNA sequences. This is referred to as *functional genomics*. Determining the role of each gene in an organism is a challenging task. Approaches that have gained much popularity are the complementary DNA (cDNA) and oligonucleotide microarray technologies. The microarray technology allows for the simultaneous measurements of the expressions of thousands of genes, or an entire genome. Through these genome-wide snapshots of an organism, microarray technology has become an important tool for developing understanding of gene function, regulation, and interaction. Microarrays are also used extensively in clinical research. The goal is to identify disease genes and to develop treatments and diagnostic tools. In this section, we review the image-processing issues with the cDNA microarray technology (cf. [Yang et al. 2000] and [Yang et al. 2001]). Interested readers are referred to http:www.affymetrics.com and http:www.rii.com for the alternative Affymetrics genechip and inkjet microarray technologies, and image-processing issues for affymetrics genechips are addressed in [Irizarry et al. 2003].

12.1.1 cDNA Microarray Images

We first review some basic genetic concepts. A gene is a segment of DNA that codes for a specific protein. DNA (deoxyribonucleic acid) is a double-stranded macromolecule, each strand a polymer of nucleotides. There are four different nucleotides: adenine (A), guanine (G), cytosine (C), and thymine (T). The two strands are linked together by hydrogen bonds between base pairs: A to T, and G to C. This complementary binding property of DNA is how information is stored and transmitted in the cell. Proteins are polymers of amino acids. There are twenty different amino acids, each encoded for by one or more triplets of the bases A, T, G, or C.

The cDNA microarray image technology is a tool geared at measuring the "activity" of a gene, that is, the protein production. The expression of a gene is a two-stage process. The first stage is *transcription* where the DNA segment is transcribed into a messenger RNA (mRNA) complementary copy of the DNA sequence. The second stage is *translation*, where mRNA is used as a blueprint for the protein.

Microarray experiments measure the level of activity of a gene at the first stage. The abundance of a specific mRNA in a cell is related to the amount of the corresponding protein being produced. In a cell at any given time, many genes will be active and many different mRNA will be present. We measure the abundance of different mRNA in a sample, *relative* to another sample. DNA probes (each corresponding to a gene, or DNA segment) are placed, or "spotted", onto a microscopic glass slide by a robotic *arrayer*. A reference sample of mRNA is labeled with a green fluorescent dye (Cy3). The sample of interest is labeled with a red dye (Cy5). The two mRNA samples are mixed and allowed to hybridize (binding of mRNA to probe DNA) onto the array. For each probe only the complementary mRNA strands will bind. The relative mRNA abundance (for each probe) is measured through the competitive hybridization of the two samples. A laser scan of the array produces two fluorescent intensity images, one corresponding to the excitation frequency of the green dye, the other corresponding to the excitation frequency of the red dye. The image intensity ratio of pixels for each probe, or spot, is proportional to the relative abundance of mRNA in the two samples. The raw microarray image data thus consist of two high-precision (16 bpp) scans. A small image subset, with 4×4 probes, is shown in figure 12.1. Comparing probe intensities between the two scans we see that the top left corner probe is more "active" (higher intensity) in the red (sample of interest) scan, whereas the bottom left corner probe is about equally expressed in both samples. In figure 12.2 a larger image example is shown. This image corresponds to a 4×4 print-tip grid. Each grid contains 19×21 probes, different probes for each grid with the exception of a few housekeeping probes. We show the sum of the red and green scan intensity images in figure 12.2. The image is highly structured, with high-intensity spots (corresponding to the probes) located on the grid. The spots are submerged in a noisy and non-stationary background (spatial systematic variation , see paragraph on *Normalization* below). The spots have a roughly circular shape, though some show significant deviation from this shape due to the experimental variation of the spotting procedure.

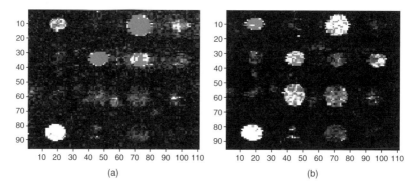

Figure 12.1   (a) Subset of green scan. (b) Subset of red scan.

Genetic Information Extraction   The relative mRNA abundance, that is, the *differential gene expression* between the two samples, is measured. We cannot get absolute measurements due to the difficulty of depositing exact amounts of DNA probes on the glass slides. In order to accurately estimate differential gene

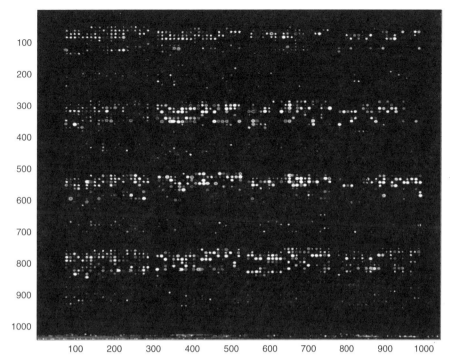

Figure 12.2   Microarray image: 4×4 grid setup, 19×21 spots per grid.

expression we have to identify the high-intensity regions in the images corresponding to each probe, and where hybridization has occurred. Moreover, we have to estimate, and correct for, the local background intensity or noise level due to nonspecific hybridization. Various methods for image segmentation, and background correction are used in the processing of microarray images.

Segmentation   Segmentation is done on the sum of the two images such that the same segmentation is used on both scans. Automatic registration of the image is used to determine the approximate centers, or the grid location, of the spots [Yang et al. 2000]. The spots are somewhat circular, and of roughly equal size. Thus, the most simplistic approach to identify the regions where hybridization has occurred is through a fixed circle segmentation (see [Eisen 1998]). A circle, with a radius chosen from the estimated grid structure, is used to define the spot regions. The apex of the circle can be adjusted locally to maximize the summed signal intensity within the circle, or spot mask. However, spot sizes and shapes often vary across the array. Differing spot sizes can result from tilted array during scanning, variations in print-tip pressure when spotting, or the quantity of probe DNA material deposited. An adaptive circle segmentation (see [Genepix 4000A, User's Guide, 1999]), allowing for differences in spot radii, can significantly improve the identification of spots. Adaptive shape segmentation techniques, such as histogram methods, mixture modeling, or seeded region growing [Yang et al. 2000], allow for noncircular spots.

Background Correction   Obtaining estimates of the local background intensity level can be a difficult task. When the arrays are noisy, and the spots are positioned close together, the background estimates will often be highly variable. One approach is to sample the local background near the identified spots [Eisen 1998]. Another method is to sample the background in the "valley-between-peaks", that is, the regions that are the most distant from the center of gravity of all surrounding spots [Genepix 4000A User's Guide, 1999]. These methods work well if the spots are clearly separated. A more robust background estimation scheme is presented in [Yang et al. 2000], and relies on image filtering operations (erosion and dilation).

Summary Statistics   An example of spot, or gene, summary statistics is the ratio of background-corrected mean intensities. Pixels in each image are summed within each identified spot. We denote by R_i the red (fluor tag) scan pixels, and by G_i the green scan pixels. The differential expression level, R/G, is then calculated as the ratio of the mean spot intensities:

$$\frac{R}{G} = \frac{\frac{1}{S}\sum_{R_i \in spot} R_i - BgR}{\frac{1}{S}\sum_{G_i \in spot} G_i - BgG},$$

where Bg refers to the estimates of the local background, and S is the number of spot pixels. The quantity studied in downstream statistical analyses, such as clustering and classification, is the vector $M = \log_2 \frac{R}{G}$ of log-ratios of estimated differential gene expressions. A log transform is applied to compress the scale, and even out the possibly skewed distribution of differential gene expressions. Other quantities of interest are measures of quality, such as spot variances, spot shapes, and product intensities $A = \log_2 \sqrt{RG}$. The product intensities, A, are indicative of how reliable the measurements of the gene expression are.

Normalization   Normalization is necessary prior to downstream analysis. The fluorescent dyes used to label the two samples have different labeling efficiencies, and there is a dye bias in scanning efficiency. Furthermore, there are spatial systematic errors across the array (see figure 12.2). It is common to use the genes that show little differential variation between samples for normalization. In some experiments, most genes are not differentially expressed, and all spots can be used for normalization. In other experiments, a set of housekeeping genes are used. M and A are simply a coordinate transformation of the background corrected spot intensities R and G. Dye-bias normalization is usually conducted on M, with respect to A. Normalization is an important, and far from resolved issue. A global normalization method (see, e.g., [Chen, Dougherty and Bittner 1997], [Genepix 4000A User's Guide, 1999]) estimates a constant factor c for each array from the arithmetic mean of the vector M. The normalized values $\tilde{M}$ are computed as $M - c$. An example of a local and nonlinear normalization scheme is that of Yang et al.

[2001]. For each spatial subarea of the array (one of the 4×4 subgrids of Fig. 12.2), we estimate a locally linear fit of M on A. The residual vector $\tilde{M}$ is computed, and used as the spatial and dye-bias–corrected differential gene expressions in subsequent analysis.

12.2   Statistical Problems in Gene Expression

A typical microarray experiment consists of at most a hundred samples of interest, with expressions measured for thousands of genes. From the processed image data a data matrix of dimension $n \times p$ is extracted, where n is the number of samples and p the number of genes. The expression of a gene j across the n samples is referred to as the gene profile, whereas the expression of genes within a sample i is called a sample profile or observation. The samples of interest can correspond to, for example, samples of healthy tissue at different time points, or samples of cancerous tissues.

Clustering   The analysis of high-dimensional and noisy gene expression data poses many challenges. The gene expression data can be used to study similarities of gene expression profiles across different samples to form a gene clustering. The clusters may be indicative of genetic pathways. Development of robust clustering techniques and validation tools is central to this problem. Parallel to gene clustering is the important application of sample classification based on all or selected gene expressions. Sample classification can have significant diagnostic value for diseases such as cancer. Feature selection, the selection of informative genes with respect to sample classes, has also received much attention. Since gene expression data tend to be sparse ($n \ll p$), feature selection is a difficult task.

In current research, there is a particular focus on the problems of gene clustering, and also sample clustering. Hierarchical clustering methods are often the preferred tools. Examples of other gene clustering methods that have appeared in the literature are k-means, partitioning around mediods (PAM), as well as novel SVD-based methods such as gene-shaving (Hastie et al. [2000b]).

Classification   For sample classification, we build predictive models for the sample classes based on all or selected gene expressions. Many classification methods have been applied to gene expression data: some traditional methods such as discriminant analysis (DA), nearest neighbors (NN), classification and regression trees (CART), and some novel and more complex methods such as support vector machines (SVMs), boosting and bagging CART, and neural nets. On most data sets, the simple and complex methods perform almost equally well, or poorly. In fact, a recent study by Dudoit, Fridlyand and Speed [2000] indicates that simple NN, or diagonal linear DA (DLDA) often results in the best test error rate performance. Gene expression data sets consist of few samples on which to build and validate models. It is possible that the use of more complex classifiers will be justified and necessary as the number and size of data sets grow.

Feature Selection   Many classifiers show improved performance with variable
or feature selection. In addition, parsimonious or sparse classification models are
often easier to interpret. This motivates gene or variable subset selection. There is
a vast literature on selection of individual genes for sample classification. Different
approaches based on T-tests, between-to-within sum of squares, mutual information, graph theory, and surprise scores all focus on the selection of genes one by
one ([Dudoit, Fridlyand and Speed 2000; Golub et al. 1999; Ben-Dor, Friedman
and Yakhini 2001; Xing and Karp 2001], and many more). Selecting genes that
act as good classifiers of, for example, tumor types is not a trivial task. The gene
expressions are often highly correlated, which makes the model selection problem
very unstable. Furthermore, the sample size n in gene expression data is usually
very small compared with the huge number of genes studied.

Gene clustering and sample classification with gene selection are in most cases
treated as separate problems, or in a directional manner (one as an aid for the
other). As an example of the first, Li and Hong [2001] cluster genes and use cluster
centroids with "soft-max" sample classification. However, there is no selection of
centroids; all of them are used for classification. An example of the latter, the
supervised gene-shaving of Hastie et al. [2000b] uses the sample class information
for improved gene clustering. Another example of a directional approach is the
supervised harvesting of expression trees of Hastie et al. [2000a]. In supervised tree
harvesting, an initial clustering is followed by the selection of cluster centroids for
classification, but the clustering remains fixed.

12.3   Model Selection in Linear Regression with Correlated Predictors

When the predictor variables are correlated, as with gene expression data, model
selection in linear regression is a difficult task. The instability of such model selection
problems is well-known (see e.g. [Breiman 1996]). Small perturbations of the data
may lead to big changes in the selected models. The predictive performance of
selected models may be similar, however. We consider the case when the number
of predictors p is very large, compared to the sample size n, as in the case of gene
expression data analysis. If the predictors are highly correlated, we approach the
model selection by first clustering the predictors, then selecting cluster centroids for
prediction of the response variable. If a predictor cluster model gives a reasonable
description of the data distribution, the cluster centroids are less correlated than
the individual predictors. This may reduce the instability in the model selection.
When $p \gg n$, and the predictors are highly correlated, using cluster centroids
as new predictor variables is reminiscent of model averaging, and the predictive
performance may be significantly improved over the individually selected models.

12.3.1 MDL or MML clustering

The commonly used minimum description length (MDL) approach to clustering is a two-stage coding scheme and appeared under minimum message length (MML) in [Wallace and Boulton 1968]. We first describe the cluster models, the number of clusters, the relative abundance of each cluster, and a cluster membership map. At the second stage, we encode for each datum its deviance from the cluster model. The cluster model includes a "centroid" for each cluster (e.g. mean or median), and an independent additive mean zero Gaussian error distribution, with an associated cluster standard deviation. Priors are assigned to all parameters of the cluster model. The number K of clusters is assumed uniformly distributed on $[1, M]$, where M is a known fixed upper bound, that is, $K \sim \frac{1}{M}$. Given K, the cluster data model is a Gaussian mixture model with parameters $\theta = (\mu, \sigma, p)^{(k)}$, $k = 1, \cdots, K$, i.e.

$$f(x) = \sum_{k=1}^{K} p_k \times \phi_k(x), \quad \phi_k(x) = \frac{1}{\sqrt{2\pi\sigma_k^2}} \exp(-\frac{1}{2\sigma_k^2}(x - \mu_k)^2).$$

Each cluster assignment is assumed equally likely, that is, we use a uniform prior $h(p) = (K - 1)!$. The cluster means μ_k are assumed to be uniformly distributed on $[-\sigma, \sigma]$, where σ^2 is the population variance. The cluster standard deviations σ_k are assumed uniformly distributed on $[0, \sigma]$. Taking the priors to be independent, the total prior equals

$$h(\mu, \sigma, p) = \frac{(K - 1)!}{2^K \sigma^{2K}}.$$

The parameter estimates are obtained via the expectation-maximization (EM) algorithm. The first stage of coding is to convey the cluster model description to the decoder by transmitting the estimates $\hat{\theta} = (\hat{\mu}, \hat{\sigma}, \hat{p})^{(k)}$. The prior distribution is used to define the code for the parameters. The MML code length can then be approximated as [Wallace and Boulton 1994]

$$MML = -\log h(\theta) + \log \sqrt{\det I(\theta)} + L(x^n|\theta).$$

We recognize this as the SIC-type approximation of the MDL mixture code length [Rissanen 1989]. In the Gaussian mixture model, with independent priors we have $\log \sqrt{\det I(\theta)} = \sum_{k=1}^{K} \frac{\sqrt{2}n_k}{\sigma_k^2}$, where n_k are the number of observations in cluster k.

At the second stage, we encode the deviance of data string x^n, from the cluster model. Each residual $r_i = \sum_{k=1}^{K} 1\{i \in b(k)\} (x_i - \mu_k)$ is computed, where $b(k)$ denotes the cluster membership map of cluster k. The r_i are encoded with a Gaussian coding scheme, with parameters $(0, \hat{\sigma}_k^2)$. If $b(k)$ is empty, has a single member, or $\hat{\sigma}_k^2 = 0$, no additional code is needed for r_i, i.e.

$$L(x^n|\hat{\theta}) = \sum_{i=1}^{n} \sum_{k=1}^{K} -1\{i \in b(k), \ |b(k)| > 1\} \ \log \phi(r_i|0, \hat{\sigma}_k^2),$$

and the total cluster MML code length is given by

$$MML = K\log(2\sigma^2) - \log(K-1)! + \sum_{k=1}^{K} \frac{\sqrt{2}n_k}{\sigma_k^2} + \qquad (12.1)$$

$$-\sum_{i=1}^{n}\sum_{k=1}^{K} 1\{i \in b(k), \ |b(k)| > 1\} \ \log\phi(r_i|0, \hat{\sigma}_k^2).$$

The extension to D-dimensional data is straightforward. Computation of the code length for the Gaussian mixture model is relatively simple since we assumed independence between all model components. Some current work has been directed toward allowing cluster dependence structure, and mixture model assumptions other than Gaussian (Baxter and Oliver [1995]).

12.3.2 Simultaneous Clustering and Regression Model Selection

MDL model selection in regression traditionally assumes that the predictor variables are known at the decoder. For the purpose of simultaneous clustering of the predictor variables and subset selection of cluster centroids for prediction of the response variable, we now assume that the predictors are not known. In this case, the predictor variables have to be transmitted to the decoder, prior to transmitting the response variable. If the predictor variables are highly correlated, and their distribution can be approximated by a Gaussian mixture model, the MDL or MML clustering code length (12.1) can be applied. By minimizing the MDL clustering code length, we form K clusters of predictor variables, and find the corresponding optimal cluster assignments, and cluster centroids. Given the clustering structure of the predictor variables, how can we efficiently encode the response variable? If the predictors are correlated, there will be many competing models that perform almost equally well for prediction or, equivalently, coding. A common strategy is to use a weighted prediction scheme for y. Below, we see that using cluster centroids as new predictors in a regression model setup is equivalent to a weighting scheme.

We have n observations, $(y, X) = (y_i|x_{i,1}, \cdots, x_{i,p})$, $i = 1, \cdots, n$. Given the MDL clustering of the predictor variables, we can view $x_m, m = 1, \cdots, p$ as noisy observations from a cluster model, with K clusters. If x_m belongs to cluster k, then observation

$$x_{i,m} = \mu_k + \delta_{i,k}, \qquad (12.2)$$

where μ_k is the k-th cluster centroid, and $\delta_{.,k}$ are independently an identically distributed (i.i.d.) $N(0, \sigma_k^2)$. The response variable generating model is given by

$$y_i = \sum_{\gamma_m=1} x_{i,m}\kappa_m + \epsilon_i^{(m)}, \qquad (12.3)$$

where $\epsilon^{(m)}$ are distributed i.i.d. $N(0, \sigma_{y,(m)}^2)$. If we plug (12.2) into (12.3), we find that the model for y equals

$$y_i = \sum_{\gamma_k = 1} \mu_k \beta_k + \epsilon_i, \tag{12.4}$$

with ϵ i.i.d. $N(0, \sigma_y^2)$ for some σ_y^2, and where β_k is a linear combination of the κ_m of the "active" predictors x_m in cluster k.

The coding of (y, X), or, equivalently, the model selection problem is a simultaneous selection of a cluster model for the predictors X, and the selection of cluster centroids in the regression model for y^n, as stated in (12.4). We use a two-part code length to describe the data (y, X). The first description length component $DL(X)$ deals with the cluster structure of the predictor variables, collected in design matrix X. We use the MDL or MML clustering code length for $DL(X)$. The second component describes the response variable, given the estimated structure of the predictors. We call this component $DL(y|X^*)$, where X^* is a $n \times K$ matrix with entries

$$(X^*)_{ik} = \mu_{ik} = \frac{1}{|b(k)|} \sum_{j=1}^p 1\{x_{ij} \in b(k)\} x_{ij},$$

that is, the estimated sample cluster centroids. Here, $b(k)$ is the set of predictor variables in cluster k. For $DL(y|X^*)$, we use the gMDL mixture code length of Hansen and Yu [2001]. gMDL has a data-dependent penalty on the model dimension and adaptively behaves like AIC or BIC depending on which one is more desirable:

$$DL(y|X^*) = \begin{cases} \frac{n}{2} \log RSS + \frac{k}{2} \log\left(\frac{\left(\frac{R^2}{1-R^2}\right)}{\left(\frac{k/n}{1-k/n}\right)}\right) + \frac{n}{2} \log(\frac{1}{1-k/n}) + \log n & \text{if } R^2 \geq k/n \\ \frac{n}{2} \log(y^T y) + \frac{1}{2} \log n & \text{otherwise,} \end{cases}$$

where $RSS = ||y - X^*(X^*X)^{-1}(X^*)^T y||^2$. The code lengths $DL(X)$ and $DL(y|X^*)$ may have very different magnitudes, if, for example, $p \gg n$. $DL(X)$ is a code length of $n \times p$ "observations" in the design matrix X. In contrast, only n observations y contribute to $DL(y|X^*)$. We want the two code lengths to have the same relative importance if we increase the sample size, or include more predictors in the selection. It is therefore more natural to consider the coding *rates*, and select the model that minimizes the following expression:

$$DL(y, X) = \frac{DL(X)}{np} + \frac{DL(y|X^*)}{n} \tag{12.5}$$

Minimizing (12.5) is not equivalent to a two-stage approach, where we first form the optimal cluster model by minimizing $DL(X)$, and then select cluster centroids for the regression model by minimizing $DL(y|X^*)$. The clustering is affected by the subsequent regression model selection, and vice versa.

If the observations X are i.i.d. samples from a one-dimensional cluster model, we need not cluster $X_{n \times p}$, that is, cluster p observations in n dimensions. Instead we compute the $1 \times p$ dimensional matrix $\bar{X}$, with elements

$$(\bar{X})_j = \frac{1}{n} \sum_{i=1}^{n} x_{ij}, \ j = 1, \cdots, p,$$

and cluster this one-dimensional data string. We thus encode $\bar{X}$ with an MDL cluster code length. After decoding, $(\bar{X})_j$ is available at the decoder. If X consists of n samples from the one-dimensional cluster model, the residuals

$$r_{ij} = x_{ij} - x_{.j}$$

are obviously independent of the clustering, and can be transmitted at a fixed cost. Clustering $\bar{X}$ rather than X may prove vital when n is large, since clustering high-dimensional data is in general difficult. The combined code length for data (y, X) is now given by

$$DL(y, X) = \frac{DL(\bar{X})}{p} + \frac{DL(y|X^*)}{n} + \text{constant},$$

where the constant refers to the code length for $X|\bar{X}$.

If X are not i.i.d. observations from a one-dimensional cluster model, the code length for $X|\bar{X}$ is not independent of the clustering. Moreover, since we intend to use the generated cluster centroids for prediction, we need to be careful in selecting the dimension in which to cluster X. It is possible that the vector $\bar{X}$ produces a clustering of predictor variables that eliminates all possibility of prediction. If some of the observations are replicates, it is natural to form a reduced dimension matrix $\bar{X}_{n' \times p}$ prior to clustering, where we take averages of x_{ij} over the replicates, and n' is the number of distinct observations. If the response variables are continuous, and there are no replications in the data set, we can reduce X to a matrix $\bar{X}$, with dimension $n' \times p$, by computing predictor variable averages for samples with similar y values. This corresponds to quantizing y to n' levels.

Let us assume we have formed a reduced dimension matrix $\bar{X}$ with dimension $d \times p$, where d is a value in $[1, n]$ chosen in some appropriate fashion. The combined code length for data (y, X) is then given by

$$DL(y, X) = \frac{DL(\bar{X})}{dp} + \frac{DL(y|X^*)}{n}. \tag{12.6}$$

In practice, we apply the k-means algorithm to estimate the K-partitioning of $\bar{X}$, rather than the EM algorithm as was done in Section 12.3.1. Since we want the two components, $DL(\bar{X})$ and $DL(y|X^*)$, to "feed back" on each other, we do not run the k-means algorithm to convergence, given K. Instead, we choose K random seeds from $\bar{X}$ and apply k-means for a fixed number of iterations $L(K)$. An ordering map for the predictor variables is sent to the decoder with a fixed code length. We then send a list of the integers p_k, which denote the number of members for each cluster k, $k = 1, \cdots, K$. We allow no cluster to be empty. The string $(p_1, \cdots, p_K)$ can thus be sent with a code based on a multinomial distribution, where we assign

$p - K$ "observations" to K "bins" [Rissanen 1989]. This code length is given by

$$DL(n_1, \cdots, n_K) = \log \frac{p!}{(p-K)!(K-1)!}.$$

Using a similar coding strategy for the cluster model parameters (μ_k, σ_k^2) as in Section 12.3.1, we end up with the following clustering code length for $\bar{X}_{d \times p}$:

$$DL(\bar{X}_{d \times p}) = \log \frac{p!}{(p-K)!(K-1)!} + K \sum_{s=1}^{d} \log(2\sigma_{(d)}^2) + \sum_{s=1}^{d} \sum_{k=1}^{K} \frac{\sqrt{2}p_k}{\sigma_{s,k}^2} \quad (12.7)$$

$$- \sum_{s=1}^{d} \sum_{j=1}^{p} \sum_{k=1}^{K} \log \phi((\bar{x}_{sj} - \mu_{ik})|\sigma_{sk}^2) \, 1\{j \subset b(k)\} + \text{constant},$$

where the constant refers to the code length for $X|\bar{X}$, and the order map for X. $\sigma_{(s)}^2$ is the total variance in dimension s, and σ_{sk}^2 is the variance for the kth cluster in dimension s. Given the K partitioning of X, we form the cluster centroids $X_{n \times K}^*$ as defined above. We apply the gMDL selection criterion to select a subset k of the K cluster centroids in the regression model for y. We present the algorithm for simultaneous predictor variable clustering and subset selection for prediction below. Here, $B(K_q)$ refers to an iteration factor, that is, the number of models with a K_q partitioning of X that are sampled.

Algorithm 12.3.1

1. Compute $\bar{X}$ with dimension $d \times p$. If we assume X is a random sample from a d-dimensional cluster model, $\bar{X}_{sj}$ is the average of x_{ij} over i, in dimension s.

2. Select an initial number of predictor variable clusters, K_q, $q = 0$.

3. Compute $DL(\bar{X}|K_q)$ (12.7), where a randomly selected K_q partition is used as seed for k-means.

4. Compute the matrix of observed cluster centroids, $X^*(K_q)$ with dimension $n \times K_q$.
Select k_q^* cluster centroids that minimize the code length $DL(y|X^*(K_q))$, where $DL(y|X^*(K_q))$ is the gMDL criterion.

5. Iterate steps 3 and 4 $B(K_q)$ times, and choose the K_q model with the smallest combined code length $\frac{DL(\bar{X}|K_q)}{dp} + \frac{DL(y|X^*(K_q))}{n}$.

6. Go to step 3, set $K_q = K_q + 1$, and $q = q + 1$. If $q = q_{stop}$, then stop. Select the q^0 that minimizes $\frac{DL(\bar{X}|K_q)}{dp} + \frac{DL(y|X^*(K_q))}{n}$. The final model for (y, X) is thus a K_{q^0} clustering of X, and selected k_{q^0} cluster centroids for the prediction of y.

In practice, we need to select the number of k-means iteration steps $L(K_q)$ for each K_q, and the number of iterations $B(K_q)$ in step 5 of the algorithm. The selection of $L(K_q)$ is not so crucial. Convergence to a *local* optimum is often achieved in fewer than 10 iterations. The choice of $B(K_q)$ is obviously a more delicate matter.

Even with a modest number of predictors p, the number of possible partitions is enormous, and we cannot perform an exhaustive search of the model space. Algorithm 12.3.1 is a "poor man's" version of a Markov chain Monte Carlo (MCMC) sampling scheme, where we use values for $B(K_q)$ that reflect the number of possible K_q partition, that is, we pick $B(K_q)$ to be an increasing function in $|K_q - p/2|$.

12.4   Simultaneous Clustering and Gene Selection

12.4.1   Optimal Scoring and MDL in Classification

The microarray problem is a classification problem, but model selection criteria in classification that are based on 0-1 loss are often intractable. It is therefore common to use an L2 loss approximation for selection. Here, we thus take the route of turning classification into regression via optimal scoring. We then appeal to the existing MDL methodology in regression discussed earlier to construct an MDL model selection criterion for classification. We restrict our attention to linear discriminant analysis (LDA). Let X be the matrix of predictor (gene) vectors. In LDA we find discriminant functions μ such that the linear combinations of feature vectors (projections onto the space spanned by the discriminant functions) $X\mu$ have maximal Between-to-Within-class sum of squares. LDA is thus an eigenvalue problem. Classification of a new observation is done in the subspace spanned by μ by assigning an observation to the closest class mean (Euclidean distance) in the subspace. Hastie, Tibshirani, and Buja [1994] discuss the familiar equivalence of LDA and regression via optimal scoring. The point of optimal scoring is to turn a categorical problem into a quantitative one. We find the discriminant functions μ via linear regression. Instead of solving the eigenvalue problem, we form a multiple response regression problem, that is, we form an $n \times C$ dummy matrix Y, and regress it on X. The jth column of Y has ith row entry "1" if sample i belongs to class $j \in \{1, \cdots, C\}$, and "0" otherwise. The simultaneous estimation of the optimal scores, and the regression coefficients can be stated as $\min_{\theta,B} ||Y\theta - XB||^2$, with constraint $\theta^T D_p \theta = I$, where D_p is a diagonal matrix of class proportions. Given θ, the minimizing B are the least squares coefficients such that

$$\min_{\theta,B} ||Y\theta - XB||^2 = \min_{\theta} Tr\{(\theta^*)^T \theta^* - \theta^T (Y^T \hat{Y})\theta\}. \tag{12.8}$$

From this follows that a third alternative to finding μ is to minimize $||\theta^* - XB^*||^2$, that is, regress the orthogonal *optimal scores* $\theta^* = Y\theta$ on X. The regression coefficient estimates B^* are proportional to the discriminant functions μ such that the lth discriminant function

$$\mu_l = \frac{1}{\sqrt{R_l^2(1 - R_l^2)}} B_l^*, R_l^2 = 1 - \frac{RSS_l(\theta_l^*, X)}{((\theta_l^*)^T \theta_l^*)}, \tag{12.9}$$

where R_l^2 is the multiple r-squared of the lth column of θ^* regressed on X. The model selection (selecting columns of X) aspect of discriminant analysis is more complex. If the selection criterion is a function of the individual RSS_l, the selection can be affected by the choice of initial optimal scores θ^*, themselves functions of X. It is then recommended to iterate between selection and updating of the optimal scores using the selected columns of X.

We construct an MDL model selection criterion for classification by applying an extension of gMDL to multiresponse regression of the orthogonal optimal scores. Since the scores are orthogonal, the closest Gaussian approximation consists of independent response models. For a C class problem, there are $C-1$ nontrivial optimal scores θ^*. We write

$$gMDL_C = \sum_{l=1}^{C-1} gMDL(\theta_l^*|X),\qquad(12.10)$$

where

$$gMDL(\theta_l^*|X) = \begin{cases} \frac{n}{2(C-1)}\log(\sum_l^{C-1} RSS_l) + \frac{k}{2}\log\left(\frac{(\frac{R_l^2}{1-R_l^2})}{(\frac{k/n}{1-k/n})}\right) + \\ +\frac{n}{2}\log(\frac{1}{1-k/n}) + log(n) & \text{if } R_l^2 \geq k/n \\ \frac{n}{2}\log((\theta_l^*)^T\theta_l^*) + \frac{1}{2}\log n & \text{otherwise.} \end{cases}$$

The shrinkage estimates of the discriminant functions equal

$$\hat{\mu}^{(l)} = \frac{\hat{\beta}_{LS}^{(l)}}{\sqrt{R_l^2(1-R_l^2)}}\,1\{R_l^2 \geq k/n\},\qquad(12.11)$$

where $\hat{\beta}$ are the optimal score regression coefficients. For some l, the estimates $\hat{\mu}^{(l)}$ may equal zero, and those discriminant functions are thus dropped from the model. Reducing the dimension in which we classify often improves the class predictive performance of the selected models [Hastie et al. 1994].

To compute gMDL$_C$, implicitly we have to estimate $(C-1)+C_c$ hyperparameters, where C_c is the number of R_l^2 that exceed k/n. When the sample size is small we may prefer to use a simplified criterion, gMDL$_{eC}$, instead. gMDL$_{eC}$ is derived under an equal-variance model for the multivariate regression problem, and independent priors on the regression coefficients of each model. The number of hyperparameters in this setup is $1 + C_c$. The simplified selection criterion is given by

$$gMDL_{eC} = \begin{cases} \frac{n(C-1)}{2}\log(RSS_{tot}) + \frac{k}{2}\sum_{l=1}^{C-1}\log\left(\frac{(\frac{R_l^2}{1-R_l^2})}{(\frac{k/n}{1-k/n})}\right) + \\ +\frac{n(C-1)}{2}\log(\frac{1}{1-k/n}) + (C-1)\log(n), & \text{if } R_l^2 \geq k/n \\ \frac{n}{2}\log(Tr\{(\theta^*)^T\theta^*\}) + \frac{(c-1)}{2}\log n, & \text{otherwise.} \end{cases}$$

Here $RSS_{tot} = \sum_{l=1}^{C-1} RSS_l$. The derivation of gMDL$_C$ and gMDL$_{eC}$ requires a lengthy discussion of the choice and form of model priors, and is omitted here to conserve space. The details can be found in [Jornsten 2001].

The optimal scoring turned the categorical problem into a quantitative one, but the response variables are nevertheless discrete. A Gaussian coding scheme may not be the most effective. The hope is that the coding redundancy induced by the approximation is independent of the model size and complexity. Then, a relative comparison of the gMDL$_C$ code lengths *between* models is still valid. In practice, we find that the Gaussian-based selection criterion performs well on simulated and real data (see Section 12.4.2 and [Jornsten 2001]).

12.4.2 Simultaneous Clustering and Classification

As discussed earlier, when the predictor variables (genes) are correlated and their number is very large compared with the sample size, model selection in regression is unstable: at one level the total number of variables selected changes quite a bit when different data sets are used; at the other level different predictors (genes) are selected when different data sets are used. A similar phenomenon occurs in classification. Using the regression model through optimal scoring, we approach model selection in classification by clustering the predictors (genes), and selecting gene cluster centroids for response-variable prediction. If a predictor (gene) cluster model describes the data well, the cluster centroids are less correlated than the individual predictors, which reduces the instability of model selection at both levels. Specifically, we achieve simultaneous predictor clustering and cluster selection for classification by using a variant of Algorithm 12.3.1. As discussed in section 12.3 for regression, we reduce the dimension of the design matrix X ($n \times p$) prior to clustering. For supervised gene clustering, we have outcome variables y that are categorical. If the within-class variation is sufficiently small, instead of clustering X, we cluster the reduced dimension matrix $\bar{X}$ with dimension $C \times p$,

$$(\bar{X})_{cj} = \frac{1}{n_c} \sum_{i=1}^{n} x_{ij} 1\{y_i = c\}, \quad c = 1, \cdots, C, \ j = 1, \cdots, p,$$

where C is the number of distinct class labels, and n_c is the number of observations from class c. The MDL code length for the gene clustering, with K clusters is thus given by

$$DL(\bar{X}|K) = K \sum_{c=1}^{C} \log(2\sigma_c^2) - \log(K-1)! + \sum_{c=1}^{C} \sum_{k=1}^{K} \frac{\sqrt{2}|b(k)|}{\sigma_{c,k}^2} + \qquad (12.12)$$

$$+ \sum_{j=1}^{p} \sum_{c=1}^{C} \sum_{k=1}^{K} -1\{j \in b(k), \ |b(k)| > 1\} \ \log \phi((\bar{x}_{cj} - \mu_{c,k})|\sigma_{c,k}^2),$$

where $b(k)$ denotes the set of genes j in cluster k. Here, σ_c^2 is the population variance for $\bar{X}$ within sample class c, $\sigma_{c,k}^2$ is the variance within class c for gene cluster k, and $\mu_{c,k}$ is the kth cluster mean within sample class c.

In classification problems with $C > 2$ we have multiple responses. The response description length of Algorithm 12.3.1 $DL(y|X^*)$ is therefore replaced by gMDL$_C$ or gMDL$_{eC}$. In addition, when we combine the code lengths we also take into account that the response is multivariate. There are $(C-1)$ optimal score regression problems for a C class problem. The coding rate we minimize with respect to the number of cluster K and active cluster k is thus

$$\frac{DL(\bar{X}|K)}{Cp} + \frac{gMDL_{(e)C}(k)}{(C-1)n}.$$

12.5   Experimental Results

12.5.1   Application to a Gene Expression Data Set

We apply our algorithm for simultaneous clustering and subset selection for classification to a publicly available gene expression data set. We perform threefold cross-validation 150 times (i.e., randomly select two thirds of the data as training 150 times) to estimate the test error rate of the selected models, and to investigate the sparseness of the classification model and instability of model selection. We also run our algorithm on the full data set, and discuss the selected model and gene clusters. For each training data set, an initial gene selection removes genes that have near-constant variation across samples. There is a sharp drop-off in the between-to-within-class (B/W) sum of squares after ten to fifteen genes. We select the T=200 largest B/W genes as a starting point, and use the S=10 largest B/W genes to compute the initial optimal scores. We run the algorithm with the number of clusters ranging from K_q=1 to 20. For each K_q, we iterate $B(K_q)$ times, where $B(K_q)$=50 for $K_q \leq 10$, $B(K_q)$=100 for K_q=11 to 20. The $B(K_q)$ were selected as a reasonable tradeoff between sufficient sampling of the model space, and computing time. We allow for up to 20 clusters or individual genes to be selected in the optimal scoring regression model, and perform exhaustive search over all possible subsets.

Model selection can be affected by the choice of initial optimal scores (the S genes). To avoid the computationally intensive exercise of iterating the algorithm, we try to pick a reasonable initial S such that iteration is not necessary. We iterated our algorithm with different values for S, and found that S=10 produces the same model in one run of the algorithm as with multiple runs. It is important to realize that the S initial genes do not drive the selection, however. These S genes are not necessarily selected in the final model, nor do they necessarily fall into different gene clusters.

The simultaneous clustering and subset selection algorithm generates "active" and "inactive" clusters. Active clusters are those that are selected in the classification model. For convenience, in this subsection we will refer to our algorithm as SimClust (simultaneous clustering and subset selection). Separate clustering followed by subset selection is referred to as SepClust, individual gene selection as IndSelect. Moreover, we also include a method where we replace the mathematical cluster centroids with the genes closest to the centroid of each cluster. We refer to this method as CenterClust. This makes the selected models more easily interpretable.

In [Dudoit, Fridlyand and Speed 2000], a comparative study of classifiers was conducted. The simple nearest neighbor (NN) and diagonal linear discriminant (DLDA) methods were found to give the best test error rate results on several gene expression data sets (including NCI60). Hence we include NN and DLDA in our cross-validation study. DLDA uses all T genes. NN is based on the k nearest neighbors, where k is selected by leave-one-out cross-validation on the training set. We also implement the supervised gene-shaving (GS) of Hastie et al. [2000b]. This method resembles our approach, if the clustering is done *separately* from the subset selection. We follow Hastie et al. and generate 8 gene-shaving clusters, with sizes chosen by the gap-statistic. Since the gene-shaving clusters are (almost) orthogonal, a simple LDA classifier is used in conjunction with supervised gene-shaving.

NCI60 data   The National Cancer Institute's anticancer drug screen data (NCI60) of Ross et al. [2000] consists of n=61 samples from human cancer cell lines. Gene expression levels were measured for p=9703 genes. The samples were grouped into 8 classes according to tumor site: 9 breast, 5 central nervous system (CNS), 7 colon, 8 leukemia, 8 melanoma, 9 non–small-lung carcinoma (NSCLS), 6 ovarian, and 9 renal. Genes that had more than 2 missing values were screened out. The remaining missing values were imputed by the mean value of 5 nearest neighbor genes. The retained data matrix is thus of dimension 61 × 5244. We run our algorithm on the full data set, with T=200 and S=10 and gMDL$_C$ as the selection criterion. The SimClust selected model consists of 8 gene clusters, 6 of which are "active". The active clusters contain 143 genes. The training error rate is 11.1%. With SepClust we get 5 gene clusters, 4 of which are active. The cluster sizes range from 12 to 78, and the active gene clusters contain 195 genes. The training error is 19.7%. DLDA and GS have training error 11.1%, and NN has training error 14.8%. In NN 2 nearest neighbors were selected. The GS clusters range in size from 2 to 8, containing 40 genes. In table 12.1 the average (over cross-validation training sets) selected models are shown. The models selected by SimClust are on average larger than the ones selected by SepClust, but smaller than the ones selected by IndSelect. SimClust active gene clusters tend to be more homogeneous within a sample class than SepClust gene clusters [Jornsten and Yu 2003]. The SimClust models exhibit the smallest variability (0.4 compared to 0.9 for SepClust and 2.0 for IndSelect). Moreover, the centroids of clusters in the cross-validation study are well correlated with the centroids selected on the full data set, with mean correlation .79 and standard deviation .06. The center genes of selected clusters are not as highly correlated with the center genes selected using the full data set. The mean correlation is .67 with standard deviation .07. For this data set, the individually selected genes on cross-validation data sets are not very strongly correlated with the genes selected using the full data set. The correlation is .42, with standard deviation .1.

In table 12.2 the cross-validation test error rates are shown, comparing SimClust, SepClust, and IndSelect, to NN, GS, and DLDA. The SimClust test error rates are comparable to NN and DLDA, with the added benefit of gene cluster information.

SepClust, CenterClust, and GS perform worse, and IndSelect performs very poorly on this data set.

NCI60	k	K	r
SimClust	6.9(.4)	9.4(.6)	.79(.06)
SepClust	3.9(.9)	4.8(.8)	
CenterClust	6.9(.4)	9.4(.6)	.67(.07)
IndSelect	9.3(2.0)	NA	.42(.10))
NN	2.2(.6)	NA	

Table 12.1 NCI60: Selected models on 150 cross-validation data sets. Average and (standard deviation) of model sizes. k is the number of selected genes, centers, or centroids. K is the the number of gene clusters. r is the mean correlation and (standard deviation) of selected genes, centers, and centroids with their counterpart on the full data set.

NCI60	mean(SD)	five-number summary
Simclust	33.7(8.2)	(14.3,28.6,33.3,38.1,61.9)
SepClust	43.4(9.2)	(15.0,38.1,42.9,52.4,71.4)
CenterClust	46.0(11.3)	(33.3,38.1,42.9,52.2,66.7)
IndSelect	56.5(10.5)	(33.3,47.6,57.1,66.7,76.2)
NN	32.9(7.1)	(14.3,28.6,33.3,38.1,58.4)
GS	45.6(11.9)	(19.0,38.1,47.6,52.4,71.4)
DLDA200	31.2(8.3)	(14.3,23.4,28.6,38.1,47.6)

Table 12.2 NCI60: Mean and standard deviation of cross-validation test error rates (%). Five number summaries (min, lower quartile, median, upper quartile, max) of cross-validation test error rates.

The cross-validation test error results are similar if we replace gMDL_C with gMDL_{eC} in the SimClust algorithm, and they are omitted to conserve space. In general, selected models with gMDL_{eC} are somewhat larger. On the full NCI60 data set the gMDL_{eC}-selected model consists of 10 clusters, 7 of which are active and contain 129 genes.

12.5.2 Simulation Studies

We perform two simulation studies where we know the truth to further assess SimClust. As comparisons, we include AIC, BIC, and AIC_C in the sense that in Algorithm 12.3.1, we use them pragmatically in place of $DL(y|X^*)$ even though AIC and AIC_C are not code lengths. We generate artificial data from the estimated model for the NCI60 data set. We also generate artificial data from a sparse model, and from a model with many weak effects. The noise level is quite high in all the simulations to reflect the nature of true gene expression data. We examine how well SimClust can adapt to these different situations, and how close the estimated model is to the true generative model. We compare the $gMDL_C$ selection criteria to AIC, BIC, and AIC_C. gMDL performs well in all the simulations because it is able to adapt to the sparse and nonsparse setups, whereas BIC and AICc cannot. The AIC, BIC, and AIC_C criteria for the independent optimal score models are

$$AIC = \sum_{l=1}^{C-1} \frac{n}{2} \log RSS(\theta_l^*, X^*) + (C-1)k^*,$$

$$BIC = \sum_{l=1}^{C-1} \frac{n}{2} \log RSS(\theta_l^*, X^*) + \frac{(C-1)k^*}{2} \log n,$$

$$AICc = \sum_{l=1}^{C-1} \frac{n}{2} \log RSS(\theta_l^*, X^*) + (C-1)\frac{n}{2}\frac{1+k^*/n}{1-(k^*+2)/n}.$$

When we assume equal variance ($gMDL_{eC}$) the criteria are given by

$$AIC_2 = \frac{n(C-1)}{2} \log RSS_{tot} + (C-1)k^*,$$

$$BIC_2 = \frac{n(C-1)}{2} \log RSS_{tot} + (C-1)k^* \log n,$$

$$AICc_2 = \frac{n(C-1)}{2} \log RSS_{tot} + \frac{n(C-1)}{2}\frac{1+k^*/n}{1-(k^*(C-1)+2)/(n(C-1))},$$

where $RSS_{tot} = \sum_{l=1}^{C-1} RSS(\theta_l^*, X^*)$. The AIC_2 criterion corresponds to the generalized cross-validation (GCV) criterion used by Hastie, Tibshirani, and Buja [1994] for model selection in classification.

Simulating from the Estimated Model We simulate 50 data sets from the estimated model (selected via $gMDL_{eC}$) with 10 clusters, 7 of which are "active", that is, selected for classification. We use the class labels $y_i, i = 1, \cdots, 61$, of the NCI60 data, and construct the X matrix of gene expression as follows. We compute

$$\bar{X}_C = \frac{1}{n_c} \sum_{i=1}^{n} 1\{y_i = c\}x_{ij}, \quad \bar{X} = \frac{1}{n} \sum_{i=1}^{n} x_{ij},$$

where n_c is the number of samples with class label c. We compute the covariance matrix of $\bar{X}_C$ and $\bar{X}$, called Σ_C and Σ respectively. For active cluster k, we generate

Σ	gMDL_C	AIC	BIC	AICc
$\hat{k}^*$	7.04	10.32	5.25	7.78
$\hat{K}$	8.29	12.57	8.24	9.21
Σ	gMDL_{eC}	AIC_2	BIC_2	AICc_2
$\hat{k}^*$	7.25	10.86	5.04	8.54
$\hat{K}$	8.24	12.36	7.86	8.86
$\Sigma/2$	gMDL_C	AIC	BIC	AICc
$\hat{k}^*$	6.94	9.76	6.72	7.80
$\hat{K}$	9.22	11.52	9.60	9.24
$\Sigma/2$	gMDL_{eC}	AIC_2	BIC_2	AICc_2
$\hat{k}^*$	7.02	9.20	6.92	8.12
$\hat{K}$	10.24	12.64	10.52	10.96

Table 12.3 Simulation study. 50 simulations from the estimated gene cluster and subset model, $k^* = 7, K = 10$. In the top two panels the NCI60 data covariance structure was used in the simulation. In the lower two panels we decrease the cluster model variance by a factor of 2.

n_c samples,

$$X_c(k) \sim N(\bar{X}_c(k), \Sigma_c(k)), \ c = 1, \cdots, C,$$

where $X_c(k)$ has dimension $n_c \times b(k)$, and $b(k)$ is the number of genes in the estimated model for cluster k. For inactive clusters k', we generate data from

$$X(k') \sim N(\bar{X}(k'), \Sigma(k')),$$

where $X(k')$ has dimension $n \times b(k')$. We also generate a test set with $m = 2500$ samples, where the m class labels have been chosen such that the relative class abundances are the same as in the NCI60 data set.

We run the simultaneous predictor clustering and classification model selection algorithm on the simulated data sets. The results are shown in table 12.3. In the top two panels the NCI60 data covariance structure was used in the simulation. We apply both gMDL_C and gMDL_{eC} and similarly both the unequal and equal variance versions of AIC, BIC, and AICc. The results show comparable results for the unequal variance criteria and the equal variance criteria (gMDL or not). So in the text below, we do not make a distinction between the two versions. The gMDL criterion is best at selecting the true number of active clusters k^* in both the unequal and equal variance cases, but underfits the number of clusters K in the data by combining inactive clusters. The latter is also true of BIC. This is an example of how the classification can have a "bad" feedback on the clustering. AIC overfits both in terms of number of clusters and number of active clusters. AICc is best at selecting the number of clusters but overfits in terms of active clusters. The test error rate performance is comparable for all criteria (figure 12.3). In the lower

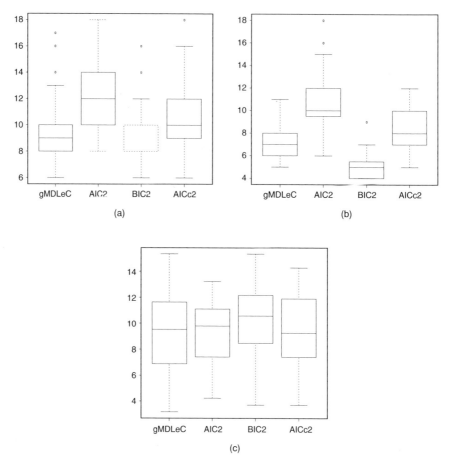

Figure 12.3 Number of clusters, selected clusters (gMDL$_{eC}$, equal variance model), and test error rates on simulated data with $n = 61, p = 200$, generated from the estimated model. (a) The number of clusters (cmp $K = 10$); (b) number of selected clusters (cmp $k^* = 7$); and (c) test error rate.

two panels we decrease the cluster model variance by a factor of 2. Now, gMDL and BIC are the best. BIC performance is much improved compared with the higher variance simulation. AIC and AICc both overfit.

In the simulation study using the estimated model, clusters $(2, 4, 7, 10)$ are almost always correctly estimated. These smaller active clusters are all good classifiers on the original NCI60 data. The large $(1, 6, 8)$ and inactive $(3, 5, 9)$ clusters are estimated with less certainty.

Sparse and Nonsparse Models   We simulate 50 data sets from models with

(a) $K = 10$ clusters, $k^* = 9$ active clusters;

(b) $K = 14$ clusters, $k^* = 4$ active clusters.

in the same fashion as above. The models used for simulations were the most and least sparse models selected (via gMDL$_{eC}$) in the 150 random splits of the cross-validation study.

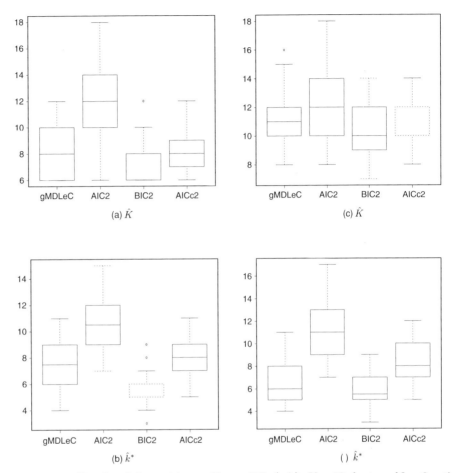

Figure 12.4   Simulated data with $n = 61, p = 200$. (a-b): $K = 10$ clusters, $k^* = 9$ active clusters. (c-d): $K = 14$ clusters, $k^* = 4$.

From the estimated model above we did not see a significant difference between versions of criteria for the unequal and equal cases. Hence we only use the equal variance model selection criteria here. As can be seen from figure 12.4, gMDL$_{eC}$ is able to adapt to the sparse, and nonsparse models (see also [Hansen and Yu 2001]). On the nonsparse model [figure 12.4(a) and (b)], AICc$_2$ overfits both in terms of the number of clusters and number of active clusters. AICc$_2$, BIC$_2$, and gMDL$_{eC}$ also select too few clusters. BIC$_2$ underfits in terms of active clusters, whereas gMDL$_{eC}$ and AICc$_2$ come closer to the true number of active clusters. gMDL$_{eC}$ gives the best test error rate, closely followed by AICc$_2$ [figure 12.5(a)].

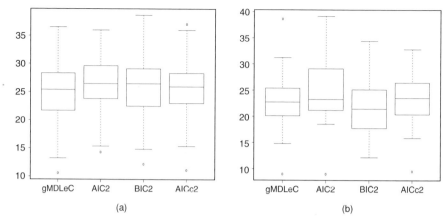

Figure 12.5 Simulated data with $n = 61, p = 200$. Test error rates. (a) $K = 10$ clusters, $k^* = 9$ active clusters. (b) $K = 14$ clusters, $k^* = 4$. Sparse model.

On the sparse model [see figure 12.4(c) and (d), figure 12.5(b)] all four criteria underfit in terms of number of clusters. The noise level in the simulation is high, so noisy inactive clusters tend to be combined. However, in terms of active clusters, gMDL_{eC} and BIC_2 perform much better than AIC_2 and AICc_2. For this model BIC_2 gives the best test error rates, closely followed by gMDL_{eC}.

In conclusion, gMDL shows comparable performance to AICc on the nonsparse model and comparable to BIC on the sparse model. For gene expression data, without prescreening of the genes, the models may be more sparse, and the ability of gMDL to adapt to the situation at hand may prove important.

Concluding Remarks

We reviewed a new MDL model selection criterion for the simultaneous clustering of explanatory variables and subset selection in linear regression by coding the explanatory variables together with the response variable. Through optimal scoring, this criterion is applied to the problem of simultaneous gene clustering and subset selection based on microarray sample classification data. This method gives sparse and interpretable classification models with competitive test error rate results, compared to some of the best methods reported in the literature, on the NCI60 gene expression data set. Similar results were also obtained on several other gene expression data sets [Jornsten and Yu 2003]. In addition, we show the model selection instability is reduced by selecting gene clusters, compared with individual gene selection. The simultaneous clustering and subset selection algorithm generates largely homogeneous gene clusters, and separates "active" clusters that are class predictive from "inactive" clusters that exhibit cross-sample variation but are not necessarily good class predictors. Moreover, we demonstrated on simulated data that gMDL in combination with the MDL/MML clustering code is able to adapt to situations with sparse or nonsparse data generative models. Finally, it is worth noting that even though we use linear discriminant analysis with our gene clustering method, any postprocessing classifier can be applied to the selected models [Jornsten 2001].

12.5.3 Acknowledgments

This research was partially supported by grants from NSF (FD01-12731) and ARO (DAAD19-01-1-0643). We also thank Mark Hansen for many helpful discussions and comments on the chapter.

References

Baxter, R.A., and J.J. Oliver (1995). MDL and MML, similarities and differences (introduction to minimum encoding inference - Part III). Technical report, Department of Computer Science, Monash University, Clayton, Victoria, Australia.

Ben-Dor, A., N. Friedman, and Z. Yakhini (2001). Class discovery in gene expression data. In *Proceedings of the Fifth Annual International Conference on Computational Molecular Biology (RECOMB)*.

Breiman, L. (1996). Heuristics of instability and stabilization in model selection. *Annals of Statistics, 24*(6), 2350–2383.

Chen Y., E.R. Dougherty, and M.L. Bittner (1997). Ratio-based decisions and the quantitative analysis of cDNA microarrays. *Journal of Biomedical Optics, 2*, 364–374.

Dudoit, S., J. Fridlyand, and T. Speed (2000). Comparison of discrimination methods for the classification of tumors using gene expression data. *Journal of the American Statistical Association, 97*(457) 77–87.

Eisen, M. (1998). Scanalyze. Available at `http://rana.stanford.edu/software`.

Genepix 4000A, User's Guide (1999). Genepix-Axon Instruments. See `http:www.axon.com`.

Golub, T.R., D.K. Slonim, P. Tamayo, C. Huard, M. Gaasenbeek, J.P. Mesirov, H. Coller, M.L. Loh, J.R. Downing, M.A. Caligiuri, C.D. Bloomfield, and E.S. Lander (1999). Molecular classification of cancer: Class discovery and class prediction by gene expression monitoring. *Science, 286*, 531–537

Hansen, M., and B. Yu (2001). Model selection and the principle of minimum description length. *Journal of the American Statistical Association, 96*(454), 746–774

Hastie, T., R. Tibshirani, D. Botstein, P. Brown (2000b). Supervised harvesting of expression trees. Technical report, Department of Statistics, Stanford University, Stanford, CA.

Hastie, T., R. Tibshirani, M. Eisen, P. Brown, D. Ross, U. Scherf, J. Weinstein, A. Alizadeh, L. Staudt, and D. Botstein (2000a). Gene Shaving: a new class of clustering methods for expression arrays. Technical report, Department of Statistics, Stanford University, Stanford, CA.

Hastie, T., R. Tibshirani, and A. Buja (1994). Flexible discriminant analysis. *Journal of the American Statistical Association, 89*, 1255–1270.

Hirji, K., C. Mehta, and N. Patel (1987). Computing distributions for exact logistic regression. *Journal of the American Statistical Association, 82*, 1110–1117.

Irizarry, R.A., B. Hobbs, F. Collin, Y.D. Beazer-Barclay, K.J. Antonellis, U. Scherf, and T.P. Speed (2003). Exploration, normalization, and summaries of high density oligonucleotide array probe level data. *Biostatistics, 4*(2), 249–264.

Jörnsten, R. (2001). Data Compression and its Statistical Implications, with an Application to the Analysis of microarray images. *Ph.D. thesis, Department of Statistics, University of California at Berkeley.*

Jörnsten, R. and B. Yu (2003). Simultaneous gene clustering and subset selection for classification via MDL. *Bioinformatics, 19*, 1100–1109.

Li, H., and, F. Hong (2001). Cluster-Rasch model for microarray gene expression data. *Genome biology, 2*(8-31), 1–13.

Li, J., and H. Zha (2002). Simultaneous classification and feature clustering using discriminant vector quantization with applications to microarray data analysis. In *Computer Society Bioinformatics Conference (CSB)*, Stanford, CA, pp. 246–255.

Rissanen, J. (1989). Stochastic complexity. Singapore: World Scientific.

Ross, D.T., U. Scherf, M. Eisen, C.M. Perou, P. Spellman, V. Iyer, S.S. Jeffrey, M, van de Rijn, M. Waltham, A. Pergamenschikov, J.C.F. Lee, D. Lashkari, D. Shalon, T.G. Myers, J.N. Weinstein, D. Botstein, and P.O. Brown (2000). Systematic variation in gene expression patterns in human cancer cell lines. *Nature Genetics, 24*, 227–234.

Tabus, J., J. Rissanen, and J. Astola (2003). Classification and feature gene selection using the normalized maximum likelihood model for discrete regression. *Signal Processing, 83*, 713–727.

Wallace, C.S., and D.M. Boulton (1968). An information measure for classification . *Computer Journal, 11*, 185–195.

Wallace, C.S., and D.M. Boulton (1994). Intrinsic classification by MML - the SNOB program. In *Proceedings of the 8th Australian Joint Conference on Artificial Intelligence.*

Xing, E., and R. Karp (2001). CLIFF: Clustering of high-dimensional microarray data via iterative feature filtering using normalized cuts. *Bioinformatics*, *17*(Suppl 1), S306–S315.

Yang, Y., M.J. Buckley, S. Dudoit, and T. Speed (2000). Comparisons of methods for image analysis on cDNA microarray data. *Journal of Computational and Graphical Statistics*, 11(1), 108–136.

Yang, Y., S. Dudoit, P. Luu, and T. Speed (2001). Normalization for cDNA microarray data. Microarrays: Optical technologies and informatics, Volume 4266 of Proceedings of SPIE (the International Society for Optical Engineering).

13 An MDL Framework for Data Clustering

Petri Kontkanen
Complex Systems Computation Group (CoSCo)
Helsinki Institute for Information Technology (HIIT) [1]
P. O. Box 9800, FIN-02015 HUT, Finland
petri.kontkanen@hiit.fi, http://www.hiit.fi/petri.kontkanen/

Petri Myllymäki
Complex Systems Computation Group (CoSCo)
Helsinki Institute for Information Technology (HIIT)
P. O. Box 9800, FIN-02015 HUT, Finland
petri.myllymaki@hiit.fi, http://www.hiit.fi/petri.myllymaki/

Wray Buntine
Complex Systems Computation Group (CoSCo)
Helsinki Institute for Information Technology (HIIT)
P. O. Box 9800, FIN-02015 HUT, Finland
wray.buntine@hiit.fi, http://www.hiit.fi/wray.buntine/

Jorma Rissanen
Complex Systems Computation Group (CoSCo)
Helsinki Institute for Information Technology (HIIT)
P. O. Box 9800, FIN-02015 HUT, Finland
jorma.rissanen@hiit.fi, http://www.mdl-research.org/

Henry Tirri
Complex Systems Computation Group (CoSCo)
Helsinki Institute for Information Technology (HIIT)
P. O. Box 9800, FIN-02015 HUT, Finland
henry.tirri@hiit.fi, http://www.hiit.fi/henry.tirri/

---

1. HIIT is a joint research institute of University of Helsinki and Helsinki University of Technology.

We regard clustering as a data assignment problem where the goal is to partition the data into several nonhierarchical groups of items. For solving this problem, we suggest an information-theoretic framework based on the minimum description length (MDL) principle. Intuitively, the idea is that we group together those data items that can be compressed well together, so that the total code length over all the data groups is optimized. One can argue that as efficient compression is possible only when one has discovered underlying regularities that are common to all the members of a group, this approach produces an implicitly defined similarity metric between the data items. Formally the global code length criterion to be optimized is defined by using the intuitively appealing universal normalized maximum likelihood code which has been shown to produce an optimal compression rate in an explicitly defined manner. The number of groups can be assumed to be unknown, and the problem of deciding the optimal number is formalized as part of the same theoretical framework. In the empirical part of the paper we present results that demonstrate the validity of the suggested clustering framework.

13.1 Introduction

Clustering is one of the central concepts in the field of unsupervised data analysis. Unfortunately it is also a very controversial issue, and the very meaning of the concept "clustering" may vary a great deal between different scientific disciplines (see, e.g., [Jain, Murty, and Flynn 1999] and the references therein). However, a common goal in all cases is that the objective is to find a structural representation of data by grouping (in some sense) similar data items together. In this chapter we want to distinguish the actual process of grouping the data items from the more fundamental issue of defining a criterion for deciding which data items belong together, and which do not.

In the following we regard clustering as a partitional data assignment or data labeling problem, where the goal is to partition the data into mutually exclusive clusters so that similar (in a sense that needs to be defined) data vectors are grouped together. The number of clusters is unknown, and determining the optimal number is part of the clustering problem. The data are assumed to be in a vector form so that each data item is a vector consisting of a fixed number of attribute values.

Traditionally, this problem has been approached by first fixing a distance metric, and then by defining a global goodness measure based on this distance metric — the global measure may, for example, punish a clustering for pairwise intra-cluster distances between data vectors, and reward it for pairwise inter-cluster distances. However, although this approach is intuitively quite appealing, from the theoretical point of view it introduces many problems.

The main problem concerns the distance metric used: the task of formally describing the desirable properties of a suitable similarity metric for clustering has turned out to be a most difficult task. Commonly used distance metrics include the Euclidean distance and other instances from the Minkowski metric family. However, although these types of metrics may produce reasonable results in cases where the the underlying clusters are compact and isolated, and the domain attributes are all continuous and have a similar scale, the approach faces problems in more realistic situations [Mao and Jain 1996].

As discussed in [Kontkanen, Lahtinen, Myllymäki, Silander, and Tirri 2000], noncontinuous attributes pose another severe problem. An obvious way to try to overcome this problem is to develop data preprocessing techniques that essentially try to map the problem in the above setting by different normalization and scaling methods. Yet another alternative is to resort to even more exotic distance metrics, like the Mahalanobis distance. However, deciding between alternative distance metrics is extremely difficult, since although the *concept* of a distance metric is intuitively quite understandable, the properties of different distance metrics are far from it [Aggarwal, Hinneburg, and Keim 2001].

A completely different approach to clustering is offered by the *model-based approach*, where for each cluster a data-generating function (a probability distribution) is assumed, and the clustering problem is defined as the task to identify these distributions (see, e.g., [Smyth 1999; Fraley and Raftery 1998; Cheeseman, Kelly, Self, Stutz, Taylor, and Freeman 1988]). In other words, the data are assumed to be generated by a finite mixture model [Everitt and Hand 1981; Titterington, Smith, and Makov 1985; McLachlan 1988]. In this framework the optimality of a clustering can be defined as a function of the fit of data with the finite mixture model, not as a function of the distances between the data vectors.

However, the difference between the distance-based and model-based approaches to clustering is not as fundamental as one might think at first glance. Namely, it is well-known that if one, for example, uses the squared Mahalanobis distance in clustering, then this implicitly defines a model-based approach based on Gaussian distributions. A general framework for mapping arbitrary distance functions (or loss functions) to probability distributions is presented in [Grünwald 1998]. The reverse holds, of course, as well: any explicitly defined probabilistic model can be seen to implicitly generate a distance measure. Consequently, we have two choices: we can either explicitly define a distance metric, which produces an implicitly defined probability distribution, or we can explicitly define a probabilistic model, which implicitly defines a distance metric. We favor the latter alternative for the reasons discussed below.

One of the main advantages of the model-based approach is that the explicit assumptions made correspond to concepts such as independence, linearity, unimodality and so on, that are intuitively quite understandable. Consequently, we can argue that constructing a sensible model is easier than constructing a meaningful distance metric. Another important issue is that the modern statistical machine-learning community has developed several techniques for automated selection of model complexity. This means that by explicitly defining the model assumptions, one can address the problem of deciding the optimal number of clusters together with the problem of assigning the data vectors to the clusters.

Nevertheless, although the modeling approach has many advantages, it also introduces some problems. First of all, the finite mixture model implicitly assumes the existence of a hidden clustering variable, the values of which are unknown by definition. Evaluating probabilistic models in this type of an incomplete data case is difficult, and one needs to resort to approximations of theoretically derived model selection criteria. Furthermore, it can also be argued that if the fundamental goal is to find a data partitioning, then it is somewhat counterintuitive to define the objective of clustering primarily as a model search problem, since clustering is a property of the data, not of the model. Moreover, if one is really interested in the model, and not a partition, then why restrict oneself to a simple finite mixture model? Bayesian or probabilistic networks, for instance, offer a rich family of models that extend the simple mixture model [Lauritzen 1996; Heckerman, Geiger, and Chickering 1995; Cowell, Dawid, Lauritzen, and Spiegelhalter 1999]. A typical survey of users of the Autoclass system [Cheeseman et al. 1988] shows that they start out using clustering, start noticing certain regularities, and then switch over to some custom system. When the actual goal is broader knowledge discovery, model-based clustering is often too simple an approach.

The model-based approach, of course, implicitly leads to clustering, as the mixture components can be used to compute the probability of any data vector originating from that source. Hence, a mixture model can be used to produce a "soft" clustering where each data vector is assigned to different clusters with some probability. Nevertheless, for our purposes it is more useful to consider "hard" data assignments, where each data vector belongs to exactly one cluster only. In this case we can compute, in practice, some theoretically interesting model selection criteria, as we shall see later. In addition, it can be argued that this type of hard assignments match more naturally to the human intuition on clustering, where the goodness of a clustering depends on how the data are globally balanced among the different clusterings [Kearns, Mansour, and Ng 1997].

In this chapter we propose a model selection criterion for clustering based on the idea that a good clustering is such that one can encode the clustering *together* with the data so that the resulting code length is minimized. In the Bayesian modeling framework this means regarding clustering as a missing data problem, and choosing the clustering (assignment of missing data) maximizing the joint probability. As code lengths and probabilities are inherently linked to each other (see, e.g., [Cover and Thomas 1991]), these two perspectives are just two sides of the same coin. But in order to formalize this clustering criterion, we need to explicitly define what we mean by minimal code length/maximal probability. In the Bayesian setting optimality is usually defined with respect to some prior distribution, with the additional assumption that the data actually come from one of the models under consideration.

The main problem with the Bayesian model-based approach for clustering stems from the fact that it implicitly assumes the existence of a latent "clustering variable," the values of which are the missing values that we want to find in clustering. We claim that determining an informative prior for this latent variable is problematic, as the variable is by definition "hidden"! For example, think of a data set of web log data collected at some website. A priori, we have absolutely no idea of how many underlying clusters of users there exist in the data, or what are the relative sizes of these clusters. What is more, we have also very little prior information about the class-conditional distributions within each cluster: we can of course compute, for example, the population mean of, say, the age of the users, but does that constitute a good prior for the age within different clusters? We argue that it does not, as what we are intuitively looking for in clustering is discriminative clusters that differ not only from each other but also from the population as a whole.

The above argument leads to the following conclusion: the Bayesian approach to clustering calls for noninformative (objective) priors that do not introduce any involuntary bias in the process. Formally this can be addressed as a problem for defining so-called *reference priors* [Bernardo 1997]. However, current methods for determining this type of priors have technical difficulties at the boundaries of the parameter space of the probabilistic model used [Bernardo 1997]. To overcome this problem, we suggest an information-theoretic framework for clustering, based on the minimum description length (MDL) principle [Rissanen 1978, 1987, 1996], which leads to an objective criterion in the sense that it is not dependent on any prior distribution; it only uses the data at hand. Moreover, it also has an interpretation as a Bayesian method with respect to a worst-case prior, and is thus a finite sample variant of the reference prior. It should also be noted that the suggested optimality criterion based on the MDL approach does not assume that the data actually come from the probabilistic model class used for formalizing the MDL principle — this is of course a sensible property in all realistic situations.

In summary, our approach is essentially model-based, as it requires an explicit probabilistic model to be defined, no explicit distance metric is assumed. This is in sharp contrast to the information-theoretic approaches suggested in [Gokcay and Principe 2002; Slonim, Friedman, and Tishby 2002], which are essentially distance-based clustering frameworks, where the distance metric is derived from information-theoretic arguments. As discussed above, with respect to the standard model-based Bayesian approach, our approach differs in that the objectivity is approached without having to define an explicit prior for the model parameters.

The clustering criterion suggested here is based on the MDL principle which, intuitively speaking, aims at finding the shortest possible encoding for the data. For formalizing this intuitive goal, we adopt the modern *normalized maximum likelihood (NML)* coding approach [Shtarkov 1987], which can be shown to lead to a criterion with very desirable theoretical properties (see, e.g., [Rissanen 1996; Barron, Rissanen, and Yu 1998; Grünwald 1998; Rissanen 1999; Xie and Barron 2000; Rissanen 2001] and the references therein). It is important to realize that approaches based on either earlier formalizations of MDL, or on the alternative *minimum message length (MML)* encoding framework [Wallace and Boulton 1968; Wallace and Freeman 1987], or on more heuristic encoding schemes (see, e.g., [Rissanen and Ristad 1994; Dom 2001; Plumbley 2002; Ludl and Widmer 2002]) do not possess these theoretical properties!

The work reported in [Dom 1995] is closely related to our work as it addresses the problem of segmenting binary strings, which essentially is clustering (albeit in a very restricted domain). The crucial difference is that in [Dom 1995] the NML criterion is used for encoding first the data in each cluster, and the clustering itself (i.e., the cluster labels for each data item) is then encoded *independently*, while in the clustering approach suggested in Section 13.2 all the data (both the data in the clusters plus the cluster indices) is encoded *together*. Another major difference is that the work in [Dom 1995] concerns binary *strings*, that is, ordered sequences of data, while we study unordered sets of data. Finally, the computational method used in [Dom 1995] for computing the NML is computationally feasible only in the simple binary case — in Section 13.4 we present a recursive formula that allows us the compute the NML exactly also in more complex, multidimensional cases.

This chapter is structured as follows. In Section 13.2 we introduce the notation and formalize clustering as a data assignment problem. The general motivation for the suggested information-theoretic clustering criterion is also discussed. In Section 13.3 the theoretical properties of the suggested criterion are discussed in detail. Section 13.4 focuses on computational issues: we show how the suggested MDL clustering criterion can be computed efficiently for a certain interesting probabilistic model class. The clustering criterion has also been validated empirically: illustrative examples of the results are presented and discussed in Section 13.5. Section 13.6 summarizes the main results of our work.

13.2 The Clustering Problem

13.2.1 Clustering as Data Partitioning

Let us consider a data set $\mathbf{x}^n = \{\mathbf{x}_1, \ldots, \mathbf{x}_n\}$ consisting of n outcomes (vectors), where each outcome $\mathbf{x}_j$ is an element of the set $\mathcal{X}$. The set $\mathcal{X}$ consists of all the vectors of the form $(a_1, \ldots, a_m)$, where each variable (or attribute) a_i takes on values on some set that can be either a continuum of real numbers, or a finite set of discrete values. A *clustering* of the data set $\mathbf{x}^n$ is here defined as a partitioning of the data into mutually exclusive subsets, the union of which forms the data set. The number of subsets is a priori unknown. The *clustering problem* is the task to determine the number of subsets, and to decide to which cluster each data vector belongs.

Formally, we can notate a clustering by using a *clustering vector* $y^n = (y_1, \ldots, y_n)$, where y_i denotes the index of the cluster to which the data vector $\mathbf{x}_i$ is assigned. The number of clusters K is implicitly defined in the clustering vector, as it can be determined by counting the number of different values appearing in y^n. It is reasonable to assume that K is bounded by the size of our data set, so we can define the clustering space Ω as the set containing all the clusterings y^n with the number of clusters being less than n. Hence the clustering problem is now to find from all the $y^n \in \Omega$ the optimal clustering y^n.

For solving the clustering problem we obviously need a global optimization criterion that can be used for comparing clusterings with different numbers of clusters. On the other hand, as the clustering space Ω is obviously exponential in size, in practice we need to resort to combinatorial search algorithms in our attempt to solve the clustering problem. We return to this issue in Section 13.5. In the following we focus on the more fundamental issue: what constitutes a good optimality criterion for choosing among different clusterings? To formalize this, we first need to explicate the type of probabilistic models we consider.

13.2.2   Model Class

Consider a set $\Theta \in \mathbb{R}^d$. A class of parametric distributions indexed by the elements of Θ is called a *model class*. That is, a model class M is defined as the set

$$M = \{P(\cdot|\theta) : \theta \in \Theta\}. \tag{13.1}$$

In the following, we use the simple finite mixture as the model class. In this case, the probability of a single data vector is given by

$$P(\mathbf{x} \mid \theta, M_K) = \sum_{k=1}^{K} P(\mathbf{x} \mid y = k, \theta, M_K) P(y = k \mid \theta, M_K), \tag{13.2}$$

so that a parametric model θ is a weighted mixture of K component models $\theta_1, \ldots, \theta_K$, each determining the local parameters $P(\mathbf{x} \mid y = k, \theta, M_K)$ and $P(y = k \mid \theta, M_K)$. Furthermore, as is usually done in mixture modeling, we assume that the variables $(a_1, \ldots, a_m)$ are locally (conditionally) independent:

$$P(\mathbf{x} \mid y = k, \theta, M_K) = \prod_{i=1}^{m} P(a_i \mid y = k, \theta, M_K) \tag{13.3}$$

The above assumes that the parameter K is fixed. As discussed above, the number of clusters can be assumed to be bounded by the size of the available data set, so in the following we consider the union of model classes $M_1, \ldots, M_n$.

The finite mixture model class is used as an illustrative example in this chapter, but it should be noted that the general clustering framework applies, of course, to other model classes as well. The benefit of the above simple mixture model class is that while it allows arbitrary complex global dependencies with increasing number of components K, from the data mining or data exploration point of view this model class is very appealing, as this type of local independence model is very easy to understand and explain.

For the remainder of this chapter, we make also the following restricting assumption: we assume that the data are discrete, not continuous, and that the possibly originally continuous variables have been discretized (how the discretization should be done is a difficult problem and forms a research area that is outside the scope of this chapter). One reason for focusing on discrete data is that in this case we can model the domain variables by multinomial distributions without having to make restricting assumptions about unimodality, normality, and so on, which is the situation we face in the continuous case. Besides, discrete data are typical of domains such as questionnaire or web log data analysis, and the demand for this type of analysis is increasing rapidly. Moreover, as we shall see in Section 13.4, by using certain computational tricks, in the multinomial case we can compute the theoretically derived objective function presented in the next section exactly, without resorting to approximations. On the other hand, although we restrict ourselves to discrete data in this chapter, the information-theoretic framework presented can be easily extended to cases with continuous variables, or to cases with both continuous and discrete variables, but this is left as a task for future work.

13.2.3   Clustering Criterion

Our optimality criterion for clustering is based on information-theoretical arguments, in particular on the MDL principle [Rissanen 1978, 1987, 1996]. This also has a perspective from the Bayesian point of view, as discussed in more detail in Section 13.3. In the following we try to motivate our approach on a more general level.

Intuitively, the MDL principle aims at finding the shortest possible encoding for the data; in other words the goal is to find the most compressed representation of the data. Compression is possible by exploiting underlying regularities found in the data — the more regularities found, the higher the compression rate. Consequently, the MDL optimal encoding has found all the available regularities in the data; if there would be an "unused" regularity, this could be used for compressing the data even further.

What does this mean in the clustering framework? We suggest the following criterion for clustering: *the data vectors should be partitioned so that the vectors belonging to the same cluster can be compressed well together.* This means that those data vectors that obey the same set of underlying regularities are grouped together. In other words, the MDL clustering approach defines an implicit multilateral distance metric between the data vectors.

How to formalize the above intuitively motivated MDL approach for clustering? Let us start by noting the well-known fact about the fundamental relationship between codes and probability distributions: for every probability distribution P, there exists a code with a code length $-\log P(\mathbf{x})$ for all the data vectors $\mathbf{x}$, and for each code there is probability distribution P such that $-\log P(\mathbf{x})$ yields the code length for data vector $\mathbf{x}$ (see [Cover and Thomas 1991]). This means that we can compress a cluster efficiently if our model class yields a high probability for that set of data. Globally this means that we can compress the full data set $\mathbf{x}^n$ efficiently if $P(\mathbf{x}^n \mid M)$ is high. Consequently, in the finite mixture framework discussed in Section 13.2.2, we can define the following optimization problem: find the model class $M_K \in M$ so that $P(\mathbf{x}^n \mid M_K)$ is maximized.

As discussed in the Introduction, the above model-based approach to clustering poses several problems. One problem is that this type of an incomplete data probability is in this case difficult to compute in practice as the finite mixture formulation (13.3) implicitly assumes the existence of a latent clustering variable y. What is even more disturbing is the fact that actual clustering y^n has disappeared from the formulation altogether, so the above optimization task does not solve the clustering problem as defined in Section 13.2.1. For these reasons, we suggest the following general optimality criterion for finding the optimal clustering $\hat{y}^n$:

$$\hat{y}^n = \arg\max_{y^n} P(\mathbf{x}^n, y^n \mid M), \tag{13.4}$$

where M is a probabilistic model class.

It is important to notice here that in this suggested framework, optimality with respect to clustering is defined as a relative measure that depends on the chosen model class M. We see no alternative to this: any formal optimality criterion is necessarily based on some background assumptions. We consider it very sensible that in this framework the assumptions must be made explicit in the definition of the probabilistic model class M. In addition to this, although in this approach we end up with an optimal data partitioning $\hat{y}^n$, which was our goal, we can in this framework also compare different model classes with respect to the question of how well they compress and partition the data.

From the coding point of view, definition (13.4) means the following: If one uses separate codes for encoding the data in different clusters, then in order to be able to decode the data, one needs to send with each vector the index of the corresponding code to be used. This means that we need to encode not only the data $\mathbf{x}^n$ but also the clustering y^n, which is exactly what is done in (13.4).

Definition (13.4) is incomplete in the sense that it does not determine how the joint data probability should be computed with the help of the model class M. In the Bayesian framework this would be done by integrating over some prior distribution over the individual parameter instantiations on M:

$$P(\mathbf{x}^n, y^n \mid M) = \int P(\mathbf{x}^n, y^n \mid \theta, M) P(\theta \mid M) d\theta \tag{13.5}$$

As discussed in the Introduction, in the clustering framework very little can be known about the model parameters a priori, which calls for objective (noninformative) priors. Typical suggestions are the uniform prior, and the Jeffreys prior. In our discrete data setting, the basic building block of the probability in (13.4) is the multinomial distribution. As the values of the clustering variable are in our approach based on (13.4) known, not hidden, it follows that instead of a sum as in (13.2), the joint likelihood of a data vector $\mathbf{x}, y$ reduces to a product of multinomials. This means that the (conjugate) prior $P(\theta)$ is a product of Dirichlet distributions. In the case of the uniform prior, all the individual Dirichlet distributions have all the hyperparameters set to 1. As shown in [Kontkanen, Myllymäki,

Silander, Tirri, and Grünwald 2000], the Jeffreys prior is in this case given by

$$
\theta \sim \mathrm{Di}\left(\frac{1}{2}\left(\sum_{i=1}^{m}(n_i-1)+1\right),\ldots,\frac{1}{2}\left(\sum_{i=1}^{m}(n_i-1)+1\right)\right)
$$
$$
\times \prod_{i=1}^{m}\prod_{k=1}^{K}\mathrm{Di}\left(\frac{1}{2},\ldots,\frac{1}{2}\right), \quad (13.6)
$$

where n_i denotes the number of values of variable a_i, K is the number of clusters, and m is the number of variables (not counting the clustering variable y). Yet another possibility is to use the prior suggested in [Buntine 1991], which is given by

$$
\theta \sim \mathrm{Di}\left(\frac{r}{K},\ldots,\frac{r}{K}\right)\prod_{i=1}^{m}\prod_{k=1}^{K}\mathrm{Di}\left(\frac{r}{Kn_i},\ldots,\frac{r}{Kn_i}\right). \quad (13.7)
$$

Properties of this prior are discussed in [Heckerman et al. 1995]. Parameter r is the so-called *equivalent sample size (ESS)* parameter that needs to be determined. Unfortunately, as can be seen in Section 13.5, the value of the equivalent sample size parameter affects the behavior of the resulting clustering criterion a great deal, and we are aware of no disciplined way of automatically determining the optimal value.

In the next section we discuss an information-theoretic framework where the joint probability of the data and the clustering can be determined in an objective manner without an explicit definition of a prior distribution for the model parameters. Section 13.4 [see (13.24)] shows how this framework can be applied for computing the clustering criterion (13.4). In Section 13.5 this information-theoretic approach to clustering is studied empirically and compared to the Bayesian alternatives.

13.3   Stochastic Complexity and the Minimum Description Length Principle

The information-theoretic minimum description length (MDL) principle developed by Rissanen [1978, 1987, 1989, 1996] offers a well-founded theoretical framework for statistical modeling. Intuitively, the main idea of this principle is to represent a set of models (model class) by a single model imitating the behavior of any model in the class. Such representative models are called *universal*. The universal model itself does not have to belong to the model class, as is often the case.

The MDL principle is one of the *minimum encoding* approaches to statistical modeling. The fundamental goal of the minimum encoding approaches is *compression of data*. That is, given some sample data, the task is to find a description or *code* of it such that this description uses the least number of symbols, less than other codes and less than it takes to describe the data literally. Intuitively speaking, in principle this approach can be argued to produce the best possible model of the problem domain, since in order to be able to produce the most efficient coding of data, one must capture all the regularities present in the domain.

The MDL principle has gone through several evolutionary steps during the last two decades. For example, the early realization of the MDL principle (the two-part code MDL [Rissanen 1978]) takes the same form as the *Bayesian information criterion (BIC)* [Schwarz 1978], which has led some people to incorrectly believe that these two approaches are equivalent. The latest instantiation of MDL discussed here is *not* directly related to BIC, but to the formalization described in [Rissanen 1996]. The difference between the results obtained with the "modern" MDL and BIC can be in practice quite dramatic, as demonstrated in [Kontkanen, Buntine, Myllymäki, Rissanen, and Tirri 2003].

Unlike some other approaches, for example, Bayesianism, the MDL principle does not assume that the model class is correct (technically speaking, in the Bayesian framework one needs to define a prior distribution over the model class M, yielding a zero probability to models θ outside this set). It even says that there is no such thing as a true model or model class, as acknowledged by many practitioners. This becomes apparent in Section 13.3.3: the MDL principle can be formalized as a solution to an optimization problem, where the optimization is done over all imaginable distributions, not just over the parametric model class M. Consequently, the model class M is used only as a technical device for constructing an efficient code, and no prior distribution over the set M is assumed.

13.3.1   Stochastic Complexity as Normalized Maximum Likelihood

The most important notion of MDL is the *stochastic complexity (SC)*. Intuitively, stochastic complexity is defined as the shortest description length of given data relative to a model class. In the following we give the definition of SC, before giving its theoretical justification in Section 13.3.2.

Let $\hat{\theta}(\mathbf{x}^n)$ denote the *maximum likelihood* estimate of data $\mathbf{x}^n$, that is,

$$\hat{\theta}(\mathbf{x}^n) = \arg\max_{\theta \in \Theta}\{P(\mathbf{x}^n|\theta, M)\}. \tag{13.8}$$

The SC is then defined in terms of the likelihood evaluated at its maximum $P(\mathbf{x}^n \mid \theta, M)|_{\theta=\hat{\theta}(\mathbf{x}^n)}$ as

$$
\begin{aligned}
SC(\mathbf{x}^n \mid M) &= -\log \frac{P(\mathbf{x}^n \mid \theta, M)|_{\theta=\hat{\theta}(\mathbf{x}^n)}}{R_M^n} \\
&= -\log P(\mathbf{x}^n \mid \theta, M)|_{\theta=\hat{\theta}(\mathbf{x}^n)} + \log R_M^n,
\end{aligned} \tag{13.9}
$$

where R_M^n is given by

$$R_M^n = \sum_{\mathbf{x}^n} P(\mathbf{x}^n \mid \theta, M)|_{\theta=\hat{\theta}(\mathbf{x}^n)}, \tag{13.10}$$

and the sum goes over all the possible data matrices of length n. The term $\log R_M^n$ is called the *regret* and since it depends on the length of data, not the data itself, it can be considered as a normalization term, and the distribution in (13.9) is called the *normalized maximum likelihood (NML)* distribution proposed for finite alphabets in [Shtarkov 1987]. The definition (13.9) is intuitively very appealing: every data matrix is modeled using its own maximum likelihood (i.e., best fit) model, and then a penalty for the complexity of the model class M is added to normalize the distribution.

13.3.2   Normalized Maximum Likelihood as a Two-Part Code

A two-part code is such that one first encodes the model to be used for coding, and then the data with the help of the model. Consequently, the total code length consists of a sum of two terms, both of which are lengths of codes produced by proper codes. In its definitional form in (13.9), NML is not a two-part code because the (minus) log regret term is subtracted from the first term.

To make this a two-part code, we use the following interpretation: The statistical event $\mathbf{x}^n$ can be broken down into two parts: the first part is the event $\hat{\theta}(\mathbf{x}^n)$ which means we are supplied with the data maximum likelihood but not the data itself; the second part is the event $\mathbf{x}^n \mid \hat{\theta}(\mathbf{x}^n)$ which then supplies us with the full data. For a simple one-dimensional Gaussian model, this means receiving the sample mean first, and then receiving the full set of data points. For distributions with sufficient statistics, the first part $\hat{\theta}(\mathbf{x}^n)$ is generally all that is interesting in the data anyway!

The stochastic complexity (13.9) can now be manipulated as follows:

$$
\begin{aligned}
SC(\mathbf{x}^n \mid M) &= -\log \frac{P(\mathbf{x}^n, \hat{\theta}(\mathbf{x}^n) \mid \theta, M)\Big|_{\theta=\hat{\theta}(\mathbf{x}^n)}}{R_M^n} \\
&= -\log P(\hat{\theta}(\mathbf{x}^n) | n, M) - \log P(\mathbf{x}^n \mid \hat{\theta}(\mathbf{x}^n), \theta, M)\Big|_{\theta=\hat{\theta}(\mathbf{x}^n)}, \quad (13.11)
\end{aligned}
$$

where

$$
P(\hat{\theta}(\mathbf{x}^n)|n, M) = \frac{P(\hat{\theta}(\mathbf{x}^n) \mid \theta, M)\Big|_{\theta=\hat{\theta}(\mathbf{x}^n)}}{\sum_{\hat{\theta}} P(\hat{\theta}(\mathbf{x}^n) = \hat{\theta} \mid \theta, M)\Big|_{\theta=\hat{\theta}(\mathbf{x}^n)}}. \quad (13.12)
$$

The normalizing term of $P(\hat{\theta}(\mathbf{x}^n)|n, M)$ is just the regret (13.10) with the summation rearranged.

The NML version of stochastic complexity is now a two-part code. The first part encodes the maximum likelihood value $\hat{\theta}(\mathbf{x}^n)$ according to the prior

$$
P(\hat{\theta}(\mathbf{x}^n)|n, M) \;\propto\; \max_{\theta} P(\hat{\theta}(\mathbf{x}^n) \mid \theta, M) . \quad (13.13)
$$

Thus the parameter space Θ has been discretized to values achieving a maximum likelihood for some sample of size n, and the prior distributed so each has its highest possible likelihood. This construction is given in Figure 13.1 for the binomial model with sample size $n = 10$. Each dashed curve gives a likelihood for a different number of, say, 1s, in the data, yielding 11 curves in all. The stochastic complexity

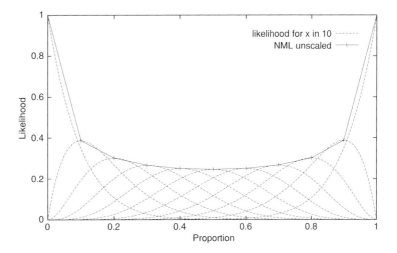

Figure 13.1   Likelihood curves for K=2, n=10.

is then computed for $\hat{\theta} = 0, 1/10, 2/10, \ldots, 9/10, 1$, which before scaling by regret yields the solid curve. NML at the discretized points $\hat{\theta}$ for different sample sizes $n = 2, 4, \ldots, 128$ is given in Figure 13.2. Notice since this is a discrete distribution, the probability at the points sums to 1, and thus the values decrease on average as $1/(n+1)$.

The second part of the two-part code encodes the *remainder of the data* given the maximum likelihood value $\hat{\theta}(\mathbf{x}^n)$ already encoded. Thus this is no longer a standard sequential code for independent data. In the one-dimensional Gaussian case, for instance, it means the sample mean is supplied up front and then the remainder of the data follows with a dependence induced by the known mean.

The ingenious nature of the NML construction now becomes apparent: *One is in effect using a two-part code to encode the data, yet no data bits have been wasted in defining the parameters θ since these also form part of the data description itself.* This two-part code appears to be a complex code length to construct in pieces. However, *one computes this two-part code length without having to explicitly compute the code lengths for the two parts.* Rather, the regret is computed once and for all for the model class and the regular sequential code for data $(-\log P(\mathbf{x}^n \mid \theta, M))$ is the basis for the computation.

One is tempted to continue this construction to interpret $P(\hat{\theta}|n, M)$ based on some reduction to a prior $P(\theta|M)$ over the full parameter space Θ, not just the maximum likelihood values for samples of size n. But this is apparently not possible in the general case. Moreover, in many cases no unique such prior exists. For typical exponential family distributions, for instance, the dimensionality of $P(\hat{\theta}|n, M)$ is less than $P(\theta|M)$ and no unique prior will exist except in a limiting sense when $n \to \infty$. We discuss this situation next.

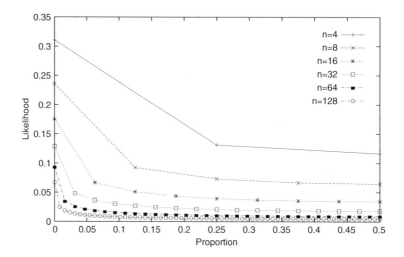

Figure 13.2 NML distribution for K=2, different n.

13.3.3 Normalized Maximum Likelihood as an Optimization Problem

There have been a number of different alternatives to NML proposed in the literature over the years. We compare some of these here. They provide us with theoretical counterparts to our experimental results.

There are different standards one might use when comparing code lengths on data.

Best case: The optimal possible value for encoding the data $\mathbf{x}^n$ according to model M is $\log 1/P(\mathbf{x}^n|\hat{\theta}(\mathbf{x}^n), M)$, which is unrealizable because $\hat{\theta}$ needs to be known.

Average of best case: Assuming a particular θ for model M holds, the average of the best case is $E_{P(\mathbf{x}^n|\theta,M)} \log 1/P(\mathbf{x}^n|\hat{\theta}(\mathbf{x}^n), M)$.

Barron et al. [1998] summarize various optimization problems with respect to these. First, one needs the code length that will actually be used, $Q(\mathbf{x}^n)$, which is the length we are optimizing.

NML is sometimes derived as the following: find a $Q(\cdot)$ minimizing the worst-case (for $\mathbf{x}^n$) increase over the best-case code-length for $\mathbf{x}^n$:

$$\min_{Q(\cdot)} \max_{\mathbf{x}^n} \log \frac{P(\mathbf{x}^n \mid \hat{\theta}(\mathbf{x}^n), M)}{Q(\mathbf{x}^n)} \tag{13.14}$$

Stochastic complexity $SC(\mathbf{x}^n)$ is the minimizing distribution here [Shtarkov 1987]. Notice this requires no notion of truth, only a model family used in building a code.

A related definition is based on the average best-case code length for θ: Find a $Q(\cdot)$ minimizing the worst-case (for θ) increase over the average best-case code length for θ,

$$
\begin{aligned}
&\min_{Q(\cdot)} \max_{\theta} E_{P(\mathbf{x}^n|\theta,M)} \log \frac{P(\mathbf{x}^n|\hat{\theta}(\mathbf{x}^n),M)}{Q(\mathbf{x}^n)} \\
&= \min_{Q(\cdot)} \max_{P(\theta|M)} E_{P(\theta|M)} E_{P(\mathbf{x}^n|\theta,M)} \log \frac{P(\mathbf{x}^n|\hat{\theta}(\mathbf{x}^n),M)}{Q(\mathbf{x}^n)} \\
&= \max_{P(\theta|M)} E_{P(\theta|M)} E_{P(\mathbf{x}^n|\theta,M)} \log \frac{P(\mathbf{x}^n|\hat{\theta}(\mathbf{x}^n),M)}{P(\mathbf{x}^n|M)} \\
&= \log R_M^n - \min_{P(\theta|M)} KL\left(P(\mathbf{x}^n|M)\|SC(\mathbf{x}^n|M)\right).
\end{aligned}
\tag{13.15}
$$

The first step is justified changing a maximum $\max_\theta$ into $\max_{P(\theta|M)} E_{P(\theta|M)}$; the second step is justified using minimax and maximin equivalences [Barron et al. 1998] since

$$
P(\mathbf{x}^n|M) = \underset{Q(\mathbf{x}^n)}{\arg\min} E_{P(\mathbf{x}^n,\theta|M)} \log \frac{P(\mathbf{x}^n|\hat{\theta}(\mathbf{x}^n),M)}{Q(\mathbf{x}^n)},
\tag{13.16}
$$

and the third step comes from the definition of $SC(\mathbf{x}^n|M)$.

This optimization then yields the remarkable conclusions for the average best case:

■ Finding a $Q(\mathbf{x}^n)$ minimizing the worst case over θ is equivalent to finding a prior $P(\theta|M)$ maximizing the average over θ, although the prior found may not be unique. One could call this a "worst-case Bayesian" analysis that is similar to the so-called *reference prior* analysis of Bernardo [1997]: a $\max_{P(\theta|M)}$ term has been added to a standard formula to minimize a posterior expected cost. However, it applies to the finite sample case, and thus is surely more realistic in practice.

■ The minimizing $Q(\mathbf{x}^n)$ must be a valid marginal $P(\mathbf{x}^n|M)$ for some joint $P(\theta|M)P(\mathbf{x}^n|\theta,M)$. Otherwise it is the closest in Kullback-Leibler divergence to the NML distribution. If for some prior $P(\theta|M)$ the induced marginal $P(\mathbf{x}^n|M)$ approaches the NML, then that prior must approach the optimal. Thus NML provides the gold standard for this average case.

■ In particular, for exponential family distributions the likelihood for the sufficient statistics of the data and the likelihood for their maximum likelihood value $\hat{\theta}(\mathbf{x}^n)$ are closely related. When the Fisher information is of full rank, a prior $P(\theta|M)$ with point mass on the set $\{\theta : \exists\mathbf{x}^n \text{ such that } \theta = \hat{\theta}(\mathbf{x}^n)\}$ can sometimes be found to make the marginal $P(\mathbf{x}^n|M)$ equal to the NML distribution. We claim this holds for the multinomial case. The minimizing $Q(\mathbf{x}^n)$ will thus be the NML in many cases.

Under certain regularity conditions, the optimizing prior approaches the Jeffreys prior when $n \to \infty$. Boundaries cause problems here because they mean part of the parameter space is of a lower dimension. For finite n in the case of the multinomial model when the boundaries are included, Xie and Barron [2000] argue for a mixture of Jeffreys priors corresponding to different dimensions being fixed. For the binomial

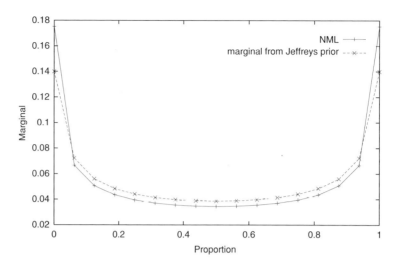

Figure 13.3   Jeffreys prior vs. NML as $P(\hat{\theta}|n=16, M)$ for binomial.

case, this corresponds roughly to mixing a Jeffreys prior with point mass at the two endpoints ($\theta = 0, 1$). NML vs. the Jeffreys prior for the binomial is given in Figure 13.3 for the case when $n = 16$.

For the multinomial for different dimension K and sample size n, NML corresponds closely to Jeffreys prior off the boundaries. The boundaries have significant additional mass. An approximate proportion for Jeffreys prior in the NML distribution is given in Figure 13.4 for the multinomial model with sample sizes $n = 10, \ldots, 1000$ and $K = 2, \ldots, 9$. This records the ratio of NML over the Jeffreys prior at a data point with near-equal counts (i.e., off the boundaries). It can be seen that the proportion very slowly rises to 1.0 and for the section here at least is sublinear in convergence. Xie and Barron use $O(1/n^{1/8})$ for their convergence rate to the Jeffreys prior for the general multinomial. This indicates just how dangerous it is to use the Jeffreys prior as a substitute for the NML distribution in practice.

13.4   Computing the Stochastic Complexity for Multinomial Data

13.4.1   One-dimensional Case

In the following we instantiate the NML for the one-dimensional multinomial case. Extension to the multidimensional model class discussed in Section 13.2.2 is relatively straightforward and is given in Section 13.4.2.

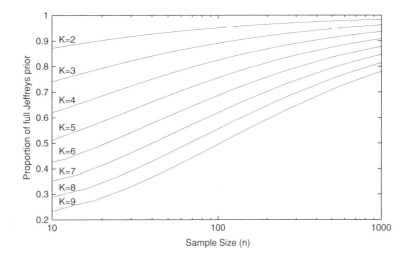

Figure 13.4   Proportion of Jeffreys prior in NML for the multinomial model.

13.4.1.1   *Multinomial Maximum Likelihood*

Let us assume that we have a multinomial variable X with K values. The parameter set Θ is then a simplex

$$\Theta = \{(\theta_1, \ldots, \theta_K) : \theta_k \geq 0, \theta_1 + \cdots + \theta_K = 1\}, \tag{13.17}$$

where $\theta_k = P(X = k)$. Under the usual assumption of independently and identically distributed (i.i.d.) data, the likelihood of a data set $\mathbf{x}^n$ is given by

$$P(\mathbf{x}^n | \theta) = \prod_{k=1}^{K} \theta_k^{h_k}, \tag{13.18}$$

where h_k is the frequency of value k in $\mathbf{x}^n$. Numbers $(h_1, \ldots, h_K)$ are called the *sufficient statistics* of data $\mathbf{x}^n$. The word "statistics" in this expression means a function of the data and "sufficient" refers to the fact that the likelihood depends on the data only through them.

To instantiate the stochastic complexity (13.9) to the single multinomial case, we need the maximum likelihood estimates of the parameters θ_k, that is,

$$\hat{\theta}(\mathbf{x}^n) = (\hat{\theta}_1, \ldots, \hat{\theta}_K) = (\frac{h_1}{n}, \ldots, \frac{h_K}{n}). \tag{13.19}$$

Thus, the likelihood evaluated at the maximum likelihood point is given by

$$P(\mathbf{x}^n \mid \hat{\theta}(\mathbf{x}^n)) = \prod_{k=1}^{K} \left(\frac{h_k}{n}\right)^{h_k}. \tag{13.20}$$

13.4.1.2 Multinomial Regret

Since the maximum likelihood (13.20) only depends on the sufficient statistics h_k, the regret can be written as

$$R_K^n = \sum_{h_1+\cdots+h_K=n} \frac{n!}{h_1!\cdots h_K!} \prod_{k=1}^K \left(\frac{h_k}{n}\right)^{h_k}, \tag{13.21}$$

where the summing goes over all the *compositions* of n into K parts, that is, over all the possible ways to choose non-negative integers $h_1,\ldots,h_K$ so that they sum up to n.

The time complexity of (13.21) is $\mathcal{O}\left(n^{K-1}\right)$, which is easy to see. For example, take case $K=3$. The regret can be computed in $\mathcal{O}\left(n^2\right)$ time, since we have

$$R_K^n = \sum_{h_1+h_2+h_3=n} \frac{n!}{h_1!h_2!h_3!} \left(\frac{h_1}{n}\right)^{h_1} \left(\frac{h_2}{n}\right)^{h_2} \left(\frac{h_3}{n}\right)^{h_3}$$

$$= \sum_{h_1=0}^n \sum_{h_2=0}^{n-h_1} \frac{n!}{h_1!h_2!(n-h_1-h_2)!} \cdot \left(\frac{h_1}{n}\right)^{h_1} \left(\frac{h_2}{n}\right)^{h_2} \left(\frac{n-h_1-h_2}{n}\right)^{n-h_1-h_2}. \tag{13.22}$$

Note that a slightly more efficient way to compute the regret would be to sum over *partitions* of n instead of compositions. A (restricted) partition of integer n into K parts is a set of K non-negative integers whose sum is n. For example, compositions $h_1=3, h_2=2, h_3=5$ and $h_1=2, h_2=5, h_3=3$ (with $n=10$) correspond to the same partition $\{5,3,2\}$. Since the maximum likelihood term in (13.21) is clearly different for every partition (but not for every composition), it would be more efficient to sum over the partitions. However, the number of partitions is still $\mathcal{O}\left(n^{K-1}\right)$, so this more complex summing method would not lead to any improvement of the time complexity. Therefore, in order to compute the stochastic complexity in practice, one needs to find better methods. This issue is addressed below.

13.4.1.3 Recursive Formula

A practical method for regret computation is derived via a clever recursion trick. The idea is to find a dependence of R_K^n and regret terms corresponding to a smaller number of values. It turns out that the *double recursive* formula (13.23) derived below offers a solution to this problem. In this formula, R_K^n is represented as a function of $R_{K^*}^n$ and $R_{K-K^*}^n$, where K^* can be any integer in $\{1,\ldots,K-1\}$. We

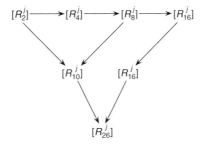

Figure 13.5   Recursive computation of R_{26}^n.

have

$$
R_K^n = \sum_{h_1+\cdots+h_K=n} \frac{n!}{h_1!\cdots h_K!} \prod_{k=1}^{K} \left(\frac{h_k}{n}\right)^{h_k} = \sum_{h_1+\cdots+h_K=n} \frac{n!}{n^n} \prod_{k=1}^{K} \frac{h_k^{h_k}}{h_k!}
$$

$$
= \sum_{\substack{h_1+\cdots+h_{K^*}=r_1 \\ h_{K^*+1}+\cdots+h_K=r_2 \\ r_1+r_2=n}} \frac{n!}{n^n} \frac{r_1^{r_1} r_2^{r_2}}{r_1!\, r_2!} \left(\frac{r_1!}{r_1^{r_1}} \prod_{k=1}^{K^*} \frac{h_k^{h_k}}{h_k!} \cdot \frac{r_2!}{r_2^{r_2}} \prod_{k=K^*+1}^{K} \frac{h_k^{h_k}}{h_k!} \right)
$$

$$
= \sum_{\substack{h_1+\cdots+h_{K^*}=r_1 \\ h_{K^*+1}+\cdots+h_K=r_2 \\ r_1+r_2=n}} \frac{n!}{n^n} \frac{r_1^{r_1} r_2^{r_2}}{r_1!\, r_2!} \left(\frac{r_1!}{h_1!\cdots h_{K^*}!} \prod_{k=1}^{K^*} \left(\frac{h_k}{r_1}\right)^{h_k} \right.
$$

$$
\left. \cdot \frac{r_2!}{h_{K^*+1}!\cdots h_K!} \prod_{k=K^*+1}^{K} \left(\frac{h_k}{r_2}\right)^{h_k} \right)
$$

$$
= \sum_{r_1+r_2=n} \frac{n!}{r_1!r_2!} \left(\frac{r_1}{n}\right)^{r_1} \left(\frac{r_2}{n}\right)^{r_2} \cdot R_{K^*}^{r_1} \cdot R_{K-K^*}^{r_2}. \tag{13.23}
$$

This formula can be used in efficient regret computation by applying a combinatoric doubling trick. The procedure goes as follows:

1. Calculate the table of R_2^j for $j = 1,\ldots,n$ using the composition summing method (13.21). This can be done in time $\mathcal{O}\left(n^2\right)$.

2. Calculate tables of $R_{2^m}^j$ for $m = 2,\ldots,\lfloor \log_2 K \rfloor$ and $j = 1,\ldots,n$ using the table R_2^j and recursion formula (13.23). This can be done in time $\mathcal{O}\left(n^2 \log K\right)$.

3. Build up R_K^n from the tables. This process also takes time $\mathcal{O}\left(n^2 \log K\right)$.

The time complexity of the whole recursive procedure given above is $\mathcal{O}\left(n^2 \log K\right)$. As an example of this method, say we want to calculate R_{26}^n. The process is illustrated in Figure 13.5. First we form the tables $R_{2^m}^j$ for $m = 1,2,3,4$ and $n = 1,\ldots,N$. Equation (13.23) is then applied to get the tables of R_{10}^j from R_2^j and R_8^j for $j = 1,\ldots,n$. Finally, R_{26}^n can be computed from the tables of R_{16}^j and R_{10}^j.

13.4.2   Multidimensional Generalization

In this subsection, we show how to compute NML for the multidimensional clustering model class (denoted here by $\mathcal{M}_T$) discussed in Section 13.2.2. Using (13.21), we have

$$
SC(\mathbf{x}^n, y^n | \mathcal{M}_T) \;=\; -\log\left(\prod_{k=1}^{K} \left(\frac{h_k}{n}\right)^{h_k} \prod_{i=1}^{m} \prod_{k=1}^{K} \prod_{v=1}^{n_i} \left(\frac{f_{ikv}}{h_k}\right)^{f_{ikv}} \right) \cdot \frac{1}{R^n_{\mathcal{M}_T, K}},
$$
(13.24)

where h_k is the number of times y has value k in $\mathbf{x}^n$, f_{ikv} is the number of times a_i has value v when $y = k$, and $R^n_{\mathcal{M}_T, K}$ is the regret

$$
R^n_{\mathcal{M}_T, K} = \sum_{h_1 + \cdots + h_K = n} \; \sum_{f_{111} + \cdots + f_{11n_1} = h_1} \cdots \sum_{f_{1K1} + \cdots + f_{1Kn_1} = h_K} \cdots
$$

$$
\sum_{f_{m11} + \cdots + f_{m1n_m} = h_1} \cdots \sum_{f_{mK1} + \cdots + f_{mKn_m} = h_K} \frac{n!}{h_1! \cdots h_K!} \prod_{k=1}^{K} \left(\frac{h_k}{n}\right)^{h_k}
$$

$$
\cdot \prod_{i=1}^{m} \prod_{k=1}^{K} \frac{h_k!}{f_{ik1}! \cdots f_{ikn_i}!} \prod_{v=1}^{n_i} \left(\frac{f_{ikv}}{h_k}\right)^{f_{ikv}}.
$$
(13.25)

Note that we can move all the terms under their respective summation signs, which gives

$$
R^n_{\mathcal{M}_T, K} = \sum_{h_1 + \cdots + h_K = n} \frac{n!}{h_1! \cdots h_K!} \prod_{k=1}^{K} \left(\frac{h_k}{n}\right)^{h_k}
$$

$$
\cdot \prod_{i=1}^{m} \prod_{k=1}^{K} \sum_{f_{ik1} + \cdots + f_{ikn_i} = h_k} \frac{h_k!}{f_{ik1}! \cdots f_{ikn_i}!} \cdot \prod_{v=1}^{n_i} \left(\frac{f_{ikv}}{h_k}\right)^{f_{ikv}}
$$

$$
= \sum_{h_1 + \cdots + h_K = n} \frac{n!}{h_1! \cdots h_K!} \prod_{k=1}^{K} \left(\frac{h_k}{n}\right)^{h_k} \prod_{i=1}^{m} \prod_{k=1}^{K} R^{h_k}_{n_i},
$$
(13.26)

which depends only linearly on the number of variables m, making it possible to compute (13.24) for cases with lots of variables provided that the number of value counts are reasonably small.

Unfortunately, (13.26) is still exponential with respect to the number of values $K, n_1, \ldots, n_m$. The situation is especially bad if the number of clusters K is big, which often is the case. It turns out, however, that the recursive equation (13.23) can also be generalized to the multidimensional case. Proceeding similarly as in (13.23), we can write

$$
R^n_{\mathcal{M}_T,K} = \sum_{h_1+\cdots+h_K=n} \left(\frac{n!}{h_1!\cdots h_K!} \prod_{k=1}^{K} \left(\frac{h_k}{n}\right)^{h_k} \prod_{i=1}^{m}\prod_{k=1}^{K} R^{h_k}_{n_i} \right)
$$

$$
= \sum_{h_1+\cdots+h_K=n} \left(\frac{n!}{n^n} \prod_{k=1}^{K} \frac{h_k^{h_k}}{h_k!} \prod_{i=1}^{m}\prod_{k=1}^{K} R^{h_k}_{n_i} \right)
$$

$$
= \sum_{\substack{h_1+\cdots+h_{K^*}=r_1 \\ h_{K^*+1}+\cdots+h_K=r_2 \\ r_1+r_2=n}} \left[\frac{n!}{n^n}\frac{r_1^{r_1}}{r_1!}\frac{r_2^{r_2}}{r_2!} \left(\frac{r_1!}{r_1^{r_1}} \prod_{k=1}^{K^*} \frac{h_k^{h_k}}{h_k!} \cdot \frac{r_2!}{r_2^{r_2}} \prod_{k=K^*+1}^{K} \frac{h_k^{h_k}}{h_k!} \right) \right.
$$

$$
\left. \cdot \prod_{i=1}^{m}\prod_{k=1}^{K^*} R^{h_k}_{n_i} \prod_{k=K^*+1}^{K} R^{h_k}_{n_i} \right], \tag{13.27}
$$

from which we get the result

$$
R^n_{\mathcal{M}_T,K} = \sum_{\substack{h_1+\cdots+h_{K^*}=r_1 \\ h_{K^*+1}+\cdots+h_K=r_2 \\ r_1+r_2=n}} \left[\frac{n!}{r_1!r_2!} \left(\frac{r_1}{n}\right)^{r_1} \left(\frac{r_2}{n}\right)^{r_2} \right.
$$

$$
\cdot \left(\frac{r_1!}{h_1!\cdots h_{K^*}!} \prod_{k=1}^{K^*} \left(\frac{h_k}{r_1}\right)^{h_k} \prod_{i=1}^{m}\prod_{k=1}^{K^*} R^{h_k}_{n_i} \right)
$$

$$
\left. \cdot \left(\frac{r_2!}{h_{K^*+1}!\cdots h_K!} \prod_{k=K^*+1}^{K} \left(\frac{h_k}{r_2}\right)^{h_k} \prod_{i=1}^{m}\prod_{k=K^*+1}^{K} R^{h_k}_{n_i} \right) \right]
$$

$$
= \sum_{r_1+r_2=n} \frac{n!}{r_1!r_2!} \left(\frac{r_1}{n}\right)^{r_1} \left(\frac{r_2}{n}\right)^{r_2} \cdot R^{r_1}_{\mathcal{M}_T,K^*} \cdot R^{r_2}_{\mathcal{M}_T,K-K^*}. \tag{13.28}
$$

That is, we can calculate multidimensional regrets using exactly similar procedures as described in Section 13.4.1.3.

In clustering applications it is typical that the number of clusters K is unknown. Therefore, in order to apply NML for clustering, one needs to evaluate multidimensional regrets with varying number of clusters. It follows that the easiest way to use the recursive equation (13.28) is to start with the trivial case $K = 1$, and then always choose $K^* = 1$. The resulting procedure is very simple and as effective as any other, provided that one wants to calculate regrets for the full range $K = 1,\ldots,K_{\max}$. On the other hand, if there is only need to evaluate NML for some fixed K (as is the case if the number of clusters is known), then one should use similar procedures as described in Section 13.4.1.3.

In practice, the recursive NML computation for the clustering case goes as follows. The goal is to calculate a $(n \times K_{\max})$ table of multidimensional regrets. The procedure starts with the calculation of another array consisting of one-dimensional regrets, since these are needed in (13.28). The size of this array is $(n \times V_{\max})$, where $V_{\max}$ is the maximum of the number of values for the variables $(a_1,\ldots,a_m)$. This array is calculated using (13.23). The time complexity of this step is clearly

$$\mathcal{O}\left(V_{\max} \cdot N^2\right).$$

The next step is to determine the starting point for the calculation of the array of multidimensional regrets. When $K = 1$, (13.26) clearly reduces to

$$R^n_{\mathcal{M}_T,1} = \prod_{i=1}^{m} R^n_{n_i}. \tag{13.29}$$

Another trivial case is $n = 0$, which gives

$$R^0_{\mathcal{M}_T,K} = 1, \tag{13.30}$$

for all K. After that, the calculation proceeds by always increasing n by 1, and for each fixed n, increasing K by 1 up to the maximum number of clusters wanted.

The interesting thing is that although the multidimensional regret (13.26) is rather complicated, the described procedure never uses it directly. The only things needed are the trivial starting cases $K = 1$ and $n = 0$, and the recursive equation (13.28). It follows that the calculation of multidimensional regrets is computationally as effective as in the single-dimensional case, which is a rather surprising but important fact.

13.5   Empirical Results

13.5.1   Clustering Scoring Methods

We have presented a framework for data clustering where the validity of a clustering y^n is determined according to the complete data joint probability in (13.4). Consequently, we obtain different clustering criteria or scoring methods by using different ways of computing this probability. The following clustering methods were empirically validated:

NML: The NML criterion given by (13.9).

UNI: The Bayesian criterion given by the marginal likelihood (13.5) over the uniform prior distribution.

JEF: The Bayesian criterion given by the marginal likelihood (13.5) over the Jeffreys prior distribution (13.6).

ESS(r): The Bayesian criterion given by the marginal likelihood (13.5) over the prior distribution (13.7). The parameter r is the equivalent sample size required for determining this prior.

The above means that ESS(r) is actually a continuum of methods, as the equivalent sample size can be any positive real number. The following alternatives were tested: ESS(0.01), ESS(0.1), ESS(1.0), ESS(10.0), and ESS(100.0).

13.5.2 Empirical Setup

In the following we wish to study empirically how the NML clustering criterion compares with respect to the Bayesian scores UNI, JEF, and ESS(r). The problem is now to find an empirical setup where these different criteria can be compared objectively. However, this turns out to be a most difficult task. Namely, at first sight it seems that an objective empirical scenario can be obtained by the following setup:

1. Choose randomly K probability distributions $P(\mathbf{x} \mid \Theta_1), \ldots, P(\mathbf{x} \mid \Theta_K)$.

2. i:=1.

3. Generate data $\mathbf{x}^n$ by repeating the following procedure n times:

   (a) Choose a random number z_i between 1 and K.

   (b) Draw randomly a data vector $\mathbf{x}_i$ from distribution $P(\mathbf{x} \mid \Theta_{z_i})$.

   (c) i:=i+1.

4. Cluster the generated data $\mathbf{x}^n$ to get a clustering y^n.

5. Validate the clustering by comparing y^n and the "ground truth" z^n.

We claim that the above procedure has several major weaknesses. One issue is that the setup obviously requires a search procedure in step 4, as the clustering space is obviously exponential in size. However, any heuristic search algorithm chosen for this purpose may introduce a bias favoring some of the criteria.

More importantly, one can argue that the "original" clustering z^n is not necessarily the goal one should aim at: Consider a case where the data was generated by a 10-component mixture model, where two of the components are highly overlapping, representing almost the same probability distribution. We claim that in this case a sensible clustering method should produce a clustering with 9 clusters, not 10! On the other hand, consider a case where all the 10 component distributions are not overlapping, but only one sample has been drawn from each of the 10 components. We argue that in this case a sensible clustering criterion should suggest a relatively small number of clusters, say 1 or 2, instead of the "correct" number 10, since with small sample sizes the variation in the data could not possibly justify the use of so many clusters (meaning a high number of parameters).

This means that the above scenario with artificial data makes only sense if the mixture components are nonoverlapping, and the amount of data is substantial. Obviously it can now be argued that this unrealistic situation hardly resembles real-world clustering problems, so that the results obtained in this way would not be very relevant. What is more, if the data are generated by a finite mixture of distributions, which means that the local independence assumptions we made in Section 13.2.2 do indeed hold, then this setup favors the Bayesian approach, as in this unrealistic case the marginal likelihood criterion is also minimax optimal. A more realistic setup would of course be such that the assumptions made would not hold, and the data would *not* come from any of the models in our model class.

The above scenario can be modified to a more realistic setting by changing the data-generating mechanism so that the assumptions made do not hold anymore. One way to achieve this goal in our local independence model case would be to add dependencies between the variables. However, this should be done in such a manner that the dependencies introduced are sensible in the sense that such dependencies exist in realistic domains. This is, of course, a most difficult task. For this reason, in the set of experiments reported here we used real-world data that were gathered in a controlled manner so that the above testing procedure could be used, although reality was used as a data-generating mechanism instead of a manually constructed mixture model. Before describing the data, let us have a look at the actual clustering procedure used in the experiments.

13.5.3   The Search Algorithm

For the actual clustering algorithm, we studied several alternatives. The best results were obtained with a simple stochastic greedy algorithm, where the number of clusters K was first fixed, and then the following procedure was repeated several times:

1. Choose a random initial data assignment.
2. Choose a random data vector.
3. Move the chosen data vector to the cluster optimizing locally the clustering score.
4. If converged, stop. Otherwise, go to step 2.

This procedure was repeated with all the possible values for K, and with all the clustering scoring methods listed in Section 13.5.1. At the end, all the clusterings of different size, produced by all the runs with all the clustering methods, were put together into a large pool of candidate clusterings. Finally, all the candidate clusterings were evaluated by using all the clustering criteria. The purpose of this procedure was to prevent the effect of chance between individual runs of the stochastic search algorithm with different criteria. It should be noted, however, that in our experiments almost all the best clusterings were found using NML as the clustering score. We believe that this tells us something important about the shape of the search space with different clustering criteria, and this interesting issue will be studied in our future research.

13.5.4   The Data

In this set of experiments, the data consisted of measured signal strength values of radio signals originating from eight WLAN access points (transmitters) located in different parts of our laboratory. As the measured signal strength depends strongly on the distance to the transmitting access point, the distribution of the data collected at some fixed point depends on the relative distances of this point and the locations of the eight access points. This means that the measurement distributions at two locations far from each other are very likely to be very different. Furthermore, as the access points are not affecting each other, the eight measured signals are at any fixed point more or less independent of each other.

Consequently, the data collected in the above manner are in principle similar to artificial data generated by a finite mixture model. Nevertheless, in real-world environments there is always some inherent noise caused by factors such as measurement errors, position and angle of reflecting or damping surfaces, air humidity, presence or absence of people, and so on. This means that these types of data resemble artificial data in the sense that the overlap between the component distributions can be controlled by choosing the locations where the measurements are made, but at the same time the data contain a realistic type of noise that was not artificially generated.

13.5.5 The Results

For this set of experiments, data were gathered at different locations situated as far from each other as possible. This means that the data-generating mechanisms were rather different, and partitioning the unlabeled data into clusters corresponding to the measurement locations was relatively easy with all the clustering methods used, if a sufficient amount of data was available. However, as we in this setup were able to control the amount of data available, we could study the small sample size behavior of the different clustering scores. A typical example of the behavior of different clustering criteria can be seen in Figures 13.6 and 13.7.

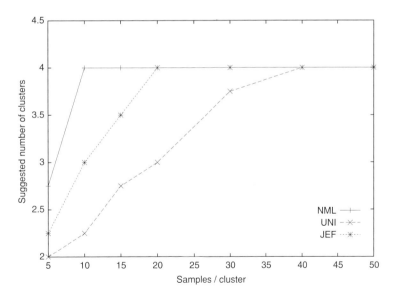

Figure 13.6 An example of the behavior of different clustering scores in the task of finding a four-cluster data partitioning, as a function of sample size per cluster.

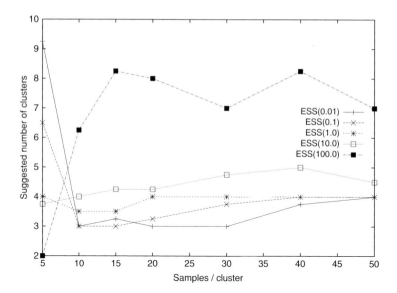

Figure 13.7   An example of the behavior of different ESS clustering scores in the task of finding a four-cluster data partitioning, as a function of sample size per cluster.

In Figure 13.6 we see a typical example of how the NML, UNI, and JEF clustering criteria behave as a function of the sample size. In this case, the correct number of clusters was four (data were gathered at four different positions), and the x-axis gives the number of data vectors collected at each of the 4 locations. The y-axis gives the number of clusters in the best clustering found with each of the three clustering criteria, where the pool of candidate clusterings was generated as described in Section 13.5.3. In this simple case, whenever the best clustering contained 4 clusters, the actual clustering y^n was perfectly consistent with the way the data were collected, that is, the clustering suggested was "correct." Obviously, whenever the suggested number of clusters was other than 4, the correct clustering was not found. The values on the y-axis are averages over several repeats of the sequential procedure consisting of data gathering, construction of the clustering candidate pool, and validation of the clustering candidates with different clustering criteria.

From Figure 13.6 we can see that with very small sample sizes (fewer than 10 samples from each cluster), NML tends to suggest fewer clusters than there actually are. However, as discussed above, this is sensible behavior as very small data sets do not justify very complex models. After a sample size of 10, the NML always finds the correct number of clusters (and, as explained above, also the correct clustering). The behaviors of the UNI and JEF scores are very similar, but they need more data to find the correct clustering.

The behavior of the ESS scores is rather interesting, as we can see in Figure 13.7. In this particular case, a relatively small equivalent sample size seems to work well: ESS(1) converges rather quickly (after seeing 20 samples per cluster) to the right level. However, the behavior is somewhat counter-intuitive with very small sample sizes as the suggested number of clusters is first close to 4, then goes down as the sample size increases to 15, after which it goes up again. A similar, but even more disturbing pattern is produced by the ESS scores with small equivalent sample size: with very small samples (fewer than 10 samples per cluster), they tend to suggest clusterings with a number of clusters that is much too high. This, of course, would lead to poor results in practice.

The ESS scores with a high equivalent sample size increase the suggested number of clusters with increasing data size up to a point, after which they start to converge to the right level. As a matter of fact, after a sufficient number of samples from each cluster, all the clustering criteria typically suggest a clustering identical, or very close, to the correct clustering. Consequently, this example shows that the interesting differences between the different clustering methods cannot be seen in low-dimensional cases if a large amount of data are available. Real-world problems are typically very high-dimensional, which means that the amount of data available is always relatively low, which suggests that the small sample size behavior of the clustering criteria observed here is of practical importance.

13.6   Conclusion

We suggested a framework for data clustering based on the idea that a good clustering is such that it allows efficient compression when the data are encoded together with the cluster labels. This intuitive principle was formalized as a search problem, where the goal is to find the clustering leading to maximal joint probability of the observed data plus the chosen cluster labels, given a parametric probabilistic model class.

The nature of the clustering problem calls for objective approaches for computing the required probabilities, as the presence of the latent clustering variable prevents the use of subjective prior information. In the theoretical part of the chapter, we compared objective Bayesian approaches to the solution offered by the information-theoretic MDL principle, and observed some interesting connections between the NML approach and the Bayesian reference prior approach.

To make things more concrete, we instantiated the general data clustering approach for the case with discrete variables and a local independence assumption between the variables, and presented a recursive formula for efficient computation of the NML code length in this case. The result is of practical importance as the amount of discrete data is increasing rapidly (in the form of webpages, web log data, questionnaires, etc.). Although the approach can be easily extended to more complex cases than the one studied in this chapter, we argue that the local independence model is important as the resulting clusters are in this case easy to analyze. It can also be said that the local independence model assumed here is complex enough, as one can obviously model arbitrarily complex distributions by adding more and more clusters.

In the empirical part of the chapter we studied the behavior of the NML clustering criterion with respect to the Bayesian alternatives. Although all the methods produced reasonable results in simple low-dimensional cases if a sufficient amount of data was available, the NML approach was clearly superior in more difficult cases with an insufficient amount of data. We believe that this means that NML works better in practical situations where the amount of data available is always vanishingly small with respect to the multidimensional space determined by the domain variables.

The difference between the NML and Bayesian approaches was especially clear when compared to the "parameter-free" approaches with either the uniform or Jeffreys prior. The equivalent sample size prior produced good results if one was allowed to manually choose the ESS parameter, but this, of course, does not constitute a proper model selection procedure, as no general guidelines for automatically selecting this parameter can be found.

In this chapter the clustering framework was restricted to flat, nonoverlapping and nonhierarchical clusterings. The approach could be obviously extended to more complex clustering problems by introducing several clustering variables, and by assuming a hierarchical structure between them, but this path was left to be explored in our future research.

Acknowledgments

This research has been supported by the Academy of Finland. The authors thank Michael Lee and Dan Navarro for their encouraging and valuable comments.

References

Aggarwal, C., A. Hinneburg, and D. Keim (2001). On the surprising behavior of distance metrics in high dimensional space. In J. V. den Bussche and V. Vianu (Eds.), *Proceedings of the Eighth International Conference on Database Theory*, Volume 1973 of *Lecture Notes in Computer Science*, pp. 420–434. Berlin: Springer-Verlag.

Barron, A., J. Rissanen, and B. Yu (1998). The minimum description principle in coding and modeling. *IEEE Transactions on Information Theory, 44*(6), 2743–2760.

Bernardo, J. (1997). Noninformative priors do not exist. *Journal of Statistical Planning and Inference, 65*, 159–189.

Buntine, W. (1991). Theory refinement on Bayesian networks. In B. D'Ambrosio, P. Smets, and P. Bonissone (Eds.), *Proceedings of the Seventh Conference on Uncertainty in Artificial Intelligence*, pp. 52–60. San Francisco: Morgan Kaufmann.

Cheeseman, P., J. Kelly, M. Self, J. Stutz, W. Taylor, and D. Freeman (1988). Autoclass: A Bayesian classification system. In *Proceedings of the Fifth International Conference on Machine Learning*, Ann Arbor, MI, pp. 54–64.

Cover, T., and J. Thomas (1991). *Elements of Information Theory*. New York: Wiley.

Cowell, R., P. Dawid, S. Lauritzen, and D. Spiegelhalter (1999). *Probabilistic Networks and Expert Systems*. New York: Springer-Verlag.

Dom, B. (1995). MDL estimation with small sample sizes including an application to the problem of segmenting binary strings using Bernoulli models. Technical report RJ 9997 (89085), IBM Research Division, Almaden Research Center, Almaden, CA.

Dom, B. (2001). An information-theoretic external cluster-validity measure. Technical report RJ 10219, IBM Research Division, Almaden Research Center, Almaden, CA.

Everitt, B. and D. Hand (1981). *Finite Mixture Distributions*. London: Chapman & Hall.

Fraley, C., and A.E. Raftery (1998). How many clusters? Which clustering method? Answers via model-based cluster analysis. *Computer Journal, 41*(8), 578–588.

Gokcay, E., and J. Principe (2002). Information theoretic clustering. *IEEE Transactions on Pattern Analysis and Machine Intelligence, 24*(2), 158–170.

Grünwald, P. (1998). *The Minimum Description Length Principle and Reasoning under Uncertainty*. Ph. D. thesis, University of Amsterdam, ILLC dissertation series 1998-03.

Heckerman, D., D. Geiger, and D. Chickering (1995). Learning Bayesian networks: The combination of knowledge and statistical data. *Machine Learning, 20*(3), 197–243.

Jain, A., M. Murty, and P. Flynn (1999). Data clustering: A review. *ACM Computing Surveys, 31*(3), 264–323.

Kearns, M., Y. Mansour, and A. Y. Ng (1997). An information-theoretic analysis of hard and soft assignment methods for clustering. In *Proceedings of the Thirteenth Annual Conference on Uncertainty in Artificial Intelligence (UAI 97)*, pp. 282–293. San Francisco: Morgan Kaufmann.

Kontkanen, P., W. Buntine, P. Myllymäki, J. Rissanen, and H. Tirri (2003). Efficient computation of stochastic complexity. In C. Bishop and B. Frey (Eds.), *Proceedings of the Ninth International Conference on Artificial Intelligence and Statistics*, pp. 233–238. Society for Artificial Intelligence and Statistics.

Kontkanen, P., J. Lahtinen, P. Myllymäki, T. Silander, and H. Tirri (2000). Supervised model-based visualization of high-dimensional data. *Intelligent Data Analysis, 4*, 213–227.

Kontkanen, P., P. Myllymäki, T. Silander, H. Tirri, and P. Grünwald (2000). On predictive distributions and Bayesian networks. *Statistics and Computing, 10,* 39–54.

Lauritzen, S. (1996). *Graphical Models.* Oxford, UK: Oxford University Press.

Ludl, M.-C., and G. Widmer (2002). Clustering criterion based on minimum length encoding. In T. Elomaa, H. Mannila, and H. Toivonen (Eds.), *Proceedings of the Thirteenth European Conference on Machine Learning,* Volume 2430 of *Lecture Notes in Computer Science,* pp. 258–269. Berlin: Springer-Verlag.

Mao, J. and A.K. Jain (1996). A self-organizing network for hyperellipsoidal clustering (HEC). *IEEE Transactions on Neural Networks 7,* 16–29.

McLachlan, G. (1988). *Mixture Models: Inference and Applications to Clustering.* New York: Marcel Dekker.

Plumbley, M. (2002). Clustering of sparse binary data using a minimum description length approach. Technical report, Department of Electrical Engineering, Queen Mary University of London. Unpublished manuscript.

Rissanen, J. (1978). Modeling by shortest data description. *Automatica, 14,* 445–471.

Rissanen, J. (1987). Stochastic complexity. *Journal of the Royal Statistical Society, 49*(3), 223–239 and 252–265.

Rissanen, J. (1989). *Stochastic Complexity in Statistical Inquiry.* Teaneck, NJ: World Scientific.

Rissanen, J. (1996). Fisher information and stochastic complexity. *IEEE Transactions on Information Theory, 42*(1), 40–47.

Rissanen, J. (1999). Hypothesis selection and testing by the MDL principle. *Computer Journal, 42*(4), 260–269.

Rissanen, J. (2001). Strong optimality of the normalized ML models as universal codes and information in data. *IEEE Transactions on Information Theory, 47*(5), 1712–1717.

Rissanen, J., and E.S. Ristad (1994). Unsupervised classification with stochastic complexity. In *Proceedings of the First US/Japan Conference on the Frontiers of Statistical Modeling: An Informational Approach,* pp. 171–182. Boston: Kluwer Academic.

Schwarz, G. (1978). Estimating the dimension of a model. *Annals of Statistics, 6,* 461–464.

Shtarkov, Y. M. (1987). Universal sequential coding of single messages. *Problems of Information Transmission, 23,* 3–17.

Slonim, N., N. Friedman, and N. Tishby (2002). Unsupervised document classification using sequential information maximization. In *Proceedings of the Twenty-fifth Annual International ACM SIGIR Conference on Research and Development in Information Retrieval,* pp. 129–136. New York: ACM Press.

Smyth, P. (1999). Probabilistic model-based clustering of multivariate and sequential data. In D. Heckerman and J. Whittaker (Eds.), *Proceedings of the Seventh International Conference on Artificial Intelligence and Statistics*, pp. 299–304. San Francisco: Morgan Kaufmann.

Titterington, D., A. Smith, and U. Makov (1985). *Statistical Analysis of Finite Mixture Distributions*. New York: Wiley.

Wallace, C., and D. Boulton (1968). An information measure for classification. *Computer Journal, 11*, 185–194.

Wallace, C. and P. Freeman (1987). Estimation and inference by compact coding. *Journal of the Royal Statistical Society, 49*(3), 240–265.

Xie, Q., and A. Barron (2000). Asymptotic minimax regret for data compression, gambling, and prediction. *IEEE Transactions on Information Theory, 46*(2), 431–445.

14 Minimum Description Length and Psychological Clustering Models

Michael D. Lee
Department of Psychology
University of Adelaide
South Australia 5005
Australia
michael.lee@adelaide.edu.au
http://www.psychology.adelaide.edu.au/members/staff/michaellee/homepage

Daniel J. Navarro
Department of Psychology
Ohio State University
1885 Neil Avenue
Columbus, Ohio 43210
USA
navarro.20@osu.edu
http://quantrm2.psy.ohio-state.edu/navarro/

Clustering is one of the most basic and useful methods of data analysis. This chapter describes a number of powerful clustering models, developed in psychology, for representing objects using data that measure the similarities between pairs of objects. These models place few restrictions on how objects are assigned to clusters, and allow for very general measures of the similarities between objects and clusters. Geometric complexity criteria (GCC) are derived for these models, and are used to fit the models to similarity data in a way that balances goodness-of-fit with complexity. Complexity analyses, based on the GCC, are presented for the two most widely used psychological clustering models: "additive clustering" and "additive trees."

14.1   Introduction

Clustering is one of the most basic and useful methods of data analysis. It involves treating groups of objects as if they were the same, and describing how the groups relate to one another. Clustering summarizes and organizes data, provides a framework for understanding and interpreting the relationships between objects, and proposes a simple description of these relationships that has the potential to generalize to new or different situations. For these reasons, many different clustering models have been developed and used in fields ranging from computer science and statistics to marketing and psychology (see [Arabie, Hubert, and De Soete 1996; Everitt 1993; Gordon 1999] for overviews).

   Different clustering models can be characterized in terms of the different assumptions they make about the *representational structure* used to define clusters, and the *similarity measures* that describe the relationships between objects and clusters.

14.1.1   Representational Assumptions

Representationally, it is possible for different types of constraints to be imposed on how objects can be grouped into clusters. Three different assumptions are shown in Figure 14.1:

(a) The partitioning approach forces each object to be assigned to exactly one cluster. This approach can be interpreted as grouping the objects into equivalence classes, and essentially just summarizes the objects, without specifying how the clusters relate to each other. For example, if the objects A through H in Figure 14.1(a) correspond to people, the partitioning could be showing which of four different companies employs each person. The representation does not allow a person to work for more than one company, and does not convey information about how the companies themselves are related to each other.

(b) The hierarchical approach allows for nested clusters. This can be interpreted as defining a tree structure, where the objects correspond to terminal nodes. For example, the hierarchical clustering in Figure 14.1(b) could be showing not just the company employing each person but also the division they work for within that company, and further subdivisions in the organizational structure. Each of these subdivisions corresponds to a branch in the tree, and the overall topology of the tree relates objects and clusters to one another.

(c) The overlapping approach imposes no representational restrictions, allowing any cluster to include any object and any object to belong to any cluster. Overlapping clustering models can be interpreted as assigning features to objects. For example, in Figure 14.1(c), the five clusters could correspond to features like the company a person works for, the division they work in, the football team they support, their nationality, and so on. It is possible for two people in different companies to support the same football team, or have the same nationality, or have any other pattern of

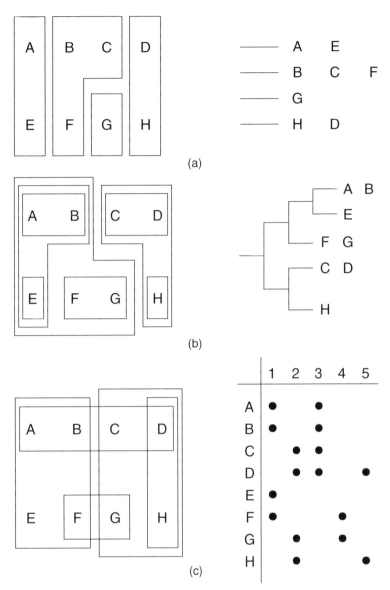

Figure 14.1   Three different representational assumptions for clustering models, showing *(left)* (a) partitioning, (b) hierarchical, and (c) overlapping structures, and their interpretation *(right)* as (a) equivalence classes, (b) tree structures, and (c) feature assignments.

shared features.

14.1.2   Similarity Assumptions

A clustering model also makes assumptions about how the similarity between objects is measured. One possibility, most compatible with partitioning representations, is to treat all objects in the same cluster as being equally similar to one another, and entirely different from objects not in that cluster. In hierarchical and overlapping representations, more detailed measures of similarity are possible. Because objects may belong to more than one cluster, various similarity measures can be constructed by considering the clusters objects have in common, and those that distinguish them, and combining these sources of similarity and dissimilarity in different ways.

14.1.3   Psychological Clustering Models

In many fields that use clustering models, most applications have relied on a relatively small range of the possible representational and similarity assumptions. Great emphasis is given to partitioning approaches like k-means clustering, and various tree-fitting approaches using hierarchical representations. Sometimes (although not always) this emphasis comes at the expense of overlapping representations, which have hierarchical and partitioning representations as special cases.

One field, perhaps surprisingly, that has a long tradition of using overlapping clustering models is psychology. In cognitive psychology, a major use of clustering models has been to develop accounts of human mental representations. This is usually done by applying a clustering model to data that describe the empirically observed similarities between objects, and then interpreting the derived clusters as the cognitive features used by people to represent the object. At least as early as Shepard and Arabie [1979, p. 91], it has been understood that "generally, the discrete psychological properties of objects overlap in arbitrary ways," and so representations more general than partitions or hierarchies need to be used.

Psychological clustering models have also considered a variety of possible similarity processes. In particular, they have drawn a useful distinction between common and distinctive features [Tversky 1977]. Common features are those that make two objects with the feature more similar, but do not affect the similarities of objects that do not have the feature. For example, think of two people with an unusual characteristic like blue hair. Having this feature in common makes these two people much more similar to each other than they otherwise would be, but does not affect the similarities between other people being considered who have 'normal' hair colors. Distinctive features, on the other hand, are those that make objects both having and not having the feature more similar to each other. For example, whether a person is male or female is a distinctive feature. Knowing two people are male makes them more similar to each other, knowing two people are female makes them more similar to each other, and knowing one person is male while the other is female makes them less similar to each other. Using common and distinctive features allows clustering models to deal with two different kind of regularities: common features capture the idea of 'similarity within', whereas distinctive features capture the notion of 'difference between'. In addition, psychological clustering models usually associate a weight with every cluster, which can be interpreted as measuring its 'importance' or 'salience'. By combining the weights of common and distinctive features in various ways, a wide range of similarity assumptions is possible.

A consequence of considering clustering models with great flexibility in both their representations and similarity measures, however, is that it becomes critical to control for model complexity. As noted by Shepard and Arabie [1979, p. 98], an overlapping clustering model that is also able to manipulate the similarity measures it uses may be able to fit any similarity data perfectly. The possibility of developing overly complicated clustering representations, of course, conflicts with the basic goals of modeling: the achievement of interpretability, explanatory insight, and the ability to generalize accurately beyond given information. In psychology, it is particularly important to control the complexity of cluster representations when they are used in models of cognitive processes like learning, categorization, and decision making. Because the world is inherently dynamic, representations of the environment that are too detailed will become inaccurate over time, and provide a poor basis for decision making and action. Rather, to cope with change, cognitive models need to have the robustness that comes from simplicity. It is this need for simple representations that makes psychological clustering models ideal candidates for minimum description length (MDL) methods.

14.1.4   Overview

This chapter describes the application of modern MDL techniques to a number of psychological clustering models. The next section provides a formal description of the clustering models considered, the common and distinctive models of similarity, and the form of the similarity data from which models are learned. Geometric complexity criteria (GCC) [Balasubramanian 1997; Myung, Balasubramanian, and Pitt 2000] are then derived for the clustering models. As it turns out, these are equivalent to Rissanen's [1996] Fisher information approximation to the normalized maximum likelihood. With the GCC measures in place, two established psychological clustering models, known as "additive clustering" and "additive trees," are considered in some detail. Illustrative examples are given, together with analysis and simulation results that assess the complexity of these models. Finally, two new psychological clustering models are described that raise different challenges in measuring and understanding model complexity.

14.2   Formal Description of Clustering Models

14.2.1   Similarity Data

Psychological clustering models are learned from similarity data, in the form of an $n \times n$ similarity matrix $\mathbf{S} = [s_{ij}]$, where s_{ij} is the similarity between the ith and jth of n objects. Usually these data are normalized to lie in the interval $[0, 1]$, and often the assumption of symmetry is made so that $s_{ij} = s_{ji}$ for all i and j pairs. Similarities are usually based on empirical measures of human performance, including ratings scales, identification tasks, sorting or grouping procedures, and a range of other experimental methodologies. It is also possible to generate psychological similarity data theoretically, using quantitative descriptions of objects. There are, for example, many methods for measuring the semantic similarity of text documents (see, e.g., [Damashek 1995; Griffiths and Steyvers 2002; Landauer and Dumais 1997; Lund and Burgess 1996]), based on the words (or sequences of characters or words) they contain. The pairwise similarities between all of the documents in a corpus could be used as the data for learning a clustering representation.

However similarity data are generated, a standard assumption (e.g., [Lee 2001; Tenenbaum 1996]) is that the similarity between the ith and jth objects comes from a Gaussian distribution with mean s_{ij}, and that the Gaussian distribution for each pair has common variance σ^2. The variance quantifies the inherent precision of the data, and can be estimated based on an understanding of the process by which the data were generated. For example, most empirical methods of collecting similarity data generate repeated measures for the similarity between each pair of objects, by having more than one person do a task, or having the same person do a task more than once. Given a set of similarity matrices $\mathbf{S}^k = [s_{ij}^k]$ provided by $k = 1, 2, \ldots, K$ data sources, the variance of the arithmetically averaged similarity matrix $\mathbf{S} = \frac{1}{K} [\sum_k s_{ij}^k] = [s_{ij}]$ can be estimated as the average of the sample variances for each of the pooled cells in the final matrix.

14.2.2   Cluster Structures

A clustering model that uses m clusters for n objects is described by a $n \times m$ matrix $\mathbf{F} = [f_{ik}]$, where $f_{ik} = 1$ if the ith object is in the kth cluster, and $f_{ik} = 0$ if it is not. When the clusters are interpreted as features, the vector $\mathbf{f}_i = (f_{i1}, \ldots, f_{im})$ gives the featural representation of the ith object. Each cluster has an associated weight, w_k for the kth cluster, which is a positive number. Generally, the cluster structure $\mathbf{F}$ is treated as the model, and the cluster weights $\mathbf{w} = (w_1, \ldots, w_m)$ are treated as model parameters.

	A	B	C	D	E
A	--				
B	17	--			
C	17	17	--		
D	05	05	14	--	
E	05	05	05	05	--

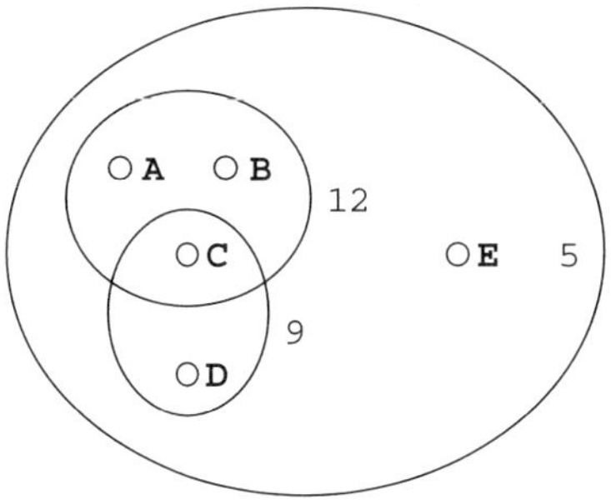

Figure 14.2 An example of an additive clustering representation and its associated similarity matrix.

14.2.3 Common Features Similarity

The common features similarity model assumes that two objects become more similar as they share more features in common, and that the extent to which similarity increases is determined by the weight of each common feature. This means that the modeled similarity between the ith and jth objects, denoted as $\hat{s}_{ij}$, is simply the sum of the weights of the common features:

$$\hat{s}_{ij} = c + \sum_k w_k f_{ik} f_{jk} \tag{14.1}$$

The "additive constant" c in (14.1) increases the similarity of each pair of objects by the same amount, and so measures the degree to which all of the objects are similar to each other. It can be interpreted as the saliency weight of a 'universal' cluster containing all objects.

Combining overlapping clusters with common features similarity corresponds to what is known as the "additive clustering" model in psychology [Arabie and Carroll 1980; Chaturvedi and Carroll 1994; Lee 2002a; Mirkin 1987, 1996; Ruml 2001; Shepard 1980; Shepard and Arabie 1979; Tenenbaum 1996]. A simple example of an additive clustering model, and the similarity matrix on which it is based, is shown in Figure 14.2. Notice that the sums of the weights of the clusters shared by each pair of objects correspond to their similarity in the matrix.

14.2.4 Distinctive Features Similarity

The distinctive features similarity model assumes that two stimuli become more dissimilar to the extent that one stimulus has a feature that the other does not. As with the common features approach, the extent to which similarity is decreased by a distinctive feature is determined by the weight of that feature. This model can be expressed as

$$\hat{s}_{ij} = c - \sum_k w_k \left| f_{ik} - f_{jk} \right|. \tag{14.2}$$

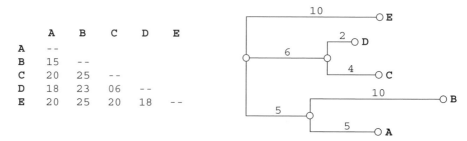

	A	B	C	D	E
A	--				
B	15	--			
C	20	25	--		
D	18	23	06	--	
E	20	25	20	18	--

Figure 14.3   An example of an additive tree representation and its associated dissimilarity matrix.

For hierarchical representations, distinctive features similarity corresponds to what is known as the "additive tree" model in psychology [Corter 1996; Johnson and Tversky 1984; Sattath and Tversky 1977; Shepard 1980; Tversky and Hutchinson 1986]. These models are usually applied to *dis*similarity data, generated by reversing the scale of similarity measures. A simple example of an additive tree model, and the dissimilarity matrix on which it is based, is shown in Figure 14.3. The model has an additive constant of 30 and seven clusters: one for each of the objects A to E, with weights 5, 10, 4, 2, and 10 respectively; one for the pair of objects A and B, with weight 5; and one for the pair of objects C and D, with weight 6. Each of these clusters corresponds to a node in the tree, and represents a feature that distinguishes between all of the objects that lie under the different branches coming from that node. Accordingly, the weights of the clusters can be interpreted as the length of the edges between nodes. This means that, in Figure 14.3, the length of the unique path between each pair of objects corresponds to their dissimilarity in the matrix.

For overlapping representations, distinctive features similarity corresponds to a discrete version of what is known as the "multidimensional scaling" model in psychology. Multidimensional scaling models (see, e.g., [Cox and Cox 1994; Shepard 1962; Kruskal 1964]) represent objects as points in a multidimensional space, so that the distance between the points corresponds to the dissimilarity between the objects. Discrete multidimensional scaling [Clouse and Cottrell 1996; Lee 1998; Rohde 2002] restricts the points to binary values, and so most of the distance metrics commonly used in the continuous version (i.e., Minkowskian metrics) reduce to the distinctive features model.

14.3   Geometric Complexity of Clustering Models

Traditionally, the complexity of clustering models in psychology has been dealt with in incomplete or heuristic ways. Most often (see, e.g., [Arabie and Carroll 1980; Chaturvedi and Carroll 1994; DeSarbo 1982; Shepard and Arabie 1979; Tenenbaum

1996]), the approach has been to find cluster structures that maximize a goodness-of-fit measure using a fixed number of clusters. More recently [Lee 2001, 2002b], the Bayesian information criterion [Schwarz 1978] has been applied, so that the number of clusters does not need to be predetermined, but the appropriate number can be found according to the goodness-of-fit achieved and the precision of the data. Both of these approaches, however, have the weakness of equating model complexity with only the number of clusters.

In general, both the representational and similarity assumptions made by a clustering model contribute to its complexity. Moving from partitions to hierarchies to overlapping clusters leads to progressively more complicated models, able to explain a progressively larger range of data. Controlling for this complexity requires more than counting the number of clusters, and needs to be sensitive to measures like the number of objects in the clusters, and the patterns of overlap or nesting between clusters. Different similarity assumptions control how the weight parameters interact, and so also affect model complexity. In addition, the complexities associated with representational and similarity assumptions will generally not be independent of one another, but will interact to create the overall complexity of the clustering model. For these reasons, it is important that psychological clustering models be evaluated against data using criteria that are sensitive to the full range of influences on model complexity.

The goal of psychological clustering is to find the best representation of empirical similarity data. The defining part of a representation is the cluster structure **F**, which encodes fixed assumptions about the representational regularities in a stimulus environment. Unlike these core assumptions, the saliency weights **w** and constant c are parameters of a particular representation, which are allowed to vary freely so that the representational model can be tuned to the data. In general, finding the best parameter values for a given set of clusters is straightforward. The difficulty is finding the best set of clusters. This involves the theoretical challenge of developing criteria for comparing different cluster representations, and the practical challenge of developing combinatorial optimization algorithms for finding the best cluster representations using these criteria .

This chapter relies on the geometric complexity criterion GCC ([Myung, Balasubramanian, and Pitt 2000]); see also [Pitt, Myung, and Zhang 2002]) for model evaluation. In the GCC, goodness-of-fit is measured by the maximum log-likelihood of the model, $\ln p\,(D \mid \theta^*)$, where $p\,(\cdot)$ is the likelihood function, D is a data sample of size N, and θ is a vector of the k model parameters which take their maximum likelihood values at θ^*. The complexity of the model is measured in terms of the number of distinguishable data distributions that the model indexes through parametric variation. The geometric approach developed by Myung, Balasubramanian, and Pitt [2000] leads to the following four-term expression:

$$\text{GCC} = -\ln p\,(D \mid \theta^*) + \frac{k}{2}\ln\left(\frac{N}{2\pi}\right) + \ln \int d\theta \sqrt{\det \mathbf{I}\,(\theta)} + \frac{1}{2}\ln\left(\frac{\det \mathbf{J}\,(\theta^*)}{\det \mathbf{I}\,(\theta^*)}\right),$$

where

$$\mathbf{I}_{ij}(\theta) = -E_\theta \left[\frac{\partial^2 \ln p(D \mid \theta)}{\partial \theta_i \partial \theta_j} \right]$$

is the Fisher information matrix of the model parameters, and

$$\mathbf{J}_{ij}(\theta^*) = - \left[\frac{\partial^2 \ln p(D \mid \theta)}{\partial \theta_i \partial \theta_j} \right]_{\theta = \theta^*}$$

is the covariance matrix of the model parameters at their maximum likelihood values.

Under the assumption that the similarities follow Gaussian distributions, with common variance estimated by $\hat{\sigma}^2$, the probability of similarity data $\mathbf{S}$ arising for a particular featural representation $\mathbf{F}$, using a particular weight parameterization $\mathbf{w}$, is given by

$$p(\mathbf{S} \mid \mathbf{F}, \mathbf{w}) = \prod_{i<j} \frac{1}{\left(\hat{\sigma}\sqrt{2\pi}\right)} \exp\left(-\frac{(s_{ij} - \hat{s}_{ij})^2}{2\hat{\sigma}^2} \right)$$

$$= \frac{1}{\left(\hat{\sigma}\sqrt{2\pi}\right)^{n(n-1)/2}} \exp\left(-\frac{1}{2\hat{\sigma}^2} \sum_{i<j}(s_{ij} - \hat{s}_{ij})^2 \right),$$

and so the log-likelihood is the sum of squared difference between the empirical data and model predictions, as scaled by the estimated precision of the data. The first term of the GCC, which measures data-fit, is simply the maximum of this log-likelihood, corresponding to the maximum likelihood–modeled similarities $\hat{s}_{ij}^*$, as follows:

$$-\ln p(\mathbf{S} \mid \mathbf{F}, \mathbf{w}^*) = \frac{1}{2\hat{\sigma}^2} \sum_{i<j}(s_{ij} - \hat{s}_{ij}^*)^2 + \text{constant} \qquad (14.3)$$

The second term of the GCC for a model with m clusters is found by noting that it uses $m+1$ parameters (including the additive constant), and that an $n \times n$ similarity matrix contains $n(n-1)/2$ observations, giving

$$\frac{m+1}{2} \ln\left(\frac{n(n-1)}{4\pi} \right). \qquad (14.4)$$

For the common and distinctive similarity models given in (14.1) and (14.2), the calculation of the second-order partial derivatives

$$\frac{\partial^2 \ln p(\mathbf{S} \mid \mathbf{F}, \mathbf{w})}{\partial w_x \partial w_y}$$

is straightforward, and allows the Fisher information matrix $\mathbf{I}(\mathbf{w})$ and the covariance matrix $\mathbf{J}(\mathbf{w})$ to be specified. As it turns out, these two matrices are identical for all of the clustering models considered here, and so the fourth term of the GCC vanishes. This makes the GCC identical to Rissanen's [1996] asymptotic approximation to the normalized maximum likelihood (see [Grünwald 2005]).

In fact, the two matrices $\mathbf{I}(\mathbf{w})$ and $\mathbf{J}(\mathbf{w})$ assume a constant value that is independent of the weight parameters, and is determined entirely by $\mathbf{F}$, which also simplifies the third term of the GCC. This constant value is conveniently written as the determinant of an $(m+1) \times (m+1)$ "complexity matrix", $\mathbf{G} = [g_{xy}]$, defined as

$$g_{xy} = \sum_{i<j} e_{ijx} e_{ijy},$$

where

$$e_{ijk} = \begin{cases} f_{ik} f_{jk} & \text{for common features,} \\ |f_{ik} - f_{jk}| & \text{for distinctive features.} \end{cases}$$

Using the complexity matrix, and assuming that, since the similarity values are normalized, the weight parameters range over the interval $[0, 1]$, the third term of the GCC is given by

$$\ln \int d\mathbf{w} \sqrt{\det \mathbf{I}(\mathbf{w})} = \ln \int_0^1 \int_0^1 \cdots \int_0^1 \sqrt{\det \left(\frac{1}{\hat{\sigma}^2} \mathbf{G} \right)} . dw_1 . dw_2 \ldots dw_{m+1}$$

$$= \frac{1}{2} \ln \det \mathbf{G} - \frac{m+1}{2} \ln \hat{\sigma}^2. \tag{14.5}$$

Putting together the results in (14.3), (14.4), and (14.5), the GCC for the clustering models is given as

$$\text{GCC} = \frac{1}{2\hat{\sigma}^2} \sum_{i<j} (s_{ij} - \hat{s}_{ij}^*)^2 + \frac{m+1}{2} \ln \left(\frac{n(n-1)}{4\pi\hat{\sigma}^2} \right) + \frac{1}{2} \ln \det \mathbf{G} + \text{constant.}$$

Strictly speaking, the GCC requires that a number of regularity conditions be met. However, Takeuchi [2000] shows that the asymptotic GCC approximation of the normalized maximum likelihood holds under a wide variety of conditions, and for a wide variety of models. While we have not checked all of the conditions, the most important ones (including positive definiteness of the Fisher information matrix) certainly hold.

14.4   Established Psychological Clustering Models

Additive clustering and additive trees are by far the most commonly used clustering models in psychology. In this section, illustrative examples of these models are provided demonstrating them being fit to similarity data using the GCC, together with analysis and simulation results based on their complexity matrices.

14.4.1   Additive Clustering

Illustrative Example   Lee and Navarro [2002] considered the similarities between nine colored shapes that combined the colors red, green, and blue with the shapes circle, square, and triangle. Twenty subjects rated the similarity of all 36 possible object pairs, presented in a random order, on a five-point scale. The final similarity matrix was arithmetically averaged across subjects, and made symmetric by transpose averaging.

Figure 14.4 shows the additive clustering representation of these data corresponding to the minimum GCC value, as found using a stochastic hill-climbing optimization algorithm [Lee 2002a]. This model explains 99.3% of the variance in the data, and each of the clusters is readily interpreted as a color or shape. Interestingly, the weights of the clusters suggest that people assigned relatively greater emphasis to common color than common shape when judging similarity. The representation also highlights the need for overlapping clusters, so that the orthogonal color and shape characteristics of the objects can both be accommodated.

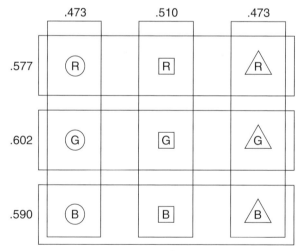

Figure 14.4   Overlapping common features representation, including cluster weights, of the colored shapes.

Interpretation of Complexity Matrix   The complexity matrix for additive clustering models is

$$
\mathbf{G} =
\begin{bmatrix}
\sum_{i<j} f_{i1}f_{j1} & \sum_{i<j} f_{i1}f_{j1}f_{i2}f_{j2} & \cdots & \sum_{i<j} f_{i1}f_{j1}f_{im}f_{jm} \\
\sum_{i<j} f_{i2}f_{j2}f_{i1}f_{j1} & \sum_{i<j} f_{i2}f_{j2} & \cdots & \sum_{i<j} f_{i2}f_{j2}f_{im}f_{jm} \\
\vdots & \vdots & \ddots & \vdots \\
\sum_{i<j} f_{im}f_{jm}f_{i1}f_{j1} & \sum_{i<j} f_{im}f_{jm}f_{i2}f_{j2} & \cdots & \sum_{i<j} f_{im}f_{jm}
\end{bmatrix}.
$$

The diagonal elements, $\sum_{i<j} f_{ik}f_{jk}$, count the number of object pairs in the kth cluster, and so measure cluster size. The off-diagonal elements, $\sum_{i<j} f_{ix}f_{jx}f_{iy}f_{jy}$, count the number of object pairs that are in both the xth and yth clusters, and so measure the overlap between clusters.

To make these ideas concrete, observe that the complexity matrix for the representation of the colored shapes in Figure 14.4 is

$$
\mathbf{G} =
\begin{bmatrix}
3 & 0 & 0 & 0 & 0 & 0 \\
0 & 3 & 0 & 0 & 0 & 0 \\
0 & 0 & 3 & 0 & 0 & 0 \\
0 & 0 & 0 & 3 & 0 & 0 \\
0 & 0 & 0 & 0 & 3 & 0 \\
0 & 0 & 0 & 0 & 0 & 3
\end{bmatrix}.
$$

Because each cluster has three objects, and hence three pairs of objects, all of the diagonal elements are three. Because each pair of clusters either has no overlap or has one object in common, no pair of clusters shares a pair of objects, and so all of the off-diagonal elements are zero.

Partitions   It is possible to show that, in general, $\mathbf{G}$ will be positive definite [Lee 2001, pp. 142-143]. This allows Hadamard's inequality (see, e.g., [Bellman 1970, pp. 129–130]) to be applied, so that the determinant is less than or equal to the product of the main diagonal,

$$
\det \mathbf{G} \le \prod_{k} g_{kk} = \prod_{k} \sum_{i<j} f_{ik}f_{jk},
$$

with equality occurring when all off-diagonal elements are zero. This suggests that partitions, which have diagonal complexity matrices, are complicated cluster structures. There are, however, two important caveats to be placed on the generality of this result [Navarro 2003]. First, while being a partition is sufficient for a diagonal complexity matrix, it is not necessary. Since the counts in $\mathbf{G}$ are of object pairs, clusters that have only one object in common also produce zero off-diagonal entries. The complexity matrix for the colored shapes in Figure 14.4 is a good example of this. Second, Hadamard's inequality requires that the product of the main diagonal elements remain constant, and so can only be used to compare cluster structures where the number of object pairs, and hence the number of objects, in each cluster is the same.

For partitions, or other cluster structures with diagonal complexity matrices, the determinant is simply the product of the diagonal elements, and so the number of objects in clusters determines model complexity. In particular, complexity is decreased by removing an object from a cluster, or by moving an object from a smaller cluster to a larger cluster.

Both of these results still hold when the universal cluster corresponding to the additive constant is included. This can be demonstrated by considering the complexity matrix $\mathbf{G}^+$ obtained when incorporating the universal cluster, which is

$$\mathbf{G}^+ = \begin{bmatrix} \mathbf{G} & \mathbf{y} \\ \mathbf{y^T} & z \end{bmatrix},$$

where $z = n\,(n-1)\,/2$ is the total number of object pairs, and $\mathbf{y}$ is a vector of the diagonal elements in $\mathbf{G}$. A standard result (see, e.g., [Magnus and Neudecker 1988, p. 23]) is that the determinant of this augmented complexity matrix can be written as

$$\det \mathbf{G}^+ = \det \mathbf{G}(z - \mathbf{y^T}\mathbf{G}^{-1}\mathbf{y}),$$

and it turns out [Lee 2001, pp. 144–145] that removing objects from clusters, or moving them from smaller to larger clusters, continues to increase complexity.

Interestingly, the reduction in complexity achieved by making clusters different sizes has a natural interpretation in terms of Shannon's [1948] noiseless coding theorem. This theorem shows that the minimum average message length needed to convey a structure is approximately given by the entropy of that structure [Li and Vitányi 1993, p. 71]. From this perspective, a partition where each cluster has the same number of objects is more complicated because each cluster is equally likely, maximizing the entropy of the representation and its message length.

Nested Clusters   A two-cluster model has complexity matrix

$$\mathbf{G} = \begin{bmatrix} a & b \\ b & c \end{bmatrix},$$

where $a \geq c$ and $b \leq c$. Since $\det \mathbf{G} = ac - b^2$ is minimized when $b = c$, the simplest possible two-cluster model is a strictly nested one. Lee [2001] follows this observation with an intuitive argument that, given a strictly nested cluster structure with i clusters, the increase in complexity from adding the $(i+1)$th cluster is minimized by making it also strictly nested. Together, these two arguments lead to the induction that strictly nested cluster structures are maximally simple additive clustering models.

Given a strictly nested cluster structure, the elementary row operation

$$
\begin{bmatrix}
1 & 0 & 0 & \cdots & 0 \\
-1 & 1 & 0 & \cdots & 0 \\
-1 & 0 & 1 & \cdots & 0 \\
\vdots & \vdots & \vdots & \ddots & \vdots \\
-1 & 0 & 0 & \cdots & 1
\end{bmatrix}
\begin{bmatrix}
a & b & c & \cdots & x \\
b & b & c & \cdots & x \\
c & c & c & \cdots & x \\
\vdots & \vdots & \vdots & \ddots & \vdots \\
x & x & x & \cdots & x
\end{bmatrix}
=
\begin{bmatrix}
a & b & c & \cdots & x \\
b-a & 0 & 0 & \cdots & 0 \\
c-a & c-b & 0 & \cdots & 0 \\
\vdots & \vdots & \vdots & \ddots & \vdots \\
x-a & x-b & x-c & \cdots & 0
\end{bmatrix}
$$

shows that $\det \mathbf{G} = (-1)^{m+1}(b-a)(c-b)\ldots x$. Since a strictly nested model is restricted to having $a > b > c > \ldots > x$, this means that the complexity of nested representation is minimized by having each successive cluster encompass one fewer object pairs than its predecessor.

General Cluster Structures   For general cluster structures, Hadamard's inequality suggests two ways of reducing model complexity. The first is to minimize the number of objects in clusters, since this minimizes the diagonal elements whose product determines the upper bound on complexity. The second is to introduce overlap between the clusters, since this creates nonzero off-diagonal elements. In general, these two strategies conflict with one another, since increasing the overlap between clusters is often best achieved by increasing their size, and reducing cluster size will often come at the expense of reducing overlap.

Navarro [2002] reported the results of a simulation study designed to explore how cluster size and overlap interact to determine complexity. This study used a sample of 10^5 randomly generated cluster structures with ten objects and six clusters, and measured their complexity, average cluster size, and average overlap. The size of a cluster containing a objects out of the total $n = 10$ was measured as the proportion of object pairs that were included, $a\,(a-1)\,/\,(n\,(n-1))$. Similarly, the overlap between two clusters containing $a \geq b$ objects, of which c were included in both, was measured as $c\,(c-1)\,/\,(b\,(b-1))$. Figure 14.5 shows the relationship between size, overlap, and complexity for a representative subsample of 10^3 of the cluster structures. Figure 14.6 shows the relationship between overlap and complexity for the 823 cluster structures with a constant average cluster size of approximately 41.6%. The basic results are that increasing size increases complexity, increasing cluster overlap decreases complexity, but that the increase due to size outweighs the decrease due to overlap.

14.4.2   Additive Trees

Illustrative Example   Johnson and Tversky [1984, table A1, lower triangular half] collected similarity data for 18 different 'risks', obtained by pooling the ratings made by subjects for each pair on a nine-point scale. Figure 14.7 shows the additive tree representation of these data, found using a stochastic search algorithm to

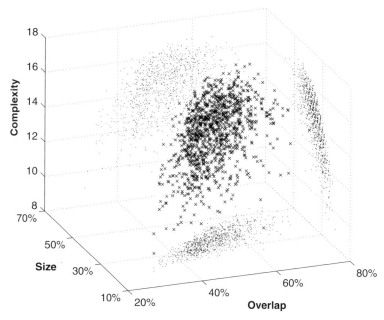

Figure 14.5 The complexity of a sample of 10^3 cluster structures with ten objects and six clusters, shown by crosses as a function of average size and overlap. The projection of each pair of measures is also shown.

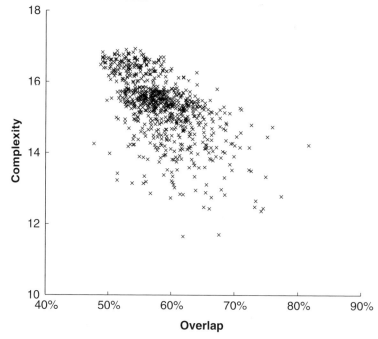

Figure 14.6 The complexity of a sample of 823 cluster structures with constant average size and variable overlap.

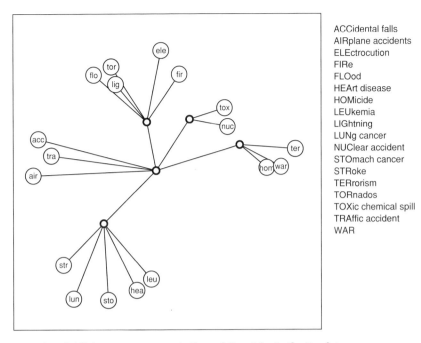

ACCidental falls
AIRplane accidents
ELEctrocution
FIRe
FLOod
HEArt disease
HOMicide
LEUkemia
LIGhtning
LUNg cancer
NUClear accident
STOmach cancer
STRoke
TERrorism
TORnados
TOXic chemical spill
TRAffic accident
WAR

Figure 14.7   Additive tree representation of the risk similarity data

minimize the GCC. The internal nodes correspond to clusters of risks that can be interpreted as (clockwise from top) 'natural disasters', 'technological disasters', 'violent acts', 'illnesses,' and 'accidents'.

It is interesting to compare this representation, which explains about 70% of the variance in the data, with previous additive tree analyses of the same data [Johnson and Tversky 1984; Corter 1996]. These previous analyses did not explicitly consider model complexity, but instead fitted 'full' trees with $(n-3) = 15$ internal nodes, explaining about 75% of the variance. Interpretation of these more complicated trees, however, is only offered for nodes near the top of tree, and basically corresponds to those concepts shown in Figure 14.7. This lack of extra interpretability suggests that the superior goodness-of-fit achieved by the more complicated trees does not come from finding additional meaningful regularities in the data.

Interpretation of Complexity Matrix   The complexity matrix for additive tree models is

$$\mathbf{G} = \begin{bmatrix} \sum_{i<j} e_{ij1} & \sum_{i<j} e_{ij1}e_{ij2} & \cdots & \sum_{i<j} e_{ij1}e_{ijm} \\ \sum_{i<j} e_{ij2}e_{ij1} & \sum_{i<j} e_{ij2} & \cdots & \sum_{i<j} e_{ij2}e_{ijm} \\ \vdots & \vdots & \ddots & \vdots \\ \sum_{i<j} e_{ijm}e_{ij1} & \sum_{i<j} e_{ijm}e_{ij2} & \cdots & \sum_{i<j} e_{ijm} \end{bmatrix}.$$

where $e_{ijk} = 1$ if the kth edge is on the unique path between objects i and j, and $e_{ijk} = 0$ if it is not. The diagonal elements count the number paths connecting objects that include each edge. The off-diagonal elements count the number of paths connecting objects that use each possible pairing of edges.

Extending Star Trees   Additive trees with a single internal (nonterminal) node are called star trees, and have complexity matrix

$$\mathbf{G}_{\text{star}} - \begin{bmatrix} n-1 & 1 & 1 & \cdots & 1 \\ 1 & n-1 & 1 & \cdots & 1 \\ 1 & 1 & n-1 & \cdots & 1 \\ \vdots & \vdots & \vdots & \ddots & \vdots \\ 1 & 1 & 1 & \cdots & n-1 \end{bmatrix}.$$

If a star tree is extended to have two internal nodes, its complexity matrix becomes

$$\mathbf{G} = \begin{bmatrix} \mathbf{G}_{\text{star}} & \mathbf{y} \\ \mathbf{y}^{\mathbf{T}} & z \end{bmatrix},$$

where z counts the number of paths that pass through the edge between the internal nodes, and $\mathbf{y} = (y_1, y_2, \ldots, y_n)^T$ is a column vector where y_i counts the number of paths that pass through both the internal edge and the edge from the terminal node representing the ith object. The determinant of this complexity matrix can be written as

$$\det \mathbf{G} = \det \mathbf{G}_{\text{star}}(z - \mathbf{y}^{\mathbf{T}} \mathbf{G}_{\text{star}}^{-1} \mathbf{y}),$$

where

$$\mathbf{G}_{\text{star}}^{-1} = \frac{1}{2(n-1)(n-2)} \begin{bmatrix} 2n-3 & -1 & -1 & \cdots & -1 \\ -1 & 2n-3 & -1 & \cdots & -1 \\ -1 & -1 & 2n-3 & \cdots & -1 \\ \vdots & \vdots & \vdots & \ddots & \vdots \\ -1 & -1 & -1 & \cdots & 2n-3 \end{bmatrix}.$$

In the simplest interesting case, the additional internal node is added to a star tree representing six objects. There are two possibilities, shown in Figure 14.8. The tree on the left divides the objects into two clusters of three. Here $z = 9$, $\mathbf{y}^{\mathbf{T}} = (3, 3, 3, 3, 3, 3)$, and so $\det \mathbf{G} = 3.6$. The tree on the right divides the objects into a cluster of four and a cluster of two. Here $z = 8$, $\mathbf{y}^{\mathbf{T}} = (2, 2, 2, 2, 4, 4)$, and so $\det \mathbf{G} = 2.2$. The tree on the left, with an equal number of objects in each cluster,

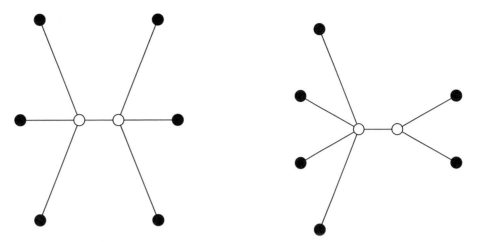

Figure 14.8   The two possible ways of adding a second internal node to a star tree representing six objects.

is more complicated.

More generally, adding an internal node to a star tree representing n objects creates one cluster with r objects, and another cluster with the remaining $(n - r)$. Here $z = r(n - r)$, the first r elements of $\mathbf{y^T}$ are $(n - r)$ and the remaining $(n - r)$ elements are r. This results in

$$\det \mathbf{G} = r(n - r) \left(1 + \frac{2r(n - r)}{(n - 1)(n - 2)} - \frac{n}{n - 2} \right),$$

which increases monotonically with $r(n - r)$. This generalizes the six-object result, showing that dividing any number of objects evenly between the two clusters leads to the greatest complexity.

General Tree Structures   The complexity matrix of an additive tree with m clusters can be represented as the result of adding $(m - 1)$ clusters to a star tree, so that

$$\mathbf{G} = \left[\begin{array}{cc} \mathbf{G}_{\text{star}} & \mathbf{Y} \\ \mathbf{Y^T} & \mathbf{Z} \end{array} \right].$$

The $(m - 1) \times (m - 1)$ matrix $\mathbf{Z}$ has both rows and columns corresponding to edges between internal nodes, counting the number of paths between objects that include each possible pairing of these edges. The $n \times (m - 1)$ matrix $\mathbf{Y}$ has rows corresponding to edges connecting terminal nodes, columns corresponding to edges between internal nodes, and elements counting the number of paths between objects that include each possible combination of these internal and terminal edges. This decomposition allows the determinant to be given as

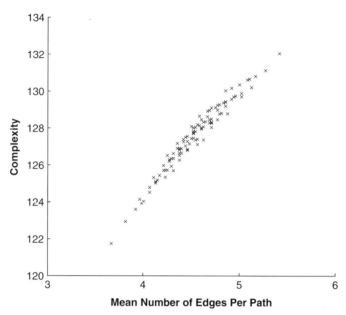

Figure 14.9 The relationship between complexity and mean edges per path for all possible additive trees with ten internal nodes, where each has three terminal nodes.

$$\det \mathbf{G} = \det \mathbf{G}_{\text{star}} \det \left(\mathbf{Z} - \mathbf{Y}^{\mathbf{T}} \mathbf{G}_{\text{star}}^{-1} \mathbf{Y} \right),$$

which depends only on $\mathbf{Y}$ and $\mathbf{Z}$ for a fixed number of objects.

To explore the relationship between the topology of additive trees and their complexity, Navarro [2002] generated all possible trees with between five and ten internal nodes, under the restriction that all internal nodes were connected to two, three, or four terminal nodes. For a given number of internal nodes, complexity was observed to increase roughly linearly with the average number of edges in the paths connecting objects, regardless of the number of terminal nodes. Figure 14.9 shows the relationship for trees of ten internal nodes with three terminal nodes each. Figure 14.10 shows the most and least complicated of these trees. The basic result is that broad trees, which have longer average path lengths, are more complicated than deep trees, which have shorter average path lengths.

14.5   New Psychological Clustering Models

This section presents two new psychological clustering models that extend the representational possibilities of additive clustering and additive trees. The first model uses a similarity measure that considers both common and distinctive

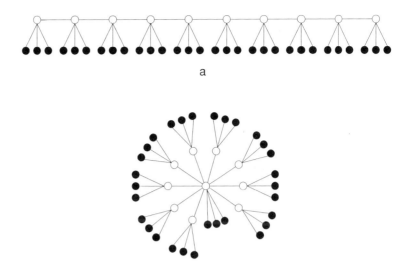

Figure 14.10   The (a) most complicated and (b) least complicated additive trees with ten internal nodes, where each has three terminal nodes.

features, while the second moves beyond clustering to incorporate continuous dimensions in its representations. Both models are demonstrated by applying them to similarity data under complexity constraints, but analyses of the complexity of these models have not been made. The study of the complexity of these models is an important area for future research.

14.5.1   Overlapping Common and Distinctive Features

Tversky [1977] proposed two similarity models combining common and distinctive features, known as the contrast model and the ratio model. Under the contrast model, similarity is measured as an additive mixture of common and distinctive features. Under the ratio model, similarity is measured as the proportion of common to distinctive features. The ratio model has a natural interpretation in terms of a Bayesian theory of generalization [Tenenbaum and Griffiths 2001], but the contrast model is more difficult to interpret, because it treats each cluster as being part common feature and part distinctive feature. To overcome this difficulty, Navarro and Lee [2002] proposed a modified version of the contrast model that designates each cluster as being either a completely common or completely distinctive feature, but allows both types of cluster in the same model.

Under this "modified contrast model" approach, similarity is measured as

$$\hat{s}_{ij} = c + \sum_{k \in CF} w_k f_{ik} f_{jk} - \sum_{k \in DF} w_k \left| f_{ik} - f_{jk} \right|, \qquad (14.6)$$

where $k \in CF$ means that the sum is taken over the common features, and $k \in DF$ means that the sum is taken over the distinctive features. The complexity matrix **G** and GCC for this similarity model can be derived in exactly the same way as the purely common and distinctive cases, by making the appropriate choice in (14.6) for each cluster.

Illustrative Example   Rosenberg and Kim [1975] collected data, later published by Arabie, Carroll, and DeSarbo [1987, pp. 62–63], measuring the similarities between 15 common kinship terms, such as 'father', 'daughter', and 'grandmother'. The similarities were based on a sorting task undertaken by six groups of 85 subjects, where each kinship term was placed into one of a number of groups, under various instructions to the subjects. A slightly modified version of this data set that excludes the term 'cousin' is considered, because it is interesting to examine how the model deals with the concept of gender, and 'cousin' is the only ambiguous term in this regard.

Table 14.1 describes the overlapping common and distinctive features clustering found by applying stochastic hill-climbing optimization to minimize the GCC. The clusters correspond to easily interpreted common and distinctive features. It has four distinctive features, dividing males from females, once-removed terms (aunt, nephew, niece, uncle) from those not once-removed, extreme generations (granddaughter, grandfather, grandmother, grandson) from middle generations, and the nuclear family (brother, daughter, father, mother, sister, son) from the extended family. It also has six common features, which correspond to meaningful subsets within the broad distinctions, such as parents, siblings, grandparents, and grandchildren. These concepts are common features since, for example, a brother and sister have the similarity of being siblings, but this does not make those who are not siblings, like an aunt and a grandson, more similar.

The kinship data provide a good example of the need to consider both common and distinctive features in the same clustering model. Common features models, such as additive clustering, are inefficient in representing concepts like 'gender', because they need to include separate equally weighted clusters for 'male' and 'female'. Distinctive feature models, on the other hand, generally cannot represent concepts like 'siblings', where the objects outside the cluster do not belong together.

Complexity Issues   The modified contrast model uses both the common and distinctive similarity measures in (14.1) and (14.2) to model similarity. This means that, in a way unlike additive clustering or additive tree models, the weight parameters of the model have different 'functional forms' [Myung and Pitt 1997] of interaction, depending on whether they are associated with a common or distinctive feature. An interesting model complexity issue raised by combining common and distinctive features, therefore, relates to the relative complexity of the two different similarity models. Some preliminary evidence [Navarro 2002, pp. 122–124], based on simulation studies, suggests that common features increase the complexity of a model more than distinctive features. Analysis of the complexity matrix for

Table 14.1 Overlapping common and distinctive features representation of the kinship terms.

Type	Objects in Cluster	Weight	Interpretation
DF	Brother, father, grandfather, grandson, nephew, son, uncle	0.452	Gender
CF	Aunt, uncle	0.298	Adult extended family
CF	Nephew, niece	0.294	Child extended family
CF	Brother, sister	0.291	Siblings
CF	Grandfather, grandmother	0.281	Grandparents
CF	Father, mother	0.276	Parents
CF	Granddaughter, grandson	0.274	Grandchildren
DF	Aunt, nephew, niece, uncle	0.230	Once-removed
DF	Granddaughter, grandfather, grandmother, grandson	0.190	Extreme generation
DF	Brother, daughter, father, mother, sister, son	0.187	Nuclear family
	Universal cluster	0.660	

the modified contrast model provides an opportunity to understand the basis and generality of this finding, and is a worthwhile area for further research.

14.5.2 Combining Features with Dimensions

Whatever representational assumptions are made, and whatever similarity measure is used, clustering models are inefficient when dealing with the inherently continuous aspects of the variation between objects. Most psychological modeling in these cases uses the "multidimensional scaling" model described earlier, where objects are represented by values along one or more continuous dimensions, so that they correspond to points in a multidimensional space. The dissimilarity between objects is then measured by the distance between their points. While dimensional representation naturally captures continuous variation, it is constrained by the metric axioms, such as the triangle inequality, that are violated by some empirical data.

It has been argued (see, e.g., [Carroll 1976; Tenenbaum 1996; Tversky 1977]) that spatial representations are most appropriate for low-level perceptual stimuli, whereas cluster representations are better suited to high-level conceptual domains. In general, though, stimuli convey both perceptual and conceptual information, and so both dimensional and clustering representations need to be combined. As Carroll [1976, p. 462] concludes: "Since what is going on inside the head is likely to be complex, and is equally likely to have both discrete and continuous aspects, I believe the models we pursue must also be complex, and have both discrete and continuous components."

In this spirit, Navarro and Lee [2003] developed a representational model that combines continuous dimensions with discrete features. Objects take values on a

(a)

```
0         2   4        8

                    6

      1   3          9

            5

                7
```

(b)

Objects in Cluster										Weight
		2		4				8		0.444
0	1	2								0.345
			3			6			9	0.331
						6	7	8	9	0.291
		2	3	4	5	6				0.255
	1		3		5		7		9	0.216
	1	2	3	4						0.214
				4	5	6	7	8		0.172
universal cluster										0.148

Figure 14.11 Representations of the numbers similarity data using the (a) dimensional and (b) clustering models.

number of dimensions, as well as potentially belonging to a number of clusters. If there are v dimensions and m features, this means the ith object is defined by a point $\mathbf{p}_i$, a vector $\mathbf{f}_i$, and the cluster weights $\mathbf{w} = (w_1, \ldots, w_m)$. The similarity between the ith and jth objects is then modeled as the sum of the similarity arising from their common features, minus the dissimilarity arising from their dimensional differences under the Minkowskian r-metric, so that

$$\hat{s}_{ij} = \left(\sum_{k=1}^{m} w_k f_{ik} f_{jk} \right) - \left(\sum_{k=1}^{v} |p_{ik} - p_{jk}|^r \right)^{\frac{1}{r}} + c.$$

Illustrative Example Shepard, Kilpatric, and Cunningham [1975] collected data measuring the "abstract conceptual similarity" of the numbers 0 through 9. Figure 14.11(a) displays a two dimensional representation of the numbers, using the city-block metric, found by multidimensional scaling. This representation explains only 78.6% of the variance, and fails to capture important regularities in the raw data, such as the fact that the number 7 is more similar to 8 than it is to 9, and that 3 is much more similar to 0 than it is to 8. Figure 14.11(b) shows an eight-cluster representation of the numbers using the same data, found by Tenenbaum [1996] using additive clustering. This representation explains 90.9% of the variance, with clusters corresponding to arithmetic concepts (e.g., $\{2, 4, 8\}$ and $\{3, 6, 9\}$) and to numerical magnitude (e.g., $\{1, 2, 3, 4\}$ and $\{6, 7, 8, 9\}$). While the clusters are appropriate for representing the arithmetic concepts, a 'magnitude' dimension seems to offer a more efficient and meaningful representation of this regularity than the five clusters used in Figure 14.11(b).

Navarro and Lee [2003] fitted combined models with between one and three dimensions and one and eight clusters to the similarity data. Because analytic results for the complexity of the combined model are not available, the Bayesian approach of selecting the most likely model given the data was used (e.g., [Kass and Raftery 1995]), based on an approximation to the log posterior found by importance sampling [Oh and Berger 1993]. The best representation under this measure contains one dimension and four clusters, explains 90.0% of the variance,

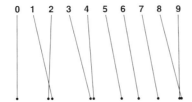

Objects in Cluster				Weight
	2	4	8	0.286
	3	6		9	0.282
	2	4	6	8	0.224
1	3			9	0.157
universal cluster				0.568

Figure 14.12   Representation of the numbers similarity data using the combined model with one dimension *(left)* and four clusters *(right)*.

and is shown in Figure 14.12. The one dimension almost orders the numbers according to their magnitude, with the violations being very small. The four clusters all capture meaningful arithmetic concepts, corresponding to "powers of two," "multiples of three", "multiples of two" (or "even numbers"), and "powers of three."

Complexity Issues   The combined model also raises interesting complexity issues related to the functional form of parameter interaction. The coordinate locations of the points interact according to the Minkowskian distance metric that is used to model similarity. In psychological applications of multidimensional scaling, particular emphasis has been placed on the $r = 1$ (city-block) and $r = 2$ (Euclidean) cases because of their relationship, respectively, to so-called 'separable' and 'integral' dimensions [Garner 1974]. Pairs of separable dimensions are those, like shape and size, that can be attended to separately. Integral dimensions, in contrast, are those rarer cases like hue and saturation that are not easily separated. Metrics with $r < 1$ have also been given a psychological justification [Gati and Tversky 1982; Shepard 1991] in terms of modeling dimensions that 'compete' for attention. Little is known about the relative complexities of these different metrics, although there is some simulation study evidence [Lee and Pope 2003] that the city-block metric is complicated, because it allows multidimensional scaling models to achieve high levels of goodness-of-fit, even for data generated using another metric. There is a need, however, for much more detailed analysis of the complexity of the combined model.

14.6   Conclusion

Clustering aims to find meaningful and predictive representations of data, and so is a fundamental tool for data analysis. One of the strengths of clustering models is that they potentially allow for great representational flexibility, and can accommodate sophisticated measures for assessing the relationships between objects. The price of these freedoms, however, is the need to control their complexity, so that they capture the regularities underlying data that are important for explanation and prediction.

This chapter has attempted to meet the challenge by treating clustering models as statistical models, and using the geometric complexity criterion for the statistical inference of model selection. Theoretically, this statistical approach offers interpretable measures of the complexity of clustering models. The results for additive clustering and additive tree models are good examples of this. Practically, the statistical approach offers a useful way of generating models from data. It compares favorably with the collections of heuristics that must otherwise be used to determine basic properties of a model, such as how many clusters it uses. The illustrative applications of the additive clustering and additive tree models are good examples of the sorts of representations that can be learned from data under complexity constraints. Finally, this chapter has also attempted to demonstrate the potential for new clustering models, and the new complexity issues they raise. Clustering models, like all good scientific models, should be developed and extended boldly, seeking general and powerful accounts of data, but also need to be evaluated and differentiated carefully, taking account of all of the complexities bound up in their generality and power.

Acknowledgments

This research was supported by Australian Research Council grant DP0211406, and by the Australian Defence Science and Technology Organisation. We thank Helen Braithwaite, Peter Grünwald, Geoff Latham, In Jae Myung, Kenneth Pope, Chris Woodruff, and the reviewers for helpful comments.

References

Arabie, P., and J.D. Carroll (1980). MAPCLUS: A mathematical programming approach to fitting the ADCLUS model. *Psychometrika, 45*(2), 211–235.

Arabie, P., J.D. Carroll, and W.S. DeSarbo (1987). *Three-Way Scaling and Clustering.* Newbury Park, CA: Sage.

Arabie, P., L.J. Hubert, and G. De Soete (1996). *Clustering and Classification.* Singapore: World Scientific.

Balasubramanian, V. (1997). Statistical inference, Occam's razor and statistical mechanics on the space of probability distributions. *Neural Computation, 9,* 349–368.

Bellman, R. (1970). *Introduction to Matrix Analysis,* 2nd edition. New York: McGraw-Hill.

Carroll, J.D. (1976). Spatial, non-spatial and hybrid models for scaling. *Psychometrika, 41,* 439–463.

Chaturvedi, A., and J.D. Carroll (1994). An alternating combinatorial optimization approach to fitting the INDCLUS and generalized INDCLUS models. *Journal of Classification, 11*, 155–170.

Clouse, D.S. and G.W. Cottrell (1996). Discrete multidimensional scaling. In *Proceedings of the Eighteenth Cognitive Science Conference*, San Diego, pp. 290–294. Mahwah, NJ: Erlbaum.

Corter, J.E. (1996). *Tree Models of Similarity and Association*. Thousand Oaks, CA: Sage.

Cox, T.F., and M.A.A. Cox (1994). *Multidimensional Scaling*. London: Chapman & Hall.

Damashek, M. (1995). Gauging similarity with *n*-grams: Language-independent categorization of text. *Science, 267*, 843–848.

DeSarbo, W.S. (1982). GENNCLUS: New models for general nonhierarchical cluster analysis. *Psychometrika, 47*, 449–475.

Everitt, B.S. (1993). *Cluster Analysis*, 3rd edition. London: Edward Arnold.

Garner, W.R. (1974). *The Processing of Information and Structure*. Potomac, MD: Erlbaum.

Gati, I., and A. Tversky (1982). Representations of qualitative and quantitative dimensions. *Journal of Experimental Psychology: Human Perception and Performance, 8*(2), 325–340.

Gordon, A.D. (1999). *Classification*, 2nd edition. London: Chapman & Hall/CRC Press.

Griffiths, T.L., and M. Steyvers (2002). A probabilistic approach to semantic representation. In W.G. Gray and C.D. Schunn (Eds.), *Proceedings of the Twenty-fourth Annual Conference of the Cognitive Science Society*, pp. 381–386. Mahwah, NJ: Erlbaum.

Grünwald, P.D. (2005). MDL Tutorial. In P.D. Grünwald, I.J. Myung, and M.A. Pitt (Eds.), *Advances in Minimum Description Length: Theory and Applications*. Cambridge, MA: MIT Press.

Johnson, E.J., and A. Tversky (1984). Representations of perceptions of risks. *Journal of Experimental Psychology: General, 113*(1), 55–70.

Kass, R.E., and A.E. Raftery (1995). Bayes factors. *Journal of the American Statistical Association, 90*(430), 773–795.

Kruskal, J.B. (1964). Multidimensional scaling by optimizing goodness of fit to a nonmetric hypothesis. *Psychometrika, 29*(1), 1–27.

Landauer, T.K., and S.T. Dumais (1997). A solution to Plato's problem: The latent semantic analysis theory of acquisition, induction, and representation of knowledge. *Psychological Review, 104*(2), 211–240.

Lee, M.D. (1998). Neural feature abstraction from judgments of similarity. *Neural Computation, 10*(7), 1815–1830.

Lee, M.D. (2001). On the complexity of additive clustering models. *Journal of*

Mathematical Psychology, 45(1), 131–148.

Lee, M.D. (2002a). Generating additive clustering models with limited stochastic complexity. *Journal of Classification, 19*(1), 69–85.

Lee, M.D. (2002b). A simple method for generating additive clustering models with limited complexity. *Machine Learning, 49*, 39–58.

Lee, M.D., and D.J. Navarro (2002). Extending the ALCOVE model of category learning to featural stimulus domains. *Psychonomic Bulletin and Review, 9*(1), 43–58.

Lee, M.D., and K.J. Pope (2003). Avoiding the dangers of averaging across subjects when using multidimensional scaling. *Journal of Mathematical Psychology, 47*, 32–46.

Li, M., and P. Vitányi (1993). *An Introduction to Kolmogorov Complexity and its Applications.* New York: Springer Verlag.

Lund, K., and C. Burgess (1996). Producing high-dimensional semantic spaces from lexical co-occurrence. *Behaviour Research Methods, Instruments, and Computers, 28*(2), 203–208.

Magnus, J.R., and H. Neudecker (1988). *Matrix Differential Calculus with Applications in Statistics and Econometrics.* New York: Wiley.

Mirkin, B. (1996). *Mathematical Classification and Clustering.* Boston: Kluwer.

Mirkin, B.G. (1987). Additive clustering and qualitative factor analysis methods for similarity matrices. *Journal of Classification, 4*, 7–31.

Myung, I.J., V. Balasubramanian, and M.A. Pitt (2000). Counting probability distributions: Differential geometry and model selection. *Proceedings of the National Academy of Sciences USA, 97*, 11170–11175.

Myung, I.J., and M.A. Pitt (1997). Applying Occam's razor in modeling cognition: A Bayesian approach. *Psychonomic Bulletin and Review, 4*(1), 79–95.

Navarro, D.J. (2002). *Representing Stimulus Similarity.* Ph. D. thesis, University of Adelaide, Australia.

Navarro, D.J. (2003). Regarding the complexity of additive clustering models [comment on Lee (2001)]. *Journal of Mathematical Psychology, 47*, 241–243.

Navarro, D.J., and M.D. Lee (2002). Commonalities and distinctions in featural stimulus representations. In W.G. Gray and C.D. Schunn (Eds.), *Proceedings of the 24th Annual Conference of the Cognitive Science Society*, pp. 685–690. Mahwah, NJ: Erlbaum.

Navarro, D.J., and M.D. Lee (2003). Combining dimensions and features in similarity-based representations. In S. Becker, S. Thrun, and K. Obermayer (Eds.), *Advances in Neural Information Processing Systems 15.* Cambridge, MA. MIT Press.

Oh, M., and J.O. Berger (1993). Integration of multimodal functions by Monte Carlo importance sampling. *Journal of the American Statistical Association,*

88, 450–456.

Pitt, M.A., I.J. Myung, and S. Zhang (2002). Toward a method of selecting among computational models of cognition. *Psychological Review, 109*(3), 472–491.

Rissanen, J. (1996). Fisher information and stochastic complexity. *IEEE Transactions on Information Theory, 42*(1), 40–47.

Rohde, D.L.T. (2002). Methods for binary multidimensional scaling. *Neural Computation,14*(5), 1195–1232.

Rosenberg, S., and M.P. Kim (1975). The method of sorting as a data-generating procedure in multivariate research. *Multivariate Behavioral Research, 10*, 489–502.

Ruml, W. (2001). Constructing distributed representations using additive clustering. In T.G. Dietterich, S. Becker, and Z. Ghahramani (Eds.), *Advances in Neural Information Processing 14*, Cambridge, MA. MIT Press.

Sattath, S. and A. Tversky (1977). Additive similarity trees. *Psychometrika, 42*, 319–345.

Schwarz, G. (1978). Estimating the dimension of a model. *Annals of Statistics, 6*(2), 461–464.

Shannon, C.E. (1948). The mathematical theory of communication. *Bell Systems Technical Journal,* 27, 623–656.

Shepard, R.N. (1962). The analysis of proximities: Multidimensional scaling with an unknown distance function. I. *Psychometrika, 27*(2), 125–140.

Shepard, R.N. (1980). Multidimensional scaling, tree-fitting, and clustering. *Science, 210*, 390–398.

Shepard, R.N. (1991). Integrality versus separability of stimulus dimensions: From an early convergence of evidence to a proposed theoretical basis. In J. R. Pomerantz and G. L. Lockhead (Eds.), *The Perception of Structure: Essays in Honor of Wendell R Garner*, pp. 53–71. Washington, DC: American Psychological Association.

Shepard, R.N. and P. Arabie (1979). Additive clustering representations of similarities as combinations of discrete overlapping properties. *Psychological Review, 86*(2), 87–123.

Shepard, R.N., D.W. Kilpatrick, and J.P. Cunningham (1975). The internal representation of numbers. *Cognitive Psychology, 7*, 82–138.

Takeuchi, J. (2000). On minimax regret with respect to families of stationary stochastic processes (in Japanese). In *Proceedings IBIS 2000*, pp. 63–68.

Tenenbaum, J. B. (1996). Learning the structure of similarity. In D.S. Touretzky, M.C. Mozer, and M.E. Hasselmo (Eds.), *Advances in Neural Information Processing Systems 8*, pp. 3–9. Cambridge, MA: MIT Press.

Tenenbaum, J.B. and T.L. Griffiths (2001). Generalization, similarity, and Bayesian inference. *Behavioral and Brain Sciences, 24*(4), 629–640.

Tversky, A. (1977). Features of similarity. *Psychological Review, 84*(4), 327–352.

Tversky, A. and J.W. Hutchinson (1986). Nearest neighbor analysis of psychological spaces. *Psychological Review, 93*(1), 3–22.

15   A Minimum Description Length Principle for Perception

Nick Chater
Institute for Applied Cognitive Science
Department of Psychology
University of Warwick
Gibbet Hill Road
Coventry
CV4 7AL
UK
N.Chater@warwick.ac.uk

Perception involves inferring the structure of the environment from sensory data. As in any process of inductive inference, there are infinitely many hypotheses about environmental structure that are compatible with sensory data. Can the perceptual system use the minimum description length (MDL) principle, which prefers hypotheses that provide a short explanation of the data, to choose between these competing explanations? This viewpoint has a long history in psychology, which can be traced back to Ernst Mach and to Gestalt psychology. This chapter considers how the MDL approach relates to apparently rival principles of perception, what types of empirical data the approach can and cannot explain, and how an MDL approach to perception might be augmented to provide an empirically adequate framework for understanding perceptual inference.

15.1   What is the Simplicity Principle?

Since Helmholtz [1925], many perceptual theorists have viewed the problem of understanding sensory input as a matter of inference (e.g., see [Gregory 1970; Marr 1982; Rock 1981]). That is, they have viewed the problem of perception as an abstract inferential problem of finding the "best" explanation of the sensory input.

The very viability of this highly abstract approach may seem in doubt: Can we really abstract away from the wealth of experimental results concerning the functioning of the perceptual system, and the detailed knowledge that is being acquired about the neurophysiology of the perceptual processing systems? The assumption in this chapter is that viewing perception as inference, and attempting to understand what kind of inference principles the perceptual system may use, is that it may provide a theoretical framework in which to organize and understand experimental and neuroscientific findings. Unless we understand, on an abstract level, *what* the perceptual system is doing, we have little hope of making sense of the psychophysical and neural data concerning *how* the perceptual system functions.

So, taking this abstract point of view, the task of the perceptual system is to find the "best" explanation of sensory input, in terms of the objects, surfaces, and lighting that may have given rise to that input. But what does it mean to be the *best* explanation? Clearly it is not just that the explanation fits the sensory input— because in perceptual problems there are invariably vast numbers of interpretations that fit the sensory data. Something other than mere "data fit" must differentiate the one (or, for rare ambiguous inputs, more than one) plausible interpretation from the plethora of implausible interpretations.

The minimum description length (MDL) principle discussed in this book provides an attractive framework for addressing the choice of interpretations. If the perceptual system follows the MDL principle, it should prefer interpretations that can be used to provide *short* descriptions of sensory data. From a purely abstract standpoint, an MDL approach to perception has a number of attractions:

- The MDL principle is widely and successfully used in statistics and machine learning, to tackle practical tasks where structure must be found in data (see, e.g., [Gao, Li, and Vitányi 2000; Quinlan and Rivest 1989; Kontkanen, Myllymäki, Buntine, Rissanen, and Tirri 2005]).

- "Ideal MDL" [Vitányi and Li 2000] can be justified on theoretical grounds as choosing explanations of data that give reliable predictions, given quite general assumptions.

- MDL is very closely related to Bayesian inference methods [Chater 1996; Vitányi and Li 2000] which are widely used in computational theories of perception [Knill and Richards 1996]

- MDL-based methods have been applied successfully in computational models of perception [Mumford 1996; Bienenstock, Geman, and Potter 1998]

These considerations suggest that the perceptual system would do well to use the MDL principle to analyze perceptual input. The question addressed here is: Does it? Or, more precisely, to what extent, and in what ways, does the MDL principle provide a productive framework for theorizing about perception?

This chapter has the following structure. The first section, *The power of simplicity: MDL-style theories of perception*, briefly outlines the MDL-type viewpoint on perception. We also describe the kinds of perceptual phenomena that this approach has been viewed as explaining. The second section, *Simplicity is not enough: Empirical challenges for MDL theories of perception*, we describe various classes of empirical phenomena that appear to pose difficulties for an MDL approaches to perception. The third section, *Where next? Prospects for an MDL approach to perception*, considers how these challenges might be addressed within an MDL framework.

15.2   The Power of Simplicity: MDL-Style Theories of Perception

The physicist and philosopher Ernst Mach [1959] proposed that the goal of perception, and for that matter the goal of science, is to provide the most economical explanation of sensory data. Thus, for example, the postulation of rigid, opaque objects may provide an economical explanation of the flow of sensory input as an observer moves through the environment. As the observer moves, the sensory input does not change in a random way—rather it unfolds predictably, given the principles of geometry and optics. The postulation of a specific three-dimensional (3D) environment provides a concise summary of these perceptual inputs. Indeed, this 3D structure also simultaneously explains other features of sensory inputs, most notably the patterns of relative disparity between the two eyes of the locations of the same objects. Common sense suggests that the world has a 3D structure, and that this gives rise to these and many other "depth cues" in the sensory input. Mach's perspective inverts this logic : the reason that we perceive a 3D world of depth at all is that this interpretation provides such an economical summary of many aspects of sensory input.

A very different example is that of color. The spectrum of light that is reflected from a surface depends on the reflectance function of the surface and the spectrum of the incident light. So the spectral properties of light bouncing off a particular green apple will differ enormously depending on the illuminant: whether the apple is in sunlight, shade, or artificial light. Yet its perceived color under these widely varying circumstances is roughly constant [Shepard 1992]. Crudely, perceived color captures aspects of the surface reflectance function of the individual surfaces and objects in the scene and this is independent of the illuminant. According to the principle of economy, the invariance of color is justified because it serves to provide an economical description of the spectra across a whole scene. The spectrum of the illuminant, combined with illuminant-invariant reflectance functions for different kinds of object or surface in the scene, provides a brief explanation of the apparently chaotic spectral variation across different parts of a scene, and over changes in illumination.

A third class of examples are the "laws of form" studied by the Gestalt psychologists (e.g., Koffka [1935]). Consider, for example, the law of common fate—that a collection of items that move coherently are seen as parts of a single object or surface. This provides an economical explanation of the movements of all the items involved—because rather than having to describe the movement of each item separately, the motion of the whole group is specified at once. In the same way, grouping by proximity, and by similarity, provides an economical way of encoding the shape, color, or other properties of many items simultaneously.

To state the same point more generally, one goal of perception is to find patterns in sensory input, and the MDL principle provides an elegant way of deciding between alternative patterns—by favoring patterns that support economical descriptions of sensory input.

In informal terms, the MDL approach to perception was proposed, as we have noted, by Mach. Mach's viewpoint was an example of positivism—roughly, the idea that the goal of science is to capture regularities in sensory experience, with the goal of making predictions about future sensory experience. A common sense version of this viewpoint is to claim that by finding the simplest explanation of past sensory experience, the perceiver or scientist is also likely to gain insight into how the real world works: what objects it contains, the nature of their causal powers, and so on. Mach took the more radical view that such apparent insight is illusory. Indeed, for Mach, that the idea that the goal of perception or science might be to find out about the nature of the world is conceptually incoherent. Unusually, for a leading physicist working well into the first part of the twentieth century, he did not believe in the reality of theoretical postulates of physics, such as atoms-these were merely convenient fictions for calculating relations between sensory experiences.

Mach's type of antirealist viewpoint, emphasizing the epistemological primacy of sensation, has not become philosophically unpopular, partly because it seems impossible to reconstruct a world of everyday objects, or scientific theoretical terms, from the language of sensation; and partly because the psychological notion of sensation has come to seem epistemologically problematic as an indubitable foundation for knowledge, given that psychological research has revealed how poorly people can access their own phenomenal experience [Dennett 1991; Laming 1997; O'Regan and Noe 2001]. This does not imply that Mach's view of the goal of perception and science, as providing economical descriptions of sensory experience, is misguided. The last twenty years has seen a substantial revival of interest in Bayesian models in the philosophy of science [Earman 1992; Horwich 1982; Howson and Urbach 1993]; and we shall see in the next section that the simplicity principle and Bayesian inference are closely related. Moreover, there may be advantages to adopting a simplicity-based view of scientific inference, over and above the strengths of the general Bayesian framework [Chater and Vitányi 2003]. Overall, I suggest that to the extent that there is an analogy between scientific inference and perception, as Mach assumed, this analogy may strengthen, rather than undermine, the case for a simplicity principle in perception.

After Mach's discussion, the case for a simplicity principle in perception was developed further by the Gestalt psychologists, in particular in relation to their formulation of laws of form, mentioned briefly above. More formal attempts to understand perception in terms of economy of representation were put forward with the development of information theory, and the developmental of formal theories of visual representation. For example, some theorists attempted to test directly the assumption that the perceptual system prefers short codes, where these are measured by optimal code lengths, given assumptions about the probability distributions over sensory inputs [Attneave 1959; Attneave and Frost 1969; Garner 1962; Garner 1974; Hochberg and McAlister 1953]. The theoretical starting point of this approach is communication theory [Shannon 1948]. This theory specifies, among other things, the code lengths that produce the briefest expected code length required to encode the output of a probability distribution. But measuring complexity relative to a probability distribution is problematic—because it ignores the instrinsic complexity of the objects being perceived. For example, suppose that in an experimental context, a participant may be presented either with a black square on a white background or a high-definition forest scene. If these have the same probability (of one half), then from an information-theoretic standpoint they have the same complexity. But this does not capture the very different perceived complexity of the two stimuli (see [Miller 1967] for more general reflections on difficulties with applying standard information theory to cognition). Moreover, outside the laboratory, we face the problem that the probability distribution over natural images is unknown—indeed, to define it would require knowledge of the full range of regularities that govern the visual world. Hence it is unclear that the information-theoretic approach is applicable, even in principle—because it bases codes on probabilities, and probabilities seem either irrelevant (as in our experimental example) or unknown.

An attractive alternative approach is to take coding, rather than probability, as the basic notion. This is the idea behind an MDL approach to perception explored in this chapter. This approach immediately deals with the case of equiprobable stimuli: the black square can be coded briefly; the forest scene will require a code of enormous complexity. The primacy of coding, rather than probability, also underpins a psychological research tradition that developed in parallel to the mathematical formulation of MDL: structural information theory [Buffart, Leeuwenberg, and Restle 1981; Restle 1970; Restle 1979; Van der Helm and Leeuwenberg 1996; Van der Helm 2000]. The aim of structural information theory is to develop a theory of representation for simple visual inputs, according to which the visual system systematically prefers interpretations that correspond to short descriptions. This approach has been concerned with a particular, and deliberately quite limited, set of coding languages and visual stimuli, so that concrete predictions can be made. In this chapter, I am concerned instead with the general claim that the perceptual system chooses the simplest representation, without commitment to a particular coding language for perceptual input. The key idea, then, is that we consider the possibility that the perceptual system aims to find the shortest representation, given some coding system for perceptual input.

15.2.1   Simplicity and Bayesian Inference

In the literature on perceptual organization [Pomerantz and Kubovy 1986], the simplicity principle is typically contrasted with the *likelihood* principle, that the perceptual system should choose the organization that corresponds to the environmental structure that has the highest probability, given the data. This type of viewpoint was proposed by Helmholtz [1925], and has been developed in parallel with the simplicity-based approach, being advocated by vision scientists [Knill and Richards 1996], as well as researchers on computational theories of human and machine vision [Geman and Geman 1984; Hinton, Ghahramani and Teh 2000; Mumford 1996].

Recent formulations of the likelihood approach use a Bayesian framework. They take the goal of perception to be to choose the perceptual hypothesis or explanation, H, which maximizes $P(H|D)$ for perceptual data, D. Using an elementary rule of probability theory, Bayes' theorem, this is equivalent to choosing the H which maximizes $P(D|H)P(H)$. This means that hypotheses about the organization of the stimulus are favored to the extent that they predict the data well (i.e., $P(D|H)$ is high), and that also have high prior probability ($P(D)$ is high).

The hypothesis, H, that maximizes this term is, of course, the same H that maximizes the logarithm of this term; and this is also the H that *minimizes* the negative of the logarithm of this term, which can be written

$$-\log_2 P(H) - \log_2 P(D|H).$$

Now by Shannon's coding theorem from information theory [Cover and Thomas 1991], we know that an optimal (binary) code length for a probability, p, is $\log_2 p$. Hence we can interpret the above terms as code lengths:

$$\text{codelength}(H) + \text{codelength}(D|H)$$

Putting all this together, we can conclude that the hypothesis, H, that maximizes likelihood can also be viewed as minimizing the code length that the hypothesis provides for the data, where that hypothesis is expressed as a two-part code. That is, the hypothesis that satisfies the likelihood principle also satisfies the simplicity principle, where simplicity is interpreted in terms of code length. This heuristic argument suggests that the simplicity and likelihood principles can be viewed as equivalent [Chater 1996; Mumford 1996]. Indeed, applying theoretical results on the relationship between a version of "ideal" MDL and Bayesian inference [Vitányi and Li 2000], it is possible to prove a "mimicry" theorem [Chater, Vitányi, Olivers, and Watson 2005]. It turns out that, for any "computable" coding language (where this is quite a mild restriction) there is a "dual" probability distribution. This dual probability distribution has the property that, for any data whatever, the hypothesis which assigns that data the shortest length using that specific coding language is also the hypothesis with the highest probability, in the dual probability distribution. Again subject to mild restrictions, the converse result holds. This mimicry theorem implies that any specific version of the simplicity principle can always be reconceptualized as a specific version of the likelihood principle, and vice versa. From this perspective, it is not surprising that the century-long debate between the simplicity and likelihood principles has not been resolved successfully by empirical evidence—because any evidence that can be explained by an account using one principle can be recast by an account using the other. [1].

The close relationship between Bayesian and MDL viewpoints in perception is particularly interesting, given the large amount of theoretical [Knill and Richards 1996], computational [Geman and Geman 1984], neuroscientific [Blakemore 1990; Rieke, Warland, de Ruyter van Steveninck, and Bialek 1997], and psychological [Weiss 1997] work that takes seriously the possibility that perception operates by Bayesian inference. Below, we shall see relations between issues that face the MDL approach to perception with related issues that have been considered in the probabilistic framework.

15.3   Simplicity is Not Enough: Empirical Challenges for MDL Theories of Perception

We have considered the prima facie attractions of an MDL approach to perception. But to understand both the principle and the challenges that it faces as a theoretical framework for perceptual theory requires facing some of the areas in which the approach does not presently seem to be adequate. In this section, we consider three challenges in turn: *the principle of least commitment, causality and independence,* and *representation and process constraints*.

15.3.1   The Principle of Least Commitment

In perceiving a stimulus, the visual system delivers a range of representations that abstract away, to varying degrees, from the details of the specific stimulus that is presented. For example, suppose that we see a somewhat noisy picture of a black square on a white background (Figure 15.1a). The perceptual system presumably represents this as a black square; and, indeed, more abstractly, as a square (Figure 15.1b). Accordingly, it will be classified as highly similar to other noisy, or less noisy, stimuli depicting squares (e.g., Figure 15.1c). Moreover, the orientation and size of the square may be separately abstracted (or perhaps thrown away) — although if the square were aligned such that its adjacent corners, rather than

---

1. There are still some possible controversies surrounding the traditional debate between simplicity and likelihood, however [Van der Helm 2000; Chater et al. 2005]. At an algorithmic level, one or other framework might appear more natural—for example, if it turns out that the brain carries out empirical sampling from probability distributions, for example, using Markov chain Monte Carlo, Gibbs sampling, or related methods, as is embodied in many neural network models, then arguably a probabilistic formulation might seem more natural. Moreover, in statistics, the relationship between MDL-type techniques and Bayesian methods is much debated. Some theorists treat these methods as identical [Wallace and Freeman 1987]; others treat MDL as fundamentally different from, and logically prior to, the Bayesian approach [Rissanen 1986, 1989].

its sides, are aligned with the perceptually salient frame of reference, then it may not be categorized as a square at all, but as a diamond (Figure 15.1d). On the other hand, of course, one could imagine instead that the perceptual system might use much less abstract codes—specifically, it might have a shape template for the precise, although stupendously arbitrary, details of that particular square. And then specifying a particular perceptual input, such as Figure 15.1a, might be merely a matter of specifying a size, rotation, translational location, and luminance,[2] for this extraordinarily precise template. Going to the opposite extreme, one could imagine that the perceptual system might choose instead an overgeneral model of its perceptual image. For example, it might use a "null" model that would assign equal probability to all possible gray-level image configurations, whether they depict black squares, faces, or pure random noise.

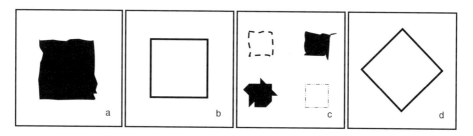

Figure 15.1   Levels of abstraction in processing a simple perceptual stimulus. (a) shows a noisy black square, which the perceptual system may, among other things, represent simple as a square (b), abstracting away from color, irregularities, and so on. (c) shows various other noisy or imperfect squares that may be classified with (a), at this level of abstraction. On the other hand, a change of orientation in relation to the natural frame of reference may lead an apparently very similar figure to be classified, instead, as a diamond (d).

From the point of view of understanding perceptual representations from the point of view of MDL, it is important that we have some way of explaining why "sensible" perceptual representations are to be preferred over these inappropriate types of overspecific or overgeneral representation.

Overgeneral models can straightforwardly be eliminated by MDL—because they do not embody all the constraints that the stimulus actually conforms with, they require excessive code length. To take a trivial example, if an image consists of uniform black, then it will have a near-zero description length in terms of a sensible model that expresses this uniformity. But in terms of the null model that we mentioned above, each "pixel" must be encoded separately, so the resulting bit-string will be enormously large (and no shorter than the code for a white noise, which would be perceived, of course, very differently).

---

2. We ignore color here to avoid complications.

Overspecific models, by contrast, are more problematic. Suppose that we have some particular set of data (in this case, visual input). Consider the ultimately overspecific model that predicts precisely that these, and no other, possible data can occur. This model provides a maximally efficient representation of the data—no information at all is required to encode the data, given the model. But this is only achieved by putting all the complexity into the specification of the model itself. But doing this does not increase the overall complexity of the encoding of the data—because, after all, encoding this hyperspecific model just *is* a matter of encoding the data, and hence the minimal code for specifying the model will be a minimal code for the data. More generally, there will typically be many overspecific models that attain minimal code length, by including essentially arbitrary features of the data as part of the model itself, and yet still function as minimal codes for the data. Intuitively, this family of models is such that the data are *typical*, and hence uncompressible, given these models. This constraint holds because if the data are not typical, then the data contain patterns that the model does not describe, and hence the models provide an inefficient representation of the data. That is, these models must extract all the *structure* from the data—but the problem of overgeneral models is that models can also encode additional, essentially arbitrary, information about the data.[3]

In statistical theory, a statistic that captures all the structure in the data is called a *sufficient* statistic. Following a suggestion of Kolmogorov, there has been recent interest in a generalization of this idea, which views models as Kolmogorov sufficient statistics (KSSs), a notion that can be formally captured [Cover and Thomas 1991; Gács, Tromp, and Vitányi 2001]. There is frequently a number of KSSs for any given data.[4] Intuition suggests that the KSS of most interest is that which makes the most modest claims about the data (i.e., where the model has the shortest code length, such that the data remain typical with respect to that model). This is the Kolmogorov *minimal* sufficient statistic (KMSS). Perhaps, then, an interesting idealization of perception is as searching not merely for short codes for visual input, but for the KMSS for that input. Thus we have an interesting principle of least commitment for perceptual theory[5]: to derive only that structure from the stimulus that is necessary to explain the data, and no more.

Consider, for example, Figure 15.2. The figure in (a) is perceived as a wire-frame cube with rigid joints. On the other hand, the joints of the figure in (b), which

---

3. In practical MDL, the focus is often on the code length associated with specifying the parameters in a model to an appropriate level of precision from which to predict the data, rather than on the code lengths of the type of model itself. If used without caution, this approach will favor overspecific models. In practice, this is rarely a problem, as overspecific models, unless chosen post hoc, will almost always be overspecific in the wrong ways, and hence encode the data poorly.

4. A recent important result by Vereshchagin and Vitanyi [2002] shows, remarkably, that the number of KSSs for any data has some, presumably very large, finite bound.

5. This term is used in a different, but perhaps related, context by Marr [1982].

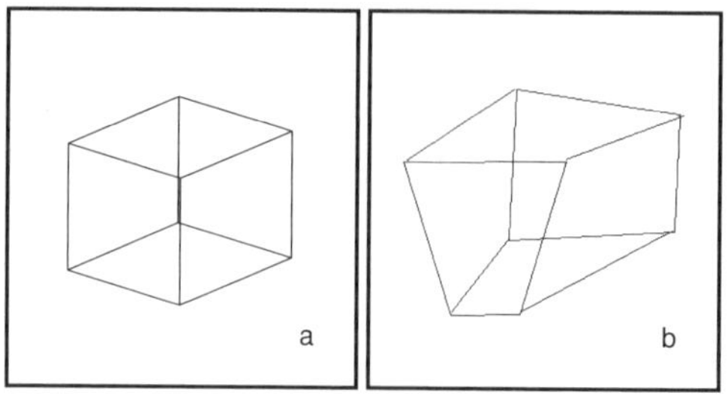

Figure 15.2 Illustration of the principle of least commitment. In (a) the highly regular 2D projection can be explained on the assumption that we are viewing a rigid cube. If the structure is nonrigid (e.g., a frame of rigid rods, attached by loose, flexible joints), then it is a causally inexplicable co-incidence that the rods happen to align to produce a 2D projection consistent with the projection of a rigid cube. The perceptual system disfavors interpretations that involve such causally inexplicable coincidences. In (b), by contrast, a nonrigid interpretation is quite natural (although joints can also be interpreted as rigid).

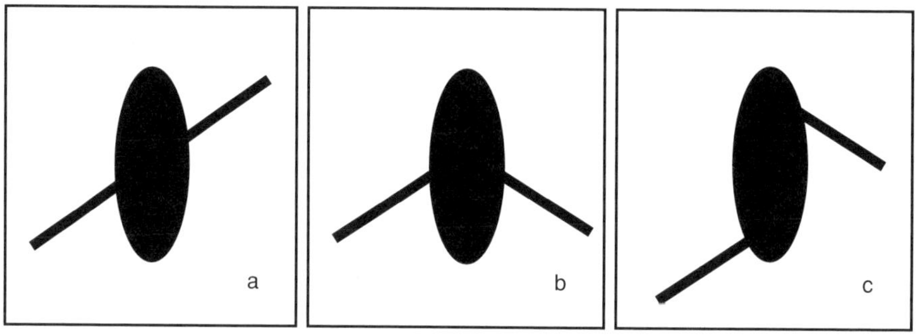

Figure 15.3 Simplicity and rigidity constraints. In (a), the alignment between the two straight lines is interpreted by the perceptual system as significant. That is, the lines are viewed as part of a single rod, occluded by the ellipse. Thus, for example, it seems natural to presume that if one rod were moved by force, the other would also move. That is, the lines are not perceived as merely aligned, but causally connected. This connection is weaker in (b), where the rods are still nonaccidentally related, by symmetry; and is weakened still further in (c) where there is no simple spatial relationship between the two rods.

is perceived as irregular, are perceived as potentially flexible. In the former case, the rigidity assumption is necessary, because if joints are flexible (and hence the whole figure is "collapsible," then it is pure coincidence that the shape happens to be aligned as a cube. The cube alignment is hence not typical with respect to a nonrigid model, which can be rejected. By contrast, in the latter case, the commitment to rigid joints is unnecessary, and hence, by the principle of least commitment we have described, it is not made. Similarly, Figure 15.3 shows how the strength of the interpretation of *attachment* between two linear bars depends on their alignment. However misaligned they are, they *could* be attached (any kind of shape linking them could be present, but occluded by the oval). But the perception of attachment is only present to the degree that this provides a short encoding of the data; if the bars were specified independently, their alignment would be mere coincidence.[6]

We have considered how wildly overgeneral and overspecific models may be eliminated. But this still leaves a huge space of intermediate models. Ultimately, one might hope that from studying the properties of natural images to which the visual system is exposed might provide predictions concerning the nature of the hierarchy of representational levels that are revealed by neuroscientific and psychological research (although, of course, it is unlikely that MDL-type constraints are the only constraints on the perceptual system—one would expect, for example, that the nature of the specific biological hardware will favor some kinds of representation over others [Chater and Oaksford 1990]).

We have also considered only the case where the perceiver has access to a single perceptual input (although this input might be of arbitrary size and temporal duration). But frequently, we do not want to treat the perceptual input in this unanalyzed way—instead, it frequently seems appropriate to view the input as consisting of several independent perceptual inputs, which must be encoded separately— for example, several different views of the same object, from different vantage points; or views of several different objects from the same category (e.g., views of various different dogs). To the extent that we can analyze the perceptual input in this way, we can further resolve the problem of overgeneral models. This is because an overgeneral model fails to explain why multiple, discrete chunks of data all fall within a smaller category. That is, the overgeneral category *animal* may be eliminated as a hypothesis explaining what one is likely to see when visiting a dog show, because it fails to explain why all the animals encountered have so much more in common than would be expected of a typical selection of animals—and this leads to excessively long codes for the representation of the specific animals seen. By contrast, the category *dog* captures these regularities neatly. But we can also readily deal with overspecific models—because multiple data points (multiple examples of dogs) will have a low probability of fitting an overspecific category. If the first dog I encounter when visiting the dog show is a dachshund, I may impute an overspecific hypothesis. But once I see other dogs, it is highly likely that I will see non-dachshunds and hence that this overspecific hypothesis can be eliminated. More generally, similar considerations may help explain how the interpretation of a particular item can be modified by the presence of other items. For example, an apparently arbitrary orientation of a square will suddenly seem significant in the presence of other items with this same orientation; an apparently arbitrary pattern of markings may suddenly become salient if this is repeated (just as an artist's scrawled signature may become salient, upon seeing it in several paintings). That is, some of the ambiguity

---

6. Strictly, this point relates to our next topic—that MDL can only exploit *causally* explicable regularities.

in determining how to interpret a specific object may be resolved by comparing it with other objects. If, as some theorists suggest, specific instances or exemplar information about past perceptual inputs are stored in memory [Hintzman 1986; Nosofsky 1991], there may be considerable scope for effects of this kind.

This point raises an interesting theoretical question concerning the granularity at which we consider sensory input in analyzing perception. At one extreme, the entire history of sensory stimulation might be treated as a single input, to be compressed; at the other extreme, very spatially and temporally local chunks of sensory information may be considered separately. This question of granularity remains an interesting issue for future research (see also Hochberg [1982] for related discussion). The possibility of breaking sensory input into discrete chunks, which must be encoded separately, also raises the possibility of applying the simplicity principle in perception to categorization—the considerations that we have just described form the basis for a theory of how categories might be learned from samples of their instances, using a simplicity principle. I do not develop these ideas here, but note that simplicity-based ideas have been pursued in building psychological models of both supervised [Feldman 2000] and unsupervised [Pothos and Chater 2002] categorization.

In this subsection, I have argued that merely finding short descriptions of sensory input is not enough. The perceptual system must also be able to separate genuine structure from mere "noise." At a technical level, the Kolmogorov sufficient statistic appears to be a valuable tool for understanding how this separation might occur; and indeed, the hierarchy of Kolmogorov sufficient statistics for sensory input might even relate to the hierarchy of representational levels computed by the perceptual system.

15.3.2 Causality and Independence

Consider the three projections of a cube, shown in Figure 15.4. The rightmost projection (c) is readily interpreted as a cube. The leftmost projection (a) is most naturally perceived as a 'pinwheel'—although it is the projection of a cube viewed precisely along an axis through diagonally opposite vertices. The middle figure, (b), is viewed from a slightly skewed version of this viewing angle—but so that one pair of axes is still aligned. This is slightly easier to interpret as a cube than (a), but is most naturally interpreted in two dimensions as two connected diamonds.

A traditional puzzle in the interpretation of 2D line drawings is that each line drawing could be generated by an infinite number of 3D structures. How does the perceptual system decide on a particular interpretation out of this infinite array of options? We assume that MDL can answer this puzzle: the preference for a cube interpretation, in, say, Figure 15.4, arises because the cube is simpler than

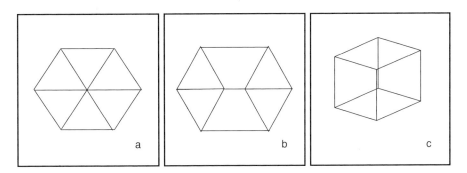

Figure 15.4 Viewpoint dependence and the perception of projections of a cube. This figure shows three projections of a wire-framed cube. The first (a) is seen from a viewpoint according to which two diagonally opposite vertices are in the same line of sight. This is a highly coincidental viewpoint, and the perceptual system disfavors such coincidences. Instead, (a) is perceived as a flat pinwheel. (b) is also projection of a cube from a coincidental viewpoint: two adjacent sides of the cube lie on the same line of sight. (b) is also not readily viewed as a cube, but as a flat structure composed of two diamonds, joined by horizontal lines. A slight misalignment between adjacent sides (c) reduces the coincidence; and also eliminates any simple alternative description in terms of a 2D pattern. Thus, (c) is readily viewed as a projection of a cube.

alternative, less symmetric, polyhedra.[7] But Figure 15.4 illustrates a more difficult problem—that some 2D projections of a cube are more readily interpreted, not as projections of a cube, but as 2D patterns.

This is prima facie puzzling for the MDL approach, because a cube seems to be a rather efficient way of specifying, say, the pinwheel pattern. We need merely specify that the cube is viewed so that two adjacent corners are precisely aligned with the axis of view to obtain the appropriate figure.[8] Though this presumably corresponds to a short code, it relies on a striking coincidence—in this case, concerning the precise alignment of the cube in relation to the viewer. There is a large class of cases of this kind, and theorists in computer vision and perception have proposed that the perceptual system dislikes interpretations that depend on coincidences of viewing angle. Constraints of this kind are known as *generic viewpoint* constraints [Biederman 1985; Binford 1981; Hoffman 1998; Koenderink and van Doorn 1979]. But from an MDL viewpoint, constraints that are viewer-dependent can, nonetheless, lead to short descriptions, and therefore it does not seem that the MDL approach alone can readily capture the perceptual system's tendency to avoid interpretations that rely on precisely specifying a viewpoint.

---

7. Symmetric figures have shorter codes because they have fewer degrees of freedom.
8. Aside from the obvious further parameters concerning size, orientation, location, type of lines used; but these must be specified, whatever underlying model is used for the geometric structure of the stimulus.

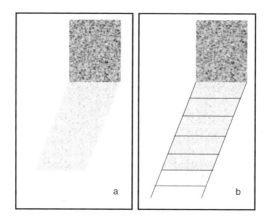

Figure 15.5 Co-incidences and the interpretation of shadows. This figure illustrates how the interpretation of a light bar as the shadow of a darker tower (a) is over-ridden when there is a patterned "path with paving slabs" that precisely coincides with this light bar (b). Intuitively, the perceptual system is biased against co-incidences; if the light bar is a shadow, then it is a striking co-incidence that it happens to line up precisely with the black outlines of the path. Therefore, in (b), the shadow interpretation is disfavored.

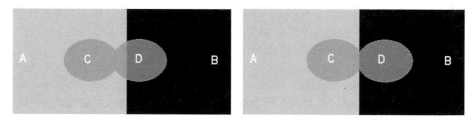

Figure 15.6 Coincidence and transparency. In the left box, the simplest interpretation is that a transparent "spectacle-shaped" object (consisting of patches C and D) lies over a pair of squares, one light gray and one black (A and B). In the right box, this transparency interpretation is impeded, because it involves a coincidental alignment between the overlaid transparent pattern and the squares, so that the indented points in the spectacle-shaped object are precisely aligned with the line between the two squares. There seems to be no causal explanation for this coincidence. Hence, the perceptual system prefers an interpretation in which A, B, C, and D are simply different colored regions, in the same plane.

The perceptual system also appears to be averse to other kinds of co-incidences. For example, Figure 15.5 illustrates how the interpretation of a light bar as the shadow of a tower (Figure 15.5a) is overridden when a patterned "path" coincides precisely with this light bar (Figure 15.5b). Intuitively, the perceptual system is, as before, biased against co-incidences; if the light bar is a shadow, then it is a striking co-incidence that it happens to line up precisely with the path. Thus, instead, the light bar in Figure 15.5b is perceived merely as a path of gray paving slabs, rather than as a shadow. Figure 15.6 shows a further example, using transparency. When the axis of symmetry of the "spectacles-shaped" object (taken from Hoffman [1998]) is precisely aligned with the division between the two background squares, then the transparency interpretation, that is otherwise so strong, disappears. The reason is that, on the transparency interpretation, there are two overlaid surfaces; and there is no apparent causal constraint that would align the patterns on these surfaces. From a causal point of view, this is mere coincidence. Notice that this kind of case is not a matter of viewpoint, and hence not a case to which the generic viewpoint constraint can directly apply. The point here is that the alignment of different parts of the figure is not arbitrary, or "generic," with respect to the causal constraints that appear to be operative.

These cases can all be viewed as indicating that the perceptual system disfavors interpretations according to which there are unexplained, or "coincidental" regularities in the input. That is, perception disfavors interpretation in which there is no *causal* explanation of why, for example, a figure has a particular alignment with the viewer, why shadows happen to line up, or why a spectacle-shaped transparent surface happens to line up precisely with the square-pattern of the surface upon which it is overlaid.

This indicates that we need to add constraints on the kinds of regularities that an MDL model can exploit— that these regularities must be causally natural. After all, the perceptual input is typically the end result of an enormously complex set of causes. The structure of the input is, of course, a product of the laws that govern this causal story; and the goal of the perceptual system is, to some extent at least, to uncover this causal story from the perceptual input. Thus, we have the constraint that the codes derived by an MDL analysis should not be merely short but must correspond to causally viable explanations of the data; codes that rely on short descriptions that are pure 'co-incidence' from a causal point of view (e.g., unexplained alignments) should be rejected.

The addition of this constraint may seem disappointing from the perspective of Mach's positivist program, in perception and in science. For Mach, the apparently somewhat opaque and metaphysical notion of causality should be avoided by science (and hence, presumably, by the cognitive system). Instead, the goal of science is to find the most economical descriptions of the available data. A positivist viewpoint can, perhaps, reconceptualize the current suggestion, without the concept of causality. If we focus not just on a single visual stimulus but over the entire history of stimuli which the perceptual system receives, cases in which co-incidences with no causal explanation will, of necessity, be rare, and hence, these regularities should be assigned long codes, and be disfavored by the MDL principle. Regularities that arise systematically and consistently must, presumably, arise from causal regularities in the perceptual input. These will be frequent, and hence will have short codes, and be preferred by MDL. Despite the possibility of this kind of hard-line MDL approach, in which causal constraints in interpreting any given input are derived from an MDL analysis over the history of perceptual input, it is also entirely possible, of course, that information about causal constraints might be derived from other sources. Thus, causal constraints may be innate [Sperber, Premack, and Premack 1995] or derived from active perceptual-motor experimentation (e.g., moving the head, adjusting a light source, or sliding a transparent sheet, which may disturb co-incidental regularities). Wherever causal constraints are derived from, however, it seems crucially important to incorporate them into a properly constrained MDL account of perception.

We have argued, in this subsection, that there appear to be substantial causal constraints on perceptual interpretations, and these constraints do not immediately arise by favoring the simplest explanation of the perceptual input. It is worth noting, too, that causal constraints are not merely important in predicting which interpretations the perceptual system favors. Rather, extracting a causal model of the external world is a critical goal of perception. This is because the ultimate utility of perception resides, of course, in its ability to drive action; and the effectiveness of action in bringing about the perceiver's objectives will critically depend on correctly perceiving which regularities in the external world are co-incidental and which are causal. Unless the perceiver can distinguish causal structure from perceptual input, it is as likely to attempt to lift a saucer by picking up the cup, as it is to attempt to lift a cup by picking up the saucer. How far the simplicity principle could support the learning of *causal* structure merely by finding the shortest description in observed data is an open question.

15.3.3   Representation and Process Constraints

A strong interpretation of an MDL approach to perception would be that the cognitive system chooses the shortest possible description of the perceptual stimulus. But this strong interpretation cannot be right, at least in general, because the search problem of finding shortest descriptions is typically intractable.[9] For some restricted codes, such as structural information theory, the search problem can be made tractable [Van der Helm and Leeuwenberg 1991]. But in most cases this is not possible. Difficult search problems arise even in the optimization calculations associated with very simple models of pixel-level correlational structure in images [Weiss 1997]; and in training Bayesian or neural networks to find structure in images [Hinton et al. 2000]. So an MDL approach to perception must make a more modest claim: that the perceptual system chooses the shortest code for perceptual data that it *can find*. Thus, the claim is that simplicity is used to choose between perceptual interpretations that are considered by the perceptual system.

Note that the space of interpretations that the perceptual system considers will be highly constrained. There will be an enormous variety of regularities that, when

---

9. Where the class of code is universal, for example, has equivalence in power to a universal programming language, then finding the shortest code is, in general, uncomputable[Li and Vitányi 1997].

encoded in an image and presented to the perceptual system, will be treated as mere random noise. To choose any of a myriad of possible examples, an "outsize" checkerboard whose black and white squares provide a binary encoding of, say, the initial 10,000 digits of π will have a short code, but will be perceptually indistinguishable from a random checkerboard.

Indeed, a critical question for an MDL model of perception is to draw on existing results from psychology and neuroscience to create realistic hypotheses about which regularities the coding language for perceptual stimuli can capture. Defining a representation or coding language makes, from this point of view, a rich set of hypotheses about the relative strengths of different perceptual interpretations; *of the hypotheses considered*, the shortest should be favored (subject to the caveats concerning causality and least commitment that we have described in the last two subsections). A second critical question is to define search processes over representations, to provide a mechanism for explaining how perception finds interpretations with short description length.[10]

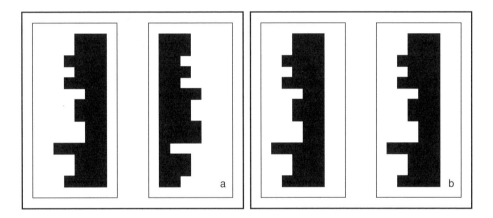

Figure 15.7 How representational format impacts the detection of simple patterns. This figure, loosely patterned on stimuli by Bayliss and Driver [1994, 1995], illustrates how a regularity that allows a stimulus to be encoded briefly may be more or less noticeable, depending on the representational format applied by the perceptual system. In both (a) and (b), there is an identity between the irregular boundaries. But in (a) the boundary is difficult to perceive because the figure/ground relation is reversed (the black shape is the figure, the white forms the background). Hoffman & Richards (1984) point out that boundaries are encoded in terms of convex protrusions of the figure into the ground. Therefore the codes that will be generated for the two irregular boundaries in (a) are very different, because what is coded as a protrusion in one boundary will be viewed as an indentation in the other (and hence will not be coded at all). By contrast, the identity of the boundaries in (b) is readily perceived.

---

10. Structural information theory is one approach to this problem, though not one we examine here.

To illustrate, consider Figure 15.7, based on stimuli used by Bayliss and Driver [1994, 1995]. Note how the identity between "boundaries" is easily perceived when they have the same figure/ground pattern—but is hard to perceive when they do not. Bayliss and Driver [1994, 1995] explain this difference by adverting to the claim of Hoffman and Richards [1984] that the edges of a figure are parsed in terms of protrusions of the figure into the ground; indentations of the figure are not encoded directly at all. This means that a boundary will be interpreted very differently depending which side of the boundary is viewed as the figure—because this will flip protrusions to indentations and vice versa. Hence, if the same boundary is present in a stimulus, but with a different figure/ground interpretation, then the codes for each will be very different, and the match between them cannot be exploited.

Figure 15.8 *Representation, figure/ground, and symmetry.* Considering each half of the figure separately, there is potential ambiguity concerning whether the black or white stripes are figure or ground. Note that the interpretation according to which the foreground stripes have a constant width is favored. Thus, we perceive white stripes in the left half of the figure, and black stripes in the right half of the figure. This makes sense, from the standpoint of the simplicity principle, only with the auxiliary assumption that the identity between the two parallel contours can only be captured if these contours are assigned to the same object (i.e., the same stripe). On this assumption, the identity between contours assigned to different stripes (in other words, between contours that are perceived as bounding a background region) cannot be captured. According to this line of reasoning, failing to capture this regularity causes the code length, with this representation, to be unnecessarily long, and hence this interpretation is disfavored by the perceptual system. Note, finally, that the symmetry in the stimulus is rather difficult to perceive. This is because perceiving this symmetry requires simultaneously representing the different figure/ground representations (white stripes on black in the left half; black stripes on white in the right half). Thus, representational and processing constraints play a substantial role in explaining which regularities the perceptual system can use to provide a short code for the stimulus.

A related example is shown in Figure 15.8. Note, first, that in the left-hand part of the figure we see white stripes against a black background, and the reverse pattern on the right-hand part of the image. A natural explanation for these figure/ground preferences is that the perceptual system prefers to postulate simpler, rather than more complex, objects. The fore-grounded stripes are simpler than the back-grounded stripes because they have parallel edges. Note, of course, that a pure MDL account would not give this preference for stripes with parallel edges—because, with the reverse segmentation, all that is required is shared contours between adjacent stripes (the left contour of one object would be shared with the right contour of an adjacent object, and so on). But the perceptual code presumably cannot capture this regularity, with the implication that this coding is not favored. Finally, note that the symmetry between the two halves of the pattern is rather difficult to exploit. One explanation for this is that symmetry can only be detected a fter segmentation of both halves of the stimulus has occurred; and simultaneously segmenting both halves of the image presents a difficult processing challenge (e.g., because the segmentations are somewhat rivalrous).

The upshot of examples such as these is that a simplicity approach to perception cannot be considered *purely* in the abstract, in the absence of constraints concerning the representations used by the perceptual system and the cognitive processes that can operate over them. The perceptual system may, if the simplicity principle is correct, aim to find the shortest code for sensory input that it can. But the perceptual system's measure of code length will be influenced by the representational units that it has available, and by the processes that allow (or do not allow) particular regularities to be exploited using those units. Moreover, the perceptual system is limited in which short codes it is able to find—some codes might be highly preferred if they could be found, but they may not typically be found (or may only be found after unusually prolonged viewing, as is frequently the experience of viewers of autostereograms). Now, it seems reasonable to suggest that the specific representations and processes that the perceptual system has evolved will be well suited to the natural environment. And, more speculatively, one might propose that, in the present framework, this might mean that the perceptual system may have representations and processes that are particularly well suited to finding short codes for regularities that occur in the natural environment. Accordingly, we should not, perhaps, be surprised that binary expansions of π are not readily detected by the perceptual system, because presumably there are no natural processes that generate this pattern; and the tendency to specify shapes in terms of convex protrusions may be adapted to the geometry of real objects [Hoffman and Richards 1984]. Indeed, it seems natural to view processes of adaptation as a process of learning over phylogenetic time; this process of learning gradually reduces the code length with which the perceptual system can represent the natural world—because perceptual systems that provide excessively long codes are less well suited to representing real perceptual input, and tend to be eliminated by natural selection. Equivalently, in a Bayesian framework, it seems natural to view one role of natural selection being to select perceptual systems with priors that are as aligned as closely as possible with the actual probability distributions in the natural world.

Overall, the MDL approach to perception must integrate with existing experimental and neuroscientific knowledge of perception. The value of the MDL approach will ultimately depend on whether this integration is smooth and productive, or forced and unhelpful.

15.4 Where Next? Prospects for an MDL Approach to Perception

We mentioned at the outset that one justification for an MDL approach to perception is that perception is a kind of inductive inference, and MDL is a normatively attractive theory of how such inference should be conducted. But this argument is only enough, in reality, to establish that MDL should be given some initial credence. We discussed, too, a number of areas (stereovision, color perception, and laws of form) where some kind of MDL framework can be applied. But whether this framework proves to be scientifically productive depends on how far it can be integrated with the psychology and neurobiology of vision, to provide specific theoretical insights, and empirical predictions.

It is also possible that technical developments in MDL-type approaches to inductive inference might be usefully applicable to understanding aspects of perception.

One intriguing idea, suggested by Paul Vitányi (personal communication, December 2001) is that not merely the Kolmogorov minimal sufficient statistic, but the other nonminimal sufficient statistics might map onto perceptual representations. Perhaps, to some approximation, we might understand the sequence of levels of representation in the perceptual system as corresponding to different Kolmogorov Sufficient Statistics. For example, suppose that we take seriously the idea that very early visual processing filters the input to remove redundancy due to highly local statistical properties of images (e.g., that, in most image locations, luminance changes smoothly, although in a few locations it changes abruptly) [Barlow 1961]. This early filtering might correspond to a (rather long) Kolmogorov sufficient statistic for the image; it throws away mere noise from the image. A slightly more abstract level of representation (e.g., representing edges, blobs, bars) might correspond to another KSS. It throws aways further "noise" of no intrinsic perceptual interest. The Kolmogorov minimal sufficient statistic represents the limit of this process—the most abstract representation that does not throw away anything other than noise. This viewpoint is not intended, of course, to be any more than an idealization of how perceptual representations might be arranged (e.g., the calculations involved in finding minimal codes are provably intractable [Li and Vitányi 1997] and hence cannot, presumably, be computed by the brain). And it is likely that perception throws away a good deal of information— that is, it is much more selective than this analysis allows. Nonetheless, it may be interesting to pursue ideas of this type, in relation to understanding the general function of multiple levels of perceptual representation.

Another interesting line of thought concerns the degree to which we can explain why the output of perception presents the world to us as "modular," that is, of consisting of discrete objects and processes. Let us suppose that, at least at the macroscopic level relevant to much of perception, the regularities in the world are naturally "parsed" into discrete chunks (e.g., objects correspond to bundles of regularities: parts of the same object tend to be made of the same thing, to be attached to each other, to move coherently, to be at roughly the same depth, etc.); and the causal interactions between objects are usually also fairly local (e.g., between a cup, the water pouring from it, and its shadow on the table). To what extent can these sorts of modular structure be uncovered from purely minimizing description length? Current theory does not appear to give clear answers here. Plausibly, if a highly modular process has given rise to perceptual input, one might suppose that a code that replays that modular causal history to reconstruct the data might provide a brief encoding (although if the data sample is insufficiently rich, this may not be true). But there will also be codes of about the same length in which that modular structure is not apparent (just as the careful modular structure of a computer program may be lost from view when it is compiled into a different language). And there might also be short codes with a different, and perhaps contradictory, modular structure. Can MDL-related ideas help to explain how modular causal structures can be inferred reliably from data alone? This seems an important question for future theoretical research—not only, indeed, in helping to understand perception, but in any domain in which MDL may be applied. We want MDL not merely to give us short codes; we want those codes to be interpretable as descriptions that correspond to a local, causal description of the structure of the system that gives rise to the data.

Most crucial for the practical usefulness of the MDL approach to perception is, of course, the degree to which it can be integrated with existing and future research on the psychology and neuroscience of perception. To what extent can neural codes be viewed as compressing sensory input (Barlow [1974], but see also Olshausen and Field [1996])? How far can interpretations of perceptual stimuli be viewed as a choice of the briefest code that can reasonably be entertained, given what is known of the perceptual representations? And, at a theoretical level, to what extent does an MDL framework for perception have advantages over alternative theoretical approaches [Leeuwenberg and Boselie 1998]? The normative appeal and descriptive elegance of an MDL framework, even over the relatively limited territory that we have discussed here, seems sufficient justification for continuing to pursue Mach's dream that perception is driven by a search for economy, that perception is a search for minimal description length.

15.5   Acknowledgments

I thank Ulrike Hahn, Peter van der Helm, Boicho Kokinov, Mark Pitt, Paul Vitányi, an anonymous reviewer, participants at the NIPS workshop on MDL, 2001, and participants at the New Bulgarian University International Summer School in Cognitive Science, 2002, for discussions about these ideas. This work was partially supported by European Commission grant RTN-HPRN-CT-1999-00065, the Human Frontiers Program, the ESRC, the Leverhulme Trust, and Mercer Oliver Wyman.

References

Attneave, F. (1959). *Applications of Information Theory to Psychology*. New York: Holt, Rinehart & Winston.

Attneave, F., and R. Frost, (1969). The determination of perceived tridimensional orientation by minimum criteria. *Perception and Psychophysics, 6*, 391–396.

Barlow, H.B. (1961). The coding of sensory messages. In W.H. Thorpe and O.L. Zangwill (Eds). *Current Problems in Animal Behaviour*, (pp. 330–360). Cambridge, UK: Cambridge University Press.

Barlow, H.B. (1974). Inductive inference, coding, perception and language. *Perception, 3*, 123–134.

Bayliss, G.C. and J. Driver (1994). Parallel computation of symmetry but not repetition in single visual objects. *Visual Cognition, 1*, 377–400.

Bayliss, G.C. and J. Driver (1995). Obligatory edge assignment in vision: The role of figure and part segmentation in symmetry detection. *Journal of Experimental Psychology: Human Perception and Performance, 21*, 1323–1342.

Biederman, I. (1985). Human image understanding: Recent research and a theory. *Computer Vision, Graphics, and Image Processing, 32*, 29–73.

Bienenstock, E., S. Geman, and D. Potter (1998). Compositionality, MDL priors, and object recognition. In M.C. Mozer, M.I. Jordan and T. Petsche (Eds.), *Advances in Neural Information Processing Systems 9*. Cambridge, MA: MIT Press.

Binford, T.O. (1981). Inferring surfaces from images. *Articial Intelligence, 17*, 205 244.

Blakemore, C. (Ed.) (1990). *Vision: Coding and efficiency*. Cambridge, UK: Cambridge University Press/

Buffart, H., E. Leeuwenberg, and F. Restle (1981). Coding theory of visual pattern completion. *Journal of Experimental Psychology: Human Perception and Performance, 7*, 241–274.

Chater, N. (1996). Reconciling simplicity and likelihood principles in perceptual organization. *Psychological Review 103*, 566–581.

Chater, N., and M. Oaksford (1990). Autonomy, implementation and cognitive Architecture: A reply to Fodor and Pylyshyn. *Cognition, 34*, 93–107.

Chater, N. and Vitányi, P. (2003). Inference to the simplest description: An inference principle in science and cognition. Unpublished manuscript.

Chater, N., P. Vitányi, C. Olivers and D.G. Watson (under review). Simplicity and likelihood principles in perception: A mimicry theorem.

Cover, T.M., and J.A. Thomas (1991). *Elements of Information Theory*. New York: Wiley.

Dennett, D. C. (1991). *Consciousness Explained*. Harmondsworth, UK: Penguin.

Earman, J. (1992). *Bayes or Bust: A Critical Examination of Bayesian Confirmation Theory.* Cambridge, MA: MIT Press.

Feldman, J. (2000). Minimization of Boolean complexity in human concept learning. *Nature 407*, 630-633.

Gács, P., J.T. Tromp, and P.M.B. Vitányi (2001). Algorithmic statistics. *IEEE Transactions in Information Theory*, 47, 2443–2463.

Gao, Q., M. Li, and P. Vitányi (2000). Applying MDL to learning best model granularity, *Artificial Intelligence 121*, 1–29.

Garner, W.R. (1962). *Uncertainty and Structure as Psychological Concepts.* New York: Wiley.

Garner, W.R. (1974). *The Processing of Information and Structure.* Potomac, MD: Erlbaum.

Geman, S., and D. Geman. (1984). Stochastic relaxation, Gibbs distribution and the Bayesian restoration of images. *IEEE Transactions on Pattern Analysis and Machine Intelligence, 6*, 721–741.

Gregory, R.L. (1970). *The Intelligent Eye.* London: Weidenfeld & Nicolson.

Helm, P. van der, and E. Leeuwenberg (1991). Accessibility: A criterion for regularity and hierarchy in visual pattern code. *Journal of Mathematical Psychology, 35*, 151.

Helm, P. van der, and E. Leeuwenberg (1996). Goodness of visual regularities: A nontransformational approach. *Psychological Review, 103*, 429–456.

Helm, P. van der (2000). Simplicity versus likelihood in visual perception: From surprisals to precisals. *Psychological Bulletin, 126*, 770–800.

Helmholtz, H. von (1925). *Physiological Optics.* Volume 3. *The Theory of the Perceptions of Vision.* Translated from the 3rd German edition, 1910. Reprint, New York: Dover.

Hinton, G.E., Z. Ghahramani, and Y.W. Teh (2000). Learning to parse images. In S.A. Solla, T.K. Leen, and K.-R. Muller (Eds.), *Advances in Neural Information Processing Systems, 12*, pp. 463–469, Cambridge, MA: MIT Press.

Hintzman, D. H. (1986). Schema abstraction in a multiple-trace memory model. *Psychological Review 93*, 411–428.

Hochberg, J. (1982). How big is a stimulus? In J. Beck (Ed.), *Organization and Representation in Perception*, pp. 191–217, Hillsdale, NJ: Erlbaum.

Hochberg, J., and E. McAlister (1953). A quantitative approach to figure "goodness." *Journal of Experimental Psychology, 46*, 361–364.

Hoffman, D.D. (1998). *Visual Intelligence: How We Create What We See.* London: Norton.

Hoffman, D.D., and W.A. Richards (1984). Parts of recognition. *Cognition 18*, 65–96.

Horwich, P. (1982). Probability and Evidence. Cambridge, UK: Cambridge University Press.

Howson, C., and P. Urbach (1993). Scientific Reasoning: The Bayesian Approach. Chicago: Open Court.

Knill, D.C., and W.A. Richards (Eds.) (1996). Perception as Bayesian Inference. Cambridge, UK: Cambridge University Press.

Koenderink, J.J., and A.J. van Doorn. (1979). The internal representation of solid shape with respect to vision. *Biological Cybernetics 32*, 211–216.

Koffka, K. (1935). *Principles of Gestalt Psychology.* London: Routledge and Kegan Paul.

Kontkanen, P., P. Myllymäki, W. Buntine, J. Rissanen, and H. Tirri (2005). An MDL framework for data clustering. In P.D. Grünwald, I.J. Myung, and M.A. Pitt (Eds.), *Advances in Minimum Description Length: Theory and Applications.* Cambridge, MA: MIT Press.

Laming, D. (1997). *The Measurement of Sensation.* Oxford, UK: Oxford University Press.

Leeuwenberg, E., and F. Boselie (1988). Against the likelihood principle in visual form perception. *Psychological Review 95*, 485–491.

Li, M., and P.M.B. Vitányi (1997). *An Introduction to Kolmogorov Complexity and Its Applications.* 2nd edition, New York: Springer-Verlag.

Mach, E. (1959). *The Analysis of Sensations* (Translated by C. M. Williams and S. Waterlow. Original edition, 1886). Reprint, New York: Dover.

Marr, D. (1982). *Vision.* San Francisco: Freeman.

Miller, G. (1967). *The Psychology of Communication.* London: Penguin.

Mumford, D. (1996). Pattern Theory: a Unifying Perspective. In D.C. Knill and W. Richards (Eds.), *Perception as Bayesian inference*, pp. 25–62. Cambridge, UK: Cambridge University Press.

Nosofsky, R.M. (1991). Tests of an exemplar model for relating perceptual classification and recognition memory. Journal of Experimental Psychology: Human Perception and Performance, 17, 3–27.

Olshausen, B.A., and D.J. Field (1996). Emergence of simple-cell receptive-field properties by learning a sparse code for natural images. *Nature, 381*, 607–609.

O'Regan, J.K., and A. Noe (2001). A sensorimotor account of vision and visual consciousness. *Behavioral and Brain Sciences 24.*

Pomerantz, J.R., and M. Kubovy. (1986). Theoretical approaches to perceptual organization: Simplicity and likelihood principles. In K.R. Boff, L. Kaufman, and J.P. Thomas (Eds.) Handbook of Perception and Human Performance. Volume 2, Cognitive Processes and Performance, pp.36-1–36-46. New York: Wiley.

Pothos, E., and Chater, N. (2002). A simplicity principle in unsupervised human categorization. Cognitive Science 26, 303-343.

Quinlan, J.R., and R.L. Rivest (1989). Inferring decision trees using the Minimum Description Length principle. *Information and Computation, 80*, 227–248.

Restle, F. (1970). Theory of serial pattern learning: Structural trees. *Psychological Review 77*, 481–495.

Restle, F. (1979). Coding theory of the perception of motion configurations. *Psychological Review 86*, 1–24.

Rieke, F., D. Warland, R. de Ruyter van Steveninck, and W. Bialek (1997). *Spikes: Exploring the Neural Code*. Cambridge, MA: MIT Press.

Rissanen, J.J. (1986). Stochastic complexity and modeling. *Annals of Statistics 14*, 1080–1100.

Rissanen, J.J. (1989). *Stochastic Complexity in Statistical Inquiry*. Singapore: World Scientific.

Rock, I. (1981). *The Logic of Perception*. Cambridge, MA: MIT Press.

Shannon, C. (1948). A mathematical theory of communication. *Bell Systems Technical Journal 27*, 379-423.

Shepard, R.N. (1992). The perceptual organization of colors: An adaptation to regularities of the terrestrial world? In J.H. Barkow, L. Cosmides, and J. Tooby (Eds.), The Adapted Mind: Evolutionary Psychology and the Generation of Culture. New York: Oxford University Press.

Sperber, D., D. Premack, and A.J. Premack (Eds.) (1995). *Causal Cognition: A Multidisciplinary Debate*. New York: Oxford University Press.

Vereshchagin, N., and P. Vitányi (2002). Kolmogorov's Structure functions with an application to the foundations of model selection. In *Proceedings of the Fourty-seventh IEEE Symposium on the Foundations of Computer Science*, pp. 751–760.

Vitányi, P., and M. Li (2000). Minimum description length induction, Bayesianism, and Kolmogorov complexity. *IEEE Transactions on Information Theory 46*, 446–464.

Wallace, C.S., and P.R. Freeman (1987). Estimation and inference by compact coding. *Journal of the Royal Statistical Society, Series B, 49*, 240–251.

Weiss, Y. (1997). Interpreting images by propagating Bayesian beliefs. In M.C. Mozer, M.I. Jordan, and T. Petsche (Eds.), *Advances in Neural Information Processing Systems 9*, pp. 908–915. Cambridge, MA: MIT Press.

16 Minimum Description Length and Cognitive Modeling

Yong Su
Department of Electrical Engineering
Ohio State University
2015 Neil Avenue Mall
Columbus, Ohio 43210–1272
USA
su.85@osu.edu
http://peekaboo.hopto.org

In Jae Myung
Department of Psychology
Ohio State University
1885 Neil Avenue Mall
Columbus, Ohio 43210–1222
USA
myung.1@osu.edu
http://quantrm2.psy.ohio-state.edu/injae/

Mark A. Pitt
Department of Psychology
Ohio State University
1885 Neil Avenue Mall
Columbus, Ohio 43210–1222
USA
pitt.2@osu.edu
http://lpl.psy.ohio-state.edu

The question of how one should decide between competing explanations of data is at the heart of the scientific enterprise. In the field of cognitive science, mathematical models are increasingly being advanced as explanations of cognitive behavior. In the application of the minimum description length (MDL) principle to the selection of these models, one of the major obstacles is to calculate Fisher information. In this study we provide a general formula to calculate Fisher information for models of cognition that assume multinomial or normal distributions. We also illustrate the usage of the formula for models of categorization, information integration, retention, and psychophysics. Further, we compute and compare the complexity penalty terms of two recent versions of MDL [Rissanen 1996, 2001] for a multinomial model. Finally, the adequacy of MDL is demonstrated in the selection of retention models.

16.1   Introduction

The study of cognition is concerned with describing the mental processes that underlie behavior and developing theories that explain their operation. Often the theories are specified using verbal language, which leads to an unavoidable limitation: lack of precision. Mathematical modeling represents an alternative approach to overcoming this limitation by inferring structural and functional properties of a cognitive process from experimental data in explicit mathematical expressions.

Formally, a mathematical model or model class[1] is defined as a parametric family of probability density functions, $f_{X|\Theta}(x|\theta)$, as a Riemannian manifold in the space of distributions [Kass and Vos 1997], with $x \in \mathcal{X}$ and $\theta \in \Omega$. $\mathcal{X}$ and Ω are the sample space and parameter space respectively. The sample space or parameter space could be a Euclidean space with arbitrary dimension. Thus the dimension of the parameter here corresponds to what is commonly referred to as the number of parameters of the model.

In modeling cognition, we wish to identify the model, from a set of candidate models, that generated the observed data. This is an ill-posed problem because information in the finite data sample is rarely sufficient to point to a single model. Rather, multiple models may provide equally good descriptions of the data. In statistics, this "ill-posedness" of model selection is overcome by reformulating the inference problem as one of making a best guess as to which model provides the closest approximation, in some defined sense, to the true but unknown model that generated the data. The particular measure of such an approximation, which is widely recognized among modelers in statistics and computer science, is *generalizability*. Generalizability, or predictive accuracy, refers to a model's ability to accurately

---

1. Strictly speaking, 'model' and 'model class' are not interchangeable. A model class consists of a collection of models in which each model represents a single probability distribution. In this chapter, however, we often use these terms interchangeably when the context makes it clear what we are referring to.

predict future, as yet unseen, data samples from the same process that generated the currently observed sample.

A formal definition of generalizability can be given in terms of a *discrepancy function* that measures the degree of approximation or similarity between two probability distributions. A discrepancy function $D(f, g)$ between two distributions, f and g, is some well-behaved function (e.g., Kullback-Leibler information divergence [Kullback and Leibler 1951]) that satisfies $D(f, g) > D(f, f) = 0$ for $f \neq g$. Generalizability could be defined as

$$\mathrm{E}^{f_T}[D(f_T, f_M)] \triangleq \int_{\mathcal{X}} D(f_T(x), f_M(\hat{\theta}(x))) f_T(x) dx, \qquad (16.1)$$

where f_T and f_M denote the probability distributions of the true and guessing models and $\hat{\theta}(x)$ is the maximum likelihood (ML) estimate of the parameter. According to the above equation, generalizability is a mean discrepancy between the true model and the best-fitting member of the model class of interest, averaged across all possible data that could be observed under the true model. The basic tenet of model selection is that among a set of competing model classes, one should select the one that optimizes generalizability [i.e., minimizes the quantity in (16.1)]. However, generalizability is not directly observable and instead, one must estimate the measure from a data sample by considering the characteristics of the model class under investigation.

Several generalizability estimates have been proposed. They include Bayesian information criterion (BIC) [Schwarz 1978] and cross-validation (CV) [Stone 1974]. In BIC, generalizability is estimated by trading off a model's *goodness-of-fit* with *model complexity*. Goodness-of-fit refers to how well a model fits the particular data set, whereas model complexity or flexibility refers to a model's ability to fit arbitrary patterns of data. The BIC criterion, which is derived as an asymptotic approximation of a quantity related to the Bayes factor [Kass and Raftery 1995], is defined as

$$\mathrm{BIC} \triangleq -\log f_{X|\Theta}(x|\hat{\theta}) + \frac{k}{2}\log(n),$$

where $\log(\cdot)$ is the natural logarithm function of base e, k is the dimension of the parameter, and n is the sample size. The first term represents a goodness-of-fit measure and the second term represents a complexity measure. From the BIC viewpoint, the number of parameters (k) and the sample size (n) are the only relevant facets of complexity. BIC, however, ignores another important facet of model complexity, namely, the functional form of the model equation [Myung and Pitt 1997]. Functional form refers to the way in which the model's parameters are combined to define the model equation. For example, two models, $x = at + b$ and $x = at^b$, have the same number of parameters but differ in functional form.

CV is an easy-to-use, sampling-based method of estimating a model's generalizability. In CV, the data are split into two samples, the calibration sample and the validation sample. The model of interest is fitted to the calibration sample and the best-fit parameter values are obtained. With these values fixed, the model is fitted again, this time to the validation sample. The resulting fit defines the model's generalizability estimate. Note that this estimation is done without an explicit consideration of complexity. Unlike BIC, CV takes into account functional form as well as the number of parameters, but given the implicit nature of CV, it is not clear how this is achieved.

The principle of minimum description length (MDL) [Barron, Rissanen, and Yu 1998; Grünwald 2005; Hansen and Yu 2001; Rissanen 1989, 1996, 2001], which was developed within the domain of algorithmic coding theory in computer science [Li and Vitányi 1997], represents a new conceptualization of the model selection problem. In MDL, both models and data are viewed as codes that can be compressed, and the goal of model selection is to choose the model class that permits the greatest compression of data in its description.[2] The shortest code length obtainable with the help of a given model class is called the *stochastic complexity* of the model class. In this chapter we focus on two implementations of stochastic complexity: a *Fisher information approximated normalized maximum likelihood* (FIA) [Rissanen 1996] and *normalized maximum Likelihood* (NML) [Rissanen 1996, 2001]. Each, as an analytic realization of Occam's razor, combines measures of goodness-of-fit and model complexity in a way that remedies the shortcomings of BIC and CV: complexity is explicitly defined and functional form is included in the definition.

The purpose of this chapter is threefold. The first is to address an issue that we have had to deal with in applying MDL to the selection of mathematical models of cognition [Lee 2002; Pitt, Myung, and Zhang 2002]. Calculation of the Fisher information can sometimes be sufficiently difficult to be a deterrent to using the measure. We walk the reader through the application of a straightforward and efficient formula for computing Fisher information for two broad classes of models in the field, those that have multinomial or independent normal distributions. Next we compare the relative performance of FIA and NML for one type of model in cognition. Finally, we present an example application of the MDL criteria in the selection of retention (i.e., memory) models in cognitive science. We begin by briefly reviewing the two MDL criteria, FIA and NML.

16.2   Recent Formulations of MDL

It is well established in statistics that choosing among a set of competing models based solely on goodness-of-fit can result in the selection of an unnecessarily complex model that overfits the data [Pitt and Myung 2002]. The problem of overfitting is mitigated by choosing models using a generalizability measure that strikes the right balance between goodness-of-fit and model complexity. This is what

---

2. The code here refers to the probability distribution p of a random quantity. The code length is justified as $\log(1/p)$ from Shannon's information theory.

both the FIA and NML criteria achieve. These two criteria are related to each other in that the former is obtained as an asymptotic approximation of the latter.

16.2.1   FIA Criterion

By considering Fisher information, Rissanen proposed the following model selection criterion [Rissanen 1996]:

$$\text{FIA} \triangleq -\log f_{X|\Theta}(x|\hat{\theta}) + C_{\text{FIA}}$$

with

$$C_{\text{FIA}} \triangleq \frac{k}{2} \log \frac{n}{2\pi} + \log \int_{\Omega} \sqrt{|I(\theta)|} d\theta, \qquad (16.2)$$

where Ω is the parameter space on which the model class is defined and $I(\theta)$ is the Fisher information of sample size one given by, e.g., [Schervish 1995],

$$I_{i,j}(\theta) = -\text{E}_{\theta} \left[\frac{\partial^2}{\partial \theta_i \partial \theta_j} \log f_{X|\Theta}(x|\theta) \right],$$

where E_{θ} denotes the expectation over data space under the model class $f_{X|\Theta}(x|\theta)$ given a θ value. In terms of coding theory, the value of FIA represents the length in "ebits" of the shortest description of the data the model class can provide. According to the MDL principle the model class that minimizes FIA extracts the most regularity in the data and therefore is to be preferred.

Inspection of C_{FIA} in (16.2) reveals four discernible facets of model complexity: the number of parameters k, sample size n, parameter range Ω, and the functional form of the model equation as implied in $I(\theta)$. Their contributions to model complexity can be summarized in terms of three observations. First, C_{FIA} consists of two additive terms. The first term captures the number of parameters and the second term captures the functional form through the Fisher information matrix $I(\theta)$. Notice the sample size, n, appears only in the first term; this implies that as the sample size becomes large, the relative contribution of the second term to that of the first becomes negligible, essentially reducing C_{FIA} to the complexity penalty of BIC. Second, because the first term is a logarithmic function of sample size but a linear function of the number of parameters, the impact of sample size on model complexity is less dramatic than that of the number of parameters. Finally, the calculation of the second term depends on the parameter range on which the integration of a non-negative quantity in the parameter space is required. As such, the greater the ranges of the parameters, the larger the value of the integral, and therefore the more complex the model.

Regarding the calculation of the second term of C_{FIA}, there are at least two nontrivial challenges to overcome: integration over multidimensional parameter space and calculation of the Fisher information matrix. It is in general not possible to obtain a closed-form solution of the integral. Instead, the solution must be sought using a numerical integration method such as Markov chain Monte Carlo

[Gilks, Richardson, and Spiegelhalter 1996]. Second, with partial derivatives and expectation in the definition of Fisher information, direct element-by-element hand calculation of the Fisher information matrix can be a daunting task. This is because the number of elements in the Fisher information matrix is the square of the dimension of the parameter. For example, with a 100-dimensional parameter, we need to find 10,000 elements of the Fisher information matrix, which would be quite a chore. Efficient computation of Fisher information is a significant hurdle in the application of MDL to cognitive modeling [Pitt et al. 2002]. This chapter presents a method to overcome it. In section 16.3, we provide a simple algebraic formula for the Fisher information matrix that does not require the cumbersome element-by-element calculations and expectations.

16.2.2 NML Criterion

FIA represents important progress in understanding and formalizing model selection. It was, however, derived as a second-order limiting solution to the problem of finding the ideal code length [Rissanen 1996], with the higher-order terms being left off. Rissanen further refined the solution by reformulating the ideal code length problem as a minimax problem in information theory [Rissanen 2001].[3] The basic idea of this new approach is to identify a single probability distribution that is "universally" representative of an entire model class of probability distributions in the sense that the desired distribution mimics the behavior of any member of that class [Barron et al. 1998]. Specifically, the resulting solution to the minimax problem represents the optimal probability distribution that can encode data with the minimum mean code length subject to the restrictions of the model class of interest.

The minimax problem is defined as finding a probability distribution or code p^* such that

$$p^* \triangleq \operatorname*{arginf}_{p} \operatorname*{sup}_{q} \mathrm{E}^q \left[\log \frac{f_{X|\Theta}(x|\hat{\theta})}{p(x)} \right],$$

where p and q range over the set of all distributions satisfying certain regularity conditions [Rissanen 2001], q is the data-generating distribution (i.e., true model), $\mathrm{E}^q[\cdot]$ is the expectation with respect to the distribution q, and $\hat{\theta}$ is the ML estimate of the parameter. Given a model class of probability distributions $f_{X|\Theta}(x|\theta)$, the minimax problem is to identify one probability distribution p^* that minimizes the mean difference in code length between the desired distribution and the best-fitting member of the model class where the mean is taken with respect to the worst-case scenario. The data-generating distribution q does not have to be a member of the model class. In other words, the model class need not be correctly specified.

---

3. Although formal proofs of the NML criterion were presented in [Rissanen 2001], its preliminary ideas were already discussed in [Rissanen 1996].

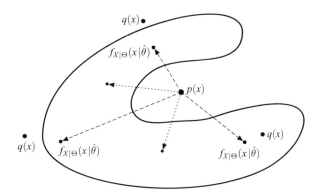

Figure 16.1   The minimax problem in a model manifold.

Similarly, the desired probability distribution, as a solution to the minimax problem, does not have to be a member of the model class. The intuitive account of the minimax problem is illustrated schematically in Figure 16.1.

The solution to the minimax problem [Shtarkov 1987] is given by

$$p^* = \frac{f_{X|\Theta}(x|\hat{\theta})}{C_f},$$

where

$$C_f \triangleq \int_{\hat{\theta}(x)\in\Omega} f_{X|\Theta}(x|\hat{\theta}(x))dx.$$

Note that p^* is the maximum likelihood of the current data sample divided by the sum of maximum likelihoods over all possible data samples. As such, p^* is called the *normalized* maximum likelihood (NML) distribution, which generalizes the notion of ML. Recall that ML is employed to identify the parameter values that optimize the likelihood function (i.e., goodness-of-fit) within a given model class. Likewise, NML is employed to identify the model class, among a set of competing model classes, that optimizes generalizability.

C_f, the normalizing constant of the NML distribution, represents a complexity measure of the model class. It denotes the *sum of all best fits* the model class can provide collectively. Complexity is positively related to this value. The larger the sum of the model class, the more complex the model is. As such, this quantity formalizes the intuitive notion of complexity often referred to as a model's ability to fit diverse patterns of data [Myung and Pitt 1997] or as the "number" of different data patterns the model can fit well (i.e., flexibility) [Myung, Balasubramanian, and Pitt 2000]. It turns out that the logarithm of C_f is equal to the minmax value of the mean code length difference obtained when the NML distribution happens to be the data-generating distribution [Rissanen 2001]. In other words, another interpretation of C_f is that it is the minimized worst prediction error the model class makes for the data generated from the NML distribution.

The desired selection criterion, NML, is defined as the code length of the NML distribution p^* (i.e., $-\log(p^*)$),

$$\text{NML} \triangleq -\log f_{X|\Theta}(x|\hat{\theta}) + C_{\text{NML}},$$

where

$$C_{\text{NML}} \triangleq \log \int_{\hat{\theta}(x) \in \Omega} f_{X|\Theta}(x|\hat{\theta}(x)) dx. \qquad (16.3)$$

As presented above, the difference between FIA and NML is in their complexity measure, C_{FIA} and C_{NML}. Since C_{FIA} can be obtained from a Taylor series expansion of C_{NML} under the assumption of large sample sizes, C_{NML} captures the full scope of model complexity, thereby being a more complete quantification of model complexity. Like C_{FIA}, C_{NML} is also nontrivial to compute. They both require evaluation of an integral, though different kinds: integration over the parameter space in C_{FIA} and integration over the data (sample) space in C_{NML}. In the next section, we provide an easy-to-use formula to calculate the Fisher information matrix when computing C_{FIA}. Calculation of C_{NML} is more challenging, and requires two steps of heavy-duty computation: step 1, maximization of the likelihood function, given a data sample, over the parameter space on which the model class is defined; and step 2, integration of the maximized likelihood over the entire data space. In practice, the first step of parameter estimation is mostly done numerically, which is tricky because of the local maxima problem. The second step is even harder as sample space is usually of much higher dimension than parameter space. Another goal of our investigation is to compare these two complexity measures for specific models of cognition to examine the similarity of their answers (see Section 16.4).

16.3   Fisher Information

As discussed in Section 16.2.1, a major challenge of applying FIA is to compute the Fisher information matrix $I(\theta)$, especially when the dimension of the parameter space is large. Although the standard formula for the Fisher information matrix has been known in the literature, it is often presented implicitly without the detail of its derivation. In this section, we show its derivation in detail and provide a unified, easy-to-use formula to compute it for a model having an arbitrary dimensional parameter defined in terms of multinomial or independent normal distributions—the two most commonly assumed distributions in cognitive modeling. The resulting formula, which is obtained under simplifying assumptions, greatly eases the computation of the Fisher information by eliminating the need for both numerical expectation and second-order differentiation of the likelihood function. We also demonstrate the application of this formula in four areas of cognitive modeling: categorization, information integration, retention, and psychophysics.

16.3.1   Models with Multinomial Distribution

We begin by defining the notation. Consider the model $f_{X|\Theta}(x|\theta)$ with a multinomial distribution. The parameter $\theta = [\theta_1, \ldots, \theta_K]^T$, and $X|\Theta = [X_1|\Theta, \ldots, X_N|\Theta]^T$. It is assumed that $\{X_n|\Theta\}$ is independent and each follows a multinomial distribution with C categories and sample size n': $X_n|\Theta \sim Mult_C(n', p_{n,1}(\theta), \ldots, p_{n,C}(\theta))$. K is the parameter dimension number, N is the random vector dimension number, and C is the number of categories. Different selection of $\{p_{n,c}(\theta)\}$ yields different models. So

$$f_{X_n|\Theta}(x_n|\theta) = \binom{n'}{x_{n,1}, \ldots, x_{n,C}} \prod_{c=1}^{C} p_{n,c}(\theta)^{x_{n,c}}$$

with respect to a counting measure on $\{(x_{n,1}, \ldots, x_{n,C}) : \sum_{c=1}^{C} x_{n,c} = n', \ x_{n,c} \in \{0, \ldots, n'\}\}$. Since $\{X_n|\Theta\}$ is independent,

$$f_{X|\Theta}(x|\theta) = \prod_{n=1}^{N} \binom{n'}{x_{n,1}, \ldots, x_{n,C}} \prod_{c=1}^{C} p_{n,c}(\theta)^{x_{n,c}}$$

$$\log f_{X|\Theta}(x|\theta) = \sum_{n=1}^{N} \left(\log \binom{n'}{x_{n,1}, \ldots, x_{n,C}} + \sum_{c=1}^{C} x_{n,c} \log p_{n,c}(\theta) \right).$$

The first and second derivatives of the log-likelihood function are then calculated as

$$\frac{\partial \log f_{X|\Theta}(x|\theta)}{\partial \theta_i} = \sum_{n=1}^{N} \sum_{c=1}^{C} \frac{x_{n,c}}{p_{n,c}(\theta)} \frac{\partial p_{n,c}(\theta)}{\partial \theta_i}$$

$$\frac{\partial^2 \log f_{X|\Theta}(x|\theta)}{\partial \theta_i \partial \theta_j} = \sum_{n=1}^{N} \sum_{c=1}^{C} \frac{-x_{n,c}}{p_{n,c}^2(\theta)} \frac{\partial p_{n,c}(\theta)}{\partial \theta_i} \frac{\partial p_{n,c}(\theta)}{\partial \theta_j} + \frac{x_{n,c}}{p_{n,c}(\theta)} \frac{\partial^2 p_{n,c}(\theta)}{\partial \theta_i \partial \theta_j}.$$

With the regularity conditions [Schervish 1995, p. 111] held for the model $f_{X|\Theta}(x|\theta)$ in question, we write one element of Fisher information matrix of sample size one as

$$\begin{aligned} I_{i,j}(\theta) &= -\mathrm{E}_\theta \left[\frac{\partial^2}{\partial \theta_i \partial \theta_j} \log f_{X|\Theta}(x|\theta) \right] \\ &= \sum_{n=1}^{N} \sum_{c=1}^{C} \frac{1}{p_{n,c}(\theta)} \frac{\partial p_{n,c}(\theta)}{\partial \theta_i} \frac{\partial p_{n,c}(\theta)}{\partial \theta_j} - \frac{\partial^2 p_{n,c}(\theta)}{\partial \theta_i \partial \theta_j} \\ &= \sum_{n=1}^{N} \sum_{c=1}^{C} \frac{1}{p_{n,c}(\theta)} \frac{\partial p_{n,c}(\theta)}{\partial \theta_i} \frac{\partial p_{n,c}(\theta)}{\partial \theta_j} \\ &= \sum_{l=1}^{NC} \frac{1}{p_l(\theta)} \frac{\partial p_l(\theta)}{\partial \theta_i} \frac{\partial p_l(\theta)}{\partial \theta_j}, \end{aligned}$$

where $p_l(\theta) \triangleq p_{n,c}(\theta)$ and $l = (n-1)C + c$. Rewriting the above result in matrix form yields

$$I(\theta) = P^T \Lambda^{-1} P \qquad (16.4)$$

with

$$
\begin{aligned}
P &\triangleq \frac{\partial\,(p_1(\theta),\ldots,p_{NC}(\theta))}{\partial\,(\theta_1,\ldots,\theta_K)} \\
\Lambda &\triangleq \mathrm{diag}(p_1(\theta),\ldots,p_{NC}(\theta)),
\end{aligned}
$$

where $\frac{\partial(p_1(\theta),\ldots,p_{NC}(\theta))}{\partial(\theta_1,\ldots,\theta_K)} = [P_{i,j}]$ is the $NC \times K$ Jacobian matrix with $P_{i,j} = \frac{\partial p_i(\theta)}{\partial \theta_j}$ and Λ is the diagonal matrix with $p_1(\theta),\ldots,p_{NC}(\theta)$ as the diagonal elements. With (16.4), to calculate $I(\theta)$, we need to evaluate only two sets of functions: $\{p_l(\theta)\}$, which are nothing but the model equations; and the first derivatives $\{\frac{\partial p_l(\theta)}{\partial \theta_k}\}$, which can easily be determined in analytic form.

Interestingly enough, (16.4) looks strikingly similar to the well-known formula for the reparameterization of Fisher information [Schervish 1995, p. 115]. There is, however, an important difference between the two. Equation (16.4) tells us how to calculate Fisher information for a given model in which the Jacobian matrix P is in general nonsquare. On the other hand, the reparameterization formula reveals how to relate Fisher information from one parameterization to another, once the Fisher information has been obtained with a given parameterization. Since the two parameterizations are related to each other though a one-to-one transformation, the corresponding Jacobian matrix P is always square for reparameterization.

In the following, we demonstrate application of (16.4) for models of categorization, information integration, and retention.

Categorization   Categorization is the cognitive operation by which we identify an object or thing as a member of a particular group, called a category. We categorize a robin as a bird, a German shepherd as a dog, and both as mammals. Since no two dogs are exactly alike, categorization helps us avoid being overwhelmed by the sheer detail of the environment and the accompanying mental operation that would otherwise be required to represent every incident we encounter as a unique event [Glass and Holyoak 1986]. Without categorization, the world would appear to us as an incidental collection of unrelated events. Further, categorization helps us make inferences about an object that has been assigned to a category. For example, having categorized a moving vehicle as a tank, we can infer that it is an all-terrain vehicle, is armored, is armed with a cannon gun mounted inside a rotating turret, and can damage the road.

In mathematical modeling of categorization, an object, often called a category exemplar, is represented as a point in a multidimensional psychological space in which the value of each coordinate represents the magnitude or presence/absence of an attribute such as height, weight, color, whether it is an animal or not, and so on. In a typical categorization experiment, participants are asked to categorize a series of stimuli, presented on a computer screen, into one or more predefined categories. The stimuli are generated from a factorial manipulation of two or more stimulus attributes. As a example, we illustrate the application of (16.4) for the generalized context model (GCM) [Nosofsky 1986].

According to the GCM model, category decisions are made based on a similarity comparison between the input stimulus and stored exemplars of a given category. Specifically, this model requires no specific restrictions on K, N, and C in computing complexity, and assumes that the probability of choosing category c in response to input stimulus n is given by

$$p_{n,c} = \frac{\sum\limits_{m \in C_c} s_{nm}}{\sum\limits_{q} \sum\limits_{p \in C_q} s_{np}},$$

where C_c is the set of all indices of the prototype stimuli in category c and

$$s_{ij} = \exp\left(-s \cdot \left(\sum_{t=1}^{K-1} w_t |x_{it} - x_{jt}|^r\right)^{1/r}\right).$$

In the above equation, s_{ij} is a similarity measure between multidimensional stimuli i and j, s (> 0) is a sensitivity or scaling parameter, w_t is a non-negative attention weight given to attribute t satisfying $\sum_{t=1}^{K-1} w_t = 1$, and x_{it} is the tth coordinate value of stimulus i. According to the above equation, similarity between two stimuli is assumed to be an exponentially decreasing function of their distance, which is measured by the Minkowski metric with metric parameter r (≥ 1). Note that the parameter θ consists of $\theta = [\theta_1, \ldots, \theta_K]^T \triangleq [w_1, \ldots, w_{K-2}, s, r]^T$.

The first derivatives of the model equation are computed as

$$\frac{\partial p_{n,c}}{\partial \theta_k} = \frac{\left(\sum\limits_{m \in C_c} \frac{\partial s_{nm}}{\partial \theta_k}\right)\left(\sum\limits_{q} \sum\limits_{p \in C_q} s_{np}\right) - \left(\sum\limits_{m \in C_c} s_{nm}\right)\left(\sum\limits_{q} \sum\limits_{p \in C_q} \frac{\partial s_{np}}{\partial \theta_k}\right)}{\left(\sum\limits_{q} \sum\limits_{p \in C_q} s_{np}\right)^2}$$

with

$$\frac{\partial s_{ij}}{\partial \theta_k} = \begin{cases} s_{ij} \cdot \frac{-s}{r} \cdot T_{ij}^{\frac{1-r}{r}} \cdot (|x_{ik} - x_{jk}|^r - |x_{iK-1} - x_{jK-1}|^r) & k = 1, \ldots, K-2 \\ s_{ij} \cdot -T_{ij}^{\frac{1}{r}} & k = K-1 \\ s_{ij} \cdot \log s_{ij} \cdot \left(\frac{-1}{r^2} \cdot \log T_{ij} + \frac{\sum_{t=1}^{K-2} w_t |x_{it} - x_{jt}|^r \log |x_{it} - x_{jt}|}{r T_{ij}}\right) & k = K \end{cases}$$

where $T_{ij} \triangleq \sum_{t=1}^{K-1} w_t |x_{it} - x_{jt}|^r$.

Using $l = (n-1)C + c$, we can easily obtain $\{p_l(\theta)\}$ and $\{\frac{\partial p_l(\theta)}{\partial \theta_k}\}$ from $\{p_{n,c}(\theta)\}$ and $\{\frac{\partial p_{n,c}(\theta)}{\partial \theta_k}\}$ derived above. Plugging these into (16.4) yields the desired Fisher information matrix.

Information Integration Models of information integration are concerned with how information from independent sources (e.g., sensory and contextual) are combined during perceptual identification. For example, in phonemic identification we might be interested in how an input stimulus is perceived as /ba/ or /da/ based on the cues presented in one or two modalities (e.g., auditory only or auditory plus visual). In a typical information integration experiment, participants are asked to identify stimuli that are factorially manipulated along two or more stimulus dimensions.

Information integration models represent a slightly more restricted case compared to categorization models. As with categorization models, the stimulus is represented as a vector in multidimensional space. K is the sum of all stimulus dimensions and N is the product of all stimulus dimensions. To illustrate the application of (16.4), consider models for a two-factor experiment (e.g., FLMP, LIM).[4] For such models, the response probability p_{ij} of classifying an input stimulus specified by stimulus dimensions i and j as /ba/ vs. /da/ can be written as

$$p_{ij} = h(\theta_i, \lambda_j), \tag{16.5}$$

where θ_i and λ_j ($i \in \{1, \ldots, I\}$, $j \in \{1, \ldots, J\}$) are parameters representing the strength of the corresponding feature dimensions. So we have $K = I+J$, $N = I \cdot J$, and $C = 2$. With the restriction on C, the above model assumes the binomial probability distribution, which is a special case of multinomial distribution so (16.4) can still be used. Now, we further simplify the desired Fisher information matrix by taking into account $C = 2$ and $\sum_{c=1}^{C} p_{n,c} = 1$ as follows:

$$
\begin{aligned}
I_{i,j}(\theta) &= \sum_{n=1}^{N} \sum_{c=1}^{C} \frac{1}{p_{n,c}(\theta)} \frac{\partial p_{n,c}(\theta)}{\partial \theta_i} \frac{\partial p_{n,c}(\theta)}{\partial \theta_j} \\
&= \sum_{n=1}^{N} \frac{1}{p_n(\theta)(1 - p_n(\theta))} \frac{\partial p_n(\theta)}{\partial \theta_i} \frac{\partial p_n(\theta)}{\partial \theta_j}
\end{aligned}
$$

with $p_n(\theta) \triangleq p_{n,1}(\theta) = p_{ij}(\theta)$, $n = (i-1)J + j$ and $\theta = [\theta_1, \theta_2, \ldots, \theta_{I+J}]^T \triangleq [\theta_1, \theta_2, \ldots, \theta_I, \lambda_1, \lambda_2, \ldots, \lambda_J]^T$. So

$$I(\theta) = B^T \Delta^{-1} B \tag{16.6}$$

with

$$
\begin{aligned}
B &\triangleq \frac{\partial \left(p_1(\theta), \ldots, p_{I \cdot J}(\theta) \right)}{\partial \left(\theta_1, \ldots, \theta_{I+J} \right)} \\
\Delta &\triangleq \operatorname{diag}(p_1(\theta)(1 - p_1(\theta)), \ldots, p_{I \cdot J}(\theta)(1 - p_{I \cdot J}(\theta))).
\end{aligned}
$$

It is worth noting that the number of diagonal elements of $\Delta \in \mathbb{R}^{N \times N}$ is one half of that of Λ in (16.4).

---

4. Fuzzy logical model of perception [Oden and Massaro 1978], linear integration model [Anderson 1981].

Applying the above results to the generic model equation (16.5), we note that since $n = (i-1)J + j$, $i \in \{1, \ldots, I\}$ and $j \in \{1, \ldots, J\}$, we have $i = \lfloor (n-1)/J \rfloor + 1$, $j = n - J \lfloor (n-1)/J \rfloor$. So

$$p_n(\theta) = h(\theta_{\lfloor (n-1)/J \rfloor + 1}, \theta_{n - J\lfloor (n-1)/J \rfloor})$$

$$\frac{\partial p_n(\theta)}{\partial \theta_k} = \frac{\partial h(\theta_{\lfloor (n-1)/J \rfloor + 1}, \theta_{n - J\lfloor (n-1)/J \rfloor})}{\partial \theta_k},$$

where $\lfloor x \rfloor \triangleq \max\{n \in \mathbb{Z} : n \leq x\}$.

Retention   Retention refers to the mental ability to retain information about learned events over time. In a typical experimental setup, participants are presented with a list of items (e.g., words or nonsense syllables) to study, and afterward are asked to recall or recognize them at varying time delays since study. Of course, the longer the interval between the time of stimulus presentation and the time of later recollection, the less likely the event will be remembered. Therefore, the probability of retaining in memory an item after time t is a monotonically decreasing function of t.

Models of retention are concerned with the specific form of the rate at which information retention drops (i.e., forgetting occurs) [Rubin and Wenzel 1996; Wickens 1998]. For instance, the exponential model assumes that the retention probability follows the form $h(a, b, t) = ae^{-bt}$ with the parameter $\theta = (a, b)$, whereas the power model assumes $h(a, b, t) = at^{-b}$. For such two-parameter models, we have the parameter dimension $K = 2$ and the number of categories $C = 2$. It is then straightforward to show in this case that

$$|I(\theta)| = \sum_{n, l=1;\ n<l}^{N} \frac{\left(\frac{\partial p_n(\theta)}{\partial \theta_1} \frac{\partial p_l(\theta)}{\partial \theta_2} - \frac{\partial p_n(\theta)}{\partial \theta_2} \frac{\partial p_l(\theta)}{\partial \theta_1} \right)^2}{p_n(\theta)(1 - p_n(\theta))p_l(\theta)(1 - p_l(\theta))}, \qquad (16.7)$$

which reduces to the previous result in [Pitt et al. 2002, Appendix A] for $K = 1$,

$$|I(\theta)| = \sum_{n=1}^{N} \frac{\left(\frac{dp_n(\theta)}{d\theta} \right)^2}{p_n(\theta)(1 - p_n(\theta))}. \qquad (16.8)$$

Close inspection and comparison of (16.7) and (16.8) strongly suggest the following form of Fisher information for the general case of $K \geq 1$:

$$|I(\theta)| = \sum_{n_1 < n_2 \cdots < n_K = 1}^{N} \frac{\left| \frac{\partial (p_{n_1}(\theta), p_{n_2}(\theta), \ldots, p_{n_K}(\theta))}{\partial (\theta_1, \theta_2, \ldots, \theta_K)} \right|^2}{\prod_{k=1}^{K} p_{n_k}(\theta)(1 - p_{n_k}(\theta))} \qquad (16.9)$$

The above expression, though elegant, is a conjecture whose validity has yet to be proven (e.g., by induction). On the other hand, one might find it computationally more efficient to use the original equation (16.6), rather than (16.9).

16.3.2   Models with Normal Distribution

For models with independent normal distribution, the form of the Fisher information formula turns out to be similar to that of the multinomial distribution, as shown in the following.

Look at a model $f_{X|\Theta}(x|\theta)$ with normal distribution. The parameter $\theta = [\theta_1, \theta_2, \ldots, \theta_K]^T$, $X|\Theta = [X_1|\Theta, X_2|\Theta, \ldots, X_N|\Theta]^T$, and $X|\Theta \sim \mathcal{N}_N(\mu(\theta), \sigma(\theta))$ with $\mu \in \mathbb{R}^N$ and $\sigma \in \mathbb{R}^{N \times N}$. Different choices of $\mu(\theta)$ and $\sigma(\theta)$ correspond to defining different models. Since $X|\Theta \sim \mathcal{N}_N(\mu(\theta), \sigma(\theta))$, we have

$$f_{X|\Theta}(x|\theta) = (2\pi)^{-\frac{N}{2}} |\sigma(\theta)|^{-\frac{1}{2}} \exp\left(-\frac{1}{2}(x - \mu(\theta))^T \sigma(\theta)^{-1}(x - \mu(\theta))\right)$$

with respect to the Lebesgue measure on $\mathbb{R}^N$. The general expression of Fisher information is then obtained as

$$I_{i,j}(\theta) = \frac{1}{2}\left(\frac{\partial^2 \log|\sigma(\theta)|}{\partial\theta_i\partial\theta_j} + \sum_{m,n=1}^{N} \sigma_{m,n}(\theta)\frac{\partial^2(\sigma(\theta)^{-1})_{m,n}}{\partial\theta_i\partial\theta_j}\right) + \frac{\partial\mu(\theta)}{\partial\theta_i}^T \sigma(\theta)^{-1}\frac{\partial\mu(\theta)}{\partial\theta_j}.$$

The above equation is derived without any supposition of independence. With the assumption that $\{X_n|\Theta\}$ is independent (i.e., σ is diagonal with the diagonal element not necessarily equal), the above result can be further simplified to

$$I_{i,j}(\theta) = \frac{\partial\mu(\theta)}{\partial\theta_i}^T \sigma(\theta)^{-1}\frac{\partial\mu(\theta)}{\partial\theta_j} + \sum_{n=1}^{N}\frac{1}{2\sigma_{n,n}(\theta)^2}\frac{\partial\sigma_{n,n}(\theta)}{\partial\theta_i}\frac{\partial\sigma_{n,n}(\theta)}{\partial\theta_j}.$$

The desired Fisher information matrix is then expressed in matrix form as

$$I(\theta) = P^T \Lambda^{-1} P \tag{16.10}$$

with

$$P \triangleq \frac{\partial\left(\mu_1(\theta), \ldots, \mu_N(\theta), \sigma_{1,1}(\theta), \ldots, \sigma_{N,N}(\theta)\right)}{\partial\left(\theta_1, \ldots, \theta_K\right)}$$

$$\Lambda \triangleq \text{diag}(\sigma_{1,1}(\theta), \ldots, \sigma_{N,N}(\theta), 2\sigma_{1,1}(\theta)^2, \ldots, 2\sigma_{N,N}(\theta)^2),$$

where P is the $2N \times K$ Jacobian matrix and Λ is a diagonal matrix. Therefore, we have obtained a computation formula for Fisher information entirely in terms of the mean vector μ and covariance matrix σ for normally distributed models. Note the similarity between the result in (16.10) and that in (16.4).

To demonstrate the application of (16.10), consider Fechner's logarithmic model of psychophysics [Roberts 1979],

$$X = \theta_1 \log(Y + \theta_2) + E$$

where $X = [x_1, \ldots, x_N]^T \in \mathbb{R}^N$ is the data sample, $Y = [y_1, \ldots, y_N]^T \in \mathbb{R}^N$ is a vector of independent variables, $\theta = [\theta_1, \theta_2]^T \in \mathbb{R}^2$ is the parameter, and $E \sim \mathcal{N}(0, c)$ is random error with constant variance $c \in \mathbb{R}$. So we have $X|\Theta \sim \mathcal{N}_N(\mu(\theta), \sigma(\theta))$, $\mu(\theta) = \theta_1 \log(Y + \theta_2)$, and $\sigma(\theta) = cI_N$, where I_N denotes the identity matrix and is not to be confused with $I(\theta)$, the Fisher information matrix. Using (16.10), the Fisher information matrix is obtained as

$$I(\theta) \;=\; P^T \Lambda^{-1} P$$

$$= \left[\begin{array}{c|c} \log(Y + \theta_2) & \frac{\theta_1}{Y+\theta_2} \\ \hline \mathbf{0} & \mathbf{0} \end{array} \right]^T \cdot \left[\begin{array}{c|c} cI_N & \mathbf{0} \\ \hline \mathbf{0} & 2c^2 I_N \end{array} \right]^{-1} \cdot \left[\begin{array}{c|c} \log(Y + \theta_2) & \frac{\theta_1}{Y+\theta_2} \\ \hline \mathbf{0} & \mathbf{0} \end{array} \right]$$

$$= \frac{1}{c} \left[\begin{array}{cc} \displaystyle\sum_{n=1}^{N} (\log(y_n + \theta_2))^2 & \displaystyle\sum_{n=1}^{N} \theta_1 \frac{\log(y_n + \theta_2)}{y_n + \theta_2} \\ \displaystyle\sum_{n=1}^{N} \theta_1 \frac{\log(y_n + \theta_2)}{y_n + \theta_2} & \displaystyle\sum_{n=1}^{N} \frac{\theta_1^2}{(y_n + \theta_2)^2} \end{array} \right],$$

where $\mathbf{0}$ denotes the null matrix of appropriate dimensions. Comparison of the above derivation with one obtained element by element in [Pitt et al. 2002] nicely illustrates why this method of computing Fisher information is preferable.

16.4   MDL Complexity Comparison

As discussed in section 16.2, the two model selection criteria of FIA and NML differ only in their complexity measure, C_{FIA} and C_{NML}. With the formula of Fisher information derived in section 16.3, the computation of C_{FIA} becomes routine work. On the other hand, C_{NML} is more challenging to calculate and an efficient computation of this quantity has yet to be devised. In certain situations, however, it turns out that one can obtain analytic-form solutions of C_{FIA} and C_{NML}. Taking advantage of these instances, we compare and contrast the two to gain further insight into how they are related to each other.

In demonstrating the relationship between C_{FIA} and C_{NML}, we consider a saturated model with a multinomial distribution (for related work, see [Kontkanen, Buntine, Myllymäki, Rissanen, and Tirri 2003]). The data under this model are assumed to be a C-tuple random vector $X|\Theta \sim Mult_C(n, \theta_1, \ldots, \theta_C)$ and $\theta = [\theta_1, \ldots, \theta_{C-1}]^T$ is the parameter.

16.4.1   Complexity of C_{FIA}

The complexity penalty term of FIA is again given by

$$C_{\text{FIA}} \triangleq \frac{k}{2} \log \frac{n}{2\pi} + \log \int_\Omega \sqrt{|I(\theta)|}\, d\theta.$$

For the saturated multinomial model, the dimension of the parameter $k = C-1$ with $\Omega = \{(\theta_1, \theta_2, \ldots, \theta_{C-1}) : \theta_c \geq 0 \; \forall c, \; \sum_{c=1}^{C-1} \theta_c \leq 1\}$. Using (16.4) of Fisher information for multinomial distribution, we have

$$
\begin{aligned}
I(\theta) &= \frac{\partial(\theta_1, \ldots, \theta_C)}{\partial(\theta_1, \ldots, \theta_{C-1})}^{T} \cdot \mathrm{diag}(\theta_1^{-1}, \ldots, \theta_C^{-1}) \cdot \frac{\partial(\theta_1, \ldots, \theta_C)}{\partial(\theta_1, \ldots, \theta_{C-1})} \\[2ex]
&= \left[\; I_{C-1} \;\middle|\; -\mathbf{1}_{(C-1)\times 1} \;\right] \cdot \left[\begin{array}{c|c} A & \mathbf{0} \\ \hline \mathbf{0} & \theta_C^{-1} \end{array}\right] \cdot \left[\begin{array}{c} I_{C-1} \\ \hline -\mathbf{1}_{1\times(C-1)} \end{array}\right] \\[2ex]
&= A + \mathbf{1}_{(C-1)\times(C-1)} \cdot \theta_C^{-1}
\end{aligned}
$$

where $\mathbf{1}_{n\times m}$ is an $n \times m$ matrix with all elements equal to one, and $A = \mathrm{diag}(\theta_1^{-1}, \ldots, \theta_{C-1}^{-1})$. The determinant of $I(\theta)$ is then calculated as

$$
\begin{aligned}
|I(\theta)| &= \begin{vmatrix} \frac{1}{\theta_1} + \frac{1}{\theta_C} & \frac{1}{\theta_C} & \cdots & \frac{1}{\theta_C} \\ \frac{1}{\theta_C} & \frac{1}{\theta_2} + \frac{1}{\theta_C} & \cdots & \frac{1}{\theta_C} \\ \vdots & \vdots & \ddots & \vdots \\ \frac{1}{\theta_C} & \frac{1}{\theta_C} & \cdots & \frac{1}{\theta_{C-1}} + \frac{1}{\theta_C} \end{vmatrix} \\[3ex]
&= \left|\begin{array}{cccc|c} \frac{1}{\theta_1} & 0 & \cdots & 0 & \frac{-1}{\theta_{C-1}} \\ 0 & \frac{1}{\theta_C} & \cdots & 0 & \frac{-1}{\theta_{C-1}} \\ \vdots & \vdots & \ddots & \vdots & \vdots \\ 0 & 0 & \cdots & \frac{1}{\theta_{C-2}} & \frac{-1}{\theta_{C-1}} \\ \hline \frac{1}{\theta_C} & \frac{1}{\theta_C} & \cdots & \frac{1}{\theta_C} & \frac{1}{\theta_{C-1}} + \frac{1}{\theta_C} \end{array}\right| \\[3ex]
&= |B| \cdot \left| \frac{1}{\theta_{C-1}} + \frac{1}{\theta_C} - \mathbf{1}_{1\times(C-2)} \cdot \frac{1}{\theta_C} \cdot B^{-1} \cdot -\mathbf{1}_{(C-2)\times 1} \cdot \frac{1}{\theta_{C-1}} \right| \\[3ex]
&= \prod_{c=1}^{C} \frac{1}{\theta_c},
\end{aligned}
$$

where $B = \text{diag}(\theta_1^{-1}, \ldots, \theta_{C-2}^{-1})$. Using Dirichlet integration, we find that

$$\int_\Omega \sqrt{|I(\theta)|} d\theta = \int_\Omega \prod_{c=1}^{C} \theta_c^{-1/2} d\theta$$

$$= \frac{\Gamma(1/2)^C}{\Gamma(C/2)},$$

where $\Gamma(\cdot)$ is the gamma function defined as $\Gamma(x) \triangleq \int_0^\infty t^{x-1} e^{-t} dt$ for $t > 0$. Finally, the desired complexity of the model is obtained as follows[5]:

$$C_{\text{FIA}} = \frac{C-1}{2} \log \frac{n}{2\pi} + \log \left(\frac{\pi^{\frac{C}{2}}}{\Gamma(\frac{C}{2})} \right) \tag{16.11}$$

In (16.11), C_{FIA} is no longer a linear function of the dimension of the parameter (i.e., $k = C-1$) due to the gamma function in the second term. This contrasts with BIC, where complexity is measured as a linear function of the dimension of the model parameter.

16.4.2 Complexity of C_{NML}

The following is the complexity penalty of NML:

$$C_{\text{NML}} \triangleq \log \int_{\hat{\theta}(x) \in \Omega} f_{X|\Theta}(x|\hat{\theta}(x)) dx$$

To obtain the exact expression for C_{NML}, we would need the analytic solution of $\hat{\theta}(x)$, which requires solving an optimization problem. The log-likelihood function is given by

$$\log f_{X|\Theta}(x|\theta) = \log \binom{n}{x_1, \ldots, x_C} + \sum_{c=1}^{C} x_c \log \theta_c.$$

The ML estimate that maximizes the above log-likelihood function is found to be $\hat{\theta}_c = \frac{x_c}{n}$ $\forall c \in \{1, 2, \ldots, C\}$. Plugging this result into the earlier equation, we obtain

$$C_{\text{NML}} = \log \left(\sum_{\substack{0 \leq x_c \leq n \\ x_1 + x_2 + \ldots + x_C = n}} \binom{n}{x_1, \ldots, x_C} \prod_{c=1}^{C} \left(\frac{x_c}{n} \right)^{x_c} \right). \tag{16.12}$$

C_{NML} can be calculated by considering all possible $\binom{n+C-1}{C-1}$ data patterns in the sample space for a fixed C and a sample size n. To do so, for each data pattern we would need to compute the multinomial coefficient and the multiplication of

---

5. The same result is also described in [Rissanen 1996], and a more general one in [Kontkanen et al. 2003].

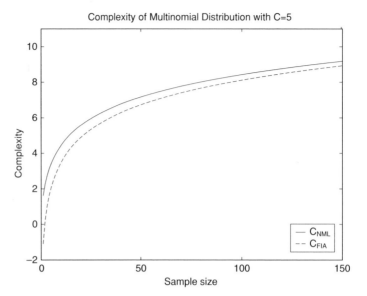

Figure 16.2   MDL complexity as a function of sample size.

C terms. There exists an elegant recursive algorithm based on combinatorics for doing this [Kontkanen et al. 2003]. Even so, (16.12) would still be computationally heavier than (16.11).

16.4.3   The Comparison

Shown in Figure 16.2 are plots of C_{FIA} and C_{NML} as a function of sample size n for the number of categories $C = 5$ (i.e., parameter dimension $K = 4$). As can be seen, the two curves follow each other closely, with C_{NML} being slightly larger than C_{FIA}. Both curves resemble the shape of a logarithmic function of n.

In Figure 16.3, we plot the two complexity measures now as a function of C for a fixed sample size $n = 50$. Again, C_{FIA} and C_{NML} are quite close and slightly convex in shape. This nonlinearity is obviously due to the functional form effects of model complexity. In contrast, the complexity measure of BIC, which ignores these effects, is a straight line. Interestingly however, the BIC complexity function provides a decent approximation of C_{FIA} and C_{NML} curves for $C \leq 4$.

To summarize, the *approximate* complexity measure C_{FIA} turns out to do a surprisingly good job of capturing the *full-solution* complexity measure C_{NML}, at least for the saturated multinomial model we examined.

16.5   Example Application

This section presents a model recovery simulation to demonstrate the relative performance of FIA and the other two selection criteria, BIC and CV. We chose three

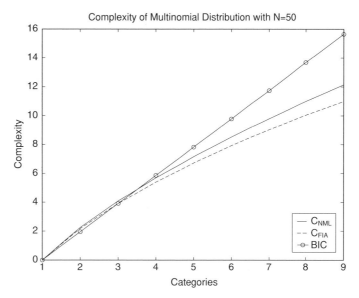

Figure 16.3   MDL complexity as a function of the number of categories.

retention models with binomial distribution   [Rubin and Wenzel 1996; Wickens 1998] so $X_k|[a,b]^T \sim Bin(n,h(a,b,t_k))$. The sample size $n=20$, the independent variable t_k was selected to be $t_k = 1,2,4,8,16$, and the success probability $h(a,b,t)$ under each model was given by

$$h(a,b,t) = \begin{cases} 1/(1+t^a) & \text{(M1)} \\ 1/(1+a+bt) & \text{(M2)} \\ t^{-b}e^{-at} & \text{(M3)} \end{cases}$$

with the range of exponential parameter to be [0,10] and [0,100] otherwise.

The complexity measure C_{FIA} of each model was computed using (16.7) and was evaluated by simple Monte Carlo integration. Its value was 1.2361, 1.5479, and 1.7675 for models M1, M2, and M3, respectively. Model M1 is the simplest with one parameter, whereas models M2 and M3 have two parameters, with their complexity difference of 0.2196 being due to the difference in functional form. For each model, we first generated 1000 random parameter values sampled across the entire parameter space according to Jeffreys' prior [Robert 2001]. For each parameter, we then generated 100 simulated data samples with binomial sampling noise added. Finally, we fit all three models to each of 100,000 data samples and obtained their best-fitting parameter values. The three selection methods were compared on their ability to recover the data-generating model. Maximum likelihood (ML), a goodness-of-fit measure, was included as a baseline.

The results are presented in Table 16.1, which consists of four 3×3 submatrices, each corresponding to the selection method specified on the left. Within each submatrix, the value of each element indicates the percentage of samples in which

Table 16.1 Model recovery rates of three retention models.

Selection Method/ Fitted Model	Data-Generating Model (C_{FIA})		
	M1 (1.2361)	M2 (1.5479)	M3 (1.7675)
ML			
M1	22%	11%	0%
M2	41%	88%	4%
M3	37%	1%	96%
BIC			
M1	91%	55%	8%
M2	4%	44%	4%
M3	5%	1%	88%
CV			
M1	52%	40%	7%
M2	28%	53%	19%
M3	20%	7%	74%
FIA			
M1	83%	37%	7%
M2	11%	62%	6%
M3	6%	1%	87%

the particular model's fit was preferred according to the selection method of interest. Ideally, a selection criterion should be able to recover the true model 100 % of the time, which would result in a diagonal matrix containing values of 100 %. Deviations from this outcome indicate a bias in the selection method.

Let us first examine the recovery performance of ML. The result in the first column of the 3 × 3 submatrix indicates that model M1 was correctly recovered only 22% of the time; the rest of the time (78%) models M2 and M3 were selected incorrectly. This is not surprising because the latter two models are more complex than M1 (with one extra parameter). Hence such overfitting is expected. This bias against M1 was mostly corrected when BIC was employed as a selection criterion, as shown in the first column of the corresponding 3 × 3 submatrix. On the other hand, the result in the second column for the data generated by M2 indicates that BIC had trouble distinguishing between M1 and M2. CV performed similarly to BIC, though its recovery rates (52%, 53%, 74%) are rather unimpressive. In contrast, FIA, with its results shown in the bottom submatrix, performed the best in recovering the data-generating model.[6]

---

6. A caveat here is that the above simulations are meant to be a demonstration, and as such the results are not to be taken as representative behavior of the three selection methods.

16.6 Summary and Conclusion

Model selection can proceed most confidently when a well-justified and well-performing measure of model complexity is available. C_{FIA} and C_{NML} of minimum description length are two such measures. In this chapter we addressed issues concerning the implementation of these measures in the context of models of cognition. As a main contribution of the present study, we provided a general formula in matrix form to calculate Fisher information. The formula is applicable for virtually all models that assume the multinomial distribution or the independent normal distribution—the two most common distributions in cognitive modeling.[7] We also showed that C_{FIA} represents a good approximation to C_{NML}, at least for the saturated multinomial probability model. This finding suggests that within many research areas in cognitive science, modelers might use FIA instead of NML with minimal worry about whether the outcome would change if NML were used instead. Finally, we illustrated how MDL performs relative to its competitors in one content area of cognitive modeling.

Acknowledgments

This research was supported by National Institutes of Health grant R01 MH57472. We thank Peter Grünwald, Woojae Kim, Daniel Navarro, and an anonymous reviewer for many helpful comments.

References

Anderson, N.H. (1981). *Foundations of Information Integration Theory*. New York: Academic Press.

Barron, A., J. Rissanen, and B. Yu (1998). The minimum description length principle in coding and modeling. *IEEE Transactions on Information Theory, 44*, 2743–2760.

Gilks, W.R., S. Richardson, and D.J. Spiegelhalter (1996). *Markov Chain Monte Carlo in Practice*. London: Chapman & Hall.

Glass, A.L., and K.J. Holyoak (1986). *Cognition*, 2nd edition, Chap. 5. New York: Random House.

Grünwald, P.D. (2005). Tutorial on MDL. In P.D. Grünwald, I.J. Myung, and M.A. Pitt (Eds.), *Advances in Minimum Description Length: Theory and*

7. The reader is cautioned that the formula should not be used blindly. In some cases, it might be more efficient to use a simpler formula. For example, instead of (16.4), sometimes it may be easier to use (16.7) for binomial models with a two-dimensional parameter.

Applications. Cambridge, MA: MIT Press.

Hansen, M.H., and B. Yu (2001). Model selection and the principle of minimum description length. *Journal of the American Statistical Association, 96,* 746–774.

Kass, R.E., and A.E. Raftery (1995). Bayes factors. *Journal of the American Statistical Association, 90,* 773–795.

Kass, R.E., and P.W. Vos (1997). *Geometrical Foundations of Asymptotic Inference.* New York: Wiley.

Kontkanen, P., W. Buntine, P. Myllymäki, J. Rissanen, and H. Tirri (2003). Efficient computation of stochastic complexity. In C.M. Bishop and B.J. Frey (Eds.), *Proceedings of the Ninth International Workshop on Artificial Intelligence and Statistics,* pp. 181–188. Society for Artificial Intelligence and Statistics.

Kullback, S., and R.A. Leibler (1951). On information and sufficiency. *Annals of Mathematical Statistics, 91,* 79–86.

Lee, M.D. (2002). Generating additive clustering models with minimal stochastic complexity. *Journal of Classification, 19,* 69–85.

Li, M., and P. Vitányi (1997). *An Introduction to Kolmogorov Complexity and Its Applications,* 2nd edition. New York: Springer-Verlag.

Myung, I.J., V. Balasubramanian, and M.A. Pitt (2000). Counting probability distributions: Differential geometry and model selection. *Proceedings of the National Academy of Sciences USA, 97,* 11170–11175.

Myung, I.J., and M.A. Pitt (1997). Applying Occam's razor in modeling cognition: A Bayesian approach. *Psychonomic Review and Bulletin, 4,* 79–95.

Nosofsky, R.M. (1986). Attention, similarity, and the identification-categorization relationship. *Journal of Experimental Psychology: General, 115,* 39–57.

Oden, G.C. and D.W. Massaro (1978). Integration of featural information in speech perception. *Psychological Review, 85,* 172–191.

Pitt, M.A. and I.J. Myung (2002). When a good fit can be bad. *Trends in Cognitive Sciences, 6*(10), 421–425.

Pitt, M.A., I.J. Myung, and S. Zhang (2002). Toward a method of selecting among computational models of cognition. *Psychological Review, 109*(3), 472–491.

Rissanen, J. (1989). *Stochastic Complexity in Statistical Inquiry.* Singapore: World Scientific.

Rissanen, J. (1996). Fisher information and stochastic complexity. *IEEE Transactions on Information Theory, 42*(1), 40–47.

Rissanen, J. (2001). Strong optimality of the normalized ML models as universal codes and information in data. *IEEE Transactions on Information Theory, 47*(5), 1712–1717.

Robert, C.P. (2001). *The Bayesian Choice,* 2nd edition, New York: Springer-

Verlag.

Roberts, F.S. (1979). *Measurement Theory with Applications to Decision Making, Utility, and the Social Sciences*. Reading, MA: Addison-Wesley.

Rubin, D.C., and A.E. Wenzel (1996). One hundred years of forgetting: A quantitative description of retention. *Psychological Review, 103*, 734–760.

Schervish, M.J. (1995). *Theory of Statistics*. Springer-Verlag.

Schwarz, G. (1978). Estimating the dimension of a model. *Annals of Statistics, 6*(2), 461–464.

Shtarkov, Y.M. (1987). Universal sequential coding of single messages. *Problems of Information Transmission, 23*, 3–17.

Stone, M. (1974). Cross-validatory choice and assessment of statistical predictions [with discussion]. *Journal of the Royal Statistical Society, Series B, 36*, 111–147.

Wickens, T.D. (1998). On the form of the retention function: Comment on Rubin and Wenzel (1996): A qualitative description of retention. *Psychological Review, 105*, 379–386.

Index